AF841592

GREENWICH LIBRARY

LAW
12001402

OXFORD MONOGRAPHS IN INTERNATIONAL LAW

General Editor: PROFESSOR VAUGHAN LOWE,
Chichele Professor of Public International Law in the University of Oxford and Fellow of All Souls College, Oxford

The Immunity of States and Their Officials in International Criminal Law and International Human Rights Law

OXFORD MONOGRAPHS IN INTERNATIONAL LAW

The aim of this series is to publish important and original pieces of research on all aspects of international law. Topics that are given particular prominence are those which, while of interest to the academic lawyer, also have important bearing on issues which touch upon the actual conduct of international relations. Nonetheless, the series is wide in scope and includes monographs on the history and philosophical foundations of international law.

RECENT TITLES IN THE SERIES

Jurisdiction in International Law
Cedric Ryngaert

The Fair and Equitable Treatment Standard in International Foreign Investment Law
Ioana Tudor

Targeted Killing in International Law
Nils Melzer

Defining Terrorism in International Law
Ben Saul

Diplomatic Protection
Chittharanjan F. Amerasinghe

Human Rights and Non-Discrimination in the 'War on Terror'
Daniel Moeckli

The Decolonization of International Law
Matthew Craven

Investment Treaty Arbitration and Public Law
Gus van Harten

International Organizations and their Exercise of Sovereign Powers
Dan Sarooshi

Peremptory Norms in International Law
Alexander Orakhelashvili

4673464

The Immunity of States and Their Officials in International Criminal Law and International Human Rights Law

ROSANNE VAN ALEBEEK
Assistant Professor, University of Amsterdam

UNIVERSITY OF GREENWICH LIBRARY

OXFORD
UNIVERSITY PRESS

This book has been printed digitally and produced in a standard specification in order to ensure its continuing availability

OXFORD
UNIVERSITY PRESS

Great Clarendon Street, Oxford OX2 6DP

Oxford University Press is a department of the University of Oxford.
It furthers the University's objective of excellence in research, scholarship,
and education by publishing worldwide in

Oxford New York

Auckland Cape Town Dar es Salaam Hong Kong Karachi
Kuala Lumpur Madrid Melbourne Mexico City Nairobi
New Delhi Shanghai Taipei Toronto

With offices in

Argentina Austria Brazil Chile Czech Republic France Greece
Guatemala Hungary Italy Japan South Korea Poland Portugal
Singapore Switzerland Thailand Turkey Ukraine Vietnam

Oxford is a registered trade mark of Oxford University Press
in the UK and in certain other countries

Published in the United States
by Oxford University Press Inc., New York

© R. Van Alebeek 2008

The moral rights of the author have been asserted

Database right Oxford University Press (maker)

Reprinted 2010

Crown copyright material is reproduced under Class Licence
Number C01P0000148 with the permission of the Controller of
HMSO and the Queen's Printer for Scotland.

All rights reserved. No part of this publication may be reproduced,
stored in a retrieval system, or transmitted, in any form or by any means,
without the prior permission in writing of Oxford University Press,
or as expressly permitted by law, or under terms agreed with the appropriate
reprographics rights organization. Enquiries concerning reproduction
outside the scope of the above should be sent to the Rights Department,
Oxford University Press, at the address above

You must not circulate this book in any other binding or cover
And you must impose this same condition on any acquirer

ISBN 978-0-19-923247-5

General Editor's Preface

The immunity of States—or more accurately of those persons who are considered the embodiment of the State, whether as sovereigns, diplomats, or some other State agency—is generally regarded as one of the oldest and most clearly established of all principles of international law. It is a principle that seems to enable the State, both metaphorically and literally, to get away with murder. This careful analysis of the development of the law on State immunity challenges that general conception and offers a new rationalization of the principles governing immunity.

Dr Van Alebeek argues for an understanding of the modern law on State immunity that recognizes that it is not merely a survival of the ancient inviolability of sovereigns, now made subject to certain limited qualifications.

She proposes a new view of this area of the law that fits more comfortably with the notion that fundamental considerations of human rights, and in particular the right to a fair trial, entail the restriction of claims to immunity.

At a time when those injured by the acts of States are more able and more willing than they have been in the past to challenge States in the courts, this study has a practical value that matches its considerable intellectual interest.

AVL
All Souls College, Oxford
October 2007

Acknowledgements

While working on this book I have spent many a day in the library. Several eureka-moments were lived thanks to inspiration found in quiet reading rooms, exploring the cases and literature that shaped the law of state immunity over the years. I would therefore first like to express my gratitude to the Law Library of the University of Leiden, the Oxford University Bodleian Law Library, the Library of the Peace Palace in The Hague, and the Library of the Camera dei Deputati in Rome, and to all the people working there.

My research has furthermore benefited greatly from the encouragement, guidance, and critical attitude of Professor John Dugard. I owe many thanks to him. I also thank Zsuzsanna Deen-Racsmány for her helpful comments on early versions of parts of this book. I thank Lady Fox, Professor Schrijver, Professor Nollkaemper, Professor Kooijmans, Professor Schermers, Professor Lammers, and Dr van Sliedregt for their insightful comments on the PhD version of this book that was defended in 2006 at Leiden University.

A huge thank you goes to all my friends and my family for their love and support throughout this project. In particular I thank Joop Nijssen for making life wonderful even on the countless eurakaless days.

Rosanne Van Alebeek
November 2007
The Hague

Contents—Summary

Contents—Outline

List of Abbreviations

AC	Appeal Cases
AD	Annual Digest
AEDPA	Antiterrorism and Effective Death Penalty Act
AFDI	Annuaire Français de Droit International
AIDI	Annuaire de l'Institut de Droit International
AJIL	American Journal of International Law
All ER	All England Law Reports
ASDI	Annuaire Suisse du Droit International
ATCA	Alien Tort Claims Act
BCCI	Bank for Credit and Commerce International
Bull. Cas.	Bulletin des ârrets de la Cour de Cassation
BYIL	British Yearbook of International Law
CB	Common Bench
Ch.	Chancery Division
Ch D	Chancery Division 1875–90
CLR	Columbia Law Review Commonwealth Law Reports
CA	Court of Appeal
Ct of Apps	Court of Appeals
DC	District Court
DLR	Dominion Law Reports
DPA	Diplomatic Privileges Act
DR	Decisions and Reports
DRC	Democratic Republic of the Congo
ECHR	European Convention for the Protection of Human Rights and Fundamental Freedoms European Court of Human Rights
EComHR	European Commission of Human Rights
EHRR	European Human Rights Reports
EJIL	European Journal of International Law
El & El	Ellis & Ellis
EPO	European Patent Office
FCAFC	Federal Court of Australia Full Court
F It	Foro Italiano
FSIA	Foreign Sovereign Immunities Act
GA	General Assembly of the United Nations
Giu It	Giurisprudenza Italiana
HL	House of Lords
HLC	House of Lords Cases
HLR	Harvard Law Review
IAC	Iraqi Airways Company

ICC	International Criminal Court
ICCPR	International Covenant on Civil and Political Rights
ICJ	International Court of Justice
ICLQ	International and Comparative Law Quarterly
ICTR	International Criminal Tribunal for Rwanda
ICTY	International Criminal Tribunal for the Former Yugoslavia
ILA	International Law Association
ILC	International Law Commission
ILM	International Legal Materials
ILR	International Law Reports
ILQ	International Law Quarterly
JDI	Journal du Droit International
JDIP	Journal du Droit International Privé et de la Législation Comparée
JICJ	Journal of International Criminal Justice
JT	Journal des Tribunaux
KAC	Kuwait Airways Corporation
KB	King's Bench
Ld Raym.	Lord Raymond
LJIL	Leiden Journal of International Law
LQR	Law Quarterly Review
LR	Law Reports
LR A & E	Law Reports: Admiralty and Ecclesiastical
LT	Law Times
NILR	Netherlands International Law Review
NJ	Nederlands Juristenblad
NJW	Neue Juristische Wochenschrift
NStZ	Neue Zeitschrift für Strafrecht
NZLR	New Zealand Law Reports
P.	Probate, Divorce & Admiralty Division 1891–1970
PB	Pasicrisie Belge
PCA	Permanent Court of Arbitration
PCIJ	Permanent Court of International Justice
PD	Probate, Divorce & Admiralty Division 1875–90
QB	Queen's Bench
QBD	Queen's Bench Division
RBDI	Revue Belge de Droit International
RdC	Recueil des Cours
RCDIP	Revue Critique de Droit International Privé
RDI	Rivista di Diritto Internazionale
RDILC	Revue de Droit International et de Législation Comparée
RDIP	Revue de Droit International Privé
RDIPP	Rivista di Diritto Internazionale Privato e Processuale
RGDIP	Revue Générale de Droit International Public
RIAA	Reports of International Arbitral Awards
ROC	Republic of China
RSDIE	Revue Suisse de Droit International et Européen

SALJ	South African Law Journal
SC	Security Council of the United Nations
SCRA	Philippine Supreme Court Reports
SCR	Supreme Court of Canada Reports
SCSL	Special Court for Sierra Leone
S Ct	Supreme Court
SIA	State Immunity Act
TC	Convention Against Torture and Other Cruel, Inhuman and Degrading Treatment or Punishment
TVPA	Torture Victim Protection Act
UK	United Kingdom
UN	United Nations
US	United States
VCCR	Vienna Convention on Consular Relations
VCDR	Vienna Convention on Diplomatic Relations
VJIL	Virginia Journal of International Law
WLR	Weekly Law Reports
YBILC	Yearbook of the International Law Commission
YLJ	Yale Law Journal
ZaöRV	Zeitschrift für ausländisches öffentliches Recht und Völkerrecht

Table of Cases

INTERNATIONAL COURTS

Arbitral Tribunals

European Commission of Human Rights

European Court of Human Rights

Inter-American Commission on Human Rights

Inter-American Court of Human Rights

International Court of Justice

International Criminal Tribunal for the Former Yugoslavia

International Military Tribunal

International Military Tribunal for the Far East

Permanent Court of International Justice

Special Court for Sierra Leone

United Nations Human Rights Committee

United Nations Secretary-General

NATIONAL COURTS

Canada

Chile

Danzig

Egypt

France

Federal Republic of Germany

Greece

Japan

Jordan

Kenya

Malaysia

Mexico

The Netherlands

New Zealand

Nigeria

Pakistan

Philippines

Poland

Romania

Senegal

South Africa

Spain

Switzerland

United Kingdom

United States

Zimbabwe

1
Introduction

Are the well-established immunity rules that shield states and their officials from foreign adjudicative jurisdiction affected by the relatively recent developments in international human rights law and international criminal law? This, in an obviously constraining nutshell, is the principal question at the basis of this study.[1] The progressive development of a normative system of international human rights law and international criminal law without the simultaneous development of international institutional enforcement mechanisms has put the question of the role of national courts in the application of these norms to the fore and has made the question as to the relation between immunity rules and human rights norms and international criminal law an immediate one.[2]

The question can be approached from two distinct perspectives. In the first place it must be questioned whether immunity rules as such are compatible with certain rights of individuals under international human rights law like the right of access to the courts, the right to a remedy, or the right to effective protection. This perspective formed the thrust of the critique on the absolute approach to the rule of state immunity half a century ago. The fact that with the increasing economic activity of states the absolute approach was seen to entail the risk of denial of justice to private individuals is one of the reasons for the prevalence of a restrictive approach to the rule today. In recent times the question is also approached from a second perspective. It is questioned whether foreign states and foreign state officials still have a right to immunity from proceedings concerning grave human rights abuses in view of certain conceptual changes in the international legal order.

It was the *Pinochet* case that put the issue of immunity and human rights in the limelight of attention. When the former head of state of Chile Augusto Pinochet visited the United Kingdom in 1998 Spanish authorities issued an international warrant for his arrest in respect of, *inter alia*, allegations of torture that took place in Chile during his time in office. He was arrested by UK authorities and Spain subsequently requested his extradition. The 1999 decision of the House of Lords

[1] The research does not extend to the question of immunity from execution of state property.

[2] This study will often employ the notion of a 'human rights exception to immunity rules' as an umbrella term for exceptions to immunity rules based on international human rights law or international criminal law.

that Pinochet did not enjoy immunity from the criminal jurisdiction of UK courts with regard to some of the acts of torture and could hence be extradited to Spain sparked of a vigorous debate on immunity and human rights both on the political and the academic level.[3]

The question, however, transcends the particulars of the *Pinochet* case. Pinochet relied on the rule of *functional* immunity that shields all (former) state officials from the jurisdiction of foreign national courts with regard to the limited class of official acts performed on behalf of the state. That rule must be distinguished from the rule of *state* immunity—that precludes the exercise of jurisdiction over the *acta jure imperii* of foreign states—and the rule of *personal* immunity—that provides comprehensive protection from foreign jurisdiction to certain categories of foreign state officials during their term of office. The present study will examine the research question in regard to all three immunity concepts.[4]

By now, this can hardly be called a virgin area of international law. In the wake of the *Pinochet* case the question as to the relation between state immunity and human rights has engaged the minds of the judges of the European Court of Human Rights in *Al-Adsani v United Kingdom*, while the relation between personal immunity and international criminal law was at the heart of the decision of the International Court of Justice (ICJ) in the *Arrest Warrant* case (*Congo v Belgium*) and the House of Lords addressed the relation between functional immunity and international human rights law in *Jones v Saudi Arabia*. These cases—the central pieces of the décor in which our examination takes place—compel the conclusion that arguments against immunity rules based on international human rights law and international criminal law have not fared particularly well in state practice.

The *Pinochet* case is deceiving in this respect. The decision has been lauded for deciding that 'l'ancien Chef d'Etat … n'est … pas à l'abri des poursuites lorsque ces actes revêtent le caractère de crimes de droit international'[5] and providing 'le critère qui permet de distinguer parmi les actes d'un gouvernant'.[6] Upon closer consideration the decision does however not bear the weight of such sweeping claims. Although it is well-nigh impossible to find a common ratio decidendi in the six individual majority opinions in the *Pinochet* case, it can be safely stated that the denial of immunity turned on the specific terms of the 1984 Convention against Torture and Other Cruel, Inhuman or Degrading Treatment or

[3] *R v Bow Street Metropolitan Stipendiary Magistrate and others, ex p Pinochet Ugarte (Amnesty International and ors intervening)* [1999] 2 All ER 97 (UK, HL, 1999) (*Pinochet* no 3).

[4] The immunity of international organizations and their officials is not included in this study.

[5] C Dominicé, 'Quelques observations sur l'immunité de juridiction pénale de l'ancien chef d'Etat' (1999) 103 RGDIP 297, 307.

[6] M Cosnard, 'Quelques observations sur les décisions de la Chambre des Lords du 25 Novembre 1998 et du 24 Mars 1999 dans l'affaire Pinochet' (1999) 103 RGDIP 309, 319.

Punishment and the particular definition of the crime of torture therein, rather than on considerations applicable to crimes against international law in general.[7]

The relation between the law of state immunity and international human rights law was an issue of debate well before 1998. From the end of the 1980s onwards proponents of a human rights exception have argued that acts that violate *jus cogens* norms cannot qualify as sovereign—*jure imperii*—acts for the purpose of the rule of state immunity. Several US courts expressed sympathy for the argument. For example, in the 1992 decision in the case of *Siderman de Blake v Republic of Argentina* the Ninth Circuit Court of Appeals considered that 'international law does not recognize an act that violates *jus cogens* as a sovereign act. A state's violation of the *jus cogens* norm prohibiting official torture therefore would not be entitled to the immunity afforded by international law.'[8] Reluctantly, the court concluded that the strictures of the 1976 Foreign Sovereign Immunities Act did not leave it any choice but to grant Argentina immunity in respect of the claim for damages for alleged torture of Jose Siderman. With the conspicuous exceptions of the Greek case of *Prefecture of Voiotia v Federal Republic of Germany* and the Italian case of *Ferrini v Federal Republic of Germany* no court has accepted a human rights exception to the law of state immunity.[9]

The paucity of positive state practice led the European Court of Human Rights to conclude in *Al-Adsani v United Kingdom* that under international law no such exception exists.[10] The Court attached great weight to the fact that the 2004 UN Convention on Jurisdictional Immunities of States and their Property does not include a human rights exception, and relied on a report of the ILC Working Group that concluded that state practice as yet did not support such an exception.[11] Eight of the seventeen judges dissented. They did not argue that the rule of state immunity does not extend to violations of *jus cogens* norms. Rather, they argued that '[t]he acceptance . . . of the *jus cogens* nature of the prohibition of torture entails that a State allegedly violating it cannot invoke hierarchically lower rules . . . to avoid the consequences of the illegality of its actions.' In respect of allegations of torture, they concluded, the rule of state immunity does not produce

[7] Convention against Torture and Other Cruel, Inhuman and Degrading Treatment or Punishment (1984) 1465 UNTS 85, reprinted in (1984) 23 ILM 1027.

[8] *Siderman de Blake v Republic of Argentina* 965 F 2d 699 (US, Ct of Apps (9th Cir), 1992) 718.

[9] *Prefecture of Voiotia v Federal Republic of Germany* (Greece, S Ct, 2000) (German trans on file with the author), discussed in M Gavouneli & I Bantekas, 'Prefecture of Voiotia v. Federal Republic of Germany', (2001) 95 AJIL 198, 202. Cf for the 1997 decision of the Court of First Instance of Leivadia, (1997) 50 Revue Hellénique De Droit International 595; and the case note by I Bantekas in (1998) 92 AJIL 765. *Ferrini v Repubblica Federale di Germania* 87 RDI 2004 539 (Italy, Corte di Cassazione, 2004). Moreover, the US has adopted an exception to the rule of state immunity in respect of certain human rights claims against a limited group of 'terrorist states', see ch 6 § 2.3.2.3 below.

[10] *Al-Adsani v United Kingdom* (2001) 34 EHRR 273, 123 ILR 24.

[11] Appendix to the 1999 Report of the Working Group of the International Law Commission on Jurisdictional Immunities of States and their Property, annexed to the Report of the ILC on the work of its fifty-first session.

any legal effect.[12] The Court however decided in majority to reject the *jus cogens* argument because it was 'unable to discern in the international instruments, judicial authorities or other materials before it any firm basis for concluding that, as a matter of international law, a State no longer enjoys immunity from civil suit in the courts of another State where acts of torture are alleged'.[13]

In its 2002 decision in the *Arrest Warrant* case, the ICJ reasoned in a comparable vein.[14] In October 2000 Congo had instituted proceedings against Belgium in respect of a dispute concerning an international arrest warrant *in absentia* issued by an investigating judge of the Brussels *Tribunal de première instance*, charging the then incumbent minister of foreign affairs of Congo, Mr Yerodia, with crimes under international law and crimes against humanity. The ICJ concluded that the Belgian arrest warrant indeed violated the personal immunity of the minister. It argued in relevant part that 'it has been unable to deduce from … practice that there exist under customary international law any form of exception to the rule according immunity from criminal jurisdiction and inviolability to incumbent Ministers for Foreign Affairs, where they are suspected of having committed war crimes or crimes against humanity'.[15] In particular, the Court rejected reliance on the principle of irrelevance of official capacity as laid down in the Charter of the Nuremberg Tribunal and the Statutes of the International Criminal Tribunal for the Former Yugoslavia (ICTY), the International Criminal Tribunal for Rwanda (ICTR) and the International Criminal Court (ICC) respectively. The Court argued that these rules did 'not enable it to conclude that any such exception exists in customary international law in regard to national courts.'[16]

In its 2006 decision in *Jones v Saudi Arabia* the House of Lords held foreign state officials sued for acts of torture committed under ostensible official authority to be protected under the same immunity cloak as foreign states.[17] According to the Law Lords, foreign states can invoke state immunity on behalf of their officials whenever these officials are sued for acts for which the state bears international responsibility under the law of state responsibility. Under reference to, *inter alia*, the *Al-Adsani* case it was concluded that the rule of state immunity knows no exception in case of torture allegations.

If these three particularly eminent courts had authoritatively settled the issues put before them there would be no point in a comprehensive study like the present one. It will therefore be no surprise that this author is not swayed by the rhetoric

[12] ibid, dissenting opinion of Judges Rozakis and Caflisch joined by Judges Wilhaber, Costa, Cabral Barreto, and Vajic, § 3. Judges Ferrari, Bravo, and Loucaides delivered separate dissenting opinions.

[13] ibid § 61.

[14] *Arrest Warrant of 11 April 2000* (*Democratic Republic of the Congo v Belgium*) (Judgment) ICJ Reports 2002 3.

[15] ibid 24, § 58.

[16] ibid.

[17] *Jones v Saudi Arabia* [2006] UKHL 26 available at <http://www.publications.parliament.uk/pa/ld/ldjudgmt.htm>.

of the *Pinochet*, *Al-Adsani*, *Arrest Warrant*, and *Jones* cases. It is not necessarily the *outcome* of the inquiries undertaken in these cases that is taken issue with. Rather, it is *the terms on which the decisions are premised* that fail to convince.

Legal arguments divide in two principal categories. We can argue what the applicable law *is* and we can argue what the applicable law *should be*. Decisions of courts must be based on the first type of argument—the state of the law arguments. This type of argument knows two variants. A state of the law argument may be focused on the scope of a rule, or it may argue that a certain rule does not apply—regardless of its scope—for example because it is trumped by another rule of international law. The second type of argument—the policy arguments—urges states to change the rules through a change of practice or conventional law.

It is noted at the outset that both type of arguments are equally valuable in a conceptual debate on the position of immunity rules in international law. Especially policy arguments that can point to a clash between the obligations under the relevant rule and *other* obligations of states under international law are forceful. The term policy argument in this study should hence be understood from the perspective of immunity rules. Policy arguments of this kind may in fact pivot on a state of the law argument on international human rights law or international criminal law. Since judges could decide that the latter legal obligation should prevail over the former, such a policy argument may in fact result in the non-application of the immunity rule. If on the other hand, the forum state is allowed to apply the immunity rule, a successful policy argument of this kind in any case obliges the forum state to compensate the private individual whose human rights are violated. Arguments that approach the research question from the first perspective identified above are in principle policy arguments. States that once adhered to an absolute approach to the rule of state immunity were convinced to change their practice on the basis of such policy arguments. The clash between the obligations owed to foreign states under the law of state immunity—albeit not in terms of *international* law as will be explained in chapter 2 of this study—and the obligation to protect the rights and interests of private individuals under international human rights law did not *change* the law of state immunity as such but *urged* states to change the law. As Lauterpacht put it: 'At a period in which in enlightened communities the securing of the rights of the individual—in all their aspects, against the state has become a matter of special and significant effort, there is no longer a disposition to tolerate the injustice which may arise whenever the state—our own state or a foreign state—screens itself behind the shield of immunity in order to defeat a legitimate claim.'[18]

It stands to reason that the respective arguments do have a different *role* in the debate. A policy argument cannot convince when the ascertainment of the scope

[18] H Lauterpacht, 'The Problem of Jurisdictional Immunities of Foreign States' (1951) 28 BYIL 220, 235.

of the rule is the subject of debate; and a state of the law argument is no persuasive rebuttal of a policy argument.

To be coherent, both the *form* of state of the law arguments and the *substance* of state of the law *and* policy arguments on the relation between the three immunity rules and developments in international human rights law and international criminal law must reflect sound international legal theory on the nature and the scope of all rules relied on. The form of an argument is only coherent when it is consistent with the epistemology of international law. This is in particular an issue for state of the law arguments on customary international law. How *can* arguments work in light of accepted theories of formation, change, and invalidation of rules of customary international law? Policy arguments are obviously not limited in this regard—although of course a policy argument that relies on the clash of different rules of international law must rely on state of the law arguments establishing the existence of these obligations. For an argument to be coherent in substance, it must proceed from a correct understanding of the substance of the rules and principles it relies on.

This study will argue that the arguments of *both* opponents *and* proponents in the debate on a human rights exception to immunity rules proceed from unarticulated—and problematic—assumptions as to the epistemology of rules of customary international law and suffer from a lack of theorization on the nature and substance of the respective immunity rules. The recent instances of judicial thinking on our research question hence warrant further inquiry into the theory of immunity rules. The study sets out to reconsider the nature and substance of the rule of state immunity, the rule of functional immunity and the rule of personal immunity in order to identify the parameters of coherent argument in a debate on the scope of these respective rules. On the basis of this analysis the study will proceed to assess the possible influence of international human rights law and international criminal law on these rules.

The ideas put forward in this work follow a study and analysis of a variety of sources. The foremost source of international immunity rules is national jurisprudence. Immunity decisions from courts all over the world are remarkably well documented, most prominently in the International Law Reports and in surveys compiled in preparation of codification efforts by international learned bodies. In addition, the availability of extensive scholarly writings in the field of immunity law has proven a valuable starting point for further research in national law reports. For the purposes of this study it is not necessary to relate the specifics of each individual jurisdiction. There will be a focus on those decisions that best illustrate the trends and developments in the field of the respective immunity rules. Thus, if we discuss the rule of state immunity, Belgian, Italian, UK, and US case law warrants special attention since knowledge of the developments in those jurisdictions in particular contributes to a better understanding of the nature and the substance of the international law rule as we know it today.

Also the national and international codifications of international law immunity rules provide valuable insights. This study draws extensively on national immunity laws like the US Foreign Sovereign Immunities Act and the UK State Immunity Act; on international conventions like the Vienna Conventions on Diplomatic and Consular Relations, the Special Missions Convention, and the recent UN Convention on Jurisdictional Immunities of States and their Property; and on the codification efforts undertaken by international learned bodies like the Harvard Research Project, the International Law Commission, the Institut de Droit International, and the International Law Association.

Finally, this study has benefited greatly from the extensive scholarly pondering on the rule of state immunity, the rule of functional immunity and the rule of personal immunity of diplomats and heads of state. The work of scholars like Anzilotti, Brownlie, Cosnard, Crawford, De Sena, and Lauterpacht—to name a few—forms the indispensable basis upon which this study builds.

A conscious choice has been made to allow for lengthy quotations from all of these sources. Many old sources are still widely referred to today—but often these references rely on interpretations of these sources by others rather than on an inquiry into the source itself. Or, we see that courts or scholars are attributed certain ideas detaching quotations from their context. Second, and this reason is less pertinent, it is believed to be the duty of every doctoral researcher—blessed with time to blow dust off old books—to share particularly cutting insights and pointed formulations of scholars or judges that have once mused upon issues that are still relevant today, in order to save them from passing into oblivion.

These sources provide the framework for the critical study of instances of state practice and scholarly thinking regarding our research question, like the *Pinochet*, *Al-Adsani*, *Arrest Warrant*, *Taylor*, and *Jones* cases—to name only the most conspicuous of relevant judicial decisions—the Belgian war crimes legislation, the resolution of the Institut de Droit International on head of state immunity, the US terrorist-state exception to state immunity and so on.

As said, the study commences with an analysis of the nature and substance of the rule of state immunity, the rule of functional immunity, and personal immunity rules. To this end, the first three chapters introduce and unravel the respective immunity concepts—that will, in fact, prove essentially distinct. The aspiration is *not* to give a complete overview of all three immunity rules. The focus is on materials that provide a particular insight into the nature and substance of these rules *or* in the common perception thereof.

Chapter 2 examines the rule of state immunity. The chapter proposes that a reformulation of the rule, in terms of the limits on the essential competence of national courts serves to distinguish the rule of restrictive immunity from the archaic notions of regal dignity and privilege that attach to an absolute approach to the rule.[19] The rule of state immunity reflects the limits on sovereignty—and hence on the competence of national courts—inherent in a legal order consisting

[19] The notion 'absence of essential competence' is borrowed from Brownlie, cf ch 2 § 3.3.1 below.

of entities equal and independent in the exercise of their territorial sovereignty. The realization that the rule of state immunity as we know it today is *not* a continuation of the rule of absolute immunity with some exceptions accepted to it, but that a qualitative difference between the two rules exists has consequences for the form and substance of coherent argument on the scope of the rule. In the first place, it is argued that a purely inductive approach to the formulation of exceptions does not convincingly settle the issue. It is argued that arguments based on logic—or reason—are in fact coherent in *form* and a persuasive rebuttal requires discussion of the merits of these arguments. The restatement of the rule in terms of essential competence however does not only expand the parameters of coherent argument. The *substance* of coherent argument must reflect a thorough understanding of the substance of the rule. In this respect it is also argued that the policy arguments as once developed against the absolute state immunity rule may not be persuasive in respect of the restrictive state immunity rule.

Chapter 3 examines the rule of functional immunity of foreign state officials. It is increasingly common to represent the rule as a corollary of the rule of state immunity *ratione materiae*. State officials are then regarded immune in respect of *sovereign* activity they have performed on behalf of the state in order to prevent that the rule of state immunity could be circumvented by suing the officials that performed the act. The chapter rejects that interpretation of the rule. The rule of functional immunity concerns the non-personal responsibility of state officials for acts of state. It is argued that in this respect 'act of state' is an autonomous concept unrelated to the concept of sovereign act of state that controls the rule of state immunity. The application of the law of state immunity to foreign state officials is only *a consequence* of the operation of the rule of functional immunity. The concept is also not related—as is argued in a second popular interpretation of the rule—to the act of state concept that features in the law of state responsibility. For the purpose of the rule of functional immunity act of state means an act that must be attributed to the state rather than to the individual that performs the act. The proposed approach to the rule and the rejection of the two approaches that currently prevail, offers a new perspective on the substance of coherent argumentation on the scope of the rule. In particular, it establishes that certain developments in the field of international criminal law are *directly* related to the rule.

Chapter 4 examines the personal immunity of foreign diplomatic agents and foreign heads of state.[20] These protected individuals are granted immunity from jurisdiction in the real sense of the word. Coherent arguments on the scope of the rule are therefore—indeed—limited to inductive reasoning on the basis of state practice on these rules. Developments in the field of international criminal law are not directly relevant in this respect. However, forceful policy arguments may be formulated against the rules of personal immunity.

[20] Personal immunities that may apply to foreign military forces are not dealt with in this study.

The restatement of the rules in terms of lack of essential competence, absence of personal responsibility, and immunity from jurisdiction prepares the ground for the examination of the relation between these rules and developments in international human rights law and international criminal law and for the critical discussion of the arguments that presently prevail in the debate on this relation. The essential differences between the three immunity concepts allow a reasoned distinction between the form and substance of arguments on the scope of the rules in chapters 5 and 6.

Chapter 5 examines the relation between the functional and personal immunity of foreign state officials and the obligations of individuals under international law. It is here that the *Pinochet* case and the *Congo v Belgium* case will be discussed in more detail. The chapter will also examine the oft-heard argument that functional and personal immunities from foreign jurisdiction do not apply to *international* courts. The decision of the Special Court for Sierra Leone (SCSL) in *Prosecutor v Taylor* deserves special consideration in this respect.[21]

Chapter 6 inquires into the relation between the immunity of foreign states and its officials and the rights of individuals under international law. Which arguments are convincing in light of our proposed understanding of the rule of state immunity and of the characteristics of international human rights law? How do the majority and minority opinions in the *Al-Adsani* case fare in this respect?

A critical discussion of what by now may be called mainstream human rights doctrine ultimately furthers the position of human rights in international law. The unqualified attack on immunity rules launched by the human rights movement risks casting a shadow over *all* human rights-based arguments against immunity rules. This study attempts to sort the wheat from the chaff.

[21] *Prosecutor v Charles Ghankay Taylor* SCSL–2003–01–I Appeals Chamber Decision on Immunity from Jurisdiction (2004), available at <http://www.sc-sl.org/>.

2

State Immunity

1 Introduction

Academic writing on the law of state immunity is profuse. So why is another examination of the nature and substance of the rule of state immunity, through the discussion of well-known case law and oftquoted scholarly works, thought warranted? The main reason is that the rule suffers from the trees-for-wood phenomenon: scholars and courts alike have tended to focus on the formulation of a workable regime for the application of the restrictive rule of state immunity while its nature and substance as a rule of international law have been steadily disregarded.

The study of the influence of human rights law on immunity rules requires examination of two preliminary questions. The current debate bears the marks of an underdeveloped legal theory as regards these two questions.

The first question that must be addressed is how arguments that immunity is not available when core human rights norms are violated may function in light of the theory of custom ascertainment. Proponents of a human rights exception tend to cast their arguments in terms of logic: in light of the developments in the field of human rights law state immunity *can* no longer be available when certain norms are violated. They argue either that the reasons underlying the rule do not require immunity to be granted, or alternatively that the rule must give way to other, more important rules or principles of international law. Opponents, on the other hand usually argue in a formalistic vein. Since customary international law follows the conjunction of a general state practice supported by *opinio juris sive necesitatis*—the argument of opponents runs—a human rights exception to immunity rules may only develop through the gradual acceptation of such exception in state immunity practice. At first blush the approach of opponents to a human rights exception seems to represent mainstream legal theory on custom formation while proponents seem to resort to a less accepted, objectivist approach to custom ascertainment. However, close consideration of the nature of the rule of state immunity may put the controversy in a different perspective.

The second question regards the substantive parameters of human rights arguments in favour of, and against, immunity rules. When can it be argued that the immunity rules conflict with obligations of states under international human

UNIVERSITY OF GREENWICH LIBRARY

rights and international criminal law? And when can arguments of logic convince in light of the substance of the international law requirements to which these rules give expression? One of the arguments of proponents of a human rights exception to state immunity is that human rights violations cannot qualify as sovereign acts for the purposes of the restrictive state immunity theory. Opponents have pointed out that the exercise of police and military power is an epitome of sovereign state activity and hence squarely covered by the theory. In essence, the controversy centres on the function of the concept of sovereignty in the law of state immunity. To be coherent both state of the law and policy arguments on the scope of the rule of state immunity must evidence a thorough understanding of the substance of the rule. Arguments of opponents *and* proponents fail to convince from this perspective.

The coherency of both the form and substance of arguments in favour of and against the human rights exception has been negatively affected by the common focus on the regime rather than the rationale of the rule in standard immunity doctrine. The purpose of this chapter is to set out the nature and substance of the rule of state immunity in order to identify the tools needed for the development and assessment of arguments in the debate on a human rights exception. In section 2 the argument is developed that the practice of formation of the rule of state immunity together with the common—and related—approach to the formulation of the rule constitute the basis of the current focus on the regime of state immunity rather than on the rule itself. Awareness of the actual circumstances of the formation of the state immunity rule will help to identify some of the premises of its development and will point us to the often-unarticulated anachronisms that still haunt the rule today. The discussion of the rule is dominated by Latin phrases like *par in parem non habet imperium*, immunity *rationae personae* versus immunity *ratione materiae*, and most importantly *acta jure imperii* versus *acta jure gestionis*. These formulas have enchanted courts and scholars alike, and although they do indeed all have some bearing on the rule, their automatic, uncritical and often misplaced restatement has prevented further examination of the foundation of the state immunity concept. 'A page of history is worth a volume of logic',[1] will prove a maxim apposite to the study of the state immunity rule. Only after untangling the web of state immunity cases and doctrine can an attempt be made to reconstruct the concept in terms of requirements imposed by international law.

In section 3 it will be argued that the rule of restrictive state immunity is essentially unrelated to the rule of absolute state immunity as it was once applied in several jurisdictions and that a qualitative difference between the two rules exists. Building on the work of the handful of scholars that recognized the flaws of conventional immunity thinking, it will be argued that in substance the state immunity rule reflects the operation of several principles of international law regarding

[1] Holmes J in *NY Trust Co v Eisner* 256 US 345 (US, S Ct, 1921) 349.

the essential competence of national courts. The rule of state immunity, as we know it today, is inherent in an international legal order consisting of states that are equal in status and independent in their exercise of state power over a certain territory. The conception of state immunity as a sort of necessary principle of the international legal order rather than an ordinary rule of customary international law has consequences for both the form and substance of arguments in the debate on the human rights exception.

2 The Rule of Restrictive State Immunity

2.1 Introduction

The origins of the modern rule of state immunity from foreign jurisdiction are commonly traced to the early nineteenth century. The 1812 decision of the US Supreme Court in the case of *The Schooner Exchange v M'Faddon*[2] is generally held to be the first judicial expression of the rule of foreign state immunity. On 30 December 1810 the French navy forcibly seized the schooner *Exchange*, a ship privately owned by US nationals and on its way from the United States to the Continent. The ship was taken to France, where it was turned into a French warship and renamed the *Balaou*. When in August of the next year the *Balaou*, under stress of bad weather, made a stop into the port of Philadelphia, the original owners of the vessel, John M'Faddon and his partner, filed a claim before a US court, asserting their right of property. Their claim was dismissed on immunity grounds, and the following words of Chief Justice Marshall have since then been quoted in virtually every treatise on state immunity:

> One sovereign being in no respect amenable to another, and being bound by obligations of the highest character not to degrade the dignity of his nation, by placing himself or its sovereign rights within the jurisdiction of another, can be supposed to enter a sovereign territory only under an express licence, or in the confidence that the immunities belonging to his independent sovereign status, though not expressly stipulated, are reserved by implication, and will be extended to him.[3]

Of course, kings, princes and the like had been shielded from foreign jurisdiction before. *The Schooner Exchange* was seen to confirm that the recognition of the existence of the sovereignty of the state as an abstract entity, separate and independent from the sovereignty from its personal ruler, entailed the development of an immunity concept shielding that artificial legal concept 'state' from foreign jurisdiction as well.[4]

[2] *The Schooner Exchange v M'Faddon* 11 US 116 (US, S Ct, 1812).

[3] ibid 137.

[4] Early literature on international law did not mention the concept of immunity of foreign states only that of personal immunity of diplomats and foreign sovereigns. Cf A Gentili, *De Legationibus*

The study of the development of the state immunity rule from its inception in the nineteenth century until the gradual but distinct prevalence of the restrictive theory of state immunity since the second half of the twentieth century provides valuable insights for the understanding of the rule as we know it today. The foreign state immunity doctrine is often depicted as having developed from an absolute rule, categorically precluding national courts from exercising jurisdiction over foreign states, to a restrictive rule that allows the exercise of jurisdiction under certain circumstances.[5] An examination of early foreign state immunity decisions however does not confirm this. The development of the state immunity rule is more complex than cursory consideration leads us to think.

Many states indeed accepted the theory of absolute state immunity at one point in time. The French *Cour de cassation*, for example, formulated an absolute foreign state immunity rule as early as 1849. It refused to engage in a claim brought by a French company against Spain with regard to the purchase of boots for the Spanish army considering that a government cannot be subjected to the jurisdiction of a foreign state in respect of its contractual obligations.[6]

The theory of restrictive immunity was however already adhered to by Italy and Belgium in the nineteenth century and adopted by several other states not long thereafter. Are these early developments but a temporary and insignificant deviation from the otherwise general and consistent acceptance of the absolute immunity rule; or should it be concluded that international law has never required national courts to grant an absolute immunity to foreign states? It will be argued in this study that early restrictive immunity practice, viewed together with the less than convinced application of the absolute immunity rule in early US and UK practice, compel reconsideration of the common theory on the development of the law of state immunity.

This conclusion is important for the next step in the argumentation developed in this section. The rule of restrictive state immunity is now widely accepted but little understood. Scholars and courts alike have focused on a practicable regime and commonly skirt important questions as to the theoretical basis of the rule. In particular, the rule of restrictive state immunity is presented as the continuation of the old absolute rule with a list of exceptions attached to it. The section will conclude with a proposal to rethink the nature and substance of the law of state immunity as we know it today.

Libri Tres (1594), ch XVI; H Grotius, *De Jure Belli ac Pacis* (1625) trans by LR Loomis (1949), ch XVIII s IV; C Van Bynkershoek, *De Foro Legatorum Liber Singularis* (1721), trans by GJ Laing (1946), ch XIII for diplomatic immunity and Van Bynkershoek ch IV and V; E De Vattel, *Le droit de gens ou principes de la loi naturelle, appliqués à la conduite & aux affaires des nations & des souverains* (1758) iii trans by CG Fenwick (*The Law of Nations*, 1983), liv IV ch VII for personal foreign sovereign immunity.

[5] Cf eg R Higgins, *Problems & Process, International Law and How We Use It* (1994) 79; R Jennings and A Watts (eds), *Oppenheim's International Law* (9th edn, 1992) i 355–63.

[6] *Gouvernement Espagnol v Casaux* Sirey 1849, Part I, 81 (France, Cour de cassation, 1849).

2.2 Development of the Rule of Restrictive State Immunity

2.2.1 Early Restrictive Tendencies

In the nineteenth century Belgium and Italy refused to grant foreign states absolute immunity from the jurisdiction of their courts.[7] The restrictive approach to state immunity proved, however, not to be an isolated Belgian and Italian caprice; it gained gradual though steady support in other jurisdictions as well. Already in 1933 Allen found, after a thorough examination of the judicial practice on foreign state immunity in several states, that

> a growing number of courts are restricting the immunity to instances in which the state has acted in its official capacity as a sovereign political entity. The current idea that this distinction is peculiar to Belgium and Italy must be enlarged to include Switzerland, Egypt, Roumania, France, Austria and Greece.[8]

Although this unequivocal statement disregards the subtleties of reality—for one, the situation before French courts was more complex than this[9]—the general idea it conveys of a spreading of Belgian and Italian practice to other jurisdictions at an early stage already, is accurate. The considerations of a Romanian court in the 1920 case of *Banque roumaine de commerce v État polonais*, for example, can indeed be seen to echo many of the views developed in the case law of the two harbinger states. The court held as follows:

> Considérant que tout État doit être considéré sous deux aspects comme conséquence de ses besoins et de ses obligations: (a) l'État qui fait des actes publics, des actes de souveraineté, de gouvernement, *jure imperii*, conséquence des besoins politiques et (b) l'État qui fait des actes civils, des actes de gestion, achète, vend, fait toute espèce de transactions *jure privato* comme conséquence des grandes attributions et des exigences de l'État moderne, cette dernière activité ayant pour effet que l'État ne se distingue pas d'un particulier; le critérium de la distinction de tels actes étant de les considérer d'après leur nature et non d'après le but qu'ils poursuivent.[10]

[7] Cf for Belgium, *L'Etat du Pérou v Kreglinger* PB 1857–2–348 (Tribunal de commerce d'Anvers and Cour de Bruxelles, 1857); *Rau, Vanden Abeele et Cie v Duruty* PB 1879–2–175 (Commercial Tribunal Ostend, 1879); *SA des Chemins de Fer liégeois-luxembourgeouis v l'Etat néerlandais* PB 1903–I–294 (Cour de cassation, 1903). For Italy cf *Morellet v Governo Danese* Giu It 1883–I–125 (Corte di Cassazione di Torino, 1882); *Guttieres v Elmilik* 11 F It 1886–I–913 (Corte di Cassazione di Firenze, 1886); *Typaldos, Console di Grecia a Napoli v Manicomio di Aversa* Giu It 1886–I–1–222 (Corte di Cassazione di Napoli, 1886). Belgian courts have applied absolute immunity in a few exceptional cases. See P De Visscher and J Verhoeven, 'L'immunité de juridiction de l'État étranger dans la jurisprudence belge et le projet de convention du Conseil de l'Europe', in *L'immunité de juridiction et d'exécution des Etats* (1969) 37, 38. Cf also EW Allen, *The Position of Foreign States before Belgian Courts* (1929) 221.

[8] EW Allen (1933) 301.

[9] M Cosnard, *La soumission des États aux tribunaux internes: Face à la théorie des immunités des États* (1996) 22. Dutch judicial practice was equally inconsistent, see H Lauterpacht (1951) 263.

[10] *Banque roumaine de commerce et de crédit de Prague v État polonais* (1924) 19 RDIP 581 (Romania, Tribunal de commerce d'Ilfov, 1920) 582–3.

Lauterpacht, in his seminal critique of the absolute doctrine of immunity, attached particular importance to the early and consistent acceptance of the restrictive theory by the Mixed Courts of Egypt because of their international composition.[11] The Egyptian case of *Monopole des Tabacs de Turquie v Régie Co-Intéressée des Tabacs de Turquie* exemplifies the gradual spreading of the ideas first developed in Italian and Belgian courts. The court in this case ruled that

> The jurisprudence of the Mixed Courts (like the jurisprudence of the Italian and Belgian Courts) is fixed in this sense, that immunity applies only to acts of sovereignty and does not apply to acts of management (*actes de gestion*) as to which the foreign State has brought its activities into the field of private rights.[12]

The question of the scope of foreign state immunity was a controversial subject in academic writings at the end of the nineteenth and beginning of the twentieth century. While eminent scholars like Anzilotti and Van Praag continued their support of the rule of absolute state immunity, a growing group of scholars—including Weiss and De Visscher—favoured a restrictive approach to the rule.[13]

Finally, it should be noted that at a very early stage, the restrictive theory was reflected in scholarly efforts to codify the immunity rule. In the 1891 Resolution of the Institut de Droit International certain proceedings against foreign states were declared admissible. *Inter alia*, courts were held to have jurisdiction regarding actions connected with a commercial or industrial establishment or railway exploited in the territory of the forum state; actions arising out of contracts concluded within that territory and actions for damages for a tort or quasi-tort there committed.[14] Also the report on the 'Competence of Courts in Regard to

[11] H Lauterpacht (1951) 255.

[12] *Monopole des Tabacs de Turquie and Another v Régie Co-Intéressée des Tabacs de Turquie* 5 AD 123, case no 79 (Egypt, Mixed CA, 1930) 124. See for other Egyptian cases S Sucharitkul, 'Immunities of Foreign States before National Authorities' (1976–I) 149 RdC 87, 137; H Lauterpacht (1951) 255; JY Brinton, 'Suits against Foreign States', (1931) 25 AJIL 50.

[13] Cf for support of the rule of absolute immunity a.o.: L Van Praag, *Juridiction et droit international public, La juridiction nationale d'après droit international public coutumier en temps de paix* (1915); D Anzilotti, 'L'esenzione degli stati stranieri dalla giurisdizione' (1910) 5 RDI 477; A Chrétien, *Principes de droit international public* (1893) i 247; E Loening, *Die Gerichtsbarkeit über fremde Staaten und Souveräne* (1903); E Nys, *Le droit international: les principes, les théories, les faits* (1904) ii 340 ; J De Louter, *Het stellig volkenrecht* (1910) i 246–7; R Provinciali, *L'immunità giurisdizionale degli stati stranieri* (1933). And for support for the rule of restrictive immunity a.o.: P Pradier-Fodéré, *Traité de droit international public européen et américain suivant les progrès de la science et de la pratique contemporaines* (1906) iii no 1589; A Weiss, *Traité élémentaire de droit international privé* (1886) v 94; A Weiss, 'Compétence ou incompétence des tribunaux à l'égard des États étrangers' (1923–I) 1 RdC 521, 536ff; L Von Bar, *The Theory and Practice of Private International Law* (2nd edn, 1892, trans by GR Gillespie); P Fiore, *Nouveau droit international public suivant les besoins de la civilisation moderne* (1869, trans by P Pradier-Fodéré) i no 514; C De Visscher, 'Les Gouvernements étrangers en justice, Reconnaissance internationale et immunités' (1922) 49 RDILC 300; N Wolfman, 'Sovereigns as Defendants' (1910) 4 AJIL 373.

[14] Institut de Droit International, Projet de règlement international sur la compétence des tribunaux dans les procès contre les Etats, souverains où chefs d'Etat étrangers (1891), (1889–92) 11 AIDI. Cf also League of Nations, Committee of Experts for the Progressive Codification of International Law, Questionnaire no 11, 'Competence of the Courts in Regard to Foreign States',

Foreign States' published by the Harvard Research Project in International Law in 1932—while acknowledging that many of the suggested rules were *de lege ferenda*—proposed a restrictive approach to the state immunity rule. The nucleus of the report can be found in article 11 that provides as follows:

> A State may be made a respondent in a proceeding in a court of another State when, in the territory of such other State, it engages in an industrial, commercial, financial, or other business enterprise in which private persons may there engage, or does an act there in connection with such an enterprise wherever conducted, and the proceeding is based upon the conduct of such enterprise or upon such an act.[15]

The 1926 Brussels Convention for the Unification of Certain Rules concerning the Immunity of State-Owned Ships assimilated the position of state-owned vessels engaged in trading activities to that of privately-owned merchant vessels.[16] Article 3 makes an exception for

> ships of war, Government yachts, patrol vessels, hospital ships, auxiliary vessels, supply ships and other craft owned and operated by the State, and used at the time a cause of action arises exclusively on Governmental and non-commercial service, and such vessels shall not be subject to seizure, attachment or detention by any legal process, nor to judicial proceedings *in rem*.

The convention received only 13 ratifications. It has however been used as a model for a number of bilateral treaties and its substantive provisions have in fact been applied by states not party to it.[17] Moreover, the mere adoption of the draft convention by the Brussels Conference on Maritime Law in 1926 evinces that the restrictive theory was not confined to the practice of a limited number of dissident states and academic theory only, but was seriously discussed, and adopted—albeit not finally ratified—in a body consisting of state representatives.

2.2.2 Prevalence of the Restrictive Doctrine

The idea that states can, under certain circumstances, be subjected to foreign jurisdiction gained ground rapidly in the second half of the twentieth century. It is the 1950 Austrian case of *Dralle v Republic of Czechoslovakia* that is commonly

Report of the Sub-Committee (Rapporteur Matsuda) (1927), (1928 special supplement) 22 AJIL 117. The report recognized the existence of two conflicting views on the issue of the immunity of foreign states acting in a private capacity (at 119). Although the report tended to favour the restrictive approach, Matsuda emphasized that 'it would be difficult to formulate any definite or precise conclusion which could be used as the basis for a uniform arrangement to be concluded between the Powers' (at 125)—an observation not shared by commission member G Diena, 128–32.

[15] Harvard Law School, Research in International Law (Reporter PC Jessup), Competence of Courts in Regard to Foreign States, (1932 supplement) 26 AJIL 451, 597. The article knows the following caveat: 'The foregoing provision shall not be construed to allow a State to be made a respondent in a proceeding relating to its public debt.'

[16] See a.o. GM Badr, *State Immunity: An Analytical and Prognostic View* (1984) 41.

[17] I Sinclair, 'The Law of Sovereign Immunity, Recent Developments' (1980–II) 167 RdC 113, 139.

hailed as the landmark of a new era. The Supreme Court, after a careful examination of the practice of various other states, famously stated that

> [t]his survey shows that today it can no longer be said that jurisprudence generally recognises the principle of exemption of foreign States in so far as concerns claims of a private character, because the majority of courts of different civilized countries deny the immunity of a foreign State, and more particularly because exceptions are made even in those countries which today still adhere to the traditional principle that no State is entitled to exercise jurisdiction over another State... [18]

The court further stated that

> [t]he classic doctrine of immunity arose at a time when all the commercial activities of States in foreign countries were connected with their political activities... Today, the position is entirely different; States engage in commercial activities and enter into competition with their own nationals and foreigners. Accordingly, the classic doctrine of immunity has lost its meaning and *ratione cessante*, can no longer be recognized as a rule of international law.[19]

This observation critically bares the immediate circumstances that gave rise to the rapid spreading of the restrictive theory at the time. The rise of state trading and the consequent increase of commercial disputes between states and individuals made the impossibility of holding foreign states accountable in domestic proceedings an acute problem. Higgins appositely noted in this respect that '[t]he developments in State immunity have been a self-generated response to the requirements of the contemporary commercial world and to notions of stability and equity in the market place.'[20]

The conversion of the common law countries to the restrictive approach was a long time coming. The United States—enacting the Foreign Sovereign Immunities Act in 1976—was the first to codify the restrictive immunity rule in national legislation.[21] Before that time US courts had commonly deferred to the State Department in state immunity questions. Although the State Department had in the 1952 Tate Letter expressed its intention to issue its suggestions as regards immunity requests of foreign states on the basis of the restrictive doctrine, the implementation of that intent left something to be desired—to say the least—and it was not until the 1976 Foreign Sovereign Immunities Act that the doctrine was recognized as a rule of international law to be applied independently by the courts. The US example was followed by the UK,[22] Singapore,[23]

[18] *Dralle v Republic of Czechoslovakia* 17 ILR 155 (Austria, S Ct, 1950) 161.

[19] ibid 163.

[20] R Higgins, 'Certain Unresolved Aspects of the Law of State Immunity' (1982) 29 NILR 265, 265.

[21] US, Foreign Sovereign Immunities Act 1976, Public Law 94–583, 90 Stat. 2891, reproduced in (1976) 15 ILM 1388.

[22] UK, State Immunity Act 1978, reproduced in (1978) 17 ILM 1123.

[23] Singapore, State Immunity Act 1979, reproduced in UN–Materials ST/LEG/SER.B.20, 28.

Pakistan,[24] South Africa,[25] Canada,[26] Australia,[27] and Argentina,[28] while the courts of New Zealand,[29] Zimbabwe,[30] Kenya,[31] and Ireland[32] have applied the restrictive theory in the absence of guidance by the legislature.[33]

The practice in India deserves separate mention. Section 86.1 of the Code of Civil Procedure provides that '[n]o Ruler of a foreign state may be sued in any court otherwise competent to try the suit except without the consent of the Central Government certified in writing by the Secretary of State'—and this provision has been interpreted to apply to proceedings against foreign states as well.[34] The Supreme Court has admitted in *Mirza Ali Akbar Kashani v United Arab Republic* that 'the effect of s. 86(1) is to modify to a certain extent the doctrine of immunity recognised by International Law'.[35]

At first blush, it may seem that the executive has full discretion in the matter. Indian courts do however exercise a certain degree of control on the reasonableness of the executive decision in specific cases. The case of *Harbhajan Singh Dhalla v Union of India* concerned a complaint by an Indian citizen who had failed to obtain permission to sue Algeria with regard to unsettled bills in respect of maintenance work undertaken by him at the Algerian Embassy and the residence of the Algerian ambassador.[36] The court, after a critical discussion of the

[24] Pakistan, State Immunity Ordinance 1981, reproduced in UN–Materials ST/LEG/SER.B.20, 20.

[25] South Africa, Foreign States Immunity Act 1981, reproduced in UN–Materials ST/LEG/SER.B/20, 34.

[26] Canada, State Immunity Act 1982, reproduced in (1982) 21 ILM 798.

[27] Australia, Foreign Sovereign Immunities Act 1985, reproduced in (1986) 25 ILM 715.

[28] Argentina, La Ley 24.488, Immunidad Jurisdiccional de los Estados Extranjeros ante los Tribunalos Argentinos (1995), reproduced in A Dickinson, R Lindsay and JP Loonan (eds), *State Immunity, Selected Materials and Commentary* (2004).

[29] *Governor of Pitcairn Islands v Sutton* [1995] 1 NZLR 426 (New Zealand, CA, 1994); 104 ILR 509.

[30] *Barker McCormac (Private) Ltd v Government of Kenya* 84 ILR 18 (Zimbabwe, S Ct, 1983).

[31] *Minister of Defence of Government of the United Kingdom v Joel Ndegwa*, 103 ILR 235 (Kenya, CA, 1983).

[32] *Government of Canada v The Employment Appeals Tribunal and Burke* 95 ILR 467 (Ireland, S Ct, 1992).

[33] Several courts have moreover declared that the restrictive theory applied *regardless* of the national legislation, cf eg *I Congreso del Partido* [1983] 1 AC 244 (UK, HL, 1981); *Inter-Science Research and Development Services Ltd v Republica Popular of Moçambique* 64 ILR 689 (South Africa, S Ct Transvaal Provincial Division, 1979); *Kaffraria Property Co v Government of the Republic of Zambia* United Nations, Materials on Jurisdictional Immunities of States and their Property (1982), ST/LEG/SER.B/20 (South Africa, S Ct Eastern Cape Division, 1980); *Zodiak International Products Inc v Polish People's Republic* 64 ILR 51 (Canada, Quebec CA, 1977); *Government of the Democratic Republic of the Congo v Venne* 64 ILR 24 (Canada, S Ct, 1972); *Ferranti-Packard Ltd v Cushman Rentals Ltd* 64 ILR 63 (Canada, Ontario High Court of Justice, 1980); *Re Royal Bank of Canada and Corriveau et al* 64 ILR 69 (Canada, Ontario High Court, 1980); *Amanat-Khan v Fredson Travel Int (No 2)* 64 ILR 734 (Canada, High Court of Ontario, 1982); *Qureshi v Union of Soviet Socialist Republics* 64 ILR 585 (Pakistan, S Ct, 1981).

[34] *Mirza Ali Akbar Kashani v United Arab Republic* 64 ILR 489 (India, S Ct, 1965).

[35] ibid 502.

[36] *Harbhajan Singh Dhalla v Union of India* 92 ILR 530 (India, S Ct, 1986).

old absolute immunity concept based on the dignity of the state, proceeds to an assessment of both the nature of the claim of the individual as well as the decision of the executive to refuse permission to subject the foreign state to judicial scrutiny in respect of that claim. The individual, the court reasoned, has a constitutional right to carry on his business and carry on trade and the claim presented to the executive was not frivolous. In cases like this, it continued, it is difficult to see what the reasons for refusal could be since the exercise of jurisdiction 'would be in conformity with the principles of international law as recognised as part of our domestic law and in accordance with our Constitution and human rights, the power given to the central Government must not be exercised arbitrarily or on whimsical grounds but upon proper reasons and grounds'. The court added that such exercise of jurisdiction would moreover 'be in consonance with human rights'.[37] In what may be a barely hidden expression of discontent with the Indian situation the court emphasized that assessment of immunity questions is not normally a power of governments but of courts. This power, the court stressed 'must be exercised in accordance with the principles of natural justice and in consonance with the principles of natural justice and in consonance with the principle that reasons must appear from the order.'[38] Thus, the power of the Indian executive in state immunity matters is practically reduced to a paper tiger.

The prevalence of the restrictive approach is reflected in several conventions and the work of international learned bodies. The European Convention on State Immunity 1972, for long the only comprehensive multilateral instrument in force dealing with state immunity, is based on a restrictive approach to the rule,[39] as is the UN Convention on Jurisdictional Immunities of States and their Property that opened for ratification in January 2005.[40] A similar approach is found in several draft conventions and resolutions on state immunity, like the Inter-American Draft Convention on Jurisdictional Immunity of States,[41] the Resolution on State Immunity of the Institut de Droit International,[42] the International Law Association's Draft Articles for a Convention on State Immunity,[43] and the

[37] ibid 536–7.

[38] ibid 538.

[39] European Convention on State Immunity and Additional Protocol (1972), reproduced in (1972) 11 ILM 470. The Convention entered in force on 11 June 1976 and is, at the time of writing this study, ratified by a mere eight states.

[40] UN Convention on Jurisdictional Immunities of States and their Property (2004), adopted by GA Resolution 59/38 (2004) based on the ILC Draft Articles mentioned in n 44 below.

[41] Inter-American Judicial Committee, Draft Convention on Jurisdictional Immunity of States (1983).

[42] Institut de Droit International, Resolution on Contemporary Problems Concerning the Jurisdictional Immunity of States (1992), (1992) 64–II AIDI 267.

[43] International Law Association, Draft Articles for a Convention on State Immunity Report of the Sixtieth Conference (1982), 5ff and 325ff as revised by the Final Report on Developments in the Field of State Immunity and Proposal for a Revised Draft Convention on State Immunity for the ILA Buenos Aires Conference in 1994, Report of the Sixty-sixth Conference (1994) 452ff.

International Law Commission's Draft Articles on Jurisdictional Immunities of States and their Property.[44]

Residues of the rule of absolute state immunity are still found in several legal systems—with Russia and China as conspicuous examples.[45] However, with the large majority of states accepting the rule of restrictive state immunity it clearly can not be said that international law requires states to grant other states immunity from their jurisdiction under *all* circumstances. As the German *Bundesverfassungsgericht* aptly put it in the 1963 *Claim against the Empire of Iran* case:

> From the practice of the courts it can no longer be deduced... that the granting of unrestricted immunity can still today be regarded as a usage followed by the great majority of States in the belief that it is legally obligatory.[46]

The application of the restrictive theory in practice is far from uniform. The demarcation problems in the application of the restrictive rule are troublesome not only for courts in practice but also—as we will see below—for the development of a cogent theory. Yet the fact that international law clearly requires states to grant such immunity in *some* cases but not in others allows the conclusion that *a* restrictive rule of foreign state immunity prevails.[47]

So how must the early Belgian and Italian case law that heralded the contours of an immunity concept, as it was to eventually prevail, be interpreted? Did these states at the time dissent from an otherwise widely accepted and firmly established rule of absolute state immunity? In 1925 an Italian court asserted that they did not. The court noted that the restrictive immunity rule applied by Italian courts did not violate a rule of international law since the discord between the judicial authorities of various states should be seen to demonstrate that a generally recognized and binding norm was lacking.[48] The view that international law never did require states to grant other states an absolute immunity from their adjudicative

[44] International Law Commission, ILC Draft Articles on Jurisdictional Immunities of States and their Property (1991), YBILC 1991 ii (part two) 13.

[45] Cf also *Kramer Italo Limited v Government of Kingdom of Belgium; Embassy of Belgium* 103 ILR 299 (Nigeria, CA, 1988). In Japan the absolute immunity rule was established in the 1928 *Matsuyama v Republic of China* case (4 AD 168, Great Court of Judicature). Only very recently Japanese courts have started indicating support for the restrictive approach to the rule, see especially *Yamaguchi v United States* (S Ct, 2002), discussed by M. Tomonori, 'Case Note on *Yamagughi v United States*' (2003) 97 AJIL 406. Cf Y Iwasawa, 'Japan's Interactions with International Law: The Case of State Immunity' in N Ando (ed), *Japan and International Law: Past, Present and Future* (1999) 123.

[46] *Claim against the Empire of Iran Case* 45 ILR 57 (Federal Republic of Germany, Federal Constitutional Court, 1963) 73.

[47] Cf H Fox, *The Law of State Immunity* (2002) 257; I Pingel-Lenuzza, *Les immunités des Etats en droit international* (1997) 359; M Cosnard (1996) 24.

[48] *Governo Francese v Serra* and *C v Ceretti ed altri* (1925) 17 RDI 540 (Italy, Appello Genova, 1925) 543.

jurisdiction finds more and more support in doctrine.[49] A closer look at the early case law in the United States and the United Kingdom further corroborates this view. The first hundred fifty years of state immunity practice in these countries is muddled by a mix up of distinct immunity concepts, the influence of constitutional principles regarding the separation of powers, and the disabling grip of the *stare decisis* rule.

2.2.3 A Closer Look at Early Absolute Tendencies

A brief discussion of the development of the absolute immunity rule in two conspicuously relevant states, the United States—where the rule allegedly originates—and the United Kingdom—where the rule proved particularly impervious to changing socio-economic circumstances—qualifies the persistent idea that the common law resolutely embraced the absolute state immunity rule from the beginning of the nineteenth century onwards. No attempt is made to give a full overview of the intricate history of US and UK state immunity jurisprudence. Only those cases have been selected that allow a sketch of some of the features that characterized the development of the rule in those countries.

2.2.3.1 The United States

The 1926 decision of the US Supreme Court in *Berizzi Bros v SS Pesaro*, upholding the immunity of a trading vessel owned by the Italian government, cited *The Schooner Exchange v M'Faddon* as precedent for the theory of absolute immunity of foreign states from the jurisdiction of US courts.[50] The court held that the principles laid down in *The Schooner Exchange*

> are applicable alike to all ships held and used by a government for a public purpose…when, for the purpose of advancing the trade of its people or providing revenue for its treasury, a government acquires, mans, and operates ships in the carrying trade, they are public ships in the same sense that warships are.[51]

The reference to the public purpose of the activities the *Pesaro* was engaged in should not be seen as a serious qualification of the absolute theory since it was held that

> there is no international usage which regards the maintenance and advancement of the economic welfare of a people in time of peace as any less a public purpose than the maintenance and training of a naval force.[52]

[49] See eg I Pingel-Lenuzza (1997) 135; M Byers, 'Al-Adsani v. Government of Kuwait and Others' (1996) 67 BYIL 537; OJ Lissitzyn, 'Sovereign Immunity as a Norm of International Law' in *Essays in Honour of Philip Jessup* (1972) 188, 190; H Steinberger, 'Zur Rechtsprechung des Bundesverfassungsgerichts zu Fragen der Immunität fremder Staaten' in B Börner, H Jahrreiß, K Stern (eds), *Einigkeit und Recht und Freiheit: Festschrift für Karl Carstens* (1984) ii 889, 901.

[50] *Berizzi Bros v SS Pesaro* 271 US 562 (US, S Ct, 1926).

[51] ibid 574.

[52] ibid.

The fact that the *Pesaro* was a merchant vessel engaged in the common carriage of merchandise for hire—like olive oil and silk—corroborates the trivial nature of the qualification. The reliance on *The Schooner Exchange* in *Berizzi Bros* has haunted the 1812 decision of the Supreme Court ever since: the roots of the absolute immunity doctrine are often traced back to it.[53]

This interpretation of *The Schooner Exchange* provides the absolute theory with a more solid basis than it actually has. The facts of this illustrious case were recapitulated in the introduction to this section. It is thought time that the two or three passages of *The Schooner Exchange* that are still widely quoted as the earliest expressions of the rule of state immunity, are considered within the broader context of Chief Justice Marshall's argumentation. In fact, the reasoning employed to support the non-exercise of jurisdiction was more akin to the theory underlying diplomatic immunity, foreign head of state immunity, and the immunity of foreign armed forces when present on the territory of the forum state, or to the rule of immunity from execution, than to a more principled rule of non-exercise of jurisdiction over disputes involving foreign state defendants. Moreover, it can be questioned whether even within the limited context of *in rem* admiralty proceedings the case forms a solid precedent for an absolute immunity of all ships in possession of foreign states.

The case concerned an action *in rem* against property in possession of the French sovereign that had entered the territorial jurisdiction of the United States. Marshall emphasized that

> [t]he jurisdiction of the nation within its own territory is necessarily exclusive and absolute. It is susceptible of no limitation not imposed by itself. Any restriction upon it, deriving validity from an external source, would imply a diminution of its sovereignty to the extent of the restriction, and an investment of that sovereignty to the same extent in that power which could impose such restriction. All exceptions, therefore, to the full and complete power of a nation within its own territories, must be traced up to the consent of the nation itself. They can flow from no other legitimate source.[54]

States, however, have agreed to restrict the exercise of their territorial jurisdiction under several circumstances. As Marshall formulated it:

> The world being composed of distinct sovereignties, possessing equal rights and equal independence, whose mutual benefit is promoted by intercourse with each other, and by an interchange of those good offices which humanity dictates and its wants require, all sovereigns have consented to a relaxation in practice, in cases under certain peculiar circumstances, of that absolute and complete jurisdiction within their respective territories which sovereignty confers....

[53] See K C Randall, *Federal Courts and the International Human Rights Paradigm* (1990) 91; J W Dellapenna, *Suing Foreign Governments and their Corporations* (1988) 3, fn 12; *Doe v United States* 860 F. 2d 40 (US, Ct of Apps (2nd Cir), 1988) 44. Cf also C De Visscher (1922) 312.

[54] *The Schooner Exchange v M'Faddon* (US, 1812) 136.

This full and absolute territorial jurisdiction being alike the attribute of every sovereign, and being incapable of conferring extra-territorial power, would not seem to contemplate foreign sovereigns nor their sovereign rights as its objects. One sovereign being in no respect amenable to another; and being bound by obligations of the highest character not to degrade the dignity of his nation, by placing himself or its sovereign rights within the jurisdiction of another, can be supposed to enter a foreign territory only under an express license, or in the confidence that the immunities belonging to his independent sovereign station [*sic*], though not expressly stipulated, are reserved by implication, and will be extended to him. This perfect equality and absolute independence of sovereigns, and this common interest impelling them to mutual intercourse, and an interchange of good offices with each other, have given rise to a class of cases in which every sovereign is understood to waive the exercise of a part of that complete exclusive territorial jurisdiction, which has been stated to be the attribute of every nation.[55]

Marshall identified the immunity of diplomats, personal sovereigns and armed forces that are admitted to the territory of a foreign state as such exceptions to the normal exercise of territorial jurisdiction. The entry into US territory of a foreign warship, he argued, should equally be assumed to occur in confidence that immunity attaches to it. Vattel wrote that

[i]t is impossible to conceive... that a prince who sends an ambassador or any other minister can have any intention of subjecting him to the authority of a foreign power; and this consideration furnishes an additional argument, which completely establishes the independency of a public minister. If it cannot be reasonably presumed that his sovereign means to subject him to the authority of the prince to whom he is sent, the latter, in receiving the minister, consents to admit him on the footing of independency; and thus there exists between the two princes a tacit convention, which gives a new force to the natural obligation.[56]

Marshall considered that it is

[e]qually impossible... to conceive, whatever may be the construction as to private ships, that a prince who stipulates a passage for his troops, or an asylum for his ships of war in distress, should mean to subject his army or his navy to the jurisdiction of a foreign sovereign. And if this cannot be presumed, the sovereign of the port must be considered as having conceded the privilege to the extent in which it must have been understood to be asked.[57]

In this respect, Marshall argued, public armed ships must be clearly distinguished from private trading vessels entering foreign territory. He explained that

[w]hen private individuals of one nation spread themselves through another as business or caprice may direct, mingling indiscriminately with the inhabitants of that other, or

[55] ibid 136–7.

[56] Quoted ibid 143 (the quotation is taken and translated from *Le droit de gens ou principes de la loi naturelle, appliqués à la conduite & aux affaires des nations & des souverains* (1758), Book IV, Ch VII, § 92).

[57] ibid.

when merchant vessels enter for the purposes of trade, it would be obviously inconvenient and dangerous to society, and would subject the laws to continual infraction, and the government to degradation, if such individuals or merchants did not owe temporary and local allegiance, and were not amenable to the jurisdiction of the country. Nor can the foreign sovereign have any motive for wishing such exemption. His subjects thus passing into foreign countries, are not employed by him, nor are they engaged in national pursuits. Consequently there are powerful motives for not exempting persons of this description from the jurisdiction of the country in which they are found, and no one motive for requiring it.... But in all respects different is the situation of a public armed ship. She constitutes a part of the military force of her nation; acts under the immediate and direct command of the sovereign; is employed by him in national objects. He has many and powerful motives for preventing those objects from being defeated by the interference of a foreign state. Such interference cannot take place without affecting his power and his dignity. The implied license, therefore, under which such vessel enters a friendly port, may reasonably be construed, and it seems to the court, ought to be construed, as containing an exemption from the jurisdiction of the sovereign, within whose territory she claims the rights of hospitality.[58]

It is important to note that the distinction between ships of war and private ships conceded in the judgment is not indicative of a preference of the restrictive over the absolute immunity theory. Marshall did discuss—though not explicitly approve—the arguments of Van Bynkershoek as regards the private property of foreign princes. The judge considered that

there is a manifest distinction between the private property of the person who happens to be a prince, and that military force which supports the sovereign power, and maintains the dignity and the independence of a nation. A prince, by acquiring private property in a foreign country, may possibly be considered as subjecting that property to the territorial jurisdiction; he may be considered as so far laying down the prince, and assuming the character of a private individual; but this he cannot be presumed to do with respect to any portion of that armed force which upholds his crown, and the nation he is entrusted to govern.[59]

However, the distinction between a prince acting (or in the above quotation 'possessing') in his private capacity, rather than in his sovereign capacity does not translate well to the sovereign state as abstract institution. Yet, since the terminology of the public–private distinction *has* shaped the development of the restrictive immunity regime, early case law concerning personal foreign sovereigns may confuse the casual observer. Where the distinction formulated by Van Bynkershoek referred to a tangible and ascertainable reality determining the applicability of immunity rules protecting certain individuals, in the field of state immunity it refers to a normative qualification at the basis of the substance of the rule, hence determining the outcome of its application.

[58] bid 144.

[59] ibid 144–5. It is noted that counsel for France did concede this point, cf 123.

Several commentators have disregarded this difference. A brief excursion into UK practice illustrates the problematic nature of the argument best. In the 1844 case of *Duke of Brunswick v King of Hanover* it was held that

> a foreign sovereign, coming into this country, cannot be made responsible here for an act done in his sovereign character in his own country; whether it be an act right or wrong... the courts of this country cannot sit in judgment upon an act of a sovereign, effected by virtue of his sovereign authority abroad, an act done not as British subject, but supposed to be done in the exercise of his authority vested in him as sovereign

and that the acts under consideration

> could not have been done, and... were not done, in any private character, but were done, whether right or wrong, in the character of the sovereign of a foreign state.[60]

In a similar vein, the capacity in which the acts were committed was held to be decisive in the case of *De Haber v Queen of Portugal*. The court concluded that

> an action cannot be maintained in an English court against a foreign potentate for anything done or omitted to be done by him in his public capacity as representative of the nation of which he is the head... To cite a foreign potentate in a municipal court, for any complaint against him in his public capacity, is contrary to the law of nations and an insult which he is entitled to resent.[61]

In part on the basis of these cases Lewis observed that it

> is of particular interest... that the initial ideas outlined in England at that time, although cast into limbo for a hundred years or so while the common law followed a most unsatisfactory path, getting itself all the while into greater difficulties and not a little disrepute, emerged triumphant only recently, thanks to the radical action of the legislature... Although it had been recognized in the middle of the 19th century that a foreign sovereign enjoyed immunity in respect of his public acts, and was entitled to assert immunity in respect of State property destined to public uses, the position had been reserved in respect of private transactions.[62]

In a similar vein, Marshall's endorsement of the distinction devised by Van Bynkershoek between the private and public character of a prince has been interpreted to reflect support for the restrictive theory of state immunity.[63]

However, we only have to place these judicial considerations in the light of, for example, the French cases of *L'Empereur d'Autriche v Lemaitre* or *Isabelle de Bourbon v Mellerio* to recognize their limited scope.[64] *L'Empereur d'Autriche v*

60 *Duke of Brunswick v King of Hanover* (1848) 2 HLC 1 (UK, HL, 1848) 17 and 18.

61 *The Haber v Queen of Portugal* 17 QB 171 (UK, Court of Queen's Bench, 1851).

62 CJ Lewis, *State and Diplomatic Immunity* (3rd edn, 1990) 16. See for a similar interpretation GM Badr (1984) 15; C De Visscher (1922) 302.

63 Cf eg GM Badr (1984) 10–13.

64 *L'Empereur d'Autriche v Lemaitre* (1874) 1 JDI 32 (France, Cour de Paris, 1872); A-C Kiss, Répertoire de la pratique française en matière de droit international public (1965) iii 269; *Isabelle de Bourbon v Mellerio* (1874) 1 JDI 32 (France, Tribunal Civil de la Seine, 1872); A-C Kiss, Répertoire

Lemaitre concerned a case against the emperor of Austria, as heir of the emperor of Mexico Maximilien, regarding a contract concluded by the latter for the commission of decorations destined to honour persons for their merit to public services. The court refused to exercise jurisdiction since

> il est de principe, à raison de l'indépendance réciproque des Etats, que les tribunaux français n'ont pas juridiction pour juger les engagements contractés par les souverains étrangers agissant comme chefs d'Etat au titre de puissance publique.[65]

In *Isabelle de Bourbon v Mellerio* immunity was refused to the former queen of Spain in a dispute concerning the purchase of jewellery for personal use. The court considered that she would only have enjoyed immunity from French jurisdiction if she had purchased the items 'en sa qualité de personne souveraine et au compte de Trésor espagnol'.[66] Notably, the nature of the act engaged in was irrelevant to the inquiry. Surely the purchase of decorations, or jewellery by a *state*—and hence with state funds—would qualify as a private act under the restrictive theory of state immunity. What are now considered private acts for state immunity purposes could very well qualify as public acts in the public–private distinction applied in cases concerning personal foreign sovereigns.

It is probable that trade engaged in by the state as an abstract entity with profits flowing to the treasury rather than to the private funds of 'the person that happens to be the prince' was not yet a familiar concept. When such an act was at issue clearly the personal sovereign had acted in his personal capacity and for his own benefit.

Also the considerations of Sir Robert Phillimore several decades later, in the 1873 case *The Charkieh* should be viewed in that perspective. He argued that

> [n]o principle of international law, and no decided case, and no dictum of jurists of which I am aware, has gone so far as to authorize a sovereign prince to assume the character of a trader, when it is for his benefit; and when he incurs an obligation to a private subject to throw off, if I may so speak, his disguise, and appear as a sovereign, claiming for his own benefit, and to the injury of a private person, for the first time, all the attributes of his character.[67]

However, the ship in question was owned by the Khedive of Egypt and the profits from the commercial carriage of goods the ship was engaged in, most likely the personal property of the Khedive.

de la pratique française en matière de droit international public (1965) iii 270. Cf also *Petau v Honore de Grimaldi, Prince de Monaco* A-C Kiss, Répertoire de la pratique française en matière de droit international public (1965) iii 269 (France, Cour de Paris, 1810).

65 *L'Empereur d'Autriche v Lemaitre* (1874) 1 JDI 32 (France, Cour de Paris, 1872); A-C Kiss, Répertoire de la pratique française en matière de droit international public (1965) iii 269.

66 *Isabelle de Bourbon v Mellerio* (1874) 1 JDI 32 (France, Tribunal de la Seine, 1872); A-C Kiss, Répertoire de la pratique française en matière de droit international public (1965) iii 270.

67 *The Charkieh* LR 4A & E 59 (UK, High Court of Admiralty, 1873) 99. It has to be noted though that the case was principally decided on the grounds that the status of the defendant did not entitle him to claim immunity in the first place.

Coming back to our discussion of *The Schooner Exchange v M'Faddon* it is noted that the notion of a merchant ship employed by a foreign sovereign *state* seems alien to the decision in *The Schooner Exchange*. Chief Justice Marshall steered his argumentation around the immunity of this latter category—whether this is the result of clever navigation or oblivion as to the prickliness of the issue remains unclear.

Some commentators have held that because the governing principle of *The Schooner Exchange* was the full jurisdiction of the territorial state rather than the immunity of the foreign state the decision forms a precedent for the restrictive rather than for the absolute immunity theory.[68] This, it is argued here, is reading too much into Chief Justice Marshall's words. In fact, *The Schooner Exchange* is a murky precedent for the absolute as well as the restrictive immunity rule. The reasoning of the decision was tailored to the specific circumstances of the physical entrance of an element of a foreign state's sovereign structure into the territory of a foreign state. The immunity of foreign armed ships was modelled on the immunity of foreign diplomats and foreign heads of state present in the territory of the forum state. Moreover, the nature of *in rem* proceedings conflates the question of immunity from jurisdiction with that of immunity from execution. The immunity of the property of a foreign state from execution is, in principle, unrelated to the question of immunity of the foreign state in a dispute in which that property may be implicated. The facts and nature of the claim at issue in *The Schooner Exchange* together compel the conclusion that the case is no precedent for claims against foreign state defendants *in personam* as in an action in contract or tort.

The defendants had urged the court to dismiss the case on more principled grounds. They had submitted, *inter alia*, that no jurisdiction may be exercised over the rights of foreign sovereigns because sovereigns are equal and a sovereign 'is the sole arbiter of his own rights. He acknowledges no superior but God alone. To his equals, he shows respect, but not submission.'[69] Marshall acknowledged the possible weight of these arguments but explicitly stated that they were not at the basis of his decision:

> The arguments in favor of this opinion which have been drawn from the general inability of the judicial power to enforce its decisions in cases of this description, from the consideration that the sovereign power of the nation is alone competent to avenge wrongs committed by a sovereign, that the questions to which such wrongs give birth, are rather questions of policy than of law, that they are for diplomatic, rather than legal discussion, are of great weight, and merit serious attention. But the argument has already been drawn to a length, which forbids a particular examination of these points.[70]

68 G M Badr (1984) 13; See also H Lauterpacht (1951) 228; I Sinclair (1980) 122.
69 *The Schooner Exchange v M'Faddon* (US, 1812) 134.
70 ibid 146.

The Schooner Exchange was based on the narrow argument that the physical entrance in foreign territory of a sovereign, his representatives, and his property is supposed to take place under (implied) license of the local sovereign and in the confidence that the normal territorial jurisdiction in regard of them will be waived.

The case of *Berizzi Bros v SS Pesaro* equally concerned *in rem* proceedings against property of a foreign state physically present in US territory. Unlike the *Exchange*, however, the *Pesaro* was not a foreign warship but was engaged in commercial trade. The court made a point of emphasizing that the ship was nevertheless employed by the Italian state rather than by its sovereign:

> the vessel, when arrested, was owned, possessed, and controlled by the Italian government, was not connected with its naval or military forces, was employed in the carriage of merchandise for hire between Italian ports and ports in other countries including the port of New York, and was so employed in the service and interest of the whole Italian nation, as distinguished from any individual member thereof, private or official.[71]

According to the court, the fact that *The Schooner Exchange* did not contain a reference to merchant ships owned and operated by a foreign government was

> not of special significance, for in 1812, when the decision was given, merchant ships were operated only by private owners, and there was little thought of governments engaging in such operations. That came much later. The decision in The Exchange v. M'Faddon therefore cannot be taken as excluding merchant ships held and used by a government from the principles there announced. On the contrary, if such ships come within those principles, they must be held to have the same immunity as war ships...[72]

Several lower courts had underlined that '[i]t is not the ownership or the exclusive possession of the instrumentality by the sovereign, but its appropriation and devotion to [public] service, that exempts it from judicial process.'[73] The Supreme Court decided in *Berizzi Bros v SS Pesaro* that a ship engaged in commercial trade could nevertheless be possessed by a foreign government and appropriated to public service. The decision was formally not foreclosed by *The Schooner Exchange*. What can be said safely though, is that *Berizzi Bros v SS Pesaro* is at odds with the spirit of Marshall's judgement. It is not clear why the non-amenability to jurisdiction of foreign publicly-owned merchant vessels that enter a territory for the purpose of trade and 'mingle indiscriminately' with the inhabitants of the territorial state is any less 'inconvenient and dangerous to society' than an entrance under similar conditions from a privately-owned merchant ship, when this difference will often not be obvious from outward appearances.[74]

[71] *Berizzi Bros v SS Pesaro* (US, 1926) 570.

[72] ibid 573–4.

[73] *The Roseric* 254 F 154 (US, DC for the District of New Jersey, 1918) 161–2. Cf also *The Attualità* 238 F 909 (US, Ct of Apps (4th Cir), 1916).

[74] Cf the case of *The Attualità*, ibid 911, where the court emphasized that there were 'many reasons which suggest the inexpediency and impolicy of creating a class of vessels for which no one

In anticipation of the discussion of the early UK jurisprudence below, it is interesting to note that the Supreme Court distinguished the reasons underlying its decision from those relied on by the UK courts. With reference to *The Parlement Belge* the court considered:

Sometimes it is said of that decision that it was put on the ground that a libel in rem under the British admiralty practice is not a proceeding solely against property, but one directly or indirectly impleading the owner—in that instance the Belgian government. But this latter was given as an additional and independent ground, as is expressly stated in the opinion...[75]

Hence, the Supreme Court made a point of distancing itself from the sanction given by the UK courts to the more principled approach advanced by the defendants in *The Schooner Exchange*.

The acceptance of the absolute theory of immunity as regards admiralty proceedings against public ships in *Berizzi Bros v SS Pesaro* already carried in it the seeds for its downfall. When the Italian government requested the Department of State in 1921 to prevent the arrest of the *Pesaro* on immunity grounds, the Department replied that it was 'of the opinion that vessels owned by a state and engaged in commerce are not entitled, within the territorial waters of another state, to the immunity accorded to vessels of war, and that notwithstanding such ownership these vessels are subject to the local jurisdiction to the same extent as other merchant vessels'.[76] When the case came before the courts, the Department of State also refused to issue a certificate that the vessel was immune from process. When the judge of first instance inquired in their position they replied that '[i]t is the view of the Department that government-owned merchant vessels... should not be regarded as entitled to the immunities accorded public vessels of war. The Department has not claimed immunity for American vessels of this character.'[77]

Although the court did not follow the Department's reasoning—in absence of clear legislative change it felt itself bound to apply the absolute immunity rule—the growing opposition of the executive can be seen to have shaped the course of subsequent court practice regarding immunity claims. Gradually, US courts

is in any way responsible.' In particular, it mentioned the limited number of ambassadors, their 'responsible character' and the 'dignity' of the sovereign, guarantees that according to the court did not apply to charter ships.

[75] *Berizzi Bros v SS Pesaro* (US, 1926) 575. See for a discussion of *The Parlement Belge* p 35–6 below.

[76] GH Hackworth, *Digest of International Law* (1941) ii 437.

[77] *The Pesaro* 277 F 473 (US, DC for the Southern District of New York, 1921) 479–80, fn 3. The State Department had already, in 1918, addressed a communication to the Attorney-General of the United States stating that 'where [government-owned] vessels were engaged in commercial pursuits, they should be subject to the obligations and restrictions of trade, if they were to enjoy its benefits and profits'. It was held that 'when a Sovereign enters into business, he submits himself to the conditions thereof' and 'if immunity were granted, American citizens as well as foreigners would be left without recourse in the Courts of just such claims as the might have against the vessels concerned... their only means for obtaining satisfaction would be through political channels—either through Congress, or through diplomacy', GH Hackworth (1941) ii 429.

started abdicating their role in determining foreign state immunity claims, deferring to the 'suggestions' of immunity filed by the executive.[78] In the 1943 case *Ex parte Peru*[79] the Supreme Court held that

[u]pon recognition and allowance of the claim by the State Department and certification of its action presented to the court by the Attorney General, it is the court's duty to surrender the vessel and remit the libelant to the relief obtainable through diplomatic negotiations... This practice is founded upon the policy, recognized both by the Department of State and the courts, that our national interest will be better served in such cases if the wrongs to suitors, involving our relations with a friendly power, are righted through diplomatic negotiations rather than by the compulsions of judicial proceedings.[80]

It concluded that '[t]he certification and the request that the vessel be declared immune must be accepted by the courts as a conclusive determination by the political arm of the Government.'[81] The influence of the diverging views of the executive on the concept of foreign state immunity can arguably already be seen in the 1945 case *Republic of Mexico v Hoffman.*[82] Although the facts of the case resemble those of the *Pesaro*, the declination of the State Department to file a suggestion of immunity was in fact followed by a refusal of the Supreme Court to grant immunity. The court famously considered that '[i]t is... not for the courts to deny an immunity which our government has seen fit to allow, or to allow an immunity on new grounds which the government has not seen fit to recognize.'[83] In an attempt to smooth the appearance of a divergence in interpretation of substantive principles the court relied on the difference between title and possession. It distinguished the case before it from *Berizzi Bros v SS Pesaro* observing that although the ship was owned by Mexico it was not actually in its possession.[84] In his interesting concurring opinion Justice Frankfurter however alluded to the possibility of regarding the decision of the court as 'an implied recession' from the *Pesaro* decision.[85] And Lauterpacht, discussing the implications of this case, cautiously observed that '[i]t is possible that instead of choosing the drastic method

[78] A 'suggestion' is a formal document that can be filed by one of the parties to the case, by a consular or diplomatic representative of an interested foreign power, or in fact by the State Department, and sets out and comments on the facts at issue. Cf AB Lyons, 'The Conclusiveness of the "Suggestion" and Certificate of the American State Department' (1947) 24 BYIL 116 for a useful overview of both procedural and substantive issues regarding the filing of suggestions by the US State Department.

[79] *Ex p Republic of Peru* 318 US 578 (US, S Ct, 1943).

[80] ibid 588–9.

[81] ibid 589. Cf already *The Navemar* 303 US 68 (US, S Ct, 1938), 74–5; 9 AD 176, case no 68. In the *Schooner Exchange v M'Faddon* the consideration that 'there seems to be a necessity for admitting that the fact might be disclosed to the court by the suggestion of the attorney for the United States' also seemed to allude to the prerogative of the executive with regard to the decision on immunity, (US, 1812) 147.

[82] *Republic of Mexico v Hoffman* 324 US 30 (US, S Ct, 1945).

[83] ibid 35.

[84] ibid 36. Cf also *The Navemar* (US, 1938); *The Beaton Park* 13 AD 83, case no 35 (US, DC for the Western District of Washington, Northern District, 1946).

[85] ibid 39 (Concurring opinion Justice Frankfurter, Justice Black joining).

of formal reversal of the established doctrine, [the court] may proceed by way of a less direct approach . . .'[86]

So how did US courts deal with claims instigated against foreign states *in personam*? It first must be noted that at this period in time cases are still rare. A careful examination of the few examples available reveals a wavering judiciary in search of principles to deal with the changing world around it. Lower courts usually did not acknowledge that *The Schooner Exchange* case and the *Pesaro* case do not support *in personam* immunity and several courts did state in no uncertain terms that a friendly foreign state cannot be sued without its consent.[87] However, the reasoning applied in some of these decisions, as well as the reasoning in cases in which immunity was granted without the assertion of such a basic principle compel the conclusion that US practice was not firmly based on the absolute state immunity doctrine. For one, courts set out to distinguish the activity of the foreign state before it from purely lucrative commercial undertakings. In *Oliver–American Trading Co v Government of the United States*, for example, it was considered that no jurisdiction could be exercised over a foreign state in regard to its operation of the railways since 'it is the practice of governments to own and operate the railways. This is not regarded by them as engaging in trade, but as the performance of a fundamental governmental function.'[88] In a similar vein, in *Kingdom of Roumania v Guaranty Trust Co of New York* the grant of immunity was supported by the consideration that 'the Kingdom of Roumania in contracting for shoes and other equipment for its armies was not engaged in business, but was exercising the highest sovereign function of protecting itself against its enemies'.[89]

Courts clearly struggled with the rule of state immunity and with criticism in doctrine increasing,[90] responsibility for the issue was eventually shifted to the executive that until 1952 ordinarily requested immunity in all actions against

[86] H Lauterpacht (1951) 269.

[87] Cf *Republic of France v Pittsburgh Steel Export Company* 1 AD 134, case no 89 (US, City Court of the City of New York, 1920); *Kunglig Jarnvagsstyrelsen v Dexter and Carpenter* 2 AD 121, case no 63, 5 AD 125, case no 80 (US, DC for the Southern District of New York & Ct of Apps (2nd Cir), 1924 & 1929); *Lamont v Travellers Insurance Co* 9 AD 207, case no 73 (US, New York Ct of Apps, 1939); *Puente v Spanish National State* 9 AD 190, case no 70 (US, Ct of Apps (2nd Cir), 1940); *Republic of China v American Express Co* 19 AD 192, case no 39 (US, Ct of Apps (2nd Cir), 1952). It is noted that government-owned corporations were not considered to be protected by the rule: *Coale et Al v Société Coopérative Suisse des Charbons, Basle et al* 1 AD 133, case no 88 (US, DC for the Southern District of New York, 1921); *United States v Deutsches Kalisyndicat Gesellschaft* 31 F 2d 199 (US, DC for the Southern District of New York, 1929) 201–2; *Hannes v Kingdom of Roumania Monopolies Institute* 9 AD 198, case no 72 (US, S Ct of New York, 1938 & 1940).

[88] *Oliver–American Trading Co v Government of the United States of Mexico* 2 AD 49, case no 21, 50 (US, Ct of Apps (2nd Cir), 1924).

[89] *Kingdom of Roumania v Guaranty Trust Co. of New York* 250 F 341 (US, Ct of Apps (2nd Cir), 1918) 345.

[90] Cf eg JY Brinton, 'Suits against Foreign States' (1931) 25 AJIL 50.

friendly foreign sovereigns.[91] In 1952 the State Department communicated with the so-called Tate Letter that it would 'hereafter be the Department's policy to follow the restrictive theory of sovereign immunity in the consideration of requests of foreign governments for a grant of sovereign immunity.'[92] Significantly, the Tate Letter did not propose to change the practice of suggestions of immunity. Moreover, the statement was merely one of intent: it did not provide criteria for the application of the restrictive theory, nor the possibility of judicial control. Subsequent practice did not in fact reflect a strict application of the restrictive theory: political considerations continued to influence executive decisions in the field. When in the case of *Chemical Natural Resources v Republic of Venezuela* the court was confronted with a suggestion of immunity although the dispute before it clearly involved commercial acts, it expressed its dismay as follows:

> Irrespective of its clear meaning, it appears that the State Department has silently abandoned the 'revised and restricted policy' set forth in the Tate Letter and has substituted a case by case foreign sovereign immunity policy, *i.e.* the State Department will recognize and suggest or fail to recognize or grant or suggest sovereign immunity *in each case* presented to it, depending (a) upon the foreign and diplomatic relations which our country has at that particular time with the other country, and (b) the best interest of our country at that particular time.[93]

It did however reluctantly follow the suggestion, holding that

> [i]f and when the State Department concludes that a foreign Nation is entitled to sovereign immunity that determination . . . is conclusive no matter how unwise or, in a particular case, how unfair or unjust the Department's determination appears to be . . .[94]

Consequently, contrary results were reached in similar situations depending on whether a suggestion was issued or not. For example in the *Victory Transport* case immunity was denied in absence of an executive determination because the contract for the carriage of grain which was at the basis of the dispute was not a public act; while in the *Isbrandtsen Tankers* case similar facts did induce the State Department to issue a suggestion of immunity.[95] The court in this case did point out that the acts of the Indian Government were most probably 'purely private

[91] *Verlinden BV v Central Bank of Nigeria* 461 US 480 (US, S Ct, 1983) 486. Cf *Sullivan v State of São Paulo* 10 AD 178, case no 50 (US, Ct of Apps (2nd Cir), 1941); *Piascik v British Ministry of War Transport* 12 AD 87, case no 22 (US, DC for the Southern District of New York, 1943); *Isbrandtsen Co, Inc v Netherlands East Indies Government (The Martin Behrman)* 14 AD 75, case no 26 (US, DC for the Southern District of New York, 1947).

[92] Letter of Jack B Tate, Acting Legal Adviser, Department of State, to Acting Attorney-General Philip B Perlman, 19 May 1952, reprinted in (1952) 26 Department of State Bulletin 984. Cf WW Bishop, 'New United States Policy Limiting Sovereign Immunity' (1953) 47 AJIL 93.

[93] *Chemical Natural Resources v Republic of Venezuela* 420 Pa 134 (US, S Ct of Pennsylvania, 1966), 159; 42 ILR 119, 122.

[94] ibid 147.

[95] *Victory Transport Inc v Comisaria Gen De Abestecimientos y Transportes* 336 F 2d 354 (US, Ct of Apps (2nd Cir), 1964); 35 ILR 110. *Isbrandtsen Tankers Inc v President of India* 446 F 2d 1198 (US, Ct of Apps (2nd Cir), 1971) 1201.

commercial decisions' but saw 'no alternative but to accept the recommendation of the State Department'.[96]

Courts acknowledged, and often sanctioned, the use of political considerations rather than legal criteria by the State Department. In *Spacil v Crowe* the court held:

When the executive branch has determined that the interests of the nation are best served by granting a foreign sovereign immunity from suit in our courts, there are compelling reasons to defer to that judgment without question. Separation-of-powers principles impel a reluctance in the judiciary to interfere with or embarrass the executive in its constitutional role as the nation's primary organ of international policy. And the degree to which granting or denying a claim of immunity may be important to foreign policy is a question on which the judiciary is particularly ill-equipped to second-guess the executive. The executive's institutional resources and expertise in foreign affairs far outstrip those of the judiciary. Perhaps more importantly, in the chess game that is diplomacy only the executive has a view of the entire board and an understanding of the relationship between isolated moves. Will granting immunity serve as a bargaining counter in complex diplomatic negotiations? Will it preclude a significant diplomatic advance; perhaps a détente between this country and one with whom we are not on the best speaking terms? These are questions for the executive, not the judiciary.[97]

It is obvious that this practice raised serious due process questions, especially since the suggestions of the State Department are beyond review by the courts.[98] In *Spacil v Crowe* the plaintiffs argued that the State Department must explicate the reasons behind its decision; only then can the judiciary properly be confident that the executive has exercised its discretion within the bounds of reasonableness. The State Department had only explained its suggestion holding that 'the public interest and United States foreign relations are best served' by the grant of immunity. The court decided that to

require the executive to enlighten us with the foundation of its decision to recognize and allow a claim of sovereign immunity might itself create a serious risk of interference with foreign relations... We can visualize situations where the disclosure that negotiations are ongoing, or even contemplated, would wreak havoc with foreign relations. We simply dare not risk this sort of interference... We hold, therefore, that the executive's decision to recognize and allow a claim of foreign sovereign immunity binds the judiciary,

[96] ibid. Cf also LM Drachsler, 'Some Observations on the Current Status of the Tate Letter' (1960) 54 AJIL 790 with reference to another case where the executive suggestion seemed issued in disregard of the Tate Letter (*Weilamann and McCloskey v The Chase Manhattan Bank* 28 ILR 165 (US, S Ct of New York, 1959) .

[97] *Spacil v Crowe* 489 F 2d 614 (US, Ct of Apps (5th Cir), 1974) 619; 63 ILR 24. See also *Rich v Naviera Vacuba SA* 295 F 2d 24 (US, Ct of Apps (4th Cir), 1961); 32 ILR 127.

[98] Even though in the late 1960s the State Department formalized the procedure by which foreign states present their immunity claims, providing for informal, quasi-judicial hearings where both sides presented written and oral arguments to the State Department's Office of the Legal Advisor.

and that no further review of the executive's action is dictated by the Administrative Procedure Act.[99]

This led one commentator to ask the following rhetorical question:

is sufficient weight being accorded to the interests of the plaintiff, when he is denied the opportunity to have his rights adjudicated as a result of the filing of a suggestion which may accord immunity neither required by international law nor consistent with previously announced State Department policy, and which is utterly beyond review?[100]

In 1976 the Supreme Court decided that the restrictive theory was applicable in the United States.[101] It was however not until the enactment of the 1976 Foreign Sovereign Immunities Act that the rule of restrictive state immunity was accepted as a legal norm the application of which was a power vested exclusively in the courts.[102]

In sum, early US state practice can hardly be regarded as support for an international law rule of absolute state immunity. Chief Justice Marshall in his opinion on *The Schooner Exchange* wrote:

In exploring an unbeaten path, with few, if any, aids from precedents or written law, the court has found it necessary to rely much on general principles, and on a train of reasoning, founded on cases in some degree analogous to this.[103]

Unlike the UK courts later, Marshall preferred to decide the case before him solely on an analogy with diplomatic and head of state immunity. A careful examination of his argumentation—as well as of that employed in the *Pesaro* case—revealed the limited basis of his decision in a physical entry of the property of a foreign state in the territory of the forum and the nature of *in rem* proceedings.[104] One can only guess as to the reasons for the apparent reluctance to base the grant of immunity on the sovereign status of a state as such. One explanation may be the uneasy existence of the immunity of the local sovereign in the national legal system. It has been questioned how a rule, devised to protect the person of sixteenth-century monarchs, has ended up shielding a democratic government from the application of the rule of law.[105] Its incorporation into US law has been called 'one of the mysteries of legal evolution'.[106] As Lauterpacht noted, the 1907 decision in *Kawananakoa v Polybank* was taken at a time in which support

[99] *Spacil v Crowe* (US, 1974) 620–1.

[100] RC Pugh and J McLaughlin, 'Jurisdictional Immunities of Foreign States' (1966) 41 New York University Law Review 25, 63. Cf for more criticism PC Jessup, 'Has the Supreme Court Abdicated One of its Functions?' (1946) 40 AJIL 168.

[101] *Alfred Dunhill of London Inc v Republic of Cuba* 425 US 682 (US, S Ct, 1976).

[102] US, Foreign Sovereign Immunities Act of 1976, Public Law 94–583, 90 Stat 2891, reproduced in (1976) 15 ILM 1388.

[103] *The Schooner Exchange v M'Faddon* (US, 1812) 136.

[104] Cf especially GM Badr (1984) 37.

[105] V Lawyer, 'Birth and Death of Governmental Immunity' (1966) 15 Cleveland-Marshall Law Review 529, 532; H Lauterpacht (1951) 233.

[106] EM Borchard, 'Government Liability in Tort' (1924–25) 34 YLJ 1, 4.

for the rule was in fact already waning.[107] Although this may not have been on Marshall's mind in 1812, it may shed some light on the later jurisprudence. It has moreover been suggested that the reluctance to accept broad constraints on US jurisdiction in *The Schooner Exchange* reflects the preoccupation of a new state to jealously protect its own rights.

Lower courts that *did* pronounce a rule of absolute state immunity *in personam* did so without much conviction and quickly moved to defer to the executive branch in foreign state immunity matters. As the Supreme Court noted in *Verlinden v Central Bank of Nigeria* '[u]ntil 1952 the State Department ordinarily requested immunity in all actions against friendly foreign sovereigns'.[108] Although the practice of deference only became fully established with the decision of the Supreme Court in *Ex parte Peru*,[109] lower courts had regularly taken into account views expressed by the executive before. Early US practice is therefore not a reflection of an international rule but rather reflects national constitutional requirements. The court in the *Victory Transport* case admitted as much:

> The [state immunity] doctrine originated in an era of personal sovereignty, when kings could theoretically do no wrong... With the passing of that era, sovereign immunity has been retained by the courts chiefly to avoid possible embarrassment to those responsible for the conduct of the nation's foreign relations.[110]

And also the court in *Heaney v Government of Spain* stated that:

> the contemporary rationale for sovereign immunity is the avoidance of possible embarrassment to those responsible for the conduct of the nation's foreign relations.[111]

2.2.3.2 The United Kingdom

Compared to the United States, in the United Kingdom judicial support for the restrictive theory developed along a different path and at a markedly different pace. Although early UK state immunity practice similarly concerned *in rem* proceedings against ships owned by foreign sovereigns, the reasoning of the courts in support of the state immunity rule differs from that developed in *The Schooner Exchange*. The UK courts did not hesitate to formulate an absolute immunity doctrine, which they then applied, as Lauterpacht noted, 'with a consistency bordering on rigidity'.[112]

The *Parlement Belge* was a packet-boat owned and possessed by the King of the Belgians. The Royal Belgian Navy used the ship as a mail packet between Ostend and Dover, but the ship was also operated in the carriage of passengers

[107] *Kawananakoa v Polybank* 205 US 349 (US, S Ct, 1907) 353. See H Lauterpacht (1951) 231.

[108] *Verlinden BV v Central Bank of Nigeria* (US, 1983) 486.

[109] *Ex p Republic of Peru* (US, 1943).

[110] *Victory Transport Inc v Comisaria Gen De Abestecimientos y Transportes* (US, 1964) 357.

[111] *Heaney v Government of Spain and Adolpho Gomero* 57 ILR 153 (US, Ct of Apps (2nd Cir), 1991) 156.

[112] H Lauterpacht (1951) 270.

and merchandise for hire. After collision with another vessel in the Port of Dover, *in rem* proceedings were brought against the ship to recover damages. Phillimore—in first instance—refused to grant immunity because the ship was partially engaged in trading activities.[113] The decision was however overturned by the Court of Appeal that asserted that since 'the ship has been mainly used for the purpose of carrying the mails, and only subserviently to that main object for the purposes of trade' immunity should be granted.[114] Several scholars have pointed out that maybe immunity would have been denied had trading been the *principal* activity of the vessel.[115] The observation is a valid one. However, the reasoning employed by the court reveals that the immunity in *in rem* proceedings was thought to be also required by the immunity enjoyed by foreign sovereigns in *in personam* proceedings. The court first considered that

> as a consequence of the absolute independence of every sovereign authority and of the international comity which induces every sovereign state to respect the independence of every other sovereign state, each and every one declines to exercise by means of any of its Courts, any of its territorial jurisdiction over the person of any sovereign or ambassador of any other state, or over the public property of a state which is destined to public use, or over the property of any ambassador, though such sovereign, ambassador, or property be within its territory, and, therefore, but for the common agreement, subject to its jurisdiction.[116]

In addition, the court found that, since the proceedings *in rem* indirectly impleaded the State as the owner of the ship, it was relevant to note that the Belgian state enjoyed an absolute immunity from the jurisdiction of the English courts in proceedings brought against it directly. 'We think'—the court held—'that he cannot be so indirectly impleaded, any more than he could be directly impleaded.'[117]

The facts of the 1919 *Porto Alexandre* case were similar to those of the US case of *Berizzi Bros v SS Pesaro* discussed above.[118] The same Court of Appeal that had emphasized the public use of the vessel in *The Parlement Belge*, disregarded these considerations in *The Porto Alexandre* and held a state-owned ship used exclusively in trading operations to be entitled to immunity. The case has been referred to as the climax of absolute immunity and the high-water mark in acceptance of the doctrine by English courts.[119]

[113] *The Parlement Belge* (1878–79) 4 PD 129 (UK, Court of Admiralty, 1879).

[114] *The Parlement Belge* (1879–80) 5 PD 197 (UK, CA, 1880) 214–15 (*per* Brett LJ).

[115] I Sinclair (1980) 126; S Sucharitkul, *State Immunities and Trading Activities in International Law* (1959) 60.

[116] *The Parlement Belge* (UK, 1880) 214–15.

[117] ibid 219.

[118] *The Porto Alexandre* [1920] P 30 (UK, CA, 1919); 1 AD 146, case no 100.

[119] S Sucharitkul (1959) 66; I Sinclair (1980) 157. The approach has been followed by lower courts and the Court of Appeal in a number of decisions, including *Compania Mercantil Argentina v United States Shipping Board* 131 LT 388 (UK, CA, 1924).

When the House of Lords finally confirmed the rule in *The Cristina* in 1938, the first cracks in the UK adherence to the absolute theory as regards *in rem* proceedings however were already visible.[120] Only Lords Atkin and Wright expressed an unqualified acceptance of the rule of absolute immunity as laid down in *The Porto Alexandre*. Lord Atkin held that

> the Courts of a country will not implead a foreign Sovereign, that is, they will not by their process make him against his will a party to legal proceedings whether the proceedings involve process against his person or seek to recover from him specific property or damages.... they will not by their process, whether the Sovereign is a party to the proceedings or not, seize or detain property which is his or of which he is in possession or control. There has been some difference in the practice of nations as to possible limitations of this second principle, as to whether it extends to property only used for the commercial purposes of the Sovereign or to personal private property. In this country it is in my opinion well settled that it applies to both.[121]

The other Lords based the grant of immunity on the ground that the ship in question was dedicated to public use and expressed serious doubts regarding *The Porto Alexandre* decision. Lord Thankerton held himself free to reconsider the case arguing that the Court of Appeal had erred in finding a precedent in *The Parlement Belge*, since that case had reference to ships used for public purposes only.[122] Lord Macmillan asserted that there was 'no proved consensus of international opinion or practice' in favour of a rule of absolute immunity applicable even to vessels engaged wholly or substantially in trading activities.[123] Finally, Lord Maugham went as far as rejecting *The Porto Alexandre* decision, giving expression to 'the most pungent judicial criticism yet given of the rule of absolute immunity'.[124]

In 1950 an interdepartmental committee was set up to discuss a possible reform of state immunity law in the UK. The decision of the Court of Appeal in *Krajina v Tass Agency* to grant immunity in a libel suit against a news agency because of its formal status of department of the Soviet State was the immediate cause for the sudden interest in the topic.[125] An interim report—reflecting a tendency to abandon the absolute immunity theory—*was* issued, but since the committee was too divided to agree on any proposals, the report was never published and the work of the committee discontinued.[126]

The thorny question of state agencies engaged in commerce came again before the courts in *Baccus SRL v Servicio Nacional del Trigo*.[127] The case concerned

[120] *The Cristina* (1938) 60 LR 147 (UK, HL, 1938).
[121] ibid 156.
[122] ibid 158–9.
[123] ibid 159–60.
[124] ibid 169–70. For the qualification see H Lauterpacht (1951) 271.
[125] *Krajina v Tass Agency* [1949] All ER 274 (UK, CA, 1949).
[126] See H Fox (2002) 112.
[127] *Baccus SRL v Servicio Nacional del Trigo* [1957] 1 QB 438 (UK, CA, 1956).

a claim for an alleged breach of contract against a department of the Spanish Ministry of Agriculture engaged in the commercial trade of rye. In a dissenting opinion Singleton LJ stated:

I cannot find that it has been almost universally recognised that if a government sets up a legal entity, something which may contract on its own behalf as a limited company does in this country, it can succeed in a claim for sovereign immunity in respect of the activities of that company or entity.[128]

The other two judges of the court, however, rejected the concept of separate legal personality and proceeded to grant the agency immunity from jurisdiction. In *Trendtex Trading Corporation v Central Bank of Nigeria*[129] immunity *was* denied to the central bank of Nigeria. While the 'separate legal personality' of an institution was still not deemed relevant, the Court of Appeal did not consider the bank a department or organ of the state.

Clearly, the *Trendtex* case effectively reduced the scope of the absolute immunity doctrine somewhat. The limiting of the scope of the state immunity rule through a redefinition of what constitutes a state is however a far cry from a conversion to the restrictive immunity doctrine. Support for a restrictive immunity rule was initially only ventilated in dissenting or concurring opinions. The rule saw its most prominent advocate in the UK judiciary in the person of Lord Denning, who in the cases of *Rahimtoola v The Nizam of Hyderabad*,[130] *Thai-Europe Tapioca Service Ltd. v Government of Pakistan*[131] and the illustrious *Trendtex* case,[132] developed a strong critique of the absolute immunity rule. In *Rahimtoola* he stated, *inter alia*, that

if the dispute concerns, for instance, the commercial transactions of a foreign government...and it arises properly within the territorial jurisdiction of our courts, there is no ground for granting immunity.[133]

The following was one of the considerations advanced in support of this conclusion:

In all civilized countries there has been a progressive tendency towards making the sovereign liable to be sued in his own courts; notably in England by the Crown Proceedings Act 1947. Foreign sovereigns should not be in any different position. There is no reason why we should grant to the departments or agencies of foreign Governments an immunity which we do not grant our own.[134]

[128] ibid 461.

[129] *Trendtex Trading Corporation v Central Bank of Nigeria* [1977] QB 529 (K, CA, 1976).

[130] *Rahimtoola v The Nizam of Hyderabad* [1958] AC 379 (UK, HL, 1957); 24 ILR 175. The other Judges emphatically disassociated themselves from Denning's views.

[131] *Thai-Europe Tapioca Service Ltd v Government of Pakistan* [1976] 1 LR 1(UK, CA, 1975).

[132] *Trendtex Trading Corporation v Central Bank of Nigeria* (UK, 1976).

[133] *Rahimtoola v The Nizam of Hyderabad* (UK, 1957) 422.

[134] ibid 418.

In *Thai-Europe* Denning argued that an exception to state immunity must be recognized in respect of proceedings regarding 'land situated in England', 'trust funds in England', 'debts incurred in England for services rendered to its property in England', and a dispute arising from 'commercial transactions with a trader in England . . . which is properly within the territorial jurisdiction of the English courts'.[135] The other two judges on the bench argued that the rule of stare decisis foreclosed the adoption of the restrictive approach by this court. In the words of Scarman LJ:

[A] rule of international law, once incorporated into our law by decisions of a competent court, is not an inference of fact, but a rule of law. It therefore becomes part of our municipal law and the doctrine of *stare decisis* applies as much to that as to a rule of law with a strictly municipal provenance . . . I think therefore that it is not open to this court to apply a new rule or view developing in the international field if it be inconsistent with a rule already incorporated into our law by a decision of the Court of Appeal or the House of Lords.[136]

In 1976, just before the Court of Appeal decision in *Trendtex*, the Privy Council held in *The Philippine Admiral* that foreign states were not immune from the jurisdiction of local courts in actions *in rem* with respect to state-owned commercial ships or cargoes, declining to follow *The Porto Alexandre* precedent. The Council qualified its decision with regard to actions *in personam*

The rule that no action in personam can be brought against a foreign sovereign state on a commercial contract has been regularly accepted by the Court of Appeal in England and was assumed to be the law even by Lord Maugham in *The Cristina*. It is no doubt open to the House of Lords to decide otherwise, but it may fairly be said to be at the least unlikely that it would do so . . . [137]

Although it admitted that 'the resulting position may be somewhat anomalous'[138] the Council insisted on applying the restrictive theory as far as it could since it held that theory to be 'more consonant with justice'[139] It moreover considered:

In this country—and no doubt in most countries in the western world—the state can be sued in its own courts on commercial contracts into which it has entered and there is no apparent reason why foreign states should not be equally liable to be sued there in respect of such transactions.[140]

[135] *Thai-Europe Tapioca Service Ltd. v Government of Pakistan* (UK, 1975) 4–5. Immunity was to be granted since the dispute did not qualify under one of the four categories.

[136] ibid 8.

[137] *The Philippine Admiral* 64 ILR 90 (UK, The Privy Council, 1975) 108. Cf also the Council's decision in *Sultan of Johore v Abubakar*, [1952] AC 318, 343 where it emphasized that '[t]heir Lordships do not consider that there has been finally established in England . . . any absolute rule that a foreign independent sovereign cannot be impleaded in our courts in any circumstances.'

[138] ibid 109.

[139] ibid 109.

[140] ibid 108.

Lord Denning did not let pass the opportunity to resume his mission in the *Trendtex* case.[141] While Stephenson LJ and Shaw LJ preferred to base their decision on the ground that the defendant bank could not be regarded as a department of the Nigerian Government, Denning considered that international law did not require states to grant immunity in cases concerning ordinary trading transactions, regardless of whether an action *in rem* or an action *in personam* was concerned. The two other judges disagreed on whether—as Scarman LJ and Lawton LJ had argued in *Thai-Europe*—the stare decisis rule precluded Denning's approach. Shaw argued it did not. He explained that

> [t]he rule of *stare decisis* operates to preclude a court from overriding a decision which binds it in regard to a particular rule of (international) law, it does not prevent a court from applying a rule which did not exist when the earlier decision was made if the new rule has had the effect in international law of extinguishing the old rule.[142]

Stephenson disagreed. He did express sympathy for the restrictive doctrine though when he concluded that because of the rule of stare decisis he felt bound to stand 'loyally but reluctantly on the old doctrine and the old decisions.'[143]

In 1978 the UK State Immunity Act (SIA) was enacted.[144] The controversy on the common law position did however continue in cases decided after the enactment but dealing with questions of immunity under the old law. In *Uganda Co. (Holdings) v Government of Uganda* Donaldson, J, held that the reasoning of the judges in *Trendtex*—as recalled not at the basis of the decision in that case—could not be reconciled with *Thai-Europe* and the established position of the absolute doctrine of immunity for actions *in personam*. The decision in the latter case was followed 'because a decision which asserts the doctrine of precedent must logically have more weight *as a precedent* than one which denies or modifies that doctrine'.[145] Moreover, the judge attached 'great weight to the forecast by the Judicial Committee of the Privy Council that the House of Lords will be unwilling to abandon the absolute rule of immunity in actions *in personam*.'[146]

[141] *Trendtex Trading Corporation v Central Bank of Nigeria* (UK, 1976).

[142] ibid 579. Also Lord Denning denied that the rule of stare decisis required the application of the absolute doctrine. He argued that since international law clearly favoured the restrictive doctrine, and since international law was automatically the law of the United Kingdom, the rule did not apply, 553. Cf for a critical discussion of that position CJ Lewis (1990) 25.

[143] ibid 572.

[144] UK, State Immunity Act 1978, reproduced in (1978) 17 ILM 1123.

[145] *Uganda Co (Holdings) v Government of Uganda* [1979] 1 LR 481 (UK, Queen's Bench Division, 1978).

[146] ibid 487.

Lord Wilberforce had in the meantime, however, already cast doubt as to the merits of this forecast. At the November 1978 meeting of the International Law Association (ILA) he stated:

> We were hoping to get the *Trendtex* case and to revolutionize the law but the parties went and settled before we could![147]

The House of Lords got its chance with *I Congreso del Partido*. The decision was given *after* the introduction of the SIA, but on the basis of the common law.[148] Lord Wilberforce argued that 'it is clear that international law, in a general way, in 1978, gave support to a "restrictive" theory of state immunity. We do not need the statute to make this good.'[149]

UK adherence to the absolute immunity doctrine gives rise to two qualifying observations. In the first place, the UK doctrine of foreign state immunity was developed in a period in which in the UK the status of a state *as such* was seen to prevent judicial scrutiny of its acts. Second, the rule of stare decisis pinned UK state immunity law to that doctrine even when thinking on the rationale of the rule developed.

The first observation regards the *basis* of the UK absolute immunity doctrine. The development of the notion of the state as an abstract institution did not immediately free the concept of the state of the honorific and often archaic features of dignity and status attaching to the personal sovereign. Even though at the time of *The Parlement Belge* the days of Louis XIV were left far behind, residues of the identification of the ruler with the state undeniably influenced legal thinking. This identification was at the basis of the development of an internal state immunity concept, and extended to foreign states. In the UK immunity of foreign states was, to a large extent, based on the same principles as the internal immunity of the forum state. The rule of absolute immunity was hence not as much based on principles of international law, but rather on principles concerned with the status of states *as such*.

The immunity of the local sovereign and the immunity of the foreign personal sovereign are commonly recognized as being at the cradle of the rule of foreign state immunity. With regard to the immunity of local sovereigns Lauterpacht remarked, for example, that

> it is probable that a substantial explanation of that [immunity] doctrine will be found in the traditional immunity of the sovereign state from suit in its own courts. The entire concept of state immunity—whether of the foreign state or of the territorial state—is a survival of the period when the sovereign, if he did justice to the subject, did so as a matter

147 Quoted in C J Lewis (1990) 24.
148 *I Congreso del Partido* (UK, 1981).
149 ibid 260.

not of duty but of grace. It is an inheritance, not as indirect as it may appear, of the principle that the personal sovereign—and subsequently the state—is *legibus solitus*.[150]

While Lalive wrote that

[h]istoriquement la notion s'explique par le fait que l'Etat s'identifiait à la personne même du souverain. La souveraineté et l'indépendance du chef de l'Etat étranger, du Prince, entraînaient, par voie de conséquence nécessaire, l'impossibilité d'attraire celui-ci devant les tribunaux étrangers.[151]

Although the two reputed factors of influence are usually treated separately, they can only be appreciated when understood as one integral process. In particular, the analogy with the immunity of the local sovereign can be seen to have facilitated the use of the analogy of personal immunity of foreign sovereigns—since a similar transposition from the immunity of the person to the abstract institution had taken place within national legal systems as well.

Notably, all three immunity concepts were thought necessary to protect the dignity of the sovereign. Lauterpacht wrote in this regard that

[t]here is a close similarity between the manner in which the 'dignity of the sovereign' was used as a justification of sovereign immunity within the state and the way in which it was relied upon for the same purpose with regard to the jurisdictional immunities of foreign states.[152]

In sum, at a time where the archaic features of the personal sovereign were projected onto the abstract institution of the state, foreign state immunity was at least partly based on the status of the state *as such* rather than on any consideration concerning the specific position of a *foreign* state. The position of the forum state before the court may be indicative of the development of legal thinking on this point and may *hence* be relevant for the determination of the position of the foreign state. If the forum state cannot be sued because of reasons perceived to be inherent in the concept of state as such this equally precludes the subjection to jurisdiction of a foreign state. Accordingly, in *The Parlement Belge* the court stated that 'the real principle on which the exemption of every sovereign from the jurisdiction of every Court has been deduced is . . . dignity'.[153]

150 H Lauterpacht (1951) 232. See similarly S Sucharitkul (1976) 96 and 115.

151 J-F Lalive, 'L'immunité de juridiction des États et des organisations internationales' (1953–III) 84 RdC 205, 213. Cf also I Sinclair (1980) 121; PD Trooboff, 'Foreign State Immunity: Emerging Consensus on Principles' (1986–V) 200 RdC 235, 252.

152 H Lauterpacht (1951) 231, cf fn 6.

153 *The Parlement Belge* (UK, 1880) 207 (*per* Esher LJ). Cf also Lord Denning in his dissent in *Rahimtoola*: 'Search as you will among the accepted principles of international law and you will search in vain for any set propositions. There is no agreed principle except this: that each State ought to have proper respect for the dignity and independence of other States.' *Rahimtoola v The Nizam of Hyderabad* (UK, 1957) 417. This mix up of state and person can be seen confirmed in an 1894 case against the Sultan of Johore. The Sultan, who was temporarily living in the UK under the name of Albert Baker was sued for breaking of his engagement to Ms Mighell. When the Sultan revealed his true identity, the court considered under reference to *The Parlement Belge* that

In a similar vein, the fact that the forum state *can* be sued is a relevant argument in the development of a restrictive approach to foreign state immunity. The Court of Cassation of Rome considered for example that

[i]t is not permissible to invoke a prerogative of immunity from jurisdiction in favour of a foreign sovereign in Italy, where even the national sovereign is subject to ordinary law of a proprietary nature.[154]

In the early Belgian case law, similar considerations are found. In the case of *SA des Chemins de Fer liégeois-luxembourgeouis v l'Etat néerlandais*,[155] mentioned above, the Court of Cassation held that

pour les Etats étrangers, comme pour l'Etat belge, la souveraineté n'est pas en jeu quand ils sont en cause, non pas comme pouvoirs, mais uniquement pour l'exercice ou la défense d'un droit privé.

In a particularly insightful vein Lalive wrote:

A l'époque où l'Etat s'identifiait avec la personne du souverain, il était compréhensible que les auteurs et la jurisprudence eussent marqué certaines hésitations [as to the restriction of immunity]. Mais aujourd'hui la situation est très différente; l'antropomorphisme étatique a été remplacé par des notions nouvelles, mieux en harmonie avec la réalité et avec la solidarité internationale. Le pouvoir politique a été transféré de la personne souveraine des gouvernants à l'Etat, entité abstraite, ensemble de services publics. Ce phénomène d'institutionnalisation du pouvoir, combiné aux faits qui ont été examinés ci-dessus, a privé de toute raison d'être la théorie de l'immunité absolue.[156]

In the UK the possibility to sue the executive before the courts was created relatively late. It is instructive to note however that the opposition against the rule of absolute state immunity in the UK indeed developed *after* the enactment of the 1947 UK Crown Proceedings Act.[157] The most influential criticism was without doubt that advanced by Lauterpacht in his seminal article published in 1951.[158] He boldly argued in favour of the abolition of the rule of state immunity

in personam proceedings against a foreign sovereign were impossible and granted him immunity from civil jurisdiction, *Mighell v Sultan of Johore* [1894] 1 QB 149 (UK, CA, 1893).

154 *Carlo d'Austria Este v Nobili* 73 Giu It 1921–I–471 (Italy, Corte di Cassazione di Roma, 1921) 473; 1 AD 136, case no 90, 136. Although this case concerned the personal immunity of a foreign sovereign, this was also the general approach in cases against states, see *Canale v Governo francese* (1937) 29 RDI 81 (Italy, Appello Genova, 1937), and especially *Government of Bolivia v Italian Association for Aeronautical Exports* 15 AD 133, case no 41 (Italy, Court of Cassation, 1948) 135. The Italian courts have continued to assimilate the position of foreign states to the position of the Italian states before it, see M Cosnard (1996) 69.

155 *SA des Chemins de Fer liégeois-luxembourgeouis v l'Etat néerlandais* (Belgium, 1903).

156 J-F Lalive (1953) 222.

157 UK, Crown Proceedings Act (1947), available at <http://www.dwp.gov.uk/advisers/docs/lawvols/greenvol/pdf/g_0101.pdf>.

158 H Lauterpacht (1951).

and an assimilation of the position of foreign sovereigns with that of the local sovereign.[159] He noted that:

[p]ublic opinion, and practical considerations do not permit too wide a gap between the law governing the immunities of the home state and the law, which many regard as increasingly artificial, unjust, and archaic, relating to the immunities of foreign states.[160]

Many agreed with Lauterpacht's assessment that '[i]t is very probable that the law of the countries—which still grant absolute immunity to foreign states, goes beyond the requirements of international law.'[161] And also the idea that foreign state immunity should not go further than the immunity of the own state under the 1947 Crown Proceedings Act found support.[162] It is further recalled that both the Privy Council in *The Philippine Admiral* and Lord Denning in *Rahimtoola* supported their plea for the restrictive approach with the consideration that there is no reason why foreign sovereigns should be in a different position from the local sovereign.[163]

With reference to scholars and courts linking different immunity concepts, Cosnard made a point of stating that the immunity of the personal foreign sovereign and the immunity of the local sovereign do not provide the rule of foreign state immunity with a foundation.[164] It is respectfully submitted that this assertion mistakes exercises in history with an exercise in logic. Of course, a distinct basis for the immunity of the local sovereign—more geared to the attributes of the state as an abstract institution—was later developed. In the United States, for example, two separate arguments can be distinguished. The first, which could deprecatingly be termed 'The King can do no wrong' theory in disguise, is derived from the view that the origin of law resides within the territorial state.[165] Justice Holmes, in the US Supreme Court decision in *Kawananakoa v Polybank*, famously based the immunity of the state 'on the logical and practical ground that there can be no legal right as against the authority that makes the law on which the right depends'.[166] A second argument was found in the 'separation of powers' doctrine. The control exercised by the judiciary over the acts of the executive in

[159] Although the theory of assimilation disregards the distinct principles applicable to the local and the foreign state, the proposal advanced by Lauterpacht arguably escapes that criticism. In § 2.3.2 below a further interpretation of Lauterpacht's proposal will be given.

[160] H Lauterpacht (1951) 221.

[161] ibid 239. Cf EJ Cohn, 'Waiver of Immunity' (1958) 34 BYIL 260, 260–1; E Lémonon (Rapporteur Institut de Droit International), L'immunité de juridiction et d'exécution forcée des Etats étrangers, Rapport et projet de Résolution définitifs, observations E Beckett, (1952) 44–I AIDI 5, 53–93.

[162] Cf BA Wortley, 'The Interaction of Public and Private International Law Today' (1954–I) 85 RdC 239, 268.

[163] Cf p 38, 39 above.

[164] M Cosnard (1996) 62.

[165] See also GG Phillimore, 'Immunité des États, au point de vue de la juridiction ou de l'exécution forcée' (1925–III) 8 RdC 413, 442–3; J-F Lalive (1953) 218.

[166] *Kawananakoa v Polybank* (US, 1907) 353.

case of judicial proceedings against the state was held to be contrary to the independence of the latter and therefore unacceptable.

It may be clear that this two-pillared basis of the internal immunity of states is as such not transposable to justify the immunity of foreign states. Cosnard therefore argued that in fact the analogy with internal immunity is a false one, not able to provide a foundation to the rule of foreign state immunity.[167] State immunity, he emphasized, has a distinct foundation in the principle of sovereign equality. So far, so good. And as far as this argument is used to criticize proposals to assimilate the position of foreign states with that of the local sovereign, or alternatively, with its position before its own courts, it is also valid.[168]

It is submitted however that the methodology of discussing the immunity of the local sovereign and the immunity of the personal sovereign, as part of the search for a sound foundation of the doctrine of immunity of foreign states, is unfortunate because it focuses on justification of the doctrine, where a focus on its explanation is to be preferred. Negating the internal immunity analogy on the basis of logical reasoning assumes the existence of a theoretically-sound basis to the foreign state immunity rule. In fact, its inception is at least partly attributable to historical fallacies. Disregard of this reality prevents one from fully grasping the process of inception of the state immunity rule. The analysis of Cosnard is, so to say, troubled by the disadvantage of hindsight. Maybe the identification of the influence of false arguments in the development of the immunity rule is a more valuable finding than the automatic restatement of the sovereign equality of states as its basis.

The proposed perspective—that of explanation rather than justification—impels the conclusion that the immunity of the local sovereign has undeniably induced and facilitated the inception of the state immunity concept in the common law countries. This approach places the examination of the link between the two rules back in history, instead of discussing the topic in light of contemporary doctrine. From this perspective it cannot but be concluded that via the analogy of the immunity of the local sovereign, 'the honorific and ceremonial features of the immunity of the sovereign in person, and their representatives, have reacted often in exaggerated forms upon the topic of State immunity in general'.[169]

Most importantly, even if the distinct basis in international law of the rule of state immunity discredits any state immunity regime based on assimilation, the limits placed on the immunity of the local sovereign *are* relevant for the immunity of foreign sovereigns—and not only because of the sociological consideration that '[p]ublic opinion, and practical considerations do not permit too wide a gap

[167] M Cosnard (1996) 73.

[168] Cf also P De Visscher and J Verhoeven (1971) 53.

[169] I Brownlie (Rapporteur Institut de Droit International), Contemporary Problems Concerning the Jurisdictional Immunity of States, Preliminary Report (1987), (1987) 62–I AIDI 13, 22.

between the law governing the immunities of the home state and the law'.[170] As was argued above, the exercise of jurisdiction over the local sovereign made clear that nothing in the quality of being a state as such could underlie the rule of foreign state immunity.

The second observation that qualifies the importance of the adherence to the absolute immunity doctrine in the UK regards the role of the stare decisis rule. At a certain point the application of the doctrine no longer reflected a belief in the principle. When the notion of dignity lost its cogency judges did start to express support—albeit cautious—for the principles of the restrictive approach. The stare decisis rule was however thought to be an obstacle to the abandonment of the absolute immunity doctrine. Already in 1958 one scholar noted in this respect that the UK courts might no longer have 'the means of finding a way out of the fetters which they have created for themselves'.[171]

2.2.4 Conclusion

A significant majority of states today supports a restrictive approach to the rule of foreign state immunity. It can therefore be safely stated that international law does not require states to grant immunity beyond the demands of the restrictive theory. It was questioned at the outset of this section whether the early developments in countries like Belgium and Italy were at the time violating international law, or that alternatively international law has never required national courts to grant an absolute immunity to foreign states. The early conversions to the restrictive approach, together with the observations regarding the early developments in the US and the UK do not make a strong case for the argument that state immunity started out as an absolute rule. Although instances of application of the absolute rule can be found in the history of civil law jurisdictions as well, if anything, the piecemeal application of the rule evidences a wavering judiciary and an unsettled and uncertain practice.[172]

The explanation for the slow adjustment of legal theory to practical reality should however not only be sought in positive factors accounting for the adherence to the absolute doctrine. The adherence to an arguably archaic absolute doctrine, or the deference to the executive, may at least to some extent be attributable to the absence of a *convincing* alternative. The next section will argue that while

[170] H Lauterpacht (1951) 221.

[171] EJ Cohn (1958) 260. CH Schreuer, *State Immunity: Some Recent Developments* (1988) 4 noted that '[a]n obvious irony in this development is the fact that common law countries have found it necessary to pass legislation in order to adjust their practice, while the civil law countries have been quite content at developing the law on a case by case basis. This reversal of the traditional patterns may at least partly be explained by the fact that stare decisis has led the common law judiciaries into dead ends, from which only formal legislation could free them.' Cf also CJ Lewis (1990) 11.

[172] Sucharitkul for example described the German practice as having followed a 'zigzag course', S Sucharitkul (1976) 146. Compare also I Sinclair (1980) 128ff; H Lauterpacht (1951) 250ff; EW Allen (1933).

the *reasons* for the limitation of state immunity are readily discernable, a *cogent theory* of the restrictive immunity rule is still lacking.

2.3 A Poorly Articulated Theory

2.3.1 Explanation over Justification

The adoption of the rule of restrictive immunity is often explained under reference to the increasing involvement of states in commercial enterprises. Legal disputes between states and individuals were on the rise and the rule of absolute immunity was increasingly felt to entail a denial of justice. It was the 'economic reality' that left 'no alternative' to states but to adopt a restrictive approach to the immunity rule.[173] In *Alfred Dunhill* the US Supreme Court explained:

> Participation by foreign sovereigns in the international commercial market has increased substantially in recent years... The potential injury to private businessmen—and ultimately to international trade itself—from a system in which some of the participants in the international market are not subject to the rule of law has therefore increased correspondingly.[174]

The considerable increase of disputes between private individuals and foreign states, because of the development of commercial activity by foreign states as well as the increasingly international character of many commercial transactions in the second half of the twentieth century, coincided with the increased interest in the rights of individuals as against the state. As Lauterpacht noted, the abandonment of the absolute approach was not only required by 'the expansion of the activities of states and the injustice and inconvenience resulting from the disregard of these developments in relation to claims of individuals', but also by the more fundamental consideration that

> [a]t a period in which in enlightened communities the securing of the rights of the individual—in all their aspects, against the state has become a matter of special and significant effort, there is no longer a disposition to tolerate the injustice which may arise whenever the state—our own state or a foreign state—screens itself behind the shield of immunity in order to defeat a legitimate claim.[175]

Courts and commentators alike have emphasized that 'it is necessary in the interest of justice to individuals having transactions with states to allow them to bring such transactions before the courts.'[176]

[173] Cf MB Feldman, 'The United States Foreign Sovereign Immunities Act in Perspective: A Founders View' (1986) 35 ICLQ 302, 302. Cf also Harvard Law School, Research in International Law (Reporter PC Jessup), Competence of Courts in Regard to Foreign States (1932 supplement) 26 AJIL 451, 473–4.

[174] *Alfred Dunhill of London Inc v Republic of Cuba* (US, 1976) 703.

[175] H Lauterpacht (1951) 235.

[176] *I Congreso del Partido* (UK, 1981) 262 (*per* Lord Wilberforce). Cf also *Hall v Bengoa* (1921) 48 JDI 270 (Egypt, Cour d'appel mixte d'Alexandrie, 1920) 272: 'l'immunité de juridiction

The idea that states should be accountable players in the market place has at times also been rationalized from the perspective of the interests of states rather than individuals. In the 1886 case of *Guttieres v Elmilik* the Court of Cassation of Florence explained that the restrictive theory facilitates the exercise of economic activity of the state since they will be trusted more as a trading partner when they can be called to respond to their obligations.[177] The absolute doctrine casts a dubious shadow on the reputation of states as trading partners. Individuals, rather than risk finding the courts closed when a dispute concerning a commercial enterprise arises, may very well refuse to deal with foreign states. Scrutton LJ sketched the following picture in *The Porto Alexandre*:

> If ships of the State find themselves left on the mud because no one will salve them when the State refuses any legal remedy for salvage, their owners will be apt to change their views. If the owners of cargoes on national ships find that the ship runs away and leaves them to bear all the expenses of salvage, as has been done in this case, there may be found a difficulty in getting cargoes for national ships.[178]

The *reasons* for the adoption of a restrictive rather than an absolute approach to the rule of state immunity are thus apparent. A more fundamental question inquires into the *theorization* of the restrictive rule. The rationale of the rule of state immunity is the independence and equality of states.[179] Lord Wilberforce formulated it as follows:

> The basis on which one State is considered to be immune from the territorial jurisdiction of the courts of another State is that of '*par in parem non habet imperium*', which

dans ce cas serait la négation de la justice puisqu'elle priverait du secours de celle-ci les individus dont les intérêts se trouvent en conflit avec les intérêts privés du dit Etat'; *The Philippine Admiral* (UK, 1975) 109: 'the restrictive theory is more consonant with justice'; *Victory Transport Inc v Comisaria Gen De Abestecimientos y Transportes* (US, 1964) 357; 35 ILR 110; *The Charkieh* (UK, 1873); *Venne v Democratic Republic of the Congo* 5 DLR (3d) 128 (Canada, Quebec Court of Queen's Bench, 1968) 143–4: 'an absolute and universal immunity could be a source of injustice'; *Zodiak International Products Inc v Polish People's Republic* (Canada, 1977) 58; *Harbhajan Singh Dhalla v Union of India* (India, 1986) discussed p 18–9 above.

[177] *Guttieres v Elmilik* 11 F It. 1886–I–913 (Italy, Corte di Cassazione di Firenze, 1886) 921.

[178] *The Porto Alexandre* (UK, 1919) 39. It should be noted however that Scrutton did not see in this an argument against immunity. He continued stating that '[t]hese are matters to be dealt with by negotiations between Governments, and not by Governments exercising their power to interfere with the property of other states contrary to the principles of international courtesy which govern the relations between independent and sovereign states.' The argument *did* prevail in the decision by the lower court in *The Pesaro*(US 1921) 481. Cf also WW Bishop (1953) 98.

[179] The concept of dignity seems to have lost most of its attraction. Already in 1951 Lauterpacht argued that '[t]hese strained emanations of the notion of dignity are an archaic survival and [...] they cannot continue as a rational basis of immunity.' Moreover, he wrote, 'the dignity of foreign states may suffer more from an appeal to immunity than from a denial of it'. H Lauterpacht (1951) 231 and 232. In a similar vein, another scholar held that '[it] would seem that as far as the dignity of a state can be the basis of any proposition, it would be that it is better preserved by compliance with international law and bearing the consequences of a failure to do so', TH Hill, 'A Policy Analysis of the American Law of Foreign State Immunity' (1981) 50 Fordham Law Review 155, 165. Cf also *Harbhajan Singh Dhalla v Union of India* (India, 1986) 537: 'One should have thought that the political relationship between the two countries would be better served and the image of a foreign State be better established if citizens' grievances are judicially investigated.'

effectively means that the sovereign or governmental acts of one State are not matters on which the courts of other States will adjudicate.[180]

The *justification* for the restrictive approach is generally held to be that the principles of equality and independence only require the grant of immunity to foreign state defendants in cases concerning acts they performed in the exercise of their sovereign authority. In 1886 the Court of Cassation of Florence considered that the independence of states does not allow acts of a state that concern the exercise of its sovereignty to be subjected to foreign jurisdiction. However, it continued,

when these high prerogatives are not involved, and the Government as a civil body, descends into the sphere of contracts and transactions so as to acquire rights and assume obligations, just as a private person might do, then the independence of the State is immaterial, for in such case it is a question solely of private acts and obligations to be governed by the rules of the general laws.[181]

Exactly *how* these principles explain the restrictive scope of state immunity is however a question conveniently ignored. Since also the absolute state immunity doctrine relied on the principles of independence and equality of states this justification requires some elaboration. The French Court of Cassation considered for example that it follows from the principle of the independence of states that

un gouvernement ne peut être soumis pour les engagements qu'il a contracté à la juridiction d'un Etat étranger; qu'en effet, le droit de juridiction qui appartient à chaque gouvernement pour juger les différends nés à l'occasion des actes émanés de lui est un droit inhérent à son autorité souveraine; qu'un autre gouvernement ne saurait s'attribuer sans s'exposer à altérer leurs rapports respectifs.[182]

A Belgian court—in one of the rare instances of application of the absolute doctrine—emphasized the principle of equality of states, considering that:

Ce principe primordial du droit international public qui proclame toutes les nations également souveraines, indépendants, et pas suite sans juridiction les unes à l'égard des autres, puisque la juridiction suppose la subordination et non point la parfaite égalité.[183]

[180] *I Congreso del Partido* (UK, 1981) 262. Cf also *Holland v Lampen-Wolfe* [2000] 1 WLR 1571 (UK, HL, 2000) 1580 (*per* Lord Cooke of Thorndon), 1581 (*per* Lord Clyde), and 1584 (*per* Lord Millett); *Special Representative of the State of the City of the Vatican v Pieciukiewicz* 78 ILR 120 (Italy, Court of Cassation, 1982) 121; *Swissair v X and Another* 82 ILR 36 (Switzerland, Federal Tribunal, 1985) 37; *Al-Adsani v United Kingdom* (ECHR, 2001) 289, § 54; 123 ILR 24.

[181] *Guttieres v Elmilik* (Italy, 1886) 920–1 (trans in GM Badr (1984) 24). Cf in a similar sense *Roumania v Pascalet* 2 AD 132, case no 68 (France, Commercial Tribunal of Marseille, 1944); *Alfred Dunhill of London Inc v Republic of Cuba* (US, 1976) 703–4.

[182] *Gouvernement Espagnol v Casaux* (France, 1849).

[183] *Gouvernement ottoman v Société de Sclessin et Deppe et Roef* PB 1877–3–28 (Belgium, Tribunal d'Anvers, 1876) 28. Cf also E Lémonon (Rapporteur Institut de Droit International), L'immunité de juridiction et d'exécution forcée des Etats étrangers, Rapport et projet de Résolution définitifs, observations E Beckett, (1952) 44–I AIDI 5, 106, Observations A de Lapradelle: 'L'égalité souveraine des États, indépendants membres de la societé internationale, ne leur permet de venir ni en demande ni en défense devant les tribunaux d'un autre État.'

The maxim *par in parem non habet imperium*—or, equals cannot exercise jurisdiction over one another—was first used in support of the *absolute* state immunity doctrine. In *The Cristina* case Lord Wright wrote that '[t]he rule may be said to be based on the principle "*par in parem non habet imperium*"—no State can claim jurisdiction over another Sovereign State.'[184] The Chilean Supreme Court argued as follows

> One of the fundamental rights of States is their right to equality.... This characteristic... determines that a sovereign State shall not be subject to the jurisdictional power of the courts of another State.[185]

A surprising continuity accordingly characterizes judicial and academic thinking on the rationales of the concept of state immunity. Anzilotti argued—in a brilliant paper on state immunity published in 1910—that the principle of equality and the maxim *par in parem non habet imperium* can only account for an absolute approach to the rule of state immunity.[186] It is not here asserted that the maxim has no place in restrictive immunity theory—in fact, it will later be argued that it does—but it must be admitted that without further theorization the restrictive approach appears to rest somewhat uncomfortably on the justifications offered.

In this regard it is interesting to consider that early restrictive immunity decisions often rationalized the absence of immunity by reference to either the 'implied waiver' or the 'double capacity' theory. These arguments have been spurned in legal theory and practice alike but appear in a different light when understood as an accommodation of the constraints of status thinking.

The implied waiver theory was, for example, relied on in the 1925 case of *Russian Trade Delegation v Tesini and Malvezzi* where the Italian Court of Cassation held that

> (a) Italian courts have no jurisdiction over foreign States, except in cases where the foreign States themselves renounce their jurisdictional immunity;

[184] *The Cristina* (UK, 1938) 162.

[185] *Senerman Rapaport v Republic of Cuba* 65 ILR 29 (Chile, S Ct, 1975) 30. Cf also *S v British Treasury* 24 ILR 223 (Poland, S Ct, 1948) 224–5; C Calvo, *Le droit international théorique et pratique* (3rd edn, 1881) i § 522; A De Cuvelier, 'De l'incompétence des tribunaux nationaux a l'égard des gouvernements étrangers' (1888) 20 RDILC 109. See especially R Provinciali (1933) for the argument that respect for the principles of independence and equality of states imposed an absolute state immunity rule. The equality and independence of states, he argued, are constitutional principles of the international legal order and the rule of absolute state immunity is hence a necessary consequence of the organization of international society in this model. The exercise of jurisdiction is the exercise of sovereignty, which implies a superior power not conceivable between subjects that are independent and equal. He therewith rejected Anzilotti's thesis discussed at the end of § 2.3.2 below. He argued that the principle of equality and independence of states requires an absolute approach to state immunity and hence qualified the absolute rule as a necessary rule, see especially 84–7.

[186] D Anzilotti (1910).

(b) Such a renunciation is implied when the foreign State invokes that jurisdiction by bringing an action before an Italian court *or when it embarks upon commercial or industrial activities in Italy.*[187]

Another illustrative case is the 1925 case of *Storelli v Governo della Repubblica francese*.[188] The Civil Court of Rome refused to grant immunity to the French government in a dispute with an Italian merchant, holding that when

the foreign State transplants itself into the national territory, it must be presumed, because of the imperative simultaneous respect for the sovereignty exercised over such territory, to consent to submit to the exercise of that sovereign's most characteristic function.[189]

Hence, a foreign state was deemed to have voluntarily submitted to the jurisdiction of the forum state in respect of commercial transaction within that state's jurisdiction. Similar reasoning can be found in early Belgian, German, Austrian, Egyptian and Greek restrictive immunity decisions.[190] The reference to implied waiver to justify the exercise of jurisdiction over commercial acts has passed into disuse. The generally accepted view is now that:

[t]here is no attraction in using the theory of 'implied consent' to aggrandise 'exceptions' to the principle of immunity, so to speak, as a flag of convenience. Waiver should in principle exist on the basis of facts indicating a real and not a presumptive consent.[191]

Another concept that features in early restrictive immunity jurisprudence is the theory of 'double capacity' or 'double personality' of a state. The theory, distinguishing between the state as a public entity and the state as a private entity for immunity purposes, was especially popular in Italian jurisprudence. In 1886 the Florence Court of Cassation stated that

once the distinction between the Government as a body politic and a civil entity is admitted, once it is recognized that even a State may, by reason of acts of pure management without offence to its political sovereignty, be made subject to the jurisdiction of foreign courts, there can be nothing more correct than that the foreign State against whom in this capacity a proceeding is brought, must be included in the category of

[187] *Rappresentanza Commerciale Russa v Ditta Tesini e Malvezzi* (1926) 18 RDI 249 (Italy, Corte di Cassazione, 1925); 3 AD 176, case no 127 (emphasis added). Cf also the note of ET Liebman, Case Comment (1926) 18 RDI 257.

[188] *Storelli v Governo della Repubblica francese* (1925) 17 RDI 236 (Italy, Tribunale di Roma, 1924); 2 AD 129, case no 66.

[189] ibid 240 (my translation).

[190] See for an overview of these cases I Sinclair (1980) 200. Cf also CF Gabba, 'De la compétence des tribunaux à l'égard des souverains et des Etats étrangers' (1890) 17 JDIP 27, 39.

[191] I Brownlie (Rapporteur Institut de Droit International), Contemporary Problems Concerning the Jurisdictional Immunity of States, Definitive Report (1987), (1987) 62–I AIDI 45, 94. Cosnard convincingly criticized the use of this construction on dogmatic grounds, arguing that the reasoning can be perfectly reversed to state that the individual has consented implicitly to waive its recourse in case of dispute, or that the forum state has waived its jurisdiction by consenting to the transactions of the defendant state on its territory: M Cosnard (1996) 327.

foreigners ... the State being, in this respect, assimilated to other persons, physical or juristic, not forming part of the Italian Kingdom.[192]

The court made a distinction between the government as a political entity (*ente politico*) and a civil entity (*ente civile)* and held that in this latter capacity the state could be made subject to jurisdiction without offence to its sovereignty. The acts emanating from these different entities were qualified as acts *d'impero* and acts *di gestioni* respectively.[193]

The critical comment by Fitzmaurice that 'a sovereign State does not cease to be a sovereign State because it performs acts which a private citizen might perform'[194] is exemplary for how this reasoning was perceived in doctrine. In the 1912 case of *Gamen Hubert v Etat Russe* the Court of Appeals of Paris rejected the double-personality concept with the following words:

There is no reason for distinguishing between ... the public personality to which foreign jurisdiction does not extend and the juristic personality which is said to be subject to such jurisdiction. All the acts of a state have but one purpose and one finality which is always political; the unity of the state does not permit such duality.[195]

Although the criticism on both theories is valid, it is regrettable that the *function* of those theories in the development of the restrictive immunity theory is disregarded. The role and position of these two concepts in restrictive immunity theory can only be understood in light of the apparent friction between the traditional status-oriented immunity theory and the development of a restrictive regime according a decisive role to the subject matter of the dispute at hand. The reference to implied waiver and double capacity may be characterized as a construction—rather than a theory—rationalizing the restriction of a right based on the sovereign status of the defendant state. Only when the defendant state is not before the foreign court in its sovereign status, or when the defendant state has voluntarily waived the rights flowing from this status, can the restrictive theory be reconciled with the equality-rationale. In other words, these arguments served to accommodate the theoretical constraints of status thinking. Scholars and courts rejecting the implied waiver and double capacity constructions generally assert that *alternatively* courts may exercise jurisdiction over non-sovereign

[192] *Guttieres v Elmilik* (Italy, 1886) 922 (trans in GM Badr (1984) 24). Cf also *Hamspohn v Bey di Tunisi* F It 1887 474 (Italy, Appello Lucca, 1887) 485–6; *Morellet v Governo Danese* (Italy, 1882) 130–1; *Canale v Governo francese* (Italy, 1937). In 1948 the Court of Cassation still relied on this distinction in *Government of Bolivia v Italian Association for Aeronautical Exports*, which was followed in a number of subsequent cases. See also N Wolfman (1910).

[193] ibid 922.

[194] G Fitzmaurice, 'State Immunity from Proceedings in Foreign Courts' (1933) 14 BYIL 101, 121. Cf also A Weiss (1923) 537; P De Paepe, 'De la compétence civile à l'égard des Etats étrangers et de leurs agents politiques, diplomatiques, ou consulaires' (1895) 22 JDIP 31, 33; C De Visscher (1922) 309; CC Hyde, *International Law, chiefly as interpreted and applied by the United States* (1945) ii 844; H Lauterpacht (1951) 224; I Sinclair (1980) 209.

[195] *Gamen Hubert v Etat Russe* (1919) RCDIP 493 (France, Cour d'Appel de Paris, 1912).

acts of foreign states because the nature of such acts does not require courts to abstain from the exercise of jurisdiction. They do not however recognize that the—admittedly somewhat strained—constructions served a legitimate goal and that the proposed *alternative* requires rethinking the theory underlying the international law rule of foreign state immunity.

2.3.2 Regime over Rationales

The application of the restrictive rule further exposes the underdeveloped theorization of its foundations. The consensus on the foreign state immunity concept is limited to the restrictive nature of the rule and does not extend to the modalities of its application. In fact, state practice is far from uniform. The application of the rule is generally seen to give rise to two distinct problems. First, there is the theoretical problem of identification of the relevant aspects of a case. Should regard be had to the purpose or the nature of an act when determining its character? Second, at a more practical level there are difficulties classifying the relevant aspects as either public or private in character.[196] The discussion of both issues reflects a poor understanding of the nature and the scope of the rule of state immunity.

The identification issue is often referred to as the nature–purpose controversy: is the qualification of acts under the restrictive theory exclusively based on the nature of the act, or may its purpose be taken into account? The classic example to explain the difference is the act of purchasing boots for the army—which is clearly not sovereign in its nature but can be said to serve a sovereign purpose.[197] The opposition against an acknowledged relevance of the purpose of state activity is hardly surprising. Schreuer aptly noted that '[o]nce we start inquiring into the underlying motives of a State partner to a transaction we will most probably end up with some political purpose somewhere.'[198] The statement of the US Supreme Court in *Berrizi Bros v Pesaro* that there was 'no international usage which regards the maintenance and advancement of the economic welfare of a people in time of peace as any less a public purpose than the maintenance and

[196] CH Schreuer (1988) 15.

[197] While a US court declared the act to be of a sovereign nature, an Italian court qualified the act as non-sovereign: *Kingdom of Roumania v Guaranty Trust Co. of New York* (US, 1918) 345; *Governo Rumeno v Trutta* 78 Giu It 1926–I 774 (Italy, 1926). Cf also *Victory Transport Inc. v Comisaria Gen. De Abestecimientos y Transportes* (US, 1964) 359, on the nature of the act as test: 'While this criterion is relatively easy to apply, it ofttimes produces rather astonishing results, such as the holdings of some European courts that purchase of bullets or shoes for the army…are private acts.' (It is noted that nowadays also the US courts agree that 'the intent of the purchasing sovereign to use the goods for military purposes does not take the transaction outside the "commercial exception" to sovereign immunity', *McDonnell Douglas Corp. v Islamic Republic of Iran* 758 F 2d 341 (Ct of Apps (8th Cir), 1985) 349.) Other diverging approaches are mentioned in the Harvard Law School, Research in International Law (Reporter PC Jessup), Competence of Courts in Regard to Foreign States (1932 supplement) 26 AJIL 451, 609ff; H Lauterpacht (1951) 222; I Sinclair (1980) 210.

[198] CH Schreuer (1988) 15.

training of a naval force'[199] is an almost grotesque confirmation of the rationality of this fear. It is therefore often firmly stated that '[a]s a means for determining the distinction between acts *jure imperii* and *jure gestionis* one should rather refer to the nature of the State transaction or the resulting legal relationships, and not to the motive or purpose of the State activity.'[200] The nature test has been incorporated in several national immunity statutes and (draft) conventions and has been approved by many courts.[201]

The agreement reached is however apparent. It has repeatedly been argued that the purpose of an act cannot be completely discarded in the qualification process since '[it] is not possible to classify the nature of any human activity without reference to its purpose.'[202] Crawford has argued that in fact the real issue is the distinction of narrow and broader aspects of a transaction. He explained that '[t]he acceptance of an offer may entail the conclusion of a contract on particular terms for the purchase of concrete for use in building barracks to house an army increased in size for particular foreign policy issues.'[203] The broader aspects of a case may be regarded irrelevant when they are too remote from the activity that is at the basis of the claim.[204] This example, however, fits the classic nature–purpose distinction quite well, and most scholars would agree that the reasons underlying the purchase do not alter the 'private' nature of the conclusion of the contract that is at the basis of the claim before the court. The real problem seems to be that in fact one must not generalize the activity in the qualification process, overemphasizing the private nature of a particular aspect of the complex of facts that is at the basis of the claim. Or, the necessity of identifying the transaction 'as precisely and narrowly as is reasonably possible' may in fact require the taking into account of the *broader* aspects of the transaction at the basis of the claim before the court—indeed to get a *full* picture of the specific activity complained of.

A quotation taken from *International Association of Machinists and Aerospace Workers v Organization of Petroleum Exporting Countries et al.* serves to illustrate this seemingly contradictory assertion. Plaintiffs brought an action against OPEC and its member states alleging that their price-setting activities were

[199] *Berrizi Bros v Pesaro* (US, 1926) 574.

[200] *Claim against the Empire of Iran Case* (Federal Republic of Germany, 1963) 80.

[201] After a fierce debate on the issue in the ILC the 2004 UN Convention now provides in art 2.2: 'In determining whether a contract or transaction is a "commercial transaction"... reference should be made primarily to the nature of the contract or transaction, but its purpose should also be taken into account if the parties to the contract or the transaction have so agreed, or if, in the practice of the State of the forum, that purpose is relevant to determining the non-commercial character of the contract or transaction'.

[202] Australian Law Reform Commission, Foreign State Immunity, Report no 24 (1984) § 49. Cf also J Crawford, 'International Law and Foreign Sovereigns: Distinguishing Immune Transactions' (1983) 54 BYIL 75, 95; *I Congreso del Partido* (UK, 1981) 272 (*per* Lord Wilberforce); *Re Canada Labour Code* [1992] 2 SCR 50 (Canada, S Ct, 1992) 73.

[203] J Crawford, 'International Law and Foreign Sovereigns: Distinguishing Immune Transactions' (1983) 54 BYIL 75, 95.

[204] See CH Schreuer (1988) 22 and J Crawford, ibid 97 for a discussion of the 'once a trader—always a trader?'—issue and the complex facts of *I Congreso del Partido* (UK, 1981).

anti-competitive and illegal under US law and claiming damages for injury caused by having to pay higher petrol prices. They argued that defendants did not enjoy immunity under the FSIA since the action was based on commercial activities as provided in section 1605(a)(2) of the Act. The court dismissed the action on immunity grounds, arguing, *inter alia*, as follows:

> [T]he determining factor is how the court defines the act or activity. An act or activity can be defined broadly, such as 'hiring of employees', an activity carried on by private parties, and thus 'commercial', or it can be defined narrowly, such as, 'employment of diplomatic, civil service or military personnel', a governmental activity. It was suggested that in determining whether to define a particular act narrowly or broadly, the court should be guided by the legislative intent of the FSIA, to keep our courts away from those areas that touch very closely upon the sensitive nerves of foreign countries.
>
> This Court agrees that this 'commercial activity' should be defined narrowly. This determination, while based partially on the factor mentioned above, is premised primarily on the recognition that a court must base its ruling on specific facts. By basing a ruling on a *generalized* view of the evidence, a court may be passing its ruling on half-truths. This Court is required to make its ruling upon the *specific* evidence presented in the evidentiary hearings and trial. From the evidence presented to this Court, it is clear that the nature of the activity engaged in by each of these OPEC member countries is the establishment by a sovereign state of the terms and conditions for the removal of a prime natural resource . . . from its territory.[205]

Control over natural resources, concluded the court, is a sovereign function and when a sovereign state establishes the terms and conditions for removal of natural resources from its territory it is performing a governmental, not a commercial activity.

Without theorization the *acta jure imperii–acta jure gestionis* distinction tends to direct the focus to the acts at the basis of a claim rather than the activity. Another—delightfully straightforward—example is found in the Dutch case of *LF and HMHK v Federal Republic of Germany*.[206] A Dutch national present on Dutch territory entered into an agreement for the sale and delivery of hashish with—what later turned out to be—a German undercover agent. The individual was arrested by the German police upon delivery in Germany and convicted by a German criminal court to a term of imprisonment of nine years. In proceedings before the Dutch courts the individual applied for an injunction ordering the FRG to return him to the Netherlands and to pay damages on the ground that the methods of investigation employed against him and the prosecution and trial were unlawful. While the individual relied on established case law that a

[205] *International Association of Machinists and Aerospace Workers v Organization of Petroleum Exporting Countries* 477 F Supp 553 (US, DC, 1979) 567; 63 ILR 284, 291. It is noted that the decision was affirmed on appeal but on act of state grounds 649 F 2d 1354 (US, Ct of Apps 9th Cir), (1981); 66 ILR 413.

[206] *LF and HMHK v Federal Republic of Germany* NJ 1987 No 955 (Netherlands, Rechtbank Haarlem, 1986); 20 NYIL 1989 285–9.

foreign state does not enjoy immunity when it enters into a legal relationship on an equal footing with individuals; the court placed the disputed contract in a broader context—thus defining the activity at hand more 'narrowly'—and found that Germany was immune from the jurisdiction of the Dutch courts since the disputed acts were performed in the exercise of a public law function.[207]

Also immunity decisions in labour disputes between a foreign state and its employees working at an embassy or consulate in the forum state cannot be explained on the basis of a strict public–private *act* distinction. Exceptions exist, of course. A French national employed as head of the visa section of a French consulate in Austria sued France in an Austrian court for breach of contract and unpaid salary. The Austrian Supreme Court considered that '[w]here a foreign State acts as the holder of private rights and concludes a contract of employment for work to be performed on the territory of the State of the forum, that foreign State can also be subjected to proceedings concerning the employment relationship. What must be examined is not the purpose of the work but the nature of the employment obligations.'[208] In general, however, courts attach importance to the question whether the proceedings would interfere with the exercise of public authority rather than to the nature of the contract under consideration alone. No agreement exists, however, as to *when* proceedings constitute an unlawful interference. Some courts regard the mere fact that an individual was employed at an embassy or consulate a sufficient reason for the grant of immunity; others inquire into the type of activities performed by the individual or the type of claim instigated.[209]

It was noted earlier that in addition to the quandary of identification of the relevant aspects, the question of classification troubles the application of the restrictive immunity rule. Many scholars have in fact questioned whether the distinction between *acta jure imperii* and *acta jure gestionis*—or that between the sovereign/public and non-sovereign/private acts of a state—forms a satisfactory formulation of the restrictive immunity rule. In 1963 Brierly noted that the distinction 'although superficially attractive as a means of keeping state immunity

[207] Cf for a more dubious case: *Heaney v Government of Spain and Adolpho Gomero* 445 F 2d 501 (US, Ct of Apps 2nd Cir, 1971), 57 ILR 153. The court qualified a contract between Spain and Mr Heaney in which the latter undertakes to generate adverse publicity against the UK with the purpose to oust the UK from Gibraltar as a strictly political or public act and granted Spain immunity in a dispute concerning payment under the contract.

[208] *French Consular Employee Claim Case* (Austria, S Ct, 1989) 86 ILR 583.

[209] See for a comprehensive overview of case law R Garnett, 'State Immunity in Employment Matters', 46 ICLQ 1997 81; H Fox, 'Employment Contracts as an Exception to State Immunity: Is All Public Service Immune?', 66 BYIL 1995 97. The 2004 UN Convention employment contracts are explicitly excluded from the definition of 'commercial transaction'. Art 11 of the Convention determines that states *are* immune in respect of employment contracts concerning personnel 'recruited to perform particular functions in the exercise of governmental authority', concerning diplomatic agents, consular officers, and persons representing them at international organizations and conferences. Moreover, they are immune if 'the subject-matter of the proceeding is the recruitment, renewal of employment or reinstatement of an individual'.

within reasonable limits, does not rest on any sound logical basis; it involves making assumptions as to what are the proper functions of government which might be justifiable assumptions according to the *laissez-faire* theories of the nineteenth-century but may seem arbitrary today in a world community which contains socialist and communist as well as capitalist states.'[210] These concerns are echoed in the observation of Brownlie that 'there is a logical contradiction in seeking to distinguish the "sovereign" and "non-sovereign" acts of a State. In attempting to apply such a distinction, municipal courts inevitably apply the ideological conceptions and policy preferences of the particular forum.'[211]

A common response to the elusive nature of the restrictive rule has been that acts should be classified according to national law standards—the *lex fori*. Thus, in *Claim against Empire of Iran* the German *Bundesverfassungsgericht* considered that 'the classification of a State's function (according to the legal nature of the act) as governmental or non-governmental must be determined according to current domestic law, as international law does not, as a rule, include criteria for such a delineation'.[212] Cosnard asserted in this respect that '[l]e principe de la qualification des activités litigieuses par la loi du for est maintenant bien établie.'[213]

The idea of forum state discretion underlies for example the distinction between private law acts and public law acts as a criterion for the application of the restrictive immunity rule, relied on in many civil law countries, and in particular in France. Already the fact that a similar classification of acts is unknown to common law countries and can therefore not be *the* criterion for distinction, indicates that this is a solution at the national, not the international level.[214] An alternative criterion—partially developed in response to the particulars of the common law system—is the test whether the act concerned could, by its very nature, equally have been committed by a private person. This test was already proposed by Weiss in 1923.[215] Several influential scholars—including Jennings and Higgins—have expressed support for this solution.[216] Although this test leaves somewhat more room for objective classification of the facts of the case

[210] JL Brierly, *The Law of Nations, An Introduction to the International Law of Peace* (H Waldock (ed), 6th edn, 1963) 250. Cf also H Lauterpacht (1951) 224: 'the distinction between acts *jure gestionis* and acts *jure imperii* cannot be placed on a sound logical basis'.

[211] I Brownlie (Rapporteur Institut de Droit International) Contemporary Problems Concerning the Jurisdictional Immunity of States, Preliminary Report (1987), 62–I AIDI 1987 13, 27. Cf also Australian Law Reform Commission, Foreign State Immunity, Report no 24 (1984), § 48; CH Schreuer (1988) 7; WTR Fox, 'Competence of Courts in Regard to "Non-Sovereign" Acts of Foreign States', 35 AJIL 1941 632.

[212] *Claim against the Empire of Iran Case* (Federal Republic of Germany, 1963), 80. Cf also *Church of Scientology Case* (FRG, Federal S Ct, 1978), 65 ILR 193, 196–7.

[213] M Cosnard (1996) 342.

[214] See R Higgins (1982) 268; Australian Law Reform Commission, Foreign State Immunity, Report no 24 (1984) § 48.

[215] A Weiss (1923) 545.

[216] R Jennings (1988) 8; R Higgins (1994) 84. Cf also Federal Republic of Germany, *Claim against the Empire of Iran Case* (1963) 80; Switzerland, Tribunal federal Suisse, *Affaire Etat de Koweït v XSA* (1994), Pratique Suisse 1994, no 3.1, 5 RSDIE 1995, 593ff.

than a strict adherence to the applicable law distinction, it is clear that ultimately national law conceptions will influence the qualification process.

Reliance on the *lex fori* in the application of the restrictive immunity rule is however far from uncontroversial. De Visscher and Verhoeven argued that, state immunity being a rule of international law, international law should define the concepts used to apply the rule, or, should at least be at the basis of such a definition.[217] And indeed, acceptation of the proposition that the forum state has discretion in classifying acts for the purpose of the application of the restrictive theory necessarily entails the negation of the existence of a rule of state immunity in international law. Crawford rightly considered that the *lex fori* principle can only mean that international law 'does not *require* immunity to be accorded to foreign State defendants... in any case'.[218] He argued that 'as soon as it is conceded that... international law does require some immunity, then international law distinguishes to that extent between immune and non-immune transactions, and the question becomes on what basis it is doing so.... The initial assumption should be that international law does allow such distinctions to be drawn, that it does not leave them to the uneven discretion of forum States.'[219] The criticism is compelling. Moreover, it may be clear that it applies with equal force to a reliance on the law of the defendant state,[220] and *a fortiori* to a reliance on a defendant state's own characterization of the act.[221] It is recalled that the thought underlying the adoption of the *lex fori* principle is that the criterion used to define the restrictive rule cannot be applied with reference to the system of law to which the rule belongs. A complete deference to *lex fori* would however deny the rule *any* basis in international law. Interestingly enough, the supporters of the *lex fori* principle are not prepared to go this far. In the *Claim against Empire of Iran* case the court stressed that '[n]ational law can only be employed to distinguish between a sovereign and a non-sovereign activity of a foreign State insofar as it cannot exclude from the sovereign sphere, and thus from immunity, such State dealings as belong to the field of State authority in the narrow and proper sense, according to the predominantly-held view of States. In this generally recognizable field of sovereign activity are included transactions relating to foreign affairs, and

[217] P De Visscher & J Verhoeven (1971) 60–1. Cf also *Airport Linz v United States* (Austria, S Ct, 2004), discussed in a case note of S Wittich (2005), 99 AJIL 248; *Dralle v Republic of Czechoslovakia*, (Austria , 1950); *Floridi v Sovexportfilm* (Italy, 1951), Annali X (1952) 115.

[218] J Crawford (1983) 78.

[219] ibid 78. Cf also CH Schreuer (1988) 33.

[220] Cf for such reliance *Etat italien v X* (Switzerland, Cour d'appel de Bâle-Ville, 1985), 42 ASDI 1986 60, 61–2.

[221] Cf *Russian Trade Delegation in Italy v Kazmann* (Italy, Court of Cassation, 1933), 7 AD 178, case no 69 where the court granted immunity to a Russian state agency engaged in commercial activity because 'trading abroad is regarded by the Russian State as a function of an essentially public character' and that 'it is so treated by the internal ordering of that State under which there is established in this respect, by the Constitution itself, a monopolistic regime, controlled by a People's Commisar'; *Feldman v Etat de Bahia* (Belgium, Cour d'appel de Bruxelles, 1907), RCDIP 1909 956.

military authority, the legislature, the exercise of police authority, and the administration of justice.'[222] And also Cosnard eventually qualified his argument that 'les États sont libre de déterminer pour leur propre compte la manière dont ils appliqueront ce principe à l'égard des autres États'[223] with the consideration that such occurs 'sous réserve de [la] compatibilité [de la loi du for] avec le droit international, afin d'éviter de trop grandes distorsions entre les décisions'.[224]

In addition to the general definitional problem, it has been argued that the public–private act distinction does in fact not account for all exceptions to the rule of state immunity. Crawford, for example, has argued that the so-called territorial tort exception cannot be explained by reference to the distinction.[225] The exception—included in almost all national legislations and international (draft) conventions—regards acts qualifying as tortious under the *lex loci delicti commissi* that are closely connected to the territory of the forum state and cause physical injury or loss or damage to property.

In sum, the problems with the identification and classification of activity for the purpose of the application of the restrictive state immunity rule are a symptom of a wider problem. The requirements of international law cannot be explained by reference to a strict public–private act distinction. The formulation of the restrictive rule as protecting states from foreign jurisdiction as regards their public acts but not as regards their private acts may be seen to detach the rule from its rationales. It must be concluded that state immunity practice reinforces the need to study the basis of the rule in international law. If the public–private act distinction is not at the heart of the rule, what is? What exactly are the requirements of international law? Ironically enough, the troubled application of the restrictive rule has only served to alienate courts and scholars even further from a principled approach to the requirements under international law. Courts and scholars alike have directed all efforts on the formulation of the applicable regime while the theory justifying and explaining this regime is often disregarded.

In a rather fatalistic vein, some scholars argued that the absolute immunity doctrine was the only sound alternative.[226] Lauterpacht came to the opposite conclusion. He advanced the view that international law did not oblige states

[222] *Claim Against the Empire of Iran Case* (Federal Republic of Germany, 1963) 81.

[223] M Cosnard (1996) 25.

[224] ibid 342. Cf also G Ress (Rapporteur International Law Association), First Report on Developments in the Field of State Immunity since 1982, Report of the Sixty-fourth Conference (1990) 393, 396–7; G Dahm, 'Völkerrechtliche Grenzen der Inländischen Gerichtsbarkeit gegenüber auslandischen Staaten', in *Festschrift für Arthur Nikisch* (1958) 153, 167; M Panebianco, *Giuridisdizione interna e immunità degli Stati stranieri* (1967) 120.

[225] Australian Law Reform Commission, Foreign State Immunity, Report no 24 (1984) § 51. Cf also J Bröhmer, *State Immunity and Human Rights Violations* (1997) 60, 140 and 222; L Caflisch, Immunité de Juridiction et Respect des Droits de l'Homme, in L Boisson de Chazournes and V Gowlland-Debbas (eds), *The International Legal System in Quest of Equity and Universality* (2001) 651, 656.

[226] G Fitzmaurice (1933) 124. Cf also C Fairman, 'Some Disputed Applications of the Principle of State Immunity' (1928) 22 AJIL 569; R Provinciali (1933).

to grant jurisdictional immunity to other states.[227] Foreign states, he argued, should be made

> accountable before otherwise competent courts in respect of claims put forward against it in the matter both of contract and tort in the same way in which the domestic state is subject to the law administered by the courts.[228]

Less drastic proposals have attempted to formulate a workable regime based on a restrictive approach to the rule of state immunity. Some scholars proposed to deny immunity as regards commercial acts rather than non-sovereign acts.[229] More popular is the breaking up of the concept of non-sovereign acts in a set of specific descriptions of different categories of activity in regard of which states may be subjected to foreign jurisdiction. All national codifications of the state immunity rule, as well as the European Convention on State Immunity, the UN Convention on the Jurisdictional Immunities of States and their Property, and most draft conventions prepared by international learned bodies have adopted this approach of a basic immunity rule with the enumeration of multiple criteria for the distinction of non-immune transactions.[230]

The formulation of multiple non-immunity criteria of course does not solve the substantive differences of opinion on the extent of immunity required in international law. Exactly because of the different accents placed by states in the inviduation process and the differences in the notion of public authority prevalent in each state, the codification of the restrictive rule in an authoritative multilateral convention has not been easy.[231] The advantage of the approach is limited to the replacement of the strained concept of public or private *acts* as the decisive criterion with a more tangible, more workable set of well-defined situations in which in no immunity is available. The multiple criteria approach to

[227] H Lauterpacht (1951) 228.

[228] ibid 226.

[229] JP Niboyet, 'Les immunités de juridiction en droit français, des états étrangers engagés dans des transactions privées' (1936) 43 RGDIP 525, 532. The distinction between commercial and other acts of states has however been rejected by many others: cf eg *Claim Against the Empire of Iran Case* (FRG, 1963) 80.

[230] A notable exception is the Resolution adopted by the the Institut de Droit International (Rapporteur I Brownlie), Resolution on Contemporary Problems Concerning the Jurisdictional Immunity of States (1992), 64–II AIDI 1992 267. The Resolution contains two sets of countervailing critera that argue in favour or against competence over foreign states. Also the ILA Draft Articles for a Convention on State Immunity hint at a somewhat different approach. Article II states that '[i]n general, a foreign State shall be immune from the adjudicatory jurisdiction of a forum State for acts performed by it in the exercise of its sovereign authority, i.e. iure imperii. It shall not be immune in the circumstances provided in article III.'

[231] In 2004 the 1991 ILC Draft Articles finally led to the adoption of the UN Convention on Jurisdictional Immunities of States and their Property (GA Resolution 59/38 (2004). The Convention must now secure sufficient ratifications in order to escape the faith of the European Convention on State Immunity that was only ratified by eight states.

the restrictive theory clearly does not solve the problem of distinction, rather, it 'replace[s] one big intractable problem by a series of smaller, easier ones'.[232]

The *disadvantages* of the multiple criteria approach may not be as readily discernable. The formulation of the rule as a basic rule of immunity with a list of exceptions to it has, however, considerable repercussions for the theory of state immunity since it detaches the rule even further from the requirements of international law. Clearly, 'the rule of international law will be one which defines, or limits, the cases where immunity from jurisdiction ought to be allowed, rather than one defining the area of non-immunity'.[233] This reality is not—to put it mildly—unequivocally reflected in the multiple criteria approach to the state immunity rule. When the rule is formulated through the listing of the widely accepted exceptions to it, it no longer has a reference to concepts that explain its basis in international law. Although it is generally emphasized that the focus on the exceptions in the multiple criteria approach is 'a matter of legislative convenience' that allows no inferences as to a general rule of international law requiring immunity,[234] and it has been argued that the exceptions are fashioned 'taking into account the reasons for according immunity or for asserting jurisdiction in that specific context',[235] Brownlie rightly remarked that '[t]here is a complete absence of reference to the indicia which favour "immunity *ratione materiae*" ... Indeed, one may suspect that some lawyers have the curious assumption that it is heretical to study the legal geography on *both* sides of the line between immunity and no immunity.'[236]

Despite all assurances to the contrary the multiple criteria approach depicts the state immunity rule as the continuation of the absolute rule with exceptions accepted to it. For example, Jessup in one of his comments on the 1932 Harvard Research Project, wrote:

> The general proposition that a State may not be made a respondent in the courts of another State is widely accepted. It is the usual point of departure in the discussion of jurists, and in the opinions of courts. The rule is said to be implicit in the principles of the independence and the equality of States. One sovereign can not exercise jurisdiction over another: *jurisdictio inhaeret, cohaeret, adhaeret imperio; par in parem non habet imperium.*
>
> ...
>
> As a fundamental rule of departure, the rule regarding State immunity persists ... Exceptions, however, have made their appearance as the necessities of modern life have changed and developed.[237]

[232] CH Schreuer (1988) 8.

[233] R Jennings (1988) 9.

[234] CH Schreuer (1988) 7.

[235] Australian Law Reform Commission, Foreign State Immunity, Report no 24 (1984) § 52.

[236] I Brownlie (Rapporteur Institut de Droit International), Contemporary Problems Concerning the Jurisdictional Immunity of States, Definitive Report (1987), (1987) 62–I AIDI 45, 49.

[237] Harvard Law School, Research in International Law (Reporter PC Jessup), Competence of Courts in Regard to Foreign States 1932 (supplement) 26 AJIL 451, 527 (comment on art 7).

The idea that the exceptions to the rule of state immunity should be derived from a close examination of state practice regarding the rule in order to identify sufficient precedents supporting a particular exception is not uncommon. The consideration of the Canadian Supreme Court in the 2002 case of *Schreiber v Canada* that '[o]ver the years, the general principle of sovereign immunity has been attenuated somewhat, and certain exceptions to the general rule have emerged',[238] may be seen to express a widespread conviction in international legal theory. The approach traces to the common law countries that once adhered to an absolute state immunity rule. We saw earlier, however, that *international law* never required states to grant other states absolute immunity from their jurisdiction. Rather, the international law rule has always been limited to the *acta jure imperii* of foreign states.

The definition of the international law rule in terms of an absolute rule with customary law exceptions accepted to it influences the debate on the human rights exception to state immunity. On the one hand the *form* of the argument of opponents of the human rights exception clearly relies on this inductive approach to the emergence of exceptions to a basic principle of state immunity. On the other hand the *substance* of arguments of both proponents and opponents suffers from the focus on the regime of the law of state immunity rather than its rationales. The debate fails to recognize the qualitative difference between the commercial activity exception and a possible human rights exception to state immunity rules. Is the grant of state immunity to a foreign state in a commercial dispute of the same nature as the grant of state immunity to a foreign state in a dispute concerning alleged abuse of police power within that state's own borders?

In section 3 below it will be explained why it is not. Here only a tip of the veil is lifted through the discussion of a particularly insightful perspective on the state immunity rule developed by Anzilotti in 1910.[239] Anzilotti noted that the absolute and restrictive immunity theory are not mutually exclusive since they do not operate on the same level. However, both the adherents of the restrictive as well as those of the absolute theory failed to convince: the first by not reasoning beyond principle and the second by insisting on reasoning from principle. The restrictive theory, he argued, only establishes the possibilities from which international law can develop limitations.[240] Italian courts, he argued, in applying the restrictive doctrine fail to acknowledge that through the practice of states an international custom of absolute immunity had developed. The adherents of an absolute theory, on the other hand, were held to mistakenly argue that that theory was rooted in the quality of the state, asserting a fundamental impossibility to exercise foreign jurisdiction over it. Under reference to the well-established immovable property

[238] *Schreiber v Canada (Attorney General)* [2002] 3 SCR 269 (Canada, S Ct, 2002) § 15, see also § 17. Cf also *Bouzari v Islamic Republic of Iran* (Canada, Ontario CA, 2004) available at <http://www.ontariocourts.on.ca/decisions/2004/june/bouzariC382.htm> 95, § 41.

[239] D Anzilotti (1910).

[240] ibid 499.

exception to state immunity, Anzilotti explained that once it is admitted that *some* exceptions to state immunity are allowed the argument that *the principle* of the equality of states *requires* state immunity as a basic rule is no longer coherent. The nature of the obligation to grant immunity from jurisdiction to foreign states, he argued, does not differ from that under other immunity rules like for example diplomatic immunity. The question is whether a state has a right to immunity with regard to those acts for which it can be subjected to the jurisdiction of another state.[241] This right, he argued, would have to be established by the collective will of states.[242] In the proposed perspective, the principles relied on by adherents of the absolute theory—the dignity, equality, and independence of sovereign states—are but the material causes of the customary practice that has formed the rule.[243]

The gist of the argument advanced by Anzilotti can be restated as an identification of the difference between necessary and voluntary immunity rules with the restrictive theory falling within the first and the absolute theory within the latter category.[244] The article did not expand on the concept of necessary immunity rules. It was taken for granted that as regards *acta jure imperii* states could not be subjected to each other's jurisdiction. It was only explained that *beyond* this impossibility, rooted in the principles of international law, states had developed a customary rule of absolute state immunity with the principles of dignity, equality, and independence of states as mere material causes of state practice. Hence, from a contemporary perspective this would compel the conclusion that the development of a restrictive immunity concept entails a qualitative and not a mere quantitative change as compared to the absolute immunity concept.[245]

Also the illustrious proposal of Lauterpacht may be seen to appear in a different light when put in this perspective. In his seminal 1951 article on state immunity Lauterpacht advocated the abolition of the rule of state immunity. He argued that there is no rule of international law that obliges states to grant jurisdictional immunity to other states—a rather bold statement indeed.[246] Instead, he proposed, a foreign state should be made accountable 'before otherwise competent courts in respect of claims put forward against it in the matter both of contract and tort in the same way in which the domestic state is subject to the law administered by the courts'.[247] It has often been remarked that Lauterpacht's proposal did not in fact amount to an abolition of the rule of state immunity.

[241] ibid 503.
[242] ibid 504.
[243] ibid 515.
[244] It recalls the distinction between natural law and voluntary law as found already in the work of H Grotius, *De Jure Belli ac Pacis* (1625) translated by LR Loomis (1949) ii 193–200. This distinction—and the fundamental difference between natural and necessary law—is further elaborated below.
[245] Cf GM Badr (1984) 134.
[246] H Lauterpacht (1951) 228.
[247] ibid 226.

Crawford, for example, pointed out that although Lauterpacht went close to abolition he 'allowed a quite extensive area of immunity in as it were, through the back door'.[248] In fact, Lauterpacht followed his proposal for abolition of the rule with the caveat that immunity must remain the rule in respect of:

1. the legislative acts of a foreign state and of measures taken in pursuance thereof;
2. the executive and administrative acts of a foreign state within its territory (e.g. alleged unjustified expulsion, exaction of dues, wrongful imprisonment or, generally, denial of justice.) In particular, no action should lie with regard to torts committed by foreign states and their organs in their own territory.
3. contracts that by virtue of private international law are outside the jurisdiction of the forum state;
4. matters to which the law of diplomatic immunity applies.[249]

If the category of acts singled out by Lauterpacht overlaps with the acts for which immunity exists under the restrictive theory this does not necessarily mean that he qualified his proposal to abolish the rule of immunity. Rather, it may suggest that the category of acts protected by the restrictive theory is in fact outside the jurisdiction of foreign courts on grounds unrelated to the classical immunity from jurisdiction concept. In this respect, the caveat 'otherwise competent courts' may very well be an allusion to these categories of residual 'immunity'.[250] Clearly, the third category is unrelated to immunity law. Lauterpacht explained that the abolition of immunity 'should not place the foreign state in a position less advantageous than that of private individuals'.[251] States would in these circumstances not enjoy immunity from the jurisdiction of foreign courts; rather these foreign courts would not be able to establish jurisdiction in the first place. Does a similar consideration not apply to the first and the second category? Admittedly, Lauterpacht himself did not elaborate on this issue. At the risk of reading too much in his words, it is argued here that Lauterpacht, with the simultaneous abolition of the rule of state immunity and formulation of the four categories, recognized the essentially different nature of the rule of absolute immunity and what is called the rule of restrictive immunity.

The problem with the standard approach to state immunity is that it employs the terminology of a voluntary immunity concept with a focus on customary obligations and marginal regard to principle while the immunity concept as applied today may very well qualify for the most part within the category of necessary obligations. Courts, although eventually willing to change their practice to adapt to economic reality, have proven unable to adapt the theory to the reality of this new practice.

[248] J Crawford (1983) 78, fn 14.

[249] H Lauterpacht (1951) 237.

[250] Apart from category 4 which refers to the separate topic of diplomatic immunity discussed in ch 4 of this study.

[251] H Lauterpacht (1951) 238.

3 The Independence and Equality of States as Limits on the Essential Competence of National Courts

3.1 Introduction

Dworkin pointedly noted that '[d]iscretion, like the hole in a doughnut, does not exist except as an area left open by a surrounding belt of restriction.'[252] The almost casual observation of Cosnard that the discretion of national courts to have regard to their *lex fori* is of course subject to 'les limites raisonnables' or even more specific to the 'compatibilité avec le droit international' affirms that the rule of restrictive state immunity *can* ultimately be defined in terms of international law.[253] The limits to the discretion are the parameters of the obligation under international law. These limits can be explained by reference to two fundamental principles of international law: the independence and equality of states.

This section will approach the requirements of international law in regard to national court proceedings against foreign states from the perspective of these two principles. The thesis advanced by Brownlie—and a handful of other scholars—that in substance the rule of state immunity as we know it today in fact reflects the operation of several principles of international law regarding the essential competence of national courts will prove convincing and relevant. In this respect, the definition of the rule adopted by the Italian *Corte di Cassazione* is particularly instructive. Foreign states, the court considered, are exempt from jurisdiction with regard 'to those relations which remain completely outside the Italian legal order or because those States act, albeit within the territory of some other States, as subjects of international law, or because they act as the holders of a power of command within their own legal order and within the limits of their own territory'.[254] This definition reveals the two distinct issues of competence cloaked under the concept of state immunity for *acta jure imperii*. On the one hand there is the division of competence between national courts—the horizontal division—based on the principle of non-interference, and inherent in the recognition of the exclusive competence of states to exercise certain powers on their territory independent from other states; on the other hand there is the division of competence between national courts and international dispute settlement procedures—the vertical division—based on the principle of equality of states, and inherent in a non-hierarchical international legal order. The reformulation of the restrictive rule of state immunity in terms of non-competence allows us to make several pertinent observations regarding the nature and substance of the

252 R Dworkin, *Taking Rights Seriously* (1977) 31.

253 See n 224 above.

254 *Campione v Peti-Nitrogenmuvek NV and Hungarian Republic* 65 ILR 287 (Italy, Court of Cassation, 1972) 300. Cf also *Kingdom of Greece v Gamet* 28 ILR 153 (Italy, Court of Cassation, 1959).

law of state immunity. In particular, it will be argued that the distinction of the concept of immunity from the concept of incompetence has consequences for the parameters of coherent arguments in the debate on a human rights exception to state immunity rules.

3.2 The Independence and Equality of States

3.2.1 Non-Interference in the Exercise of Sovereign Authority

It is sometimes argued that since the notion at the root of sovereignty is superiority the term is ill-fitted to describe the state in its relations with other states.[255] It may be clear, however, that such reasoning confuses the internal and external aspect of sovereignty. External sovereignty does not regard absolutist power of states in the international legal order; it is but the other side of the medal of internal sovereignty when recognized by other states. In fact it reflects the co-existence of and cooperation between states on a basis of juridical equality rather than superiority, since states are essentially equal in their sovereign status. The notion of external sovereignty serves to secure the independent exercise of the competences attributed to the state under international law and guarantees states the right to respect for one's statehood.

Judge Alvarez famously wrote in the *Corfu Channel* case that

> [b]y sovereignty, we understand the whole body of rules and attributes which a state possesses in its territory, to the exclusion of all other states, and also in relation with other states.[256]

It may be more instructive to say that international law recognizes a bundle of competences that all states possess—including a body of exclusive territorial competences—and that the notion of sovereignty serves to establish that states have the right to exercise these competences independently and on a basis of equality with other states. As Judge Huber explained in the *Palmas Islands* case:

> Sovereignty in the relations between States signifies independence. Independence in regard to a portion of the globe is the right to exercise therein to the exclusion of any other State, the functions of a State. The development of the national organisation of States during the last few centuries and, as a corollary, the development of international law, have established this principle of the exclusive competence of the State in regard to its own territory in such a way as to make it the point of departure in settling most questions.[257]

[255] JL Brierly, 'The Shortcomings of International Law' (1924) 5 BYIL 4, 12. Cf also L Henkin, 'The Mythology of Sovereignty' in RSJ MacDonald (ed), *Essays in Honour of Wang Tieya* (1994) 351, 352.

[256] *Corfu Channel Case* (*United Kingdom v Albania*) (Merits), ICJ Reports 1949 4, Individual Opinion Judge Alvarez 39, 43.

[257] *Island of Palmas Case* (*Netherlands v United States*) 2 RIAA 829 (PCA, 1928) 838. Crawford used a combination of the two definitions: '[i]n its most common modern usage, sovereignty is the

This right to an independent and exclusive exercise of certain powers with regard to a certain portion of the globe has as a necessary corollary the obligation of states *not* to exercise those powers within the territory of other states without their consent, *and* to refrain from interfering in the exercise of another state's powers that qualify as exclusive under international law. The principle that '[e]very State has the right to independence and hence to exercise freely, without dictation by any other State, all its legal powers, including the choice of its own form of government' is clearly mirrored in the principle that '[e]very State has the duty to refrain from intervention in the internal or external affairs of any other State.'[258]

Territorial boundaries provide a clear-cut limit for the exercise of *imperium*. When the Dutch police wishes to continue its pursuit of a criminal suspect that takes refuge in Belgian territory it will need to cooperate with Belgian authorities to accomplish the arrest. It needs little explanation that the abduction of Adolf Eichmann by Israeli authorities from Argentine soil with the purpose of putting him on trial in Israel violated the territorial integrity and the sovereignty of Argentina. More subtle however, is the limit put on the exercise of *imperium* within a state's own territory so as not to interfere with another state's exercise of *imperium*. The principle of non-interference imposes that states may not exercise their exclusive state authority as regards issues that fall within the exclusive authority of another state. The independence of a state may be illusory when other states—even though not physically crossing borders to substitute the authority of the state with theirs—can order it to adopt or abandon a certain policy as regards the exercise of its exclusive territorial authority through the exercise of jurisdiction by their courts. Moreover, the assessment of responsibility of the state for damages resulting from alleged wrongdoings committed in the course of exercise of state authority by the courts of a foreign state implies an authority over the sovereign activity of the state that a foreign state does not have. The equality and independence of states forbids courts to exert their jurisdiction so as to require a foreign state to exercise its *imperium* in a certain way, or to order them to indemnify those that suffered damages from the exercise of *imperium*. State immunity can be seen to be the device developed to prevent the interference in the exclusive state authority as recognized by international law by the exercise of foreign adjudicative jurisdiction.[259]

term for the "totality of international rights and duties recognized by international law" as residing in an independent territorial unit—the State', J Crawford, *The Creation of States in International Law* (1979) 26 quoting the *Reparation for Injuries Case*.

[258] Articles 1 and 3 of the 1949 ILC Draft Declaration on Rights and Duties of States, YBILC 1949 286, 287.

[259] Even when states have agreed to certain international dispute settlement procedures with regard to alleged violations of international standards applicable to the exercise of exclusive territorial competences—like diplomatic protection as regards the treatment of aliens and human rights tribunals as regards the treatment of individuals generally—claims can usually only be instigated after local remedies have been exhausted.

The isolation of the *acta jure imperii–acta jure gestionis* distinction from the concept of *imperium* protected in international law is arguably responsible for the confusion on the so-called territorial tort exception. This exception is included in almost all (draft) codifications of the rule of state immunity at the national and international level. The basic tenet of the exception is that state immunity is excluded for acts qualifying as tortious under the *lex loci delicti commissi* that are closely connected to the territory of the forum state and cause physical injury or loss or damage to property.[260] The FSIA for example provides in § 1605 (a) (5) that foreign states are not immune from US jurisdiction in cases

> in which money damages are sought against a foreign state for personal injury or death, or damage to or loss of property, occurring in the United States and caused by the tortious act or omission of that foreign state or of any official or employee of that foreign state while acting within the scope of his office or employment; except this paragraph shall not apply to:
>
> (a) any claim based upon the exercise or performance or the failure to exercise or perform a discretionary function regardless of whether the discretion be abused, or
> (b) any claim arising out of malicious prosecution, abuse of process, libel, slander, misrepresentation, deceit or interference with contract rights.[261]

Article 12 of the UN Convention on Jurisdictional Immunities of States and their Property formulates the exception as follows:

> Unless otherwise agreed between the States concerned, a State cannot invoke immunity from jurisdiction before a court of another State which is otherwise competent in a

[260] Formulation of the exception in the various (draft) codifications differs as regards the territorial nexus requirement and the type of injury or damage for which the foreign state may be held accountable. See especially Report no 24, § 115 on the limitation to loss or damage to *tangible* property only. In light of the strict territorial nexus requirement the *lex loci delicti commissi* will almost always be the law of the forum state, cf CH Schreuer (1988) 53; Report of the ILC on the work of its thirty-sixth session (1984), YBILC 1984 ii (part two), 66, § 3.

[261] US, Foreign Sovereign Immunities Act of 1976, Public Law 94–583, 90 Stat. 2891, reproduced in (1976) 15 ILM 1388. See for other examples s 5 of the UK State Immunity Act 1978, reproduced in (1978) 17 ILM 1123; s 13 of the Australian FSIA, reproduced in (1986) 25 ILM 715; s 6 of the Canadian SIA, reproduced in (1982) 21 ILM 798; art 2 of the Argentinean immunity statute, La Ley 24.488, Immunidad Jurisdiccional de los Estados Extranjeros ante los Tribunalos Argentinos (1995), reproduced in A Dickinson, R Lindsay and JP Loonan (eds), *State Immunity, Selected Materials and Commentary* (2004); s 6 of the South African FSIA, reproduced in UN-Materials ST/LEG/SER.B.20, 34; art 11 of the European Convention on State Immunity, reproduced in (1972) 11 ILM 470; art 12 of the UN Convention on Jurisdictional Immunities of States and their Property (2004) (based on art 12 of the ILC Draft Articles on Jurisdictional Immunities of States and their Property (1991), YBILC 1991 ii (part two) 13; art III F of the Draft Articles for a Convention on State Immunity, Report of the Sixtieth Conference (1982), p 5ff and 325ff as revised by the Final Report on Developments in the Field of State Immunity and Proposal for a Revised Draft Convention on State Immunity for the ILA Buenos Aires Conference in 1994, Report of the Sixty-sixth Conference (1994) 452ff; art II (e) of the Resolution of the Institut de Droit International on Contemporary Problems Concerning the Jurisdictional Immunity of States (1992), (1992) 64–II AIDI 267. The Pakistan Ordinance does not contain the exception, while art 6(e) of the Inter-American Draft Convention on Jurisdictional Immunity of States is limited to *commercial* torts.

proceeding which relates to pecuniary compensation for death or injury to the person, or damage to or loss of tangible property, caused by an act or omission which is alleged to be attributable to the State, if the act or omission occurred in whole or in part in the territory of that other State and if the author of the act was present in that territory at the time of the act or omission.

The exception is not uncontroversial. Several states argue that it violates the rule that states are immune for their *acta jure imperii*. The classic case applying the *acta jure imperii–acta jure gestionis* distinction to claims concerning torts allegedly committed within the territory of the forum state is the Austrian *Holubek* case.[262] Plaintiff in this case brought an action for damages for negligence against the US alleging his car had been damaged by negligent driving of a car owned by the US. The Austrian Supreme Court rejected a plea for state immunity on the following consideration:

an act must be deemed to be a private act where the State acts through its agencies in the same way as a private individual can act...

By operating a motor car and using public roads the defendant moves into spheres in which private individuals also move. In these spheres the parties face one another on a basis of equality, and there is no indication here of any supremacy and subordination.[263]

During the hearings preceding the enactment of the FSIA it was explained that the classic example qualifying under section 1605(a)(5) would be an accident caused by a vehicle owned by a foreign embassy and driven by an official or employee acting within the scope of his duties.[264] Moreover, the discretionary function exception secures the independent exercise of, for example, the consular activities of foreign states that would qualify as *acta jure imperii* under the traditional approach to the issue. So what *is* the difference between the territorial tort exception and the *acta jure imperii–acta jure gestionis* approach to territorial torts advanced in the *Holubek* case?

The case of *Letelier v Chile* elucidates this point.[265] In 1976 Orlando Letelier—Chilean ambassador and foreign minister during the Allende regime—and his aide Ronni Moffitt—a US national—were killed in Washington by a car bomb. A US investigation revealed that the men responsible for the assassination were connected to the government in Chile. Relatives of the two men filed a civil action for damages against the Republic of Chile. Chile denied any involvement in the death of Letelier and Moffitt, but argued that even if it were involved the court

[262] *Collision with Foreign Government-Owned Motor Car (Austria) Case* 40 ILR 73 (Austria, S Ct, 1961).

[263] ibid 75 and 77. Cf also *Ciniglio v Ambasciata d'Indonesia e Compagnia di Assicurazioni Intercontinentale* (1968) 4 RDIPP 104 (Italy, Pretore di Roma, 1966); 65 ILR 268.

[264] Statement of Monroe Leigh, Legal Advisor of the State Department, Jurisdiction of U.S. Courts in Suits Against Foreign States: Hearings on H.R. 11315 Before the Subcomm. on Admin. Law and Governmental Relations of the House Comm. On the Judiciary, 94th Cong, 2d Sess 24, 27.

[265] *Letelier v Chile* 488 F Supp 665 (US, DC for the District of Columbia, 1980).

could not establish jurisdiction under the FSIA since the act does not cover political assassinations because of their public, governmental character. The argument was rejected by the court. There is no indication, it held,

> that the tortious acts to which the Act makes reference are to only be those formerly classified as 'private', thereby engrafting onto the statute...the requirement that the character of a given tortious act be judicially analysed to determine whether it was of the type heretofore denoted as *jure gestionis*, or should be classified as *jure imperii*.[266]

The acts on which the claim was based moreover did not qualify under the discretionary function exception. An act that is discretionary, the court held, is one in which 'there is room for policy judgment and decision'.[267] The court concluded:

> Whatever policy options may exist for a foreign country, it has no 'discretion' to perpetrate conduct designed to result in the assassination of an individual or individuals, action that is clearly contrary to the precepts of humanity as recognized in both national and international law.[268]

Also the Canadian Supreme Court has rejected the argument that the territorial tort exception of the 1982 Canadian State Immunity Act only applies to *acta jure gestionis*. It emphasized that the exception does not depend on the nature of the act on which the claim is based. The court pointed out that if this were different, victims of the worst breaches of basic rights would be deprived of any possibility of redress in national courts.[269]

From the traditional perspective the conclusion of the court in the *Letelier* case could be paraphrased as a refusal to allow the *acta jure imperii–acta jure gestionis* distinction in through the back door—after all, under the *Holubek* criteria the assassination of Letelier by Chilean secret agents probably qualified as an *acta jure imperii* of the Chilean government.[270] However, keeping in mind the natural limits of a state's *imperium* it is more appropriate to say that the territorial tort exception as included in almost all national codifications of the state immunity rule, as well as in the European Convention on State Immunity and the UN Convention on the Jurisdictional Immunities of States and their Property *is* the reflection of the *jure imperii–jure gestionis* distinction.[271] A state may only

[266] ibid 671.

[267] ibid 673. Under reference to jurisprudence on the Federal Tort Claims Act: *Dalehite v United States* 346 US 15 (US, S Ct, 1953) 36.

[268] ibid. Cf also *Helen Liu v The Republic of China* 892 F 2d 1419 (US, Ct of Apps (9th Cir), 1989).

[269] *Schreiber v Canada (Attorney General)* (Canada, 2002) §§ 30–37, § 37. Cf the difference with the pre-State Immunity Act approach in *Carrato v United States of America* 90 ILR 229 (Canada, Ontario High Court, 1982).

[270] Cf n 226 above for the widespread view that the *acta jure imperii–acta jure gestionis* distinction is not relevant to the territorial tort exception.

[271] See R Quadri, *La giurisdizione sugli stati stranieri* (1941) 127 for an early consideration of this issue and a plea for the *Letelier*—and hence the territorial tort exception—approach. Cf however *Carrato v United States of America* (Canada, 1982) where it was decided that the seizure of assets in Canada without authorization of Canadian authorities by a receiver appointed by a US

legitimately exercise its sovereign authority on the territory of another state with that state's consent. The performance of consular acts like the issuance of passports and visa is an obvious example of such extra-territorial exercise of *imperium* with consent. The state that has consented to this exercise of *imperium* cannot exercise jurisdiction over that exercise as long as it stays within the bounds of the agreement.[272] Since the exercise of *imperium* on foreign territory is dependant on permission to exercise a certain well-defined function, it is possible to construct a foreign state's authority by reference to legal standards. The bounds of the national law of the territorial state do not determine the authority of foreign states. For example, the issuance of a passport in violation of the law of the territorial state is still an exercise of sovereign authority. However, if the activity of a foreign state *in itself*—hence independent of the way in which the activity was exercised—violates the law of the territorial state, there is at least a strong presumption that the territorial state cannot have consented to that.

Two final observations are called for. In the first place it is noted that the 1994 *Alicog v Kingdom of Saudi Arabia* case establishes an important caveat on the use of the territorial tort exception in US courts. It may be clear that compared to claims concerning commercial activity, tort suits carry a considerable risk of frivolous claims. The case concerned two former servants of Prince Saad of the Kingdom of Saudi Arabia who sued, among others, the Kingdom of Saudi Arabia for private imprisonment and acts of serious physical and mental abuse allegedly inflicted upon them by Saudi state officials when they accompanied the Prince on a visit to the United States in 1991.[273] The court acknowledged that '[t]he law has imposed limits on the exception for discretionary functions.'[274] It moreover considered that '[k]idnapping, private imprisonment, and assassination are all beyond the scope of legitimate diplomatic operations and are not protected by the discretionary function exception, and courts have jurisdiction over a government committing those acts.'[275] Although the court ruled that '[t]he kingdom would

court to collect taxes due to be paid to US authorities was an illegal, but nevertheless public act of the US government.

[272] See *Alexeeff v Rappresentanza Commerciale dell'Unione delle Republiche Sovietiche Socialiste (URSS)* (1933) Temi Emiliana 266 (Italy, 1933) 271–2. Cf also *Yamaguchi v United States* (Japan, 2002) where the court decided that taking off and landing of US military aircraft at the Yokota Air Base in Tokyo, Japan 'is a public activity *par excellence* of the US armed forces and clearly an act *jure imperii*', discussed by M Tomonori in a case note in (2003) 97 AJIL 406–11. Cf also *Presidenza Consiglio dei ministri e Stati Uniti d'America v Federazione italiana lavoratori dei trasporto della provincia di Trento and others* (2001) 37 RDIPP 1019 (Italy, Corte di Cassazione, 2000); *Airport Linz v United States* (Austria, 2004).

This must be distinguished from the discussion in how far states can rely on the law of diplomatic immunity. Cf J Salmon and S Sucharitkul (1987); JC Barker, 'State Immunity, Diplomatic Immunity and Act of State: A Triple Protection against Legal Action?' (1998) 47 ICLQ 950.

[273] *Alicog v Kingdom of Saudi Arabia* 860 F Supp 379 (US, DC for the Southern District of Texas, 1994).

[274] ibid 383.

[275] ibid.

not be immune if the consular officers committed serious physical abuse'[276] it refused to hear the case because plaintiffs had failed to show sufficient evidence of the allegations at hand. The court considered that 'testimony is vague at best, with no specification of who did precisely what to whom, where, and on what occasion. Six months of enslavement and torture... must have some detail, some objective residue somewhere... If the damage were serious enough to warrant judicial scrutiny, there must have been hospital records, pictures, scars, or testimony from others about the extent of harm... If... the plaintiffs have no evidence of abuse, only allegations, this court cannot provide redress.'[277] Jurisdiction can hence not be created by mere allegations that qualify under one of the exceptions to the FSIA but requires at least some substantiation: as a preliminary hurdle plaintiffs will have to present a credible, well-documented claim.

The second observation is more fundamental and prepares us for the next section. As was stated earlier, apart from a division of competences between national courts, state immunity reflects a division of competences between national courts and international dispute settlement procedures. This second limit on the essential competence of national courts is bound to clash with an unabridged application of the territorial tort exception. The most obvious example would be the reliance on the exception as regards activity of a foreign state in the course of an armed conflict with the forum state. We will see below that the concept of *acta jure imperii* is also used for the acts that a state performs as a subject of international law. Fox considered in this regard that '[w]here the forum State's territory is occupied by force by another State the principles of independence and equality are set aside and the law of armed conflict rather than the law of peace applies. Matters falling within the law of armed conflict are classified as acts in the exercise of sovereign authority and as such, if compensation is sought, reparation for war damage is made by direct negotiation between States on the international plane. Therefore a claim made in peacetime for personal injuries or tangible damage occurring during a previous armed conflict or period of occupation of the forum State territory by the defendant State relates to matters *jure imperii* and hence is immune.'[278] War is the paradigm example. But what about a terrorist attack like that carried out by French secret agents against the *Rainbow Warrior* ship within New Zealand territory? The fact that international law standards are violated is clearly not enough. Surely the inclusion of such standards in international law cannot deprive an individual of judicial recourse it previously had. The mere applicability of international legal standards to the activity at hand does not mean that a state has acted as a subject of international law for state immunity purposes. A more delicate question is whether national courts are competent

[276] ibid 384.
[277] ibid.
[278] H Fox (2002) 316.

when the international law aspects of a particular act may be said to dominate the private law aspects.

3.2.2 Rights and Obligations under International Law

A second category of state immunity decisions gives expression to the vertical division of competences between national courts and international dispute settlement procedures. In *Campione v Petit-Nitrogenmuvek NV and Hungarian Republic* the Italian *Corte di Cassazione* considered that when states act as subjects of international law—a competence, in contrast to those discussed in section 3.2.1, not territorially limited[279]—the ensuing relations remain completely outside the Italian legal order.[280] Anzilotti stated in this regard that the fact that states are not subject to the jurisdiction of other states as regards their relations under international law does not need evidence: it has always been recognized by all as an evident and inherent truth, as an irrecusable logical consequence of the concept of international law.[281]

This is not the place for a discussion of the principle of equality of states and its role in the international legal order as such.[282] For our purposes it suffices to state that it is uncontroversial that 'the principle of juridical equality is formally established as one of the basic principles of international law'.[283] As an organizational principle of the international legal order it has consequences for the enforcement of the rights and obligations under international law. The equality of states would be incompatible with one state exercising its jurisdiction over acts of another state that are governed by rules of international law. It is here that the operation of the principle of equality of states is properly expressed through the maxim *par in parem non habet imperium*.

It must be noted at the outset that this aspect of the rule of state immunity bears some resemblance to the international dispute settlement rule. States cannot be subjected to international adjudication without their consent.[284] Some scholars

[279] Cf eg *In re Savini and Others* 4 AD 166, case no 106 (Italy, CA of Rome, 1927) 167: 'in certain historical circumstances and in the course of events of an international character, especially if these result from war, a State may exist outside its natural boundaries and still preserve the character of a person in public international law in its relations with other States and particularly in its relations with the State whose hospitality it enjoys'.

[280] See n 254 above.

[281] D Anzilotti (1910) 477: 'è cosa che non ha bisogno di essere dimostrata e che da tutti e sempre è stata riconosciuta come una verità evidente di per se stessa, come una conseguenza logica irrecusabile dello stesso concetto del diritto internazionale.'

[282] Cf PH Kooijmans, *The Doctrine of the Legal Equality of States: An Inquiry into the Foundations of International Law* (1964).

[283] R Jennings and A Watts (eds) (1992) i 340, § 107.

[284] Cf *Case of the Monetary Gold Removed from Rome in 1943* (*Italy v France, United Kingdom and United States*), ICJ Reports 1954 10, 32 where the ICJ referred to the 'well-established principle of international law embodied in the Court's Statute, namely, that the Court can only exercise jurisdiction over a State with its consent'.

have drawn a general parallel between the rule and the law of state immunity. Jennings, for example, noted

the similarity of the principle of the jurisdictional immunity of States before domestic courts of other States, and the consensual principle of jurisdiction of international courts... This relationship is not always evident from the text books, nor indeed remarked by commentators. But jurisdictional immunity in the absence of waiver, and jurisdiction created by consent, are the obverse and reverse of the same coin. In either case it is State sovereignty that is the underlying *rationale* and historical cause.[285]

Crawford considered the international dispute settlement rule 'the nearest direct analogue in international law to the rule of State immunity'.[286] In his influential article *International Law and Foreign Sovereigns: Distinguishing Immune Transactions* Crawford identified the rule as one of three rules underlying the notion of restrictive immunity. He put the following question to his readers:

With respect to transactions not within the jurisdiction of the forum State under international law, how is the forum State in a *better* position than an international judicial forum in asserting jurisdiction against a foreign State defendant?[287]

Crawford argued that the rule 'implies that certain disputes involving States are to be settled on the international plane, not by subjecting the defendant State to the compulsory jurisdiction of some municipal court'.[288]

It is proposed to formulate the relation between the two rules somewhat differently. National courts are—in principle—not the appropriate forum to decide disputes regarding the rights and obligations of foreign states under international law: *par in parem non habet imperium*. Rather, states must rely on international dispute settlement mechanisms. The jurisdiction of international courts and tribunals over such disputes *is* of course *a priori* appropriate. The international dispute settlement rule only reflects the absence of supreme authority in international law: consent is necessary to allow the exercise of this *a priori* appropriate jurisdiction. The rule undoubtedly strengthens the vertical aspect of the law of state immunity but is not directly, or even indirectly, related to it.

The operation of the vertical aspect of the law of state immunity is most obvious when a claim requires a court to decide a dispute that is formulated in terms of rights and obligations under international law.[289] More common is however the claim of an individual formulated in terms of rights and obligations under

[285] R Jennings (1988) 3–4. Cf also the discussion of the Third Report on the Jurisdictional Immunities of States and their Properties (Special Rapporteur S Sucharitkul) in the ILC, YBILC 1981 i 55, 57–8, § 15.

[286] J Crawford (1983), 80.

[287] ibid.

[288] Cf also J Crawford, 'Execution of Judgments and Foreign Sovereign Immunity' (1981) 75 AJIL 820, 856; Australian Law Reform Commission, Foreign State Immunity, Report no 24 (1984), § 40.

[289] Cf *Arab Republic of Syria v Arab Republic of Egypt* 91 ILR 289 (Brazil, S Ct, 1982).

national law as regards the exercise of a competence of a state regulated under international law. An example is found in the case of the *Kingdom of Greece v Gamet.*[290] Following the 1947 Treaty of Peace with Italy, the Greek government had issued a decree that all shares in Greek companies owned by Italian citizens or companies were to be deposited so as to be at the disposal of the Greek government and were to remain blocked for the time being. The French plaintiff in this case claimed before the Italian courts that some of the shares thus deposited were in fact hers. It was held that since the acts of the Greek state that were the subject of plaintiff's complaint had been in execution of the Italian Peace Treaty, Greece was exempt from jurisdiction. The court crucially considered that if a state operates on the territory of another state it is exempted from jurisdiction for 'acts of a public character performed in the exercise of the sovereign power of the State acting outside its own territory as a subject of international law. In such cases, the legal relations are outside the ambit of the municipal law which applies in the territory in which the foreign State operates.'[291]

Without doubt, claims of individuals alleging responsibility in tort of a foreign state with regard to acts committed in the course of armed conflict either on the territory of the forum state or on the territory of a third state, are the most relevant instances of application of the principle for the purpose of this study. In the 1968 case *Ministry of Foreign Affairs v Federici and Japanese State*[292] it was concluded that the Italian courts lacked competence to decide a claim of an Italian national for compensation for the acts of the Japanese occupation forces in China during the Second World War. After the armistice between Italy and the Allied Powers in September 1943, Mr Federici, an Italian national resident in China, refused to swear allegiance to the Italian 'Repubblica Sociale' successor to the Fascist government in Northern Italy and allied to Germany and Japan. Japanese military authorities interned him in a concentration camp and seized his valuables. After the surrender of Japan in January 1946 the 'Japanese Liaison Office with the Commission for the Settlement of Allied Claims' in Shanghai provided him with a declaration recognizing his right to claim US$ 638,050 from the Japanese state. When payment of the sum did not come off, Federici eventually brought a claim against Japan before an Italian court. In 1963 the Tribunal of Rome held the Japanese State liable to pay the debt since it qualified the recognition of debt as an act of a private law nature. The 1968 case concerned the decision on the third party opposition proceedings against that judgement brought by the Italian Ministry of Foreign Affairs. The court first criticized the approach taken in the 1963 judgement holding that 'the public or private nature of a legal obligation . . . is to be deduced from its legal basis and from any other evidence proving either that the parties have concluded a transaction and that civil responsibility

[290] *Kingdom of Greece v Gamet* (Italy, 1959).

[291] ibid. Cf moreover *X v Federal Republic of Germany* 65 ILR 10 (Austria, S Ct, 1963).

[292] *Ministry of Foreign Affairs v Federici and Japanese State* 65 ILR 275 (Italy, Tribunal of Rome, 1968).

is involved, or alternatively that the legal relationship is based on acts which by their very nature lie outside the sphere of such responsibility and are governed by other legal rules'.[293] The declaration, the court held, did not change the legal relationship resulting from requisitions in Shanghai in 1943 and the recognition of debt should not have been separated from the underlying legal act which was clearly part of a public law relationship. The court held furthermore that

> relationships arising from acts of sovereignty performed by States (especially those relating to activities of troops during military operation) can exist only and directly between States as subjects of international law even when those relationships concern damage caused to *individuals* and not to the State.[294]

The court considered that '[t]he legal relationship upon which the contested judgement was pronounced lies outside the competence of Italian courts.'[295] 'Such relationships' the court explained, 'are regulated under international law and through diplomatic channels... In cases such as these the protection of the individual's interests is entrusted to the State, which is responsible for their protection with regard to the actions of a foreign State, in accordance with international law.'[296] Consequently '[t]his is a case of inter-State relations, subject to international law and concerning the exclusive rights of the States themselves rather than those of the wronged individual.'[297]

A Dutch case regarding German activity in Belgium during the First World War gave rise to similar considerations.[298] A vessel with a cargo of coal belonging to Mr De Booy, a Dutch merchant, was destroyed by German military authorities on Belgian soil. In default proceedings before a Dutch District Court in 1916, Germany was ordered to pay damages.[299] The ensuing developments are quite complex. When the Dutch government was informed of the judgment it took proceedings of a summary nature before the President of the District Court to have the execution of the judgment stayed pending decision on a formal claim to have it definitively annulled. The government was of the opinion that the judgement was contrary to international law since it regarded acts of a foreign state in the exercise of its sovereign belligerent powers.[300] The president found

[293] ibid 276–7.

[294] ibid 278.

[295] ibid.

[296] ibid.

[297] ibid 278–9.

[298] *De Booij v het Duitsche Rijk, the Government of Holland Intervening* 1 AD 124, case no 84 (The Netherlands, DC of Amsterdam, 1920). See for a detailed discussion of the case and related developments EW Allen (1933) 110; CCA Voskuil, 'State Immunity and the Law of Civil Procedure and Execution in the Netherlands' in TD Gill and WP Heere (eds), *Reflections on Principles and Practice of International Law* (2000) 223, 226–9.

[299] *De Booij v het Duitsche Rijk* NJ 1917 13 (The Netherlands, Rechtbank Rotterdam, 1916).

[300] Cf also L Van Praag, 'Vonnis en Beslag tegen een Vreemden Staat' (1917) Weekblad van het Recht 10036, 3:1–4:1.

for the government and ordered a stay of execution.[301] The government further instigated a claim for annulment through third-party opposition against the original judgment. We will not enter into the particularities of the case here. It is only noted that the Dutch Supreme Court did eventually consider that the 1916 decision of the District Court violated international law because it regarded a claim on account of acts committed by the German state in its capacity under public law.[302]

Foreign states acting on the territory of the forum state thus enjoy immunity when they have acted as a subject of international law. As was explained in the previous section, the principle may thwart the operation of the territorial tort exception. The Italian case of *The Ditta Pomante v Federal Republic of Germany* illustrates the tension between the two rules.[303] After the Italian declaration of war on Germany on 13 October 1943 German armed forces removed timber from the sawmill of the firm of Pomante in Roseto degli Abruzzi. Later, the German military command entered into contract with the plaintiff for the supply of timber to the German armed forces. It can not be said however that the plaintiff entered into the contract out of free will. He was compelled to return to the sawmill under very dangerous working circumstances and at the risk of the lives of 150 workmen to produce the timber while exposed to heavy air raids. The German authorities never paid for the materials supplied or the materials removed and claim was made for reparation. The court considered that Germany had demanded supply as an Occupying Power in the exercise of its sovereign powers—a situation to which article 52 of the 1907 Hague Convention is applicable. The court rejected the argument of plaintiff that the contract was entered into on the basis of equality. The court considered that 'the powers with which the foreign State acted, not the form which the relationship may have taken' are decisive 'for a State's acts are not characterized according to the methods which were used'.[304]

In sum, activity that cannot be qualified as the exercise of sovereign authority in terms of exclusive competence may deserve that qualification when placed within the context of international law.[305] Exactly *when* an act loses the

[301] *De Staat der Nederlanden v (1) de Booij (2) het Duitsche Rijk* NJ 1917 133 (The Netherlands, Rechtbank Rotterdam, 1917).

[302] *De Booij v (1) den Staat der Nederlanden (2) het Duitsche Rijk* 1 AD 124 (The Netherlands, Hoge Raad, 1924) 128; NJ 1924 535. Cf also *NV Limburgsch Landbouw Syndicaat (Wijk-Maastricht) v het Duitsche Rijk* NJ 1917 12 (Rechtbank Maastricht, 1916).

[303] *The Ditta Pomante v Federal Republic of Germany* 40 ILR 64 (Italy, Civil Court of l'Aquila, 1960).

[304] ibid 68.

[305] Cf in particular *Russian Trade Delegation v Société Française Industrielle et Commerciale des Pétroles (Groupe Malopolska)* 9 AD 245, case no 83 (France, Civil Tribunal of the Seine, 1940) and *Société Française Industrielle et Commerciale des Pétroles v Russian Trade Delegation* 11 AD 145 case no 77 (France, CA of Paris, 1941). Cf also *Urrutia and Anollobieta v Martiarena* 8 AD 237 case no 94 (Belgium, Court of Brussels, 1937); *Oder-Neisse Property Expropriation Case* 65 ILR 127 (Germany, Superior Provincial Court Munich, 1975).

character of territorial tort and becomes a matter for conflict resolution on the international level may not be immediately obvious. As said, the applicability of the law of armed conflict is the paradigm example. Notably, the UK State Immunity Act provides in section 16.2 that the exceptions to state immunity do not apply 'to proceedings relating to anything done by or in relation to the armed forces of a State while present in the United Kingdom'. In a similar vein, article 31 of the European Convention states that '[n]othing in this Convention shall affect any immunities or privileges enjoyed by a Contracting State in respect of anything done or omitted to be done by, or in relation to, its armed forces when on the territory of another Contracting State.' The Explanatory Report on the Convention clarifies that '[t]he Convention is not intended to govern situations which may arise in the event of armed conflict'.[306]

During repeated discussions on the territorial tort exception several members of the ILC suggested that the exception should be seen to be limited to insurable risks like traffic accidents or negligent, unintentional injury or damage to property. This would exclude in particular criminal and political offences from the scope of article 12. It was argued that the peaceful settlement of such disputes by negotiations through diplomatic channels is preferable.[307] The interpretation of article 12 as applying to insurable risks only would reduce the scope of the provision to the reach of the classic *Holubek* formulation. It would entail the grant of sovereign immunity whenever a foreign state violates outside the boundaries of its own territory on purpose and with vile intent rules that can normally be applied by the national court.[308] In his eighth and final report Sucharitkul left the issue unresolved. On the one hand he considered it questionable whether national courts were the best forum to solve disputes concerning the liability of foreign states for acts that qualify as *acta jure imperii*—argued under the *Holubek* approach to the term. On the other hand he considered the local remedies rule an argument in favour of the exercise of jurisdiction over such disputes by national courts in order to avoid any implication of denial of justice. The indeterminate conclusion that '[a] balanced approach is vital to a meaningful solution to this problem' leaves us guessing as to the criterion for distinction preferred by the ILC.[309] In the Commentary on the 1991 Draft Articles we do read that article 12 does not apply to situations involving armed conflict, but the UN Convention does not contain a specific article to that effect.[310]

[306] *Explanatory Report on the European Convention on state immunity and the additional protocol* (2nd edn, 1985) 39.

[307] Cf eg S Sucharitkul (Special Rapporteur ILC), Sixth Report on the Jurisdictional Immunity of States and their Property, YBILC 1984 ii (part one) 5, 11, § 17; Report of the Commission on the Work of its Thirty-fifth Session, YBILC 1983 ii (part two), 19–20, § 86–91.

[308] The *Letelier* case is then an example of what should not qualify under art 12. Cf for this approach (in a case concerning activity on the high seas) *The National Navigation Cy of Egypt v Tavoularidis* (1930) 57 JDI 203 (Egypt, Tribunal mixte d'Alexandrie, 1927).

[309] S Sucharitkul (Special Rapporteur ILC), Eighth Report on the Jurisdictional Immunities of States and their Property, YBILC 1986, ii (part one) 21, 27, § 17.

[310] International Law Commission, ILC Draft Articles on Jurisdictional Immunity of States and their Property (1991), YBILC 1991 ii (part two) 13, 46. Article 26 of the UN Convention

It is suggested that the vertical division of competences must be distinguished from the question whether certain disputes are better solved on the international level as a policy option. The relevant question should be whether the powers under scrutiny are governed by international law either *a priori*, or because states agree *afterwards* to settle the dispute on the international level.[311] Notably, the applicability of rules of international law to the acts of the foreign state, or the impact of the dispute on interstate relations does *as such* not affect the character of the dispute for the purpose of the vertical division of competences. The *a priori* incompetence of national courts is at issue when a foreign state is called to account for *acts committed as a subject of international law*. The application of this criterion is of course far from straightforward. What if a state claims to have acted under the rules of self-defence, reprisal, or humanitarian intervention? Difficult cases are not further explored here.[312] For the purposes of this study it suffices to note the conceptual difference.

The *Letelier* case is a conspicuous example of a dispute that was not *a priori* outside the competence of the national courts. While the assassination of Letelier violated norms of international law, the act retained its significance under national law as well. The competence over national law claims in regard of this type of dispute can only be affected by settlement on the international level. The *a priori* competence of the national courts may operate as a sword of Damocles and be an impetus to settle the damages on the interstate level.[313] The intricate question whether states may move to settle claims of their nationals even when these national would prefer to take their case to court falls outside the scope of this study; the conclusion is limited to the assumption that interstate settlement *is* an option. Claims that ask courts to reconsider the terms of such settlement fall outside the essential competence of national courts.[314]

3.2.3 *Acta Jure Imperii:* A Coherent Concept After All

The principle of independence of states requires states not to exercise adjudicatory jurisdiction over the exclusive competences of other states. The principle of

does provide that '[n]othing in the present Convention shall affect the rights and obligations of States Parties under existing international agreements which relate to matters dealt with in the present Convention as between parties to those agreements', securing thus the prevalence of Status of Forces Agreements over general state immunity rules.

[311] A distinct question—and one outside the scope of this study—is whether there are limits on the power of states to take issues out of national law into the international arena, and whether there are limits on the power of states to dispose of individual claims in such process.

[312] Cf for support for the exercise of jurisdiction in such cases J Crawford (1983) 111; HD Collums, 'The *Letelier* Case: Foreign Sovereign Liability for Acts of Political Assassination' (1981) 21 VJIL 251, 267.

[313] Cf in this respect the Report of the Commission on the work of its Thirty-fifth Session, YBILC 1983 ii (part two), 19–20, § 91, where it was stated that the territorial tort exception 'intended to expedite diplomatic negotiations.'

[314] In this respect the definition of the territorial tort exception in the ILC Draft Articles on Jurisdictional Immunities of States and their Property (YBILC 1991 ii 2 (part two) 13, 44) and the 2004 UN Convention on Jurisdictional Immunities of States and their Property is significant. Art 12 provides that states are not immune in respect of territorial torts '[u]nless otherwise agreed between the States concerned'.

equality of states moreover requires that states do not exercise adjudicatory jurisdiction over the rights and obligations of other states in disputes exclusively governed by international law. The rule of state immunity can hence be defined as the prohibition to exercise jurisdiction over a foreign state's exercise of authority under international law.

It is important to note that competence is claimed *not* whenever a court qualifies the activity of a foreign state in legal terms, but only when that characterization implies that the forum state has jurisdiction over the exercise of the activity. In that case, the proceedings in fact turn on the rights and obligations of the foreign state. The rule of state immunity therefore only applies when a foreign state is either nominally, or factually a defendant in the case. Hence, state immunity is still an immunity *ratione personae* and should not be confused with the act of state or non-justiciability doctrines that find their basis in certain national legal systems. As a Dutch court put it in a case against a private entrepreneur—accused of conspiracy in the crime of genocide and violation of the laws and practices of war because of, *inter alia*, the supply of nerve gas and other materials for the production of chemical weapons to the state of Iraq:

> Although it is inevitable for the court in this case to give a judgment on the persons that have been included in the indictment as perpetrators concerning the principle offenses, this is not considered to be an exercise of jurisdiction, because this cannot lead to a conviction or the implementation of coercive measures against these persons.[315]

Or, as Von Bar asserted already in 1889: 'the Courts are free to consider and pronounce an opinion upon the exercises of sovereign power by a foreign Government, if the consideration of those acts of a foreign Government only constitutes a preliminary to the decision of a question of private rights which in itself is subject to the competency of the Court of law. In fact in such a case the Court is merely dealing with premises on which its judgment in the private suit is to proceed.'[316] *Oppenheim's International Law* formulates it as follows: 'the courts of one state do not, as a rule, question the validity or legality of the official acts of another sovereign state or the official or officially avowed acts of its agents, at any rate *insofar as those acts involve the exercise of the state's public authority, purport to take effect within the sphere of the latter's own jurisdiction and are not in themselves contrary to international law.*'[317] Often, the rule is even said to be circumscribed

[315] *Van Anraat* (The Netherlands, 2005) English transl available at <http://zoeken.rechtspraak.nl/Default.aspx>. The reasoning of the District Court of Amsterdam and the Court of Appeal of Amsterdam in *Republic of the South Moluccas v Royal Packet Shipping Company* 17 ILR 143, case no 39 (1950, 1951), where the act of state doctrine was attributed international law status, was hence not followed.

[316] L Von Bar (1892) 1121. Cf also E Zitelman, *Internationales Privatrecht* (1897) i 378–80; FA Mann, 'The Sacrosanctity of the Foreign Act of State' (1943) 59 LQR 42, 155, 171.

[317] R Jennings and A Watts (eds) (1992) i 365, § 112 (emphasis added). Cf also PM Dupuy, *Droit international public* (5th edn, 2000) 422ff; I Brownlie, *Principles of Public International Law* (6th edn, 2003) 319; Article 3 of the 1993 Resolution of the Institut de Droit International

by the potentially broader concept of the *ordre public* of the forum state,[318] or, as the ICTY held in *Prosecutor v Furundžija*,[319] by *jus cogens* norms—the *ordre public* of the international legal order.

A foreign state can of course be the factual or proper defendant when it is not the defendant *eo nominee* in a case. The UK case of *Buck v Attorney General* is a case in point.[320] After the coming to independence of Sierra Leone in 1961 a group of residents of the former colony sought to challenge the formal validity of a British Order-in-Council that was issued as part of the creation of the constitution of Sierra Leone before the UK courts. Diplock LJ emphatically distinguished the case from cases where the validity of the foreign law came into question *incidentally* as a necessary matter for decision in the course of adjudicating private rights and obligations.[321] The Court of Appeal found that the very subject matter of the claim put before it was the invalidity of a foreign constitution. The validity of the foreign law was hence the *central* issue of dispute and the court consequently refused to entertain the action.[322] It was in the course of this decision that the court considered that 'the application of the doctrine of sovereign immunity does not depend upon the persons between whom the issue is joined, but upon the subject-matter of the issue'.[323] It is the *object of the claim*—namely the *invalidation* rather than the *non-recognition* of a foreign act of state—that distinguishes *Buck* from the typical act of state doctrine case.[324]

The more obvious example is the case in which a foreign state official is sued for acts committed in an official capacity.[325] The 1848 decision of the UK House of Lords in *Duke of Brunswick v King of Hanover* is an early exponent of this category of cases. When the King of Hanover issued a decree to depose the Duke of Brunswick and replace him with the Duke of Cambridge, removing him from his land and title, the deposed Duke filed a claim before the English courts. The Lords famously considered that

> a foreign sovereign... cannot be made responsible for an act done in his sovereign character in his own country... the courts of this country cannot sit in judgment upon an act of a sovereign, effected by virtue of his sovereign authority abroad, an act not done as a

on The Activities of National Judges and the International Relations of their State (Rapporteur B Conforti), (1993) 65–I AIDI 444, 446.

[318] Cf eg P Weil, 'Le contrôle par les tribunaux nationaux de la licéité internationale des actes des États étrangers' (1977) 23 AFDI 9 and French doctrine in general.

[319] *Prosecutor v Furundžija*, IT–95–17/1, Trial Chamber, Judgment (ICTY, 1998) § 155.

[320] *Buck v A-G* [1965] Ch 745 (UK, CA, 1964).

[321] ibid 770.

[322] ibid 768.

[323] ibid 770.

[324] Cf in this respect also *National Institute of Agrarian Reform v Terry Kane* (1963–II) 2 ILM 658 (US, District CA of Florida, Third District, 1963); *Société Algérienne de Commerce Alco et Autres v Sempac et Autres* (1978) 105 JDI 904 (France, Cour de Cassation, 1978); 65 ILR 73.

[325] A comprehensive discussion of the position of foreign state officials will follow in ch 3 below.

British subject, but supposed to be done in the exercise of his authority vested in him as a sovereign.[326]

Also the 1897 decision of the US Supreme Court in *Underhill v Hernandez* should be cited in this respect.[327] The plaintiff in this case was an American national who was in charge of the waterworks of the Venezuelan city of Bolivar in 1892. He alleged that he had been prevented from leaving the city and forced to operate the waterworks for the benefit of the revolutionary forces and brought suit for damages against the head of the army of the revolutionary government of Venezuela. The court dismissed the case with the famous consideration that

> Every sovereign state is bound to respect the independence of every other sovereign state, and the courts of one country will not sit in judgment on the acts of the government of another done within its own territory. Redress of grievances by reason of such acts must be obtained through the means open to be availed of by sovereign powers as between themselves.[328]

Since the 'acts of the defendant were the acts of the Government of Venezuela' they were 'not properly subject to adjudication in the courts of another government'.[329]

Rather than as support for the immunity of foreign acts of state *Underhill* and *Duke of Brunswick* should be understood from the narrow perspective of claims against individuals that performed an act on behalf of a foreign state and in the exercise of the state's sovereign authority. Though commonly regarded as the earliest articulation of the act of state doctrine, the *Underhill* decision can in fact be seen as an early precedent for the rule of functional immunity of state officials and the consequent applicability of the rule of state immunity.[330] It is now firmly established that the rule of state immunity may apply to cases in which a foreign state is the *factual* or *proper* defendant before the court. In *Esnault-Pelterie v The AV Roe Cy Ltd* a French court formulated it thus:

> la règle de l'indépendance réciproque des Etats doit s'appliquer non seulement aux demandes dirigées contre le Gouvernement lui-même, mais encore à celles introduites contre les agents, mandataires, ou cocontractants de ce Gouvernement, à raison des actes qu'ils accomplissent en cette qualité, ou en vertu des ordres dudit Etat.[331]

326 *Duke of Brunswick v King of Hanover* (UK, 1848) (*per* Lord Cottenham).

327 *Underhill v Hernandez* 168 US 250 (US, S Ct, 1897).

328 ibid 252. Cf also *Hatch v Baez* 7 Hun 596 (US, New York S Ct, 1876) 599: 'the courts of one country are bound to abstain from sitting in judgment on the acts of another government done within its own territory'.

329 ibid 254.

330 Cf in fact *Banco Nacional de Cuba v Sabbatino* 376 US 398 (US, S Ct, 1964) 430.

331 *Esnault-Pelterie v The AV Roe Cy Ltd* (1925) 52 JDI 702 (France, Tribunal Civil de la Seine, 1925); A-C Kiss, Répertoire de la pratique française en matière de droit international public (1965) iii 236. A variant of this first type of case is the suit of private individuals in respect of property they hold as a mandatory or agent of a foreign state. Cf *Twycross v Dreyfuss* 5 Ch D 605 (UK, CA, 1877); *De Keller v Maison de la Pensée Française* (1955) 82 JDI 118 (France, Tribunal Civil de la Seine, 1954).

Cases like *Chuidian v Philippine National Bank*,[332] *Jaffe v Miller*,[333] and *Propend Finance Pty Ltd v Sing*[334]—to name a few—prove that the principle is now entrenched in the law of state immunity.

If it is the act that is seen to be immune rather than the state, the law of state immunity acquires definite traits of the act of state and non-justiciability doctrines. In this regard it may be noted that in *Pinochet no 3* Lord Millett considered that '[g]iven its scope and rationale [the rule of state immunity *ratione materiae*] is closely similar to and may be indistinguishable from aspects of the Anglo-American 'Act of State doctrine.'[335] In the subsequent decision of the House of Lords in *Holland v Lampen-Wolffe* Millett again stressed that state immunity 'is a subject-matter immunity. It operates to prevent the official and governmental acts of one state from being called into question in proceedings before the courts of another.'[336] State immunity *is* a subject matter immunity indeed. However, the subject matter of the dispute—or the nature of the claim—hinges on the status of the defendant. The *mise en cause* of a foreign state—nominally or factually—*does* control the application of the rule.

This study repudiates the widespread conviction that the reliance on the notion of *acta jure imperii* in the law of state immunity 'does not rest on any sound logical basis'.[337] This does *not*, however, mean that the notion provides in and of itself sufficient guidance to national courts applying the law.[338] In particular, while the core of the concept of 'exclusive state competences' is apparent, states do clearly not agree on its exact contours. At first blush, the idea of a distinction between the rule and its application conflicts with accepted theories of customary international law formation. A further inquiry into the nature of the obligations in the field of the law state immunity hence is called for.

3.3 The Nature of the Law of State Immunity: A Qualitative Difference Between the Absolute and the Restrictive Approach

3.3.1 The Essential Competence of National Courts

Immunity presupposes jurisdiction. The concept operates to shield certain persons, objects, and institutions from the normal functioning of the local jurisdiction of the forum state.[339] The immunity of a diplomatic agent from the

332 *Chuidian v Philippine National Bank* 912 F 2d 1095 (US, Ct of Apps (9th Cir), 1990).

333 *Jaffe v Miller and Others* 95 ILR 446 (Canada, Ontario CA, 1993).

334 *Propend Finance Pty. Ltd v Sing* 111 ILR 611(UK, CA, 1997).

335 *Pinochet* no 3, 172.

336 *Holland v Lampen-Wolfe* (UK, 2000) 1584 (*per* Lord Millett).

337 Cf n 210 above.

338 Cf in this sense D Anzilotti (1910) 496.

339 Cf a.o. S Sucharitkul (Special Rapporteur ILC), Preliminary Report on Jurisdictional Immunity of States and their Property, YBILC 1979 ii (part one) 227, 238, § 53; S Sucharitkul (Special Rapporteur ILC), Third Report on Jurisdictional Immunity of States and their Property, YBILC 1981 ii (part one) 125, 129, § 9; Report of the Commission on the Work of its Forty-third

jurisdiction of the courts of the receiving state is paradigmatic. When the restrictive rule of state immunity is approached from the perspective of the obligations imposed by the independence and equality of states the question presents itself, however, whether 'immunity from jurisdiction' is an accurate description of the rule. Immunity appears as an inherent limit on the sovereign powers of states; not as the non-exercise of an existing power. A grant of immunity implies that states are exempted from the exercise of authority by the court while in most cases covered by the restrictive immunity rule that authority is in fact absent. This study embraces in this regard a term introduced by Brownlie in his reports for the Institut de Droit International: the independence and equality of states delimits 'the essential competence of national courts'.[340]

The argument that the law of state immunity should be understood from the perspective of the incompetence of the forum state rather than the immunity of the defendant state is not new. Already in 1922 De Visscher noted in this respect:

> Il est manifeste qu'il ne s'agit pas ici d'un privilège comportant de la part de la juridiction saisie l'abandon de l'une de ses attributions normales: l'abstention n'implique chez elle que la reconnaissance des limites naturelles et infranchissables assignées à toute juridiction interne par le principe supérieur du respect des souverainetés.[341]

Some thirty years later the idea was taken up by the French scholars Niboyet and Freyria, who set out to distinguish 'immunités de juridiction' from 'incompétence d'attribution'.[342] Niboyet analysed the problem of the inherent connotations of the concept of immunity in very clear words:

> Il semble qu'on pourrait apporter un peu plus de clarté à la matière des immunités de juridiction en droit international privé, si l'on faisait une distinction qui n'apparaît pas généralement, bien qu'elle s'impose, entre la compétence territoriale et la compétence d'attribution. La confusion généralement faite a pour conséquence de faire ranger dans la compétence territoriale des cas qui appartiennent, en réalité, à la compétence d'attribution, c'est-à-dire de les considérer comme des immunités de juridiction.[343]

Immunity from jurisdiction, he explained, is accorded because of the quality of certain defendants. It is

Session, YBILC 1991 ii (part two) 12, 23, § 1; GM Badr (1984) 83; *Victory Transport Inc v Comisaria Gen De Abestecimientos y Transportes*, (US, 1964) 360.

[340] Cf n 355 above.

[341] C De Visscher (1922) 323.

[342] JP Niboyet, 'Immunité de juridiction et incompétence d'attribution' (1950) 39 RCDIP 139; C Freyria, 'Les limites de l'immunité de juridiction et d'exécution des Etats étrangers' (1951) 40 RCDIP 207; C Freyria, 'Les limites de l'immunité de juridiction et d'exécution des Etats étrangers' (1951) 40 RCDIP 449.

[343] ibid 139. The seeds for the argument developed in this article can already be found in JP Niboyet (1936) 538. Cf also S Sucharitkul, (1976) 141.

la qualité du défendeur, et cette qualité seule, [qui] fait obstacle à la compétence des tribunaux français, parce que, sans elle, le litige serait de ceux dont ils peuvent connaître normalement. Il est fait échec aux règles de la compétence territoriale des tribunaux...[344]

Certain disputes, however, are not within the 'attributions de juger' of national courts. The refusal to exercise jurisdiction rests on the lack of *compétence d'attribution* rather than immunity from jurisdiction. The ideas of Niboyet were taken up by Freyria, albeit with a distorting twist.[345] Where Niboyet had argued that restrictive state immunity decisions in fact reflected considerations related to incompetence *ratione materiae* (or, *compétence d'attribution*), Freyria argued that the state immunity concept had become redundant since 'l'organisation de la compétence d'attribution de nos tribunaux judiciaires français' already sufficiently protected foreign states from French jurisdiction.[346] He emphasized that the rules that command the *compétence d'attribution* as regards governmental acts are rules of French national law that apply equally to the French government as to foreign governments.[347] Although Niboyet had also referred to the national law principles of attribution of competence between French courts, considering that '[e]n droit interne, un tribunal civil ne peut pas connaître de la validité d'un acte administratif qui relève du Conseil d'Etat, seul qualifié pour juger l'administration française',[348] his argument was not based on this consideration but related to it in a comparative vein. Crucially he considered that

les tribunaux français ne sont pas incompétents en vertu d'une immunité de juridiction parce que leur compétence est totalement étrangère à la qualité du défendeur, mais découle uniquement de la nature de l'acte, acte essentiellement administratif du pays étranger, ne peuvent être apprécié par les tribunaux d'un autre pays, sans que ceux-ci ne s'érigent, se qui serait contraire à l'indépendance des Etats en contrôleurs de leur propre activité.[349]

...

un tribunal national ne peut juger une collectivité publique étrangère qui ne relève pas de lui. Cela sort totalement de ses attributions. Il ne faut donc pas croire qu'à défaut des immunités de juridiction les tribunaux civils auraient, dans l'ordre international, la plénitude de juridiction à l'égard des collectivités étrangères: cela se heurterait à un principe fondamental, celui de l'indépendance des Etats et du respect des diverses souverainetés. S'il existe, en droit interne, plus ou moins respecté, un principe de la séparation des pouvoirs, il n'y a pas moins, en droit international, depuis plus longtemps, une séparation des divers pouvoirs nationaux.[350]

[344] JP Niboyet (1950) 141.
[345] The article was published in two parts, C Freyria (1951); C Freyria (1951).
[346] C Freyria (1951) 450.
[347] ibid 460: 'Nos tribunaux ne seront juges ni de la régularité juridique des actes de notre administration ni de celle des actes des administrations étrangères.'
[348] JP Niboyet (1950) 142.
[349] ibid.
[350] ibid 143. Cf further P De Visscher and J Verhoeven (1971).

Hence, while Freyria related a mere practical reality from an essentially French perspective, Niboyet argued from principle and from the perspective of international law.[351]

Italian courts have indicated that state immunity decisions in fact reflect that the relations underlying the claim at hand remain completely foreign to the Italian legal order, either because the foreign state has acted as a subject of international law or because it has acted as the holder of *imperium* over a certain territory.[352] Several scholars have stressed that the question of immunity may only arise as regards relations that *are* subject to the national legal order of the forum state. The formulation of state immunity in terms of relations that are outside the national legal order serves to establish that the law of state immunity is in fact unrelated to the concept of immunity from jurisdiction.[353]

The idea that the law of state immunity regards incompetence of the forum state, rather than immunity of the defendant state was further developed in the work of Brownlie as Rapporteur of the Institut de Droit International. His reports on the *Contemporary problems concerning the jurisdictional immunity of States* proceed from the view that 'the concept of "immunity" is far from helpful. It tends to describe a result. However, so far as it indicates a conceptual foundation it is rather misleading.'[354] Brownlie stressed that state immunity decisions in fact reflect principles of public international law related to the essential competence of national courts. In the 2003 edition of *Principles of International Law* he explained that when state immunity is based on the principle of non-interference 'the national court has no competence to assert jurisdiction: it is a matter of the essential competence of the local courts in relation to the subject-matter'.[355]

Also the 1996 study of Cosnard concluded that '[s]i la juridiction n'existe pas, en vertu des limites imposées par le droit international, le refus de juger ne peut être fondé sur la théorie des immunités de l'État, puisque l'immunité suppose la

[351] It has been argued that also Niboyet argued from the peculiarities of the French legal system only: eg P De Visscher and J Verhoeven, ibid 52; G Van Hecke, 'Notes Critiques sur la Théorie de la Non-Justiciabilité' in *Nouveaux itinéraires en droit: Hommage à François Rigaux* (1993) 517, 517–18.

[352] Cf n 254 above.

[353] See in particular G Morelli, *Diritto processuale civile internazionale* (2nd edn, 1954) 189ff.

[354] I Brownlie (Rapporteur Institut de Droit International), Contemporary Problems Concerning the Jurisdictional Immunity of States, Definitive Report (1987), (1987) 62–I AIDI 45, 46. See also I Brownlie (Rapporteur Institut de Droit International), Contemporary Problems Concerning the Jurisdictional Immunity of States, Preliminary Report (1987), (1987) 62–I AIDI 13; I Brownlie (Rapporteur Institut de Droit International), Contemporary Problems Concerning the Jurisdictional Immunity of States, Supplementary Report (1989), (1989) 63–I AIDI 13; I Brownlie, (Rapporteur Institut de Droit International), Contemporary Problems Concerning the Jurisdictional Immunity of States, Memorandum (1991), (1991) 64–I AIDI 80; Institut de Droit International (Rapporteur I Brownlie), Contemporary Problems Concerning the Jurisdictional Immunity of States, Plenary Session (1992), (1992) 64–II AIDI 214; Institut de Droit International, Resolution on Contemporary Problems Concerning the Jurisdictional Immunity of States (1992), (1992) 64–II AIDI 267.

[355] I Brownlie (2003) 320.

juridiction.' Rather, he observed, '[i]l s'agit là d'une *absence de pouvoir*, non d'une abstention d'exercer un pouvoir de juger existant au préalable.'[356]

In sum, while foreign diplomatic agents or foreign states in the early common law period were indeed exempted from the jurisdiction of the courts, this notion does not accurately describe the operation of the rule of state immunity today. Although in exceptional cases foreign states are shielded from otherwise existing jurisdiction—for example in defamation proceedings[357]—the rules based on the independence and equality of states regard the division of essential competence rather than exemption from jurisdiction. It is not that a rule of immunity from jurisdiction may not apply in the absence of essential competence. In fact, immunity from jurisdiction may preclude courts from inquiring into the nature of the acts complained of and hence from determining their essential competence. However, the rule of state immunity does not apply *indistinctly* from the question of essential competence, rather it *is* a question of essential competence.[358]

The formulation of state immunity in terms of lack of competence has always met resistance of mainstream state immunity doctrine. In particular, the notion of competence has been held to be incompatible with the accepted role of waiver in the law of state immunity:

> Although it is sometimes expressed in jurisdictional terms, immunity is not, strictly speaking, a question of jurisdiction in the sense that the court lacks any power to deal with either the subject-matter or the person before it. Jurisdiction can never be acquired by consent, but even the most absolute theory of sovereign immunity admits that it may be waived.[359]

In sum 'if the courts were to lack competence in cases of this kind, it is not easy to see how the foreign State could "attribute" the wanting jurisdiction by means of this waiver'.[360] In fact, the advocates of the non-competence theory tend to agree. De Visscher noted in this regard:

> L'interdiction faite aux tribunaux de statuer sur les actes de puissance publique d'un Etat étranger a son fondement dans l'intérêt commun des Etats; elle est de ordre public international. A ce titre elle assigne à la compétence des tribunaux internes une limite absolue, limite imposée, non par l'idée d'une faveur personnelle, mais par un principe permanent et supérieur aux intérêts engagés dans le litige. Vainement l'Etat étranger cité en justice

[356] M Cosnard (1996) 377 (cf in general 376–89).

[357] Cf ibid 399–400.

[358] This argument must be distinguished from that advanced by Badr. Badr relied on the concept of primary jurisdiction when he argued that the lack of jurisdiction of national courts over *acta jure imperii* was not the result of the sovereignty and independence of foreign states but resulted from a lack of jurisdictional contacts between those acts and the territory of the forum state, GM Badr *(*1984) 80 and 92–3.

[359] *Cargo ex the Ship Atra v Lorac Transport Ltd* 84 ILR 700 (Canada, CA, 1986) 708.

[360] HF Van Panhuys, 'In the Borderland between the Act of State Doctrine and Questions of Jurisdictional Immunities' (1964) 13 ICLQ 1193, 1199. Cf also YBILC 1981 i 55, 57, § 14: 'if the court declined jurisdiction because it lacked competence, neither waiver nor consent could remedy the defect'.

offrirait-il ici de renoncer à l'immunité de juridiction; cette renonciation serait dépourvue d'effet, non pas qu'un Etat ne puisse, dans un cas particulier, se désister de l'exercice d'un droit souverain, mais parce qu'il ne peut dépendre d'un Etat de conférer aux tribunaux d'un autre Etat une compétence qui leur est refusée pour des raisons d'ordre public international et d'intérêt permanent et que leur propre loi n'a pu, par conséquent, leur accorder.[361]

While Niboyet considered:

[s]i un Etat, hypothèse d'école, acceptait d'être jugé par nos tribunaux pour un véritable acte de caractère gouvernemental, nous pensons que nos tribunaux ne seraient pas obligés de statuer, car les Etats ne sont pas faits pour se juger les uns les autres en pareille matière.[362]

Is it true that jurisdiction can never be acquired by consent? It seems that in the analysis of this question two distinct aspects of jurisdiction are confused by both critics and defendants of the 'non-competence rather than immunity' thesis. The absence of consent is an inherent part of the limit on the competence of national courts imposed by the principle of independence and equality of states. Just as a state may agree to the jurisdiction of an arbitral tribunal, it may agree to the jurisdiction of a foreign national court.[363] This does not create essential but exceptional competence of the national court. While thus international law no longer forms an obstacle, the question arises whether the jurisdictional rules applicable in the forum state allow the use of the national judicial system in cases that do not fall within its essential competence. Obviously, the national law rules on jurisdiction and competence are impervious to the consent of the defendant in a particular case. It is this jurisdiction that may never be acquired by consent.[364]

3.3.2 Why the Distinction between Immunity from Jurisdiction and Lack of Essential Competence is Relevant

It is sometimes argued that the reference to non-competence instead of immunity is merely a question of terminology.[365] That is disputed here. Although of course the label used cannot change the nature of the rule, the use of *different* labels for

[361] C De Visscher (1922) 321.

[362] JP Niboyet (1936) 539. Cf also A Weiss (1923) 535; G Morelli (1954) 191; G Morelli (1958) 128.

[363] P De Visscher and J Verhoeven (1971) 57–8. Cf L Renault, 'Un litige international devant la cour de cassation de France' (1881) 13 RDILC 22 on the *Phare case* (*France v Nicaragua*).

[364] Cf eg *Socialist Libyan Arab Popular Jamahiriya v Libyan American Oil Company (LIAMCO)* (1981) 37 ASDI 217 (Switzerland, Tribunal Fédéral Suisse, 1980) 223; *République du Guatemala v Société internationale de négoce de café et du cacao SINCAFC et autres* (1991) 80 RCDIP 378 (France, Cour de Cassation, 1990); *Consorts Duvalier et autres v État haïtien et autres* (1991) 80 RCDIP 386 (France, Cour de Cassation, 1990).

[365] G Ress (Rapporteur International Law Association), First Report on Developments in the Field of State Immunity since 1982, Report of the Sixty-Fourth Conference (1990) 393, 403. Ress states that Brownlie himself admits that it is just a question of terminology. This is however a misrepresentation of Brownlie's words. Brownlie merely said that even though state immunity is in

related rules does evince their *distinct* nature. Terminology hence serves a purpose. The qualitative difference between the absolute and restrictive approach to state immunity has consequences for the parameters of coherent argument on the scope of the law of state immunity. The distinction of non-competence and immunity from jurisdiction frees the restrictive rule from some inherited connotations that have until now influenced the *form* as well as the *substance* of arguments in the debate on the human rights exception.

3.3.2.1 The *form* of coherent argument

The question as to the influence of international human rights law on the law of state immunity pivots in essence on the epistemology of international law. Except for the argument that the rule of state immunity is *trumped* by hierarchically higher *jus cogens* rules, and the argument that states that engage in grave human rights breaches *forfeit* any rights they may have under international law, state of the law arguments regard the substance and scope of the rule of state immunity. How is the substance of rules of customary international law ascertained and how do these rules change? Much of the controversy between proponents and opponents of the human rights exception to the state immunity rule turns on the form of the reasoning on the ascertainment of the rule. This section sets out to identify the controversy and through a brief excursion into the theory of custom formation it eventually chooses sides in the debate.

Custom is usually held to follow the conjunction of two elements: an objective element—a general and consistent state practice—and a subjective element—the *opinio juris sive neccesitatis*. The International Court of Justice formulates it as follows:

> for a new customary rule to be formed, not only must the acts concerned 'amount to a settled practice', but they must be accompanied by the *opinio juris sive necessitatis*. Either the States taking such action or other States in a position to react to it, must have behaved so that their conduct is 'evidence of a belief that this practice is rendered obligatory by the existence of a rule of law requiring it'.[366]

Customary international law is of course not static. Many scholars have reflected on the conceptual problem inherent in the subjective element of the definition of custom formation. The 'chronological paradox'[367] of 'the mysterious phenomenon of customary law which is deemed to be a source of law only on condition

fact a matter of non-competence, he would continue to use the conventional terminology of state immunity.

[366] *Case Concerning Military and Paramilitary Activities in and against Nicaragua* (*Nicaragua v United States of America*) (Merits), ICJ Reports 1986 14, 108–9, § 207. The citation explicitly refers to *North Sea Continental Shelf* (*Federal Republic of Germany v Denmark, Federal Republic of Germany v The Netherlands*) (Judgment), ICJ Reports 1969 3, 44, § 77.

[367] M Byers, *Custom, Power and the Power of Rules, International Relations and Customary International Law* (1999) 130.

that it is in accordance with law'[368] was first identified by Kelsen.[369] Although it is often argued that this formula cannot account for the development and change of rules of customary international law,[370] it seems that the *opinio juris* requirement kicks up more dust in legal theory than it does in practice. In the *Nicaragua* case the International Court of Justice—discussing the principle of non-intervention—held:

> Reliance by a State on a novel right or an unprecedented exception to the principle might, if shared in principle by other States, tend towards a modification of customary international law.[371]

The thorny question whether acts contrary to established practice but clearly part of a developing modification of a customary rule are as much a violation of international law as acts contrary to an established and unchanging rule of customary international law has not been considered by the ICJ. However, the quote from the *Nicaragua Case* as well as the reference in the *North Sea Continental Shelf* Judgement to 'emergent rules of customary international law'[372] do not evince a strenuous dwelling on the hurdles to the development of custom as identified in theory.[373]

The arguments advanced in support of a human rights exception to state immunity rules however do not rely on the emergence of precedents. Rather, they purport to rely on logic: the changes in the international legal order brought about by international human rights law and related concepts like universal jurisdiction, *jus cogens* norms, and *erga omnes* obligations, are said to have affected the basis of the law of state immunity in international law. For one, it is argued that 'states...are clearly prohibited from extreme human rights violations and cannot claim that such behaviour falls within its sovereign domain' it is hence submitted that 'the reasons for sovereign immunity apply poorly to the case of extreme human rights violations'.[374] In this perspective, the few precedents available *reflect* rather than *constitute* the change.

Opponents of a human rights exception attack proponents on the form of their argument. For example, in *Al-Adsani v UK* the European Court of Human Rights considered that

[368] H Lauterpacht, 'Sovereignty over Submarine Areas' (1950) 27 BYIL 376, 395.

[369] H Kelsen, 'Théorie du Droit International Coutumier' (1939) 1 Revue Internationale de la Théorie du Droit 253, 263. F Geny, *Méthode d'interprétation et sources en droit privé positif* (2nd edn, 1919), 367, had noted the same problem with regard to national legal systems.

[370] Cf M Byers (1999) 131.

[371] *Case Concerning Military and Paramilitary Activities in and against Nicaragua* (ICJ, 1986) 109, § 207.

[372] *North Sea Continental Shelf* (ICJ, 1969) 39, § 63.

[373] I Brownlie, *The Rule of Law in International Affairs, International Law at the Fiftieth Anniversary of the United Nations* (1998) 21.

[374] HM Osofsky, 'Foreign Sovereign Immunity from Severe Human Rights Violations: New Directions for Common Law Based Approaches' (1998) 11 New York International Law Review 35, 52.

> [n]otwithstanding the special character of the prohibition of torture in international law, the Court is unable to discern in the international instruments, judicial authorities or other materials before it any firm basis for concluding that, as a matter of international law, a State no longer enjoys immunity from civil suit in the courts of another State where acts of torture are alleged. In particular, the Court observes that none of the primary international instruments referred to (Article 5 of the Universal Declaration of Human Rights, Article 7 of the International Covenant on Civil and Political Rights and Articles 2 and 4 of the United Nations Convention against Torture) relates to civil proceedings or to State immunity.[375]

The Court moreover referred to a report of the Working Group on Jurisdictional Immunities of States and their Property of the International Law Commission that acknowledged that

> while national courts had in some cases shown some sympathy for the argument that States were not entitled to plead immunity where there had been a violation of human rights norms with the character of *jus cogens*, in most cases (including those cited by the applicant in the domestic proceedings and before the Court) the plea of sovereign immunity had succeeded.[376]

The Court considered that the amendment to the FSIA introducing an exception to state immunity for state sponsored terrorism, only seems to confirm that 'the general rule of international law remained that immunity attached even in respect of claims of acts of official torture'.[377] Moreover, it was held that the decision of the House of Lords in *Pinochet* no 3 should be distinguished since it concerned the immunity from criminal jurisdiction of a former head of state who was at the material time physically within the United Kingdom. It was concluded that despite the growing recognition of the overriding importance of the prohibition of torture it

> does not accordingly find it established that there is yet acceptance in international law of the proposition that States are not entitled to immunity in respect of civil claims for damages for alleged torture committed outside the forum State.[378]

From the perspective of the two-tier formula of custom-formation the reasoning of proponents of a human rights exception to state immunity indeed fails to convince. In the absence of an explanation of the epistemological approach the use of reason in the identification of the substance of a rule may be conceived as confounding the *is* with the *ought*. Thus, the arguments of proponents seem tainted with the vices of natural law theory.

Kelsen's discussion of the difference between natural law and positive law may serve to illustrate this point. Kelsen distinguished two normative systems based

[375] *Al-Adsani v United Kingdom* (ECHR, 2001) 291, § 61.
[376] ibid 291, § 62.
[377] ibid 292, § 64.
[378] ibid § 66.

on two different types of basic norms. On the one hand there is the static system in which norms are valid by virtue of their content. In his words:

> Their content has an immediately evident quality that guarantees their validity, or, in other terms: the norms are valid because of their inherent appeal. This quality the norms have because they derive from a specific basic norm...[t]he binding force of [which] is itself self-evident, or at least presumed to be so...[A]ll the particular norms of such a system are *obtainable by means of an intellectual operation*.[379]

In a dynamic normative system, on the other hand, norms cannot be obtained from the basic norm by intellectual operation since their validity does not derive from their content. Rather,

> [a] norm forms part of a dynamic system if it has been created in a way that is—in the last analysis—determined by the basic norm.[380]

In sum, where the basic norm in a static system is a value from which norms are then derived, in a dynamic system the basic norm is the fundamental rule according to which the norms of the system are to be created. The difference is that between natural and positive law. Legal orders, Kelsen argued, are always systems of the dynamic kind.[381]

At this point, a pertinent observation presents itself: the scepticism towards a possible human rights exception to immunity rules resonates the apprehension with naturalist tendencies in international legal thinking. It is argued here that the *form* of the arguments of proponents of a human rights exception *can* however be distinguished from natural law reasoning. It is submitted that the two-tier formula of custom formation does not account for all rules of customary international law. Diplomatic immunity is a classic example of a customary rule. Although initially the theory of representation was a popular explanation for the law of diplomatic immunity—considering diplomats as an extension of the state and hence anchoring the law in the principle of sovereignty—it is now generally accepted that the rule is based on the general practice of states while the practice finds its material cause in the importance of free and independent performance of diplomatic duties—*ne impediatur legatio*. In contrast, the formula fits the restrictive rule of state immunity rather uncomfortably. If the independence and equality of states imposes limits on the essential competence of national courts, these limits appear *inherent* in an international legal order based on these principles. What does it *mean* that the sovereignty and equality of states represents the 'basic constitutional doctrine of the law of nations'?[382] In particular it must be questioned whether rules that are necessary to preserve these constitutional principles have the same epistemological qualities as other rules of customary

[379] H Kelsen, *General Theory of Law and State* (1945) 112 (emphasis added).
[380] ibid 113.
[381] ibid.
[382] I Brownlie (2003) 287.

international law. What is the role of state practice and consent when a rule is *based* on the independence and equality of states?

The following consideration in the *Gulf of Maine* case may be seen to corroborate the idea of two categories of customary rules with different epistemological qualities. The Court held in relevant part:

> A body of detailed rules is not to be looked for in customary international law which in fact comprises a limited set of norms for ensuring the co-existence and the vital co-operation of the members of the international community, together with a set of customary rules whose presence in the *opinio juris* of States can be tested by induction based on the analysis of a sufficiently extensive and convincing practice, and not by deduction from preconceived ideas.[383]

It has been argued that the first class of rules may be determined deductively and includes rules 'qui seraient en quelque sorte nécessaires, dictées par les exigences de la coexistence entre Etats, et constitueraient un irréductible noyau dur du droit coutumier'.[384] It is submitted here that at least the rules that *inhere* in the principle of independence and equality of states together with the *pacta sunt servanda* rule are necessary rules of international law. The latter rule is the paradigm example. As Brierly explained:

> consent cannot of itself create an obligation; it can do so only within a system of law which declares that consent duly given . . . shall be binding on the party consenting. To say that the rule *pacta sunt servanda* is itself founded on consent is to argue in a circle. A consistent consensual theory again would have to admit that if consent is withdrawn, the obligation created by it comes to an end.[385]

Of course, the limits on the essential competence of national courts are less absolute: they do not inhere in the existence of an international legal order as such—but in the existence of an international legal order composed of independent and equal territorial states. Such an order is unthinkable without limits on the essential competence of states. These limits are hence *necessary incidents* of the constitutional principles of the international legal order. Other examples are the prohibition of aggression and the principle of non-intervention. The ILC referred to the prohibition of aggression as 'a conspicuous example' of *jus cogens*.[386] Arguably it is more than that. Although it is the content of the norm that justifies its *jus cogens* character the qualification *jus cogens* is not inherent in the norm but follows from the normal law creation process.[387] Can one however conceive of an international legal order based on the equality and independence of states

383 *Delimitation of the Maritime Boundary in the Gulf of Maine Area* (*Canada v United States of America*) (Judgment), ICJ Reports 1984 246, 299, § 111.

384 S Sur, *La coutume internationale, sa vie, son oeuvre* (1990) ii.

385 JL Brierly (1963) 53.

386 Report of the ILC on the work of its seventeenth session, YBILC 1966 ii 169, 247.

387 Cf eg R Higgins (1994) 21; JI Charney, 'Universal International Law' (1993) 87 AJIL 529, 542.

without a prohibition of aggression? In this regard it is interesting to note that the ICJ has termed respect for territorial integrity 'an *essential foundation* of international relations [between independent States]'[388] just as the principle of non-intervention that was even more pointedly qualified 'a *corollary* of the principle of the sovereign equality of states'.[389]

The argument recalls Judge Tanaka's reasoning in the *South West Africa Cases*.[390] Contrasting a 'formalistic' with a 'teleological or sociological and conceptual' interpretation of international law the Judge found that enlarged rules of standing inhered in the nature of the rules at issue in the case. He cautioned, however, that his approach was not to 'deduce' rules from 'mere necessity or desirability' but from 'the *raison d'être* and the theoretical construction' of the framework of rules applicable to the case. The rule thus 'deduced' reflected 'the reasonably assumed intention of the parties' and logic hence found a limit in voluntarism.[391]

The content of the restrictive immunity rule has an immediate evident quality—to use Kelsen's terminology—because it can be derived from the principle of independence and equality of states by means of an intellectual operation. However, the validity of the general principle from which this specific rule can be obtained is not self-evident. Equality and independence are not inherent rights of states but fundamental principles on which the present international legal order is based. As one scholar once noted '[t]he concept of an international community made up of sovereign States is the basis of our intellectual framework for international law.'[392] The restrictive state immunity rule has an inherent appeal not because it corresponds to a certain value, but because it is inherent in an accepted constitutional principle.

[388] *Corfu Channel Case* (*United Kingdom v Albania*) (Merits), ICJ Reports 1949 4, 35 (emphasis added). See also *North Sea Continental Shelf* (ICJ, 1969) 28–9, § 37 and K Marek, 'Le problème des sources du droit international dans l'arrêt sur le plateau continental de la mer du Nord' (1970) 6 RBDI 55, 60. It should also be noted that in the *Continental Shelf Case* (*Libya Arab Jamahiriya v Malta*) (Application to Intervene, Judgment) the ICJ considered that '[i]t is of course axiomatic that the material of customary international law is to be looked for *primarily* in the actual practice and *opinio juris* of States...', ICJ Reports 1984 3, 290, § 80 (emphasis added). Quoted again in *Case Concerning Military and Paramilitary Activities in and against Nicaragua* (ICJ, 1986) 97, § 183.

[389] ibid 106, § 202. The *Concise Oxford Dictionary of Current English* (9th edn, 1995) defines 'corollary', in relevant part, as: 1 (a) a proposition that follows from (and is often appended to) one already proved (b) an immediate deduction. 2 (often foll by *of*) a natural consequence or result.

[390] *South West Africa Cases* (*Ethiopia v South Africa*; *Liberia v South Africa*) (Second Phase), ICJ Reports 1966 6, 248, Dissenting Opinion Judge Tanaka. Cf 277ff.

[391] While the Court did not follow Judge Tanaka at the time, it can be argued that the decision in the *Barcelona Traction* case sanctioned Judge Tanaka's reasoning after all, cf *The Barcelona Traction, Light and Power Company, Limited* (*Belgium v Spain*) (Second Phase), ICJ Reports 1970 3, 32, discussed in ch 6 § 1 of this study.

[392] C Schreuer, 'The Waning of the Sovereign State: Towards a New Paradigm for International Law?' (1993) 4 EJIL 447, 447.

What does this mean for the ascertainment of the scope of the rule? In particular, what is the relation between state practice and the scope of the law of state immunity? Can it be maintained that state immunity is 'a general principle which the inductive method has shown to be limited in the practice of States by the operation of several exceptions',[393] if it is at the same time agreed that '[i]mmunity operates as long as there is a legal basis for it' and that '[i]n the absence of such basis there is no immunity'?[394] It is submitted that it cannot. Since the principle of independence and equality of states is not the material but the formal cause of the rule a critical discussion of state practice in light of these principles is possible.

Of course, as Anzilotti already argued almost a century ago, states may agree to grant *more* immunity than required by these principles. He distinguished, in this respect, necessary from voluntary immunity rules. A general and consistent state practice may establish a voluntary state immunity rule beyond the necessary immunity inherent in the limits of the essential competence of national courts that is in its nature comparable to the law of diplomatic immunity. In this respect, some considerations of Chief Justice Marshall in *The Schooner Exchange* may also be recalled. The judge emphasized that states had consented to 'a relaxation in practice' of their absolute and complete territorial jurisdiction because the 'mutual benefit' of states 'is promoted by intercourse with each other, and by an interchange of those good offices which humanity dictates and its wants require'.[395] However, with the possible exception of state immunity from defamation claims, state practice does not evidence the acceptance of such a voluntary state immunity concept.

State practice purports to give effect to the limitations on essential competence imposed by the principles of independence and equality of states. While state practice is an important indicator of the agreed scope of the requirements flowing from these principles, a rational discussion on the scope of the law of state immunity is possible as long as this practice is said to purport to give effect to these principles. This perspective also explains the distinction between the rule of state immunity and its application—introduced in section 3.2.3. It is recalled that normal custom requires a general and consistent state practice. In the *Asylum* case,[396] the state practice regarding diplomatic asylum was held not to satisfy this requirement. The Court explained that

> [t]he facts... disclose so much uncertainty and contradiction, so much fluctuation and discrepancy in the exercise of diplomatic asylum and in the official views expressed on

[393] Report of the Commission on the work of its thirty-fifth session, YBILC 1983 ii (part two) 17, 26, § 11.

[394] S Sucharitkul (Special Rapporteur ILC), Fourth Report on the Jurisdictional Immunities of States and their Property, YBILC 1982 ii (part one) 199, 207, § 33 and restated in Report of the Commission on the work of its thirty-fifth session, YBILC 1983 ii part two) 17, 27.

[395] *The Schooner Exchange v M'Faddon* (US, 1812) 136.

[396] *Asylum Case* (*Columbia v Peru*), ICJ Reports 1950 266.

different occasions, there has been so much inconsistency in the rapid succession of conventions on asylum, ratified by some States and rejected by others, and the practice has been so much influenced by considerations of political expediency in the various cases, that it is not possible to discern in all this any constant and uniform usage, accepted as law...[397]

Scholars at times note the apparent tension between this requirement and the reality of the law of state immunity. Jennings noted in this respect that there may '[n]o doubt... be problems in attempting to derive a rule of international law from the practice which differs so much from one municipal jurisdiction to another. Yet it is difficult to see how immunity can be denied the status of a rule of international law.'[398] The perspective on the law of state immunity as a necessary incident of an international community consisting of independent and equal states allows a reasoned explanation of this state of affairs. The absence of uniform practice does not regard the rule of state immunity but rather the interpretation of the requirements flowing from the principles of independence and equality of states, or, the assessment of the question when proceedings in a foreign court would violate these principles.

More in general, it should be noted that in this area of law the existence of *opinio juris* as to the material state practice is not self-evident. In the *North Sea Continental Shelf Cases* the ICJ considered that there was no evidence that the available state practice on the delimitation of continental shelf boundaries according to the equidistance principle was supported by *opinio juris*. The fact that many states were parties to the 1958 Geneva Convention on the Continental Shelf that laid down the equidistance principle in article 6, made that these states were 'acting actually or potentially in the application of the Convention' rather than because they felt legally compelled to draw them in this way by reason of a rule of customary law obliging them to do so. It concluded that '[f]rom their action no inference could legitimately be drawn as to the existence of a rule of customary international law in favour of the equidistance principle.'[399] In the field of state immunity considerations *other* than the requirements under international law may be seen to underlie state practice.

For one, it is often pointed out that states 'may accord immunity as a matter of comity, deference or strategy'.[400] This is only reinforced by the hope to receive reciprocal treatment when the roles are reversed. Although it is commonly emphasized that the principle of reciprocity has operated as a motor for the development of the restrictive theory, it must be realized that this 'ripple effect' requires a first stone.[401] Since the principal bearer of the duty and the possible bearer of

[397] ibid 277.

[398] R Jennings (1988) 4–5. Cf A Orakhelashvili, *Peremptory Norms in International law* (2006) 337 for the argument that there is indeed no customary international law on state immunity.

[399] *North Sea Continental Shelf* (ICJ, 1969) 43, § 76.

[400] J Crawford (1983) 78. Cf also S Sucharitkul (1976) 119.

[401] For the term 'ripple effect' cf GM Badr (1984) 135.

the right is not the principal bearer of the negative consequences of the grant of immunity, reciprocity operates as a motor when the immunity rule *is* moving towards a more restrictive interpretation but operates as a powerful brake to the start of this process.

Moreover, the codification of the rule of state immunity in national legislation means that state immunity decisions often reflect the strictures of national rather than international law. National legislation 'inevitably... reflects the differing constitutional laws, or a particular view of the relationship between municipal law and international law'.[402] As Lord Wilberforce noted in *I Congreso*, 'to argue from the terms of a statute to establish what international law provides is to stand the accepted argument on its head'. He cautioned that 'if one State chooses to lay down by enactment certain limits, that is by itself no evidence that those limits are generally accepted by States. And particularly enacted limits may be (or presumed to be) not inconsistent with general international law—the latter being in a state of uncertainty—without affording evidence what that law is.'[403] In sum, a national court decision may, in the words of Borchard, only be evidence of what international law is *not*.[404]

If a certain application of the rule cannot be explained by reference to either the necessary or the voluntary state immunity concept, the limitation of the jurisdiction of the court has a national law character and qualifies as international comity. One example is the application of stricter jurisdictional standards in proceedings against foreign states: it is generally agreed that international law does not require states to impose stricter standards in commercial disputes with a foreign state defendant.[405]

In brief, there *is* room for reason in the ascertainment of the law of state immunity. The analysis of the influence of international human rights law on the law of state immunity and hence the arguments in favour or against a human rights exception to state immunity rules cannot be limited to the standard inductive approach to the identification of exceptions to the rule. It may for instance be argued that the principles of independence and equality of states are not violated when jurisdiction is exercised over human rights violations of foreign states. In chapter 6 we will see that scholars that argue that human rights violations do not constitute sovereign acts for the purpose of the restrictive theory adopt this approach—albeit without articulating a justification for the form of their arguments. Moreover, it may be argued that the role of the principles that underlie the rule of state immunity has changed. In this respect regard may *inter alia* be had to the state practice on other rules that give expression to these principles—like

402 R Jennings (1988) 6.

403 *I Congreso del Partido* (UK, 1981) 260.

404 Quoted in JL Kunz, 'The Nature of Customary International Law' (1953) 47 AJIL 662, 668.

405 CH Schreuer (1988) 36; J Crawford (1983) 109.

the rule of exhaustion of local remedies and the international dispute settlement rule.[406]

Sucharitkul argued that

the method of approach and conduct of studies is inevitably an inductive one... rules of international law on the topic must of necessity be based on the practice of the courts of various countries, large and small, and on the case-laws of various types of municipal legal systems.

The law of nations on the subject under examination is to be found in the customary rules of international law as evidenced by the practice of States.'[407]

General studies on the rule of state immunity usually proceed from a basic rule of immunity, and formulate a list of exceptions to this rule.[408] The exceptions are then derived from the perusal of state practice with regard to immunity law for the existence of precedents supporting this type of exception to state immunity. The limits of the area of non-immunity however are not necessarily drawn inductively. In his influential study on state immunity for the Institut de Droit International Brownlie commented that

the subject of State Immunity has acquired an hermetic quality which creates an unfortunate isolation from the general framework of international law principles.[409]

This is a critical observation. The isolation of the subject of state immunity is, however, only a practical reality, that cannot detract from the inextricable link between state immunity and principles of international law. Hence, state immunity decisions have acquired a hermetic quality, not the state immunity concept.

To sum up, the finding that the rule of restrictive state immunity is—in principle—a necessary incident of the independence and equality of states has consequences for the legitimacy of the form of arguments on the scope of the rule. In particular, it should be acknowledged that there is room for arguments based on 'reason' or 'logic' in the debate on the human rights exception and that hence the *form* of arguments of proponents of a human rights exception appears rational.

[406] It should be noted that the proposed approach to ascertainment of the substance of the requirements under international law is to some extent comparable to, but in essence distinct from, the ideas developed by Crawford in the course of his extensive work on the rule of state immunity. Cf J Crawford (1983); Australian Law Reform Commission, Foreign State Immunity, Report no 24 (1984).

[407] S Sucharitkul, 'Developments and Prospects of the Doctrine of State Immunity, Some Aspects of Codification and Progressive Development' (1982) 29 NILR 252, 259.

[408] A prominent exception to this practice is the Resolution of the Institut de Droit International on Contemporary Problems Concerning the Immunity of States in Relation to Questions of Jurisdiction and Enforcement (1992) that proposed two sets of countervailing criteria for the determination of the applicability of the state immunity rule in a particular case, Institut de Droit International, Resolution on Contemporary Problems Concerning the Jurisdictional Immunity of States (1992), (1992) 64–II AIDI 267.

[409] I Brownlie (Rapporteur Institut de Droit International), Contemporary Problems Concerning the Jurisdictional Immunity of States, Preliminary Report (1987), (1987) 62–I AIDI 13, 17.

It must in conclusion be noted that also from another perspective the form of arguments of opponents is questionable. The recognition of the basis of the law of state immunity in the principle of independence and equality of states does not only *expand* the range of possible arguments in the debate. The emphasis on the absence of state practice to support the human rights exception represents the issue as a mere progression of the trend of limiting the immunity of states from foreign jurisdiction. It implies that states have shown a willingness to limit the privilege of immunity for commercial disputes and must now decide whether a similar limit will be accepted for gross human rights violations. The argument disregards the qualitative difference between the absolute and the restrictive approach to state immunity. The comment that it is state immunity 'which is the exception to jurisdiction and not jurisdiction which is the exception to a basic rule of immunity'[410] is valid as far as it criticizes the formulation of the restrictive rule as a basic rule of immunity with exceptions accepted to it. Indeed, the grant of immunity in the area of non-immunity under the restrictive rule would be an exception to the jurisdiction of the forum. This, however, is not true with the grant of state immunity in the area of immunity under the restrictive rule.

3.3.2.2 The *substance* of coherent argument

State of the law arguments based on logic and reason must proceed from an understanding of the rule of state immunity. When an argument exceeds the boundaries of logic it is no longer coherent in a discussion of what *is* the law and can only qualify as a policy argument on what *ought* to be the law. The argument that *jus cogens* violations do not qualify as sovereign acts under the rule of state immunity must hence be tested against the *acta jure imperii* concept set out in section 3.2 of this chapter.

Policy arguments may be equally incoherent when they fail to reflect the rationales of both human rights law and state immunity law. The argument that obligations under state immunity law clash with obligations under international human rights law should properly reflect the nature and substance of the respective obligations. In this respect, policy arguments against a voluntary state immunity rule may not convince when relied on in the debate on the scope of a necessary rule. In particular, the arguments of proponents of the human rights exception are influenced by the connotation of privilege, or of immunity as a shield from justice, that attaches to voluntary rules—but *not* to necessary rules.

In this respect, proponents often refer to Lauterpacht's characterization of state immunity as 'an archaic and cumbersome doctrine of controversial validity and usefulness'[411] or to his argument that '[a]t a period in which in enlightened

[410] R Higgins (1982) 271. Cf eg I Sinclair (1980) 113, 215; I Brownlie (Rapporteur Institut de Droit International), Contemporary Problems Concerning the Jurisdictional Immunity of States, Definitive Report (1987), (1987) 62–I AIDI 45, 147 (observations of S Sucharitkul); *McDonnell Douglas Corp. v Islamic Republic of Iran* (US, 1985) 348.

[411] H Lauterpacht (1951) 247.

communities the securing of the rights of the individual, in all their aspects, against the state has become a matter of special and significant effort, there is no longer a disposition to tolerate the injustice which may arise whenever the state... screens itself behind the shield of immunity in order to defeat a legitimate claim.'[412] Another popular quotation is that taken from the dissenting opinion of Justice Musmanno in the *Chemical Resources* case. The judge had argued against the grant of immunity to Venezuela in a commercial dispute, pungently stating that

> [t]he sovereign immunity doctrine... is no longer a healthy manifestation of society. It is, in fact, an excrescence on the body of the law, it encourages irresponsibility to world order, it generates resentments and reprisals. Sovereign immunity is a stumbling block in the path of good neighborly relations between nations, it is a sour note in the symphony of international concord, it is a skeleton in the parliament of progress, it encourages government toward chicanery, deception and dishonesty. Sovereign immunity is a colossal effrontery, a brazen repudiation of international moral principles, it is a shameless fraud.[413]

The disregard for the distinction between necessary and voluntary immunity rules, or, for the qualitative difference between the restrictive and the absolute approach to state immunity, is reflected in judicial and academic thinking on the law of state immunity. The idea that also the restrictive rule of state immunity prevents access to an otherwise available court is widespread. In this respect it is interesting to note that the US Supreme Court still explicitly relies on *The Schooner Exchange v M'Faddon* arguing that 'foreign sovereign immunity is a matter of grace and comity on the part of the United States'.[414] While this reasoning *was* coherent in the context of the grant of immunity to the schooner *Exchange* in 1812, it is obviously less convincing in the context of the contemporary restrictive immunity concept. We will see in chapter 6 of this study that the term 'state immunity from jurisdiction' induces circular reasoning. Courts and scholars alike argue that state immunity is an exception to the normal territorial jurisdiction of the forum state *because* it is *called* immunity from jurisdiction. Restrictive immunity however can not be seen to shield states from the normal judicial process. The Legal Advisor to the US State Department aptly put it when he explained that 'the purpose of sovereign immunity in modern international law is not to protect the sensitivities of 19th-century monarchs or the prerogatives of the 20th century state'.[415] Since there is a qualitative difference between the absolute and the restrictive theory of state immunity the forceful arguments

[412] ibid 235.

[413] *Chemical Natural Resources v Republic of Venezuela* 42 ILR 119 (US, 1966) Dissenting Opinion of Musmanno JJ, 122.

[414] *Verlinden BV v Central Bank of Nigeria* (US, 1983), 486.

[415] Statement of Monroe Leigh, Legal Advisor of the State Department, Jurisdiction of US Courts in Suits Against Foreign States: Hearings on HR 11315 Before the Subcomm on Admin Law and Governmental relations of the House Comm On the Judiciary, 94th Cong, 2d Sess 24, 27.

formulated some fifty years ago against the absolute state immunity rule form no authority for delimiting state immunity beyond the logical limits imposed by the principles of independence and equality of states. In fact—as was explained in section 2.3.2 above—Lauterpacht explicitly recognized that his arguments did not affect the prohibition to exercise jurisdiction over foreign states in regard to several categories of acts. Most pertinently, he emphasized that 'no action should lie with regard to torts committed by foreign states and their organs in their own territory. These must be left either to judicial remedies within that foreign state or to appropriate diplomatic action in accordance with the accepted practice of diplomatic protection of citizens abroad.'[416]

3.3.2.3 Conclusion

Both Anzilotti and Lauterpacht recognized that so-called 'immunity' rules can be divided in rules that define the sovereignty of the forum and rules that operate as an exception to that sovereignty. Anzilotti used in this regard the insightful terms 'necessary' and 'voluntary' immunity rules, while Lauterpacht—in what was arguably a purist approach to the issue—did not regard the former rules state immunity rules at all.

In 1950 Niboyet urged state immunity doctrine to clearly distinguish the state immunity concept from the immunity *ratione personae* of diplomats and heads of state:

> Comme l'anatomiste, il doit procéder à toutes sortes de coupes et séparer les tissus les uns des autres pour restituer à chacun son originalité propre.[417]

This section has set out why the distinction of these concepts is indeed important. In anticipation of chapter 6 of this study it was explained that the debate on the human rights exception is shaped by a failure to distinguish the anatomy of the two concepts. The acknowledgement of the inherent quality of the law of state immunity both *expands* and *limits* the parameters of coherent arguments in the debate. While on the one hand arguments based on logic and reason do—quite exceptionally—have a proper role to play in the ascertainment of the scope of the law of state immunity, on the other hand coherent arguments must appreciate the basis of the contemporary state immunity concept in the principles of independence and equality of states.

4 Conclusions

The study of the history of the state immunity concept reveals a troubled regime and a poorly articulated foundation. Judicial and academic thinking on the rule

[416] H Lauterpacht (1951) 238.
[417] JP Niboyet (1950) 158.

of state immunity has severed the rule from its rationales. Courts and scholars alike have focused on the formulation of the exceptions to the rule, rather than on the theory underlying that rule. In particular, the difference between the absolute immunity theory and the restrictive immunity theory is commonly approached as merely quantitative, rather than qualitative in character.

A coherent debate on a human rights exception to the rule of state immunity must reflect a thorough understanding of the nature, substance, and scope of that rule. This chapter set out to develop the tools for the determination of parameters of coherent argument in the debate on the influence of human rights law on the rule of state immunity. To this end, the rule was approached from the perspective of the principles of the independence and equality of states. The sovereignty of states—and hence the essential competence of their courts—finds its limit in the sovereignty of other states. The principle of independence would be violated if a national court would claim competence over the exercise of exclusive competences of a foreign state. Moreover, the principle of equality would be violated if a national court would claim competence over the determination of rights or obligations of a foreign state under international law.

On the basis of these findings it was argued that the epistemological qualities of the restrictive rule of state immunity are distinct from those of ordinary rules of customary international law. In contrast to voluntary immunity rules—like the rule of diplomatic immunity—state practice is not formative of such a necessary state immunity rule. The rule is inherent in an international legal order based on the independence and equality of its members. As long as legislation or jurisprudence is said to give effect to the wants of the principles of independence and equality of states there is room for logic in the ascertainment of the requirements of international law without lapsing into natural law reasoning. The *form* of coherent state of the law arguments is hence not limited to inductive reasoning, not even if it is an argument as to the scope of the rule of state immunity. The particular nature of the restrictive state immunity rule does however not only *expand* the range of coherent argument. The *substance* of coherent state of the law *and* policy arguments must reflect the theoretical foundations of the rule.

3
Functional Immunity

1 Introduction

The functional immunity of (former) foreign state officials is often approached as a corollary of the rule of state immunity. The reasoning of the UK Court of Appeal in *Propend Finance v Sing* is typical in this respect:

> The protection afforded by the [SIA] to States would be undermined if employees, officers or... 'functionaries' could be sued as individuals for matters of State conduct in respect of which the State they were serving had immunity. [The relevant provision of the SIA] must be read as affording individual employees or officials of a foreign State protection under the same cloak as protects the State itself.[1]

From this perspective, the question as to the influence of international human rights law and international criminal law on the immunity of foreign state officials is in fact a question as to the scope of the rule of state immunity applicable to the foreign home state. In this regard, the approach of the House of Lords in the *Pinochet* case is conspicuous. The former head of state of Chile had invoked immunity from the jurisdiction of the UK courts as regards, *inter alia*, allegations of torture committed during his term of office. Lord Browne-Wilkinson paraphrased the central question to be 'whether international law grants state immunity in relation to the international crime of torture'.[2] Differentiation between cases involving foreign states and cases involving foreign state officials is then only possible from the perspective of developments in the field of international human rights law or international criminal law—as in fact was proposed in the *Pinochet* case—*not* from the perspective of the concept of immunity itself. A separate treatment of the immunity of state officials hence appears unnecessary.

Section 2 of this chapter proposes a different view on the rule of functional immunity. If state officials are considered immune because their home state would have been immune had it been sued instead, the rule of state immunity appears as a veritable act of state immunity. However, the rule of state immunity applies only when a national court is asked to exercise its jurisdiction over a foreign state.

[1] *Propend Finance Pty Ltd v Sing* (UK, 1997) 669.

[2] *R v Bow Street Metropolitan Stipendiary Magistrate and others, ex p Pinochet Ugarte (Amnesty International and others intervening)* (UK, 1999) (*Pinochet* no 3) 111.

This chapter will argue that in fact, many functional immunity decisions offer support for the assertion that the law of state immunity only applies if the foreign state is the nominal or factual defendant in the proceedings. If state immunity is to be a rule anchored in the principles of independence and equality of states, rather than a rule protecting 'the sensitivities of 19th-century monarchs or the prerogatives of the 20th century state'[3] it should not be allowed to lapse into a rule of act of state immunity. Recent judicial and academic thinking on the rule of functional immunity evidences that this danger in fact looms large. This chapter will argue that the application of the rule of state immunity to foreign state officials should be seen to rely on a premise regarding the legal position of the state official concerned. Functional immunity—it will be argued—is not directly related to the immunity of the state but rather regards an autonomous rule of international law concerning this premise. Foreign state officials do not incur responsibility in their personal capacity for acts committed as arm or mouthpiece of their home state. Such acts must be regarded as acts of the state rather than as acts of the official and are termed official acts. State officials can only be called to account in regard to these acts in their official capacity. A suit against an official in regard of such acts would therefore involve impleading the foreign sovereign. The suggestion that the rules on state immunity determine the position of state officials before foreign national courts will hence prove deceiving. Rather, state immunity may be applied to cases involving foreign state officials as a consequence of the operation of the rule of functional immunity.

Section 3 will contrast this conception of the rule of functional immunity with two other conceptions that feature—ever more prominently—in academic and judicial thinking on the rule. Most prominent is the act of state immunity argument as accepted in *Propend Finance v Sing* and confirmed by the House of Lords in its 2006 decision in *Jones v Saudi Arabia*.[4] In addition it is sometimes argued that foreign state officials enjoy functional immunity in respect of all acts that can be imputed to their home state. It stands to reason that the arguments in the debate on functional immunity and human rights are shaped by the conception participants have of the applicable rules. The influence of both alternative conceptions of the rule on the debate will be analysed and contrasted with the conception proposed in this study.

This chapter sets out the nature and substance of the rules determining the competence of national courts over (former) foreign state officials in order to identify the tools needed for the development and assessment of state of the law and policy arguments in the debate on a possible human rights (or rather,

[3] Statement of M Leigh, Legal Adviser of the State Department, Jurisdiction of US Courts in Suits Against Foreign States: Hearings on HR 11315 Before the Subcommittee on Administrative Law and Governmental relations of the House Committee on the Judiciary, 94th Cong, 2d Sess 24, 27.

[4] *Jones v Saudi Arabia* (UK, 2006).

international crimes) exception to these rules. It prepares the ground for the critical discussion of the various arguments in the current debate that will follow in chapter 5.

2 Which Came First—The Chicken or the Egg? State Immunity as a Consequence of Functional Immunity Rather than Functional Immunity as a Corollary of State Immunity

2.1 Kelsen's Act of State Immunity Argument

Kelsen rationalized the immunity of state officials from the jurisdiction of foreign national courts in the following terms:

> No state is allowed to exercise through its own courts jurisdiction over another state unless the other state expressly consents... Since a state manifests its legal existence only through acts performed by human beings in their capacity as organs of the state, that is to say, through acts of state, the principle that no state has jurisdiction over another state must mean that a state must not exercise jurisdiction through its own courts over acts of another state unless the other state consents. Hence the principle applies not only in case a state as such is sued in a court of another state but also in case an individual is the defendant or the accused and the civil or criminal delict for which the individual is prosecuted has the character of an act of state.[5]

The immunity of the foreign state official thus appears as a logical consequence of the principle of state immunity. It was as a consequence of the rule of state immunity, Kelsen argued, that state officials could not be held personally responsible for acts that can be imputed to the state. It is not difficult to see that the argument necessarily relies on the concept of act of state immunity. If the law of state immunity is understood from the concept of the direct or indirect implication of a foreign state—as proposed in chapter 2 of this study—the reasoning advanced by Kelsen acquires a problematic circularity.

Chapter 2 explained that the principle of equality and independence of states limits the essential competence of national courts. These principles are compromised if jurisdiction is exercised, either directly or indirectly, over the exclusive competences of a foreign state. The implication of the foreign state is a prerequisite for the application of the law of state immunity. If not the nominal defendant,

[5] H Kelsen, *Principles of International Law* (RW Tucker (ed), 2nd edn, 1966) 358. Cf also H Kelsen, *Principles of International Law* (1952) 235; H Kelsen, 'Collective and Individual Responsibility for Acts of State in International Law' (1948) Jewish Yearbook of International Law 226; H Kelsen, 'Will the Judgment in the Nuremberg Trial Constitute a Precedent in International Law?' (1947) 1 ILQ 153; H Kelsen, *Peace Through Law* (1944); H Kelsen, 'Collective and Individual Responsibility in International Law with Particular Regard to the Punishment of War Criminals' (1943) 31 California Law Review 530.

a state is impleaded when it is the *proper* or *factual* defendant in a case before a foreign court. If a national court is asked to declare the legislation of a foreign state invalid *even within the territory of that state* such an implication is inherent in the claim. However, if compensation is asked for alleged tortious activity of a foreign state official that can be attributed to a foreign state the implication is not immediately obvious. Can it be said that the state is the factual defendant when one of its officials is sued *in his personal capacity* for acts (ostensibly) committed in an official capacity? Only when that official cannot bear responsibility in his personal capacity or when the case clearly sets out to affect the rights and obligations of the state through the implication of its official can it be said that such proceedings in fact implead the home state. In the argument advanced by Kelsen the absence of personal responsibility is however only the *consequence* of the applicability of the law of state immunity. The implication of the state is hence irrelevant for the operation of the law of state immunity. Kelsen clearly advanced a broader rule of act of state immunity, protecting the foreign state even from proceedings that do not purport to exercise jurisdiction over it but merely question the legality of acts that can be imputed to it. As he himself put it: 'The immunity from the jurisdiction of another State is not, as this principle is usually formulated, attached to the very "person" of the State . . . but to the acts of the State as the acts performed by the government, at its command, or with its authorization.'[6]

2.2 Non-Personal Responsibility as an Autonomous Principle *Preceding* State Immunity

The application of the rule of state immunity to foreign state officials can be explained in different terms. As a rule, foreign state officials do not incur personal responsibility for acts committed under the authority of their home state. That this principle is distinct from the law of state immunity is already clear from the fact that state officials may be immune in cases where the state—under the restrictive approach to state immunity—is not. A claim for payment of, say, pencils ordered for the office—a pure *actum jure gestionis* for the purposes of the law of state immunity—cannot be recovered from the personal bank account of the state official that happens to have placed the order.[7] Upon closer consideration, the functional immunity of foreign state officials concerns this non-personal responsibility for acts committed as the arm or as mouthpiece of the home state.

[6] H Kelsen (1944) 82–3.

[7] Discussing the extent of the functional immunity of former diplomats under art 39.2 of the VCDR Denza aptly notes that '[t]here will undoubtedly be some cases where the sending State may under restricted rules of state immunity be subject to local jurisdiction whereas its diplomatic agent remains immune on an indefinite basis under Art 39.2 because the acts in question were performed in the exercise of his functions as a member of the mission.' E Denza, *Diplomatic Law, A Commentary on the Vienna Convention on Diplomatic Relations* (2nd edn, 1998) 363.

The non-personal responsibility of state officials for acts committed on behalf of the state may be seen to be an autonomous principle that *precedes* in its operation the application of the rule of state immunity to the facts of a case. While under the reasoning proposed by Kelsen the individual state official cannot be *held* personally responsible; in the autonomous variant the individual state official *bears* no responsibility in his personal capacity. An Italian court formulated the principle as follows:

> for acts done by them in their public capacity diplomatic agents and subordinate personnel cannot be made personally responsible, for the reason that it is not the diplomatic agent or the member of his staff but the foreign State for which they act which has to be regarded as responsible.[8]

In this regard, Anzilotti explained that acts performed by diplomatic agents in the exercise of official functions are 'facts legally imputable not to him but to another subject'.[9] Or, as Conforti commented, 'the agent cannot be summoned to appear in court to account for them civilly or criminally, not because he is accorded immunity, but because they are not *his* acts.'[10]

The application of the law of state immunity to cases involving foreign state officials is often premised on the absence of personal responsibility of the state official that happened to have performed the act. Where a claim against a state official personally is not possible, the state is regarded the factual—if not the nominal—defendant when a claim against that official is instigated nevertheless.

2.2.1 Functional Immunity as the Non-Personal Responsibility for Official Acts

2.2.1.1 The principle identified

When a state official contracts on behalf of the state the non-personal involvement is most obvious. A case in point is *Monnaie v Caratheodorou Effendi* which concerned a claim instigated against the former Ottoman Ambassador in Brussels for the payment of the costs of a new heating system installed at the Embassy. The Belgian court rejected the claim arguing in relevant part:

> les fournitures dont il s'agit ont été incontestablement commandées pour compte du gouvernement ottoman, et en vue de permettre à celui-ci l'exercice de son droit

[8] *Società Arethusa Film v Reist* 22 ILR 544 (Italy, Tribunal of Rome, 1953) 546.

[9] D Anzilotti, 'Case Comment' (1915) 9 RDI 217, 219 (my translation): 'fatti che non a lui, ma ad un altro subietto debbono essere giuridicamente riferiti.' Cf also D Anzilotti, 'Case Comment' (1912) 6 RDI 501, 501; A Cavaglieri, 'Règles générales du droit de la paix' (1929–I) 26 RdC 311, 470; A Malintoppi, 'Su l'esenzione giurisdizionale degli agenti diplomatici' (1954) 37 RDI 118, 121; A Malintoppi, 'Attività imputabile a Stato estero e responsabilità personale dell'individuo-organo' (1955) 38 RDI 84; P Cahier, *Le droit diplomatique contemporain* (1962) 253 and 308.

[10] B Conforti, *Diritto internazionale* (3rd edn, 1987) 220 (emphasis added) (my translation): 'L'agente non può essere citato in giudizio per rispondere penalmente o civilmente, non perché gli sia riconosciuta una immunità ma perché non si tratta di atti suoi.' Cf in similar terms B Conforti, *Diritto internazionale* (6th edn, 2002) 229.

de représentation et de légation dans notre pays: que seul ledit gouvernement en tire profit; ... le défendeur *ne pourrait donc être tenu personnellement de ce chef*...[11]

The *McLeod*—or *Caroline*—case is the classic example of the non-personal responsibility principle in practice. During the Canadian Rebellion of 1837 British forces violently captured the vessel *The Caroline* while it was on the US side of the border between the two countries. Within the US and especially along the Canadian border sympathy with and even support for the cause of the rebels existed. The British government maintained that the vessel was being used as a means of transport for the rebels as well as for the deliverance of supplies to them. The vessel was set afire and abandoned to the current that eventually led it to descend the Niagara Falls. In the course of this operation two Americans were killed. The incident sparked a diplomatic row. The US considered the attack 'an offense to the sovereignty and the dignity of the United States, being a violation of their soil and territory' and demanded reparation. The UK emphasized that it concerned an act of necessary self-defence. The negotiations that ensued concentrated on the applicable principles of international law: the law of neutrality, the principle of non-interference, and the rules on self-defence.[12] One issue was added to the negotiations when in November 1840 McLeod—a British national—was arrested while visiting New York. He was believed to have been one of the officials taking part in the seizure of the *Caroline* and was indicted for murder and arson.

On 13 December 1840 the British Minister at Washington, Fox, protested the arrest in a letter to the American Secretary of State, Forsyth. He argued that McLeod had been arrested for acts for which he did not bear individual responsibility since they had been performed on orders from and under the authority of the British state. Only after a change of administration in March 1841 did the United States prove receptive to the British arguments. In that same month the new Secretary of State, Webster, communicated the executive's position in a letter to the Attorney-General, the pertinent part of which reads as follows:

it raises a question entirely public and political, a question between independent nations; and... individuals connected in it cannot be arrested and tried before the ordinary

[11] *Monnaie v Caratheodorou Effendi* JT 1903 col 764 (Belgium, Tribunal civil de Bruxelles, 1903) (emphasis added). Cf also *Mellerio v Isabelle de Bourbon* (1874) 1 JDI 32 (France, Tribunal civil de la Seine, 1872) ; A-C Kiss, *Répertoire de la pratique française en matière de droit international public* (1965) iii, 270; *L'Empereur d'Autriche v Lemaitre* (France, 1872); *Répertoire de la pratique française en matière de droit international public* (1965) iii, 269; *Angelo-Poulos v Ferton* Sirey 1809–11 2, 514 (France, Cour de Paris, 1811); *Bernet et autres v Herran, Dreyfus-Scheyer et autres*, A-C Kiss, *Répertoire de la pratique française en matière de droit international public* (1965) iii, 237 (France, Cour de Paris, 1880); *Bradford v Director General of Railroads of Mexico* 3 AD 182, case no 132 (US, Court of Civil Appeals of Texas (El Paso) 1925); Lord McNair, *International Law Opinions* (1956) i, 192.

[12] Cf RY Jennings, 'The *Caroline* and *McLeod* Cases' (1938) 32 AJIL 82.

tribunals, as for the violation of municipal law. If the attack on the *Caroline* was unjustifiable, as this Government has asserted, the law which has been violated is the law of nations; and the redress which is to be sought is the redress authorized, in such cases, by the provisions of that code.

...

That an individual forming part of a public force and acting under the authority of his Government, is not to be held answerable, as a private trespasser or malefactor, is a principle of public international law sanctioned by the usages of all civilized nations, and which the Government of the United States has no inclination to dispute.

...

whether the process be criminal or civil, the fact of having acted under public authority, and in obedience to the orders of lawful superiors, must be regarded as a valid defence; otherwise, individuals would be holden responsible for injuries resulting from the acts of Government, and even from the operations of public war.[13]

In the absence of the appropriate legal tools the US Government however proved incapable of compelling the State of New York to release McLeod. He was eventually acquitted upon proof of alibi in October 1841. The issue was again discussed in the correspondence between the British Foreign Secretary Lord Ashburton and Webster in the run-up to the Webster–Ashburton Treaty that settled the *Caroline* incident. In a letter dated 28 July 1842 Lord Ashburton wrote:

Individuals have been made personally liable for acts done under the avowed authority of their Government; and there are now many brave men exposed to personal consequences for no other cause than having served their country. That this is contrary to every principle of international law it is useless for me to insist.

He inquired whether

the Government of the United States is now in a condition to secure in effect and in practice the principle which has never been denied in argument, that *individuals acting under legitimate authority are not personally responsible for executing the orders of their Government.*[14]

The US did not dispute the principle invoked. Webster acknowledged that

for an act committed by the command of his sovereign... an individual cannot be responsible, in the ordinary courts of another State. It would regard it as a high indignity if a citizen of its own, acting under its authority, and by its special command, in such cases, were held to answer in a municipal tribunal, and to undergo punishment, as if the behest of his Government were no defense or protection to him.

[13] Letter Webster, 15 March 1841, 29 British & Foreign State Papers, 1139, partly cited in RY Jennings, ibid 94.

[14] Letter Lord Ashburton, 28 July 1842, 30 British & Foreign State Papers, 195, cited in RY Jennings, ibid 95 (emphasis added).

Webster further wrote that it was because of peculiarities of the US legal system that the release of McLeod had not been immediate. '[P]ersons arrested on charges of high crimes', he explained 'can only be discharged by some judicial proceeding.'[15]

Also the British Law Officers confirmed McLeod's non-personal responsibility for the *Caroline* incident. When some years after his release from prison McLeod pressed for compensation for his imprisonment through the British Government, the Foreign Office sought advice of the Law Officers on the merits of the claim. Their Report reads in relevant part:

> The principle of International Law that an individual doing a hostile act authorised and ratified by the government of which he is a member cannot be held individually answerable as a private trespasser or Malefactor, but that the act becomes one for which the State to which he belongs is in such case alone responsible, is a principle too well established to be now controverted...[16]

The principle of non-personal responsibility for acts committed under authority of a foreign state is still regularly recognized in state practice. An example can be found in the *travaux préparatoires* on article 39.2 of the Vienna Convention on Diplomatic Relations. While diplomatic immunity ends with the end of the accreditation of the diplomatic agent the article provides that 'with respect to acts performed by such a person in the exercise of his functions as a member of the mission, immunity shall continue to subsist'. The discussions within the ILC on this provision evince that such acts were considered '*not really private acts at all but acts of the sending State*'.[17] This in fact is the rule of functional immunity as it applies to *all* (former) foreign state officials.[18]

While consular agents are, during their term of office, arguably protected by a personal immunity 'in respect of acts performed in the exercise of their consular functions', their immunity is often explained with reference to the functional

[15] Letter Webster, 6 August 1842, 30 British & Foreign State Papers, 201. This 'peculiarity' was in fact remedied before long. In August 1842 the United States Congress enacted a law allowing federal judges to discharge any person proved to have acted under the commission, order, or sanction of a foreign power. Cf 30 British & Foreign State Papers, 202–3.

[16] Report Law Officers (1854) FO 83.2209, cited in RY Jennings, ibid 97.

[17] Chairman J Zourak on the rationale of art 30.2 of the Draft Report on the Law Relating to Diplomatic Intercourse and Immunities (now art 39.2 VCDR), YBILC 1957 i 217, § 22 (emphasis added).

[18] Cf B Conforti (2002) 242; G Morelli, *Diritto processuale civile internazionale* (2nd edn, 1954) 201; A Cavaglieri, *Corso di diritto internazionale* (2nd edn, 1932) 329. The process of qualification of an act as official for functional immunity purposes *is* different when an official operates on the territory of the forum state, as is further explained in § 2.2.1.2 and 2.2.1.3 below. See *Former Syrian Ambassador to the German Democratic Republic* 115 ILR 595 (Federal Republic of Germany, Federal Constitutional Court, 1997), for the anomalous argument that art 39.2 secures some special diplomatic immunity: ch 4 § 2.1.2.1 below; cf also M Tomonori, 'The Individual as Beneficiary of State Immunity: Problems of the Attribution of *Ultra Vires* Conduct' (2003) 29 Denver Journal of International Law and Policy 101, 121.

immunity for official acts.[19] Thus, an Italian court considered that the issue of a passport by a foreign consul '*constitute[s] an activity of the sending State and not of the consul personally*'.[20]

Likewise, a German court considered a report issued by New Scotland Yard according to which the Church of Scientology was guilty of criminal offences against its members 'direct State conduct' that could '*not be attributed as private activities*' to the Head of New Scotland Yard in his personal capacity only because he happened to be authorized to issue the report.[21] In a comparable case against the Chief of the German Federal Police, a Dutch court considered that a report of the German Police on the Church of Scientology 'can only be regarded as an *act done in his official capacity and not as a private person*'.[22]

The Philippine case of *Sanders et al v Veridiano et al* concerned a claim for libel. The claim was instigated by two US officials employed at the US Naval Base against their superiors—also US officials employed at the Base. In a dispute over the terms of the employment of claimants official correspondence between the superiors described the character and functioning of the claimants in terms these latter considered to be libellous. The Supreme Court reasoned that as the foreign state officials sued in this case had 'acted on behalf of that government, and within the scope of their authority, *it is that government, and not the petitioners personally, that is responsible for their acts*.'[23]

In the 1997 decision of the ICTY in *Prosecutor v Blaškić* the principle at hand was discussed in some detail.[24] Croatia had challenged the legal power and authority of the Tribunal to issue compulsory orders to Croatian state officials

[19] Art 43.1 1963 Vienna Convention on Consular Relations (VCCR) 596 UNTS 261.

[20] Re *Rissmann* (1971) 54 RDI 702 (Italy, Tribunale di Genova, 1970); 71 ILR 577, 581. In a similar vein another Italian court stressed that a diplomatic agent is not personally responsible for acts committed as the organ of the state—like the engagement of contractual obligations on the part of the state: *Soc Vivai industriali Roma v Legazione dell'Arabia Saudita* (1955) 38 RDI 79 (Italy, Tribunale di Roma, 1953).

[21] *Church of Scientology Case* (Federal Republic of Germany, 1978) 198 (emphasis added).

[22] *Church of Scientology in the Netherlands Foundation and Others v (1) Herold and (2) Heinrich Bauer Verlag* 65 ILR 380 (The Netherlands, DC of Amsterdam, 1980) 381–2 (emphasis added).

[23] *Sanders v Veridiano* 162 SCRA 88 [1988] (Philippines, S Ct, 1988) (emphasis added); 102 ILR 148. Cf also *United States of America and Others v Guinto, Valencia and Others, United States of America and Others v Ceballos and Bautista, United States of America, Lamachia and Others v Rodrigo and Genove* 102 ILR 132 (Philippines, S Ct, 1990) especially 139; and *Baer v Tizon* (Philippines, S Ct, May 1974); *Wylie v Rarang* (Philippines, S Ct, May 1992); *United States of America v Reyes* (Philippines, S Ct, March 1993) available at <http://www.lawphil.net/judjuris/judjuris.html>.

[24] *Prosecutor v Blaškić* IT–95–14, Judgment on the Request of the Republic of Croatia for Review of the Decision of Trial Chamber II of 18 July 1997 (ICTY, Appeals Chamber, 1997). In the *Krstić* case the Appeals Chamber decided that subpoenas to give evidence of what a state official saw or heard at a time when he was a state official and in the course of exercising his official functions were not covered by the rule of functional immunity. The crucial question, it appears, is whether the state official must be deemed to have been summoned *as the state*. The appeals chamber argued that '[u]nlike the production of State documents, the State cannot itself provide evidence which only such a witness could give': *Prosecutor v Krstić* IT–98–33, Decision on Application for Subpoenas (ICTY, Appeals Chamber, 2003) § 20–8, cf especially § 24–5.

to produce certain documents. The Appeals Chamber agreed that the tribunal could not address subpoenas or other binding orders to state officials acting in their official capacity. 'Such officials', it held, 'are mere instruments of a State and their official action can only be attributed to the State. They cannot be the subject of sanctions or penalties for conduct that is not private but undertaken on behalf of a State. In other words, State officials cannot suffer the consequences of wrongful acts *which are not attributable to them personally* but to the State on whose behalf they act: they enjoy so-called "functional immunity".'[25]

In sum, foreign state officials enjoy functional immunity in regard to official acts. Acts committed as a mere arm or mouthpiece of a foreign state are acts of that state rather than acts of the officials personally. Accordingly, state officials cannot be called to account for them in their personal capacity.

2.2.1.2 The principle explained in terms of international law: presumption of authority

It is often argued that functional immunity derives from the principle of respect for the internal organization of the foreign state.[26] One Italian court referred in this regard to 'the principle of international law of respect for the internal legal organisation of every state by all other states, from which derives the obligation for all of them to consider the activity of the organs of foreign states as activity imputable to the state itself and not to the physical persons of its functionaries, and thus to not attach civil or criminal consequences of a personal character to the activity of these functionaries—to the extent that they qualify as agents who performed acts within their functions'.[27] However, as Balladore Pallieri aptly pointed out, this reasoning fails to account for the application of the rule of functional immunity in cases where the state official does in fact incur personal responsibility under the laws of his home state.[28]

The non-personal responsibility for official acts is of course a principle widely recognized in national legal systems. In *international* law however the principle acquires an extra dimension. In most national legal systems state officials may be sued in their personal capacity for ultra vires conduct, as well as for serious mistakes in the performance of their mandate. The Philippine Supreme Court, for example, explains that as a general rule state officials 'can be held personally

[25] ibid § 38 (emphasis added).

[26] Cf eg G Morelli(1954) 201ff; G Morelli, *Nozioni di diritto internazionale* (7th edn, 1967) 215ff. Cf also T Perassi, *Lezioni di diritto internazionale* (1955) 105; A Tanzi, *L'immunità dalla giurisdizione degli agenti diplomatici* (1991) 9.

[27] *Soc Vivai industriali Roma v Legazione dell'Arabia Saudita* (Italy, 1953) 82 (my translation): 'principio di diritto internazionale... rispetto dell'organizzazione giuriddica interna di ogni Stato da parte di tutti gli altri Stati, da cui discende l'obbligo per ciascuno di essi di considerare l'attività degli organi di Stati stranieri come attività imputabile agli Stati stessi e non alle persone fisiche dei suoi funzionari, e quindi non ricollegare all'attività di questi ultimi—in quanto agenti nella loro qualifica—consequenze civili o penali di carattere individuale.'

[28] G Balladore Pallieri, *Diritto internazionale pubblico* (8th edn, 1962) 371ff.

accountable for acts claimed to have been performed in connection with official duties where they have acted ultra vires or where there is showing of bad faith.'[29] Moreover, generally applicable normative limits are often seen to circumscribe the protective mandate of state officials. In the United States, state officials can for example be sued in their personal capacity for constitutional torts committed under the colour of law.[30]

As regards foreign state officials a comparable inquiry is typically not made. That acts performed under ostensible authority but in excess of actual authority *are* attributable to the person of the state official is equally true for foreign state officials. The difference lies in the tools available to courts to determine such a discrepancy. In a Canadian case against US state officials the court explicitly stated that '[t]he illegal and malicious nature of the acts alleged do not of themselves move the actions outside the scope of the official duties of the responding defendants.'[31] As regards the act of a foreign consul committed within the territory of his home state a French court considered that even if they were ultra vires '[o]nly the courts of the country which the Consul represents are competent to deal with such abuse of power.'[32] In general it can be said that *ostensible authority is accepted as actual authority.*

The principle of respect for the internal organization of the foreign state can hence not adequately explain the rule of functional immunity of foreign state officials. Other theories have been advanced. Quadri, for example, has based the rule on the obligation not to interfere in the constitutional life of foreign states; while Seyersted based it on the protection of the organic jurisdiction of states.[33]

[29] *Chavez v Sandiganbayan* 193 SCRA 282 [1991] (Philippines, S Ct, 1991).

[30] The US Supreme Court had already held in *Ex p Young* 209 US 123 (1908) 159–60 that when a state official acts under a state law in a manner that violates the Federal Constitution he 'comes into conflict with the superior authority of that Constitution, and he is in that case stripped of his official or representative character and is subjected *in his person* to the consequences of his individual conduct. The State has no power to impart to him any immunity from responsibility to the supreme authority of the United States' (emphasis added). This case was however limited to actions for prospective injunctive relief. In *Bivens v Six Unknown Federal Narcotics Agents* 403 US 388 (1971) the Supreme Court recognized a civil remedy for individuals whose constitutionally or legally protected rights had been violated by persons acting under colour of law. Also relevant in this regard is 42 USC 1983 that provides a civil action for deprivation of rights (the section reads in relevant part: 'Every person who, under color of any statute, ordinance, regulation, custom, or usage, of any State or Territory or the District of Columbia, subjects, or causes to be subjected, any citizen of the United States or other person within the jurisdiction thereof to the deprivation of any rights, privileges, or immunities secured by the Constitution and laws, shall be liable to the party injured in an action at law, suit in equity, or other proper proceeding for redress…'). The Supreme Court has emphasized that no 11th amendment immunity is available in personal capacity suits, even when the alleged act has been performed in an official capacity, cf *Hafer v Melo* 502 US 21 (1991).

[31] *Jaffe v Miller and Others* (Canada, 1993) 460.

[32] *Boyer v Aldrète* 23 ILR 445 (France, Tribunal Civil de Marseille, 1956) 446. The relevance of the situs of the act will be explained in § 2.2.1.3 below.

[33] R Quadri, *Diritto internazionale pubblico* (5th edn, 1968) 614; F Seyersted, 'Jurisdiction over Organs and Officials of States, the Holy See and Intergovernmental Organisations,' (1965) 14 ICLQ 31, 33.

Roughly stated, both scholars argued—albeit it in different terms—that the relation between a state and its officials is within the exclusive competence of that state.[34] Balladore Pallieri himself argued that the rule did not inhere in any principle but simply concerned a rule of customary international law.[35] We cannot dwell here on the particulars of each of these theories. The theories of Quadri and Seyersted are arguably too categorical. For one, as will be argued in the following section, the acts of state officials that operate within the territory of the forum state are subject to a less marginal review.

It is suggested here that it is not as much the relation between the state and its officials that is within the exclusive competence of the state, but rather the mandate and directions given to state officials while exercising the authority of the state under international law. Accordingly, if a foreign state inquires into that mandate it purports to exercise jurisdiction over an exclusive competence of another state. The presumption of authority is hence an aspect of the law of state immunity. The ICTY in *Prosecutor v Blaškić* reasoned along these lines. The Tribunal held that

> customary international law protects the internal organization of each sovereign State: it leaves it to each sovereign State to determine its internal structure and in particular to designate the individuals acting as State agents or organs. Each sovereign State has the right to issue instructions to its organs, both those operating at the internal level and those operating in the field of international relations, and also to provide for sanctions or other remedies in case of non-compliance with those instructions. The corollary of this exclusive power is that each State is entitled to claim that acts or transactions performed by one of its organs in its official capacity be attributed to the State, so that the individual organ may not be held accountable for those acts or transactions.[36]

It should be emphasized that this does *not* mean that the functional immunity of the foreign state official as such is part of the law of state immunity. The non-personal responsibility for acts that are in law the acts of the state is an autonomous principle. The law of state immunity merely influences the operation of that principle. In the application of the rule of functional immunity the foreign state is not as much immune in respect of the *act* as in respect of the *instructions preceding that act*. As long as state officials perform acts in their official capacity within the context of the exercise of state authority under international law they are presumed to have acted as a mere arm or mouthpiece of their home state.

The substantive rather than procedural character of functional immunity has consequences for the scope of the rule. In the first place, the immunity is not dependent on an official's term of office. It applies to former and incumbent

[34] Cf eg F Seyersted, ibid 33: 'The organic jurisdiction of a state implies that all its relations with—and all relations between and within—its organs and officials as such are governed by the public law and by the executive and judicial organs of that State and not by the public or private law or the organs of any other State.'

[35] G Balladore Pallieri(1962) 371ff.

[36] *Prosecutor v Blaškić* (ICTY, 1997) § 41. Cf also § 43.

officials alike. With regard to officials that operate abroad it must be noted moreover that the functional immunity applies not only between the receiving and the sending state but *erga omnes*, as regard all third states.

The rule of functional immunity does of course not oblige courts to blindly accept *any* claim of a foreign state that an official has acted under its authority. A court may independently inquire into the reasonableness of such claim. Certain acts are so inherently personal that it cannot reasonably be claimed that they were performed under authority of a state. It is hard to dispute, for instance, that a head of state that murders the proverbial gardener in a fit of rage was committing anything but a purely private crime. Likewise, the veil of state authority could not convincingly cover the trade in narcotic substances for purely private benefit.[37] That such a purely private act is committed during the exercise of an official's functions does not make a difference.[38] In sum, the claim that acts should be attributed to the state rather than to the state official personally cannot be frivolously relied on by foreign states to protect their state officials.

The UK case *Re P (No 2)* provides an illustrative example of the limits of the argument.[39] When the German wife of a US diplomat in London started divorce proceedings in Germany, she applied to the High Court in London for restraining orders in order to prevent the father from taking their two children with him to the US. The High Court upheld the argument advanced by the father and the United States—intervening in the proceedings—that it lacked jurisdiction because both the father and the children possessed diplomatic immunity and dismissed the application.[40] Immediately after that judgment and upon the end of the term of office of the father, the children were removed to the United States. The mother then commenced proceedings in the High Court seeking a declaration that the father had wrongfully removed the children from the United Kingdom. The father and the USA—which again intervened—argued that the English courts lacked jurisdiction on the ground that the father had returned to the US with the children on the orders of the US Government and claimed that therefore 'his act was one performed in the exercise of his functions as a member of the US diplomatic mission in the UK and that he was entitled to immunity under article 39.2 VCDR'. That claim was resolutely—and rightly—rejected by the court.[41]

[37] *United States v Noriega* 746 F Supp 1506 (US, DC for the Southern District of Florida, 1990) 1519; *United States v Noriega* 117 F 3d 1206 (US, Ct of Apps (11th Cir), 1997). Although the case was primarily decided on the ground that Noriega had not been recognized as a head of state, the courts did in addition note the non-official character of the crimes at issue. Cf also *Jiminez v Aristeguieta* 311 F 2d 547 (US, Ct of Apps (5th Cir), 1962).

[38] Cf eg *L v The Crown* 68 ILR 175 (New Zealand, S Ct, Auckland, 1977). Cf however *Commonwealth v Jerez* 457 NE2d 1105 (US, 1983) 1109; and *Yugoslav Consul Immunity Case* 73 ILR 689 (Germany, Supreme Provincial Court of Bavaria, 1973).

[39] *Re P (No 2)* 114 ILR 485 (UK, High Court, Family Division; CA, Civil Division, 1998).

[40] *Re P (No 1)* 114 ILR 478 (UK, High Court, Family Division, 1997).

[41] *Re P (No 2)* (UK, 1998) 495. See § 3.3 below for a discussion of the second part of this case which concerned the remarkable decision that the former diplomat *was* covered by the law of state immunity.

The international law rule of functional immunity does *neither* entail that all acts that *can* be attributed to the state qualify as official acts. The rule that ostensible authority presumes actual authority is premised on the exercise of authority under international law. As regards foreign state officials that exercise exclusive competences on the territory of the forum state, the scope of authority necessarily depends on an agreement between the home state and the forum state. (See section 2.2.1.3 below). Moreover, when a home state defeats the presumption of authority, an act may no longer qualify as official for functional immunity purposes (See section 2.2.1.4 below). In both cases the ultra vires conduct nevertheless may be attributable to the foreign state.

2.2.1.3 Inherent limits of the presumption of authority

The rule that ostensible authority presumes actual authority only applies if foreign state officials act within the context of the exercise of state authority under international law. It was explained in chapter 2 of this study that with this we mean *not* that a state acts *in accordance* with international law but rather that it acts *in the capacity of (externally) sovereign state.* Two distinct situations were identified. States act in such capacity when they exercise exclusive territorial competences, *or* when they operate within the context of international law.[42] Accordingly—unless the international law element comes into play—the rule that only the home state may determine the scope of an official's authority finds its limit in territorial boundaries. Authority to exercise sovereign activity in the territory of a foreign state is by definition dependent on the consent of the foreign territorial state. Outside the territory where the home state exercises exclusive competence, the authority of a state official that performs sovereign activity is also defined by the agreement between the sending and receiving state on the scope of his functions. If the official acts within the agreed limits of the sovereign function the presumption of authority applies since the foreign state has been allowed to act within its authority under international law. If not, the principle of functional immunity applies without this presumption. In sum, as regards acts within the territory of the forum state an independent inquiry into the scope of the mandate of the foreign state official may be undertaken.

Let us take a look at the relevant state practice. The position of foreign state officials that exercise sovereign authority abroad is best discussed on the basis of consular immunity practice. Since diplomatic agents enjoy an almost absolute personal immunity during their term of office, only cases against *former* diplomatic agents will normally discuss the rule of functional immunity. The immunity of the consular officer is however much more limited and cases against consular officers are in general instructive on the rule. Article 43.1 of the 1963 Vienna Convention on Consular Relations provides that

[42] Cf ch 2 § 3.2.

> [c]onsular officers and consular employees shall not be amenable to the jurisdiction or administrative authorities of the receiving state in respect of acts performed in the exercise of their consular functions.

While arguably article 43.1 regards the immunity *ratione personae* of a consular officer rather than his immunity *ratione materiae* the article is often said to provide functional immunity—or immunity for official acts—to consular officers rather than any form of personal immunity.[43] The case law based on article 43.1 is therefore often phrased in terms of the rule of functional immunity.

The state practice on libel claims against foreign consular officers illustrates that the mandate of a consular officer is not unilaterally determined by the sending state but also depends on the consent of the receiving state. The French case *Zizianoff v Bigelow*[44] concerned a US consular officer in Paris. Princess Zizianoff brought a libel claim against the officer who had informed the press that the princess' application for a visa was rejected because she was considered an international spy. The US claimed that the French courts were not competent to deal with the claim since its officer had acted in the performance of his duties when furnishing the information. The Court of Appeal rejected that claim holding that 'the conduct complained of could in no way be associated with the performance of his official duties'. It argued in particular that the comments 'whether considered apart from or in association with the official function itself, constitute a grave offence calculated to prejudice private interest, and are personal in character. This offence can be clearly separated from the official

[43] See eg I Brownlie(2003) 355; LT Lee, *Consular Law and Practice* (1991) 484; Y Dinstein, *Consular Immunity from Judicial Process, With Particular Reference to Israel* (1966) 23 and 25; R Jennings and A Watts (eds)(1992) i 1144; Third Restatement, § 463, Reporters note 1, and Comment a; Harvard Law School, Research in International Law (Reporter Q Wright) Legal Position and Functions of Consuls (1932 supplement) 26 AJIL 189, 339; J Zourek (Special Rapporteur ILC) First Report on Consular Intercourse and Immunities, YBILC 1957 ii 71, 99, and Second Report on Consular Intercourse and Immunities, YBILC 1960 ii 10; Report of the ILC on the work of its Thirteenth session, YBILC 1961 ii 88, 117; *Rubin v Console della Repubblica di Panama* (1978) 61 RDI 565 (Italy, Corte di Cassazione, 1978); *Church v Ferraino* (1987) 23 RDIPP 325 (Italy, Corte di Cassazione, 1986).

The provision then secures functional immunity for those acts that states can only engage in with the consent of the territorial state. A consular officer may act on behalf of his home state without engaging in a typical consular function—just as a diplomatic agent may perform an official act that is not a specific function of the diplomatic mission. A conspicuous example is the signing of a rental contract for the consular—or diplomatic—premises. Art 53.4 VCCR sees to this broader rule of functional immunity in general providing that although the immunity of a consular officer ceases when his term of office has come to an end 'with respect to acts performed by a consular officer or a consular employee in the exercise of his functions, immunity from jurisdiction shall continue to subsist without limitation of time'.

It could be argued that even for as far as the *scope* of art 43.1 overlaps with the *scope* of the rule of functional immunity, the use of the latter term to describe the former rule is inapposite because of the distinct *nature* of the two rules. Art 43.1 could be seen to secure immunity from jurisdiction in respect of acts performed in the exercise of consular functions. This obstacle to jurisdiction renders an inquiry into the functional immunity of the consular again redundant.

[44] *Princess Zizianoff v Kahn and Bigelow* 4 AD 384, case no 266 (France, Tribunal correctionnel of the Seine, CA of Paris, Court of Cassation, 1927–28); (1929) 23 AJIL 172.

function performed by Bigelow and in no way involves an examination of the said function'.[45]

A similar case came before the US courts a few decades later. A Venezuelan national in political exile in the US brought an action for libel against the Consul General of Venezuela in New York.[46] Plaintiff alleged that the consul had published articles in Venezuelan newspapers that reflected negatively on his social, moral, political, and professional standing and was circulating copies of those articles via mailing lists and in the consulate. The court in considering whether the defamatory acts could be seen to form part of the consul's functions emphasized the importance of the specific mandate as agreed for the specific state official before it. It held that 'a consul's duties are commercial but... they may be enlarged by special authority. To be effective such an enlargement must, however, "be recognized by the government within whose dominions he assumes to exercise it".'[47] The Venezuelan Ambassador in his letter to the Secretary of State asserted that the consul's mandate had indeed been enlarged and that the official had acted upon specific request of the Venezuelan authorities. In fact, the ambassador stressed 'he would have been remiss in carrying out his official instructions had he failed to do so.'[48] The court did not agree. It regarded the fact that the relevant letter had been submitted to it without comment by the State Department as a further indication that no enlargement of functions had been recognized and that the acts complained of fell outside the limits of the consul's mandate.

It was stated above that as long as the official that is allowed to exercise sovereign activity on the territory of a foreign state acts within the agreed limits of that sovereign function the presumption of authority applies. In other words, foreign states have a discretion to exercise the sovereign function in accordance with their policy preferences. This discretion is most visible in those cases where a consular officer is considered protected by immunity even when the performance of a typical consular function has violated the law of the receiving state. The Italian court in the *Rissmann* case famously considered the activity of the Consul of Germany in Genoa to have been performed within the exercise of

[45] ibid 386. The Attorney-General in this case explicitly stated that the 'French courts cannot be bound by the opinion of the Government of the United States which thinks that Consul Bigelow has acted within the scope of his duties' ((1929) 23 AJIL 172, 177).

[46] *Arcaya v Páez* 23 ILR 436 (US, DC for the District of New York, Ct of Apps (2nd Cir), 1956 and 1957). Cf also *Mario Cardile v Amílcar Bresso et al* 8 AD 403, case no 192 (Argentina, Federal S Ct, 1937); and *Kovtunenko v U Law Yone* 31 ILR 259 (Burma, S Ct, 1960). It is recalled that *Boyer v Aldrète* (France, 1956) (n 32 above) concerned a libel action concerning activity outside the receiving state. Cf *Difference Relating to Immunity from Legal Process of a Special Rapporteur of the Commission on Human Rights (The Cumaraswamy Case)* Advisory Opinion, ICJ Reports 1999 62, for an example of speech as 'official act' for the purpose of the immunity of an official of an international organization.

[47] ibid 441.

[48] ibid 442.

his functions even though he had violated Italian criminal law.[49] The Consul had issued a passport and travel documents for a minor resident in Italy and assisted her to leave Italy in order to join her father, a German national resident in Germany. While the minor was a German national under German law and a German court had entrusted guardianship to her father, under Italian law she was an Italian national and an Italian court had entrusted her to her mother, resident in Genoa. Criminal proceedings were instituted against the Consul. In an official memorandum the German Embassy in Rome objected that Rissmann had acted in the exercise of his functions and invoked consular immunity on his behalf. In response to the claim of immunity the court first considered the nature of the concept of consular immunity. It held that

> functional immunity... finds its justification in the general principle according to which the consul's acts, even though they may be valid within the legal system of the receiving State and thus produce legal consequences therein, constitute an activity of the sending State and not of the consul personally, since, in the exercise of his office he is accountable to his government. Such an immunity is not, therefore, merely procedural. It is based on a principle of substantive law and continues even after his tour of office has terminated.[50]

With regard to the acts violating Italian criminal law the court considered that

> there can be no doubt that Rissmann, in issuing her with a German passport, was carrying out a true and proper official act as Consul
>
> ...
>
> It should not be forgotten that Consuls, being State agents operating abroad, do not exceed the scope of their functions when they act in accordance with the laws of their country which they must comply with in so far as these laws are to be applied abroad.
>
> ...
>
> There can be no doubt that the German Federal Republic, in the aforementioned memorandum of its Embassy in Rome had fully assumed responsibility for the Consul's action, as it complied with the provisions of the German legal system to which Rissmann's conduct was required to conform.[51]

The Court of Cassation affirmed the decision underlining that the agent had acted 'within the limits of his functions' carrying out 'acts proper to his office'.[52]

[49] *Re Rissmann* (Italy, 1970), (1973) 9 RDIPP 121 (Corte di Cassazione, 1972). See 71 ILR 577 for both decisions. The decision of the Court of Cassation is hardly more than an affirmation of the decision of the Tribunal of Genoa.

[50] 71 ILR 577, 581.

[51] ibid 582–3.

[52] ibid 583. See for a critical note on the *Rissmann* case, L Condorelli, (1976) 2 Italian Yearbook of International Law 339. He was of the opinion that the German consul had acted in contempt of Italian laws and regulations and had jeopardized a specific order of an Italian judge 'thus placing himself outside the limits of his functions'. Consular functions, he argued, should be exercised with respect for laws of the receiving state (341). To support his argument Condorelli approvingly referred to art 21 of the Harvard Draft Convention on the Legal Position and Functions of Consuls, Harvard Law School, Research in International Law (Reporter Q Wright) Legal Position and Functions of Consuls, (1932 supplement) 26 AJIL 189, 338, that laid down that 'the receiving

Similar reasoning can be found in the US case of *State of Indiana v Ström*.[53] Criminal suit was brought against Ström, a Swedish consul in the US, for supplying a passport to a Swedish national who was accused of murder in the US, thus allowing him to return to Sweden. The court held in relevant part:

> There is no doubt that consuls... are immune from certain actions even if those actions violate the local criminal laws of the receiving State... even though a consul covered by the [Vienna Convention on Consular Relations] violates a local or State law he is immune from prosecution if the actions which violated the laws were performed by him in the exercise of his consular functions.

The court considered that in supplying the passport Ström had indeed performed an act in the exercise of his consular functions.

However, while the violation of the national law of the receiving state does not exclude the official character of an act *per se*, a violation that cannot be explained by the discretion of a foreign state in the exercise of a conspicuous consular activity is not likely to be accepted as an official act. A coherent distinction for example can be made between the acts at issue in the *Rissmann* and *Ström* cases and the German *Tabatabai* case where it was held that 'the importation of narcotic substances... which occurred without the authorization of the receiving State is not to be classified as one of the official functions of a special envoy'.[54]

Moreover, several cases indicate that the accepted functions of consular officers may be considered circumscribed by normative limits. The US case *Gerritsen v De La Madrid* relied heavily on the definition of consular functions provided in article 5 of the VCCR.[55] The case concerned a civil suit against several Mexican consular officers on allegations of having unlawfully impeded a protest against the Mexican President near the Consulate in Los Angeles. The allegations included striking with a heavy metal object, threatening with a club and gun, kidnapping and interrogating the protester, forcibly taking his leaflets and camera. The officers' claim that the alleged acts qualified as official acts for which they enjoyed immunity was rejected. The court considered that the consular functions at issue in the case were explicitly circumscribed by normative limits in article 5 VCCR. Subcategory a and m of this article provide that consular functions consist of 'protecting in the receiving State the interests of the sending State and its nationals..., within the limits permitted by international law' and 'performing any other functions entrusted to a consular post by the sending State which

state decides subject to diplomatic intercourse by the sending state whether the act was done in the performance of... [official] functions.'

[53] *State of Indiana v Ström* (US, Court of Lake County, Criminal Division, 1988) reported in LT Lee(1991) 501. Cf also *Risk v Halvorsen and Others* 98 ILR 125 (US, Ct of Apps (9th Cir), 1991)—a civil case comparable on the facts to the *Rissmann* case; *R v Bonadie* (Canada, Ontario Court of Justice, 1996) discussed in EG Lee et al, 'Consular Immunity, Alleged Criminal Activity of a Consular Officer' (1996) 34 Canadian Yearbook of International Law 293.

[54] *Tabatabai* 80 ILR 389 (Germany, Provincial Court, 1983).

[55] *Gerritsen v De La Madrid* 101 ILR 478 (US, Ct of Apps (9th Cir), 1987).

are not prohibited by the laws and regulations of the receiving State'. The court concluded that since the suppressing of the freedom of speech on political matters violates international law, and assault with a deadly weapon and kidnapping violate US penal laws, the alleged acts could not have been performed in the exercise of consular functions.[56]

In a similar vein, the Swiss government relied on the definition of the functions in the Vienna Convention on Diplomatic Relations to support its argument that acts of espionage could not be covered by the functional immunity of former diplomats laid down in article 39.2. Article 3.1(d) provides that it is the function of a diplomatic mission to 'ascertain [. . .] by all lawful means conditions and developments in the receiving State, and report [. . .] thereon to the Government of the sending State.' The Swiss government argued that hence 'l'obtention de renseignements par des voies illégales, soit l'espionnage, ne fait pas partie des fonctions de la mission.'[57]

Arguably, the rules of international law limit the scope of consular functions in general. It is in this regard interesting to note that the normative limit relied on in *Gerritsen* recalls the limits formulated in *Letelier v Chile* and *Liu v China* on the discretionary function exception to the territorial tort exception of the FSIA.[58] The FSIA provides that although foreign states are not immune in regard to territorial tort claims, immunity *is* available if a claim is based on the exercise or performance—or the failure to exercise or perform—a discretionary function of the foreign state. In this regard the courts inquire in the first place whether the government employee that performed the act had any discretion to act or if there was an element of choice as to appropriate conduct, and second whether the decisions were grounded in social, economical, and political policy.[59] In *Letelier v Chile* the court held that '[w]hatever policy options may exist for a foreign country, it has no 'discretion' to perpetrate conduct designed to result in the assassination of an individual or individuals, action that is clearly contrary to the precepts of humanity as recognized in both national and international law.'[60] Since the protection of discretionary function in the FSIA is similar to the protection of discretion in the exercise of consular functions, a similar argument may be formulated as regards consular immunity.[61] While violations of the type at issue in *Letelier* are obviously not taken within the context of the exercise of consular functions, the same is not true, for example, for the issuance of visa on the

[56] ibid 481–2.

[57] Avis de droit de la Direction du droit international public du Département politique fédéral (1979), (1980) 36 ASDI 210, 211. Cf this to an earlier opinion to the opposite effect published in (1964) 21 ASDI 171.

[58] *Letelier v Chile* (US, 1980); *Helen Liu v The Republic of China* 892 F 2d 1419 (US, Ct of Apps (9th Cir), 1989). Cf ch 2 § 3.2.1 above.

[59] Cf *Risk v Halvorsen* (US, 1991).

[60] *Letelier v Chile* (US, 1980) 673.

[61] Cf *Risk v Halvorsen* where both questions were treated in one case and in similar vein.

basis of discriminatory criteria. This intricate question will be further discussed in chapter 6 of this study.

As stated above, if the act of a foreign state official on the territory of the foreign state is not performed within the exercise of consular—or diplomatic—functions this does not automatically mean that the rule of functional immunity does not apply to the facts of the case. Many cases against consular officers are in fact decided on the basis of the rule of functional rather than consular immunity. The case against the former Ottoman Ambassador in Brussels who was sued for the payment of the costs of a new heating system installed at the Embassy was noted earlier in this chapter. The court dismissed the claim arguing that the materials had been ordered on behalf of the Ottoman government and were only of profit to that government. The former Ambassador could not be held personally accountable for the unpaid bill.[62] This type of reasoning is also often applied to incumbent consular officers that contract on behalf of their home state.[63] Consular officers contracting on behalf of the state are in this respect not treated differently from other foreign state officials doing so. When the commanding officer of the US Rest and Recuperation Office in Sydney was sued in regard of a contract he signed on the provision of a civilian clothing hire service for members of the US Forces that come to Sydney for rest and recuperation, the Australian court noted that '[i]t is clear beyond all argument that Major Boyd did not contract in a personal capacity when he signed the [contract].'[64] It emphasized that 'what was done through or in name of the United States R. & R. Office was done for the purposes of the foreign state itself'.[65]

Also outside the field of contracts is the non-personal involvement of foreign state officials acting within the territory of the forum state regularly recognized. When a claim requires a state official to perform an act—or refrain from performing an act—in his public capacity the non-personal involvement is evident.[66] In personal tort claims this may be so if the acts complained of are clearly performed on behalf of the home state. The facts of the Philippine case of *Sanders et al v Veridiano et al* were set out above. US officials had complained that correspondence of their superiors concerning their dismissal was libellous. The Supreme Court concluded that '[g]iven the official character of the above-described letters, we have to conclude that *the petitioners were, legally speaking, being sued as officers of the United States government. As they have acted on behalf of that government,*

[62] *Monnaie v Caratheodorou Effendi* (Belgium, 1903). Cf also Lord McNair (1956) i 192, discussing a 1823 opinion of the UK Law Officers of the Crown on the non-personal responsibility of the Spanish ambassador in London for contracts passed for the Spanish government.

[63] *Landley v Republic of Panama* 9 AD 441, case no 175 (US, DC for the Southern District of New York, 1940).

[64] *Grunfeld and Another v United States of America and Others* 52 ILR 332 (Australia, New South Wales, S Ct, Sydney, 1968) 334.

[65] ibid 335. Cf also *Syquia et al v Lopez et al* 18 ILR 228 (Philippines, S Ct, 1949).

[66] Cf *Johnson v Major-General Howard M. Turner et al* 21 ILR 103 (Philippines, S Ct, 1954); *Baer v Tizon* (Philippines, 1974) available at <http://www.lawphil.net/judjuris/judjuris.html>.

and within the scope of their authority, it is that government, and not the petitioners personally, that is responsible for their acts.'[67] *United States v Ceballos* regarded a claim against state officials working for the Office of Special Investigations of the US Air Force stationed in the Philippines.[68] During a buy-bust operation the officials had arrested a Philippine national employed as a barracks boy at the Air Base on suspicion of a drugs-related offence. When a charge was filed against him on the basis of the testimonies of these officials he was dismissed from his job. He commenced proceedings for damages against the individual state officials. The Philippine Supreme Court noted that the officials were charged with the function of preventing the distribution, possession and use of prohibited drugs and prosecuting violations of the relevant rules. The court argued that it could therefore 'not for a moment be imagined that they were acting in their private or unofficial capacity when they apprehended and later testified against the complainant.'[69] In sum, when foreign state officials have clearly acted as the arm or mouthpiece of their home state the rule of functional immunity applies to them regardless of the place where the act is performed.[70]

The forum state however may apply its national law standard to ascertain whether foreign state officials acting within its territory—diplomatic agents and consular officers excluded—*have* in fact acted as arm or mouthpiece. At the same time as *United States v Ceballos* the Philippine Supreme Court decided *United States v Alarcon Vergara*.[71] A number of Philippine nationals had filed a complaint for damages for injuries allegedly sustained as a result of the arrest (for theft) performed by US state officials. The parties gave conflicting accounts of the events. The arrested individuals claimed that the officials had used excessive violence arresting them and that they had been seriously injured by the bites of dogs that had been unleashed upon them by the officials. The officials disputed that the arrest was irregular. They argued that while the dogs had indeed bitten the detainees when these resisted the arrest, they had called off the dogs and medical care had been provided immediately. The court considered that on the facts before it, it could not come to the same conclusion as in *United States v Ceballos*.

[67] *Sanders v Veridiano* (Philippines, 1988).

[68] *United States v Ceballos* (Philippines, 1990) 143.

[69] ibid 143–4. Cf also *Capitaine Saabrok v la Société maritime auxiliare de transports* (1922–23) 18 RDIP 743 (France, Cour d'appel de Rennes, 1919); *Lakhowsky v Gouvernement fédéral suisse et de Reynier (colonel)* (1921) 48 JDI 179 (France, Cour de Paris, 1921) 181.

[70] Cf however *Advokaat v Schuddinck and the Belgian State* 2 AD 133, case no 68 (The Netherlands, DC of Dordrecht, 1923) 133–4; *Saorstat and Continental Steamship Company, Ltd. v Rafael de las Morenas* 12 AD 97, case no 25 (Ireland, S Ct, 1944) 99. Cf also *Polish Officials in Danzig Case* 6 AD 130, case no 64 (Danzig, High Court, 1932). The bearing of this latter case on the rule of functional immunity is however dubious, cf P De Sena, *Diritto internazionale e immunità funzionale degli organi statali* (1996) 196.

[71] *United States v Alarcon Vergara* (Philippines, S Ct, 1990) consolidated case under *United States of America and Others v Guinto, Valencia and Others, United States of America and Others v Ceballos and Bautista, United States of America, Lamachia and Others v Rodrigo and Genove* (Philippines, 1990).

It stated that '[t]he contradictory factual allegations in this case deserve...a closer study of what actually happened to the plaintiffs. The record is too meagre to indicate if the defendants were really discharging their official duties or had actually exceeded their authority when the incidence in question occurred.'[72] It concluded that further inquiry was required in order to determine the capacity in which the officials were acting at the time of the incident.

In *Wylie v Rarang* the Philippine Supreme Court made clear that the standard applicable to Philippine state officials in order to determinate the capacity in which an act is committed is equally applicable to foreign state officials.[73] A US state official claimed that an article published in a daily bulletin published by the US Naval Base station (in the Philippines) constituted false, injurious and malicious defamation tending to impeach her honesty, virtue and reputation and exposing her to public hatred, contempt and ridicule. She sued the person responsible for publication of the bulletin and the commanding officer of the Base—who had approved the publication—in their personal capacities for alleged tortious acts in publishing a libellous article. The defendants of course argued that the publication was made in the performance of their official functions. The court summarized the issue in dispute as the question whether 'American naval officers who commit a crime or tortious act while discharging official functions [are] still covered by the principle of state immunity from suit'. The court did not think so. In a rather emotional vein it stated that '[k]illing a person in cold blood on patrol duty, running over a child while driving with reckless imprudence on an official trip, or slandering a person during office hours could not possibly be covered by the immunity agreement. Our laws and, we presume, those of the United States do not allow the commission of crimes in the name of official duty.'[74] The sued officials were held liable for damages in their personal capacities.

This approach was confirmed in *United States of America v Reyes*.[75] One US state official employed at the Joint United States Military Assistance Group based in the Philippines claimed that another official had had her subjected to an oppressive and discriminatory search on her body, bags and car *in excess of authority*. The United States intervened in the proceedings and objected the exercise of jurisdiction of the Philippine courts. In particular it argued that 'even if the...act were ultra vires [the defendant] would still be immune from suit for the rule that public officers or employees may be sued in their personal capacity for ultra vires and tortious acts is "domestic law" and not applicable in International Law'. It claimed that 'the application of the immunity doctrine does not turn

[72] ibid 145.

[73] *Wylie v Rarang* (Philippines, 1992).

[74] ibid. The court refers to a case concerning a Philippine state officials: *Chavez v Sandiganbayan* (Philippines, 1991). Cf also *Liang v The Philippines* (Philippines, S Ct, January 2000) available at <http://www.lawphil.net/judjuris/judjuris.html> for the same approach in a case against an official of an international organization.

[75] *United States of America v Reyes* (Phillipines, 1993).

upon the lawlessness of the act or omission attributable to the foreign national for if this were the case, the concept of immunity would be meaningless as inquiry into the lawlessness or illegality of the act or omission would first have to be made before considering the question of immunity; in other words, immunity will lie only if such act or omission is found to be lawful'.[76] The court however, held on to its domestic law standard. It argued in relevant part: 'The cloak of protection afforded the officers and agents of the government is removed the moment they are sued in their individual capacity. The situation usually arises where the public official acts without authority or in excess of the powers vested in him. It is a well-settled principle of law that a public official may be liable in his personal capacity for whatever damage he may have caused by his acts done with malice and in bad faith, or beyond the scope of his authority or jurisdiction.'[77]

Foreign state officials not acting within the exercise of sovereign authority under international law incur personal responsibility for the commission of such crimes *even if committed under government orders*. The *Staschynskij* case is a conspicuous example.[78] In 1959 the KGB agent Staschynskij killed two political exiles in Munich (Germany). He was prosecuted and convicted for murder by the German *Bundesgerichtshof*. The court explicitly acknowledged that Staschynskij had acted on orders of his superiors, stating even that the murders had been ordered by the highest echelons in the Soviet government.[79] The court considered in relevant part:

> Diese besonderen Umstände staatlich befohlener Verbrechen befreien die Tatbeteiligten keineswegs von der strafrechtlichen Schuld. Jede staatliche Gemeinshaft darf und muß verlangen daß such jedermann von Verbrechen, auch von unter Mißbrauch staatlicher Befugnisse geforderten, bedingungslos fernhält. Andernfalls wäre jede Ordnung aufgelöst und den politischen Verbrechen das Tor geöffnet. Der innere Grund des Schuldvorwurfs liegt darin, daß der Mensch auf freie, verantwortliche, sittliche Selbstbestimmung angelegt und deshalb befähigt ist, sich für das Recht und gegen das Unrecht zu entscheiden, sein Verhalten nach den Normen des rechtlichen Sollens einzurichten und das rechtlich Verbotene zu vermeiden . . .[80]

[76] ibid.

[77] ibid.

[78] The *Staschynskij* Case 18 Entscheidungen des Bundesgerichtshof in Strafsachen 87 (Federal Republic of Germany, Bundesgerichtshof, 1962).

[79] ibid 88–9.

[80] ibid 94. Cf for similar cases the 2004 decision of the Court of Appeal of Qatar jailing two Russian agents for the murder of a former Chechen leader in Qatar. The trial judge explicitly stated that the men had acted on orders of the Russian government; the decision of the German Bundesgerichtshof in 2004 confirming the decisions of the Berlin landsgericht, the Leipzig Bundesrichter convicting former Libyan agents for a bomb attack at the nightclub La Belle in Berlin by the Libyan secret services in 1986; The 2004 decision of the Argentinean Supreme Court (24–08–2004, case A.533.XXXVIII) confirming an earlier decision of a Buenos Aires trial court (20–11–2000) convicting the former Chilean secret agent Enrique Arancibia Clavel to life in prison for the murder of Chile's former Commander-in-Chief of the Army and former Vice President of the Republic General Prats and his wife by a car bomb in Buenos Aires in 1974; in 2005 Italy issued

The famous *Rainbow Warrior* incident equally concerned secret service officials committing a crime on the territory of a foreign state. In 1985 two violent explosions took place on board of the Greenpeace ship the *Rainbow Warrior*. At the time of the explosions the ship lay in the port of Auckland (New Zealand), from where it would have left to protest against French nuclear experiments in the Pacific. A Dutch photographer died in the attack. New Zealand authorities soon arrested and subsequently convicted two French secret agents to ten years imprisonment each for complicity in manslaughter and wilful damage to a ship.[81] The French government fiercely contested their conviction. France emphasized that the ship had been sunk upon instructions of the French government and that it was willing to undertake reparations for the consequences of the action. The diplomatic conflict that evolved, and of which the position of the two agents was but one aspect, was eventually put to the Secretary-General of the UN in order to obtain a ruling.[82] In its memorandum to the Secretary-General, France requested the release of its agents on the basis that they could not be held personally responsible for the attack on the ship. It wrote:

> France is ready to assume, as regards New Zealand and the victims of the incident, all responsibilities, incumbent upon it, in place of the persons having acted on its behalf, as done, for example, by the British Government in respect of the United States Government when the vessel 'Caroline' was destroyed by a British commando unit...[83]

New Zealand, for its part, noted that the acts of the agents were criminal under New Zealand law and stressed that it did not accept 'that military personnel acting under official orders are exempt from personal responsibility for criminal acts. "Superior orders" is not a defence in New Zealand law, nor is it a defence in the legal systems of most countries'.[84]

Although the Secretary-General did not discuss the issue of personal responsibility as such, his decision that the agents were to be held in solitary seclusion within a French military facility on an isolated island outside Europe for at least three years does not—to put it mildly—*support* the thesis that no such responsibility arises in respect of acts of this kind.[85]

arrest warrants for 22 alleged CIA agents accused of kidnapping an Islamic cleric in Milan in order to bring him to Egypt for interrogation, without the consent of the Italian authorities.

[81] The agents concerned were not the principal actors but had provided logistical support for the operation.

[82] United Nations Secretary-General, Ruling on the *Rainbow Warrior* Affair between France and New Zealand (1986), (1987) 26 ILM 1346ff.

[83] ibid 1366.

[84] ibid 1351 and 1357.

[85] ibid 1346, and 1369–70. Cf G Apollis, 'L'affaire du "Rainbow Warrior"' (1987) 91 RGDIP 10; J Charpentier, 'L'affaire du Rainbow Warrior' (1985) 31 AFDI 210 for support for the application of the *McLeod* principles to the *Rainbow Warrior* Case. The accord, commented Apollis, arranged the release of the 'agents malchanceux...a des conditions draconnienes' (43). It is noted that a dispute on the accord evolved later, *inter alia* because the agents were not held on the island

The *Rainbow Warrior* incident—together with other examples of personal responsibility for unauthorized acts on foreign territory[86]—is commonly relied on in doctrine in support of the argument that the principles laid down in the *McLeod* case are no longer good law.[87] This argument is rejected here. The facts of the two incidents are indeed deceivingly similar. Both concerned the violent destruction of a vessel on the territory of a foreign state causing bodily harm and casualties in the process. It is however important to see that the rule of functional immunity allows distinction between the two cases. The *McLeod* case arose in the context of a dispute between British governed Canada and the United States on the principles of neutrality. The UK argued that the attack constituted necessary self-defence while the US saw it as foreign power invading their boundary with an armed force. Under such circumstances the qualification of the act under national law loses its relevance. States exercise their authority under international law when they are engaged in boundary disputes or interstate armed conflict.[88]

This rule supersedes the distinction between lawful and unlawful combatants. Lawful combatants do not incur responsibility under the domestic law of the adversary state even though acts of warfare would normally qualify as murder, arson, battery, or destruction of property. That privilege does not befall *unlawful* combatants.[89] Combatants are lawful when they wear distinctive emblems and wear their arms openly—combatants 'may try to become invisible in the landscape, but not in the crowd'[90]—and act furthermore in accordance with the laws and principles of war. The distinction applies irregardless of the question whether or not the combatants are part of the regular armed forces of a

for the agreed period, cf G Palmisano, 'Sulla Decisione Arbitrale Relativa alla Seconda Fase del Caso "Rainbow Warrior"' (1990) 73 RDI 874.

[86] Cf in addition to political murders as in the *Staschynskij* case also the practice of aerial intrusions discussed in OJ Lissitzyn, 'The Treatment of Aerial Intruders in Recent Practice and International Law' (1953) 47 AJIL 559, 565, fn 30; M Bothe, 'Die strafrechtliche Immunität fremder Staatsorgane' (1971) 31 ZaöRV 246.

[87] See eg L Migliorino, 'Giurisdizione dello Stato territoriale rispetto ad azione non autorizzate di agenti di Stati stranieri' (1988) 71 RDI 784, 796. Cf before the *Rainbow Warrior* case already M Miele, *L'immunità giurisdizionale degli organi stranieri* (2nd edn, 1961) 191.

[88] The principle of non-personal responsibility *was* arguably stated in overbroad terms. It is recalled that the UK Law Officers asserted that 'an individual doing a hostile act authorised and ratified by the government of which he is a member cannot be held individually answerable as a private trespasser or Malefactor, but that the act becomes one for which the State to which he belongs is in such case alone responsible'. Here it is argued that this principle is limited to acts performed in the context of the exercise of state authority under international law.

[89] A Rosas, *The Legal Status of Prisoners of War: A Study in International Humanitarian Law Applicable in Armed Conflict* (1976) 305; C Rousseau, *Le droit des conflits armés* (1983) 63; F Kalshoven, 'The Position of Guerrilla Fighters under the Law of War' (1972) 11 Revue de Droit Pénal Militaire et de Droit de la Guerre 73ff; RR Baxter, 'So-Called "Unprivileged Belligerency": Spies, Guerrillas and Saboteurs' (1951) 28 BYIL 323.

[90] D Binschedler-Robert, 'A Reconsideration of the Law of Armed Conflicts' in *The Law of Armed Conflicts: Report of the Conference on Contemporary Problems of the Law of Armed Conflict, 1969* (1971) 1, 43.

foreign state acting under government orders.[91] However, the rule of functional immunity *does* apply to unlawful combatants in uniform whose acts form part of the military activities. The activity of spies and saboteurs is not regulated under the laws and principles of war and their fate is similar to that of foreign secret agents committing crimes outside the context of armed conflict—like in the *Staschynskij* and *Rainbow Warrior* cases. The US Supreme Court rightly stated in *Ex parte Quirin*:

> [T]hose who during time of war pass surreptitiously from enemy territory into our own, discarding their uniforms upon entry, for the commission of hostile acts involving destruction of life or property, have the status of unlawful combatants punishable as such by the military commission.
>
> ...
>
> entry upon our territory in time of war by enemy belligerents, including those acting under the direction of the armed forces of the enemy, for the purpose of destroying property used in prosecuting the war, is a hostile and warlike act. It subjects those who participate in it without uniform to the punishment prescribed by the law of war or unlawful belligerents.[92]

The same is true for unlawful combatants that have violated the laws of war while pursuing their private impulses. War crimes committed by the regular armed forces committed as part of the military strategy of the state are however subject to a different regime. The conviction of McLeod for murder and arson ignored the exclusive applicability of international law to the facts of the case as well as the non-personal responsibility of state officials for acts within the context of the exercise of state authority under international law.

The attack on the *Rainbow Warrior* did of course violate the territorial sovereignty of New Zealand and hence the Charter of the United Nations and international law in general. The qualification of the act under international law did not however *supersede* the applicability of national law to the incident. In other words, as long as national law is applicable to the facts of the case—and the state official was not exercising exclusive competences with the consent of the forum state—it cannot be said that the state official has acted within the context of the exercise of state authority under international law.[93]

The proposed distinction admittedly entails a slippery slope. The line is the same as the line between the territorial tort exception and the vertical division of

[91] Y Dinstein, 'Unlawful Combatants and War Criminals' in Y Dinstein and M Tabory (eds), *International Law at a Time of Perplexity, Essays in Honour of Shabtai Rosenne* (1989) 103, 105.

[92] *Ex p Quirin* 317 US 1 (US, S Ct, 1942) 35–6 and 37. Cf also *Mohamed Ali v Public Prosecutor* [1969] AC 430 (Privy Council, 1968) in which members of the Indonesian armed forces were convicted of murder committed in Singapore (then part of Malaysia) in civilian clothes.

[93] The idea that for example the *Staschynskij* case regarded the exercise of jurisdiction over sovereign activity is therefore rejected in this study. Cf M Bothe, 'Die strafrechtliche Immunität fremder Staatsorgane' (1971) 31 ZaöRV 246; I Seidl-Hohenveldern, 'Immunität ausländischer Staaten in Strafverfahren und Verwaltungsstrafverfahren' in H Conrad, et al (eds), *Gedächtnisschrift Hans Peters* (1967) 915, 922 for this argument.

competences discussed in chapter 2 § 3.2.2 of this study. The examples of hard cases discussed there equally trouble the application of this aspect of the rule of functional immunity. We will see moreover in chapter 5 of this study that the experience of the two World Wars led states to formulate limits on the rule of functional immunity.

It has at times been argued that the rule of functional immunity does not apply when state officials purport to exercise state authority within the territory of a foreign state without the required authorization.[94] This finding however needs specification. The basic principle is indeed that states may not exercise sovereign authority on the territory of another state without that state's consent. It seems obvious that acts that violate this principle do not have to be recognized as official acts for functional immunity purposes and that foreign state officials may be called to account for them in their personal capacity. Van Praag already noted in 1915, that if the consul 'sort de sa compétence, cet acte (quelle qu'en soit la qualification dans le pays qui l'e envoyé) constitue une atteinte à l'autorité de l'Etat où il réside; dans cet Etat en effet il ne lui est pas permis d'accomplir des actes officiels qui ne sont pas de sa compétence'.[95]

Whether a foreign state official *is* effectively called to account depends however on whether a particular act in fact constitutes a violation of the national law of the state whose territorial sovereignty has been violated or whether only an interstate norm has been violated. When the official has committed a common crime under national criminal law the violation of national law is in principle distinct from the violation of international law. The *Staschynskij* and *Rainbow Warrior* cases are conspicuous examples in this regard. State officials are then held accountable in their personal capacity under the national law of the forum state—unless of course states agree to absolve the officials from punishment in a political solution of the dispute. When however the only violation is that of the territorial integrity of the forum state because of the unauthorized exercise of state authority this is not the case. The pivotal question then is whether the violation of international law is *also* a violation of national law so that the distinct qualifications of the one violation exist alongside each other. This is not self-evident. The example of Switzerland that has criminalized *all* unauthorized exercise of sovereign authority on Swiss territory stands out. Article 271 paragraph 1 of the Swiss Penal Law provides:

> Wer auf schweizerischem Gebiet ohne Bewilligung für einen fremden Staat Handlungen vornimmt, die einer Behörde oder einem Beamten zukommen, wer solche Handlungen für eine ausländische Partei oder eine andere Organisation des Auslands vornimmt, wer solchen Handlungen Vorschub leistet, wird mit Gefängnis, in schweren Fällen mit Zuchthaus bestraft.[96]

[94] Cf M Miele (1961); L Migliorino (1988).

[95] L Van Praag, *Juridiction et droit international public, La juridiction nationale d'après droit international public coutumier en temps de paix* (1915) 328.

[96] The prohibition was first included in the Swiss Penal Law in 1935, (1935) 51 Amtliche Sammlung 482. Cf J Outry, *Verletzung der Schweizerischen Gebietshoheit durch verbotene Handlungen für einen fremden Staat* (1951).

If only interstate norms have been violated the individual state officials may not be punished for their behaviour. In this context states necessarily exercise authority under international law.[97]

It is moreover interesting to note that in the *Staschynskij* case the court did not explicitly state that it did not recognize the cloak of foreign state authority for unauthorized acts on its territory. The issue of individual responsibility was approached in an abstract manner. The fact that the orders had been given by a *foreign* state seemed irrelevant. The individual responsibility of Staschynskij was approached as a question as to the possible scope of the cloak of state authority in general.[98] The argument that state officials of the forum state would not be able to hide behind the protective shield of their mandate in similar circumstances was relied on both in the *Staschynskij* case and in the *Rainbow Warrior* case. The national law standard seemed at least an *additional* argument on which to base the absence of functional immunity also in these cases. It could even be argued that the unauthorized exercise *as such* is not a sufficient criterion and that the national law standard applies to cases concerning foreign state officials that do and that do not violate the territorial sovereignty of the forum state alike.

In sum, foreign state officials that commit crimes or personal torts within the territory of the forum state are likely to be held responsible in their individual capacity. If state officials act outside the context of the exercise of state authority under international law the (national) ultra vires standard may be applied to determine the capacity in which an act was performed. The argument of the United States in *United States of America v Reyes* is not convincing. The standard applied does not affect the law of *state* immunity: a comparison to the US legal system itself, where violation of the US constitution exposes US state officials to individual responsibility, is enlightening in this respect.

2.2.1.4 Defeat of presumption

The rule of functional immunity explicitly regards *a presumption* of authority. This presumption may be defeated by the home state. Two types of defeat are feasible. In the first place, states may declare that in a specific case, a specific state official has acted without authority (an *a posteriori*—ad hoc defeat). Second, states may agree—in the form of a rule of international law—that certain activity may never be cloaked by the authority of a state (an *a priori*—general defeat). In both cases the act is not 'in law an act of the state rather than of the official that

[97] The argument of M Bothe (1971) 260–1 that functional immunity is only not available when a *serious* violation of the territorial sovereignty is at issue confuses practice with principle. Trivial violations will often not violate the national law of the territorial state or be solved at the diplomatic level.

[98] Interestingly enough Staschynskij was not convicted as 'perpetrator' (Tater) but as 'accomplice' (Tatgehilfe). The fact that he acted under orders of the Soviet government and in particular under their pressure and with fear of reprisals if he failed to obey, was considered ground to mitigate the punishment, The *Staschynskij* Case (Federal Republic of Germany, 1962) 94–6.

happened to perform the act'. Accordingly, the act is not official in character and the state official incurs responsibility in his personal capacity.

A Posteriori–Ad Hoc A home state may of course declare that despite the *ostensible* exercise of authority, its official did *in fact* exceed his authority performing a certain act. Such a declaration defeats the presumption of authority that may attach to that act.[99] The 1997 case of *Phaneuf v Government of Indonesia and Mawardi* and the 2004 case of *Velasco v Government of Indonesia and Mawardi*, for example, concerned a selling of false promissory notes by an Indonesian state official allegedly in name of the National Defense Security Council of the Republic of Indonesia.[100] When the notes were traded for promissory notes issued by a Syria based financier defendant Mawardi—then Indonesia's ambassador to Syria—took part in the signing ceremony and allegedly confirmed the authority of the Indonesian state official, as well as the governmental nature of the promissory notes. The notes were later discovered to be worthless and an action was brought to enforce payment on the notes against Indonesia and Mawardi. The court in the *Phaneuf* case did not know whether Mawardi had acted within the scope of his authority but stressed that if he had acted without authority the FSIA does not shield him from suit in his individual capacity. The court in the *Velasco* case had a statement of the Indonesian government at its disposal in which it was confirmed that Mawardi had acted without authority. Accordingly, the court concluded that the FSIA did not protect Mawardi from suit. However, since the ambassador had been sued in his official capacity rather than in his individual capacity the claim against him was to be dismissed.

The defeat of the presumption is technically not 'a waiver of immunity'. Waiver of immunity for real official acts is not possible.[101] The use of the term in practice may be apposite when the person concerned also relies on *personal* immunity rules. For example, when the former president of the Philippines and his wife were sued in the US courts on embezzlement claims the Aquino government wrote in a diplomatic note that 'the Government of the Philippines hereby *waives* any residual sovereign, head of state, or diplomatic immunity that the former President Ferdinand Marcos and his wife Imelda Marcos may enjoy under international and U.S. law, including, but not limited to, Article 39(2) of the Vienna Convention on Diplomatic Relations, by virtue of their former offices in

[99] The claim must of course be a reasonable one. It is for example unthinkable that the earlier introduced Ottoman ambassador would incur personal responsibility for the costs of the installation of the new heating system at the Embassy upon a declaration of the Ottoman Empire that the signing of contracts for essential maintenance of the Embassy building fell outside the ambassador's mandate.

[100] *Phaneuf v Government of Indonesia and Mawardi* 106 F 3d 302 (US, Ct of Apps (9th Cir), 1997); *Velasco v Government of Indonesia and Mawardi* 370 F 3d 392 (US, Ct of Apps (4th Cir), 2004).

[101] As far as a personal capacity suit is concerned. A state can of course waive immunity, or in the terms of ch 2 § 3.3.1 'accept jurisdiction', when the state itself is the defendant.

the Government of the Philippines'.[102] While the term waiver was an adequate response to Marcos' reliance on the US head of state immunity rules, the use of the term in regard to article 39.2 VCDR immunity is unfortunate.

A Priori–General The rule that the acts of foreign state officials in the ostensible exercise of state authority are presumed to have been performed under actual state authority may be limited in its scope by a general and consistent state practice accepted as law. In other words, states may agree on the international level that certain acts can never be cloaked by state authority. Just as normative limits on the authority of state officials are provided within most national legal systems, states may develop universally applicable normative limits. In a parallel with, for example, the 11th Amendment jurisprudence in the United States, it could accordingly be agreed that state officials may never be authorized to violate 'constitutional norms' of the international legal system.[103] The acceptance of universal limits curbs the influence of the rule of state immunity on the application of the rule of functional immunity. It will be argued in chapter 5 of this study that the development of the principle of individual responsibility in the wake of second World War can be understood from this particular perspective.

2.2.1.5 Conclusion and final observations

Foreign state officials enjoy functional immunity in respect of official acts. Official acts are acts that cannot be attributed to the person of the state official. These acts are in law the acts of the state. Accordingly, (former) foreign state officials do not bear responsibility in their private or personal capacity for official acts performed on behalf of and under authority of their home state. This principle forms the pivot of the international law rule of functional immunity. In national legal systems the principle is usually circumscribed by normative limits on the scope of authority of state officials. In international law, the principle is complemented by the rule that as long as the acts are performed within the context of the exercise of state authority under international law, ostensible authority passes for actual authority. The home state may defeat—*a posteriori* or *a priori*—the presumption of authority attaching to the actions of its officials.

The rule of functional immunity is at times defined in terms of the official capacity in which the state official has acted. The official capacity in this definition

[102] *In re Mr And Mrs Doe, Witnesses Before the Grand Jury* 860 F 2d 40 (US, Ct of Apps (2nd Cir), 1988) 43. The term is likewise used by courts: *In re Grand Jury Proceedings, John Doe No 700* 817 F 2d 1108 (US, Ct of Apps (4th Cir), 1987); *In re Mr And Mrs Doe, Witnesses Before the Grand Jury* (US, 1988); *Paul v Avril* 812 F Supp 207 (US, DC for the Southern District of Florida, 1993) 210; *Marcos and Associates v Chambre d'Accusation Geneva* 82 ILR 53 (Switzerland, Federal Tribunal, 1987).

[103] *Ex p Young* 323 US 670 (US, S Ct, 1944). Cf for a similar argument J Fitzpatrick, 'The Claim to Foreign Sovereign Immunity by Individuals Sued for International Human Rights' (1994) 15 Whittier Law Review 465, 469; T Lininger, 'Overcoming Immunity Defenses to Human Rights Suits in U.S. Courts' (1994) 7 Harvard Human Rights Journal 177, 186.

however is often approached as a factual rather than legal concept. Official capacity is then linked to the concept of attribution of acts to the state under the law of state responsibility. Official acts are contrasted with private acts that the state official commits in a purely private capacity. The gardener killed in a fit of rage is the textbook example of this latter category of acts. This approach however does not incorporate the territorial limits on the exercise of exclusive state competence, nor the possibility of the acceptance as international law of normative limits on the authority of state officials. It was explained above that the concept of 'ostensible authority' should be understood from the perspective of the exercise of state authority under international law. Moreover, the concept may be circumscribed by rules of international law. Not all acts that can be attributed to the state are hence official acts, and private acts are not merely 'frolics of the individual's own'.[104]

Although a legal approach to the term *is* possible the danger of confusion with the factual approach looms large. In addition to the law of state responsibility, the factual approach is for example commonly used in the definition of offences or torts that are necessarily committed *in an official capacity*.[105] It is therefore better to avoid the terminology altogether and to say that functional immunity applies when acts have been committed *as* state official instead of *in the capacity of* state official. Or even better, that the rule of functional immunity is not concerned with the capacity in which an act is committed but rather with the capacity in which an official may be sued.[106]

Functional immunity applies *ratione materiae* rather than *ratione personae*. While an immunity *ratione personae* like diplomatic immunity constitutes a classic immunity from jurisdiction, functional immunity constitutes an exemption from the law *in a personal capacity*. The term 'immunity' may in fact not be the most apposite to describe the phenomenon at hand. Beckett wrote in this regard that if proceedings were brought against a former foreign head of state in respect of official acts 'he has a defence to the action (i.e. that he is not personally liable for such acts) but not a claim to immunity.'[107]

The distinction between non-responsibility for official acts and an exemption from jurisdiction has been most elaborately discussed in the context of the law of diplomatic immunity. Dinstein, for one, fiercely rejected the distinction. He pointed out that the concept of non-liability entails immunity from the law of the

[104] Cf for this term CA Whomersley, 'Some Reflections on the Immunity of Individuals for Official Acts' (1992) 41 ICLQ 848, 856.

[105] Cf art 1 of the Convention Against Torture and Other Cruel, Inhuman and Degrading Treatment (1984) 1465 UNTS 85, reprinted in (1984) 23 ILM 1027.

[106] Cf *Hafer v Melo* (US, 1991) for similar reasoning applied in a case concerning the internal immunity of US state officials.

[107] E Lémonon (Rapporteur Institut de Droit International) L'immunité de juridiction et d'exécution forcée des États étrangers, Rapport et projet de Résolution définitifs, Observations E Beckett, (1952) 44–I AIDI 5, 60.

receiving state.[108] This, he argued, does not correspond with the legal position of diplomatic agents. For one, the sending state may decide to waive the immunity of its (former) diplomatic agent. 'Waiver of diplomatic immunity *ratione personae*', he wrote, 'will be entirely meaningless unless local courts are able, as a consequence, to try the case of the diplomatic offender. And evidently trial is possible only on the assumption that a crime has been committed.'[109] In support of his qualification of non-liability for official acts as a misguided concept Dinstein relied on two famous UK cases. He recalled that Lord Hewart CJ considered in *Dickinson v Del Solar* that '[d]iplomatic agents are not, in virtue of their privileges as such, immune from legal liability for any wrongful acts . . . Diplomatic privilege does not import immunity from legal liability, but only exemption from local jurisdiction.'[110] This was reaffirmed in *Empson v Smith* where Lord Diplock LJ commented that '[i]t is elementary law that diplomatic immunity is not immunity from legal liability but immunity from suit.'[111] Dinstein finally relied on article 41.1 of the Vienna Convention that underlines the duty of the persons enjoying privileges and immunities under the Convention to respect the laws and regulations of the receiving state.[112]

This criticism is not convincing. In brief rebuttal the ideas developed above may benefit from a final polish. With respect to article 41.1 it should be noted that a distinct difference exists between the duty of the diplomatic agent to respect the local laws and regulations when exercising his official functions on foreign territory and the possibility to hold him personally—hence not in his capacity as state official—responsible for the acts thus performed. Article 41.1 is perfectly compatible with a distinction between official and non-official acts: when an agent performs official acts he is under a duty to respect the local laws and regulations *as* official acting on behalf of the foreign state and can be held responsible for them in that capacity only.

More pertinently, the assertion that there can be no principle of non-personal liability for official acts because diplomatic immunity can be waived evinces an unfortunate failure to distinguish the nature and operation of these two concepts. Dinstein was right in pointing out that during their term of office the functional immunity of diplomatic agents is merely 'eclipsed by the shadow of the personal immunity'.[113] As Morelli explained, the rule of diplomatic immunity is a unitary rule of a procedural nature. It is not limited—as has been argued in Italian doctrine in particular—to non-official acts.[114] This does of course *not*

[108] Y Dinstein, 'Diplomatic Immunity from Jurisdiction *Ratione Materiae*' (1966) 15 ICLQ 76, 80.

[109] ibid.

[110] *Dickinson v Del Solar* [1930] 1 KB 376 (UK, King's Bench Division, 1929) 380; 5 AD 299, case no 190, 299.

[111] *Empson v Smith* [1965] 2 All ER 881 (UK, CA, 1965) 886; 41 ILR 407, 414.

[112] Y Dinstein (1966b) 81.

[113] ibid 79.

[114] G Morelli (1954) 201–4. Cf for Italian doctrine ch 4 § 2.1.1 below.

mean that the principle of non-personal responsibility for official acts does not *apply* but merely that the procedural immunity stops the court from reaching the issue of functional immunity. Despite the acknowledgement of the existence of two distinct rules Dinstein failed to limit his plea to a unitary treatment of the rule of diplomatic immunity. He criticized the concept of non-personal liability with arguments derived from the law of state immunity. The statements of Lords Hewart and Diplock relate to diplomatic immunity. Their authority cannot be relied upon to dismiss the principle of non-personal liability for official acts. A waiver of diplomatic immunity does—at least in theory—not preclude the dismissal of a case on the basis of the concurrent operation of substantive rules regarding the personal liability of foreign state officials for official acts. As was explained before, the concept of waiver does not agree with the rule of functional immunity. Of course, a state can waive its *own* immunity when the claim against the state official can be qualified as actually impleading the foreign state. Or, a state can proclaim that the official concerned did not act under its authority or within the limits of his official mandate. This is however not a waiver of immunity, but a (*a posteriori* and ad hoc) defeat of the presumption of authority. Would it have been possible for the Ottoman government to *waive* the functional immunity of its former Ambassador in Brussels in regard to a claim for the payment of the costs of the new heating system installed at the Embassy? It may be clear that it was not. The waiver of the substantive immunity from personal liability for acts performed as an arm or mouthpiece of a foreign state is conceptually inconceivable.

2.2.2 The Application of the Law of State Immunity as a Consequence of the Implication of the State

The application of the law of state immunity in cases against foreign state officials can be explained from the perspective of the rule of functional immunity. In 1925 a French court considered that 'la règle de l'indépendance réciproque des Etats doit s'appliquer non seulement aux demandes dirigées contre le Gouvernement lui-même, mais encore à celle introduites contre les agents, ou cocontractants de ce Gouvernement à raison des actes qu'ils accomplissent en cette qualité, ou en vertu des ordres dudit Etat'.[115] If an individual has acted *as* an agent of a foreign state a claim in respect of such act is in fact a claim against that foreign state. Or as the Philippine Supreme Court formulated it in *Syquia v López*, when a foreign state official defendant has acted within the scope of his official duties as agent of a foreign state 'the real party defendant in interest is the government of [that state]'

[115] *Esnault-Pelterie v The AV Roe Cy Ltd* (France, 1925). Cf *Bernet et autres v Herran, Dreyfus-Scheyer et autres* (France, 1880).

and 'the...action must be considered as one against [that] government'.[116] In a similar vein the US court in *Lyders v Lund* considered that '[i]n actions against the officials of a foreign state not clothed with diplomatic immunity, it can be said that suits based upon official, authorized acts, performed within the scope of their duties on behalf of the foreign state, and for which the state will have to respond directly or indirectly in the event of a judgment, are actions against the foreign state.'[117]

Although not the nominal defendant, the state is hence often considered the factual defendant in cases against a foreign state official that does not bear personal responsibility. If a state official is explicitly sued in his official capacity the non-personal involvement of the official is already stated in the suit. As a US court considered in *Rios v Marshall* 'insofar as [the foreign official] is sued in his official capacity as agent of the instrumentality, he is equally protected by principles of foreign sovereign immunity'.[118] If not, the non-personal responsibility in respect of the act at issue may be relied on to determine that capacity. When a state official does not bear responsibility in his personal capacity, the action *can* only be directed against the official in his official capacity, and hence against his home state. In *Kline v Kaneko* another US court explained that when a foreign state official is sued for acts performed in 'the execution of his official duties' he '*can* be sued *only* in his official capacity, and the protections of the FSIA are available to him'.[119] Or as the Philippine Supreme Court held in *Sanders v Veridiano* 'the petitioners were, *legally speaking*, being sued as officers of the United States government'.[120] Even where a claim has been explicitly directed against a foreign state official in a personal capacity, courts may approach a suit as an official capacity suit—and dismiss the claim on the ground of state immunity—when they find that the claim regards acts that were taken on behalf of the state.[121] It stands to reason that when in such suits the act concerned is not covered by the

[116] *Syquia et al v López et al* (Philippines, 1949) 231. Cf *Johnson v Major-General Howard M Turner et al* (Philippines, 1954).

[117] *Lyders v Lund* 5 AD 321, case no 211 (US, DC for the Northern District of California, 1929). Cf *Landley v Republic of Panama* (US, 1940).

[118] *Rios v Marshall* 530 F Supp 351 (US, DC for the Southern District of New York, 1981) 371. Cf eg *Junquist et al v Sheikh Sultan Bin Khalifa Al Nayhan et al* 940 F Supp 312 (US, DC for the District of Columbia, 1996). The crown prince of Abu Dhabi Sheikh Khalifa was sued in his official capacity in respect of acts committed by his son in an individual capacity. The court held the FSIA to be applicable and concluded that since the acts complained of were personal acts of the son of the crown prince, not acts of the state, none of the exceptions to immunity applied.

[119] *Kline and Others v Kaneko and Others* 685 F Supp 386 (US, DC for the Southern District of New York, 1988) 389 (emphasis added); 101 ILR 497. Cf also *Capitaine Saabrok v la Société maritime auxiliare de transports* (France, 1919); *Lakhowsky v Gouvernement fédéral suisse et de Reynier (colonel)* (France, 1921) 181.

[120] *Sanders v Veridiano* (Philippines, 1988) (emphasis added); cf also 102 ILR 148.

[121] Cf *Sanders v Veridiano* ibid; *El-Fadl v Central Bank of Jordan* 75 F 3d 668 (US, Ct of Apps for the District of Columbia Circuits, 1996).

restrictive rule of state immunity because it is an *acta jure gestionis*, it is the state, not the state official personally that is the subject of the ruling of the court.[122]

Some suits are however personal capacity suits perforce. Penal suits are a conspicuous example, but we may also think of suits against a state official *after* he has left office, or suits explicitly directed against the personal estate of the state official. When such a personal capacity suit regards activity for which the defendant does not bear individual responsibility the claim should be declared inadmissible because instigated against the wrong defendant. As Van Praag already argued in respect of former foreign state officials: 'l'action fondée sur une telle responsabilité est elle pour ce motif non-recevable'.[123]

Notably, it may be argued that it is *not at all* possible to sue a state official that lacks the capacity to represent the state in law, in an official capacity. Only certain state officials have the capacity to represent the state in law. The application of the rule of state immunity to, for example, a foreign head of state sued in his official capacity is uncontroversial. In fact, most codifications of the law of state immunity explicitly include the head of state in his official capacity in the definition of the state for the purpose of the application of the rule.[124] Exactly which officials share this capacity is a controversial question outside the scope of this study.[125]

[122] Cf *Nashashibi v The Consul-General of France in Jerusalem* 26 ILR 190 (Jordan, Supreme Court of Cassation, 1958). When M Akehurst, 'Jurisdiction in International Law' (1972–73) 46 BYIL 145, 242 argues that agents of a state cannot claim immunity in respect of acts *jure gestionis* he surely proceeds from the assumption that they are sued in their official capacity.

[123] L Van Praag (1915) 331.

[124] See eg UK SIA Section 14 sub (a): 'references to a State include references to the sovereign or other head of that State in his public capacity'; Canadian State Immunity Act 1985, Section 2 'foreign state includes any sovereign or other head of the foreign state or of any political subdivision of the foreign state while acting as such in a public capacity'; Australia Foreign States Immunities Act 1985, art 3.3. (b) 'a reference in this Act to a foreign State includes a reference to the head of a foreign State, or of a political subdivision of a foreign State, in his or her public capacity'. See already Art II and III Resolution IDI 1891 ((1892) 11 AIDI 436); Arts 1(a) and 7–12 of the Harvard Research Draft on the Competence of Courts in Regard to Foreign States, Harvard Law School, Research in International Law (Reporter PC Jessup) Competence of Courts in Regard to Foreign States, (1932) 26 AJIL 451, 475 and 476. Cf also *O'Hair v Wojtyla* 81 ILR 607 (US, DC for the District of Colombia, 1979) 608; *The Republic of the Philippines v Marcos* 806 F 2d 344 (US, Ct of Apps (2nd Cir), 1986) 360; *Junquist v Nahyan* (US, 1996).

[125] Art 1(b) (iv) of the UN Convention on Jurisdictional Immunities of States and their Property reads: 'State means... representatives of the State acting in that capacity'. In the ILC Commentary we read that 'this category of beneficiaries of State immunity encompasses all the natural persons who are authorized to represent the state in all its manifestations... Thus, sovereigns and heads of State in their public capacity would be included under this category... Other representatives include heads of Government, heads of ministerial departments, ambassadors, heads of mission, diplomatic agents and consular officers, in their representative capacity.' Report of the Commission to the General Assembly on the Work of its Forty-third Session, YBILC 1991 ii (part two) 18, § 17. It is however controversial whether diplomatic and consular officers can be sued in their representative capacity: cf eg J Salmon and S Sucharitkul, 'Les missions diplomatiques entre deux chaises: immunité diplomatique ou immunité d'État?' (1987) 33 AFDI 163, 167; *Hénon v Egyptian Government and British Admiralty* 14 AD 78, case no 28 (Egypt, Civil Tribunal of the Mixed Courts, 1947); *De Decker v Mac Gregor* PB 1956–3–5 (Belgium, Tribunal Civil de Léopoldville, 1955); *Dame Mellerio v Consul général du Portugal* (1969) 58 RCDIP 533 (France, Cour de Cassation, 1969). Cf however: *Mallavel v Ministre des Affaires étrangères français* 65 ILR

The fact that most codifications are limited to the head of state in this respect is at least a forceful *a contrario* argument against the extension to other state officials. Here we should note that in the absence of representative quality a claim against a foreign state official in his official capacity is arguably inadmissible because instigated against the wrong defendant.

This difference in approach is illustrated by the comparison of the reasoning in the German *Church of Scientology Case* with the reasoning employed by a Dutch court in a case almost identical on the facts. The Dutch case of *Church of Scientology in the Netherlands Foundation and Others v (1) Herold and (2) Heinrich Bauer Verlag* concerned the publication of an article that the plaintiff considered to be insulting.[126] Apart from the publishing company (defendant 2) the Chief of the German Federal Police (defendant 1) was sued because the article was allegedly based on a report of the German police. In the German case a similar complaint was filed against the Head of New Scotland Yard. The finding of the German court that in regard to the conduct complained of the foreign state official sued had been 'acting as the expressly appointed agent of the British State' and that '[t]he acts of such agents constitute direct State conduct and cannot be attributed as private activities to the person authorized to perform them in a given case' was followed by the application of the law of state immunity.[127] In the Dutch case the chief of police argued in comparable terms that 'in his official capacity, he should in law be identified with the German Federal Republic'.[128] The Dutch court, however, held the rules of state immunity not to apply. Since the defendant was considered not to have the capacity to represent the Federal Republic, the Federal Republic had not been duly summoned and 'exceptions under international law limiting the Dutch Court's jurisdiction over sovereign states and assimilated parties do not apply to him.'[129] Instead, the claim was declared inadmissible. The court considered that in the proceedings before it the defendant could only be held responsible as a private person, not in his official capacity. The court reasoned that since '[t]he act imputed by the plaintiffs to Defendant (1), whether committed by him personally or, under his responsibility, by the division headed by himself...can only be regarded as an act done in his official capacity and not as a private person.... it follows that the claim of the plaintiffs... is brought against the wrong defendant, and that their claim addressed to this defendant in his official capacity is, for this reason, inadmissible. This is not altered by the

303 (Italy, Pretore di Roma, 1974); *Caisse Industrielle d'Assurance Mutuelle v Consul Général de la République Argentine* 45 ILR 381 (France, Tribunal de Grande Instance of the Seine, 1964); *Consular Premises (Greece)* 6 AD 338, case no 187 (Greece, Court of Athens, 1931); *Nashashibi v The Consul-General of France in Jerusalem* (Jordan, 1958).

126 *Church of Scientology in the Netherlands Foundation and Others v (1) Herold and (2) Heinrich Bauer Verlag* (The Netherlands, 1980).

127 *Church of Scientology Case* (Federal Republic of Germany, 1978).

128 *Church of Scientology in the Netherlands Foundation and Others v (1) Herold and (2) Heinrich Bauer Verlag* (The Netherlands, 1980) 381.

129 ibid 381.

allegation of the plaintiffs during the course of the proceedings that Defendant (1) committed the acts in question in dereliction of his official duties.'[130]

The practical result of the German and Dutch decision is the same but the cases differ crucially in their theoretical approach. Both the German and the Dutch court agreed that the police officers could not be held responsible personally for the official acts at the basis of the dispute before them. Whereas the German court took this fact to mean that the claim *was in fact directed* against the foreign state, dismissing the claim on state immunity grounds, the Dutch court concluded that the claim *should have been brought* against the foreign state, declaring the claim against the police officer inadmissible.[131] The Dutch court proceeded from the assumption that foreign state officials, apart from those that can represent the state in law, can only be brought before the courts with regard to acts for which they bear personal responsibility.

Anyway, leaving aside the critical intermezzo, it can be stated that the application of the law of state immunity to foreign state officials can be explained in the terms set out above. The rule of functional immunity is a necessary first step in the application of the law of state immunity to foreign state officials. The rule ascertains the status of the defendant before the court. If the case before the court—explicitly or necessarily—concerns an official capacity suit, the foreign state is the real party to the dispute. The statement of an Australian court that applied the law of state immunity in a case against a foreign state official that 'an entitlement to sovereign immunity is not limited to the foreign sovereign himself' is hence rejected here.[132] The entitlement to state immunity *is* limited to the foreign state, but that state may be implicated in suits against its officials in an official capacity. It is submitted that this is the context in which the consideration regarding individual state officials and the law of state immunity in *Oppenheim's International Law* must be placed. The text reads in relevant part that an '[i]ndividual may claim state immunity when sued in respect of activities on behalf of the state since in such circumstances that person can be regarded as impleading the state.'[133]

2.3 Final Observations

De Sena—in one of the most comprehensive studies on the functional immunity of foreign state officials—has argued that no unitary principle underlies

[130] ibid 381–2. It has been argued that the court's reasoning in this case should be explained by the fact that it was no longer possible to apply the rule of state immunity since the Judge of the Roll had failed to strike out the case on that ground. Cf CCA Voskuil, 'State Immunity and the Law of Civil Procedure and Execution in the Netherlands' in TD Gill and WP Heere (eds), *Reflections on Principles and Practice of International Law* (2000) 223, 243–4.

[131] In a case instigated by Scientology against a German state official in the US courts the German approach was followed: cf *Heller v Caberta*, case no 8:00CV–1528–T–27 (US, Ct of Apps (11th Cir), 9 May 2002).

[132] *Grunfeld and Another v United States of America and Others* (Australia, 1968) 334.

[133] R Jennings and A Watts (eds)(1992) i 346.

functional immunity practice.[134] He strongly opposes the idea that functional immunity necessarily follows when an individual acts in his quality of agent of the state. According to De Sena the fact that an individual has acted in such quality assumes a different relevance in different contexts. In the previous sections this study has attempted to explain the rule of functional immunity from the perspective of a unitary binding principle. It was argued that functional immunity applies when a foreign state official has acted under the authority of his home state. Although the thesis of De Sena can not be dealt with here in any detail it will prove useful to examine some of his arguments in the light of the findings of the present study.

De Sena sets out to distinguish the treatment of foreign state officials on the basis of factors extraneous to the quality in which an act was committed. First he points out that the treatment of foreign state officials that perform non-authorized acts within foreign territory depends on whether a violation of national law *independent* of the violation of the territorial sovereignty of the foreign state has occurred.[135] He argues that if no such independent violation is at issue, the treatment of the official tends to be absorbed in the violation of international law, while in the case of an independent violation the individual responsibility of the individual is the rule. In regard to both situations he points out that the fact that the state official has acted in his official capacity does not of itself impose functional immunity. Second, as regards internationally *legal* activity De Sena moreover distinguishes between the exercise of functions that are internationally protected and of functions that are not.[136] As examples of the first category he discusses head of state immunity, diplomatic immunity and consular immunity. He moreover points out that the immunity of consular officers confounds with the immunity of the state when they are called to account in respect of acts that are not typical consular acts.[137] A third important distinction he proposes is that between crimes against international law where the imputability of international responsibility to the state is in substance irrelevant—though the question of imputability of the act may form a constituent of the definition of the crime, as in the case of torture—and those crimes where such imputability constitutes the context in which the individual responsibility necessarily inserts itself.[138] The crime of genocide and crimes against humanity in general are examples of the second category. The ascertainment of the individual responsibility for these crimes involves necessarily an inquiry into the overall government

[134] P De Sena (1996) cf especially 96–104.

[135] ibid 109.

[136] ibid 191.

[137] ibid 235.

[138] ibid 139. Also in P De Sena, 'Immunity of State Organs and Defence of Superior Orders as an Obstacle to the Domestic Enforcement of International Human Rights' in B Conforti and F Francioni (eds), *Enforcing Human Rights in Domestic Courts* (1997) 367; P De Sena, 'Immunità di ex-capi di Stato e violazioni individuali del divieto di tortura: sulla sentenza del 24 Marzo 1999 della Camera dei Lords nel caso *Pinochet*' (1999) 82 RDI 933.

policy of which they are by definition the expression. National courts, De Sena argues, may prosecute foreign state officials that have committed international crimes of the first category, but will in principle refrain from prosecuting those involved in crimes of the second category. The rare examples of prosecution of foreign state officials for such crimes in national courts—like the *Eichmann*,[139] *Barbie*,[140] *Demjanjuk*,[141] *Finta*,[142] and *Karadžić*[143] cases—must, according to De Sena, be understood in the context of action undertaken by the international community in respect of these crimes: the establishment of the Nuremberg Tribunal as part of the systematic dismantling of the overall organization of the German state, and the establishment of the ad hoc international criminal tribunal for the former Yugoslavia.

The differences in treatment identified by De Sena are not however incompatible with a unitary approach to the rule of functional immunity. In respect of the category of unauthorized acts on foreign territory it must at the outset be noted that De Sena proceeds from the factual rather than the legal official capacity concept. The argument that the official capacity in which an act is performed does not impose functional immunity when crimes that violate the territorial sovereignty of a foreign state are at issue proceeds from a mistaken conception of the operation of the rule of functional immunity. Only if the authorized exercise of sovereign activity is at issue or if the actions of the foreign state officials do not come within the context of national law does the rule of functional immunity apply to acts committed by foreign state officials within the territory of the forum state. More specifically, the distinction that De Sena identified within this category of acts arguably confuses practice with legal principle. The fact that no jurisdiction is exercised over foreign state officials that have violated the territorial sovereignty of the forum state may be explained by the fact that such a violation is not criminalized in the national legal system. More importantly, the fate of the individual state official will in such cases often be included in the diplomatic settlement of the controversy between the states involved. The non-exercise of jurisdiction is hence within the discretion of the forum state rather than imposed by legal principle.[144]

Also the distinction between the exercise of functions that are and functions that are not specifically protected by international law can be explained from

[139] *Israel v Eichmann* 36 ILR 5 (Israel, DC of Jerusalem, 1961), confirmed by the Supreme Court 36 ILR 277 (1962).

[140] *Féderation National des Déportées et Internés Résistants et Patriotes and Others v Barbie* 78 ILR 125, (1985) 78 ILR 124, (1988) 100 ILR 330 (France, Court of Cassation (Criminal Chamber) 1985 and 1988).

[141] *Demjanjuk v Petrovsky* 79 ILR 538 (US, Ct of Apps (6th Cir), 1985).

[142] *Regina v Finta* 93 ILR 424 (Canada, High Court of Justice, 1989).

[143] *Kadic v Karadžić* 70 F 3d 232 (US, Ct of Apps (2nd Cir), 1995); (1995) 34 ILM 1595.

[144] De Sena admits in fact that the non-exercise of jurisdiction over foreign state officials that commit a violation that is absorbed by the violation of the territorial sovereignty is not a legal principle but an expression of the discretion of the forum state: P De Sena (1996) 125.

the inherent limits of the rule of functional immunity. If a foreign state official exercises exclusive competences within the territory of the forum state the exact limits of the agreed function are essential to determine whether the activity was authorized by the forum state or not. Moreover, if it concerns authorized sovereign activity the presumption of authority applies, as a result of which the court must refrain from questioning the actual mandate of the state official. Lastly, even though the rule of consular immunity overlaps with the rule of functional immunity it must not be forgotten that the rules have a different character. In sum, the different reasoning identified by De Sena is not a reflection of a difference in the applicable principles. Rather, it reflects the limited applicability of the presumption of authority to acts performed within the context of the exercise of sovereign authority under international law only.

The final distinction identified by De Sena attributes characteristics to the rule of functional immunity that may in fact be evidence of legal or policy concerns unrelated to that rule. The distinction is a very real one. The adjudication of certain international crimes indeed requires explicit qualification of the acts of a foreign state. While the qualification of the activity of a foreign state in terms of international law is not a problem *as such*—think of cases like the Japanese *Shimoda* case,[145] or prosecutions of private individuals or companies for international crimes[146]—this may be different when such qualification *creates* the competence over the (former) foreign state officials impleaded. Since the absence of functional immunity for international crimes is an exception to the normal horizontal division of competences between national courts, courts may understandably be somewhat apprehensive to adjudicate allegations of international crimes that involve highly controversial qualifications of foreign state activity. The Nuremberg Tribunal, the ICTY and the ICTR are conspicuous examples of the existence of international consensus on the legal qualification of the activity of a particular state, but also in the *Pinochet* case the UK courts were blessed with the existence of broad international consensus as to the merits of the allegations. Chapter 5 of this study will discuss the issue in some more detail and will explain why the distinction between two types of international crimes, as proposed by De Sena, is instrumental but should not be seen to represent a schismatic application of the rule of functional immunity.[147]

In sum, it is argued that a unitary explanation of the rule of functional immunity does exist. (Former) foreign state officials do not incur personal responsibility for official acts. These acts are in law the acts of the foreign state. As long as

[145] *Shimoda et al v The State* (Japan, Tokyo DC, 1963) trans in (1964) 8 Japanese Annual of International Law 231; 32 ILR 626.

[146] Cf eg *Doe v UNOCAL* 395 F 3d 932 (US, Ct of Apps (9th Cir), 2002); *Van Anraat* case (The Netherlands, 2005). Domestic law principles may of course compel courts to exercise restraint, cf *R v Jones* [2006] UKHL 16 (UK, HL, 2006) § 30, available at <http://www.publications.parliament.uk/pa/ld/ldjudgmt.htm>.

[147] Cf ch 5 § 2.3.1.4 below.

their acts are performed within the context of exercise of state authority under international law they are presumptively committed on behalf of the state. This argument is fundamentally distinct from Kelsen's act of state argument. In fact, the arguments reason in exact opposite directions. Where this study premises the application of the law of state immunity on the autonomous principle that state officials do not bear individual responsibility for official acts and hence can be sued only in their official capacity in their regard; Kelsen argues that the law of state immunity must apply to all acts performed by state officials that can be attributed to the state and that *therefore* the state official cannot be held personally responsible. As said before, this latter argument cannot be explained from the principles on which the law of state immunity is said to be based. From the perspective of the equality and independence of states Kelsen's argument acquires a problematic circularity. Only if the state official concerned is not personally responsible can it be said that a claim against him necessarily impleads the state. Kelsen regarded this non-personal responsibility however a *consequence* of the law of state immunity. This section has set out that the chicken-and-egg-riddle *can* be decided in favour of the rule of functional immunity. And since a decision in favour of the law of state immunity necessarily relies either on the dubious concept of act of state immunity *or* on circular reasoning it is argued that it *should*.

3 The Influence of the 'Act of State' Confusion in Contemporary Functional Immunity Thinking on the Debate on the Human Rights Exception

3.1 Introduction

The previous section argued that state officials enjoy functional immunity in regard to acts that are in law acts of the state rather than of the official personally. Contemporary doctrine and jurisprudence however rely increasingly on essentially different 'act of state' concepts to define the rule of functional immunity. Functional immunity is held to attach to 'acts attributable to the state', as well as to 'sovereign acts of the state'.[148] The dominant tendency is the rationalization of the rule in terms of the application of the law of state immunity *ratione materiae*. The conception of the rule of functional immunity inevitably determines the arguments relied on and the position taken in the debate on functional immunity and human rights. This section sets out the two alternative act of state concepts and their hold on the discussion on 'the human rights exception'. It will be explained how these concepts differ from the act of state concept advanced in this study and why this latter concept should prevail.

[148] In addition, US courts have in human rights suits linked the rule to the act of state concept of the US act of state doctrine. This will be discussed in ch 5 § 2.3.1.3 of this study.

3.2 'Act of State' as 'Act Attributable to the State'

It is often said that official acts for functional immunity purposes are acts performed by a foreign state official that can be attributed to his home state. Denza for example writes in regard to the functional immunity of article 39.2 VCDR:

> [T]he correct test to be applied... is one of imputability. If the conduct in question is imputable or attributable to the sending State—even if it did not expressly order or sanction it—then continuing immunity ratione materiae should apply. The diplomat remains immune because his own sending State is really responsible.[149]

In the same vein, it is argued that functional immunity applies whenever the home state is responsible under the law of state responsibility. In the words of Salmon 'chaque fois que la responsabilité de l'Etat... est retenue, cet acte de l'Etat doit être couvert par l'immunité'.[150] Under the rules of state responsibility an act of a state official is attributed to the state—and considered an act of state—whenever that official has acted in his official capacity, even if he exceeded his competence according to internal law or contravened instructions concerning his activity.[151] Discussing the immunity of former foreign heads of state Watts—under explicit reference to the concept of attribution in the law of state responsibility—considered that

> [a] Head of State clearly can commit a crime in his personal capacity; but it seems equally clear that he can, in the course of his public functions as Head of State, engage in conduct which may be tainted by criminality or other forms of wrongdoing. The critical test would seem to be whether the conduct was engaged in under the colour of or in ostensible exercise of the Head of State's public authority. If it was, it must be treated as official conduct, and so not as a matter subject to the jurisdiction of other States *whether or not* it was wrongful or illegal under the law of his own State.[152]

[149] E Denza, 'Ex Parte Pinochet: Lacuna or Leap?' (1999) 48 ICLQ 949, 951; E Denza(1998) 363. Cf also *Former Syrian Ambassador to the German Democratic Republic* (Federal Republic of Germany, 1997) discussed in ch 4 § 2.1.2.1 below. Because of the peculiar interpretation of art 39.2 this case is not an example of the 'attribution' argument in general.

[150] J Salmon, *Manuel de droit diplomatique* (1994) 465. Cf on this 'parallelism' also YBILC 1999 ii (part two) annex, § 23.

[151] Cf the commentary of the ILC, to arts 4 and 7 of the ILC Articles on State Responsibility, ILC Report on the work of its fifty-third session (2001) A/56/10. Even 'manifest incompetence' would not impede the imputability to the state: YBILC 1975 ii 61, § 1. Cf for early examples *Union Bridge Company Claim (United States v Great Britain)* 6 RIAA 138 (Arbitral Tribunal (Great Britain—United States) 1924); *Caire case (France v United Mexican States)* 5 RIAA 516 (French—Mexican Claims Commission, 1929); *Youmans case (United States v United Mexican States)* 4 RIAA 110 (US–Mexico General Claims Commission, 1926). Cf also T Meron, 'International Responsibility of States for Unauthorized Acts of their Officials' (1957) 23 BYIL 85; L Condorelli, 'L'imputation à l'État d'un fait internationalement illicite: solutions classiques et nouvelles tendances' (1984–VI) 189 RdC 9.

[152] A Watts, 'The Legal Position in International Law of Heads of State, Heads of Government and Foreign Ministers' (1994–III) 247 RdC 13, 56.

In its 2006 decision in *Jones v Saudi Arabia* the House of Lords explicitly linked the law of state responsibility and the law of state immunity.[153] Lord Hoffmann stated that 'the circumstances in which a state will be liable for the act of an official in international law mirror the circumstances in which the official will be immune in foreign domestic law'.[154] Referring to, *inter alia*, articles 4 and 7 of the ILC Articles on State Responsibility and the commentary thereto,[155] he pointed out that this rule also applies when the state official has not been acting in accordance with his instructions or authority.[156]

Under this approach official acts—or acts of state—are usually contrasted with personal acts, or official conduct with private conduct.[157] The applicability of the rule of functional immunity then depends on the question 'whether the act in question was an official one, done on behalf of the State, or whether it was a frolic of the individual's own'.[158]

Clearly, under the attribution approach the definition of the rule of functional immunity in terms of the official capacity in which an act is performed proceeds from the *factual* rather than the *legal* interpretation of this notion.[159] The responsibility of the state arises not only regardless of the ultra vires character of an act, but also when the state official did not act within the context of the authority of the state under international law. It is good to realize that under this approach the attack on the *Rainbow Warrior* by French secret agents, murders committed by secret agents like Staschynskij and the assault of US nationals by Mexican consular officers qualify as official acts. This conception of the rule does not, therefore, account for certain instances of exercise of jurisdiction over foreign state officials.

The difference with the act of state concept advanced in this study is apparent. In the perspective proposed in section 2 of this chapter imputability is a necessary but not sufficient requirement for the qualification of an act as in law the act of the state. As the ICTY pointed out in the *Blaškić* case 'official action can *only* be attributed to the State'.[160] It was pointed out above that acts performed outside the context of exercise of state authority under international law as well as acts that violate internationally agreed normative limits on the concept of 'act of state' may still be attributable to the state but are equally attributable to the person of the foreign state official. There is, in sum, an area between official acts and 'frolics of the individual's own'.

Many of the scholars that adopt the imputability reasoning *have* argued that functional immunity is not available for international crimes. Crucially, however,

[153] *Jones v Saudi Arabia* (UK, 2006) .
[154] ibid § 74. Cf also § 12.
[155] See for the commentary ILC Report on the work of its fifty-third session (2001) A/56/10.
[156] ibid § 78.
[157] Cf eg ibid 57 and 89.
[158] CA Whomersley (1992) 856.
[159] Cf § 2.2.1.5 above for the distinction.
[160] *Prosecutor v Blaškić* (ICTY, 1997) § 38 (emphasis added).

their argument is not that those crimes do not qualify as official acts. Rather, they argue that an exception to the rule of functional immunity has developed in customary international law. For instance, both Salmon and Watts have argued that the rule of individual responsibility for international crimes means that functional immunity may not be available in respect of these crimes *irregardless of their official nature*.[161] In fact, from their theoretical perspective the argument that international crimes do not qualify as official acts has highly undesirable consequences. The equation of official acts with acts attributable to the state creates a vicious circle in which an act must be official for functional immunity purposes in order to trigger the responsibility of the home state under international law. Bothe argued for instance that it 'darf nicht verkannt werden, daß dann, wenn man ein bestimmtes Verbrechen nicht als Amtshandlung gelden lassen will, die unmittelbare völkerrechtliche Verantwortlickeit des Heimatsstaates des handelnden Staatsorgans entfällt.'[162] In reaction to the individual opinions of three Lords in the *Pinochet* case that the alleged torture did not qualify as an official act, a number of scholars argued that the violation of human rights by state officials *should* be considered an official act since it would otherwise be impossible to assert the international responsibility of the home state for that act.[163] When a few years later the ICJ considered in the *Arrest Warrant* case that state officials not protected by personal immunity may be sued in respect of acts committed 'in a private capacity' during their period in office, Cassese lashed out at the Court. He pointed out that international crimes 'are not as a rule "private acts" '... These crimes are *seldom* perpetrated in [a private] capacity... Indeed, individuals commit such crimes by making use (or abuse) of their official status. It is primarily through the position and rank they occupy that they are in a position to order, instigate, or aid and abet or culpably tolerate or condone such crimes as genocide or crimes against humanity or grave breaches of the Geneva Conventions. In the case of torture (not as a war crime or a crime against humanity), the 'instigation or consent or acquiescence of a public official or other person acting in an official capacity' is one of the objective requirements of the crime.'[164] In response to the consideration in the concurring opinion of Judges Higgens, Kooijmans and Buergenthal that international crimes do *not* qualify as official acts, Cassese noted disapprovingly that this would mean that the crimes for which von Ribbentrop (Reich Minister for Foreign Affairs from 1938 to 1945) was sentenced to death by the Nuremberg Tribunal should be regarded as 'private acts'.[165]

These cases will be discussed in detail in chapter 5 of this study. Here it suffices to ask the reader to consider the following questions: Who says the ICJ proceeded

[161] J Salmon (1994) 468; A Watts (1994) 82 and 84.

[162] M Bothe (1971) 255.

[163] Cf ch 5 n 208 below.

[164] A Cassese, 'When May Senior State Officials Be Tried for International Crimes? Some Comments on the *Congo v Belgium* Case' (2002) 13 EJIL 853, 868.

[165] ibid 870. Cf for similar criticism ch 5 n 211 below.

from the same conception of the rule of functional immunity as Cassese? Would it not be possible that it referred to acts performed in an official capacity in a *legal* sense, as proposed in this study? The principle of individual responsibility then exerts its influence at the phase of qualification of the act. This difference in perspective severs the link between the qualification of the act for functional immunity purposes and the law of state responsibility. The harsh criticism of Cassese and co would then be premature—to say the least.

In conclusion it must be pointed out that the conception of functional immunity in terms of acts attributable to the state lacks a convincing rationale. *Why* would a state official be immune as soon as his acts can be attributed to the state? The criterion of attribution was relied on by Kelsen in his act of state immunity argument.[166] However, Kelsen formulated his argument from the perspective of an absolute state immunity rule. Obviously, the act of state concept on which the argument operated is no longer coherent from the perspective of the restrictive state immunity rule. Nowadays, the rationale of Kelsen's argument requires reliance on the sovereign nature of the act.

3.3 'Act of State' as 'Sovereign Act': A Contemporary Version of Kelsen's Act of State Immunity Argument

It was already stated in the introduction to this chapter that the question of functional immunity of foreign state officials is today often presented as a question of state immunity *ratione materiae*. Roughly, it is argued that the law of state immunity covers foreign state officials if an act is attributable to the home state and the latter would have been immune had it been sued instead. As a consequence, it is sometimes argued that foreign state officials are immune in respect of official, public acts.[167]

Over the years courts and scholars have often *rationalized* the rule of functional immunity in terms of the immunity of the home state in respect of official acts. A conspicuous example is provided by the reasoning of the Italian Court of Cassation in *Rubin v Console della Repubblica di Panama*.[168] The court held the rule of functional immunity to constitute 'the application of the recognition of the 'extraneousness' of the official acts of the consul, in so far as he acts as an agent of the foreign State, in respect to the legal order of the territorial State. It is a real and genuine defect in the jurisdiction of the territorial State over disputes connected with such acts.'[169] Article 39.2 VCDR has been explained in comparable terms. Dinstein wrote for example that '[o]fficial diplomatic acts...enjoy

[166] Cf § 2.1 above.

[167] Cf eg H Fox (2002) 509.

[168] *Rubin v Console della Repubblica di Panama* (Italy, 1978).

[169] ibid 567 (my translation): 'Questo principio costituisce applicazione del riconoscimento della estraneità degli atti ufficiali del console, in quanto organo dello Stato estero, rispetto all'ordinamento dello Stato territoriale, e si sostanzia in un vero e proprio difetto di giurisdizione

permanent exemption from the jurisdiction of local courts because they are imputed to the foreign State, and that State is entitled to immunity in respect of its own acts.'[170] In that same vein, Rapporteur Reeves on the Harvard Research Project on Diplomatic Privileges and Immunities argued that '[i]nsofar as the member acts in his official capacity, his immunity confounds itself with that of the sending state itself and depends... upon the intrinsic nature of the act performed. International law imposes upon the courts of the receiving State an incompetence *ratione materiae* in the case of public acts... Immunity for official acts... applies to all public acts, by whomsoever performed, and to all state agents, whether diplomatic or otherwise.'[171] He further considered that 'immunity for official acts is an exemption from both the jurisdiction and the law of the receiving state, and, as a manifestation of the immunity of the sending state acting in a public capacity, it imposes an incompetence *ratione materiae* upon the receiving state'.[172]

Obviously, this reasoning does not reflect the non-personal responsibility of state official in respect of official acts. It is moreover underinclusive since in fact functional immunity extends beyond the acts covered by the law of state immunity.[173] Much *more* problematic is however the *reverse* reasoning that regards the state official immune whenever the acts can be attributed to the home state and that state is immune in their regard.

An early version of this argument—of which, as discussed above, Kelsen was a staunch defender—was formulated by the Committee of Experts for the Progressive Codification of International Law in 1927. It wrote that '[t]he inability of courts to exercise jurisdiction in regard to a sovereign act of a foreign Government... should apply where the defendant is sued personally for acts done by him in his capacity as a public official—though he no longer retains that capacity at the time of the proceedings—or under powers conferred on him by a foreign State.'[174]

A more recent—though only tentative—example of such argumentation is provided by the Canadian case of *Jaffe v Miller*.[175] Mr Jaffe alleged that US state officials had laid false criminal charges against him and had had him kidnapped from Canada to face these charges after having unsuccessfully tried to obtain

di quest'ultimo per le controversie connesse con tali atti'. Cf further *Church v Ferraino* (Italy, 1986).

170 Y Dinstein (1966b) 83.

171 Harvard Law School, Research in International Law (Reporter JS Reeves) Diplomatic Privileges and Immunities, (1932 supplement) 26 AJIL 15, 99.

172 ibid 137.

173 Cf § 2.2 above.

174 League of Nations, Committee of Experts for the Progressive Codification of International Law, Questionnaire no 11, Competence of the Courts in Regard to Foreign States, Report of the Sub-Committee (Rapporteur Matsuda) (1927), (1928 special supplement) 22 AJIL 117, 125.

175 *Jaffe v Miller and Others* (Canada, 1993). Cf also *Walker et al v Bank of New York Int* 104 ILR 277 (Canada, CA for Ontario, 1994).

his extradition. He brought a civil claim before the Canadian courts against the officials who were working in the Office of the Attorney General of the State of Florida. The officials brought a motion to dismiss the claim on grounds of immunity from jurisdiction under the Canadian State Immunity Act 1985. Their claim that state officials were included in the definition of a 'foreign state' under section 2 of the Act was acknowledged by the court.[176] It held that 'the acts that the personal responding parties performed were within the scope of their duties as functionaries of the State of Florida, and they are entitled to state immunity if immunity is available to the State of Florida'.[177] The court emphasized that '[t]he illegal and malicious nature of the acts alleged do not of themselves move the actions outside the scope of the official duties of the responding defendants'.[178] This part of the court's reasoning is still reconcilable with the thesis that the applicability of the law of state immunity is a consequence of the rule of functional immunity—albeit that it suffers from the underinclusiveness-deficiency. In an attempt to explain the rationale of this extension of the doctrine of state immunity the court however also stated that 'to confer immunity on a government department of a foreign state but to deny immunity to the functionaries who in the course of their duties performed the acts, would render the *State Immunity Act* ineffective. To avoid having its action dismissed on the grounds of state immunity, a plaintiff would have only to sue the functionaries who performed the acts.'[179] Although the case was clearly concerned with official capacity suits against foreign state officials, the decision at least implies that in general no jurisdiction can be exercised over foreign state officials that acted under colour of law if immunity would be available had the claim been brought directly against the state instead.

In less uncertain terms, the US court in *Herbage v Meese* approached the functional immunity of foreign state officials as a question of state immunity *ratione materiae* in respect of foreign sovereign activity.[180] In *Chuidian v Philippine National Bank* the court had considered 'a suit against an individual acting in his official capacity the practical equivalent of a suit against the sovereign directly'.[181] It pointed out that excluding individuals from the protection of the FSIA 'would amount to a blanket abrogation of foreign sovereign immunity by allowing litigants to escape the effect of the FSIA by artfully pleading complaints against individual officials, rather than the foreign state in question'.

[176] Section 2 (b) provides that '[i]n this Act...any government of the foreign state or of any political subdivision of the foreign state, including any of its departments, and any agencies of the foreign state.'

[177] *Jaffe v Miller and Others* (Canada, 1993) 469.

[178] ibid 460. The Court approvingly cited *Herbage v Meese* 98 ILR 101 (US, DC for the District of Columbia, 1990), affirmed without reasons 946 F 2d 1564 (1991).

[179] ibid 458–9.

[180] *Herbage v Meese* (US, 1990).

[181] *Chuidian v Philippine National Bank* (US, 1990) 1101–2.

Thus, the FSIA would be undermined by 'a peculiar variant of forum shopping'. The court emphasized that a 'bifurcated approach to sovereign immunity was not intended by the Act'.[182] Subsequently, in *Herbage v Meese* the court considered that it is not possible to sue a foreign state official in his private capacity in respect of acts performed while engaged in sovereign activity. Herbage was a British national sentenced to imprisonment by the US courts and extradited from the United Kingdom to the United States. He sued the UK law enforcement officers involved in his extradition alleging that these state officials had engaged in a conspiracy to deprive him of his constitutional rights by providing false information to a London magistrate who had him arrested and extradited on the basis of that information. Herbage asserted that his action was 'directed against the British defendants, *solely*, in their individual capacity, and that the complaint is not directed *per se*, against the British Government'.[183] The court responded that 'the actions…are ones that those defendants could have taken only in their official capacities. These officials were acting as law enforcement officers. Indeed it is difficult to see how these persons could be sued, and held potentially responsible, in their individual capacities for actions they took at the behest of their government or at the very least "under color of law".'[184] It was concluded that when a state official acts as an agent of the state he qualifies under the FSIA. Pertinently, the court held that 'the standard for determining whether immunity is warranted does not depend on the identity of the person or entity so much as on the *nature of the act* for which the person or entity is claiming immunity.'[185] 'There can be no doubt', it continued, 'that the acts by the British defendants…are "sovereign or governmental in nature"…. these defendants were performing official government functions, classically belonging to the discretion of the executive, and classically immune from suit. The FSIA bars Herbage's claims against the British defendants because his allegations would require an adjudication of the propriety and legality of the acts of British authorities in the performance of their official duties.' The court explicated that there exists no *ultra vires* exception to the immunity under the FSIA holding that '[t]he FSIA is absolute in this regard, no matter how heinous the alleged illegalities.'[186] It will be explained in chapter 5 of this study that subsequently US courts have in fact devised a line of reasoning to avoid the automatic application of the FSIA to foreign state officials sued for serious human rights violations committed under color of law.[187]

English courts have most explicitly regarded the capacity in which the foreign state official is—or can—be sued irrelevant. The individual (concurring) opinions in the 1957 decision of the House of Lords in *Rahimtoola v Nizam of*

[182] ibid 1102–3.
[183] *Herbage v Meese* (US, 1990) 106–7.
[184] ibid 107.
[185] ibid 107.
[186] ibid 108.
[187] Cf ch 5 § 2.3.1.3 below.

Hyderabad illustrate the difference between the application of the law of state immunity when a suit implicates the foreign state and the application of the law of state immunity irregardless of such implication.[188] When in 1948 Indian troops invaded Hyderabad, money was transferred from the account of the Nizam of Hyderabad and his government at the Westminster Bank in London by the Nizam's Finance Minister—one of the persons entitled to operate the account—into the name of Rahimtoola—then High Commissioner for Pakistan in the UK—who received it on the instructions of the Foreign Minister of Pakistan. The Minister had however acted without authority. The Nizam issued a writ against, *inter alia*, Rahimtoola, claiming payment of the money. Rahimtoola asked the writ to be set aside on the ground that the action sought to implead Pakistan, or sought to interfere with the rights or interests of the Government of Pakistan in the money. The Bank had transferred the money to Rahimtoola under reference of his official position and his title was also shown on the credit advice. Rahimtoola made affidavits saying that he had been instructed to accept the transfer by the then foreign minister of Pakistan and that he had accepted as an agent for his government. He explicitly stated that he only accepted as High Commissioner and that he would have never accepted the money as a private person. All Lords agreed that the rule of state immunity was applicable to the facts of this case. With disregard of the many subtleties of the arguments advanced by the Lords it can be roughly stated that where Lords Viscount Simonds, Reid, Cohen and Somervell of Harrow based their decision on the finding that the proceedings impleaded Pakistan;[189] Lord Denning explicitly denied the relevance of such implication, reasoning in terms that compare with act of state immunity instead. He famously considered that

> at the present time sovereign immunity should not depend on whether a foreign government is impleaded, directly or indirectly, but rather on the nature of the dispute. Not on whether 'conflicting rights have to be decided', but on the nature of the conflict. Is it properly recognizable by our courts or not? If the dispute brings into question, for instance, the legislative or international transactions of a foreign government, or the policy of its executive, the court should grant immunity if asked to do so, because it does offend the dignity of a foreign sovereign to have the merits of such a dispute canvassed in the domestic courts of another country.[190]

The other Lords all explicitly distanced themselves from Lord Denning's opinion. Lord Denning's reasoning should be understood in light of his zealous advocacy of a restrictive approach to state immunity.[191] The focus on the nature of the act rather than the implication of the state has been crucial in the gradual shift

[188] *Rahimtoola v Nizam of Hyderabad* (UK, 1957).

[189] The Lords, *inter alia* considered that 'the interests or property of the State are to be the subject of adjudication' (ibid 178 *per* Lord Viscount Simonds); 'the agent would merely be defending the action on behalf of his principal' (ibid 184 *per* Lord Reid).

[190] ibid 200.

[191] Cf ch 2 § 2.2.3.2 above.

from an absolute to a restrictive approach in the United Kingdom. From that particular perspective the reasoning of Lord Denning can only be praised. However, if we look at the two opinions from the perspective of the rationale of the application of the rule of state immunity in cases against foreign state officials—severing the reasoning from the historical context of the decision—it may be clear from the argument developed in this study this far, that this author prefers the majority approach. Lord Denning *was* right in criticizing the focus on the particularities of English law in the argumentation developed by the other Lords. It is a strange proposition of international law indeed that would depend for its application on the finer points of national law like whether the principal of a transferee can sue in his own capacity in name for cash at the bank—a point that, as Denning pointed out, loomed large in the reasoning of the majority.[192] However, this does *not* in itself warrant recourse to a pure act of state immunity argument in which the capacity in which a state official can be sued is irrelevant. The question whether Rahimtoola had acted and accepted as an agent and was hence only accountable in his official capacity should be—and can be—determined on the basis of an objective standard. Did the state official act on behalf of his home state or did he become obliged in his personal capacity?

Also the 1964 decision of the UK Court of Appeal in *Zoernsch v Waldock and Another* evidences the tendency of some judges to see the immunity of foreign state officials as a mere corollary of the law of state immunity.[193] In a case concerning the functional immunity of members of the European Commission on Human Rights the judges drew parallels with the functional immunity of foreign state officials. Wilmer LJ stayed close to the majority reasoning in *Rahimtoola*. He stated that '[i]nsofar as he acts in an official capacity, his acts are the acts of the foreign sovereign whom he represents.' A state official cannot be sued for acts performed in his official capacity, he continued, '[f]or this would involve impleading the foreign sovereign.'[194] Diplock L.J. rationalized the immunity of foreign state officials somewhat differently. He argued that '[t]he immunity of an envoy from suit or legal process arises from the duties owed by states to one another in international law.... acts done by him in his official capacity... are acts done on behalf of his Government. His Government being a foreign sovereign Government, under principles of English law which are so well know that I refrain from citing authority, is immune from the jurisdiction of the English courts. The propriety of its acts cannot be examined in a municipal court unless it consents to waive its immunity. *A foreign sovereign Government... can only act through agents, and the immunity to which it is entitled in respect of its acts would be illusory unless it extended also to its agents in respect of acts done by them on its behalf.* To sue an envoy in respect of acts done in his official capacity would be, in effect,

[192] ibid 195–6.
[193] *Zoernsch v Waldock and Another* 41 ILR 438 (UK, CA, 1964).
[194] ibid 444.

to sue his government.'[195] Diplock LJ did not use the sweeping terms of Lord Denning. His reasoning does however border on an act of state immunity argument and the allusion to Kelsen may be obvious.

The 1997 decision of the English Court of Appeal in *Propend Finance Ltd v Sing* can be regarded as a full endorsement of the reasoning advanced by Kelsen. The court did not in any way rely on the argument that the act complained of was an act of the foreign state rather than of the foreign state official in his private capacity. Rather, it rationalized the immunity of the state official completely in terms of (the efficacy of) the law of state immunity. The court considered that '[t]he protection afforded by the Act of 1978 to states would be undermined if employees, officers, (or as one authority puts it, "functionaries") could be sued as individuals for matters of State conduct in respect of which the State they were serving had immunity. Section 14(1) must be read as affording to individual employees or officers of the foreign State protection under the same cloak as protects the State itself.'[196]

This approach was confirmed by the House of Lords in the 2006 case of *Jones v Saudi Arabia*.[197] Referring to the case law just discussed it stated that as a rule 'the foreign state is entitled to claim immunity for its servants as it could if sued itself. The foreign state's right to immunity cannot be circumvented by suing its servants or agents.'[198]

A 1998 decision of the English High Court illustrates the absurd consequences such an approach may have. The details of the case *Re P (No 2)* were discussed earlier in this chapter. We saw that the court decided that the US diplomat had not acted in the exercise of his functions removing his children from UK territory to the United States. In addition to the functional immunity argument, the defendant and the United States intervening argued that 'since the act was one ordered by the State and in respect of which the State was immune from the jurisdiction of the English courts, the father benefited from the State immunity of the United States'.[199] Under reference to *Propend Finance* the court sanctioned this argumentation. It considered that since 'the agent of a foreign State will enjoy immunity in respect of his acts of a sovereign or governmental nature' and since the US government insisted that the children were removed on explicit orders

[195] ibid 450–1.

[196] *Propend Finance Pty Ltd v Sing* (UK, 1997) 669. S 14.1 of the SIA reads: 'The immunities and privileges conferred by this Part of this Act apply to any foreign or commonwealth State other than the United Kingdom, and references to a State include references to—

(a) the sovereign or other head of that State in his public capacity;
(b) the government of that State; and
(c) any department of that government,

but not to any entity (hereafter referred to as a "separate entity") which is distinct from the executive organs of the government of the State and capable of suing or being sued.'

[197] *Jones v Saudi Arabia* (UK, 2006) .

[198] ibid § 10.

[199] *Re P (No 2)* (UK, 1998). See § 2.2.1.2 above.

of the government, the taking of his children at the end of his mission 'was an act of a governmental nature and is as such subject to State immunity from legal process'.[200]

The *Re P* case has been criticized for its complete deferral to the foreign state in the ascertainment of the nature of the act.[201] The general underlying approach of applying state immunity when governmental activity is at issue seems however not to stir much controversy. In the cases discussed above the focus has shifted from the determination of the actual defendant to the determination of the immunity of the state.[202] This shift may be understood as part of the more general trend in state immunity law to downplay the ascertainment of the status of the defendant and rely on the corrective force of the restrictive rule instead. The implication of the state in the proceedings is irrelevant: all focus is on the nature of the activity before the court. Fox remarked in this respect that 'the immunity *ratione materiae* of both diplomat and head of state is identical to the immunity of the State'.[203] Bluntly put, the approach does away with the rule of functional immunity. The immunity of foreign state officials is included in the concept of state immunity *ratione materiae* in what constitutes a contemporary version of Kelsen's act of state immunity argument.

The application of the law of state immunity in what are personal capacity suits perforce already evinces the irrelevance of the implication of the state. This observation is of academic value only. As long as the foreign state official is not personally responsible in respect of the acts at issue the difference is that between an inadmissible claim and the grant of state immunity.

Clearly, the gap between the act of state concept advanced in this study and the act of state concept of the state immunity *ratione materiae* approach is less pronounced than that discussed in the previous section. If a state official exceeds his competence while exercising sovereign functions abroad, the state immunity *ratione materiae* approach leaves in theory the possibility to exercise jurisdiction over the state under the territorial tort exception. Moreover, if a state declares that a particular individual has not acted under its authority, exercise of jurisdiction is equally possible. In fact, since foreign state officials that perform acts within the context of a state's exercise of authority under international law are presumed to have acted on behalf of the state, the application of the law of state immunity to cases where the exercise of state authority under international law is at issue seem to overlap neatly.

[200] ibid 495. The CA dismissed the appeal since the declaration sought served no useful purpose and prolonged proceedings may be contrary to the interests of the children.

[201] See eg JC Barker, 'State Immunity, Diplomatic Immunity and Act of State: A Triple Protection against Legal Action?' (1998) 47 ICLQ 950, 957.

[202] Cf CA Whomersley (1992) 850. Cf also *Schmidt v Home Secretary of the United Kingdom, the Home Secretary of the Metropolitan Police and Jones* 103 ILR 322 (Ireland, High Court, 1994).

[203] H Fox, 'The Pinochet Case No 3' (1999) 48 ICLQ 687, 696.

However, exactly for the topic under consideration in this study a gap between the two concepts *does* exist. The *Pinochet* case is a conspicuous example of how the conception of the rule of functional immunity in terms of state immunity *ratione materiae* may include too much under the operation of the rule. The case is discussed in detail in chapter 5 of this study. Here that discussion is briefly anticipated in order to demonstrate the decisive influence of the conception of immunity on the arguments advanced and the position taken in the debate on functional immunity in respect of gross human rights violations. The question of the immunity of the former head of state of Chile in respect of the alleged acts of torture was approached as an inquiry into the scope of the state immunity of Chile. Lord Hope, for example, pointed out that 'the sovereign or governmental acts of one state are not matters upon which the courts of other states will adjudicate'.[204] It was therefore important, he argued, to qualify the alleged acts as private or governmental in nature. Also Lord Millett considered the question to be one as to the scope of state immunity *ratione materiae*. This immunity, he argued, 'is a subject-matter immunity. It operates to prevent the official and governmental acts of one state from being called into question in proceedings before the courts of another, and only incidentally, confers immunity on the individual.... it is closely similar to and may be indistinguishable from aspects of the Anglo-American Act of State doctrine.'[205]

As was pointed out in the introduction of this chapter, from this conception of the rule differentiation between cases involving foreign states and cases involving foreign state officials is only possible from the perspective of developments in the field of human rights law or international criminal law. Some Lords pointed out that Pinochet would in any case be immune in civil proceedings. Lord Hutton, for example, argued that since Chile would be entitled to state immunity would a claim be brought against it on the basis of these allegations, Pinochet could equally claim immunity under the principle stated in *Jaffe v Miller*.[206] The Lords therefore tried to establish an exception to the law of state immunity for criminal law proceedings against foreign state officials in respect of the international crime of torture.

The individual opinions of the Lords will be discussed in detail in chapter 5 of this study. Here it is pointed out that the conception of the rule of functional immunity prevalent in the *Pinochet* case crucially limited the possible arguments against the grant of immunity to the former dictator. A (former) foreign state official is necessarily immune whenever his home state would be immune in respect of activities performed by that official that are attributable to the home state. This was evidenced by the 2006 decision of the House of Lords in *Jones v Saudi*

[204] *Pinochet* no 3, 146, referring to *I Congreso del Partido* [1981] 2 All ER 1064 (UK, HL, 1981) 1070.
[205] ibid 171. He repeated this in *Holland v Lampen-Wolfe* (UK, 2000) 1584 (*per* Lord Millett).
[206] ibid 167.

Arabia.[207] A UK national that had allegedly been severely tortured by Saudi state officials in a Saudi prison had instigated a civil claim against Saudi Arabia and Lieutenant Colonel Abdul Aziz—his alleged torturer. The House of Lords found that Abdul Aziz was necessarily entitled to the same immunity as Saudi Arabia since the alleged acts of torture would be attributable to Saudi Arabia under the rules of state responsibility.[208]

Under the approach advanced in this study functional immunity—and hence the possible applicability of the law of state immunity—is defeated whenever states agree that state officials may incur individual responsibility while engaged in the exercise of sovereign activity. From this perspective the absence of functional immunity in respect of crimes against international law is obvious.

3.4 Concluding Observation

The parameters of coherent argument in the debate on functional immunity in respect of gross human rights violations depend on the nature and the scope of the rule of functional immunity. This section has argued that the current debate is confused by the 'act of state' concepts prevalent in the law of state responsibility and the law of state immunity.

Since the reliance on the two alternative concepts is not 'general and consistent'—it seems limited to common law legal systems for now—this study regards it an interpretation of a rule of international law that is open to criticism. The case law relied on in this study establishes that a different approach is possible, and this chapter has attempted to establish why that approach should prevail. It must of course be acknowledged that the law of state immunity *ratione materiae* as understood in § 3.2 and 3.3 may be in the process of developing into a rule of customary international law. However, it must be realized that the extension of the law of state immunity to include cases in which states are in no way impleaded would require reliance on a different rationale than the equality and independence of states. The application of the law of state immunity regardless of the implication of the state seems to rest on an overbroad interpretation of the scope of the law of state immunity.

In chapter 2 we cited Niboyet—'comme l'anatomiste, il doit procéder à toutes sortes de coupes et séparer les tissus les uns des autres pour restituer à chacun son originalité propre'[209]—to support our argument that the law of state immunity should be clearly distinguished from the immunity *ratione personae* of diplomats and heads of state. The functional immunity of foreign state officials must be approached with the same anatomical outlook. The application of the law of state immunity to cases involving foreign state officials should be understood from

[207] *Jones v Saudi Arabia* (UK, 2006).
[208] Cf for a discussion of this case ch 5, § 2.3.1.2.
[209] JP Niboyet (1950) 158.

the perspective of—necessary—official capacity suits. The application shields the underlying concept of functional immunity but should never be confused with it.

4 Conclusions

This chapter has explained that foreign state officials enjoy functional immunity in respect of official acts. Official acts are acts performed as an arm or mouthpiece of a state in respect of which the state official that happened to perform the act does not incur personal responsibility. These acts are in law acts of the state. The idea that 'State officials (and arguably former State officials) enjoy immunity *ratione materiae* for their official acts from the jurisdiction of the courts of other States, where the effect of the proceedings would be to undermine or render nugatory the immunity of the employer State'[210] is in itself not incompatible with the perspective proposed in this study. However, it must be realized that the immunity of the state is only undermined if a suit against the foreign state official is an official capacity suit. Application of the law of state immunity is hence only warranted when the claim (necessarily) regards the official in his official capacity and the foreign state is *in fact* the defendant. As long as a state official performs acts in the context of state authority under international law his acts are presumed to have been committed on behalf of the home state. When however an act is performed outside that context, an independent inquiry into the mandate of the official may be undertaken. This explains the relevance of the limits of the function of diplomatic and consular agents (exclusive competences) as well as the relevance of the exclusive applicability of international law to certain acts (rights and obligations under international law). A state may of course always defeat the presumption of authority attaching to particular acts. It may in the first place declare that contrary to appearances certain acts were in fact committed in excess of an official's mandate (*a posteriori*, ad hoc defeat). Most pertinent to our research question is the possibility that states agree on the international level—in the form of a rule of international law—that certain acts are always committed in excess of mandate (*a priori*, general defeat).

[210] C Wickremasinghe, 'Immunities Enjoyed by Officials of States and International Organizations' in MD Evans (ed), *International Law* (2003) 387, 403.

4

Personal Immunity

1 Introduction

A limited group of state officials enjoys a comprehensive personal immunity from the jurisdiction of foreign national courts during their term of office. This chapter inquires into the personal immunity rules applicable to diplomatic agents and heads of state. Unlike the rule of state immunity and the rule of functional immunity, these rules do not need reformulation in order to understand the nature and the substance of requirements under international law. This is not to say that there are no controversies as to the scope of personal immunity rules. These controversies manifest themselves, however, on an essentially distinct level. Section 2 examines some controversial issues regarding the material and formal scope of diplomatic and head of state immunity. In particular, the analogous application of the rule of head of state immunity to ministers of foreign affairs in the *Arrest Warrant* case warrants critical commentary.[1] The decision of the ICJ in that case moreover impels reconsideration of the obligations of third states under personal immunity rules.

The chapter concludes with a brief analysis of the nature of personal immunity rules in section 3. This section prepares the ground for the chapters 5 and 6 to follow. What are the parameters of coherent argument on the scope of these rules? In contrast with the rule of state immunity and the rule of functional immunity diplomatic immunity and head of state immunity are immunities from jurisdiction in the proper sense of the word. The rules apply independently from the essential competence of the court or the individual responsibility of the defendant. The rules are moreover conspicuous examples of customary international law that relies on state practice and *opinio juris* for its formation. Accordingly, the scope of these rules can only be determined through straightforward inductive reasoning on the basis of state practice. In the absence of changing practice proponents of a human rights exception to personal immunity rules must rely on hierarchy of norms arguments. If these arguments fail to convince the debate on the relation between international criminal law and international human rights

[1] *Arrest Warrant of 11 April 2000* (ICJ, 2002) (further referred to as *Arrest Warrant* Case).

law and personal immunity rules necessarily takes the form of an exchange of policy arguments.

2 The Scope of Diplomatic and Head of State Immunity

This section gives a brief overview of both the material scope (who is obliged to do what) and the formal scope (who can claim the correlated right) of the rules of diplomatic and head of state immunity respectively. The scope of the law of diplomatic immunity is relatively uncontroversial—although some uncertainty exists as to the position of ad hoc diplomatic missions. Head of state immunity is more ambiguous. In particular, the immunity from civil jurisdiction and the analogous application of the rule to heads of government and ministers of foreign affairs are controversial issues.

2.1 Diplomatic Agents

2.1.1 Material Scope of the Immunity

The inviolability of diplomatic agents—or messengers, or heralds as they were originally called—is one of the oldest rules of international law. Already in the practice of the Hittites, Babylonians, Egyptians, Greek and Romans the person of the diplomatic agent was regarded as sacred and inviolable.[2] The immunity they enjoy from the jurisdiction of the receiving state is of a more recent date. In the early Renaissance ambassadors were often subjected to civil suit and sometimes even arrested and subjected to criminal law suits. In particular, it was sometimes held that an ambassador could be brought before the local courts with regard to commercial transactions undertaken by him after he embarked on his mission. Gentili, for example, wrote in 1594 that 'an ambassador should be subject to legal procedure on every contract which he enters into during his embassy'.[3] It has been argued that this doctrine and practice relied on a misinterpretation of Roman law, in which a revived interest existed at the time. Roman civil law was

[2] See M Ogdon, *Juridical Bases of Diplomatic Immunity, A Study in the Origin, Growth and Purposes of the Law* (1936) 8; LS Frey and ML Frey, *The History of Diplomatic Immunity* (1999) for an overview of early examples. Cf also G Tenékidès, 'Droit international et communautés fédérales dans la Grèce des cités' (1956–II) 90 RdC 469; C Phillipson, *The International Law and Custom of Ancient Greece and Rome* (1911); DJ Hill, *A History of Diplomacy in the International Development of Europe* (1911) i 11ff.

The principle of inviolability is now laid down in art 29 of the Vienna Convention on Diplomatic Relations, 500 UNTS 95: 'The person of a diplomatic agent shall be inviolable. He shall not be liable to any form of arrest or detention. The receiving state shall treat him with due respect and shall take all appropriate steps to prevent any attack on his person, freedom or dignity.'

[3] A Gentili, *De Legationibus Libri Tres* (1594), trans by GJ Laing (Three Books on Embassies, 1924), Book II, Chapter XVI, nr 115. Cf also the Spanish and Portuguese legislation to this effect described in M Ogdon (1936) 46.

predominantly concerned with the position of provincial *legati* rather than foreign diplomats. This distinction was however disregarded by several Renaissance scholars, holding the exceptions developed in Roman law to the immunity of *legati* applicable to foreign ambassadors.[4]

Although the practice in this field has not developed along clear and consistent lines it is fair to say that the reliance on Roman law to promote a restrictive immunity for foreign diplomats gradually passed out of use. The state system that emerged in late-Renaissance Europe was dominated by notions of ceremony, dignity and comity. More and more the ambassador was seen to be the direct representative, or even the personification of the monarch that had sent him. The criminal immunity of ambassadors even when a crime against the receiving state had been committed, was accepted at an early stage. For example, when, in 1584, it was found out that the Spanish ambassador in England, Mendoza, had partaken in a conspiracy against Queen Elizabeth, he was not arrested but remanded to his sovereign.[5] Today diplomatic agents enjoy an almost absolute immunity from the civil jurisdiction of the receiving state as well.[6]

The theory of representation—that would root the rule in the same principles that underlie the immunity of the state—is no longer accepted.[7] The well-nigh absolute immunity from jurisdiction that diplomatic agents enjoy in the state in

[4] M Ogdon, ibid 42.

[5] See for other examples M Ogdon, ibid 56. Cf E Denza (1998) 229 for a succinct overview of developments.

[6] The English Diplomatic Privileges Act 1708 (Anne's Law) already did not allow actions against foreign diplomats in respect of their commercial activity. In the famous case of *Taylor v Best* decided in 1854, Jarvis CJ had held that 'if the privilege does attach, it is not, in the case of an ambassador or public minister, forfeited by the party's engaging in trade, as it would... in the case of an ambassador's servant. If an ambassador or minister, during his residence in this country, violates the character in which he is accredited to our court by engaging in commercial transaction, that may raise a question between the government of this country and that of the country by which he is sent; but he does not thereby lose the general privilege which the law of nations has conferred upon persons filling that high character.' *Taylor v Best* 14 CB 487 (UK, 1854) 519. Cf also *Magdalena Steam Navigation Company v Martin* 2 El & El 94 (UK, 1859) 116, where Campbell CJ concluded that '[i]t certainly has not hitherto been expressly decided that a public minister duly accorded to the Queen by a foreign State is privileged from all liability to be sued here in civil actions; but we think that this follows from well established principles.' Italy was one of the last countries to deny diplomatic immunity for private acts. Cf *Ricorrente Rinaldi* (1915) 9 RDI 215 (Italy, Corte di Cassazione di Roma, 1915); *Comina v Kite* (1924) 16 RDI 173 (Italy, Corte di Cassazione di Roma, 1922). In reaction to this latter case the diplomatic corps in Rome complained to the Italian Foreign Office, reproduced in The Harvard Draft Convention on Diplomatic Privileges and Immunities, Harvard Law School, Research in International Law (Reporter JS Reeves), Diplomatic Privileges and Immunities, (1932 supplement) 26 AJIL 15, 105. The Italian Court of Cassation finally converted to the rule of absolute immunity, cf *De Meeüs v Forzano* (1940) 32 RDI 93 (Italy, Corte di Cassazione, 1940); cf earlier *Harrie Lurie v Steinmann* (1928) 20 RDI 528 (Italy, Tribunale di Roma, 1927).

[7] Cf eg *Aldona S v Royaume Uni* (1963) 90 JDI 191 (Poland, S Ct, 1948): 'the immunity of State has a different juridical basis from that of diplomatic agents. The immunity of representatives of a foreign State has the object of safeguarding their liberty in the exercise of their functions, whilst the immunity of the State is juridically based on the democratic principle of their equality.' See differently S Sucharitkul (1976) 97 who wrote that '[i]n the ultimate analysis, the basis of diplomatic immunity can now be regarded as identifiable with that of sovereign or State immunities.'

which they exercise their functions is today considered necessary to ensure the free and independent performance of diplomatic functions—*ne impediatur legatio*. Vattel already commented that

ambassadors and other public ministers are necessary instruments in the maintenance of that general society of Nations and of that mutual intercourse between them. But they can not accomplish the object of their appointment unless they are endowed with all prerogatives necessary to perform the duties of their charge safely, freely, faithfully and successfully. Consequently, [nations are obliged] to accord them all the rights they require and all the privileges necessary for the performance of their duties.[8]

The French *Cour de Cassation* formulated the generally accepted rationale of diplomatic immunity as follows:

Si chaque fois que l'agent diplomatique agit comme personne privée, il tombe sous la juridiction des tribunaux français, ses créanciers pour peu qu'il en ait, le traqueront sans miséricorde et pourront entraver, tantôt par des demandes légitimes, tantôt par des mauvaises chicanes, l'exercice de sa mission; on retombe ainsi dans l'inconvénient que le droit des gens voulait éviter: *ne impediatur legatio*.[8a]

Diplomatic immunity—with its functionality rationale—is not to be confused with the concept of functional immunity. It was explained in chapter 3 of this study that all (former) state officials enjoy functional immunity in respect of official acts. Diplomatic immunity is more comprehensive. It applies to diplomatic agents sued in respect of official and non-official acts alike. The *ne impediatur legatio* rationale extends to the 'private' acts of diplomatic agents because, as the Italian Court of Cassation put it in *De Meeüs v Forzano*, private acts 'constitute the necessary basis for the exercise of public activities'.[9]

The rule does not affect the liability of the diplomatic agent. As Lord Diplock emphasized in *Empson v Smith* '[i]t is elementary law that diplomatic immunity is not immunity from legal liability but immunity from suit'.[10] Since personal liability is lacking in regard to official acts it has at times been argued that diplomatic immunity applies only to the non-official acts of diplomatic agents. Kunz, for example, reasoned that 'the exemption from local jurisdiction of diplomatic agents pertains exclusively to the private acts of diplomatic agents. Their exemption from local jurisdiction for their official acts has nothing to do with diplomatic privileges and immunities; their official acts are "acts of State" and are legally imputed not to them but to the sending State.'[11] This reasoning has been

[8] E De Vattel (1758) iii trans by CG Fenwick (*The Law of Nations*, 1983) 376.
[8a] Errembault de Dudzeele (France, Cour de cassation, 1891) 18 JDI 1891 137.
[9] *De Meeüs v Forzano* (Italy, 1940) 94 (my translation): 'costituiscono il substrato materiale necessario per lo svolgimento delle attività pubbliche', cf also 9 AD 423, case no 164.
[10] *Empson v Smith* (UK, 1965) 886; 41 ILR 407, 414. Cf also *Dickinson v Del Solar* (UK, 1929) 380; 5 AD 299, case no 190, 299.
[11] JL Kunz, 'Privileges and Immunities of International Organizations' (1947) 41 AJIL 828, 838.

especially popular in Italian doctrine and case law.[12] The argument disregards, however, the logical order in which the two issues should be considered by the courts. The rule of functional immunity requires an inquiry into the nature of the alleged acts. Diplomatic immunity should therefore be seen to apply *in precedence* of functional immunity. As Morelli pointed out, diplomatic immunity prevents *any* finding on the merits, positive or negative.[13] One Italian court explained that on the procedural plane *priority—not prevalence*—was given to the rule of diplomatic immunity.[14] Accordingly, while the rule of diplomatic immunity does not *entail* non-liability; this does *not* mean that the principle of non-personal liability may not be cloaked by the rule. Dinstein aptly put it when he wrote that during a diplomatic agent's term of office, functional immunity is 'eclipsed by the shadow of the personal immunity'.[15] The activity of a diplomatic agent may only be examined if a prima facie case is made that one of the—very limited—exceptions to the rule applies.

The immunity of diplomatic agents accredited to a permanent diplomatic mission is authoritatively codified in the 1961 Vienna Convention on Diplomatic Relations.[16] The Convention was mainly a codification of existing diplomatic

[12] Cf *Società Arethusa Film v Reist* (Italy, 1953) 546; D Anzilotti, 'Case Comment' (1912) 6 RDI 501, 501; D Anzilotti, 'Case Comment' (1915) 9 RDI 217, 219; A Cavaglieri, 'Règles générales du droit de la paix' 1929–I 26 RdC 311, 470; T Perassi, 'Su l'esenzione degli agenti diplomatici dalla giurisdizione' (1940) 32 RDI 95; A Malintoppi (1954) 121; A Malintoppi (1955) 90; L Condorelli, 'Le immunità diplomatiche e I principi fondamentali della Costituzione' (1979) 24–I Giurisprudenza Costituzionale 455, 456; In the third edition of his *Diritto internazionale* (1987, 221) Conforti still writes that it is for the private acts of diplomatic agents that the real and genuine immunity from jurisdiction is foreseen—a formulation that no longer appears in the sixth edition (2002) (cf 230). Cf also M Adatci and C De Visscher (Rapporteurs Institut de Droit International), Rapport sur l'Interprétation de l'article 7, al. 4, du Pacte de la Société des Nations (Privilèges et Immunités Diplomatiques des Agents de la Société des Nations), (1924) 31 AIDI 1, 9–10; H Kelsen (1952) 229–31.

[13] G Morelli (1954) 201–4. Cf also A Tanzi (1991) 10.

[14] *Soc Vivai Industriali v Legazione dell'Arabia Saudita* (Italy, 1953) 84. The court hence sided with Morelli and rejected the approach of the scholars mentioned under n 12.

[15] Y Dinstein (1966b) 79.

[16] Vienna Convention on Diplomatic Relations (1961) 500 UNTS 95. The Convention was prepared within the ILC, see ILC Draft Articles Concerning Diplomatic Intercourse and Immunities, YBILC 1958 ii 16. Earlier attempts to codification are: The Vienna Regulations (1815); The Règlement sur les immunités diplomatiques of the Institut de Droit International (1895), reproduced and trans as Appendix 3 to the Harvard Draft Convention on Diplomatic Privileges and Immunities, Harvard Law School, Research in International Law (Reporter JS Reeves), Diplomatic Privileges and Immunities, (1932 supplement) 26 AJIL 15, 162ff; The Project of the American Institut de Droit International on Diplomatic Agents (Project no 22 1925), reproduced as Annex 5 to the Harvard Draft Convention on Diplomatic Privileges and Immunities, ibid 168ff; The Project of the International Commission of American Jurists (1927), reproduced as Appendix 6 to the Harvard Draft Convention on Diplomatic Privileges and Immunities, ibid 171ff; The Havana Convention on Diplomatic Officers (1928), 86 LNTS 111, and reproduced as Appendix 7 to the Harvard Draft Convention on Diplomatic Privileges and Immunities, ibid 175ff; The Harvard Draft Convention on Diplomatic Privileges and Immunities, Harvard Law School, Research in International Law (Reporter JS Reeves), Diplomatic Privileges and Immunities, (1932 supplement) 26 AJIL 15.

practice but also contains some provisions that constituted 'a progressive development of the law'.[17] Since then the Convention has been ratified by some hundred and eighty states and it can by now be safely stated that it reflects customary law in the field.[18] The material scope of diplomatic immunity from jurisdiction will therefore be discussed on the basis of the relevant provisions of the Vienna Convention.[19]

Article 31.1 of the Convention lays down the rule on immunity from jurisdiction:

> A diplomatic agent shall enjoy immunity from the criminal jurisdiction of the receiving State. He shall also enjoy immunity from its civil and administrative jurisdiction, except in the case of:
>
> (a) a real action relating to private immovable property situated in the territory of the receiving State, unless he holds it on behalf of the sending State for the purposes of the mission.
> (b) an action relating to succession in which the diplomatic agent is involved as executor, administrator, heir or legatee, as a private person and not on behalf of the sending State.
> (c) an action relating to any professional or commercial activity exercised by the diplomatic agent in the receiving State outside his official functions.

While the principle of inviolability does not exclude coercive measures to prevent the commission of crimes in exceptional circumstances, the immunity from the criminal jurisdiction of the courts of the receiving state in respect of committed crimes is absolute.[20] The only sanction available to the receiving state is to declare a diplomatic agent persona non grata in accordance with article 9 of the Convention. The sending state must then either recall the diplomatic agent concerned or terminate his functions with the mission.

[17] Cf R Jennings and A Watts (eds) (1992) i 1070, § 490.

[18] In this sense eg J Dugard, *International Law, A South African Perspective* (2000) 192; I Brownlie, (2003) 351. Already in 1969 the Supreme Court of Chile held that '[t]he fact that the Republic of China has not yet ratified the Vienna Convention does not prevent the application of Article 31 in our country because it is a principle of international law, common and customary, that this provision has crystallized, being only an expression of it', *MH v Embassy of the Republic of China* 70 ILR 394 (Chile, SCt, 1969). Cf also *Case Concerning United States Diplomatic and Consular Staff in Tehran* (*United States of America v Iran*) (Judgment), ICJ Reports 1980 3, 40, § 86.

[19] The issue of ad hoc diplomatic missions is further discussed at § 2.1.2.2 below.

[20] Cf for the limited exception to the principle of inviolability eg arts 6.3 and 16 of the Resolution of the Institut de Droit International (1895), reproduced as Appendix 3 to the Harvard Research Draft Convention on Diplomatic Immunities, Harvard Law School, Research in International Law (Reporter JS Reeves), Diplomatic Privileges and Immunities, (1932 supplement) 26 AJIL 15, 162; YBILC 1957 i 97, 209–10 and ii 131, 138; YBILC 1958 ii 97. The ICJ remarked in this regard that the principle did not mean 'that a diplomatic agent caught in the act of committing an assault or other offence may not, on occasion, be briefly arrested by the police of the receiving State in order to prevent the commission of the particular crime' *Case Concerning United States Diplomatic and Consular Staff in Tehran* (ICJ, 1980) 40, § 86.

The immunity from civil jurisdiction, on the other hand, is subject to three exceptions. Their scope is however very limited. Diplomatic agents are immune in respect of all the normal day-to-day activity in which they engage. It is this aspect of diplomatic immunity that most obviously negatively affects the interests of the citizens of the receiving state.[21] Even though immunity and impunity are formally distinct, in practice diplomatic immunity is often a critical stumbling block to a judicial settlement of civil disputes.

The receiving state can of course ask the sending state to waive the immunity of its diplomatic agent. Though a personal immunity, diplomatic immunity is not a personal right of the diplomatic agent. Rather, it appertains to the sending state. That state—and not the diplomatic agent—can hence dispose of the right.[22] Sending states are, however, not generally complaisant in this respect. Notably, a resolution annexed to the Final Act of the Vienna Conference on Diplomatic Relations urging states to adopt a benevolent waiver policy in respect of civil claims, did not enjoy wide support.[23]

In principle, the rule of diplomatic immunity entails rights and obligations for the sending and the receiving state only. It applies, in other words, not *erga omnes*. Third states are only obliged to accord inviolability and such other immunities as may be required to ensure the transit of diplomatic agents that proceed to take up or return to their post or return to the sending state.[24] The same obligations apply in respect of diplomatic agents that are present in the territory of a third state due to *force majeure*, the textbook example being the forced landing or diversion of an aircraft.[25] It will be explained in section 2.3 below that the decision of the International Court of Justice in the *Arrest Warrant* case compels reconsideration of conventional wisdom regarding the obligations of third states under personal immunity rules.

2.1.2 Formal Scope of the Immunity

2.1.2.1 Diplomatic agents during their term of office

The immunity rules introduced above are those that apply to diplomatic agents—ie the head of the mission and members of the diplomatic staff.[26] Diplomatic agents

[21] In ch 6 § 3.4 of this study it will be argued that the immunity from penal jurisdiction may affect the rights of other individuals as well.

[22] Art 32.1 of the Convention provides that '[t]he immunity from jurisdiction of diplomatic agents . . . may be waived by the sending State'.

[23] Resolution II on 'Consideration of Civil Claims' annexed to the Final Act. The resolution recommends that a sending state waives immunity 'in respect of civil claims of persons in the receiving State when this can be done without impeding the performance of the functions of the mission'. It moreover states that 'in the absence of waiver the sending State should use its best endeavours to bring about a just settlement of claims'.

[24] Art 40.1 VCDR.

[25] Art 40.4 VCDR.

[26] Art 1.e VCDR. The rules on diplomatic immunity apply to members of the family of the diplomatic agent forming part of his household, provided that they are not nationals of the receiving state, cf arts 37.1 and 40.1 VCDR. The Vienna Convention does not provide a more precise definition of the individuals that may be covered by this rule. In general practice it is accepted that

that are nationals of the receiving state or permanently resident in that state however are *not* covered by the rule. Such an agent is only immune (and inviolable) 'in respect of official acts performed in the exercise of his functions', unless the receiving state grants additional privileges and immunities.[27]

The receiving state must give an explicit *agrément* for the person the sending state proposes to accredit as head of the mission. *Agrément* may be withheld without giving reasons. As a general principle, the rest of the staff of the mission may be freely appointed by the sending state, with the general caveat that the receiving state has the discretion to declare a particular diplomatic agent *persona non grata*—also *ahead of* the arrival of the agent, effectively blocking the appointment of that person to the mission.[28] A specific caveat applies to persons having the nationality of the receiving state. Such persons may only be appointed as a member of the diplomatic staff of a mission with the consent of the receiving state.[29] Having regard to the circumstances and conditions in the receiving state and the needs of the particular mission the receiving state may moreover require that the size of the mission be kept within limits considered reasonable and normal *by the receiving state* and may, on a non-discriminatory basis, refuse to accept officials of a particular category.[30]

Diplomatic immunity ends when a diplomatic agent ends his functions as a member of the mission in the receiving state. The immunity in respect of acts performed by the agent in the exercise of his functions subsists however—as laid down in article 39.2 of the Convention. It was explained in chapter 3 of this study that this immunity is not a privilege peculiar to diplomatic agents. It regards the rule of functional immunity applicable *erga omnes* and to all (former) state officials alike. This immunity *ratione materiae* only gains relevance after the diplomatic agent has ended his duties in the receiving state but clearly existed all along, cloaked by the more comprehensive concept of diplomatic immunity *ratione personae*.[31]

The German *Bundesverfassungsgericht* has suggested otherwise. In a case against the former Syrian Ambassador to the German Democratic Republic it approached article 39.2 as an exclusive privilege part of the law of diplomatic immunity.[32] The case concerned the following. In 1983 a bomb exploded in

at least the spouse of a diplomat and his children below the age of majority are included. Beyond this minimum states apply different rules.

[27] Art 38.1 VCDR. In addition a different—more restrictive—regime applies to private servants and members of the administrative, technical and service staff, cf arts 37 and 38.2 VCDR.

[28] Arts 7 and 9 VCDR.

[29] Art 8.2 VCDR.

[30] Art 11 VCDR.

[31] Y Dinstein (1966b) 79. Cosnard remarked in this regard that 'la fonction change de rôle: d'attributive, elle devient distributive', M Cosnard (1996) 59.

[32] *Former Syrian Ambassador to the German Democratic Republic* (Federal Republic of Germany, 1997). Cf also M Tomonori (2003) 121.

West Berlin, causing one casualty and several serious injuries. The terrorist group which carried out the attack had been allowed to briefly store the explosives at the Syrian Embassy in the German Democratic Republic, in accordance with the specific instructions from the Syrian government to its Ambassador 'to do everything possible to assist the group'. The Ambassador refused to transport the explosives to West Berlin with the Embassy bag, but did not prevent the terrorist from taking the explosives and arranging the transport themselves, and did not alert the West German authorities. After reunification of the two Germanies an arrest warrant was issued against the—by then former—Ambassador charging him with being an accessory to murder and the causing of an explosion.

The court accepted that the Ambassador had acted in the exercise of his official functions as a member of the mission. It argued that article 39.2 shields former diplomatic agents from the jurisdiction of the former receiving state in respect of acts that are attributable to the sending state. 'Judicial proceedings', it reasoned, 'come, in their effects, close to proceedings against the sending State... [diplomatic immunity] serves to protect the sending State itself.'[33] An exception for serious crimes was considered incompatible with the 'meaning of *diplomatic immunity*' since that immunity applies exactly when the diplomatic agent violates the law of the receiving state. 'If a criminal act was never considered as official', the court argued, 'there would be no substance to continuing immunity'.[34] It was asserted that since the law of diplomatic immunity is a self-contained regime, sanctions against a diplomatic agent are limited to those foreseen in diplomatic law.[35]

The court concluded that the former Ambassador could nevertheless be sued before the German courts. As a consequence of the characterization of article 39.2 as part of diplomatic immunity the scope of the protection granted became more limited *as well as* more comprehensive. Diplomatic law, the court pointed out, does not apply *erga omnes*. It only prevents the exercise of jurisdiction by the courts of the receiving state.[36]

[33] Ibid 605–6. Interestingly, the court relied on the dubious use of the concept of immunity *ratione materiae* in the field of state immunity to replace the concept of immunity *ratione materiae* as it originates in the law of functional immunity (606).

[34] ibid 606 (emphasis added).

[35] ibid 607–8.

[36] ibid 610–12. This—within the context of the chosen approach coherent—argument was supported by unfortunate reasoning. The court considered: 'Were this continuing immunity to apply *vis-à-vis* third States, the diplomat would be subject to the jurisdiction of the third State for his official acts during the period of his office, but suddenly immune with respect to the same official acts upon termination of the mission. Consequently, according to Article 39(2), second sentence, of the VCDR, immunities would no longer just continue to subsist, but would actually come into existence with worldwide effect. The proposition that a diplomat should enjoy a wider immunity after the termination of his mission than before contradicts the basic conception of the law of diplomatic immunity enshrined in Article 39(2) of the VCDR' (612–13). However, if art 39.2 *were* to apply *erga omnes*, the immunity for official acts of course applied *erga omnes* before the end of the functions as well.

It must first be pointed out that even within the given parameters the court's reasoning is not convincing. Did the court mean to argue that foreign states are immune in respect of incidental criminal activity undertaken outside the scope of normal functions of a diplomatic mission but on orders of the state? This author would argue that in this respect there is no difference between an order to a secret agent—as in the *Letelier* case—and an order to a diplomatic agent.[37]

More pertinent however is the critique that the reasoning proceeds from the wrong parameters. It is commonly agreed that article 39.2 VCDR is *not* part of diplomatic law. Rather, it lays down the rule of functional immunity as it applies *erga omnes* and to all foreign state officials alike. While diplomatic immunity indeed applies regardless of the nature of the act, it was explained in chapter 3 of this study that normative limits *do* apply to the rule functional immunity. It is hard to see how the alleged crimes of the former Syrian Ambassador could qualify as official. The alleged crimes were not performed within the context of the exercise of state authority under international law and do hence not fall within the discretion of the sending state.[38]

2.1.2.2 *Ad hoc* diplomatic missions

In the course of their international relations states frequently resort to sending ad hoc diplomatic missions abroad. One should think of bilateral or multilateral negotiations between government officials or the representation at ad hoc conferences, government trade delegations, and official visits of high ranking state officials like a minister of foreign affairs meeting his foreign counterpart, or a head of government invited to attend a funeral abroad in his official function. Before the institute of permanent diplomatic missions gradually gained ground from the second half of the fifteenth century onwards, ambassadors were always persons on a temporary mission, proposing peace or strategic alliance against a common enemy, seeking military support and so on.[39] With increasing international cooperation and technological developments facilitating swift travel, shuttle diplomacy regained prominence over the twentieth century.[40]

[37] *Letelier v Chile* (US, 1980), cf ch 2 § 3.2.1 above.

[38] Cf for critical comments on the case eg B Fassbender, 'Case Comment' (1998) 92 AJIL 74; K Doehring and G Ress, 'Diplomatische Immunität and Drittstaaten, Überlegungen zur erga omnes Wirkung der diplomatische Immunität und deren Beachtung im Fall der Staatensukzession' (1999) 37 Archiv des Völkerrechts 68.

[39] Even though temporary missions could last for several years, their duration was always dependent on the fulfilment of the specific objective they had been sent for. The Italian free states started sending permanent missions and this practice quickly spread to other European states. It has been observed that before that, representative institutions within the Roman Empire—the *legati*—and the Christian Church resembled the later permanent diplomatic missions. Cf M Ogdon (1936) 23.

[40] M Bartoš, 'Le statut des missions speciales de la diplomatie ad hoc' (1963–I) 108 RdC 425, 440.

Scholars generally agree that 'clear and comprehensive rules of customary international law' on the immunity of temporary diplomatic missions are lacking.[41] In 1969 the General Assembly adopted the Special Missions Convention—modelled on the 1961 Vienna Convention.[42] The Convention failed to secure widespread support and the provisions granting the same immunity to temporary missions as to permanent missions are not accepted as representing customary international law.[43] The principal problem with the Special Missions Convention is that it treats all technical, administrative, and political missions alike.[44] Early codifications of the law of diplomatic immunity commonly included both permanent and temporary diplomatic agents[45] and it cannot be denied that a form of diplomatic immunity *does* in fact apply to ad hoc political missions accredited to the receiving state.[46] In particular, it is generally agreed that diplomatic immunity applies to all official missions abroad of the head of state, the head of government, and members of the cabinet—with the minister of foreign affairs as conspicuous example.[47]

41 R Jennings and A Watts (eds) (1992) i 1127, § 533. Cf also M Bartoš, ibid 434; MR Donnarumma, *La diplomazia ad hoc* (1968); MR Donnarumma, 'La Convention sur les missions speciales' (1972) 8 RBDI 34, 79; P Cahier, *Le droit diplomatique contemporain* (1962) 362; MH Ryan, 'The Status of Agents on Special Missions in Customary International Law' (1978) 16 Canadian Yearbook of International Law 157, 160; I Brownlie (2003) 357.

42 United Nations Convention on Special Missions (1969), Annex to UNGA Resolution 2530 (XXIV) of 8 December 1969, 1400 UNTS 231. The Convention was based on the ILC Draft Articles on Special Missions, YBILC 1967 ii 347–68 and entered into force 21 June 1985.

43 Cf art 31.

44 In this sense J Salmon (1994) 546; MH Ryan (1978) 186; M Waters, *The Ad Hoc Diplomat: A Study in Municipal and International Law* (1963) 170. Arguably, the Convention fails moreover to reflect the differences in functionality considerations applicable to temporary missions as compared to permanent missions. Art 37 extends the immunity rules to family members accompanying the diplomatic agent just like art 37 VCDR.

45 In the commentary to the Harvard Draft Convention on Diplomatic Privileges and Immunities (Reporter JS Reeves) we read that the convention applies to every 'diplomatic group, whatever be the permanency of its tenure or its official rank (embassy, legation, special missions)... The term is broad enough to include special missions of a political or ceremonial character which are accredited to the government of the receiving state. Members of special missions probably enjoy the same privileges and immunities as those of permanent missions.' (1932 supplement) 26 AJIL 15, 42. Cf also arts 2 and 12 of the Règlement sur les immunités diplomatiques of the Institut de Droit International (1895), reproduced and translated as Appendix 3 to the Harvard Draft Convention on Diplomatic Privileges and Immunities, ibid 162ff; Arts 2 and 14 of the Project of the American Institut de Droit International on Diplomatic Agents (Project no 22 1925), reproduced as Annex 5 to the Harvard Draft Convention on Diplomatic Privileges and Immunities, ibid 168ff; Arts 2 and 14 of the Project of the International Commission of American Jurists (1927), reproduced as Appendix 6 to the Harvard Draft Convention on Diplomatic Privileges and Immunities, ibid 171ff; Arts 2 and 9 of the Havana Convention on Diplomatic Officers (1928), 86 LNTS 111 and reproduced as Appendix 7 to the Harvard Draft Convention on Diplomatic Privileges and Immunities, ibid 175ff.

46 Notably, the ILC stated that the articles on immunity and privileges reflected an already existing obligation, not mere courtesy: YBILC 1967 ii 347, 358.

47 Cf Gore-Booth (ed), *Satow's Guide to Diplomatic Practice* (5th edn, 1979) 157.

2.2 Heads of State

2.2.1 Material Scope of the Immunity

Heads of state enjoy an absolute immunity from foreign criminal jurisdiction. While some scholars have argued that the immunity only applies when a head of state is present on foreign territory or even only when a head of state is present on foreign territory while on an official visit, the immunity is today commonly accepted to apply without such restrictions.[48] In other words, the absolute immunity from criminal jurisdiction of foreign heads of state applies *erga omnes*—as does the rule ensuring their inviolability. Most of the recent state practice deals with the influence of international criminal law on the scope of the immunity and will be later examined in chapter 5 of this study.[49]

In comparison, the extent of the head of state's immunity from foreign civil jurisdiction is subject to considerable academic and judicial controversy. Some argue that no such immunity *ratione personae* exists, others that this is limited to official visits of a head of state abroad, and a third group maintains that this immunity is at least subject to certain exceptions.

Early case law involving foreign heads of state did not support a rule of personal immunity from civil jurisdiction.[50] It is recalled that in *The Schooner Exchange* Chief Justice Marshall alluded to the double capacity of personal sovereigns. He suggested that 'there is a manifest distinction between the private property of the person who happens to be the prince, and that military force which supports the sovereign power, and maintains the dignity and the independence of a nation. A prince, by acquiring private property in a foreign country, may possibly be considered as subjecting that property to the territorial jurisdiction; he may be considered as so far laying down the prince, and assuming the character of a private individual; but this he cannot be presumed to do with respect to any portion of that armed force, which upholds his crown, and the nation he

[48] See eg H Fox (2002) 441; A Watts, (1994) 54; J Salmon (1994) 599; P Cahier (1962) 338; H Damian, *Staatenimmunität und Gerichtszwang, Grundlagen und Grenzen der völkerrechtlichen Freiheit fremder Staaten von inländischer Gerichtsbarkeit in Verfahren der Zwangvollstreckung oder Anspruchsicherung* (1985) 76; *Bacchelli v Commune di Bologna* F It 1978 I, 804 (Italy, Corte di Cassazione, 1978) reproduced in (1978–79) 4 IYBIL 137; *Marcos and Marcos v Federal Department of Police* 102 ILR 198 (Switzerland, Federal Tribunal, 1989) 202; *R v Bow Street Metropolitan Stipendiary Magistrate and others, ex p Pinochet Ugarte (Amnesty International and others intervening)* (UK, 1999) (*Pinochet* no 3); Institut de Droit International, Resolution on the Immunities from Jurisdiction and Execution of Heads of State and of Government in International Law (Résolution sur les immunités de juridiction et d'exécution du chef d'Etat et de gouvernement en droit international), (2001), (2000–01) 69 AIDI 743. Cf for early doctrine and state practice eg D Anzilotti, (1910) 519; L Oppenheim, *International Law, A Treatise* (2nd edn, 1912) 590; L Van Praag (1915) 447.

[49] Cf ch 5 § 2.3.2.1 below.

[50] Cf eg C Calvo, *Le droit international théorique et pratique* (5th edn, 1896) iii 287ff, § 1461ff.

is entrusted to govern.'[51] Other early state immunity cases also alluded to this distinction. In chapter 2 of this study we saw that claims against the state were often instigated against the personal foreign sovereign in his public capacity. The fact that the courts in *Duke of Brunswick v King of Hanover* and *De Haber v Queen of Portugal* thought it important to emphasize that the foreign sovereign was not sued in a private capacity allows the tentative conclusion that *were this otherwise* no immunity would be available.[52] French courts equally emphasized the public capacity of the head of state, or the public authority exercised by him when granting immunity to foreign heads of state before them. In the 1870 case of *Ministère Public v Dlle Masset*, a French national with a commercial enterprise in Russia, sued the Russian Tsar for damages suffered from alleged illegal seizures, arrests, and vexation committed by the Russian police on Russian territory. Unsurprisingly the court refused to engage in the claim brought before it, reasoning as follows:

> Considérant que l'indépendance réciproque des Etats est consacrée par le droit des gens; que chaque Etat est souverain sur son territoire, y exerce la justice qui est un attribut de la souveraineté et délègue à des tribunaux cette justice, investie des droits de juridiction et de commandement nécessaires pour rendre et faire exécuter ses décisions; Qu'il suit de ces principes qu'on ne peut citer devant les tribunaux d'un pays le souverain d'un autre pays, non plus que les agents de la puissance publique qu'il représente; Que prétendre les soumettre à la justice, c'est-à-dire au droit de juridiction et de commandement du juge d'un pays étranger, ce serait évidemment violer une souveraineté étrangère et blesser en cette partie le droit des gens.[53]

The operation of a state's justice system within its own territory was considered an attribute of state sovereignty and no foreign state nor the agents that represent that state could be sued before the French courts in respect to it. Two years later the same court heard a case against the emperor of Austria, as heir of the emperor of Mexico Maximilien, involving a contract concluded by the latter for the commission of decorations destined to honour persons for their merit to the public services. The court again refused to exercise jurisdiction considering

> qu'il est de principe, à raison de l'indépendance réciproque des Etats, que les tribunaux français n'ont pas juridiction pour juger les engagements contractés par les souverains étrangers *agissant comme chefs d'Etat au titre de la puissance publique.*[54]

[51] *The Schooner Exchange v M'Faddon* (US, 1812) 144–5. It is noted that counsel for France did concede this point, cf 123.

[52] Cf ch 2 p 25 above.

[53] *Ministère Public v Dlle Masset* A-C Kiss, *Répertoire de la pratique française en matière de droit international public* (1965) iii 269 (France, Cour de Paris, 1870).

[54] *L'Empereur d'Autriche v Lemaitre* (France, 1872); A-C Kiss, *Répertoire de la pratique française en matière de droit international public* (1965) iii 269, no 456, 270 (emphasis added). Cf also *Petau v Honore de Grimaldi, Prince de Monaco* (France, 1810).

The 1916 case of *Wiercinski v Seyyid Ali Ben Hamond* did in fact make clear that foreign heads of state were not entitled to additional immunity *ratione personae* from civil proceedings before French courts.[55] The former Sultan of Zanzibar had failed to satisfy the bills of a masseur. When civil proceedings were instigated against him, he argued that as a former sovereign he enjoyed the same immunity as a reigning sovereign and that the French courts should therefore refuse to exercise jurisdiction over the claim. The court rejected the analogy argument but critically added

que même cette justification fût-elle produite, ce moyen ne saurait être accueilli; qu'en effet si le principe de l'indépendance réciproque des Etats exclut la juridiction des Tribunaux français à l'égard des souverains étrangers... cette exception doit être restreinte au cas où le souverain est assigné à raison d'engagements contractés *en qualité de chef du gouvernement*, les motifs qui la justifient n'existant pas au dehors de ce cas, mais elle ne peut être étendue à ceux où le souverain a agi ainsi que dans l'espèce *comme personne privée et dans un intérêt personnel*...[56]

The services rendered to the Sultan were hence qualified as belonging to the private rather than the public sphere and immunity was held to be absent even if he would be able to rely on the same measure of protection after as before his abdication. The same flows from the following considerations of the Court of Algiers in *Ben Aïad v Bey de Tunis*

suivant un principe de droit international universellement admis, les souverains et chefs d'Etat participent de l'indépendance de l'Etat dont ils sont les représentants; Att. que placés en quelque sorte au-dessus des lois de tout Etat étranger, ils ne peuvent être soumis à aucune juridiction autre que celle de leur propre nation; Att. que cette règle ne souffre *d'exception que lorsque*: 1 *seuls les intérêts privés sont en litige* ; 2 lorsque le chef d'Etat a lui-même renoncé à se prévaloir des prérogatives de sa souveraineté.[57]

In a similar vein, the Italian *Corte di Cassazione* refused to grant immunity to the Emperor of Austria.[58] The court held that the claim before it did not relate to acts done by the Emperor as head of state but rather to acts of a private nature that arose in Italy.

The cited cases only support immunity from civil jurisdiction to foreign heads of state when they have acted in their official capacity as head of state. This immunity however does not follow from *ratione personae* considerations but

[55] *Wiercinski v Seyyid Ali Ben Hamond* (1917) 44 JDI 1465 (France, Tribunal civil de la Seine, 1916); A-C Kiss, *Répertoire de la pratique française en matière de droit international public* (1965) iii 270, no 457.

[56] ibid 1465–6.

[57] *Ben Aïad v Bey de Tunis* (1914) JDI 1290 (France, Cour d'Alger, 1914) 1291; A-C Kiss, *Répertoire de la pratique française en matière de droit international public* (1965) iii 271, no 460. Cf also *Bey de Tunis v Mahmoud ben Aïad*: A-C Kiss, *Répertoire de la pratique française en matière de droit international public* (1965) iii 272, no 461 (France, Cour d'appel de Paris, 1893).

[58] *Carlo d'Austria Este v Nobili* (Italy, 1921).

concerns functional immunity *ratione materiae* and the consequent application of the law of state immunity as discussed in chapter 3 of this study.

It was in the common law countries that the idea of immunity *ratione personae* from civil proceedings was first developed. This immunity was seen to protect a foreign head of state regardless of the private nature of the acts involved, the private purpose of his travels abroad and even when travelling incognito. Thus, when in 1894 the Sultan of Johore—who was temporarily living in the UK under the name of Albert Baker—was sued for breaking of his engagement to Ms Mighell, he was granted immunity from the civil jurisdiction of the UK courts upon revealing his true identity.[59]

Today, the 1978 UK SIA provides a wide immunity from civil jurisdiction to foreign heads of state. Section 20.1 provides that:

> subject to the provisions of this section and to any necessary modifications, the Diplomatic Privileges Act 1964 shall apply to
>
> a. a sovereign or other Head of State;
> b. members of his family forming part of his household; and
> c. his private servants,
>
> as it applies to the head of a diplomatic mission, to members of his family forming part of his household and to his private servants.

The Diplomatic Privileges Act gives effect to the 1961 Vienna Convention on Diplomatic Relations and section 20 hence declares the rules on diplomatic immunity equally applicable to foreign heads of state.[60] Accordingly, the very limited exceptions of article 31 of the VCDR apply. While the analogical application of article 31.1.c VCDR allows foreign heads of state to be sued in relation to professional or commercial activity not related to their official functions and exercised in the UK, this exception does not regard day-to-day commercial transactions but continuous commercial or professional activity. A foreign head of state refusing to pay for services rendered to him in his personal capacity, like the famous example of the massages of the Sultan of Zanzibar, would be immune from the jurisdiction of the UK courts.

It should further be pointed out that section 20 applies regardless of the official or private nature of the visit of the head of state, or in fact regardless of presence within UK territory whatsoever. While section 20.1 of the UK SIA originally provided for the application of the Diplomatic Privileges Act 1964 to a sovereign or other head of state *who is in the United Kingdom at the invitation or with the consent of the government of the United Kingdom*, it was later amended to cover all

[59] *Mighell v Sultan of Johore* (UK, 1893). See also *Statham v Statham and the Gaekwar of Baroda* [1912] P 92 (UK, Probate, Divorce and Admiralty Provision, 1911); *Sayce v Ameer Ruler of Bahawalpur State* [1952] 2 QB 390 (UK, CA, 1952).

[60] Cf also *BCCI v Price/Waterhouse (A Firm) and Others* 111 ILR 604 (UK, High Court, Chancery Division, 1996).

foreign heads of state whether in the UK or not and whether on official business or not.[61]

Section 36 of the 1985 Australian Foreign States Immunities Act is modelled on section 20.1 SIA, while the legislation of South Africa,[62] India,[63] and Malaysia[64] does not even allow for the exceptions applicable to diplomatic immunity.

In the United States the issue of civil suit against foreign heads of state has generated a considerable body of judicial decisions, which in turn has provoked a lively scholarly debate. US scholars have commented that head of state immunity is 'at best [an] amorphous legal doctrine whose very existence is not entirely settled in U.S. law and whose reach is almost completely uncertain'.[65] Since the rule has not been codified in the 1976 FSIA the pre-FSIA practice of conclusive executive suggestions of immunity subsists.[66] The State Department proceeds from the principle that all persons it recognizes as the legitimate head of a foreign state enjoy absolute immunity from the civil jurisdiction of US courts.[67] In 1965 the head of state of Saudi Arabia, King Faisal Bin Abdull Aziz Al-Saud was named as defendant in a civil suit before US courts. The State Department made its position clear in a letter to the Attorney-General:

> King Faisal Bin Abdull Aziz Al-Saud is the Head of State of the Kingdom of Saudi Arabia and as Head of State is not subject to the jurisdiction of any foreign Court without his consent. In these circumstances, the Department of State recognizes and allows the immunity of King Faisal from suit in the above named cases and requests that the appropriate United States Attorney be instructed to appear and file with the Court a supplemental suggestion of immunity to that effect.[68]

[61] Cf *Pinochet* no 3, 113 (*per* Lord Browne-Wilkinson).

[62] s 4.1 of the 2001 Diplomatic Immunities and Privileges Act 37.

[63] s 86 of the Code of Civil Procedure provides that '[n]o Ruler of a foreign state may be sued in any court otherwise competent to try the suit except without the consent of the Central Government certified in writing by a Secretary to that Government.' s 87a.1.b defines 'ruler' as 'the person who is for the time being recognized by the Central Government to be the head of that State'.

[64] Art 181.2 of the Constitution. Cf also *Village Holdings Sdn Bhd v Her Majesty the Queen in Right of Canada* 87 ILR 223 (Malaysia, High Court, 1987).

[65] K Highet et al, 'Lafontant *v* Aristide' (1994) 88 AJIL 528, 531. See for similar observations S Varughese George, 'Head of State Immunity in the United States Courts: Still Confused After All These Years' (1995) 64 Fordham Law Review 1051; JL Mallory, 'Resolving the Confusion over Head of State Immunity: The Defined Rights of Kings' (1986) 86 CLR 169; PE Bass, 'Ex-Head of State Immunity: A Proposed Tool of Foreign Policy' (1987) 97 YLJ 299. Cf also *Doe v United States* 860 F 2d 40 (US, Ct of Apps (2nd Cir), 1988) 44, where the court considered that '[t]he scope of this immunity is in an amorphous and undeveloped state.'

[66] One of the drafters of the FSIA commented in this regard: 'Frankly, we forgot about it, or didn't know enough about it at the time, during those two or three critical years when the statute was being formulated.' Remarks Mark Feldman, 'Foreign Governments in United States Courts' (1991) 85 ASIL Proceedings 251, 276. Cf in particular *Lafontant v Aristide* 844 F Supp 128 (US, DC for the Eastern District of New York, 1994); and *Tachiona v Mugabe* 169 F Supp 2d 259 (US, DC for the Southern District of New York, 2001).

[67] We will see in § 2.2.2.1 below that the US head of state immunity doctrine extends to *former* heads of state.

[68] Letter dated 14 September 1965, partly reproduced in (1966) 60 AJIL 100, 101.

In comparable terms the State Department argued in favour of the grant of immunity to Jean-Bertrand Aristide.[69] A claim had been instigated against Aristide for extrajudicial killing by the widow of Lafontant, a well-known Haitian politician, who had been arrested and jailed after a thwarted coup d'état to prevent the president-elect Aristide from taking office. It was alleged that, a few months later, Aristide ordered a member of the armed forces of Haiti to execute Lafontant. Although two days after the execution took place Aristide was exiled from Haiti following a successful military coup, the United States continued to recognize him as the lawful head of state of Haiti and never recognized the military regime installed in Haiti. The US Justice Department stated in a suggestion of immunity letter that

> [t]he United States has an interest and concern in this action against President Aristide insofar as the action involves the question of immunity from the Court's jurisdiction of the head-of-state of a friendly foreign state. The United States' interest arises from a determination by the Executive Branch of the Government of the United States, in the implementation of its foreign policy and in the conduct of its international relations, that permitting this action to proceed against President Aristide would be incompatible with the United States' foreign policy interests.[70]

Courts, as a rule, accept the suggestions of immunity the State Department issues to this effect.[71] In this respect, the US approach to the doctrine of head of state immunity is in fact fairly consistent. Theory, however, is muddled by several judicial considerations on the scope of the doctrine in legal terms. In the first place, courts have considered the doctrine of head of state immunity applicable in cases involving *former* foreign heads of state.[72] Secondly, courts have intimated that an independent judicial application of the rule of the head of state immunity might proceed from a less absolute concept of immunity from

[69] *Lafontant v Aristide* (US, 1994).

[70] ibid 131.

[71] Cf in addition to the cases against Faisal Bin Abdull Aziz Al-Saud and Aristide, *Psinakis and Others v Marcos and Others* 81 ILR 605 (US, DC for the Northern District of California, 1975), 1975 Digest of United States Practice in International Law 344; *Estate of Silme G Domingo v Ferdinand Marcos*, no C82–1055v (US, DC for the Western District of Washington, 1982), in (1983) 77 AJIL 305; *Saltany v Reagan* 702 F Supp 319, 886 F 2d 438 (US, DC for the District of Columbia and Ct of Apps District of Columbia Circuit, 1988, 1989), 87 ILR 680; *Gerritsen v de la Madrid* (US, 1986); *Anonymous v Anonymous* NYS 2d 776 (US, New York State Ct of Apps, 1992); *Alicog v Kingdom of Saudi Arabia* (US, 1994); *Guardian F. v Archdiocese of San Antonio*, case no 93–CI–11345 (US, DC for the District of Texas, 1994); *First American Corp v Sheikh Zayed Bin Sultan Al-Nahyan* 948 F Supp 1107 (US, DC for the District of Columbia, 1996); *Tachiona v Mugabe* (US, 2001); *Abiola v Abubakar* 267 F Supp 2d 907 (US, DC for the Northern District of Illinois, 2003); *Wei Ye v Jiang Zemin*, no 03–3989 F 38 2004 WL 1984430 (US, Ct of Apps (7th Cir), 2004). Cf for cases in which no suggestion was issued *Doe v Karadžić* 866 F Supp 734 (US, DC for the Southern District of New York, 1994); *United States v Noriega* (US, 1997); *Flatow v Islamic Republic of Iran* 999 F Supp 1 (US, DC for the District of Columbia, 1998).

[72] Cf § 2.2.2.1 below.

civil jurisdiction. While in *Alicog v Kingdom of Saudi Arabia* the suggestion of immunity was considered to be granted '[*u*]*nder a doctrine of customary international law*', other courts have qualified the doctrine 'a matter of grace and comity, rather than a matter of right'.[73] In *In re Grand Jury Proceedings, John Doe No 700* one court considered that 'heads of state are immune at least as to authorized official acts taken while the ruler is in power'.[74] In the 1988 case of *Doe v United States* the court considered that 'there is respectable authority for denying head-of-state immunity to a former head-of-state for private or criminal acts in violation of American law'[75] while in the 1990 decision of *United States v Noriega* the court stated that 'there is ample doubt whether head of state immunity extends to private or criminal acts in violation of US law'.[76] These decisions suggest that *were* the practice of executive suggestions of immunity relinquished the judiciary might prefer a more restrictive approach to the doctrine.

The current practice of the issuance of suggestions of immunity in any suit against a head of a friendly foreign state has stirred academic debate. It is commonly argued that the practice raises the same due process questions as the pre-FSIA state immunity practice and that there is no reason why courts should not make independent head of state immunity decisions on the basis of a judicial standard. As one scholar put it, 'justifications are based on the same exaggerated concerns about pre-FSIA sovereign immunity'.[77] The closing of the Bank for Credit and Commerce International (BCCI) due to fraud in 1992 impelled a wave of support for a more restrictive approach to head of state immunity. The closure had a considerable impact on many US citizens who lost their jobs or their savings in the process. The trustees of a US bank owned by BCCI brought a civil suit before the US courts against, *inter alia*, Sheikh Zayed bin Sultan Al-Nahyan, the head of state of Abu Dhabi, who owned 77 per cent of the BCCI. Sheikh Zayed moved for dismissal of the case on the basis of head of state immunity. With the very real prospect of a suggestion of immunity being issued by the State Department, the concerned chairman of the House Banking Committee called for a hearing on the matter.[78] In memoranda submitted to the Committee Dellapenna and Lowenfeld argued in favour of a more restrictive approach to the head of state immunity doctrine. When after an initial settlement the case did proceed, the State Department did indeed file a suggestion of immunity on

[73] *Flatow v Islamic Republic of Iran* (US, 1998); *Lafontant v Aristide* (US, 1994) 132.

[74] *In re Grand Jury Proceedings, John Doe No 700* (US, 1987) 1110.

[75] *Doe v United States* (US, 1988) 45.

[76] *United States v Noriega* (US, 1990) 1519; and the reference to that quotation in *United States v Noriega* (US, 1997).

[77] S Varughese George (1995) 1067.

[78] Hearing before the Committee on Banking Finance and Urban Affairs on 'Head of State Immunity', House of Representatives, 103rd Congress, 9 December 1993: Serial No 103–104.

behalf of Sheikh Zayed Bin-Sultan Al Nahyan as the head of state of Abu-Dhabi, which the court accepted as conclusive and barred the claim of the trustees.[79]

Some critics have proposed to include the doctrine of head of state immunity in the FSIA. In this respect, the suggestion of immunity practice has been contrasted with the approach of the court in *Hilao v Marcos*.[80] The State Department did not intervene on behalf of Marcos when a claim was instigated against the former president of the Philippines by victims of alleged human rights abuses. The court had recourse to the FSIA in order to decide Marcos' claim to immunity. Comparing the approach of the court in *Hilao v Marcos* with that in *Lafontant v Aristide* scholars argued that the doctrine of head of state immunity was unsettled.[81] The *Hilao v Marcos* case was seen as judicial support for the application of the FSIA to heads of state and several scholars proposed to amend the FSIA to that affect, abolishing the practice of executive interference.[82]

This line of reasoning is however flawed. *Hilao v Marcos* did not concern head of state immunity. Rather it applied to the former president of the Philippines the functional immunity standard applicable to all former state officials alike. This is not a coherent alternative for the currently prevalent suggestion of immunity practice. The proposal to incorporate head of state immunity under the FSIA in fact boils down to a proposal to abolish head of state immunity altogether. Such proposal should at least acknowledge the uncontroversial international law rules on the position of foreign heads of state on official visits.

In civil law jurisdictions the scope of head of state immunity from civil jurisdiction is equally unsettled. Practice is scarce and definite conclusions inevitably rickety. The Austrian Supreme Court in the 1964 *Prince of X Road Accident* case held that the *acta jure imperii–acta jure gestionis* distinction did not apply to cases involving foreign heads of state. The court refused to engage the claim of an Austrian national against a foreign head of state held responsible for a road accident in Austria.[83]

In 1988 a Belgian court considered that President Mobutu of Zaire could rely on the rule of head of state immunity in a suit instigated by a company whose expropriated property was now private property of Mobutu.[84]

In spite of the earlier mentioned 1916 case of *Wiercinski v Seyyid Ali Ben Hammond*, the 1957 case *Ex-Roi d'Egypte Farouk v SARL Christian Dior* and the 1963 case *Jean Dessès v Prince Farouk et Dame Sadek* implied that French courts

[79] *First American Corp et al v Sheikh Zayed Bin Sultan Al-Nahyan et al* (US, 1996) 1119.

[80] *Hilao v Marcos (In re Estate of Ferdinand Marcos Human Rights Litigation)* 25 F 3d 1467 (US, Ct of Apps (9th Cir), 1994). See ch 5 § 2.3.1.3 for a more detailed discussion of this case.

[81] S Varughese George (1995) 1052 speaks of 'divergent approaches to head-of-state immunity claims.

[82] Cf JL Mallory (1986) 193; K Highet et al (1994) 532.

[83] *Prince of X Road Accident Case* 65 ILR 13 (Austria, S Ct, 1964). It is by now common knowledge that the case involved the Prince of Liechtenstein, cf J Salmon (1994) 598.

[84] *Mobotu v SA Cotoni* 91 ILR 259 (Belgium, Civil Court of Brussels, 1988). The case was however decided on other grounds.

acknowledged an absolute immunity from civil suit for heads of state in office.[85] The respective cases followed disputes involving purely private commercial acts of sitting foreign heads of state coming to the courts *after* abdication. Both courts denied the claim to head of state immunity but could be seen to intimate that immunity *would* have been available if the person concerned had still been in office. The more recent decision of the Court of Appeal of Paris in *Mobutu and Republic of Zaire v Société Logrine* did however restore the *Wiercinski* case principle. A French company that got an order to supply tents for the celebration of the sixtieth birthday of President Mobutu of Zaire brought a claim against Mobutu when payment was not made for the services supplied. Mobutu claimed that 'he should benefit from jurisdictional immunity since the order in dispute relates to the organization of a public celebration which is a matter of national sovereignty involving the exercise of sovereign powers'.[86] The court, emphasizing the private capacity in which the contract was concluded and the private character of the celebration concerned, resolutely rejected the claim to head of state immunity.

The guidance provided by treaty law on the issue is limited and generally unhelpful. Article 21.1 of the 1969 Special Missions Convention provides that a head of state who leads a special mission enjoys the facilities, privileges and immunities accorded by international law to heads of state on an official visit. The ILC Draft Articles on Jurisdictional Immunities evade the issue in a similar vein. Initially a provision on the scope of the personal immunity of heads of state was in fact included in proposals for the Draft. It was proposed that the exceptions applicable to diplomatic immunity from civil jurisdiction would be equally applicable to foreign heads of state. When it proved impossible however to reach consensus the thorny issue was removed from the Draft altogether. Article 3.2 of the 2004 Convention on Jurisdictional Immunities of States and their Property reflects the final Draft of the ILC and provides that '[t]he present Convention is without prejudice to privileges and immunities accorded under international law to heads of State *ratione personae*.'[87] In other words, 'existing customary is left untouched'.[88] The conclusion that head of state immunity *ratione personae*—which *is* head of state immunity—is not affected by the rules on state immunity *ratione materiae* leaves us empty-handed.

[85] *Ex-Roi d'Egypte Farouk v SARL Christian Dior* (1957) 84 JDI 716 (France, Cour d'Appel de Paris, 1957), A-C Kiss, *Répertoire de la pratique française en matière de droit international public* (1965) iii 271, no 459; *Jean Dessès v Prince Farouk et Dame Sadek* (1964) 91 JDI 285 (France, Tribunal de la Seine, 1963), 65 ILR 37. Cf JL Mallory (1986) 177.

[86] A claim supported by the Republic of Zaire: *Mobutu and Republic of Zaire v Société Logrine* 113 ILR 481 (France, CA of Paris, 1994).

[87] UN Convention on Jurisdictional Immunities of States and their Property, adopted by GA Resolution 59/38 (2004).

[88] ILC, Report of the Commission to the General Assembly on the work of its forty-third session, YBILC 1991 ii (part two) 12, 22.

Doctrine is equally divided. Cahier would recognize an absolute immunity for heads of state from civil jurisdiction *only* when present on the territory of the forum state.[89] In *Satow's Guide to Diplomatic Practice* it is considered that although the civil immunity of heads of state is probably absolute 'certain exceptions to full immunities may be said to be inherently justifiable, even if it cannot be said that they are fully supported by extensive practice... If the foreign sovereign engages in a trading venture or in speculative investment, it may be justifiable to subject him to civil suit or to deny him tax exemption on his profits.'[90] Salmon argued that the immunity only applies to heads of state present within the territory of the forum state. In addition, he underlined the controversy on the immunity from civil jurisdiction of heads of state on an official visit. Possibly, such immunity is subject to the three exceptions applicable to diplomatic immunity from civil jurisdiction.[91] Watts argued otherwise. While he considered that the exceptions are most likely applicable to a head of state abroad on a private visit, he insisted that a head of state enjoys absolute immunity from the civil jurisdiction of a state he visits on an official visit.[92]

Finally, the Resolution on *Immunities from Jurisdiction and Execution of Heads of State and of Government in International Law* adopted by the Institut de Droit International in 2001, adopts a restrictive approach. Article 3 provides that '[i]n civil and administrative matters, the Head of State does not enjoy any immunity from jurisdiction before the courts of a foreign State, unless that suit relates to acts performed in the exercise of his or her official functions... Nonetheless, nothing shall be done by way of court proceedings with regard to the Head of State while he or she is in the territory of that State, in the exercise of official functions.'[93]

The uncertain scope of head of state immunity from civil jurisdiction reflects the uncertain rationale of the rule. While it is often argued that the immunity protects the exercise of the functions of heads of state just like diplomatic immunity protects the exercise of diplomatic functions,[94] the scope of the rule exceeds in fact the wants of such functionality rationale. It is not the difference in scope between diplomatic immunity and head of state immunity *as such* that impels this conclusion. The *functions* of a head of state are clearly different from the *functions* of diplomatic agents. Heads of state may act on behalf of the state in all international intercourse—*jus repraesentationis omnimodae*.[95] The Legal Bureau of the Canadian Ministry of Foreign Affairs pointed out in a

[89] P Cahier (1962) 340ff. Cf also D Anzilotti (1910) 519; L Van Praag (1915) 446.

[90] Gore-Booth (ed) (1979) 19.

[91] J Salmon (1994) 595ff.

[92] A Watts (1994) 65.

[93] Institut de Droit International, Resolution on the Immunities from Jurisdiction and Execution of Heads of State and of Government in International Law (Résolution sur les immunités de juridiction et d'exécution du chef d'Etat et de gouvernement en droit international), (2001), (2000–01) 69 AIDI 743.

[94] Cf eg *Psinakis and Others v Marcos and Others* (US, 1975) fn 1.

[95] Cf A Watts (1994) 26.

memorandum that 'it might...be said that even greater respect is owed to the dignity of the visiting sovereign or Head of State, since his own diplomatic envoys in the host state are clearly inferior to him. Applying these principles to the visit of a Head of State, it is clear that the Government of Canada must, in accordance with international law and practice, afford to the Head of State and to his family and suite *at least* the privileges, immunity and inviolability provided for in the Vienna Convention on Diplomatic Relations.'[96] As Watts aptly put it, the head of state is 'the representative *par excellence* of his State' and is therefore in many respects 'an *a fortiori* case'.[97] In addition to this formal difference in status, the exposure of a head of state to media attention and the related risk of frivolous claims may justify a more extensive protection of the head of state compared to the state's diplomatic agents.

To ensure the undisturbed exercise of his functions, a head of state would however *only* need protection when abroad on an *official* visit. Verhoeven pointed out that in contrast to a diplomatic agent the 'droit de représentation [d'un chef d'Etat] n'est pas limité par une accréditation particulière et est opposable *erga omnes*, ce qui explique qu'il ait droit dans tout Etat étranger à un traitement privilégié'.[98] This is true. But it does *not* explain the protection of foreign heads of state on holidays abroad. The *ne impediatur legatio* rationale does not guarantee the actual undisturbed exercise of the diplomatic function by any specific diplomatic agent but rather ensures—on a more abstract level—that the diplomatic function can *in theory* be exercised without disturbance. A diplomatic agent therefore only enjoys immunity from the jurisdiction of the state in which he exercises his official functions. A diplomat of state A, accredited to state B, who is caught committing a crime while on holiday in state C can be arrested and brought to trial before the courts of state C without diplomatic immunity being an issue. There is no reason whatsoever to shield the diplomatic agent from the jurisdiction of third states in whose territory he stays for purely private purposes.

In contrast, the immunity *ratione personae* of foreign heads of state is not similarly abstracted from the person of the office holder. On the contrary. We saw above that the principle of inviolability and head of state immunity from criminal jurisdiction apply regardless of the official or private purpose of a visit, and even regardless of entry of foreign territory altogether. Since it can never be necessary for the exercise of the functions of a head of state to travel abroad for private purposes, the rationale of immunity granted to a head of state must lie elsewhere.

[96] Memorandum of 31 January 1981, reproduced in (1981) 10 Canadian Yearbook of International Law 324, 325.

[97] A Watts (1994) 40. Cf also M Miele (2002) 231. *Estate of Silme G Domingo v Ferdinand Marcos* (US, 1982).

[98] J Verhoeven (Rapporteur Institut de Droit International), Les immunités de juridiction et d'exécution du chef d'Etat et de gouvernement en droit international, Rapport provisoire (2000), (2000–01) 69 AIDI 482, 511.

The functionality rationale protects the exercise of the function in general, *not* the exercise of the function by an individual in particular.

The finding of the rapporteur of the Institut de Droit International that the 'considérations de "souveraineté" ont clairement cédé aujourd'hui le pas à des besoins strictement fonctionnels: comme pour les agents diplomatiques, c'est le souci de permettre au chef d'État d'exercer en toute indépendance ses fonctions qui explique fondamentalement le traitement privilégié qui lui est accordé par le droit international' is hence not shared by this author.[99] It is a great pity that this flawed conception—protection of the person rather than the office—is equally at the basis of the decision of the ICJ in the *Arrest Warrant* case. The facts of this case are related in section 2.2.2.3 below. For now it suffices to quote the Court on its interpretation of the functionality rationale. The Court stated, in relevant part:

> if a Minister for Foreign Affairs is arrested in another State on a criminal charge, he or she is clearly thereby prevented from exercising the functions of his or her office. The consequences of such impediment to the exercise of those official functions are equally serious, regardless whether the Minister for Foreign Affairs was, at the time of arrest, present in the territory of the arresting State on an 'official' visit or a 'private' visit ...[100]

In this vein, the Court should find the arrest of an ambassador while on a holiday outside either sending or receiving state equally unacceptable.

On closer consideration it cannot but be concluded that the head of state immunity rule reflects remnants of the majestic dignity that once attached to kings and princes as well as remnants of the idea of the incarnation of the state in its ruler. Or, the rationale underlying the rule is an arguably somewhat archaic, but nonetheless very real relic of the personal sovereignty with which a head of state was once endowed.[101] Watts noted in this respect that

> the mystique of sovereignty, whether of States or their Heads, is much diminished. Nevertheless, the earlier close identity of the law governing the position of States with that of Heads of States, with both aspects being informed by notions of 'sovereignty', has left its mark on current legal ideas relating to the position of Heads of States... Heads of States *are* still in a special position as the supreme representatives of, and in some respects the personal manifestations of, their States.[102]

The Swiss case of *Marcos and Marcos v Federal Department of Police* acknowledged this rationale. The court considered that '[c]ustomary international law grants such privileges *ratione personae* to Heads of State as much to take account of their functions and *symbolic embodiment of sovereignty* as by reason of their *representative character* in inter-State relations.'[103] Also *Oppenheim's International Law* notes that the immunity of heads of state does in fact not assimilate diplomatic

[99] ibid 508.
[100] *Arrest Warrant* Case, 20, § 55.
[101] Cf M Miele (1961) 122.
[102] A Watts (1994) 36.
[103] *Marcos and Marcos v Federal Department of Police* 1 (Switzerland, 1989) (emphasis added).

immunity. Head of state immunity, it is argued, is not functional in character. Rather, the maxim *par in parem non habet imperium* must be seen to underlie the rule.[104] While this finding is not further explained, it seems clear that *Oppenheim* rationalizes the scope of the rule by reference to the idea of the manifestation of the state in the person of the head of state.

The controversy on the scope of head of state immunity from civil jurisdiction can be traced to a disagreement on the hold of this *personal manifestation of sovereignty* rationale, as we will call it. The functionality rationale can only bear the weight of a comprehensive immunity from civil jurisdiction during official visits. This is to say, acts of exercise of jurisdiction, dependant on the presence of an individual on the territory of the forum state, may not be performed when a foreign head of state visits the forum state on official business. A general immunity from civil jurisdiction for private acts *may* exist but it should be realized that it is a remnant of a somewhat archaic conception of sovereignty. While this archaic form of immunity is clearly accepted in the field of criminal jurisdiction, in the field of civil jurisdiction this is less clear. The stray from a strict functionality rationale meets more opposition in the field of civil law than in the field of criminal law because of the direct negative consequences for private individuals. Gabba wrote that '[l]a qualité de souverain n'est pas une fonction publique dont sont investis les fonctionnaires publics. C'est une qualité inhérente à la personne du chef de l'Etat, qui le pénètre complètement, de sorte que le prince est sacré et inviolable dans toutes les manifestations de son activité.'[105] In a pungent reaction, Weiss rhetorically questioned whether 'n'y a-t-il pas un véritable anachronisme à soutenir, en plein XXe siècle, que la dignité conférée au souverain le place en dehors de l'humanité, ou tout au moins que sa personnalité s'absorbe et se confond dans l'Etat, dont les destinées reposent entre ses mains?'[106] Immunity for private acts, Weiss argued, 'est *en droit* impossible à justifier, et dans tous les cas elle constituerait un très grave danger.'[107]

The personal immunity of a foreign head of state may of course be waived. Like diplomatic immunity, head of state immunity appertains to the state and not to the head of state personally.[108] It has been suggested that since the head of state is the ultimate authority within the state he, unlike the diplomatic agent or any other state official, may be thought to have the capacity to waive his own immunity.[109] It is, however, arguable that the decision to waive immunity should in principle be taken by the government as a whole, even though the head of

[104] R Jennings and A Watts (eds) (1992) i 1091, § 499.

[105] CF Gabba (1890) 36.

[106] A Weiss (1923) 528.

[107] ibid 530.

[108] There are no examples of cases where a foreign state has actually waived the immunity of its head of state. Cf the following cases dealing with the waiver immunity of a former head of state, *In re Grand Jury Proceedings, John Doe No 700* (US, 1987) 1111; *Doe v United States* (US, 1988) 45; *Paul v Avril* (US, 1993) 211.

[109] P Cahier (1962) 342; A Watts (1994) 67.

state may be competent to communicate this decision. Particularly, the head of state should not be considered able to waive the immunity against the wish of the government of the state he represents.[110] Waiver is only effective moreover when exercised by the government recognized by the executive as the legitimate government of the state concerned. Thus, the waiver of the immunity of Aristide by the government in power in Haiti was not recognized by the US court that was seized of the dispute between Aristide and the widow of a political opponent arguably executed on his orders.[111]

2.2.2 Formal Scope of the Immunity

2.2.2.1 Heads of state in office

Each state determines for itself *who* is to fulfil the office of head of state and *what* are the exact powers attached to it. Both the nature of the office—elective or hereditary—and the scope of the functions differs vastly from state to state. The office entails largely symbolic functions when in the hands of European royalty or the German or Italian president; while in France or the US it entails real substantive power. For the purposes of head of state immunity these differences are irrelevant. Heads of state should all be treated alike.[112] The rule does however not apply to heads of entities that do not qualify as sovereign state.[113] Moreover, it may happen that a state does not recognize as head of state the person that *de facto* holds the office in a foreign state—we saw above that the US government refused to recognize the military regime installed in Haiti after the overthrow of President Aristide as the government of Haiti and continued to recognize Aristide as the lawful head of state instead. Even though states have in general abandoned the practice of recognition of foreign governments, *non-recognition* of a particular regime, for example after a violent coup against the democratically-elected government, is still feasible. It should finally be noted that courts—especially in

[110] Cf in this sense, J Verhoeven (Rapporteur Institut de Droit International), Les immunités de juridiction et d'exécution du chef d'Etat et de gouvernement en droit international, Rapport provisoire (2000), (2000–01) 69 AIDI 482, 533–4.

[111] *Lafontant v Aristide* (US, 1994) discussed above.

[112] Cf A Watts (1994) 26; M Miele (1961) 121. *Mirza Ali Akbar Kashani v United Arab Republic* (India, 1965) 500–01. At the end of the nineteenth century there were still writers that argued for a distinction between monarchs and presidents, see for an overview D Anzilotti (1910) 521 fn 3. In the 1992 edition of *Oppenheim's International Law,* Jennings and Watts still express support for such distinction. In § 454 (1042) we read that as far as immunity from jurisdiction on private visits is concerned there may be grounds for distinguishing presidents from monarchs because presidents lack the personal quality of sovereignty.

[113] Cf eg *Colonel HH Raja Sir Harinder Singh Barar Bans Bahadur v Commisioner of Income Tax, Punjab* 64 ILR 523 (India, S Ct, 1971) 528 (Indian princely states were considered not to possess international personality and their rulers were hence not entitled to head of state immunity); *Ric Arafat e altro* F It 1986 II, 277 (Italy, Corte di Cassazione, 1985) (the PLO was not considered a sovereign state and Arafat hence not entitled to head of state immunity); *Bacchelli v Commune di Bologna* (Italy, 1978), 137 (Grand Master of the Order of Santa Maria did not qualify as head of state); *First American Corp. et al v Sheikh Zayed Bin Sultan Al-Nahyan et al* (US, 1996) 1121.

common law countries—often defer to the executive in the determination of the question whether a particular person qualifies as head of state.[114]

Head of state immunity only applies to heads of state in office. Upon abdication a former head of state can only rely on the rule of functional immunity as applicable to *all* (former) foreign state officials. They are no longer shielded from foreign jurisdiction by any personal immunity, unless of course they are sent on special diplomatic missions by their home state.[115] Verhoeven gave a confusing twist to this reality writing that '[u]ne doctrine relativement ancienne considérait que le chef d'Etat qui n'est plus en fonction perd tous les privilèges et immunités don't il jouissait lorsqu'il était en exercice... De nos jours, la doctrine dominante paraît néanmoins considérer que l'immunité de juridiction subsiste pour ce qui concerne les actes "publics"(—de la fonction).'[116] The consideration that heads of state lose all immunity when they leave office is obviously not incompatible with the operation of the rule of functional immunity. Comparing apples with pears, Verhoeven veils the essentially distinct nature of the two rules.

It should be noted here moreover that the Resolution adopted by the Institut de Droit International contains a puzzling definition of the scope of the rule of functional immunity. Functional immunity applies to acts that are in law the acts of the foreign state. 'Official acts' are acts performed in the exercise of one's functions. While the English translation of article 13.2 of the Resolution employs the classic formulation that no immunity is available 'except in respect of acts which are performed in the exercise of official functions and relate to the exercise thereof'; the original French text states that no immunity is available 'sauf lorsqu'il y est assigné ou poursuivi en raison d'actes qu'il a accomplis durant ses fonctions et qui participaient de leur exercise'. In comparison, the French version of article 39.2 of the Vienna Convention reads that 'l'immunité subsiste en ce qui concerne les actes accomplis par cette personne dans l'exercice de ses fonctions comme membre de la mission' and also article 3 of the Resolution itself employs the classic formulation 'sauf lorsqu'il est assigné en raison d'actes qu'il a accomplis dans l'exercice de ses fonctions officielles' setting out the scope of head of state

[114] Cf s 21.1 UK State Immunity Act (1978); s 17.c South African Foreign States Immunity Act (1981); s 40.1.c Australian Foreign Sovereign Immunities Act (1985); s 13.1.c Canadian State Immunity Act (1982); s 18.a Pakistan State Immunity Ordinance (1981); s 18.a Singaporean State Immunity Act 1979. S 87.a.1.b Indian Code of Civil procedure (1908) provides in less strict terms that 'every court shall take notion of the fact... that a person has or has not been recognized by the central government to be the head of the state'. Cf for a comprehensive discussion of this aspect of the formal scope of the rule of head of state immunity A Watts (1994) 21; J Verhoeven (Rapporteur Institut de Droit International), Les immunités de juridiction et d'exécution du chef d'Etat et de gouvernement en droit international, Rapport provisoire (2000), (2000–01) 69 AIDI 482, 497–503.

[115] It should be noted that courts may of course refuse to engage claims against former foreign heads of state on grounds independent of any rule of immunity. Cf eg *Consorts Duvalier et autres v État haïtien et autres* (France, 1990).

[116] J Verhoeven (Rapporteur Institut de Droit International), Les immunités de juridiction et d'exécution du chef d'Etat et de gouvernement en droit international, Rapport provisoire (2000), (2000–2001) 69 AIDI 482, 536.

immunity from civil jurisdiction. Arguably, the French text of article 13.2 includes more than mere official acts. The reports of the Rapporteur nor the records of the discussions between the members of the Institut preceding the adoption of the Resolution offer an explanation for the anomaly of article 13.2.

In the United States suits against former heads of state may be dismissed on the basis of the head of state immunity doctrine.[117] It should, however, be recalled that executive suggestions of immunity are binding on the US judiciary. Accordingly, this practice reflects US national rather than international law.

Former heads of states *may* enjoy extra protection as a matter of courtesy. In *Oppenheim's International Law* we read that '[n]othing, of course, prevents a state from granting to a foreign ex-Head of State the same privileges as it grants to a current Head of State, but international law does not exact any such courtesy.'[118] This position is shared by most scholars.[119] It has in this respect been pointed out that the grant of immunity from jurisdiction may in fact constitute an effective foreign policy tool.[120] Chapters 5 and 6 of this study will argue, however, that the extension of immunity beyond the requirements of international law may clash with contemporary obligations of states under international criminal law and international human rights law.

2.2.2.2 Family members

It is highly questionable whether the rule of head of state immunity extends its protection to the family members of a foreign head of state. In 1915 Van Praag noted that doctrine on this question was 'divisé'.[121] Verhoeven commented in 2000 that this was not much less so today.[122] State practice is scarce and far from univocal. A Belgian court considered in a 1988 case concerning a civil claim instigated against the Zairian president Mobutu, his wife and his children that in contrast to the head of state itself, his family members could not rely on a rule of immunity from jurisdiction.[123] The Swiss Federal Tribunal considered in the 1989 case of *Marcos and Marcos v Federal Department of Police* that

[117] Cf *Abiola v Abubakar* (US, 2003); *Wei Ye v Jiang Zemin* (US, 2004). Cf also JC Barker, 'The Future of Former Head of State Immunity After Ex Parte Pinochet' (1999) 941 for the suggestion that former heads of state continue to be protected by a degree of *personal* immunity from jurisdiction.

[118] R Jennings and A Watts (eds) (1992) i 1043–44, § 456, fn 3.

[119] Cf Gore-Booth (ed) (1979) 10; A Watts (1994) 90. The Act for the Protection of Foreign Officials and Official Guests of the United States 1972 includes in the definition of foreign officials benefiting from the act not only heads of state but also 'any person who has previously served in that capacity', (1973) AJIL 67 622.

[120] PE Bass (1987) 316ff.

[121] L Van Praag (1915) 451.

[122] J Verhoeven (Rapporteur Institut de Droit International), Les immunités de juridiction et d'exécution du chef d'État et de gouvernement en droit international, Rapport provisoire (2000), (2000–01) 69 AIDI 482, 530.

[123] *Mobutu v SA Cotoni* (Belgium, 1988).

> Customary international law has always granted to Heads of State, as well as to the members of their family and their household visiting a foreign State, the privileges of personal inviolability and immunity from criminal jurisdiction... This jurisdictional immunity is also granted to a Head of State in a private capacity and also extends, in such circumstances, to the closest accompanying family members as well as to the senior members of his household staff. Accordingly, such persons cannot be the subject of criminal proceedings or even of a summons to appear before a court...[124]

The consideration was however limited to criminal jurisdiction and did not consider the immunity of heads of state and their family members when *not* on the territory of the forum state.

The UK State Immunity Act provides a very extensive immunity to family members forming part of the household of a foreign head of state, as well as to private servants. Under section 20.1.b and c these individuals have a right to the same immunity as family members and servants of diplomatic agents on the Vienna Convention of Diplomatic Relations.[125] In contrast, the Australian Foreign States Immunities Act limits the application of the law of diplomatic immunity to the spouse of the head of state.[126]

It must be noted at the outset that since US practice relies on executive rather than judicial decision-making it is questionable whether it reflects legal standards. Arguably, comity and political expedience considerations control the executive actions in this area. The US State Department is likely to file a suggestion of immunity to shield a head of state's spouse from US jurisdiction. In the *Estate of Silme G Domingo v Ferdinand Marcos* and *Kline v Cordero de la Madrid* a suggestion of immunity was issued for the wife of the president of the Philippines and the wife of the president of Mexico respectively, barring the civil suits instigated against them while they were not present on the territory of the US.[127] It is not clear whether other family members would enjoy a similar protection.[128] The only example of a suggestion of immunity in regard to a family member of a head of state other than the spouse can be found in the case of *Kilroy v Windsor* that involved a claim against the Prince of Wales, heir to the British throne.[129] Although the letter from the State Department to the Attorney-General requesting that the Department of Justice file a suggestion of immunity stated that Prince

[124] *Marcos and Marcos v Federal Department of Police* (Switzerland, 1989) 201.

[125] Cf § 2.2.1 above.

[126] Australian Foreign States Immunities Act (1985) s. 36.2. The Australian Law Reform Commission had considered in Report 24, 103, § 163 that 'there seems to be no reason to extend similar immunities to members of the family (other, perhaps, than the spouse) or to the retinue of the head of state... as the United Kingdom act does.'

[127] *Estate of Silme G Domingo v Ferdinand Marcos* (US, 1982); *Kline v Cordero de la Madrid* (US, 1989). Cf also *Kline and others v Kaneko and others* (US, 1988) 392.

[128] It is noted that in *Junquist et al v Sheikh Sultan Bin Khalifa Al Nayhan et al* (US, 1996) the State Department had not issued a suggestion in respect of the grandson of the ruler of Abu Dhabi.

[129] *Kilroy v Windsor* 81 ILR 605 (US, DC for the Northern District of Ohio, 1978).

Charles was 'a member of the sovereign's immediate family and household', the principal argument in favour of such a suggestion seemed to be another. The State Department explained that it regarded the visit of the prince 'a special diplomatic missions' and that it considered him 'an official diplomatic envoy while present in the United States on that special missions.'

With the possible exception of the spouse of a head of state it is probably right to say that the enjoyment of privileges and immunities of family members of heads of state is a matter of international comity rather than of established international law.[130] As regards family members that are not present within the territory of the forum state or that are present on a private visit this conclusion is widely shared.[131] But even as regards family members that accompany a head of state on an official visit the analogy with family members of diplomatic agents accredited to a permanent mission is not convincing. Diplomatic agents reside within the territory of the foreign state in which they exercise their functions and are therefore *naturally* accompanied by family members on their mission. The protection of these family members may hence be considered necessary to secure the independent exercise of the diplomatic functions.[132] The same is not true for family members of heads of state. Family members that are invited to join the head of state on an official visit abroad would qualify as a member of a special mission and hence be protected by immunity in that capacity.

2.2.2.3 Heads of government and ministers of foreign affairs?

Article 15 of the *Resolution on Immunities from Jurisdiction and Execution of Heads of State and of Government in International Law* of the Institut de Droit International provides that

1. The Head of Government of a foreign State enjoys the same inviolability, and immunity from jurisdiction recognised, in this Resolution, to the Head of State...
2. Paragraph 1 is without prejudice to such immunities to which other members of the government may be entitled on account of their official functions.[133]

Verhoeven had argued in his *Rapport provisoire* that both the head of government and the minister of foreign affairs are protected by the immunity regime applicable to heads of state and earlier drafts of article 15 had extended head of

[130] Cf YBILC 1989 ii 102–3 (Commentary on art 4); and art 5 of the Resolution on Immunities from Jurisdiction and Execution of Heads of State and of Government in International Law of the Institut de Droit International ((2000–01) 69 AIDI 743) for the argument that even the spouse cannot rely on a right.

[131] Cf A Watts (1994) 80–1; R Jennings and A Watts (eds) (1992) i 1039–40, § 453.

[132] It is noted that art 1.1 of the 1973 Convention on the Prevention and Punishment of Crimes against Internationally Protected Persons, including Diplomatic Agents does include accompanying family members of a head of state in the definition of 'internationally protected person'.

[133] Institut de Droit International, Resolution on the Immunities from Jurisdiction and Execution of Heads of State and of Government in International Law (Résolution sur les immunités de juridiction et d'exécution du chef d'Etat et de gouvernement en droit international), (2001), (2000–01) 69 AIDI 743.

state immunity to heads of government and ministers of foreign affairs alike. The proposal for the Resolution was only revised after the deliberations of the Institut in Plenary Session.[134] The records of the deliberations do not reveal definite explanations for the revision. It seems likely that the Institut did not want to burn its fingers on the question as to the scope of the immunity applicable to ministers of foreign affairs that was the principal question in the *Congo v Belgium* litigation before the ICJ at the time the Resolution was adopted. However, in view of the *Rapport provisoire*, the non-inclusion of ministers of foreign affairs in the Resolution is not value-free. A solid *a contrario* argument may be based on the *change* of position of the Institut de Droit International. While the initial report of Verhoeven supported the position of The Congo in the proceedings before the ICJ, the changes laid down in the final resolution can be relied on in support of the position of Belgium.[135] It is therefore regrettable that the Institut did not disclose the debates that must have preceded the revision.

Half a year later the ICJ issued its decision in the *Arrest Warrant* case.[136] The Court ruled that the issuance of an international arrest warrant by a Belgian investigating judge against the incumbent minister of foreign affairs of the Democratic Republic of the Congo, with respect to war crimes and crimes against humanity allegedly committed within the territory of the Congo, had violated the immunity from criminal jurisdiction and the inviolability attached to the office of ministers of foreign affairs under international law. The Court did not define the immunity in terms of head of state immunity. The conclusion of the Court that ministers of foreign affairs enjoy an absolute immunity from foreign criminal jurisdiction regardless of the nature of the act or the nature of the visit abroad can however be seen to equate the position of ministers of foreign affairs with that of heads of state at least in respect of criminal proceedings.

Neither the reasoning underlying the Resolution of the Institut nor the reasoning employed by the ICJ in support of its conclusions is particularly convincing. The extension of head of state immunity to heads of government and ministers of foreign affairs is far from uncontroversial—to say the least. In his authoritative article Watts had argued that '[a]lthough it may well be that a Head of State, when on a private visit to another State, still enjoys certain privileges and immunities, it is much less likely that the same is true of heads of governments

[134] Cf art 15 of the *Projet de Résolution* (2001), Institut de Droit International (Rapporteur J Verhoeven), Les immunités de juridiction et d'exécution du chef d'Etat et de gouvernement en droit international, Plenary Session (2001), (2000–01) 69 AIDI 601, 600 and 606, and J Verhoeven, (Rapporteur Institut de Droit International), Les immunités de juridiction et d'exécution du chef d'Etat et de gouvernement en droit international, Rapport provisoire (2000), (2000–01) 69 AIDI 482, 544, § 42; with art 15 of the *Projet de Résolution Révisé No 1*, Institut de Droit International (Rapporteur J Verhoeven), Les immunités de juridiction et d'exécution du chef d'Etat et de gouvernement en droit international, Plenary Session (2001), (2000–01) 69 AIDI 601, 640.

[135] Cf the Dissenting Opinion of Judge Van den Wyngaert in the *Arrest Warrant* Case, § 21. The discrepancy between the preliminary report and the final resolution is all the more intriguing considering the nationality of the Rapporteur.

[136] *Arrest Warrant* Case.

and foreign ministers'. He explained that '[a]lthough they may be accorded certain special treatment by the host State, this is more likely to be a matter of courtesy and respect for the seniority of the visitor, than a reflection of any belief that such treatment is required by international law.'[137] Accordingly, Watts confirmed the argument advanced by Cahier thirty years earlier that these officials enjoy personal immunity *only* when they are on an official visit abroad. This position is shared by most commentators.[138]

The 1973 Convention on the Prevention and Punishment of Crimes against Internationally Protected Persons, including Diplomats distinguishes the position of heads of state from that of heads of government and ministers of foreign affairs. Article 1 provides that for the purposes of the Convention 'internationally protected person' means

- Head of State, including any member of a collegial body performing the functions of a Head of State under the constitution of the State concerned, a Head of Government or a Minister for Foreign Affairs, *whenever any such person is in a foreign State*, as well as members of his family who accompany him;
- any representative or official of a State or any official or other agent of an international organization of an intergovernmental character *who, at the time when and in the place where a crime against him*, his official premises, his private accommodation or his means of transport *is committed, is entitled pursuant to international law to special protection* from any attack on his person, freedom or dignity, as well as members of his family forming part of his household.

Also article 21 of the 1969 *Convention on Special Missions* intimates a difference between the position of heads of state on the one hand and that of heads of government and ministers of foreign affairs on the other. The article reads as follows:

1. The Head of the sending State, when he leads a special mission, shall enjoy in the receiving State or in a third State the facilities, privileges and immunities accorded by international law to Heads of State on an official visit.
2. The Head of the Government, the Minister for Foreign Affairs and other persons of high rank, when they take part in a special mission of the sending State, shall enjoy in the receiving State or in a third State, in addition to what is granted by the present Convention, the facilities, privileges and immunities accorded by international law.

The draft articles of the ILC that preceded the convention had used the formulation of the now second paragraph to the position of heads of state and other high ranking persons alike, but the General Assembly chose to distinguish the position of heads of states and adopted the bipartite formulation of article 21.[139] The article *does* seem to acknowledge that all three functions enjoy special

[137] A Watts (1994) 109.

[138] P Cahier (1962) 346. Cf also R Jennings and A Watts (eds) (1992) i 1046, § 459; MH Ryan (1978) 193; J Salmon (1994) 539; A Cavaglieri(1932) 321–2.

[139] ILC Draft Articles on Special Missions, YBILC 1967 ii 347ff, 359.

protection under international law.[140] However, as Watts pointed out, the article does not necessarily see to jurisdictional immunity.[141] Also within the context of their work on the Draft Articles on Jurisdictional Immunities of States and their Property, the ILC distinguished between the three functions. While it considered at one point that their draft did 'not prejudge the extent of immunities granted by States to heads of Government and ministers for foreign affairs',[142] article 3.2 of the Draft Articles *only* provides thus in respect of *heads of state*. It should moreover be pointed out that in a previous report the Commission had in fact stated that if privileges and immunities were granted to foreign ministers this was on the basis of comity rather than on the basis of established rules of international law.[143]

State practice is particularly scarce. Judicial practice of only a handful of jurisdictions is available. In 1961 the *Cour d'Appel de Paris* denied immunity to a minister of state of Saudi Arabia who was in Paris as a member of a delegation at a UN conference and was sued in respect of a lease of a flat in Paris.[144] The court implied however that immunity *would have been* available *had* the claim concerned a minister of foreign affairs instead. This indirect recognition of personal immunity of ministers of foreign affairs is however not terribly instructive since the case concerned an official visit.

The other relevant case law comes from US courts. Upon suggestions of immunity filed by the State Department courts have granted immunity to a head of government,[145] and to two ministers of foreign affairs.[146] While the deferral to the executive, of course, casts a doubt on the relevance of the decisions for the ascertainment of customary international law,[147] courts *have* stated that they granted the immunity in conformance with rules of customary international law.[148] In fact, in cases where the State Department had filed suggestions of immunity in respect to *other* foreign state officials courts have refused to follow the suggestions noting that '[t]he government...seeks to expand the head-of-state doctrine to encompass all government officials of a foreign state

140 Cf M Bartoš (1963) 438.

141 A Watts (1994) 108 fn 243.

142 YBILC 1991 ii 22 (Commentary on art 3).

143 YBILC 1989 ii 102–3 (Commentary on art 4).

144 *Ali Ali Reza v Grimpell* 47 ILR 275 (France, CA of Paris, 1961).

145 *Saltany and Others v Reagan and Others* (US, 1988).

146 Cf *Tachiona v Mugabe* (US, 2001), affirmed on diplomatic immunity grounds: *Tachiona v United States* 386 F 3d 205 (US, Ct of Apps (2nd Cir), 2004); *Chong Boon Kim v Kim Yong Shik and David Kim* 81 ILR 604 (US, CA (1st Cir), 1963), 58 AJIL 1964 186. It is interesting to note that in *Tachiona v Mugabe* the court qualified such decisions as head-of-state immunity decisions.

147 Not because statements of the executive are not relevant for the formation of custom, but because these statements do not always purport to be based on international law.

148 Cf in addition to the cases mentioned above also *Estate of Silme G Domingo v Ferdinand Marcos* (US, 1982) 306 where the court noted that '[u]nder customary rules of international law, recognized and applied in the United States, the head of a foreign government, its foreign ministers, and those designated by the head of state or members of his official party are immune from the jurisdiction of the United States federal and state courts'; and *Kilroy v Windsor* (US, 1978) 606.

to whom the State Department chooses to extend immunity. There is no precedent for such a radical departure from past custom.'[149] It should finally be noted that in the *Tachiona v Mugabe* case the court could be seen to qualify the scope of the suggestion filed by the executive noting that '[t]he Government's assertion of head-of-state immunity as to Mugabe extended to Mudenge, *travelling as Foreign Minister and as a member of Mugabe's official entourage* at the time he was served.'[150] In fact, both the *Tachiona* case, as the *Chong Boon Kim* case, concerned the service of process on ministers of foreign affairs while on official business in the US.[151] There is room left to argue that ministers of foreign affairs are *not* immune while in US territory on a private visit.

The available conventions and case law hardly constitute a general and consistent state practice formative of a rule of customary international law extending immunity beyond the diplomatic immunity available to special missions. So how did the Institut de Droit International and the ICJ support their conclusions as to the scope of the immunity of heads of government and foreign ministers? The reasoning of the ICJ is most revealing in this respect. The Court commenced its argument stating that 'in international law it is firmly established that . . . certain holders of high-ranking office in a State, such as the Head of State, the Head of Government and Ministers for Foreign Affairs, enjoy immunities from jurisdiction in other States, both civil and criminal.'[152] Referring to the Vienna Conventions on Diplomatic and Consular Relations and to the Convention on Special Missions, it considered that '[t]hese conventions . . . do not . . . contain any provision specifically defining the immunities enjoyed by Ministers for Foreign Affairs. It is consequently on the basis of customary international law that the Court must decide the questions relating to the immunities of such Ministers'.[153] The Court then embarked on a most intriguing argumentation. After it had pointed out that customary international law granted immunity to ministers of foreign affairs, *not* for their personal benefit but to ensure the effective performance of their functions, the Court proposed that '[i]n order to determine the extent of these immunities, the Court must therefore first consider the nature of the functions exercised by a Minister for Foreign Affairs.'[154] The Court considered that the minister of foreign affairs is in charge of a government's diplomatic activities and represents the state in international negotiations. Like the head of state and the head of government he is presumed to have full powers to act on behalf of the state by virtue of his office, hence without the need to present

[149] *Republic of the Philippines v Marcos* 665 F Supp 793 (US, DC for the Northern District of California, 1987) 797–8. Cf also *El-Hadad v Embassy of the United Arab Emirates* 69 F Supp 2d 69 (US, DC for the District of Columbia, 1999) 82 fn 10; F 3d 29 (2000).

[150] *Tachiona v Mugabe* (US, 2001).

[151] The case of *Saltany v Reagan* did concern a civil claim instigated against a foreign head of government while not present within US territory.

[152] *Arrest Warrant* Case, 20–1, § 51.

[153] ibid 21, § 52.

[154] ibid § 53.

letters of credence.[155] To fulfil these duties, the Court considered, the minister is required to travel abroad frequently and he 'must be in a position freely to do so whenever the need should arise'.[156] Accordingly, the Court concluded, 'the functions of a Minister for Foreign Affairs are such that, throughout the duration of his or her office, he or she when abroad enjoys full immunity from criminal jurisdiction and inviolability. That immunity and inviolability protect the individual concerned against any act of authority of another State which would hinder him or her in the performance of his or her duties.'[157]

The *form* of argumentation of the Court is remarkable. The scope of the law argument of the Court falls short in light of the limits of coherent argument on the ascertainment of customary international law discussed in chapter 2 of this study. In complete disregard of state practice—notably even the limited practice that *was* available—the Court derived the scope of immunity from an assessment of what is necessary to protect the functions of a minister of foreign affairs. The argumentation of the Court should have been preceded by proof of the existence of a rule of customary international law providing immunity to ministers of foreign affairs on functionality considerations. When such a rule is accepted, the rationale of the rule may indeed be helpful in the determination of its scope if uniform state practice is lacking. In this sense Ogdon argued in 1936 that

> [i]f a question confronting a domestic court calls for the solution of a problem pertaining to a matter of diplomatic immunity where no universally accepted practice points to the existence of a decisive and applicable rule, the tribunal may feel itself free to apply the standard of what is necessary and adequate as a test in determining the existence or scope of the immunity that is sought.[158]

In the absence of proof that a rule of customary international law exists the Court can only be seen to approach the *ne impediatur legatio* principle not as a *material cause* of custom but rather as a *formative source*. The immunity of ministers of foreign affairs thus acquires the unmistakable flavour of a necessary rule of international law. In chapter 2 it was explained that the form of such argument is not necessarily flawed—in particular it was argued that the minimum scope of the rule of state immunity can thus be ascertained. In the field of the immunities we discuss in this chapter, the reasoning is however clearly out of place.

In her dissenting opinion Judge Van den Wyngaert criticized the decision of the Court on this point. She pointed out that:

> It is not sufficient to compare the *rationale* for the protection from suit in the case of diplomats, Heads of State and Foreign Minister to draw the conclusion that there is a rule of customary international law protecting Foreign Ministers: identifying a common *raison d'être* for a protective rule is one thing, elevating this protective rule to the status of

155 Cf art 7.2.a of the 1969 Vienna Convention on the Law of Treaties.
156 *Arrest Warrant* Case, 22, § 53.
157 ibid § 54.
158 M Ogdon (1936) 206.

customary international law is quite another thing. The Court should have first examined whether the conditions for the formation of a rule of customary law were fulfilled in the case of incumbent Foreign Ministers...

In the brevity of its reasoning, the Court disregards its own case law on the subject on the formation of customary international law. In order to constitute a rule of customary international law, there must be evidence of state practice (*usus*) and *opinio juris* to the effect that this rule exists.[159]

The blunt statement of the rule by the Court is unfortunate, but not insuperable. That ministers of foreign affairs are protected by a form of diplomatic immunity in order to be able to exercise their functions *is* widely accepted.[160] Much more problematic is the *substance* of the Court's argumentation. The Court argued that

no distinction can be drawn between acts performed by a Minister for Foreign Affairs in an 'official' capacity, and those claimed to have been performed in a 'private capacity', or, for that matter, between acts performed before the person concerned assumed office as Minister for Foreign Affairs and acts committed during the period of office. Thus, if a Minister for Foreign Affairs is arrested in another State on a criminal charge, he or she is clearly thereby prevented from exercising the functions of his or her office. The consequences of such impediment to the exercise of those official functions are equally serious, regardless whether the Minister for Foreign Affairs was, at the time of arrest, present in the territory of the arresting State on an 'official' visit or a 'private' visit... Furthermore, even the mere risk that, by travelling to or transiting another State a Minister for Foreign Affairs might be exposing himself or herself to legal proceedings could deter the Minister from travelling internationally when required to do so for the purposes of the performance of his or her official functions.[161]

The issuance of the arrest warrant with the purpose to enable the arrest of Yerodia on Belgian territory was hence held to violate the personal immunity of the minister *even though the warrant was explicitly qualified in respect of official visits*.[162]

The conclusion that the functions of a minister of foreign affairs require a full immunity from foreign criminal jurisdiction *whenever* the minister is abroad stretches the functionality argument too far. It was argued earlier that the *ne*

[159] *Arrest Warrant* Case, Dissenting Opinion Judge Van den Wyngaert, 143, § 11 and § 12. Cf also M Kamto, 'Une troublante 'immunité totale' du ministre des affaires étrangères' (2002) 35 RBDI 518, 519–23.

[160] Cf ch 4 § 2.1.2.2 above.

[161] *Arrest Warrant* Case, 20, § 55.

[162] ibid 29, § 70. See on qualification also 27, § 65 and 28–9, § 68. The Belgian investigating judge issuing the warrant noted the following: 'Pursuant to the general principle of fairness in judicial proceedings, immunity from enforcement must, in our view, be accorded to all State representatives welcomed as such on to the territory of Belgium (on 'official visits'). Welcoming such foreign dignitaries as official representatives of sovereign States involves not only relations between individuals but also relations between States. This implies that such welcome includes an undertaking by the host State and its various components to refrain from taking any coercive measures against its guest and the invitation cannot become a pretext for ensnaring the individual concerned in what would be labelled a trap. In the contrary case, failure to respect this undertaking could give rise to the host State's international responsibility.' (28–9, § 68).

impediatur legatio rationale does not guarantee the actual undisturbed exercise of the functions by any specific individual but rather ensures—on a more abstract level—that the functions can *in theory* be exercised without disturbance. A diplomatic agent therefore only enjoys immunity from the jurisdiction of the state in which he exercises his official functions. Of course, the arrest in state A of the ambassador of state B accredited in state C hinders the exercise of the diplomatic functions by this particular ambassador. The exercise of the diplomatic function does however not require travels in third states—other than transit states—and the rule of diplomatic immunity based on the functionality rationale does not extend its protection to diplomatic agents travelling in third states. The Court decided otherwise in respect of ministers of foreign affairs. The arrest of such a person while on a private visit abroad, the Court considered, clearly prevents him from exercising the functions of his office.[163]

The interpretation of the scope of the rule seems to be inspired by the scope of the rule of head of state immunity, even though in the *Arrest Warrant* case the analogy remained largely unarticulated. The reports of the Institut de Droit International are more instructive in this respect. Verhoeven rhetorically wondered '[p]ourquoi faire au chef de gouvernement un sort different du chef de l'Etat, alors qu'il exerce souvent des functions internationals bien plus étendues que ce dernier?' The same, he argued, goes for the minister of foreign affairs.[164] It is hard to see, he concluded after a discussion of the functions of these three offices, how 'une distinction puisse sérieusement être établie entre eux'.[165]

The analogy is based on a flawed understanding of the rationale of the rule of head of state immunity. It is in this respect interesting to note that Verhoeven considered that a difference of treatment of heads of state on the one hand and heads of government, and—as he initially argued—ministers of foreign affairs

[163] It is noted that in their Joint Separate Opinion Judges Higgins, Kooijmans and Buergenthal did explicitly recognize that ministers of foreign affairs are not entitled to the same immunities as Heads of State but found the absolute immunity from criminal jurisdiction to inhere—as the court did—in the functionality rationale. They argued in relevant part that ministers of foreign affairs 'may not be subjected to measures which would prevent effective performance of the functions of a Foreign Minister. Detention or arrest would constitute such a measure and must therefore be considered an infringement of the inviolability and immunity from criminal process to which a Foreign Minister is entitled', 87–8, § 81–4.

The decision of the court has an obvious effect on judicial and doctrinal thinking. UK judges, for example, refused to issue a warrant for arrest on allegations of crimes against international law in respect of the head of state of Zimbabwe and the minister of defence of Israel Shaul Mofaz because of the personal immunity of these foreign state officials, cf C Warbrick, 'Immunity and International Crimes in English Law' (2004) 53 ICLQ 769. Cf also eg C Wickremasinghe (2003) 400: 'It now seems that serving Heads of Government and serving Ministers for Foreign Affairs enjoy immunity from jurisdiction *ratione personae* under international law to a similar extent as Heads of State, since they perform comparable functions in representing their States in international relations.'

[164] J Verhoeven (Rapporteur Institut de Droit International), Les immunités de juridiction et d'exécution du chef d'Etat et de gouvernement en droit international, Rapport provisoire (2000), (2000–01) 69 AIDI 482, 543 § 42.

[165] ibid 545 § 43.

on the other 'peut se concevoir dans un système qui fonde exclusivement ce statut sur la "représentativité" du chef de l'Etat, lequel en incarne en quelque sorte la personnalité juridique. Elle ne se comprend guère si une justification purement fonctionnelle est conférée aux privilèges et immunités dont il bénéficie, ainsi que cela ne paraît pas contestée dans la pratique contemporaine.'[166] Since Verhoeven considered the rule of head of state immunity to protect nowadays 'des besoins strictement fonctionnels' he could not but argue that the same rule had to extend to heads of government and ministers of foreign affairs who in practice often have more extensive international functions as heads of state.[167]

It was explained in section 2.2.1 of this chapter that the scope of head of state immunity can in fact *not* be explained on the basis of the functionality rationale. It was argued that the scope of the rule of head of state immunity can only be understood from the perspective of archaic notions of dignity of kings and princes and the incarnation of the state in the person of its ruler. These considerations do not apply with the same force to heads of government and ministers of foreign affairs. In *Oppenheims's International Law* we read that the head of government 'does not represent the international *persona* of the state in the same way in which the Head of State does'.[168] Watts elaborated on this theme stating that 'heads of government and foreign ministers . . . do not symbolize or personify their States in the way that Heads of States do. Accordingly, they do not enjoy in international law any entitlement to special treatment by virtue of qualities of sovereignty or majesty attaching to them personally.'[169] The argument against equating the immunity of heads of government and ministers for foreign affairs with the immunity of heads of state is therefore a strong one. In anticipation of chapter 6 of this study it is noted moreover that the scope of personal immunities should be narrowly interpreted in view of the conflicting rights of individuals under international human rights law. Heads of government and ministers of foreign affairs are the ultimate example of ad hoc diplomatic agents that are covered by a form of personal diplomatic immunity. This immunity protects them while on official visits abroad. Head of state immunity extends beyond that. Since the rule is *not* strictly based on functionality considerations the position of the head of government and the minister of foreign affairs cannot be determined by analogy with the position of the head of state.

[166] ibid 543, § 42. Cf also 498.

[167] Cf p 180 above.

[168] R Jennings and A Watts (eds) (1992) i 1033, § 445.

[169] A Watts (1994) 102. Judge Van den Wyngaert, argued in her Dissenting Opinion that '[f]oreign Ministers do not "impersonate" the State in the same way as Heads of State, who are the State's alter ego', § 16. Cf also the Dissenting Opinion of Judge Al-Khasawneh. The Judge argued that in contrast with heads of state, the minister of foreign affairs 'does not, in any sense, personify the State' and immunity from criminal jurisdiction does not apply on private visits, § 2 and 4. In addition, the Judge noted that in contrast to diplomatic agents the host state cannot influence *who* occupies the post of minister of foreign affairs and cannot declare such a person *persona non grata*, § 1.

On the specific facts of the *Arrest Warrant* case this study would hence conclude differently than the ICJ.[170] Ministers of foreign affairs cannot be equated to heads of state. Their personal immunity only applies during official visits abroad. As long as Belgium clearly states that it will not act upon the warrant during such official visits of the minister—as in fact it did[171]—its actions may not be in accordance with comity but they are not in violation of international law. If—as The Congo claimed[172]—the warrant hindered official travel of its minister, this cannot be ascribed to the arrest warrant but only to a mistaken interpretation thereof.

2.3 The *Arrest Warrant* Case: Obligations of Third States under Personal Immunity Rules

The decision of the ICJ in the *Arrest Warrant* case forces us to reconsider the obligations of third states under personal immunity rules.[173] Belgium was found to have violated the immunity of the Congolese minister of foreign affairs on two separate accounts. It was explained above that the *issuance* of the arrest warrant violated Yerodia's immunity from Belgian jurisdiction. In addition, however, the Court engaged the question whether the *international circulation* of the warrant constituted a separate violation of the immunity.

The arrest warrant was communicated to Interpol in June 2000 but Belgium did not request an Interpol red notice until after the abdication of Yerodia as minister for foreign affairs. Belgium argued that the circulation of the warrant did not violate the sovereignty of DRC because the warrant had no legal effect on foreign territory. It stated that

> the warrant does not create any obligations for the authorities of any other State to arrest Mr. Yerodia in the absence of some further step by Belgium completing or validating the arrest (such as a request for the provisional detention of Mr. Yerodia), or the issuing of an arrest warrant by the appropriate authorities in the State concerned following a request to do so, or the issuing of an Interpol Red Notice.[174]

The Court did not agree. Since the circulation of the arrest warrant was 'to establish a legal basis for the arrest of Mr. Yerodia . . . abroad and his subsequent extradition to Belgium' the 'nature and purpose' of the warrant was such that it 'effectively infringed' the immunity of Yerodia. The Court considered that even in the absence of 'further steps' by Belgium the 'mere international circulation of

[170] See A Cassese (2002) 855 for support for this part of the decision. Cf ch 5 § 2.3.1 below for an analysis of the decision on the question whether the immunity of ministers of foreign affairs is available when a minister is charged with war crimes and crimes against humanity.

[171] *Arrest Warrant* Case, 23 and 25, § 65, 68 and 70.

[172] ibid 26, § 71.

[173] *Arrest Warrant* Case.

[174] ibid 27, § 66.

the warrant... could have resulted... in his arrest while abroad'. The circulation of the warrant was therefore held to constitute a violation of the rights of DRC.[175] Judges Higgins, Kooijmans, and Buergenthal further explained in their Separate Opinion that '[a]n international arrest warrant, even though a Red Notice has not yet been linked... is already a statement of willingness and ability to act and as such may be perceived as a threat so to do at a moment of Belgium's choosing.'[176]

Upon close consideration of the Court's reasoning it can only be concluded that the circulation was not held to violate the immunity from *Belgian* jurisdiction but rather the immunity Yerodia enjoyed from *foreign* jurisdictions. The considerations are *therefore* applicable to diplomatic and head of state immunity alike.[177] Accordingly, in the view of the Court, personal immunity rules do not only oblige states to refrain from establishing jurisdiction over certain individuals; they also oblige states not to request other states—regardless of whether such request has binding force—to violate these rules. The exercise of functions can be impeded by actions of third states that do not have jurisdiction over the territory.

This author is not completely persuaded by the argument. In fact, the dissent of Judge Van den Wyngaert on this point carries some force. According to the judge the personal immunity from foreign jurisdictions would only be violated if Belgium asserted 'enforcement jurisdiction'. The circulation of the warrant, she subsequently argued, does not qualify as such since the warrant could not be enforced in third countries without validation by the authorities of the state where the person mentioned in the warrant is found.[178] This is true—this author cares to add—for non-binding and binding requests alike. The requesting state does not in any way assert enforcement jurisdiction by issuing a binding request for arrest or extradition. The receiving state is merely confronted with two competing obligations under international law. Whether or not the immunity from jurisdiction of the visiting official is violated depends entirely on the actions of the receiving state. Arguably, the argument that the international circulation of an arrest warrant entails the responsibility of the requesting state under international law because it induces a *risk* that the receiving state reacts positively to the non-binding request, together with the *risk* that a requesting state moves to a binding request and the *risk* that the receiving state gives prevalence to the

[175] ibid 29–30, § 70 and 71.

[176] ibid Joint Separate Opinion Judges Higgins, Kooijmans, and Buergenthal, 84, § 69. The judges however did not agree with the majority on the appropriate remedy. They argued that 'the illegal consequences attaching to the warrant... ceased' when Yerodia abdicated, 88, § 89.

[177] The court focuses on the risk of arrest in a state where the person enjoys immunity. Had the court considered that the warrant violated the immunity from *Belgian* jurisdiction the decision would not apply to diplomatic agents that are not immune from Belgian jurisdiction.

[178] *Arrest Warrant* Case, Dissenting Opinion Judge Van den Wyngaert, 180–2, § 78. Cf also Judge Oda 'It bears stressing that the issuance of an arrest warrant by one State and the international circulation of the warrant through Interpol have no legal impact unless the arrest request is validated by the receiving State... There is... some doubt whether the Court itself properly understood this... The crucial point in this regard is *not* the issuance or international circulation of an arrest warrant but the response of the State receiving it.' Dissenting Opinion Judge Oda, 52, § 13.

obligations towards the requesting state in violation of its obligations towards the home state of the foreign official, stretches the material scope of personal immunity rules too far.

3 Concluding Remarks

Diplomatic immunity and head of state immunity extend to acts that fall squarely within the essential competence of the forum state, and do not entail immunity from legal liability. In contrast to state immunity and functional immunity, diplomatic immunity and head of state immunity are veritable *immunities from jurisdiction*. The classic definition of such immunity is that it obliges courts to refrain from the exercise of *otherwise available* jurisdiction. In chapter 2 of this study it was explained that it is better stated that an immunity from jurisdiction *applies distinctly from* jurisdictional or liability questions. While the normal jurisdictional rules do logically deserve consideration before the rule of personal immunity—even though in practice courts do not necessarily follow this logical order[179]—the procedural immunity from jurisdiction prevents the courts from an inquiry into their essential competence or the substantive liability of the defendant.

The rules moreover are conspicuous examples of rules of customary international law and are hence—in the terms introduced by Anzilotti and set out in chapter 2 of this study—voluntary rather than necessary immunity rules.[180] This is not to say that the *function* of the law of diplomatic immunity is trivial

[179] In the *Arrest Warrant* case the ICJ for example did not engage the question whether Belgium could exercise universal jurisdiction *in absentia* over Mr Yerodia. Several judges however expressed their dissatisfaction with the order in which the Court approached the issues, cf ch 5 § 1 below.

[180] Cf also H Grotius (1625) ii, 193–200. Even though the rule of head of state immunity may reflect the idea of personification of the state in its ruler, it cannot be said that the rule has a necessary character since the personification concerns a fiction that is not a constitutional principle of the international legal order.

In this regard it is also interesting to note that in the *Case Concerning United States Diplomatic and Consular Staff in Tehran* (*United States of America v Iran*) (Provisional Measures) the ICJ rationalized the rule of inviolability of diplomatic agents in natural law terms. The Court held 'there is no more fundamental prerequisite for the conduct of relations between States than inviolability of diplomatic envoys and embassies, so that throughout history nations of all creeds and cultures have observed reciprocal obligations for that purpose; and [...] the obligations thus assumed, notably those for assuring the personal safety of diplomats and their freedom from prosecution, are essential, unqualified, and *inherent in their representative character and their diplomatic function*'. ICJ Reports 1979 7, 19, § 38 (emphasis added). This type of reasoning was common when Von Pufendorf wrote in 1672 that ambassadors 'are inviolable by the very law of nature. For, since persons of that kind are necessary, in order to win or to preserve peace, which the very law of nature bids us embrace in all honourable ways, it is well understood that the same law has also provided for the safety of those persons without whom the end which it orders cannot be obtained'. S Von Pufendorf, *Elementorum jurisprudentiae universalis libri duo* (1672), trans by W Abbott Oldfather (Oxford 1931) ii Book I, Definition XII, 166–7. It is questionable, however, whether the reasoning can convince in light of the theory of custom formation set out in ch 2 of this study.

compared to the law of state immunity—indeed the International Court of Justice considered in the *Teheran Hostages Case* that 'the institution of diplomacy, with its concomitant privileges and immunities, has withstood the test of centuries and proved to be an instrument *essential* for effective co-operation in the international community, and for enabling States, irrespective of their differing constitutional and social systems, to achieve mutual understanding and to resolve their differences by peaceful means'.[181] The function of the law of head of state immunity—the protection of the dignity of the office of head of state—does compare somewhat meagrely to that of both diplomatic and state immunity.

There is no need to dwell on the question as to the parameters of coherent arguments on the influence of international human rights law and international criminal law on rules of personal immunity. The scope of the rules can only be ascertained inductively—although in the absence of uniform state practice the material cause of the state practice may serve as a guiding principle. Arguments that proceed from reason or logic are hence necessarily policy arguments. In addition, state of the law arguments may argue that personal immunity rules are invalidated or forfeited as long as this is consistent with the epistemology of international law. In respect of a forfeiture argument it must however be realized that personal immunities do not concern personal rights. The argument that the office holder forfeits his rights under the rule when he engages in certain behaviour is hence not coherent in form.

While the debate on the influence of international human rights law and international criminal law on personal immunity rules is not seriously troubled by misconceptions of the nature and substance of the immunity rules, it arguably fails to focus its attention on the most pressing issue. On the basis of the discussion of the nature and substance of personal immunities rules it should be possible to develop forceful human rights-based policy arguments against these rules. Just like the rule of absolute immunity, the rules of diplomatic immunity and head of state immunity may shield an otherwise liable person from the normal jurisdiction of the forum state and may therefore deprive private individuals from their day in court. Accordingly, obligations under personal immunity rules may clash with the obligation to guarantee the right of access to court and the right to equality before the law. Personal immunities entail an additional problem. Since these immunities also apply to serious crimes committed on the territory of the forum state, the obligations under these rules moreover may clash with the obligations of states to secure respect for human rights within their territory. Under the European Convention of Human Rights, for example, states may have positive obligations to secure the effective respect for the rights under the Convention also in the sphere of the relations of individuals between themselves. The European

[181] *Case Concerning United States Diplomatic and Consular Staff in Tehran* (*United States of America v Iran*) (Provisional Measures), ICJ Reports 1979 7, 19, § 39 (emphasis added). It is in fact recalled that even *jus cogens* norms are in principle developed through the customary process.

Court of Human Rights has for example decided that when 'fundamental values and essential aspects of private life are at stake... [e]ffective deterrence is indispensable'.[182] Personal immunities—especially diplomatic immunity—are at times deliberately used as a cloak for the commission of crimes. But more in general it must be realized that the lack of deterrence may underlie lawless behaviour also in a less spiteful sense. Even neglect of rules that may seem relatively trivial—like traffic regulations—may seriously violate the rights of others. Can a state allow such 'lawless' creatures on its territory without violating its obligations under the ECHR? Should it not at least make sure beforehand that immunity does not equal impunity? These policy arguments have arguably yet to be realized to their full potential. It will be argued later in this study that the assessment of the European Court of Human Rights, that the right of access to court is not violated by immunity rules that form part of international law, does not satisfactorily deal with the tension between the rights and interests of states and the rights and interests of private individuals inherent in immunities of states and its officials.[183] The danger of a clash of interests looms particularly large in respect of personal immunity rules. It will be argued in chapter 6 of this study that there is room for coherent policy arguments calling for a reconsideration of the balance of interests reflected in the rules set out above.

[182] *X and Y v The Netherlands* Series A-91, 8 EHRR 235 (ECHR, 1985).

[183] *Al-Adsani v United Kingdom* (ECHR, 2001); *Fogarty v United Kingdom* 34 EHRR 302, 123 ILR 53 (ECHR, 2001); *McElhinney v Ireland* 34 EHRR 322, 123 ILR 73 (ECHR, 2001). Cf ch 6 § 3.2 below.

5

The Immunity of State Officials in the Light of Obligations of Individuals under International Law

1 Introduction

International law consists of the body of principles and rules that states agree apply within the international legal order. States are accordingly the natural subjects of international law. Some of the rules of international law may however, in addition, regulate the legal position of non-state entities. While initially states only set out to delimit their competing sovereignties, more and more rules regulate the cooperation between states, and states have even assumed uniform standard setting in areas that do not concern interstate relations at all. Chapter 6 of this study discusses the development of rules recognizing *rights of individuals* under international law. This chapter focuses on the fact that states can also, as the Permanent Court of International Justice already noted in the *Jurisdiction of the Courts of Danzig* Case, create *obligations for individuals* through international agreement.[1] It stands to reason that such obligations can equally develop under customary international law.

It is no coincidence that the early examples of individual responsibility under international law—piracy, slavery, violence against diplomatic agents, illegitimate warfare[2]—all concerned actions of individuals with detrimental transnational

[1] *Jurisdiction of the Courts of Danzig* (Advisory Opinion) PCIJ Series B no 15 (1928) 17–18.

[2] Most commentators qualify these offences as crimes against international law (cf eg H Kelsen (1944) 75–8). Friedmann argued in this regard that '[t]here has always been an "international criminal law," of modest and ill-defined proportions.' W Friedmann, *The Changing Structure of International Law* (1964) 167. Brownlie, however, argued that these examples concern 'the punishment, under national law, of acts in respect of which international law gives a liberty to all states to punish, but does not itself declare criminal', I Brownlie (2003) 303, cf in this sense also G Schwarzenberger, 'The Problem of an International Criminal Law' (1950) 3 Current Legal Problems 263, 270. For piracy see eg H Halleck, *International Law* (3rd edn, 1893) i 54; *United States v Klintock* 18 US 144 (US, S Ct, 1820); *United States v Pirates* 18 US 184 (US, S Ct, 1820). Cf for other examples KC Randall, 'Universal Jurisdiction under International Law' (1988) 66 Texas Law Review 785, 791–8. For slavery see KC Randall, 798–800; *United States v The La*

consequences that were generally not committed under state authority and were hence not attributable to a state.[3] International law imposed obligations directly on the individual *only* if no state responsibility could be established.

Over the past century, however, this traditional framework proved no longer adequate to serve the needs of the international community. The experience of the two world wars precipitated the development of the principle of individual responsibility for the most serious violations of international law independent of the question of state responsibility. The Nuremberg Tribunal famously defended this decisive turn in international law holding that:

> Crimes against international law are committed by men, not by abstract entities, and only by punishing individuals who commit such crimes can the provisions of international law be enforced.[4]

Article 6 of the Nuremberg Charter provided for individual responsibility for crimes against peace, war crimes, and crimes against humanity, and today the principle is firmly established in the international legal order.[5] Let us take a closer look at this development.

In the nineteenth century states had started to codify and develop rules on aspects of interstate warfare in conventional law. In 1864 at a conference in Geneva the delegates of 16 European nations adopted the Convention for the Amelioration of the Condition of the Wounded in Armies in the Field.[6] Four years later the Declaration of St Petersburg called on States not to use arms that cause unnecessary suffering and prohibited the use of certain explosive projectiles

Jeune Eugenie 26 F Cas 832 (US, Circuit Court for the District of Massachusetts, 1822) 843. For violence against diplomats see: *Respublica v Longchamps* 1 US 111 (US, Pennsylvania S Ct, 1784); *United States v Ortega* 24 US 467 (US, S Ct, 1826). Cf on illegitimate warfare eg H Kelsen (1944) 77.

3 Cf in respect of the crime of piracy eg WE Hall, *A Treatise on International Law* (7th edn, 1917) 268–9.

4 *Nuremberg Judgment* (International Military Tribunal, 1946), reprinted in (1947) 41 AJIL 172, 221. Cf L Oppenheim (ed), *The Collected Papers of John Westlake* (1914) 269–70 for a very similar rationalization: 'The men who form a state are not allowed to disclaim their part in the offences alleged against it...And this is just. Whatever is done or omitted by a state is done or omitted by the men who are grouped in it, or at least the deed or the omission is sanctioned by them. a state is not a self-acting machine. The impulse which its wheels receive can only be a human impulse...'

5 Agreement for the Prosecution and Punishment of Major War Criminals of the European Axis and Establishing the Charter of the International Military Tribunal, Annex, 1951 82 UNTS 279.

6 Declaration Renouncing the Use, in Time of War, of Explosive Projectiles under 400 Grammes Weight (1868), reprinted in D Schindler and J Toman (eds), *The Laws of Armed Conflict: A Collection of Conventions, Resolutions and other Documents* (4th edn, 2004) 91. The Convention followed the inception of the International Committee of the Red Cross in 1863—or the International Committee for the Relief of the Military Wounded as it was called until 1876. Cf G Best, *Humanity in Warfare: The Modern History of the International Law of Armed Conflicts* (1980) for earlier developments.

that 'uselessly aggravate the sufferings of disabled men'.[7] The Declaration stated that a balance needed to be achieved between 'the necessities of war' and 'the requirements of humanity'. The Peace Conferences at The Hague in 1899 and 1907 adopted conventions defining the laws and customs of warfare and several declarations forbidding or limiting certain practices, including attacks on surrendered soldiers, the bombardment of undefended towns, the use of dumdum bullets, of 'projectiles the sole object of which is the diffusion of asphyxiating or deleterious gases', and of weapons 'calculated to cause unnecessary suffering'.[8] In the preamble of these Conventions it was moreover stated that '[u]ntil a more complete code of the laws of war is issued, the High Contracting Parties think it right to declare that, in cases not included in the Regulations adopted by them, populations and belligerents remain under the protection and empire of the principles of international law, as they result from the usages established between civilized nations, from the laws of humanity, and the requirements of the public conscience.'[9] Although the First World War had revealed an immeasurable and disheartening gap between the theory of war-law and the practice of warfare, states continued to elaborate their conventional obligations by the 1925 Geneva Protocol on Chemical and Bacteriological Warfare prohibiting the use of asphyxiating and poisonous gases, and the two 1929 Geneva Conventions relating to the treatment of prisoners of war and the wounded and the sick.[10]

In addition to these early rules of international humanitarian law—*jus in bello*, the law of armed conflict, or the law of war as it was initially termed—the end of the First World War prompted efforts to prohibit the resort to war altogether—*jus ad bellum*. To this effect the General Treaty for the Renunciation of War—better known as the Kellogg–Briand Pact—was concluded in 1928.[11]

It can accordingly be conceded that at the start of the Second World War many of the *norms* under which the Nuremberg Tribunal would later judge the conduct of individuals were unquestionably part of international law. However, the *individual responsibility under international law* for the violations of these norms *of state officials acting under government orders* is clearly a distinct question.

Let us start with the second of these two issues. In early twentieth century doctrine the question of individual responsibility for war crimes is often seen to pivot on the distinction between lawful and unlawful belligerency. It was explained in

[7] Declaration of St Petersburg (1968), reprinted in *Conventions and Declarations between the powers concerning war, arbitration and Neutrality* (1915).

[8] Hague Convention II 1899, and Hague Convention IV 1907 on the Laws and Customs of War on Land, reprinted in *Conventions and Declarations between the powers concerning war, arbitration and Neutrality* (1915).

[9] This is commonly known as 'the Martens Clause', cf A Cassese, 'The Martens Clause: Half a Loaf or Simply Pie in the Sky?' (2000) 11 EJIL 187.

[10] Protocol for the Prohibition of the Use of Asphyxiating, Poisonous or Other Gases, and of Bacteriological Methods of Warfare, 94 LNTS 65; Convention Relative to the Treatment of Prisoners of War, 118 LNTS 343.

[11] The General Treaty for the Renunciation of War (1928) 94 LNTS 57.

chapter 3 of this study that while acts of warfare would normally violate provisions of national law prohibiting murder, assault, destruction of property and the like, lawful combatants do not incur personal responsibility under the national law of the adversary state. *Unlawful* combatants befalls a different fate. Combatants that do not wear a distinctive emblem or those that violate the laws and principles of war in any other way are *in principle* punishable under the national law of the adversary state. Accordingly, the Institut de Droit International wrote in its 1880 Manual of the Laws of War on Land that '[i]f any of the [rules on warfare] be violated, the offending parties should be punished, after a judicial hearing, by the belligerent in whose hands they are.'[12]

Many commentators at the time did not question how the concept of unlawful belligerency related to the 'act of state' doctrine of the *McLeod* case—or the rule of functional immunity.[13] Hereshoff Bartlett formulated this position in the following terms:

> Pending hostilities the armed forces have authority to do all that the laws of war permit, but they have no right to violate those laws with impunity and transgress them. To do so places them on a level with bandits and outlaws and deprives them of the protection which the laws of nations and the articles of war extend to justifiable warfare... punishable... irrespective of the fact whether the offender was an officer or soldier acting under the dominion of his sovereign.[14]

The only issue that was seen to possibly interfere with the individual responsibility of unlawful combatants was the principle of *respondeat superior*.[15] This principle is however clearly distinct from the principle of non-personal responsibility

[12] Institut de Droit International, Manual of the Laws of War on Land 1880, (1881–82) AIDI 174. Art 84 of the Manual therefore provided: 'Offenders against the laws of war are liable to the punishments specified in the penal law.'

[13] Cf eg JW Garner, 'Punishment of Offenders against the Laws and Customs of War' (1920) 14 AJIL 70; L Renault, 'De l'application du droit pénal aux faits de guerre' (1918) 25 RGDIP 5; CA Hereshoff Bartlett, 'Liability for Official War Crimes' (1919) 35 LQR 177.

[14] CA Hereshoff Bartlett, ibid 178–9.

[15] Latin for 'let the master answer': the responsibility for actions by subordinates taken in the execution of superior orders lies exclusively with the superior. Cf in general on the different views on this issue JW Garner (1920) 70. L Oppenheim, *International Law, A Treatise* (AD McNair (ed) 4th edn, 1926) ii 410–11, § 253 stated that '[v]iolations of rules regarding warfare are war crimes only when committed without an order of the belligerent Government concerned. If members of the armed forces commit violations *by order* of their Government, they are not war criminals, and may not be punished... In case members of forces commit violations ordered by their commanders, the members may not be punished, for the commanders are alone responsible, and the latter may, be punished as war criminals on their capture by the enemy'; WE Hall (1917) 439; L Renault (1918) 26–8. In the sixth edition Oppenheim's *International Law* changed position. We read: 'The fact that a rule of warfare has been violated in pursuance of an order of the belligerent Government or of an individual belligerent commander does not deprive the act in question of its character as a war crime; neither does it, in principle, confer upon the perpetrator immunity from punishment by the injured belligerent. A different view has occasionally been adopted... but it is difficult to regard it as expressing a sound legal principle.' L Oppenheim, *International Law, A Treatise* (H Lauterpacht (ed) 6th edn, 1940) ii 253–4, § 253.

for acts of state. It shifts the responsibility to the commander—irrespective of the authority with which that commander had acted.

This reasoning does not convince. It is recalled that state officials are not personally responsible for acts committed as arm or mouthpiece of their home state, and that they are assumed to have thus acted when they exercise state authority under international law. Unlawful combatants that engage in espionage or sabotage—like in *Ex parte Quirin*—do not qualify as such.[16] Also unlawful combatants that have violated the rules of warfare acting on individual impulses can be easily excluded from the rule. The individual responsibility of these two categories for crimes under the national law of the adversary state is uncontroversial. However, what is the position of unlawful combatants violating international law while engaged in military activities and while acting under orders of a foreign government? The lawful–unlawful combatant distinction is a distinct principle that does not replace the act of state principle. If the *McLeod* principle no longer applied to acts violating the rules of war this needed at least to be supported by forceful arguments.

Several scholars writing in the first half of the previous century *did* in fact argue that soldiers violating the rules of war while participating in military operations on orders of their government did not incur individual responsibility. These scholars agreed that '[i]nternational law had long recognized the right of a belligerent to put on trial and summarily execute members of the armed forces of the enemy who were found guilty of violations of the laws of war' but limited this rule to violations '*not part of military operations*'.[17] In other words, international law did not allow the prosecution of state officials employed by a state wilfully conducting its military operations in violation of the rules of warfare.[18]

The second—less fundamental—issue is whether individuals that act in contravention of the laws of war violate *international law* or only *national law*. International humanitarian law in principle only obliged states. Article 3 of the 1907 Hague Convention, for example, provides as follows: 'A belligerent party

[16] Cf for *Ex p Quirin* (US, 1942) ch 3 p 128 above.

[17] Ch G Fenwick, 'The Progress of International Law During the Past Forty Years' (1951-II) 79 RdC 1, 62–3 (emphasis added). Cf also GA Finch, 'Jurisdiction of Local Courts to Try Enemy Persons for War Crimes' (1920) 14 AJIL 218; G Manner, 'The Legal Nature and Punishment of Criminal Acts of Violence Contrary to the Laws of War' (1943) 38 AJIL 407; A Verdross, *Völkerrecht* (1937) 298; H Kelsen (1944) 79ff. Finch referred to several decisions of the US Supreme Court confirming this (eg *Dow v Johnson* 100 US 158 (1879)). While Hereshoff Bartlett argued that the fact that the Supreme Court in these cases did not allow prosecution of *lawful* combatants meant that prosecution of *unlawful* combatants *was* possible ('Liability for Official War Crimes' (1919) 35 LQR 177, 186–7), Finch rightly pointed out that the Supreme Court did not allow prosecutions that alleged the commission of acts in violation of the laws of war.

[18] Röling later distinguished these two categories of unlawful combatants in those that commit 'individual criminality' (crimes committed for selfish reasons against the instructions of the own government) and those that commit 'system criminality' (crimes committed on government orders or encouragement in order to serve the war effort): BVA Röling, 'The Significance of the Laws of War' in A Cassese (ed), *Current Problems of International Law, Essays on UN Law and on the Law of Armed Conflict* (1975) 133, 137–8.

which violates the provisions of the said Regulation shall, if the case demands, be liable to pay compensation. It shall be responsible for all acts committed by persons forming part of its armed forces.' In order to ensure the compliance of their obligations on the international level states did proceed to codify the laws of war in military penal codes—the 1863 US Lieber Code being the most prominent example.[19] Scholars do not agree on the question whether before Nuremberg it was accepted that international law imposed obligations directly on the individual.[20]

The 1919 Versailles Treaty did not settle these controversies conclusively. The precedent value of the treaty is in particular limited because Germany consented to the attribution of individual responsibility to its state officials for the violation of the laws of war.[21]

What did the Treaty provide? After the First World War the Allied Powers established a Commission of Fifteen to study the possibility of prosecution and punishment of war criminals. The Commission reported to the Versailles Peace Conference that '[a]ll persons belonging to enemy countries, however high their position may have been, without distinction of rank, including Chiefs of States, who have been guilty of offences against the laws and customs of war or the laws of humanity, are liable to criminal prosecution.'[22] It recommended the establishment of an international tribunal to prosecute individuals suspected of violations of the laws and customs of war or the laws of humanity.[23]

The US members of the Commission opposed the report on several grounds and annexed reservations to it.[24] In the first place the US delegates thought

[19] Instructions for the Government of Armies of the United States in the Field, Prepared by F Lieber, promulgated as General Orders No. 100 by President Lincoln, 24 April 1863, reprinted in D Schindler and J Toman (eds) (2004) 3.

[20] Cf eg G Manner (1943) 415; RR Baxter (1951), 343–4; H Kelsen (1944) 101–4.

[21] Cf eg H Kelsen (1994) 110. It is further noted that art 3 of the 1922 Washington Treaty relating to the Use of Submarines and Noxious Gases in Warfare provided that 'any person in the service of any Power who shall violate any of those rules, whether or not such person is under orders of a governmental superior, shall be deemed to have violated the laws of war and shall be liable to trial and punishment as if for an act of piracy and may be brought to trial before the civil or military authorities of any Power within the jurisdiction of which he may be found'. The provision is not limited to nationals of states party to the treaty and is hence either a violation of international law or an indication of changing international law on this point.

[22] Commission on the Responsibility of the Authors of the War and on Enforcement of Penalties, Report Presented to the Preliminary Peace Conference, March 29, 1919, reprinted in (1920) 14 AJIL 95, 117. Cf also the the Joint Declaration of France, UK and Russia on 24 May 1915 warning Turkish leaders that they were personally responsible for the Armenian Massacres: 'En présence de ces nouveaux crimes de la Turquie contre l'humanité et la civilisation, les gouvernements alliés font savoir publiquement à la Sublime-Porte qu'ils tiendront personnellement responsable desdits crimes tous les membres du gouvernement ottoman ainsi que ce des agents qui se trouveraient impliqués dans ces pareils massacres', (1915) 22 RGDIP Documents 215.

[23] Ibid 121–4.

[24] Annex II to the Report, Memorandum of Reservations presented by the Representatives of the United States to the Report of the Commission on Responsibilities, (1920) 14 AJIL 127. Cf also the reservations of the Japanese delegates: Annex III to the Report, Reservations by the Japanese Delegation, (1920) 14 AJIL 51.

prosecution should be limited to violations of the laws and customs of war since the laws and principles of humanity are not 'a certain standard to be found in books of authority and in the practice of nations'.[25] Second, they opposed the prosecution of heads of state. Under reference to the *Schooner Exchange* case they argued that a head of state is only responsible to his own country. To hold otherwise, they held, would be 'denying the very conception of sovereignty'.[26] The delegates underlined that their observations *only* applied to incumbent heads of state—'proceedings against [a head of state who has abdicated or has been repudiated by his people] might be wise or unwise, but in any event they would be against an individual out of office and not against an individual in office and thus in effect against the state'.[27] Finally, and most fundamentally, the delegates cautioned that a newly established international tribunal amounted to the exercise of *ex post facto* jurisdiction. They knew, they wrote, 'of no international statute or convention making a violation of the laws and customs of war—not to speak of the laws or principles of humanity—an international crime, affixing a punishment to it, and declaring the court which has jurisdiction over the offence'.[28] They therefore suggested that 'the machinery at hand'—meaning the national courts of the states affected, or, if more states are affected by the same crime, a tribunal made up of the competent courts of these states—should be utilized to prosecute the suspects of war crimes rather than 'an international tribunal with a criminal jurisdiction for which there is no precedent, precept, practice or procedure'.[29]

The Peace Conference reached a compromise. The Versailles Treaty did eventually provide for the creation of a special tribunal to prosecute the ex-emperor William II of Hohenzollern for 'a supreme offence against international morality and the sanctity of treaties'.[30] In addition, the Treaty provided for the prosecution of persons 'accused of having committed acts in violation of the laws and customs of war' before the military tribunals of the Allied powers.[31]

Practice failed however to live up to these promises. The Netherlands—where the emperor had taken refuge after the war—refused to hand William over to the Allied Powers,[32] while Germany was eventually allowed to prosecute other suspected war criminals itself which resulted in the commonly agreed mock proceedings known as the Leipzig Trials.[33]

[25] ibid 133–4 and 144, quotation at 134.
[26] ibid 136.
[27] ibid 136. Cf also 147–8.
[28] ibid 146.
[29] ibid 140–2 and 145–7, quotation at 142.
[30] Treaty of Peace between the Allied and Associated Powers and Germany (Treaty of Versailles) 1919, Art 227. Notably, the US did not ratify the Treaty because of the inclusion of this article.
[31] ibid art 228.
[32] Cf eg E Decaux, 'Le statut du chef d'État déchu' (1980) 26 AFDI 101, 112.
[33] Cf WA Schabas, *An Introduction to the International Criminal Court* (2nd edn, 2004) 3–4.

The Second World War again incensed the discussion on the individual responsibility of government officials for the waging of war. Already in 1943 the Allied Powers had stated their intent to bring the Nazi war criminals to justice after the war.[34] At the end of the Second World War the controversy between those that advocated summary execution of the German political and military leaders and those that insisted on a trial was decided in favour of the latter when on 8 August the London Agreement for the Prosecution and Punishment of the Major War Criminals of the European Axis was signed, to which the Charter establishing the International Military Tribunal—better known as the Nuremberg Tribunal—was annexed.[35] The Tribunal tried the major war criminals only. It convicted nineteen of the twenty-four Nazi leaders indicted and imposed the death sentence in twelve cases. Lower ranking officials were prosecuted by Allied military tribunals on the basis of Control Council Law no 10 and the International Military Tribunal for the Far East was established to prosecute crimes against international law committed on the Eastern front.[36]

The defendants in the Nuremberg Trials argued that by ignoring the distinction between norm, and subject of the norm, their prosecution violated the *nullum crimen sine lege* principle. In the context of the individual responsibility for crimes against peace, for example, defendants argued that the Kellogg–Briand Pact 'does not expressly enact that such wars are crimes, or set up courts to try those who make such wars'. The Tribunal rejected the argument reasoning that

> [t]he defendants . . . must have known of the Treaties signed by Germany, outlawing the recourse to war for the settlement of international disputes, they must have known that they were acting in defiance of all international law when in complete deliberation they carried out their designs of invasion and aggression. On this view of the case alone, it would appear that the maxim has no application to the present facts.[37]

In an *a fortiori* argument the Tribunal relied on the concept of individual responsibility for war crimes. It argued that since 1907 the prohibitions of the Hague Convention

[34] The Moscow Declaration signed by Roosevelt, Stalin, and Churchill on 1 November 1943, Declaration of German Atrocities, 1 November 1943, reprinted in (1944 Supplement) 38 AJIL 3, 7–8.

[35] Agreement for the Prosecution and Punishment of Major War Criminals of the European Axis, and Charter of the International Military Tribunal, Annex, 1951 82 UNTS 279. Cf also The United Nations Commission for the Investigation of War Crimes, Draft Convention for the Establishment of a United Nations War Crimes Court, Doc C 50(1) 30 September 1944.

[36] Control Council Law no 10, adopted 20 December 1945, reprinted in *Trials of War Criminals before the Nuremberg Military Tribunals under Control Council Law No 10* (1946–49) (1949–53) 23; Charter of the International Military Tribunal for the Far East, adopted 19 January 1946, amended 26 April 1946, reprinted in CI Bevans (ed), *Treaties and other international agreements of the United States of America, 1776–1949* (1968–76) iv 20.

[37] *Nuremberg Judgment* (International Military Tribunal, 1946) 217.

have...been crimes punishable as offenses against the law of war; yet the Hague Convention nowhere designates such practices as criminal, nor is any sentence prescribed, nor any mention made of a court to try and punish offenders. For many years past, however, military tribunals have tried and punished individuals guilty of violating the rules of land warfare laid down by this Convention. In the opinion of the Tribunal, those who wage aggressive war are doing that which is equally illegal, and of much greater moment than a breach of one of the rules of the Hague Convention.[38]

The defendants had further argued that 'international law is concerned with the actions of sovereign States, and provides no punishment for individuals; and further that where the act in question is an act of State, those who carry it out are not personally responsible, but are protected by the doctrine of the sovereignty of the State'.[39] The Tribunal equally disposed of that argument:

That international law imposes duties and liabilities upon individuals as well as upon States has long been recognized. In the recent case of *Ex Parte Quirin*...persons were charged during the war with landing in the United States for purposes of spying and sabotage. The late Chief Justice Stone, speaking for the Court, said: 'From the very beginning of its history this Court has applied the law of war as including that part of the law of nations which prescribed for the conduct of war, the status, rights, and duties of enemy individuals.'...Many other authorities could be cited, but enough has been said to show that individuals can be punished for violations of international law.

...

The principle of international law, which under certain circumstances, protects the representative of a state, cannot be applied to acts which are condemned as criminal by international law. The authors of these acts cannot shelter themselves behind their official position in order to be freed from punishment in appropriate proceedings.[40]

The Tribunal referred to article 7 of the Nuremberg Charter that provides that

[t]he official position of defendants, whether as Heads of State or responsible officials in Government Departments, shall not be considered as freeing them from responsibility or mitigating punishment.

And stated that

[h]e who violates the laws of war cannot obtain immunity while acting in pursuance of the authority of the State if the State in authorizing action moves outside its competence under international law.[41]

The Tribunal hence proceeded as if the principles applied by it were firmly established principles of international law. With reference to the many national prosecutions of foreign soldiers for war crimes committed for example during the First World War or the Franco–German war of 1870–71, many scholars agreed.[42]

[38] ibid 218–19. [39] ibid 220.
[40] ibid 220–1. [41] ibid 221.
[42] Cf L Oppenheim (1952) ii 192, § 52*h*; Q Wright, 'The Law of the Nuremberg Trial' (1947) 41 AJIL 38; HS Levie, *The Code of International Armed Conflict* (1986) ii 858.

The trials were however not uncontroversial. Several commentators argued that the prosecution of individuals for crimes against international law *did* compromise the *nullum crimen sine lege* principle since the distinction between violations of international law and individual criminal responsibility for these violations was disregarded.[43] This author is persuaded by the latter position. The Nuremberg Tribunal and its supporters relied on state practice regarding the prosecution of unlawful combatants either for war crimes committed on private impulse or for the crime of espionage and sabotage. The fact that these categories of unlawful combatants could be prosecuted under the domestic law of an enemy state for war crimes is however no precedent for the prosecution of 'system criminality'.[44] While individual responsibility under international law for war crimes committed on the authority of a state was indeed called for—crimes against international law *are* committed by men rather than abstract entities—a rule of customary international law to that effect had yet to be established.

Whatever the merit of the criticism at the time, more than half a century later the key principles underlying the Nuremberg Charter *are* firmly established in international law. The principle of individual responsibility for crimes against international law and the principle of irrelevance of official capacity for the establishment of such responsibility was first confirmed in 1946 in a unanimously adopted resolution of the General Assembly 'affirming the principles of international law recognized by the Charter of the Nuremberg Tribunal and Judgment of the Tribunal'.[45] Since then they have been restated in the International Law Commission's 1950 Principles of International Law Recognized in the Charter of the Nuremberg Tribunal and in the Judgment of the Tribunal,[46] and its 1954 Draft Code of Offences Against the Peace and Security of Mankind and 1996 Draft Code of Crimes against the Peace and Security of Mankind,[47] in the statutes of the International Criminal Tribunal for the Former Yugoslavia (ICTY) and the International Criminal Tribunal for Rwanda (ICTR),[48] in the 1998

[43] Cf eg H Kelsen (1947); GA Finch, 'The Nuremberg Trial and International Law' (1947) 41 AJIL 20; FB Schick, 'The Nuremberg Trial and the International Law of the Future' (1947) 41 AJIL 770.

[44] Cf for the term n 18 above.

[45] Affirmation of the Principles of International Law recognised by the Charter of the Nüremberg Tribunal, UN GA Resolution 95(I), 11 December 1946, UN Doc A/64/Add 1 (1946), reprinted in D Schindler and J Toman (eds) (2004) 1263.

[46] Reprinted in D Schindler and J Toman (eds) (2004) 1265, Principle 3.

[47] Art 1 of the 1954 draft, YBILC 1954 ii (part two); Art 7 of the 1996 draft, YBILC 1996 ii (part 2).

[48] Art 7 of the Statute of the International Criminal Tribunal for the Former Yugoslavia, (1993) 32 ILM 1192. The Tribunal has on several occasions confirmed that the principle of irrelevance of official capacity is firmly established in customary international law Cf *Prosecutor v Furundžija* (ICTY, 1998) § 140; *Prosecutor v Milosević* IT–02–54, Trial Chamber, Decision on Preliminary Motions (2001), § 28–33; Art 6 of the Statute of the International Criminal Tribunal for Rwanda, (1994) 33 ILM 1598.

Rome Statute of the International Criminal Court (ICC)[49] and in the Statute of the Special Court for Sierra Leone (SCSL).[50] The principles now apply in regard of a broad range of crimes—including those committed in internal conflicts. The inclusion of a minimum of humane treatment in armed conflict *not* of an international character in common article 3 of the Geneva Conventions was a crucial step towards a change in nature of international humanitarian law.[51] Change persisted and culminated in a string of decisions by the ICTY further closing the gap between the regimes applicable to international and internal conflicts. The Appeals Chamber in the *Tadić* case commented in this respect that

> [a] State-sovereignty-oriented approach has been gradually supplanted by a human-being-oriented approach. Gradually the maxim of Roman law hominum causa omne jus constitutum (all law is created for the benefit of human beings) has gained a firm foothold in the international community as well. It follows that in the area of armed conflict the distinction between interstate wars and civil wars is losing its value so far as human beings are concerned.[52]

In the wake of the Nuremberg Trials it became accepted that national courts may exercise criminal jurisdiction over crimes against international law under the principle of universal jurisdiction—hence regardless of the *locus delicti* and the nationality of the victim and the suspect.[53] This development warrants brief discussion since it is at the basis of the increase of cases in which the question of immunity of foreign state officials may arise.

In the 1950 *Wagener* case the Italian Supreme Military Tribunal considered that the laws and customs of war 'due to their highly ethical and moral content,

[49] Arts 25 and 27.1 of the Rome Statute of the International Criminal Court, (1998) 37 ILM 999.

[50] Art 6 of the Statute of the Special Court for Sierra Leone, available at <http://www.sc-sl.org>.

[51] Cf also 1968 UN General Assembly Resolution 2444 (XXIII), 1977 Protocol II to the Geneva Conventions.

[52] *Prosecutor v Tadić*, IT–94–1, Appeals Chamber, Decision on the Defence Motion for Interlocutory Appeal on Jurisdiction (ICTY, 1995), § 96–7, quotation at § 97.

[53] The basis of jurisdiction of the Nuremberg Tribunal itself was not entirely clear. The Tribunal considered that the nations that established the Tribunal were doing 'together what any one of them might have done singly', *Nuremberg Judgment* (International Military Tribunal, 1946), 216. Some argued that this meant the Tribunal based its jurisdiction on the universality principle. The UN Secretary-General stated in a 1949 Report on the Tribunal that the prosecutions may imply that *all states* have jurisdiction over crimes against international law but that no definite conclusions could be drawn as yet: The Charter and the Judgment of the Nuremberg Tribunal: History and Analysis, UN Doc A/CN.4/5 (1949), cf AR Carnegie, 'Jurisdiction over Violations of the Laws and Customs of War' (1963) 39 BYIL 402, 415–24. But since the relevant crimes were also committed on the territory of the Allied Powers and directed against their nationals and property jurisdiction could also be based on the territoriality and passive personality principle. Moreover, it is often argued that the Allied Powers could exercise territorial jurisdiction over the crimes since they were acting as the sovereign of Germany, cf G Schwarzenberger (1950) 290–1; H Kelsen (1947) 153, 167; L Oppenheim (1952) ii 580–1. Cf for this argument also FA Mann, 'The Present Legal Status of Germany' (1947) 1 ILQ 314 and the reasoning of the Tribunal itself *Nuremberg Judgment* (International Military Tribunal, 1946) 216. Cf KC Randall (1988) 785, 807–10 for the references to the universality principle in decisions under Control Council Law no 10.

have a universal character, not a territorial one...The solidarity among nations, aimed at alleviating in the best possible way the horrors of war, gave rise to the need to dictate rules which do not recognise borders, punishing criminals wherever they may be.'[54] In the French *Barbie* case the court stated that crimes against humanity 'by reason of their nature...do not simply fall within the scope of French municipal law but are subject to an international criminal order to which the notion of frontiers and extradition rules arising therefrom are completely foreign'.[55] And the Supreme Court of Israel explained in the *Eichmann* case that 'these crimes constitute acts which damage vital international interests; they impair the foundations and security of the international community; they violate the moral values and humanitarian principles that lie hidden in the criminal law systems adopted by civilised nations... they involve the perpetration of an international crime which all the nations of the world are interested in preventing.'[56]

The recent rise in interest in the universality principle as a basis for the exercise of criminal jurisdiction has provoked a debate on the *limits* of the principle.[57] With reference to the *Lotus* case it is sometimes argued that states do not at all need a permissive rule of international law for the exercise of adjudicative jurisdiction in respect of cases relating to acts which have taken place abroad. The Permanent Court of International Justice (PCIJ) had stated in this respect that '[f]ar from laying down a general prohibition to the effect that states may not extend the application of their laws and the jurisdiction of their courts to persons, property and acts outside their territory, it leaves them in this respect a wide measure of discretion which is only limited in certain cases by prohibitive rules; as regards other cases, every State remains free to adopt the principles which it regards as best and the most suitable.'[58] However, the reasoning of the Court already encountered criticism at the time and does certainly not reflect international law today.[59] It is generally accepted that international law protects states from exorbitant claims to jurisdiction of other states by listing the legal bases of

[54] *General Wagener Case* Rivista Penale 1950 II 753 (Italy, Supreme Military Tribunal, 1950) 757 (unofficial translation).

[55] *Fédération Nationale des Déportés et Internés Résistants et Patriotes and Others v Barbie* (France, 1983 and 1984) 130. (The Court of Cassation approvingly cited the words of the Court of Appeal).

[56] *Attorney-General of Israel v Eichmann* (Israel, 1962) 291–3. Cf also *Demjanjuk v Petrovsky* (US, 1985).

[57] Notably, even the core of the universality principle is not uncontroversial. Several courts and scholars defend the view that universal jurisdiction only exists when states have agreed to the exercise of such jurisdiction. See eg HA Kissinger, 'The Pitfalls of Universal Jurisdiction' (July/August 2001) Foreign Affairs 86; Dissent of Lord Browne-Wilkinson to the Princeton Principles on Universal Jurisdiction (2001), available at <http://www.princeton.edu/~lapa/unive_jur.pdf> (fn 20); Individual opinions of Lords Hope and Philips in *R v Bow Street Metropolitan Stipendiary Magistrate and others, ex p Pinochet Ugarte* (UK, 1999), (further referred to as *Pinochet* no 3).

[58] *Case of the SS Lotus* (*France v Turkey*) (1927), PCIJ Reports, Series A, no 9, 19.

[59] Cf JL Brierly, 'Règles générales du droit de la paix' (1936–IV) 58 RdC 1, 146–8; H Lauterpacht (1970) i 488–9; FA Mann, 'The Doctrine of Jurisdiction in International Law' (1964–I) 111 RdC 1, 35–6.

jurisdiction. As Mann put it, a state must establish 'the intimacy and legitimacy of its interest in, the facts in issue'.[60]

It is in this respect good to recall that before Nuremberg, the exercise of jurisdiction over non-nationals committing crimes against non-nationals outside a state's territory was only accepted for the crime of piracy. This was not inherent in the qualification of piracy as a crime against international law but can be explained by the *sui generis* jurisdictional aspects of the crime. As Judge Moore aptly noted in the *SS Lotus Case*:

> the scene of the pirate's operations is the high seas, which it is not the right or duty of any nation to police, he is denied the protection of the flag which he may carry, and is treated as an outlaw, as the enemy of all mankind—*hostis humani generis*—whom any nation may in the interest of all capture and punish.[61]

In other words, since pirates do not operate within the territorial jurisdiction of any state they are likely to escape punishment if not *all* states are recognized to have a legitimate interest in their arrest.

It is sometimes argued that today the nature of crimes against international law establishes sufficient interest in all states and that consequently universal jurisdiction can be exercised *in absentia*—the absolute universality principle, or the unilateral universality principle as Reydams has termed it.[62] There is however increasing support for the viewpoint that courts can only prosecute crimes against international law on this basis if the alleged perpetrator is present on the soil of the forum.[63] In *Prosecutor v Furundžija* the ICTY explicitly stated both the

[60] FA Mann, *Studies in International Law* (1973) 80; M Akehurst (1972–73) 167.

[61] *Case of the SS Lotus* (*France v Turkey*) (1927), PCIJ Reports, dissenting opinion Judge Moore, 70. Cf also V Lowe, 'Jurisdiction' in MD Evans (ed), *International Law* (2003) 329, 343.

[62] See A Cassese (2002) 859–65 (a year later Cassese argued however against absolute universal jurisdiction, cf A Cassese, 'The Belgian Court of Cassation v. the International Court of Justice: the *Sharon and others* Case' (2003) 1 JICJ 437, 452); *Public Prosecutor v Sokolovic* 2001 NJW 2728 (Germany, Bundesgerichtshof, 2001), (cf also *Public Prosecutor v Jorgic* 1999 NStZ 236 (Germany, Bundesgerichtshof, 1998)); *Ordonnance du 6 novembre 1998* (1999) 118 JT 308 (Belgium, Juge d'instruction VanderMeersch) 308, discussed in L Reydams, 'Case Note' (1999) 93 AJIL 700; *Re Sharon and Yaron* 127 ILR 110 (Belgium, Court of Cassation (Second Chamber), 2003). Cf for the terminology, L Reydams, *Universal Jurisdiction, International and Municipal Legal Perspectives* (2003) 38–42.

[63] Reydams has argued in this respect that the 'unilateral universality principle has an intrinsically arbitrary character. The totally random determination of the forum… runs counter to the fundamental principle of the predictability of criminal law. [It] also does not adequately protect the interests of States which are more directly concerned [It] erodes the very concept of jurisdiction.' L Reydams, (2003) 223–5, quotation at 224. The condition of presence is also often mentioned without entering the discussion: ES Kobrick, 'The Ex Post Facto Prohibition and the Exercise of Universal Jurisdiction over International Crimes' (1987) 87 CLR 1515, 1519; CC Joyner, 'Arresting Impunity: The Case for Universal Jurisdiction in Bringing War Criminals to Accountability' (1996) 59 Law & Contemporary Problems 153, 165 and 170; M Cosnard, 'Quelques observations sur les décisions de la Chambre des Lords du 25 Novembre 1998 et du 24 Mars 1999 dans l'affaire Pinochet' (1999) 103 RGDIP 309, 323. Even Randall seemed to qualify his assertions in this way, cf KC Randall (1988) 840. Cf for support in state practice art 689 of the French Code of Criminal Procedure and two French laws providing jurisdiction over crimes against international law

seriousness of the crime and the presence on the territory to underlie the principle of universal jurisdiction:

> [O]ne of the consequences of the jus cogens character bestowed by the international community upon the prohibition of torture is that every State is entitled to investigate, prosecute and punish or extradite individuals accused of torture, *who are present in a territory under its jurisdiction*. Indeed, it would be inconsistent on the one hand to prohibit torture to such an extent as to restrict the normally unfettered treaty-making power of sovereign States, and on the other hand bar States from prosecuting and punishing those torturers who have engaged in this odious practice abroad. This legal basis for States' universal jurisdiction over torture bears out and strengthens the legal foundation for such jurisdiction found by other courts in the inherently universal character of the crime.[64]

Several ICJ judges discussed the issue in some detail in the *Arrest Warrant* case.[65] Judge Guillaume represented the sceptical school. He emphatically stated that 'at no time has it been envisaged that jurisdiction should be conferred upon the courts of every State in the world to prosecute such crimes, whoever their authors and victims and irrespective of the place where the offender is to be found. To do this would, moreover, risk creating total judicial chaos. It would also encourage the arbitrary for the benefit of the powerful, purportedly acting as agent for an ill-defined "international community". Contrary to what is advocated by certain publicists, such a development would represent not an advance in the law but a step backward.'[66] Judges Higgins, Kooijmans and Buergenthal and dissenting Judge Van den Wyngaert represented the more liberal view. The first three cautioned that reliance on state practice to determine the limits of international law may in this case be deceiving since states are not required to use the jurisdiction allowed by international law.[67] After the perusal of doctrine and state practice they concluded that international law does not impose a precondition of

committed in the former Yugoslavia and Rwanda discussed in B Stern, 'Case Note' (1999) 93 AJIL 700; Dutch war crimes legislation (Wet Internationale Misdrijven); *Bouterse* NJ 2002 77 (The Netherlands, Hoge Raad, 2001) § 8; *Guatemala Genocide Case* (2003) 42 ILM 686 (Spain, S Ct, 2003) 697ff, § 8 and 9; *Peruvian Genocide Case* (2003) 42 ILM 1200 (Spain, S Ct, 2003); *Regina v Finta* (Canada, 1989).

[64] *Prosecutor v Furundžija*, (ICTY, 1998) § 156.

[65] *Arrest Warrant of 11 April 2000* (ICJ, 2002) (further referred to as *Arrest Warrant* Case). The Congo complained that a Belgian arrest warrant for its minister for foreign affairs for crimes against international law violated the personal immunity of the minister. It moreover complained that the issuance of an arrest warrant for an individual not present on your territory could not be based on the universality principle. The Court avoided this latter question deciding the immunity question only. The judges that did engage the question argued that the Court denied therewith the logical order of the questions and argued that question of jurisdiction should have been answered first. The question is now again before the Court, cf *Certain Criminal Proceedings in France* (*Republic of the Congo v France*), Application of 9 December 2002, available at <http://www.icj-cij.org>.

[66] ibid Separate Opinion Judge Guillaume, 43, § 15. Cf also the Individual Opinion of Judge Rezek, 94, § 10 and the Declaration of Judge Ranjeva, 55ff, § 5ff.

[67] ibid Joint Separate Opinion of Judges Higgins, Kooijmans and Buergenthal, 76, § 45.

presence on the forum's territory to the exercise of universal jurisdiction.[68] For the purposes of this study it is not necessary to take a position in the debate—the controversy merely serves to sketch the background against which our research question arises.

The exercise of (non-unilateral) universal jurisdiction is at times *mandatory*. States have concluded several multilateral conventions in which they undertake the obligation to prosecute persons found within their territory suspected of committing the crime defined in those conventions. The 1948 Genocide Convention only obliged states that have *territorial* criminal jurisdiction over alleged perpetrators to exercise that jurisdiction,[69] but subsequent conventions moreover included the obligation to prosecute suspects of crimes against international law present within a state's territory on the basis of the principle of universal jurisdiction. The 1949 Geneva Conventions provide the first example of the so-called *aut dedere aut judicare* principle. Signatory states are obliged to either extradite persons present within their territory suspected of committing 'grave breaches' of the Conventions to another state or to prosecute them in their own courts.[70] The example of the Geneva Conventions was later followed in multilateral conventions related to specific crimes, the most prominent being the 1984 Convention Against Torture and Other Cruel, Inhuman and Degrading Treatment or Punishment (Torture Convention or TC).[71] Article 5.2 of the Convention provides that

[68] ibid at p 79, § 54. Cf also the Dissenting Opinion of Judge Van den Wyngaert, 169–73, § 52–8.

[69] Art 6 of the Convention on the Prevention and Suppression of the Crime of Genocide, 78 UNTS 277, provides that 'persons charged with genocide... shall be tried by a competent tribunal of the State in the territory of which the act was committed, or by such international penal tribunal as may have jurisdiction with respect to those Contracting Parties which shall have accepted its jurisdiction'.

[70] Art 49 of the First Geneva Convention for the Amelioration of the Condition of the Wounded and Sick in Armed Forces in the Field (1949) 75 UNTS 31 (1950); Art 50 of the Second Geneva Convention for the Amelioration of the Wounded , Sick and Shipwrecked Members of the Armed Forces at Sea (1949) 75 UNTS 85 (1950); Art 129 of the Third Geneva Convention Relative to the Treatment of Prisoners of War (1949) 75 UNTS 135 (1950); Art 146 of the Fourth Geneva Convention Relative to the Protection of Civilian Persons in Time of War (1949) 75 UNTS 287 (1950).

[71] Convention against Torture and Other Cruel, Inhuman and Degrading Treatment or Punishment (1984) 1465 UNTS 85, reprinted in 23 ILM 1984 1027. Cf also the 1971 Montreal Convention for the Suppression of Unlawful Acts against the Safety of Civil Aviation, the 1973 Hague Convention for the Suppression of Unlawful Seizure of Aircraft, the 1973 Convention on the Prevention and Punishment of Crimes against Internationally Protected Persons including Diplomatic Agents, the 1979 International Convention Against the Taking of Hostages, the 1980 Convention on Physical Protection of Nuclear Material, and the 1997 International Convention for the Suppression of Terrorist Bombings. Although the relevant provisions of these conventions are all worded in slightly different terms, the general mechanism of all conventions is that states undertake to establish the criminal offence at issue in their national law and to exercise jurisdiction, also on basis of universal jurisdiction.

Each State Party shall... take such measures as may be necessary to establish its jurisdiction over [...] in cases where the alleged offender is present in any territory under its jurisdiction and it does not extradite him pursuant to article 8 to any State mentioned in paragraph 1 of this article.

While article 7.1 lays down that:

The State Party in the territory under whose jurisdiction a person alleged to have committed [acts of torture] is found shall in the cases contemplated in Article 5, if it does not extradite him, submit the case to its competent authorities for the purpose of prosecution.

Although exceptionally national courts have claimed that the universality principle under international law serves as a jurisdictional basis for the exercise of jurisdiction, it is more generally agreed that implementing legislation is required, even if the principle is included in a convention to which the state is a party, as a French court held with regard to the universal jurisdiction laid down in the Geneva Conventions 'ces dispositions revêtent un caractère trop général pour créer directement des règles de compétence en matière pénale'.[72] The enactment of national legislation conferring universal jurisdiction on national courts has

[72] *Javor et autres* (France, Cour d'Appel de Paris, 1994), available at <http://www.trial-ch.org>. See for an example of the first approach *Ordonnance du 6 novembre 1998* (Belgium) 308 regarding the Belgian request for extradition of Pinochet from the UK of 6 November 1998. Although at the time the Belgian law only provided universal jurisdiction over war crimes committed in international and non-international armed conflicts, it was held that the extradition request could be based on universal jurisdiction over crimes against humanity under customary international law. The court reasoned as follows: 'we find that, before being codified in a treaty or statute, the prohibition on crimes against humanity was part of customary international law and of international *jus cogens*, and this norm imposes itself imperatively and *erga omnes* on our domestic legal order... Customary international law is equivalent to conventional international law and is directly applicable in the Belgian legal order... Hence, it follows that even in the absence of a treaty, national authorities have the right—and in some circumstances the obligation—to prosecute the perpetrators independently of where they hide... For these reasons we find that, as a matter of customary international law, or even more strongly, as a matter of *jus cogens*, universal jurisdiction over crimes against humanity exists, authorizing national judicial authorities to prosecute and punish the perpetrators in all circumstances.' Trans by L Reydams, '*In re* Pinochet, Belgian Tribunal of First Instance of Brussels' (1999) 93 AJIL 700, 702–3. Cf Loi relative à la répression des infractions graves aux Conventions internationales de Genève du 12 août 1949 et aux Protocols I and II du 8 juin 1977, additionnels à ces Conventions, 16 June 1993, Moniteur Belge, 5 August 1993. Later, in 1999 this law has been amended to enable courts to exercise jurisdiction over perpetrators of genocide and crimes against humanity, as defined in the Statute of the ICC: Loi relative à la répression des violations graves de droit international humanitaire, 10 February 1999, Moniteur Belge, 23 March 1999, reproduced in (1999) 38 ILM 918 (cf ns 295–6 below for further amendments).

The controversy was at the basis of the dissent of Lord Millett to the majority opinion in *Pinochet* no 3 that torture only became an extra-territorial offence against the law of the United Kingdom after the entry into force of the 1984 Criminal Justice Act implementing the 1984 Torture Convention on 29 September 1988, and that hence the double criminality rule in extradition law only allowed extradition to Spain for acts committed after that date. Cf R Van Alebeek, 'The *Pinochet* Case: International Human Rights Law on Trial' (2000) 71 BYIL 29, 31 for examples and arguments that support the majority view; ES Kobrick (1987) Cf differently R O'Keefe, 'Customary International Crimes in English Courts' (2001) 72 BYIL 293. Cf in general R Higgins (1994) 59.

however not kept pace with the developments in international customary law, or even with the obligations undertaken by states in international conventional law.[73] The legislation enacted by some states after the Second World War was limited to crimes committed in that war and did not provide courts with a general competence to deal with crimes against international law committed abroad. Only in a handful of cases did national courts actually exercise universal jurisdiction, and these trials—like the Israeli *Eichmann* case, the French *Barbie* case, the Canadian *Finta* case, and the Australian *Polyukhovich* case—all concerned Nazi crimes.[74]

This only changed when the interest in international criminal law was sparked by the establishment of the ICTY and ICTR in the beginning of the 1990s. Several states amended their legislation in order to be able to prosecute suspected war criminals from the former Yugoslavia and Rwanda that took refuge within their borders. Cases were for example instigated in Austria, Belgium, Denmark, France, Germany, The Netherlands, Sweden, and Switzerland. In other states, like Spain and Italy, the renewed interest in international criminal law led prosecutors to investigate crimes committed during the military regimes in South America. The establishment of the ICC in 1998 further boosted the introduction of national legislation that makes prosecution of crimes against international law possible.[75]

It should at this point be noted that the concept of individual responsibility for crimes against international law also seems to extend to the civil responsibility of perpetrators. The individual civil responsibility under international law has for example found expression in the Statute of the ICC. Article 75.2 provides that '[t]he Court may make an order directly against a convicted person specifying appropriate reparations to, or in respect of, victims, including restitution, compensation and rehabilitation.'[76]

Moreover, the universality principle has also started to affect judicial and academic thinking on the scope of civil jurisdiction of national courts. The issue of individual civil responsibility under international law came before the courts in

[73] R Van Elst, 'Implementing Universal Jurisdiction Over Grave Breaches of the Geneva Conventions' (2000) 13 LJIL 815 gives an overview of the (lack of) implementation of the mandatory principle of universal jurisdiction in the four Geneva Conventions of 1949.

[74] *Polyukhovich v The Commonwealth* 172 CLR 501 (Australia, High Court of Australia, 1991). *Attorney-General of Israel v Adolf Eichmann* (Israel, 1962); *Fédération Nationale des Déportés et Internés Résistants et Patriotes and Others v Barbie* (France, 1983, 1984, 1985, 1988); *R v Finta* (Canada, 1989).

[75] The Rome Statute, A/CONF 183/9 Cf for overview of state practice eg Redress, *Universal Jurisdiction in Europe, Criminal prosecutions in Europe since 1990 for war crimes, crimes against humanity and genocide* (1999); International Law Association, report by MT Kamminga, *The Exercise of Universal Jurisdiction in Respect of Gross Human Rights Offences: Final Report* (2000); ICRC website. Cf however *Habré* 125 ILR 569 (Senegal, CA of Dakar, Court of Cassation, 2000, 2001) for a recent example of a state that has not implemented the necessary legislation to comply with its obligations under the 1984 Torture Convention.

[76] See also rules 94 to 98 of the Rules of Procedure and Evidence, ICC-ASP/1/3.

the 1984 US *Filártiga* case.[77] The plaintiffs in this case relied on the Alien Tort Claims Act which provides that

> The district courts shall have original jurisdiction of any civil action by an alien for a tort only, committed in violation of the law of nations or a treaty of the United States.[78]

A claim was instigated by the parents of a Paraguayan boy tortured to death by a Paraguayan police officer in Paraguay during the Stroessner regime against the alleged perpetrator who had immigrated to the United States. The court stated that 'for purposes of civil liability, the torturer has become—like the pirate and the slave trader before him—*hostis humanis generis*, an enemy of all mankind'.[79] The decision of the court to award the plaintiffs over $10 million dollar damages launched the statute—passed into oblivion after its enactment in 1789—into the modern world of transborder human rights litigation.[80] In 1992 the Torture Victim Protection Act (TVPA) was enacted to remedy the gap left by the ATCA as regards the protection of US nationals.[81] Section 2 of the Act provides, in relevant part, as follows:

(a) Liability—An individual who, under actual or apparent authority, or colour of law, of any foreign nation—
    (1) subjects an individual to torture shall, in a civil action, be liable for damages to that individual; or
    (2) subjects an individual to extrajudicial killing shall, in a civil action, be liable for damages to that individual's legal representative, or to any person who may be a claimant in an action for wrongful death.

Although the US Supreme Court has decided in 2004 that the ATCA only applies to a narrow class of international norms that can be established with sufficient specifity, claims against foreign state officials for human rights violations committed abroad are still possible.[82]

The US approach to civil jurisdiction over extra-territorial torts cannot be said to receive widespread support.[83] Especially civil law countries know strict jurisdictional limits for the establishment of civil jurisdiction, but also the House of Lords rejects the broad assertion of civil jurisdiction by US courts.[84] While we

[77] *Filártiga v Peña-Irala* 630 F 2d 876 (US, Ct of Apps (2nd Cir), 1980).

[78] 28 USC § 1350 (1982), originally the Judiciary Act of 1789, ch 20 § 9 (b), 1 Stat 73, 77.

[79] *Filártiga v Peña-Irala* (US, 1980) 890.

[80] *Filártiga v Peña-Irala* 577 F Supp 860 (US, DC for the Eastern District of New York, 1984).

[81] 28 USC § 1350.

[82] *Sosa v Alvarez-Machain* (2004) 43 ILM 1390 (US, S Ct, 2004), cf ch 6 § 1 below. Cf on the question of universal civil jurisdiction also *Ferrini v Repubblica Federale di Germania* (Italy, 2004) § 9 and § 12, and the discussion thereof in A Gattini, 'War Crimes and State Immunity in the *Ferrini* Decision' (2005) 2 JICJ 224, 238ff.

[83] Cf *Arrest Warrant Case*, Joint Separate Opinion of Judges Higgins, Kooijmans and Buergenthal, § 48.

[84] Cf *Jones v Saudi Arabia* (UK, 2006) § 20, §98. Cf for the common law doctrine of the transitory tort R. Phillimore, *Commentaries upon International Law* (3rd edn, 1889) 4; JM Blum and RG Steinhardt, 'Federal Jurisdiction over International Human Rights Claims: The Alien Tort Claims

can say that these limits are under review in respect of extra-territorial activity that amounts to a crime against international law,[85] the customary international law status of the principle of universal civil jurisdiction is far from clear.[86]

This is the roughly sketched context in which our research question arises. *How do the individual responsibility for crimes against international law and related developments in international criminal law affect the functional and personal immunity of foreign state officials?*[87]

The discussion can be conducted on two distinct levels. In the first place, it can be questioned whether functional or personal immunity *is available* in respect of allegations of crimes against international law. What is the state of the law on this question? Three recent judicial decisions—the *Pinochet* case, the *Arrest Warrant* case and the *Taylor* case—pivoted on this question.[88]

In the *Pinochet* case the House of Lords was asked to decide whether a former head of state enjoys functional immunity from foreign national jurisdiction in respect of torture allegations. This chapter will argue that the extension of the principle of individual responsibility for crimes against international law to crimes committed under the cloak of state authority and the principle of the irrelevance of official capacity *directly* target the rule of functional immunity of state officials. The House of Lords reasoned in different terms. This chapter links the reasoning of the House of Lords in the *Pinochet* case to the findings of chapter 3 of this study. It sets out to prove that many arguments on the scope of the rule of functional immunity in light of developments in international criminal law—including those relied on in the *Pinochet* case—proceed from a flawed conception of the functional immunity of state officials.

The decision of the International Court of Justice (ICJ) in the *Arrest Warrant* Case and the decision of the SCSL in *Prosecutor v Taylor* both concerned personal immunities of foreign state officials. The Nuremberg Charter did not deal with procedural immunity from jurisdiction. The question did in fact only surface after the establishment of the ICC. This study agrees with the conclusion of the ICJ in the 2002 *Arrest Warrant* case that personal immunities apply also in respect of allegations of crimes against international law. The decision in the 2004 *Taylor* case distinguished jurisdiction exercised by *national* courts from that exercised

Act after *Filártiga v Peña-Irala*', in RG Steinhardt and A D'Amato (eds), *The Alien Tort Claims Act: An Analytical Anthology* (1999) 49, 58.

[85] Cf the Hague Conference on Private International Law, Preliminary Draft Convention on Jurisdiction and Foreign Judgments in Civil and Commercial Matters adopted by the Special Commission (1999), art 18.3 and the commentary on that art in the Report on the Preliminary Draft Convention on Jurisdiction and Foreign Judgments in Civil and Commercial Matters (P Nygh and F Pocar), Prel Doc No 11 (2000), available at <http://www.hcch.net>.

[86] Cf further DF Donovan and A Roberts, 'The Emerging Recognition of Universal Civil Jurisdiction', (2006) 100 AJIL 142.

[87] It is noted that this study does not engage the question which acts qualify as crimes against international law.

[88] *Pinochet* no 3; *Arrest Warrant* Case; *Prosecutor v Charles Ghankay Taylor*, (SCSL, 2004).

by *international* courts. It was concluded that since the SCSL is an international criminal court it *can* establish jurisdiction over a sitting head of state. This chapter disputes the premises of the decision in the *Taylor* case. The decision is based on a questionable interpretation of the principle of irrelevance of official capacity, on a questionable interpretation of an ambiguous obiter statement of the ICJ in the *Arrest Warrant* case and on circular reasoning as regards the nature of the jurisdiction of international courts.

In addition to the *scope* of the rules of functional and personal immunity, we must inquire into the *validity* of these rules. One popular argument that will be considered in particular is that crimes against international law *trump* the immunity rules protecting state officials from foreign jurisdiction because of their *jus cogens* nature.

The second level on which we can approach the research question is that of policy. Policy arguments do not assert that the developments in international human rights law and international criminal law *have changed* the immunities of foreign state officials; they assert that states *should change* these immunities in view of these developments. The discussion of policy arguments in this study is limited to the question whether the present scope of the immunity rule *violates* other rules of international law. If immunity *is* still available to foreign state officials it can be questioned whether the obligations states have under the immunity rules are compatible with their obligations under international criminal law. Since in case of competing legal obligations, judges may decide that one should prevail over the other, policy arguments of this sort could result in the non-application of the immunity rule.

2 State of the Law Arguments

2.1 Introduction

Are state officials shielded from foreign jurisdiction in respect of allegations of crimes against international law? What is the state of international law on this question? Two lines of inquiry must be pursued. The developments in international criminal law may have effect on the *validity* as well as the *scope* of the immunity rules protecting foreign state officials. The question as to the scope of the rules distinguishes between the functional and the personal immunity of foreign state officials.

2.2 The Normative Hierarchy Theory: Voidance of the Rules in View of International Criminal Law?

The first line of inquiry examines the argument that *jus cogens* norms of international criminal law take precedence over the hierarchically lower rules of personal and functional immunity. The argument was first developed in support of a human rights exception to the rule of state immunity—as we will see in chapter 6 below.[89] It relies on the principle that *jus cogens* rules invalidate rules of international law that are in conflict with them.[90] Kamto, for example, wrote that since the prohibition of torture is a *jus cogens* norm 'sauf à considérer que le principe de l'immunité du ministre des affaires étrangères est également une norme du *jus cogens*... l'interdiction de la torture... doit prévaloir sur la règle de l'immunité'.[91]

The argument is problematic because it requires sliding from the *jus cogens* nature of the prohibition of certain conduct to the nature of the rule allowing or requiring enforcement of that prohibition in foreign national courts. As Lord Hoffmann pointedly wrote in *Jones v Saudi Arabia*: 'To produce a conflict with... immunity, it is therefore necessary to show that the [substantive *jus cogens* prohibition] has generated an ancillary procedural rule which, by way of exception to... immunity, entitles or perhaps requires states to assume... jurisdiction over other states in cases in which torture is alleged.'[92]

It is in this respect interesting to note that Kamto argued that 'l'immunité d'un ministre des Affaires étrangères en exercice tombe devant cette exigence partagée par tous les États de combattre l'impunité en sanctionnant effectivement ses crimes éventuels qui entreraient dans la catégorie des crimes "les plus graves"'.[93] In contrast to the above quotation this latter statement does indeed refer to two opposing obligations. However, for the argument to work it must be established that the obligation to prosecute crimes against international law is of a *jus cogens* nature. Accordingly, Judge Al-Khasawneh—dissenting from the majority opinion in the *Arrest Warrant* case—formulated the argument as follows:

> *The effective combating of grave crimes* has arguably assumed a *jus cogens* character reflecting recognition by the international community of the vital community interests and values it seeks to protect and enhance. Therefore when this hierarchically higher norm comes into conflict with the rules on immunity, it should prevail.[94]

[89] Ch 6 § 2.2 below.

[90] For the concept of *jus cogens* see ch 6 § 1 below.

[91] M Kamto, 'Une troublante "immunité totale" du ministre des affaires étrangères' (2002) 35 RBDI 518, 528. Cf also A Bianchi, 'Immunity versus Human Rights: The *Pinochet* Case' (1999) 10 EJIL 237, 262; A Bianchi, 'Individual Accountability for Crimes against Humanity: Reckoning with the Past, Thinking of the Future' (1999) 19 SAIS Review 97. The argument was advanced in *Wei Ye v Jiang Zemin* (US, 2004), but the court felt obliged to give effect to the executive's suggestion of head of state immunity.

[92] *Jones v Saudi Arabia* (UK, 2006).

[93] ibid.

[94] *Arrest Warrant* Case, Dissenting Opinion of Judge Al-Khasawneh, 98, § 7 (emphasis added).

It must, in the first place, be pointed out that mandatory universal jurisdiction is for now still only of a conventional nature.[95] It can hence not be said that states have an obligation under customary international law to prosecute all individuals present within its territory that are suspected of any crime against international law.[96] The obligation to prosecute can therefore not be of a *jus cogens* character. But also as far as permissive universal jurisdiction is concerned, there is no support in international law that it classifies under the very select group of *jus cogens* norms.

The only obligations that effectively precede obligations under immunity rules are obligations imposed by the Security Council of the United Nations (SC) under Chapter VII of the UN Charter. Article 103 of the Charter provides that '[i]n the event of a conflict between the obligations of the Members of the United Nations under the present Charter and their obligations under any other international agreement, their obligations under the present Charter shall prevail.'[97] In respect of the ICTY and the ICTR Gaeta put it as follows:

> [T]he Statutes of the two ad hoc Tribunals provide for a derogation from the legal regulation of personal immunities contained in customary international law. Admittedly, these Statutes do not envisage any such derogation explicitly. However, they lay down the obligation of all UN Member States to cooperate with the International Tribunals, in particular by executing arrest warrants. This obligation, being based on a Security Council binding resolution made under Chapter VII of the UN Charter, by virtue of Article 103 of the UN Charter takes precedence over customary and treaty obligations concerning personal immunities. Consequently, whenever a Member State to which the International Tribunal issues an arrest warrant enjoining the detention of the Head of State of another UN member who happens to be on its territory executes the arrest warrant, by doing so it does not breach any customary or treaty obligations vis-à-vis the foreign State concerned.[98]

[95] Cf § 1 above. Cf § 3 below for the argument that these conventional obligations do not extend to individuals clothed with personal immunity.

[96] There is an argument that exercise of *territorial* criminal jurisdiction *is* obligatory. This has however more to do with obligations owed to individuals under human rights law than with obligations owed to other states under international criminal law and is therefore discussed in ch 6 § 3.4 below.

[97] While the Security Council can impose obligations on states when acting outside Chapter VII, the obligation to violate the normal rules of personal immunity can in fact only be imposed under Chapter VII, cf p 277 below.

[98] P Gaeta, 'Official Capacity and Immunities' in A Cassese, P Gaeta, JRWD Jones (eds), *The Rome Statute of the International Criminal Court: A Commentary* (2002) 975, 989.

It is in this respect interesting to note that upon the establishment of the ICTY the Swiss government saw itself forced to qualify the immunities granted to participants to the Conference on the former Yugoslavia in Geneva.[99]

2.3 The Scope of the Immunity of State Officials in View of Individual Responsibility for Crimes against International Law

2.3.1 Functional Immunity

2.3.1.1 Introduction

In chapter 3 of this study it was explained that there is considerable confusion as regards the act of state concept that controls the rule of functional immunity.[100] It was argued that state officials enjoy functional immunity from the jurisdiction of foreign courts in respect of acts committed as the arm or mouthpiece of their home state. These acts are acts of the state that cannot be attributed to state officials in their personal capacity and officials can accordingly not be called to account for them in that capacity. Because the determination of the mandate of state officials is within the exclusive competence of the home state, state officials are *assumed* to have acted on behalf of the state whenever they have acted within the context of the exercise of state authority under international law.

Two *different* act of state concepts feature however in academic and judicial thinking on the rule of functional immunity. State officials are seen to enjoy functional immunity whenever the state would enjoy state immunity had it been sued instead—act of state as public act—or alternatively state officials are seen to enjoy functional immunity whenever they are sued in respect of an act that can be attributed to the state—act of state as act attributable to the state. Accordingly, the application of the rule is not concerned with the capacity in which the state official can be sued. The absence of individual responsibility only *follows* the application of the rule of functional immunity.

The conception of the rule of functional immunity crucially affects the parameters of coherent legal argument on the scope of this rule. In chapter 3 a tip of the veil was lifted. This section elaborates on the influence of the three distinct conceptions of the rule on the possibility to establish the criminal and civil responsibility of (former) foreign state officials for crimes against international law. It will be argued that the principle of individual responsibility for crimes against international law and the principle of irrelevance of official capacity directly affect the assumption that an official has acted within the scope of his mandate. States have, in other words, agreed on universal limits on the mandate of state officials. Crimes against international law do not qualify as acts of the state rather than

[99] Cf L Caflisch, 'La Pratique Suisse en matière de droit international public 1998 no 7.2' (1999) 9 RSDIE 682, 690–1.

[100] This section builds on the findings of ch 3 and assumes that the reader is familiar with the reasoning developed therein.

acts of the individual that performs the act, and hence are not official acts for the purpose of the rule of functional immunity. In other words, the rationale of the rule of functional immunity does not extend to these acts.

Under the two alternative conceptions, however, crimes against international law normally qualify as acts of state for the purposes of the rule of functional immunity. Developments in international criminal law can only effect an exception to the immunity for official acts. Immunity is then lacking *in spite of* the rationale of the rule.

At first blush the question whether the absence of functional immunity for crimes against international law exists *in spite of* or *within* the rationale of the rule may seem of purely academic interest. This is true, in fact, as long as the attributability to the state criterion is not linked to the act of state immunity rationale. However, the conception of functional immunity as being in fact state immunity *ratione materiae* does limit the possible scope of an exception for crimes against international law to criminal proceedings. If the exception were to extend to civil proceedings this would amount to a *general* exception to the rule of state immunity *ratione materiae* in respect of allegations of crimes against international law. In other words, under this conception there is no rational distinction between the state and the state official for the purpose of civil responsibility.

This section sets out with a discussion of the reasoning developed from the perspective of the two alternative conceptions of the rule of functional immunity. The *Pinochet* case will provide an insightful example of the consequences of a particular definition of act of state for functional immunity purposes.[101] Subsequently, the position advanced in this study will be defended.

2.3.1.2 An exception for crimes against international law *in spite of* the rationale of the rule

If official acts are acts that can be attributed to the state, crimes against international law committed by state officials are, as a rule, official acts. Thus, after subscribing to attributability as the critical test for official acts Barker stated that '[t]o deny the official character of such offences is to fly in the face of reality.'[102] Consequently, immunity for crimes against international law can only be removed by a separate rule establishing an exception.[103]

The same is true if official acts are acts in respect of which the state would enjoy immunity had it been sued instead. The exercise of police authority or the waging of war are necessarily 'governmental' activities for the purposes of the rule of state immunity. In this sense, Jescheck noted 'das Völkerstrafrecht hat es in erster Linie mit staatlichen Hoheitsakten zu tun'.[104] Or, as Lord Millett formulated it in *Pinochet* no 3, acts of torture are 'official and governmental acts

[101] *Pinochet* no 3.

[102] JC Barker (1999) 943.

[103] Cf eg D Akande, 'International Law Immunities and the International Criminal Court' (2004) 98 AJIL 407, 414.

[104] H-H Jescheck, *Die Verantwortlichkeit der Staatsorgane nach Völkerstrafrecht, eine Studie zu den Nürnberger Prozessen* (1952) 166.

by any standard'.[105] From this perspective Fox was right to point out that the absence of immunity for international crimes 'can only be brought about by the introduction of an exception to state immunity from criminal proceedings in respect of the individuals who commit the crimes.'[106]

Many authors have argued that such an exception does in fact exist. As Gaeta put it:

> [A]ll state officials, including those at the highest level, are not entitled to functional immunity in criminal proceedings—either of a national or international nature—if charged with such offences as war crimes and crimes against humanity...
>
> It is apparent that this customary rule constitutes an exception to the general rule granting functional immunity to State organs for acts they perform in their official capacity. Clearly, the relationship between the two rules is one of *lex specialis* to *lex generalis*.[107]

Most of the Law Lords decided *Pinochet* no 3 adhered to the act of state immunity conception of the rule of functional immunity, or on an amalgam of the act of state immunity and attributability conception. A closer look at the Pinochet saga will teach us how this fact influenced the scope of the refusal of immunity to the former head of state of Chile.

On 17 October 1998 Augusto Pinochet Ugarte was arrested in the United Kingdom while ill in a London hospital. More than twenty-five years after Pinochet commanded the violent military coup that evicted the government of President Allende on 11 September 1973, the Spanish judge Garzon decided that it was time to end the impunity of the man often held responsible for the acts of systematic and widespread human rights violations that characterized the military regime in Chile. A Spanish international warrant of arrest had been issued on 16 October and was eventually followed by a second international warrant and an official extradition request by the Spanish government pursuant to the 1957 European Convention on Extradition.[108] On the basis of these international warrants, UK Metropolitan Magistrates issued two provisional warrants for Pinochet's arrest under section 8(1) of the UK Extradition Act 1989. The first warrant alleged the murder of Spanish citizens in Chile, while the second warrant included allegations of torture, hostage taking, and murder. Applications were made on behalf of Pinochet for judicial review and habeas corpus in respect of the

[105] *Pinochet* no 3, 172 (*per* Lord Millett).

[106] H Fox (1999) 696.

[107] P Gaeta (2002) 982–3. Cf eg A Verdross, *Die völkerrechtswidrige Kriegshandlung und der Strafanspruch der Staaten* (1920); A Verdross and B Simma, *Universelles Völkerrecht, Theorie und Praxis* (3rd edn, 1984) 773; G Dahm, 'Völkerrechtliche Grenzen der Inländischen Gerichtsbarkeit gegenüber ausländischen Staaten' in *Festschrift für Arthur Nikisch* (1958) 153, 170; M Bothe (1971) 254; A Watts (1994) 13, 82 and 84; J Salmon (1994) 468; A Cassese (2002) 870ff; D Akande (2004); S Wirth, 'Immunities, Related Problems, and Article 98 of the *Rome Statute*' (2002) 12 Criminal Law Forum 429; JC Barker (1999) 943–4.

[108] European Convention on Extradition (1957), CETS no 24. Incorporated in UK law by the European Convention on Extradition Order 1990 as amended by the Extradition Act 1989. The Spanish request was followed by an extradition request from the French, the Belgian, and the Swiss government.

two warrants.[109] The central question to be answered by the courts was whether Pinochet, head of state when he allegedly committed these crimes, could invoke the rule of functional immunity as a shield against the allegations.[110]

Section 20.1 of the 1978 UK State Immunity Act (SIA) controlled the debate. The section provides that:

subject to the provisions of this section and to any necessary modifications, the Diplomatic Privileges Act 1964 shall apply to

(a) a sovereign or other Head of State;
(b) members of his family forming part of his household; and
(c) his private servants,

as it applies to the head of a diplomatic mission, to members of his family forming part of his household and to his private servants.

The Diplomatic Privileges Act 1964 (DPA) gives effect to the 1961 Vienna Convention on Diplomatic Relations in English law (VCDR). The relevant provision in the Pinochet trial was article 39.2 of the Convention, which provides as follows:

When the functions of a person enjoying privileges and immunities have come to an end, such privileges and immunities shall normally cease at the moment when he leaves the country, or on expiry of a reasonable period in which to do so, but shall subsist until that time, even in case of armed conflict. However, with respect to acts performed by such a person in the exercise of his functions as a member of the mission, immunity shall continue to subsist.

Article 39.2 VCDR reflects the rule of functional immunity under international law. UK legislation hence allowed the courts to decide the immunity question in accordance with international law.

Pinochet had his fate decided in a veritable courtroom-drama consisting of four acts. After a judgment of the Divisional Court,[111] appeal was made to the

[109] See for a comprehensive overview of the facts of the case *Pinochet* no 3, 101–4 (*per* Lord Browne-Wilkinson).

[110] In *Pinochet* no 3 a *second* question became central to the proceedings. Because the majority did not regard torture criminal under UK law until s 134.1 of the Criminal Justice Act 1988 incorporating the Torture Convention in UK law came into force on 29 September 1988, the number of extradition crimes was reduced significantly. It is further noted that it *could* have been argued on behalf of Pinochet that an extradition request cannot be merely based on the principle of universal jurisdiction since the exercise of jurisdiction on that basis requires the presence of the suspect on the territory of the forum state. Cf on this question also J Dugard, Opinion in the *Boutserse* case (on file with the author) § 5.6.5. However, the Spanish court did observe that Spain had a legitimate interest because at least fifty Spanish subjects disappeared or were killed in Chile during the *Pinochet* regime, implying that jurisdiction could in addition be based on the passive personality principle: *Case 1/98* (Spain, Audiencia Nacional, criminal division, plenary session, 1998), cf M Del Carmen Márquez and J Alcaide Fernández, 'Case Note' (1999) 93 AJIL 690, 691.

[111] *R v Bow Street Metropolitan Stipendiary Magistrate and others, ex p Pinochet Ugarte* [1998] All ER (D) 509 (UK, The Divisional Court of the Queen's Bench Division, 1998). Lord Bingham of Cornhill CJ, Collins and Richards JJ unanimously quashed both warrants.

House of Lords. The learned Lords had to decide the case twice. The first decision of 25 November 1998[112] was set aside by a House of Lords Committee on 17 December 1998 because the Appellate Committee had been improperly constituted.[113] A final judgment was given on 24 March 1999.[114] All seven members of the House of Lords delivered individual opinions. A 6–1 majority decided that there could be no immunity for a former head of state for the torture allegations under consideration. It is however impossible to derive a common ratio decidendi from the six majority opinions. The opinions are divided on several critical issues. In addition, some of the opinions suffer from internal inconsistencies.

The decision has been lauded as providing 'le critère qui permet de distinguer parmi les actes d'un gouvernant'.[115] Another commentator summarized the decision as follows: 'l'ancien Chef d'Etat, en principe au bénéfice de l'immunité de juridiction pénale pour ses actes de fonction, n'est cependant pas à l'abri des poursuites lorsque ces actes revêtent le caractère de crimes de droit international'.[116] In the opinion of this author, the acclaim is in want of some qualification.

Only three Lords agreed unequivocally that there is no immunity from criminal jurisdiction for crimes against international law. But two of them—Lord Hope and Lord Philips—relied on the Torture Convention to establish the universal jurisdiction that makes this rule applicable to cases before national courts as well. Only Lord Hutton can be said to have recognized the absence of functional immunity from the jurisdiction of national courts in respect of all crimes against international law. Lord Saville of Newdigate and Lord Browne-Wilkinson based their refusal to grant immunity exclusively on the specific terms of the Torture Convention. Finally, the opinion of Lord Millett did not purport to rely on the Torture Convention but his argument seems limited to crimes against international law that can only be committed by a state official under the colour

[112] *R v Bow Street Metropolitan Stipendiary Magistrate and others, ex p Pinochet Ugarte (Amnesty International and others intervening)* [1998] 4 All ER 897 (UK, HL, 1998); [1998] 3 WLR 1456 HL (*Pinochet* no 1). The majority allowed the appeal (Lords Nicholls of Birkenhead, Steyn, and Hoffmann; Lords Slynn of Hadley and Lloyd of Berwick dissenting).

[113] Lord Hoffmann had failed to disclose his close links with Amnesty International; an intervener in the case. *R v Bow Street Metropolitan Stipendiary Magistrate and others, ex p Pinochet Ugarte* [1999] 1 All ER 577 (UK, HL, 1999); [1999] 2 WLR 272, (*Pinochet* no 2). See on this TH Jones, 'Judicial Bias and Disqualification in the Pinochet Case' (1999) Public Law 391.

[114] *Pinochet* no 3. The majority allowed the appeal but did significantly reduce the number of extradition crimes (Lords Browne-Wilkinson, Hope of Craighead, Hutton, Saville of Newdigate, Millett, and Philips of Worth Matravers; Lord Goff of Chieveley dissenting). On 2 March 2000 the UK Home Secretary Jack Straw decided that General Pinochet's ill-health made him unfit to stand trial before the English courts and that he was allowed to return to Chile. On the basis of a medical report the Home Secretary decided that Pinochet would not be extradited to Spain. See on this Straw's Letter to the Spanish Ambassador. Straw stated that: 'The principle that an accused person should be mentally capable of following the proceedings, instructing his lawyers and giving coherent evidence is fundamental to the idea of a fair trial', sub 20.

[115] M Cosnard (1999) 319.

[116] C Dominicé, 'Quelques observations sur l'immunité de juridiction pénale de l'ancien chef d'Etat' (1999) 103 RGDIP 297, 307. Cf also S Wirth, 'Immunity for Core Crimes? The ICJ's Judgment in the *Congo v Belgium* Case' (2002) 13 EJIL 877, 892.

of law. In order to ascertain the precedent value of the *Pinochet* case it is therefore necessary to closely scrutinize each individual opinion. The scope of the refusal of immunity can only be grasped when the personal parameters of functional immunity and international criminal law of each Lord are revealed.[117]

Lord Goff of Chieveley delivered the only dissent on the immunity issue. As to the nature of the protection available to Pinochet, Lord Goff agreed with Watts that the 'critical question' in the application of the rule of functional immunity is 'whether the conduct was engaged in under colour of or in ostensible exercise of the Head of State's public authority'.[118] He added that '[i]n this context, the contrast is drawn between governmental acts, which are functions of the head of state, and private acts, which are not.'[119] He asserted that any exclusion of 'state immunity' in respect of crimes of torture should be derived from the Torture Convention, since the principle of irrelevance of official capacity is only 'concerned with international responsibility before international tribunals, and not with the exclusion of state immunity in criminal proceedings before national courts'.[120]

Article 1.1 of the Torture Convention defines torture as

> any act by which severe pain or suffering, whether physical or mental, is intentionally inflicted on a person for such purposes as obtaining from him or a third person information or a confession, punishing him for an act he or a third person has committed or is suspected of having committed, or intimidating or coercing him or a third person, or for any reason based on discrimination of any kind, when such pain or suffering is inflicted by or at the instigation of or with the consent or acquiescence of a public official or other person acting in an official capacity. It does not include pain or suffering arising from, inherent in or incidental to lawful sanctions.

According to Lord Goff the argument on the influence of the Torture Convention runs as follows:

> since torture contrary to the convention can only be committed by a public official or other person acting in an official capacity, and since it is in respect of the acts of these very persons that states can assert state immunity ratione materiae, it would be inconsistent with the obligations of state parties under the convention for them to be able to invoke state immunity ratione materiae in cases of torture contrary to the convention.[121]

He did not accept that argument. In the first place, he held that a waiver of state immunity by treaty must always be express.[122] Equally adamant was his

[117] Fox rightly noted that 'the evaluation of the full implications of the case will take years': H Fox (1999) 687. My assessment and appreciation of the reasoning of the Lords has changed on several points since the publication of R van Alebeek (2000).

[118] *Pinochet* no 3 119, referring to A Watts (1994-III) 56.

[119] ibid 199.

[120] ibid 120–1.

[121] ibid 122.

[122] ibid 123.

rejection of the argument that the Convention removes immunity by implication. Because treaties are the result of extensive negotiations, compromise, and even horse-trading, the text of the treaty itself, and the travaux préparatoires are the only safe guide to its terms. In other words, Lord Goff rejected the idea that the terms of a treaty must necessarily be 'logical' or 'effective'. Moreover, he argued that 'state immunity' is not inconsistent with the obligations of state parties to the Convention. He asserted that

> in the majority of cases which may arise under the convention, no question of state immunity will arise at all, because the public official concerned is likely to be present in his own country. Even when such a question does arise, there is no reason to assume that state immunity will be asserted by the state of which the alleged torturer is a public official; on the contrary it is only in unusual cases . . . that this is likely to be done.[123]

Lord Goff hence concluded that the argument that the 'state immunity' is excluded by an implied term in the Torture Convention or waived by the states ratifying the Torture Convention is 'contrary to principle and authority, and indeed to common sense'.[124]

The opinion of Lord Saville of Newdigate is unambiguous in its exclusive reliance on the terms of the Torture Convention. A former head of state, Lord Saville noted, is immune for acts done 'in his official capacity as head of state'.[125] His subsequent reasoning reveals that he proceeded from the premise that for the purposes of the rule of functional immunity act of state means either act attributable to the state or governmental act. According to the Lord there was no exception to immunity for the international crime of torture before the coming into existence of the Torture Convention.[126] He concluded however that since the ratification of the Torture Convention by the UK on 8 December 1988 Pinochet could no longer rely on the defence of immunity in respect of allegation of torture since from that date onwards Spain, Chile and the UK were all parties to the Convention.

According to Lord Saville torture within the definition of article 1.1 of the Torture Convention automatically qualifies under the rule of functional immunity:

> So far as the states that are parties to the convention are concerned, I cannot see how, as far as torture is concerned, this immunity can exist consistently with the terms of that convention. Each state party has agreed that the other state parties can exercise jurisdiction over alleged official torturers found within their territories . . . and thus, to my mind, can hardly simultaneously claim an immunity from extradition or prosecution that is necessarily based on the official nature of the alleged torture.[127]

[123] ibid 127.
[124] ibid 123.
[125] ibid 168.
[126] ibid 168.
[127] ibid 169. Inherent in this argument is the conception of act of state as act attributable to the state, or governmental act.

He pointed out that he 'did not reach this conclusion by implying terms into the Torture Convention, but simply by applying its express terms'.[128] Although acts of torture would normally qualify for protection under section 20 SIA he considered the 'unequivocal terms of the Torture Convention' to qualify as an express waiver.[129]

Lord Browne-Wilkinson considered the immunity for official acts performed in the exercise of the functions of head of state to be the equivalent of state immunity *ratione materiae.* His reasons for refusal to grant Pinochet 'state immunity' appear somewhat ambiguous. The opinion reasons in two minds. First we read that 'long before the Torture Convention state torture was an international crime in the highest sense'.[130] Lord Browne-Wilkinson noted in this regard that '[t]he jus cogens nature of torture justifies states in taking universal jurisdiction over torture wherever committed'.[131] Later on, however, he held that torture could not be described as 'a fully constituted international crime' until the Convention provided states with universal jurisdiction to try alleged torturers.[132] The same ambiguity is also reflected in the reasons for denying immunity. At the outset Lord Browne-Wilkinson wondered—in a sweeping rhetorical question—'[h]ow [it can] be for international law purposes an official function to do something which international law itself prohibits and criminalises.'[133] The basis of his decision is however arguably much smaller. The Lord actually based his *decisive* argument against the grant of immunity—as he himself admitted—on the specific terms of the Torture Convention:

> Immunity ratione materiae applies not only to ex-heads of state and ex-ambassadors but to all state officials who have been involved in carrying out the functions of the state... if the implementation of the torture regime is to be treated as official business sufficient to found an immunity for the former head of state, it must also be official business sufficient to justify immunity for his inferiors who actually did the torturing. Under the convention the international crime of torture can only be committed by an official or someone in an official capacity. They would all be entitled to immunity. Therefore, the whole elaborate structure of universal jurisdiction over torture committed by officials is rendered abortive and one of the main objectives of the Torture Convention... will have been frustrated... all these factors together demonstrate that the notion of continued immunity for ex-heads of state is inconsistent with the provisions of the Torture Convention.[134]

In spite of the extensive reference to concepts of international criminal law and *jus cogens* Lord Browne-Wilkinson hence accorded a decisive role to the Torture Convention. This is corroborated by the fact that he held the immunity to be unavailable since 8 December 1988.[135]

[128] ibid 169.
[129] ibid 170.
[130] ibid 109.
[131] ibid 109.
[132] ibid 114.
[133] ibid.
[134] ibid 114–15.
[135] ibid 115.

The construction relied on to justify the conclusion of absence of immunity makes the opinion internally inconsistent. Lord Browne-Wilkinson considered that after 8 December organizing and authorizing torture could not be done 'in any capacity which gives rise to immunity ratione materiae because such actions were contrary to international law.'[136] The acts of torture under consideration did not therefore qualify for protection under section 20 SIA. However, within the conception of the rule of functional immunity advanced by the Lord the notion of official act controls the rule of state immunity *ratione materiae.* The parameters of coherent argument inherent in the conception advanced by Lord Browne-Wilkinson require the formulation of an exception in spite of the official character of acts.[137]

Lord Hope of Craighead wrote an intricate opinion. He saw the application of the rule of immunity protecting Pinochet to turn on the distinction between 'private acts on the one hand or governmental acts done in the exercise of his authority as head of state on the other'. He considered act of state for the purpose of functional immunity to be either act attributable to the state—'[t]he critical test would seem to be whether the conduct was engaged in under colour of or in ostensible exercise of the head of State's public authority'[138]—or governmental act—'[t]he sovereign or governmental acts of one state are not matters upon which the courts of other states will adjudicate.'[139]

Lord Hope asserted that there is not as yet a general exception to the immunity from jurisdiction of national courts for crimes against international law.[140] He expressed agreement with the analysis of Lord Slynn of Hadley in *Pinochet* no 1 who considered that

> it is necessary to find provision in an international convention to which the state asserting, and the state being asked to refuse, the immunity of a former head of state for an official act is party; the convention must clearly define a crime against international law and require or empower a state to prevent or prosecute the crime, whether or not it is committed within its jurisdiction and whether or not committed by one of its nationals; it must make it clear that a national court has jurisdiction to try a crime alleged against a former head of state, or that having been a head of state is no defence and that expressly or impliedly the immunity is not to apply so as to bar proceedings against him.[141]

Accordingly, Lord Hope set out to inquire whether the Torture Convention made 'it clear that a former head of state has no immunity in the courts of a state which

[136] ibid.

[137] The reasoning of Lord Browne-Wilkinson on this point (and of Lords Hutton and Philips who also argued that crimes against international law are not official acts) has been criticized in doctrine, but on the basis of arguments not accepted in this study, cf n 208 below.

[138] ibid 146. Refers to A Watts (1994–III) 13, 56.

[139] ibid referring to *I Congreso del Partido* [1983] AC 244 (UK, HL, 1981) 262.

[140] ibid 147.

[141] *Pinochet* no 1, 914, 1474 (*per* Lord Slynn of Hadley).

has jurisdiction to try the crime?'[142] Since there is no express provision to this regard it must be questioned whether immunity is removed by necessary implication. Lord Hope concludes that it is not. Among other things he considered that '[t]he risk to which former heads of state would be exposed on leaving office of being detained in foreign states upon an allegation that they had acquiesced in an act of official torture would have been so obvious to governments that it is hard to believe that they would ever have agreed to this.'[143]

However, Lord Hope then *returned* to considerations of customary international law to come to a final conclusion on the immunity issue:

> Nevertheless there remains the question whether the immunity can survive Chile's agreement to the Torture Convention if the torture which is alleged was of such a kind or on such a scale as to amount to an international crime.[144]

He underlined that it is an accepted part of international law that 'individuals who commit international crimes are internationally accountable for them'.[145] Once it is accepted that national courts can exercise jurisdiction over crimes against international law committed abroad Lord Hope considers this principle to apply to national court proceedings as well:

> In my opinion, once the machinery which it provides was put in place to enable jurisdiction over such crimes to be exercised in the courts of a foreign state, it was no longer open to any state which was a signatory to the convention to invoke immunity ratione materiae in the event of allegations of systematic or widespread torture committed after that date being made in the courts of that state against its officials or any other person acting in an official capacity.
>
> ...
>
> I would not regard this as a case of waiver. Nor would I accept that it was an implied term of the Torture Convention... It is just that the obligations which were recognised by customary international law in the case of such serious international crimes by the date when Chile ratified the convention are so strong as to override any objection by it on the ground of immunity materiae to the exercise over crimes committed after that date which the United Kingdom had made available.[146]

It now proves that Lord Hope's earlier finding that this principle does not apply to national courts was dependent on his restrictive approach to the question of jurisdiction over crimes against international law. Since the allegations against Pinochet concerned not incidental acts of torture but torture committed in pursuance of a policy to commit systematic torture as an instrument of government and hence concerned crimes against international law, immunity did not extend to him.

142 *Pinochet* no 3, 148.
143 ibid 148–51, quotation at 151.
144 ibid 151.
145 ibid 151.
146 ibid 152.

Lord Hope's conclusion relies on an interaction between the Torture Convention and the concept of crimes against international law. In contrast to Lords Saville and Browne-Wilkinson, he did not rely on the definition of the crime of torture in the Torture Convention. Rather, he relied on the establishment of universal jurisdiction over the crime of torture, and hence over torture amounting to a crime against international law, by the Torture Convention. He considered that the date as from which immunity *ratione materiae* was lost was 30 October 1988, which was the date that Chile's ratification of the Torture Convention took effect, since from that date onwards Chile 'was deprived of the right to object to the extra-territorial jurisdiction which the United Kingdom was able to assert over these offences'.[147]

The scope of the refusal of immunity by Lord Philips is difficult to grasp. This study argues that this scope is similar to that of the refusal by Lord Hope, but due to some internal inconsistencies the opinion is open to a different interpretation.

Lord Philips approached the immunity issue in a distinct manner. He argued that there is no customary international law rule granting immunity from criminal jurisdiction for official acts. It should first be explained that Lord Philips did 'not consider that s 20 of the 1978 Act has any application to conduct of a head of state outside the United Kingdom'. He held this conduct to be 'governed by the rules of public international law'.[148] He argued that there is no custom on the question of immunity from criminal jurisdiction for official acts since criminal jurisdiction used to be territorial and it 'seems inherently unlikely... that a foreign head of state should commit a criminal offence in the performance of his official functions while on a visit and subsequently return after ceasing to be head of state. Certainly this cannot have happened with sufficient frequency for any custom to have developed in relation to it.'[149]

Lord Philips considered that '[i]f immunity from [a novel type of extra-territorial criminal jurisdiction] is to be established it seems to me that this can only be on the basis of applying the established general principles of international law... rather than any specific rule of relating to immunity from criminal process.'[150] He proposed to consider whether the claimed immunity was supported by the principle of equality of states and the related rule that one state will not adjudicate over the governmental acts of another and the principle of non-intervention in the internal affairs of other states.

The first principle, he argued, applies in civil proceedings against foreign state officials since 'to sue an individual in respect of the conduct of the state's business is, indirectly, to sue the state'. Lord Philips hence considered Pinochet to be immune had the cases concerned civil proceedings in respect of the allegations of torture.[151] He did not however think that this reasoning has application to

147 ibid.
148 ibid 192.
149 ibid 183.
150 ibid 185.
151 ibid 186 and 182.

criminal proceedings that regard the personal responsibility of the individual.[152] As regards the second principle he developed the following argument:

> [N]o established rule of international law requires state immunity ratione materiae to be accorded in respect of prosecution for an international crime. International crimes and extra-territorial jurisdiction in relation to them are both new arrivals in the field of public international law. I do not believe that state immunity ratione materiae can co-exist with them. The exercise of extra-territorial jurisdiction overrides the principle that one state will not intervene in the internal affairs of another. It does so because, where international crime is concerned, that principle cannot prevail. An international crime is as offensive, if not more offensive, to the international community when committed under colour of office. Once extra-territorial jurisdiction is established, it makes no sense to exclude from it acts done in an official capacity.[153]

At first sight, it seems that Lord Philips denied immunity *ratione materiae* to all crimes against international law.[154] However, on closer consideration, this is less clear. The argument pivots on the existence of extra-territorial jurisdiction. In combination with the, seemingly passing, assertion that it is not clear whether international customary law recognizes universal jurisdiction in respect of international crimes,[155] it could well be argued that the Torture Convention is indispensable for his conclusion on immunity. Lord Philips' opinion should then be read in the light of his restrictive approach to the question of universal jurisdiction.

However, the obiter dictum that no immunity *ratione materiae* is available for acts of genocide either introduces uncertainty since the Genocide Convention does not provide for universal jurisdiction.[156] This would seem to contradict the finding that he requires a conventional basis for the exercise of jurisdiction. Lord Philips omitted to pinpoint a date as from which immunity is no longer available and leaves us to guess which of the above considerations he himself considered to be decisive. This study considers it likely that the reference to the Genocide Convention is based on the understandable but false assumption that that convention provides for universal jurisdiction over the crime of genocide. The Torture Convention *is* then at the basis of the opinion of Lord Philips.[157]

[152] ibid.

[153] ibid 189–90.

[154] Cf for this view eg CM Chinkin, 'Regina v. Bow Street Stipendiary Magistrate, Ex parte Pinochet Ugarte (No. 3)' (1999) 93 AJIL 703, 705 fn 15; A Bianchi (1999) 249; N Bhuta, 'Justice Without Borders? Prosecuting General Pinochet' (1999) 23 Melbourne University Law Review 499, 524–6. Although less explicit, a similar interpretation can be found in R Bank, 'Der Fall Pinochet: Aufbruch zu neuen Ufern bei der Verfolgung von Menschenrechtsverletzungen?' (1999) 59 ZaöRV 677, 698–9.

[155] *Pinochet* no 3, 188–9.

[156] ibid 189–90. Cf n 69 above.

[157] In his individual opinion in *Jones v Saudi Arabia and Abdul Aziz* & *Mitchell a.o. v Al-Dali a.o.* [2005] QB 699 (UK, CA, 2004), Lord Philips confirms this interpretation of his words. He stated that in the Pinochet case he had 'held that to claim immunity *ratione materiae* in respect of torture was incompatible with Chile's agreement to the Torture Convention', § 123.

One other obiter dictum renders the opinion of Lord Philips internally incoherent. Lord Philips notes in conclusion that if the 1978 SIA *does* oblige the grant of immunity to Pinochet in respect of all acts committed in performance of his functions as head of state he does 'not believe that those functions can, as a matter of statutory interpretation, extend to actions that are prohibited as criminal under international law'.[158] This finding is however not compatible with his earlier finding that acts of torture are official acts for the purposes of civil proceedings. Also the consideration that '[t]he only conduct covered by [the Torture Convention] is conduct which would be subject to immunity ratione materiae, if such immunity were applicable'[159] is not coherent if torture is not considered an official act.

The scope of the refusal of immunity by Lord Millett is debatable. Many commentators have argued that Lord Millett denied immunity for international crimes in general.[160] And indeed, several of the considerations found in the part in which he discusses developments in international criminal law point in that direction. After a discussion of article 7 of the Nuremberg Charter, the Nuremberg Judgment and the 1946 Principles of International Law adopted by the United Nations General Assembly he argued that it 'is no longer possible to deny that individuals could be held criminally responsibility [sic] for war crimes and crimes against peace and were not protected by state immunity from the jurisdiction of national courts'.[161] However, the part of his opinion that explicitly deals with the immunity question seems to base the denial of immunity on a somewhat smaller basis. He stated:

> The definition of torture . . . is in my opinion entirely inconsistent with the existence of a plea of immunity ratione materiae. The offence can be committed *only* by or at the instigation of, or with the consent or acquiescence of, a public official or other person acting in an official capacity. The official or governmental nature of the act, which forms the basis of the immunity, is an essential ingredient of the offence. No rational system of criminal justice can allow an immunity which is co-extensive with the offence.[162]

And continued:

> If the respondent's arguments were accepted, [the provision implementing the obligations of the Torture Convention] would be a dead letter. Either the accused was acting in a private capacity, in which case he cannot be charged with an offence under the section; or he was acting in an official capacity, in which case he would enjoy immunity from prosecution.[163]

[158] *Pinochet* no 3, 192.
[159] ibid 190.
[160] Cf eg R Wedgwood, 'International Criminal Law and Augusto Pinochet' (2000) 40 VJIL 829, 841; CM Chinkin (1999) 705 fn 15; N Bhuta (1999) 524–5. Cf also *Jones v Saudi Arabia and AbdulAziz* & *Mitchell a.o. v Al-Dali a.o.* (UK, 2004) § 52 (*per* Mance LJ).
[161] *Pinochet* no 3, 174.
[162] ibid 178–9.
[163] ibid 179.

He stressed that the acts involved 'were official and governmental or sovereign acts by any standard'.[164] The Torture Convention did not, therefore, affect the possible qualification of acts of torture under section 20 SIA as such. Moreover, he did not regard the ratification of the Torture Convention to entail a waiver of immunity since 'there was no immunity to be waived'.[165] Rather, Lord Millett concluded that

> The offence is one which could only be committed in circumstances which would normally give rise to the immunity. The international community had created an offence for which immunity rationae materiae could not possibly be available. International law cannot be supposed to have established a crime having the character of a jus cogens and at the same time to have provided an immunity which is co-extensive with the obligation it seeks to impose.[166]

However, not all crimes against international law can only be committed in an official capacity.[167] It could even be asserted that although formally Lord Millett did not explicitly rely on the entry into force of the Torture Convention, it is unclear whether the status of the perpetrator is inherent in the definition of torture or whether it is a limitation specific to the Torture Convention.[168] In this latter case Lord Millett's conclusion *in fact* relies on the Torture Convention.[169]

It should finally be noted that Lord Millett explicitly stated that there is a difference between civil and criminal proceedings in respect of alleged torture:

> acts which attract state immunity in civil proceedings because they are characterised as acts of sovereign power may, for the very same reason, attract individual criminal liability... I see nothing illogical or contrary to public policy in denying the victims of state sponsored torture the right to sue the offending state in a foreign court, while at the same time permitting (and indeed requiring) other states to convict and punish the individuals responsible if the offending state declines to take action.[170]

Lord Hutton—finally—can be said to have actually based the denial of immunity on the qualification of torture as a crime against international law. The 'crucial question for decision', argued Lord Hutton, 'is whether, if committed, the acts of torture... alleged against Senator Pinochet were carried out by him in the

[164] ibid 172.
[165] ibid 179.
[166] ibid.
[167] Cf eg *Kadic v Karadžić* (US, 1995) 239–41.
[168] Although the ICTY Statute does not explicitly include this element, the ICTY has held that the definition of torture in the Torture Convention is now part of customary international law, cf eg *Čelebići* Case, IT–96–21 Trial Chamber, Judgment (ICTY, 1998) § 452–9. The Tribunal did however hold that '[i]n the context of international humanitarian law, this requirement must be interpreted to include officials of non-State parties to the conflict', ibid § 473. In the ICC Statute and the Report of the Preparatory Commission for the International Criminal Court on the Elements of Crimes (PCNICC/2000/INF/3/Add.2) there is again no mention of the status-requirement.
[169] Cf in this sense eg R Bank (1999) 695.
[170] *Pinochet* no 3, 179.

performance of his functions as head of state.'[171] After a comprehensive review of relevant developments in international law, and the principles of individual responsibility and irrelevance of official capacity in particular, he concluded that

> since the end of the 1939–45 war there has been a clear recognition by the international community that certain crimes are so grave and so inhuman that they constitute crimes against international law and that the international community is under a duty to bring to justice a person who commits such crimes. Torture has been recognised as such a crime.[172]

Subsequently he held that since there is no jurisdiction to try Pinochet for acts of torture prior to 29 September 1988:

> it is unnecessary to decide when torture became a crime against international law prior to that date, but I am of opinion that acts of torture were clearly crimes against international law and that the prohibition of torture had acquired the status of ius cogens by that date.[173]

Lord Hutton considered that the alleged acts of torture do not qualify for protection under the rule of functional immunity.

> ...I do not consider that Senator Pinochet or Chile can claim that the commission of acts of torture after 29 September 1988 were functions of the head of state. The alleged acts of torture by Senator Pinochet were carried out under colour of his position as head of state, but they cannot be regarded as functions of a head of state under international law when international law expressly prohibits torture as a measure which a state can employ in any circumstances whatsoever and has made it an international crime.[174]

Lord Hutton did allude to the Torture Convention in his final conclusion but this does not seem to be relevant to his conclusion in any way.[175] This is also clear from the fact that he adopted the date of 29 September 1988 for the immunity issue; not because that date is relevant with regard to immunity but only because there was no jurisdiction prior to that date. On 29 September 1988 the Torture Convention had not been ratified by the United Kingdom nor Chile. Customary international law considerations alone must therefore have been sufficient for Lord Hutton to deny immunity for the torture allegations.

Lord Hutton *could* be seen to argue in the vein proposed in the next section—albeit with a less developed view on the rationale of the rule of functional immunity—*were it not for his argument on Pinochet's immunity from civil proceedings*. He held that under international law both Chile and Pinochet could claim immunity if sued in civil proceedings with respect to the acts involved.

[171] ibid 155.
[172] ibid 163.
[173] ibid 164.
[174] ibid 165. Cf also 166.
[175] See differently H Fox (1999) 697.

Pinochet, he argued, could do so under the principle stated in *Jaffe v Miller*.[176] This obiter consideration evinces that Lord Hutton did not consider the individual responsibility of Pinochet for crimes of torture to affect the rationale of the rule of functional immunity. The finding that for the purposes of criminal proceedings these acts do not qualify as official acts is therefore not coherent within the conception of the rule of functional immunity relied on.

So what is the precedent value of the *Pinochet* case? After the examination of the individual opinions one cannot but conclude that the common denominator of the majority judgment is confined to the outcome of the case. The scope of the denial of immunity to Pinochet is limited by two factors. One factor is the role of the Torture Convention in at least four of the six majority opinions. Three Lords—maybe four if we include Lord Millett—did argue that there is no functional immunity from criminal jurisdiction in respect of crimes against international law that can be tried on the basis of universal jurisdiction. Only the opinions of Lord Saville and Lord Browne-Wilkinson reason in a different vein. However, Lord Hope and Lord Philips consider national courts to have extraterritorial jurisdiction over crimes against international law only if the relevant states have concluded a convention to that effect. The non-immunity hence takes effect only upon the ratification of a convention that allows the exercise of universal jurisdiction. Accordingly, the Torture Convention played a crucial role in the denial of immunity by Lords Hope and Philips. Moreover, in contrast with Lord Hutton and Lord Hope, Lord Philips did not base his opinion on the principle of irrelevance of official capacity. Rather, he argued that there is no immunity from criminal jurisdiction for acts committed in an official capacity at all. Finally, two Lords based their refusal of immunity on *another* aspect of the Torture Convention. Lords Saville and Browne-Wilkinson argued that the obligations of the Torture Convention are incompatible with the continued existence of a rule of functional immunity in respect of torture allegations because the crime of torture is co-extensive with the rule of functional immunity.

Reliance on the Torture Convention seriously limits the scope of the decision. First, not all crimes against international law are supported by a convention granting universal jurisdiction. Moreover, the explicit limitation to state officials in the definition of torture is a peculiarity not applicable to all crimes against international law. The fact that, for example, there is no convention allowing state parties to exercise universal jurisdiction over the crime of genocide means that the opinions of Lords Hope and Philips are no precedent in proceedings concerning the prosecution of (former) foreign state officials for this crime. Moreover, the fact that non-state actors can commit genocide means that the opinions of Lords Saville and Browne-Wilkinson are no precedent either. Finally, the precedent value of all four opinions is limited to state parties of the Torture Convention. It

[176] *Pinochet* no 3, 167. Cf for *Jaffe v Miller and Others* (Canada, 1993), ch 3 § 3.3 above.

cannot but be concluded that Iraqi or Zimbabwean nationality would have protected General Pinochet from extradition.

The second factor that limits the scope of the denial of immunity to Pinochet is inherent in the conception of the rule of functional immunity that was at the basis of the reasoning of the Lords—and hence applies to all judicial and academic thinking that proceeds from this conception. The Lords clearly proceeded from an identification of the rule of functional immunity with the rule of state immunity *ratione materiae*. While some Lords did consider that the acts of torture were not official acts, in the light of their further reasoning it is fair to say that this is internally inconsistent with the conception of the rule of functional immunity that they relied on. This has inevitable consequences for the functional immunity from civil jurisdiction. Although only Lords Hutton, Millet and Philips explicitly stated that Pinochet would have enjoyed immunity had he been sued in civil proceedings instead, this conclusion is inherent in *all* six majority opinions. Within the parameters of the conception it is impossible to distinguish between the state and the state official. The state official is shielded from the civil jurisdiction of foreign national courts because, as the Court of Appeal formulated it in *Propend Finance*, '[t]he protection afforded by the [SIA] to States would be undermined if employees, officers or... "functionaries" could be sued as individuals for matters of State conduct in respect of which the State they were serving had immunity.'[177]

Accordingly, the 2006 decision of the House of Lords in *Jones v Saudi Arabia* reflects the only logical consequence of the conception of functional immunity prevalent in the *Pinochet* case.[178] Two joined actions were at the basis of the *Jones* case. Both actions concerned allegations of systematic torture in prisons in Saudi Arabia and were instigated against the state of Saudi Arabia, as well as against the individual state officials allegedly responsible for the torture. The Court of Appeal had allowed a distinction between the position of the state and the position of the individual officials, holding the former immune from its jurisdiction but the latter not.[179] The House of Lords disagreed. It stated that as a rule 'the foreign state is entitled to claim immunity for its servants as it could if sued itself. The foreign state's right to immunity cannot be circumvented by suing its servants or agents.'[180] This rule, it held, applies whenever a state is responsible for an act of its official under international law. Lord Hoffmann wrote in this respect that '[i]t has until now been generally assumed that the circumstances in which a state will be liable for the act of an official in international law mirror the circumstances in which the official will be immune in foreign domestic law. There is a logic in this

[177] *Propend Finance Ltd v Sing* (UK, 1997) 669.

[178] *Jones v Saudi Arabia* (UK, 2006).

[179] The decision of the Court of Appeal (2004) is further discussed at p 254ff below. Cf also *Jones v Saudi Arabia and Abdul Aziz* 2003 WL 22187644 QBD (UK, High Court, 2003).

[180] *Jones v Saudi Arabia* (UK, 2006).

assumption: if there is a remedy against the state before an international tribunal, there should not also be a remedy against the official himself in a domestic tribunal.'[181] Referring to, *inter alia*, articles 4 and 7 of the ILC Articles on State Responsibility and the commentary thereto,[182] he pointed out that this rule also applies when the state official has not been acting in accordance with his instructions or authority. To hold otherwise 'would produce an asymmetry between the rules of liability and immunity'.[183]

Consequently, the applicants were forced to argue that, more in general, immunity *ratione materiae* could not be claimed in respect of torture allegations. The substance of this argumentation, and the House of Lord's rejection thereof, will be discussed in chapter 6 of this study.

The idea that functional immunity of foreign state officials protects the governmental acts of their home states is increasingly echoed in judicial and academic thinking.[184] The rule of state immunity is applied regardless of the status of the defendant before the court. It was explained in chapter 3 of this study that this concerns an unfortunate revival of Kelsen's act of state immunity concept. This study proposes a different approach.

2.3.1.3 An exception *within* the rationale of the rule

The rule of functional immunity of foreign state officials entails a presumption. State officials are not personally responsible for acts committed within the context of exercise of state authority under international law because they are presumed to have committed these acts *as the state*. Accordingly, they cannot be called to account in regard of these acts in their personal capacity. The non-personal responsibility of officials that have acted as the arm or mouthpiece of the state is a principle common to all national legal systems. The international law variant of this rule does not allow states to determine whether a foreign state official has acted ultra vires since the determination of the mandate of a state official is part of the exclusive competence of the home state. As long as the official acts within the context of state authority under international law he is presumed to have acted within the scope of his mandate.

Chapter 3 of this study has explained why the two alternative act of state concepts fail to convince. In the first place, while all acts covered by the rule of functional immunity can be attributed to the home state, not all acts that can be attributed to the state are covered by the rule of functional immunity. For one, the forum state *is* allowed to determine the limits of the mandate of foreign

[181] ibid § 74. Cf also § 12.

[182] See for the commentary ILC Report on the work of its fifty-third session (2001), A/56/10.

[183] ibid § 78.

[184] See ch 3 § 3.3 above. Cf recently eg the opinions of the *amici curiae* in *Prosecutor v Charles Ghankay Taylor* (SCSL, 2004), P Sands and A Macdonald, *Submissions of the Amicus Curiae on Head of State Immunity*, available at <http://www.icc-cpi.int/library/organs/otp/Sands.pdf> § 108; D Orentlicher, *Submission of the Amicus Curiae on Head of State Immunity* (on file with the author).

state officials operating on its territory. Acts that fall outside the mandate—like the example of assassinations carried out by secret service agents on foreign territory—do not qualify as official acts. In addition, the home state may always declare that a certain official has acted ultra vires and can hence be sued before the courts of the forum state. These ultra vires acts may however be attributable to the home state.[185] Attributability is hence not the correct criterion to determine the official nature of an act for the purpose of the functional immunity rule. More problematic even is the position that functional immunity is really state immunity *ratione materiae* shielding the governmental acts of the home state from scrutiny by foreign national courts. The criterion of governmental acts includes both too much and too little. Too little because state officials can not in fact be held personally responsible for acts committed on behalf of the state that are *not* of a governmental character. Too much because state practice evinces that international law does not protect governmental acts from foreign judicial scrutiny as such. Rather, the determination of the sovereign status of the defendant—nominally or factually—can be seen to *always* precede the application of the rule of state immunity.

The concept of individual responsibility under international law dates from well before the twentieth century. The novelty of the Versailles Treaty and in particular of the Nuremberg Charter was that this concept was extended to individuals acting under state authority. The principle of irrelevance of official capacity can only be understood against the background of the act of state defence that shields state officials from foreign jurisdiction in respect of acts committed within the context of the exercise of state authority under international law. In the absence of the principle it could be argued that only individuals that act *outside* the context of state authority incur individual responsibility for crimes against international law because, as a rule, international law obliges states to regard acts committed within the exercise of state authority under international law as acts of state rather than as personal acts of the individual who performed the acts under the cloak of state authority. The principle spells out what the list of crimes for which individuals incur personal responsibility in fact already evinces—and is accordingly more explanatory or declaratory than constitutive in nature. State officials can be sued in their personal capacity for crimes against international law.

It is in this respect noteworthy that the principle of irrelevance of official capacity is formulated in the terms of the rule of functional immunity. As the Nuremberg Charter formulates it:

> The official position of defendants, whether as Heads of State or responsible officials in Government Departments, shall not be considered as *freeing them from responsibility*.[186]

[185] Cf ch 3 § 2.2.1.3 & 2.2.1.4 above.

[186] Art 7 Nuremberg Charter (emphasis added). Cf in particular the ICTY Statute, the ICTR Statute, and the SCSL Statute, that provide for the principle of individual responsibility and

The principle of individual responsibility for state crimes and the principle of irrelevance of official capacity hence directly target the functional immunity of state officials. The principle is not an exception to the rule that state officials are immune in respect of official acts. Acts are official in nature only when the act is exclusively attributable to the state and the official does not incur individual responsibility in their regard. The acceptance of individual responsibility for crimes against international law defeats the presumption that individuals have acted *as the state* whenever they act within the context of state authority under international law in respect of a limited category of atrocious crimes. In other words, the acceptance of individual responsibility for these crimes committed under the ostensible authority of a state may be regarded as a collective, *a priori*, defeat of the presumption of authority. The principle relied on in the *McLeod* case is not superseded. Rather, states have agreed on normative limits for the qualification of acts as official for functional immunity purposes. Functional immunity ends where individual responsibility begins. Crimes against international law hence do not qualify as official acts (or acts of state) under the rule of functional immunity.[187] Prosecution does not violate the sovereignty of the home state. The forum state is not required to determine a limit on the mandate of the accused foreign state official since the home state has agreed to a universal limit on authority.[188]

Since the principle defines the scope of the rule of functional immunity rather than that it provides an exception to that rule it is impossible to distinguish international courts from national courts for the purpose of its application. The ICTY rightly noted in the *Blaškić* case that 'under [the norms of international criminal law prohibiting war crimes, crimes against humanity and genocide] those responsible for such crimes cannot invoke immunity from *national or international jurisdiction* even if they perpetrated such crimes while acting in their official capacity'.[189]

irrelevance of official capacity in one art under the heading of 'individual responsibility', arts 7, 6, and 6 respectively. See for references footnotes 35, 48, and 50 above.

[187] Cf Q Wright (1947) 71; H Lauterpacht, 'The Subjects of the Law of Nations' (1947) 63 LQR 438, 442–3.

[188] Notably, international law exceptionally allows the conclusion that a foreign state official was not exercising state authority under international law, which is crucially different from the conclusion that a foreign state official was acting ultra vires. The argument that state officials are not immune in respect of ultra vires acts—cf M Tomonori (2003)—disregards the crucial role of the principle of individual responsibility for crimes against international law. The functional immunity rule in fact prevents states determining the mandate of foreign state officials that exercise state authority under international law.

[189] *Prosecutor v Blaškić* (ICTY, 1997) § 41 (emphasis added). Cf also *Prosecutor v Milosević* (ICTY, 2001) § 33 where the lack of immunity from the jurisdiction of the ICTY in that case is equalled to the lack of immunity from the jurisdiction of the House of Lords in the *Pinochet* case. In the *Krstić* case, however, the Tribunal refrained from stating the position before national courts, *Prosecutor v Krstić* (ICTY, 2003) § 26.

It has been argued that in the *Arrest Warrant* Case the International Court of Justice denied that the principle of irrelevance of official capacity applies to national courts. The contested paragraph of the decision reads as follows:

> The Court has carefully examined State practice, including national legislation and those few decisions of national higher courts, such as the House of Lords or the French Court of Cassation. It has been unable to deduce from this practice that there exists under customary international law any form of exception to the rule according immunity from criminal jurisdiction and inviolability to incumbent Ministers for Foreign Affairs, where they are suspected of having committed war crimes or crimes against humanity.
>
> The Court has also examined the rules concerning the immunity or criminal responsibility of persons having an official capacity contained in the legal instruments creating international criminal tribunals, and which are specifically applicable to the latter [refers to article 7 Nuremberg Charter and progeny]. It finds that these rules likewise do not enable it to conclude that any such exception exists in customary international law in regard to national courts.
>
> Finally, none of the decisions of the Nuremberg and Tokyo international tribunals, or of the International Criminal Tribunal for the Former Yugoslavia, cited by Belgium deal with the question of the immunities of incumbent Ministers for Foreign Affairs before national courts. The Court accordingly notes that those decisions are in no way at variance with the findings it has reached above.[190]

Cassese has held that the court here states that the principle of irrelevance of official capacity only applies to international criminal tribunals and that 'no such an exception exists in customary international law in regard to national courts'.[191] A similar criticism is also implicit in the dissenting opinion of Judge Van den Wyngaert. She complained that the Court had taken 'an extremely minimalist approach by adopting a very narrow interpretation of the "no-immunity-clauses" in international instruments'.[192] She argued that the Court had failed to recognize the customary international law status of the principle of individual accountability and had consequently failed to balance the 'two divergent interests in modern international (criminal) law: the need of international accountability for such crimes as torture, terrorism, war crimes and crimes against humanity and the principle of sovereign equality of States, which presupposes a system of immunities'.[193]

The Court's words can, however, be read differently. The conclusion that 'any such exception' does not exist in customary international law in regard to national courts clearly refers to the 'exception to the rule according immunity from criminal jurisdiction and inviolability to incumbent Ministers for Foreign Affairs', *not*

[190] *Arrest Warrant* Case, 24, § 58.

[191] A Cassese (2002) 865. Cf in similar sense J Salmon, 'Libres propos sur l'arrêt de la C.I.J. du 14 Février 2002 dans l'affaire relative au *mandat d'arrêt du 11 Avril 2000 (RDC c Belgique)*' (2002) 35 RBDI 512, 514–15.

[192] *Arrest Warrant* Case, Dissenting Opinion Judge Van den Wyngaert, 153, § 27.

[193] ibid 155–7, § 28, quotation at 141, § 5.

to the principle of irrelevance of official capacity. While the reference to 'national courts' may add to the confusion of a casual reader—in fact this author was indignant about the audacity of the argument after a first glance at the judgment—it is not unthinkable that the Court merely set out to distinguish substantive from procedural immunity in this paragraph. As it states a little further on:

> Immunity from criminal jurisdiction and individual criminal responsibility are quite separate concepts. While jurisdictional immunity is procedural in nature, criminal responsibility is a question of substantive law.[194]

In this reading of the judgment the Court *did* recognize the customary international law status of the principle of irrelevance of official capacity but did not regard this principle to affect rules of personal immunity—the position defended in this study. In fact, Judge Van den Wyngaert herself—as well as dissenting judge Al-Khasawneh—acknowledged that the distinction between substantive and procedural immunities underlies the decision of the Court.[195]

This study does not engage the question of universal civil jurisdiction,[196] but *if* national courts can establish civil jurisdiction over crimes against international law committed by foreign state officials it should be recognized that the absence of functional immunity necessarily extends to civil proceedings.[197] If an individual cannot be regarded to have acted as a mere arm or mouthpiece of a foreign state in the performance of a particularly despicable act he incurs responsibility for the act in his personal capacity. It makes no sense to argue that the question whether an act qualifies as an act of state depends on the type of proceedings involved. When an individual can be prosecuted and convicted for the commission of a certain crime because the crime is not an act of state but an act *also* attributable to the individual personally, he can necessarily be ordered to pay damages from his personal estate to indemnify the victims of his crime in civil proceedings.

The act of state defence is not commonly discussed in national court proceedings concerning foreign war criminals. All national prosecutions of foreign war criminals that have acted under the cloak of state authority confirm, however, implicitly the pertinence of the principle of irrelevance of official capacity to national court proceedings.[198]

The defence was exceptionally raised in the 1960s Israeli *Eichmann* case. Eichmann was prosecuted on allegations of crimes against humanity committed in Germany during the Second World War. The alleged acts, he argued, were acts of the German state for which he, as an organ of that state, could not be held

194 *Arrest Warrant* Case, 25, § 60.

195 Cf p 271 below.

196 Cf § 1 above.

197 The two issues can in fact be considered separately, as the ICJ states in the *Arrest Warrant* Case: 'absence of immunity does not imply jurisdiction', 24, § 59.

198 Cf in a similar sense, A Cassese (2002) 870–1; D Akande (2004) 413.

personally responsible. The Israeli Supreme Court formulated the argument as follows:

The theory of 'Act of State' means that the act performed by a person as an organ of the State... must be regarded as an act of the State alone. It follows that only the latter bears responsibility therefore, and it also follows that another State has no right to punish the person who committed the act, save with the consent of the State whose mission he performed. Were it not so, the first State would be interfering in the internal affairs of the second, which is contrary to the conception of the equality of States based on their sovereignty.[199]

In order to overcome the defence, the court set out to establish limits on the concept of state sovereignty. It cited approvingly the statement of Kunz that '[a]ny *a priori* or unlimited political concept of sovereignty must, with inescapable logic, lead to the non-existence of international law as law. Sovereignty is, therefore, essentially a relative notion; its content depends on the stage of development of international law.'[200] The court held that

there is no basis for the doctrine when the matter pertains to acts prohibited by the law of nations, especially when they are international crimes of the class of 'crimes against humanity'... Of such odious acts it must be said that in point of international law they are completely outside the 'sovereign' jurisdiction of the State that ordered or ratified their commission, and therefore those who participated in such acts must personally account for them and cannot shelter behind the official character of their task or mission...

...

international law postulates that it is impossible for a State to sanction an act that violates its severe prohibitions, and from this follows the idea which forms the core of the concept of 'international crime', that a person who was a party to such a crime must bear individual responsibility for it. If it were otherwise, the penal provisions of international law would be a mockery.[201]

The court concluded with the words of the district court

The very contention that the systematic extermination of masses of helpless human beings by a Government or régime could constitute 'an act of state', appears to be an insult to reason and a mockery of law and justice.[202]

The act of state defence was hence rejected by reference to the principle of individual responsibility for crimes against international law. States agree that these crimes fall necessarily outside the protective cloak of state authority. Individuals

[199] *Attorney-General of Israel v Adolf Eichmann* (Israel, 1962) 308–9. Cf for the decision in first instance *Attorney-General of Israel v Adolf Eichmann* (Israel, 1961).

[200] JL Kunz, 'The Nottebohm Judgment (Second Phase)' (1960) 54 AJIL 536, 545.

[201] *Attorney-General of Israel v Adolf Eichmann* (Israel, 1962) 309–10.

[202] ibid 312.

sued in respect of allegations of committing such crimes must answer in their personal capacity.[203]

It should finally be realized that the criticism on the conclusion that crimes against international law do not qualify as official acts for functional immunity purposes is always formulated from the perspective of the *alternative* act of state concepts. When the concept of official act controls not only the application of the rule of functional immunity but also the law of state responsibility and the definition of certain crimes against international law the argument that individuals that commit crimes against international law act not in an official but in a private capacity 'would constitute a remedy more harmful than the wrong it was intended to remedy.'[204]

Several scholars have pointed out that the denial of official act status necessarily means that the state does not bear international responsibility for the act concerned. In this vein, Bothe cautioned that 'wenn man ein bestimmtes Verbrechen nicht als Amtshandlung gelten lassen will, die unmittelbare völkerrechtliche Verantwortlichkeit des Heimatstaates des handelnden Staatsorgans entfällt'[205] and Barker argued that 'to deny the official character of such acts would be to remove any liability which the State might have under both international law and municipal law for the acts of its officials.'[206]

In addition, scholars have argued that crimes that can only be committed by individuals acting in an official capacity—like the crime of torture—necessarily qualify under the rule of functional immunity. As Lord Millett noted in the *Pinochet* case: 'Either the accused was acting in a private capacity, in which case he cannot be charged with an offence under the section; or he was acting in an official capacity, in which case he would enjoy immunity from prosecution.'[207]

[203] Cf also: *Ordonnance du 6 novembre 1998* (Belgium) 308; *Bouterse* R 97/163/12 Sv & R 97/176/12 Sv, (Netherlands, Gerechtshof Amsterdam, 2000) § 4.1 and 4.2: The court held that 'the commission of very grave punishable offences such as those in question cannot be regarded as the official duties of a head of state'. The terse reasoning of the court however does not reveal the argumentation underlying this conclusion. The immunity question was not discussed by the Supreme Court since the conclusion that the Dutch courts did not have jurisdiction over the alleged crimes because of the principle of non-retroactivity of penal legislation precluded the question, *Bouterse* NJ 2002 77 (Netherlands, Hoge Raad, 2001). In the *Cavallo* case a former Argentinean state official argued that he could not be extradited by Mexico to Spain to stand trial on accusations of crimes against international law committed during the military regime in Argentina from 1976 to 1983 because 'he was a member of the armed forces and obeying orders'. The Mexican Supreme Court dealt with the argument as being a superior order argument rather than one of functional immunity. It rejected the argument stating that 'international legislation and international doctrine have considered that when dealing with crimes against humanity or injury to humanity, responsibility is not waived on the grounds of acting on superior orders'. *Decision on the Extradition of Ricardo Miguel Cavallo* (2003) 42 ILM 888 (Mexico, S Ct, 2003) 908.

[204] M Spinedi, 'State Responsibility v. Individual Responsibility for International Crimes: *Tertium Non Datur*?' (2002b) 13 EJIL 895, 897.

[205] M Bothe (1971) 255 and 262.

[206] JC Barker (1999) 943.

[207] *Pinochet* no 3, 179 (*per* Lord Millett). Cf also the 2006 decision of the House of Lords in *Jones v Saudi Arabia* § 19, § 79.

The argument that crimes against international law do not qualify as an official act for the purposes of the rule of functional immunity has been said to rely on an artificial distinction between the official nature of the act of torture as defined in the Torture Convention and the official nature required for qualification of the acts under section 20 SIA.[208]

Many scholars have criticized the reasoning of the ICJ in the *Arrest Warrant* Case on these grounds. The Court held in an obiter dictum that a former foreign state official may, as far as acts committed during his period of office, only be tried 'in respect of acts committed during that period of office *in a private capacity*'.[209] Salmon pungently noted that '[l]a formule adoptée par la Cour—dont il faut esperér qu'elle fut le fruit d'une inadvertance—est donc particulièrement regrettable. C'est l'éléphant dans le magasin de porcelaine. Il est certain, en tout état de cause, qu'elle ne représente en rien le droit coutumier international. Si elle estimait que des crimes de guerre et contre l'humanité devaient être considerés comme des actes privés, elle se devait de le dire. En s'abstenant, elle prolonge et envenime la controverse.'[210] Cassese wrote in this respect that '[i]t is... hardly imaginable that a foreign minister may perpetrate or participate in the perpetration of an international crime "in a private capacity"... This would mean, for example, that the crimes for which Joachim von Ribbentrop (Reich Minister for Foreign Affairs from 1938 to 1945) was sentenced to death, namely crimes against peace, war crimes and crimes against humanity, should be regarded as "private acts"...'[211]

[208] Cf for this criticism of the *Pinochet* case but also more in general eg D Akande (2004) 414, fn 46; O Dörr, 'Statliche Immunität auf dem Rückzug?' (2003) 41 Archiv des Völkerrechts 201, 214; R Bank (1999) 693; JC Barker (1999) 943: J Bröhmer, 'Diplomatic Immunity, Head of State Immunity, State Immunity: Misconceptions of a Notorious Human Rights Violator' (1999) 12 LJIL 361, 370; I Buffard and U Kriebaum, 'Der Fall Pinochet: Für und wider die Immunität (I Buffard, Argumente für die Immunität)' in W Karl and U Brandl (eds), *Völker- und Europarecht* (2000) 25, 39–41; and the doctrine mentioned in n 211 below. Cf also E Denza (1999) for a discussion of this issue.

[209] *Arrest Warrant* case, 25, § 61 (emphasis added). Cf also the Joint Separate Opinion of Judges Higgins, Kooijmans and Buergenthal, 88, § 85 the judges argued that 'serious international crimes cannot be regarded as official acts'.

[210] J Salmon (2002) 517.

[211] A Cassese (2002) 866–70, 868 and 870. Cf also A Cassese (2003) 437 and 444; S Wirth (2002); M Spinedi (2002b); M Frulli, 'The ICJ Judgment on the Belgium v Congo Case (14 February 2002): a Cautious Stand on Immunity from Prosecution for International Crimes' (2002) 3 German Law Journal available at <http://www.germanlawjournal.com>; C McLachlan, '*Pinochet* Revisited' (2002) 51 ICLQ 959, 959; P Gaeta, '*Ratione Materiae* Immunities of Former Heads of State and International Crimes; The *Hissène Habré* Case' (2003) 1 JICJ 186, 189–91; The briefs of the *amici curiae* in SCSL, Appeals Chamber, *Prosecutor v Charles Ghankay Taylor* (2004), P Sands and A Macdonald (2004) available at <http://www.icc-cpi.int/library/organs/otp/Sands.pdf> § 113; D Orentlicher (2004) (on file with the author); CPR Romano and A Nollkaemper, 'The Arrest Warrant Against the Liberian President, Charles Taylor' (June 2003) ASIL insights, <http://www.asil.org/insights/insigh110.htm>. Dissenting Judge Van den Wyngaert noted in this respect that '[i]t is highly regrettable that the International Court of Justice has not, like the House of Lords in the *Pinochet* case, qualified this statement. It could and indeed should have added that war crimes and crimes against humanity can never fall into this category. Some crimes under international law... can for practical purposes, only be committed with the means and mechanisms of

The apparent tension between the requisites of the law of torture, the law of state responsibility and the rule of functional immunity exists however only under a defective interpretation of the latter rule. The immunity for acts performed in the exercise of official functions is more than the words used to define it. In chapter 3 of this study it was explained that there is a difference between a legal and a factual approach to the concept of acts committed in an official capacity. For purposes of the application of the rule of functional immunity the official capacity in which an act is committed is established from an internal, theoretical perspective; while the official capacity requirement in the rules of state responsibility and the definition of crimes concerns an external, factual perspective. Acts committed in the *apparent* or *ostensible* exercise of official functions do not qualify under the rule of functional immunity when there was no actual authority to act; while such apparent or ostensible exercise of official functions *is* sufficient for qualification under the definition of torture and the establishment of state responsibility.[212]

The reliance on the possibility of attribution to the state to establish the official nature of an act includes too much under the rule of functional immunity. It should at this point be recalled that the murder of Staschynskij, the bombing of the *Rainbow Warrior*, or the activity of foreign diplomatic or consular agents outside their particular functions for that matter, are not official acts for the purpose of the rule of functional immunity either. The alternative for official acts is *not* purely personal acts that cannot be attributed to the state. The alternative is acts for which a state official cannot hide behind the authority of the foreign state.

In sum, acting in an official capacity from the factual perspective of the definition of certain crimes under international law or the imputability of acts to the foreign state under the rules of state responsibility is distinct from acting in an official capacity from the theoretical perspective of the rule of functional immunity, that is, from the perspective of performing acts that are in law the acts of the foreign state only. To avoid confusion the notion 'acts performed in an official capacity' may be best reserved for the definition of the former rules, while the notion of 'acts for which an official can be sued in his official capacity only' better reflects the nature of the protection available to state officials.[213] It is

a State and as part of a State policy. They cannot, from that perspective, be anything other than "official" acts.' § 36.

[212] Cf on the concurrence of individual and state responsibility A Nollkaemper, 'Concurrence between Individual Responsibility and State Responsibility in International Law' (2003) 52 ICLQ 615. A different question is whether the ICJ should have explicitly stated that crimes against international law do not qualify as official acts. Cf in this sense B Stern, 'Immunities for Heads of State: Where Do We Stand?' in M Lattimer and P Sands (eds), *Justice for Crimes against Humanity* (2003) 73, 105–6.

[213] Cf *Hafer v Melo* (US, S Ct, 1991) 26: the Supreme Court held that the immunity of the state official turns on 'the capacity in which the state official is sued, not the capacity in which the official inflicts the alleged injury'.

the non-imputability to the state official in his personal capacity, rather than the imputability to the state that determines qualification under the rule.[214]

Although US courts do not adopt the approach advanced in this study—they have devised a *third* alternative act of state concept that controls the applicability of the FSIA to foreign state officials and the application of the rule of functional immunity—US case law provides an insightful example of how to distinguish the official capacity that immunizes state officials from the official capacity that is necessary to establish state responsibility and is part of the definition of certain crimes.

In the case of *Herbage v Meese*—discussed in chapter 3 of this study—the court held that officials could not be held personally responsible for actions taken on behest of a foreign state or at least 'under colour of law'.[215] It moreover considered that the acts of the defendants were of a sovereign nature. Accordingly, the defendants qualified for protection under the FSIA. The court underlined that there exists no ultra vires exception to the immunity under the FSIA holding that '[t]he FSIA is absolute in this regard, no matter how heinous the alleged illegalities.'[216] The court hence relied on a mix of the two alternative conceptions of act of state.

Scholars pointed out that *Herbage v Meese* would make the ATCA a dead letter since acting under 'colour of law' would trigger the working of the FSIA while 'colour of law' requirements are essential to make out many violations of human rights norms.[217] Torture, summary execution, extrajudicial killing, disappearance, arbitrary detention and systematic racial discrimination are all crimes that can only be committed by a 'public official or other person acting in an official capacity'. And although non-state actors can violate international law as well, it remains the case that once individuals *are* state actors having acted under the colour of law they seem protected by the FSIA.[218]

[214] It is noted that the Resolution on Immunities from Jurisdiction and Execution of Heads of State and of Government in International Law ((2000–01) 69 AIDI 743) of the Institut de Droit International attempts to avoid the question whether crimes against international law qualify as official acts. Art 13 of the Resolution provides that former heads of state only enjoy immunity 'in respect of acts which are performed in the exercise of official functions and relate to the exercise thereof. Nevertheless, he or she may be prosecuted and tried when the acts alleged constitute a crime under international law'. Cf eg remarks of Salmon (J Verhoeven, (Rapporteur Institut de Droit International), Les immunités de juridiction et d'exécution du chef d'Etat et de gouvernement en droit international, Réponses et observations des membres de la Commission, (2000–01) 69 AIDI 554, 575) and Treves (Institut de Droit International (Rapporteur J Verhoeven), Les immunités de juridiction et d'exécution du chef d'Etat et de gouvernement en droit international, Plenary Session (2001), (2000–01) 69 AIDI 601, 672) for the background of this formulation. However, since art 3 of the Resolution provides that incumbent heads of state are only immune from civil proceedings if the 'suit relates to acts performed in the exercise of his or her official functions' the question remains pertinent.

[215] *Herbage v Meese* (US, 1990). Cf ch 3 § 3.3 above.

[216] ibid 108.

[217] Cf eg J Fitzpatrick, 'The Future of the Alien Tort Claims Act of 1978: Lessons from in Re Marcos Human Rights Litigation' (1993) 67 St John's Law Review 491, 507.

[218] Cf on non-state actors and international law *Kadic v Karadžić* (US, 1995) 239–41.

In order to avoid the catch-22 subsequent courts have abandoned the terminology used in *Herbage* and have relied on reasoning developed within the context of the act of state doctrine instead. In the case of *Filártiga v Peña-Irala* the court had held that while an 'action by a state official in violation of the Constitution and laws of the Republic of Paraguay, and wholly unratified by that nation's government' could not properly be characterized as an act of state this 'does not strip the tort of its character as an international law violation, if in fact it occurred under color of government authority'.[219] Similarly, in *Forti v Suarez-Mason* the court considered that '[o]fficial action is not necessarily the governmental and public action contemplated by the act of State doctrine.'[220]

The *Trajano v Marcos* case incorporated this technique in the FSIA test.[221] The case concerned a suit against Marcos–Manotoc, the daughter of the former president of the Philippines Marcos, who was accused of several crimes including torture, summary execution and disappearance. The defendant claimed to be entitled to state immunity under the FSIA because the challenged acts were premised on her authority as a government agent. The court rejected her claim holding that the defendant acted on her own authority since the alleged acts were not taken within any official mandate. Crucially, the court linked this conclusion to an earlier decision. The court considered the conclusion that the defendant was not protected by the FSIA 'consistent with our earlier decision that the same allegations against former President Marcos are not nonjusticiable "acts of state"...In so holding, we implicitly rejected the possibility that the acts set out in Trajano's complaint were public acts of the sovereign.'[222]

This approach was confirmed in *Hilao v Marcos*.[223] The court in this case rejected the argument that the FSIA immunizes alleged acts of torture and execution by a foreign official. In the first place, it was held that 'where the officer's powers are limited by statute, his actions beyond those limitations are considered individual and not sovereign actions'.[224] Marcos' alleged human rights violations were held not to have been taken 'within any official mandate and were therefore not the acts of an agency or instrumentality of a foreign state within the meaning of the FSIA'.[225] Further, it was held that the court's previous decision that Marcos' acts were not protected by the act of state doctrine implicitly rejected the possibility that the acts were public acts of a sovereign.[226]

219 *Filártiga v Peña-Irala* (US, 1980) 890.

220 *Forti v Suarez-Mason* 672 F Supp 1531 (US, DC for the Northern District of California, 1987) 1546. Cf also eg *Paul v Avril* (US, 1993) 212.

221 *Trajano v Marcos (In re Estate of Ferdinand E. Marcos Litigation)* 978 F 2d 493 (US, Ct of Apps (9th Cir), 1992).

222 ibid 498, fn 10, referring to *Trajano v Marcos* 878 F 2d 1439 (US, Ct of Apps (9th Cir), 1989).

223 *Hilao v Marcos* (US, 1994). Cf also eg *Cabiri v Assasie-Gyimah* 921 F Supp 1189 (US, DC for the Southern District of New York, 1996).

224 ibid 1470–71, quotation at 1470.

225 ibid 1472.

226 ibid 1471. The court refers to *Trajano v Marcos* (US, 1992) 498 fn 10.

The case of *Helen Liu v The Republic of China* demonstrates that a disqualification of an act as official act does equally not affect the responsibility of the foreign state employing the state official in respect of that act.[227] The case concerned a claim of the widow of Henry Liu against the Republic of China (ROC) for the shooting and killing of her husband in California by two gunmen acting on orders of the Director of the Defence Intelligence Bureau of the ROC. The court found that no state immunity was available to the ROC since the exception of § 1605(a)(5) applied. The section provides that foreign states are not immune from US jurisdiction in cases

> in which money damages are sought against a foreign state for personal injury or death, or damage to or loss of property, occurring in the United States and caused by the tortious act or omission of that foreign state or of any official or employee of that foreign state while acting within the scope of his office or employment; except this paragraph shall not apply to:
>
> (a) any claim based upon the exercise or performance or the failure to exercise or perform a discretionary function regardless of whether the discretion be abused, or
> (b) any claim arising out of malicious prosecution, abuse of process, libel, slander, misrepresentation, deceit or interference with contract rights.

The ROC argued that the Director of the Defence Intelligence Bureau had acted on a personal grudge against Liu and had accordingly not acted within the scope of his employment since the murder of Liu had not been authorized nor sanctioned by the ROC and violated internal Chinese law. These alleged facts, though probably sufficient to deny the Director a right to invoke the FSIA when a claim should be instigated against him, did not remove the responsibility of the ROC for the acts.

In sum, even if foreign state officials act under colour of law and in the official capacity required by several definitions of crimes and the rules of vicarious state responsibility this does not mean that the relevant act qualifies as an official act for the purpose of functional immunity. The distinction applied by the US courts makes it possible to sue a foreign state official in a personal capacity for acts for which the state bears vicarious liability.

The act of state concept that controls the immunity of foreign state officials from the jurisdiction of the US courts does *not* however rely on the principle of individual responsibility for crimes against international law.[228] Rather, it seems to rely on the factual possibility to isolate the acts of the defendant from the acts of the home state. If an act is clearly performed in the exercise of sovereign authority, concerns the official policy of a foreign state, or is ratified by a foreign state it is not unlikely that the defendant would be allowed the protection of the

[227] *Helen Liu v The Republic of China* (US, 1989).

[228] Cf also FL Kirgis, 'Alien Tort Claims, Sovereign Immunity and International Law in US Courts' (1988) 82 AJIL 323, 329.

FSIA.[229] The 1995 decision in *Xuncax and Others v Gramajo* and *Ortiz v Gramajo* explicitly confirmed the controlling role of the foreign state in the qualification under the FSIA.[230] The plaintiffs in these cases sought compensatory and punitive damages from Gramajo, the former minister of defence of Guatemala, for injuries sustained at the hand of Guatemalan military forces. The challenged acts included summary execution, disappearance, torture, arbitrary detention and cruel, inhuman and degrading treatment in *Xuncax*, and kidnap, torture, and sexual abuse in *Ortiz*. Gramajo relied on the FSIA in defence to the allegations. The court considered that 'such immunity would in any event be unavailable in suits against an official arising from acts that were beyond the scope of the official's authority'. The fact that the Guatemalan government had not characterized the actions as officially authorized was considered a factor relevant to the outcome of the case.[231]

The so-called 'Flatow Amendment' to the terrorist state exception in the 1976 Foreign Sovereign Immunities Act confirms that crimes against international law *can* qualify as acts of state for the purpose of the applicability of the FSIA to individual state officials. In 1996 the Antiterrorism and Effective Death Penalty Act (AEDPA) amended the Foreign Sovereign Immunities Act to include an exception for certain human rights violations. The exception provides redress for US nationals who seek money damages against a foreign state designated 'state sponsor of terrorism' by the State Department 'for personal injury or death that was caused by an act of torture, extrajudicial killing, aircraft sabotage, hostage taking, or the provision of material support or resources... for such an act if such act or provision of material support is engaged in by an official, employee, or agent of such foreign state while acting within the scope of his or her office, employment, or agency'.[232] A mere five months later an amendment to the AEDPA was enacted. The amendment allows for non-economic and punitive damages against an official, employee or agent of a foreign state designated as 'terrorist' and made

[229] In *Kadic v Karadžić* (US, 1995) the court considered that the act of state doctrine only applies when a claim concerns an act related to the 'officially approved policy of a state', 250.

Commenting on the possible friction between the Torture Victim Protection Act and the act of state doctrine Senator Specter considered that '[t]he act of state doctrine does not provide a shield from liability under this act. This doctrine precludes US courts from sitting in judgment on the official public acts of a sovereign government... Because this doctrine applies only to public acts, and no foreign government commits torture as a matter of official policy, this doctrine cannot be violated by allowing a cause of action for torture.' In addition, the FSIA, 'would not normally provide a defense to an action under this act'. This would only be so, he argued, when the state official had an 'agency relationship' with the foreign state requiring that the state 'admit some knowledge or authorization of relevant acts', 138 Cong Rec S2668 (daily ed 3 March 1992). Cf also the House Report, HR Rep No 367, 102d Cong, 2d Sess 5 (1992), reprinted in 1992 USCCAN 84, 88; Senate Report on the TVPA, S Rep 102–249, 102d Cong, 1st Sess at 8 (1991).

[230] *Xuncax and Others v Gramajo* and *Ortiz v Gramajo* 886 F Supp 162 (US, DC, District of Massachusetts, 1995); 104 ILR 165.

[231] ibid 176, fn 10.

[232] § 1605 (7) FSIA. Antiterrorism and Effective Death Penalty Act, Pub L No 104–32, 110 Stat 1214 (1996). Cf ch 6, p 314–15 and p 354–7 below.

clear that the state sponsored terrorism exception to the FSIA applies to claims against foreign states and foreign state officials alike.[233] The amendment lays down that such an official

> while acting within the scope of his or her office, employment, or agency shall be liable to a United States national or the national's legal representative for personal injury or death caused by acts of that official, employee, or agent for which the courts of the United States may maintain jurisdiction under section 1605(a)(7) of title 28, United States Code, for money damages which may include economic damages, solatium, pain, and suffering, and punitive damages if the acts were among those described in section 1605(a)(7).

It further provides that

> [n]o action shall be maintained under this action... if an official, employee, or agent of the United States, while acting within the scope of his or her office, employment, or agency would not be liable for such acts if carried out within the United States.

The *Flatow* case concerned a claim brought by the parents of a US college student killed in a suicide attack on a bus passing through the Gaza strip, claimed by a faction of the Palestine Islamic Jihad.[234] In accordance with the amendment the court held the state sponsored terrorism exception to extend to state officials that have acted as agents in the implementation of state policy.

It is clear that the amendment proceeds from the assumption that individual state officials accused of 'state sponsored terrorism' are in principle covered by the FSIA. Hence, crimes against international law can be 'acts of state' for the purpose of the rule of immunity of foreign state officials from the jurisdiction of the US courts.

The US approach recalls the theory on the prosecution of war crimes before the concept of individual responsibility for crimes committed under the authority of the state was established and Röling's distinction between 'individual' and 'system' criminality.[235] However, as long as the foreign state does not object to the exercise of jurisdiction over its (former) official the US courts are prepared to accept limits of the mandate of senior state officials who would most probably have been assumed to exercise state authority under the 'old' approach.[236]

[233] Civil Liability for Acts of State Sponsored Terrorism, Pub L 104–208, div A, title I, Sec 101(c) (title V, Sec 589), Sept 30, 1996, 110 Stat 3009–121, 3009–172. Cf HR Conf Rep 863, 104th Cong, 2nd sess 1996 reprinted at 1996 USCCAN 924. In *Flatow v Islamic Republic of Iran* 1998) 13 it was explained that '[i]nterpretation in pan materia is... the most appropriate approach to the construction of both provisions... The amendment should be considered to relate back to the enactment of 28 U.S.C. §1605(a)(7) as if they had been enacted as one provision,... and the two provisions should be construed together and in reference to one another.'

[234] *Flatow v Islamic Republic of Iran* (US, 1998).

[235] Cf n 18 above.

[236] Cf eg *Doe et al v Lumintang*, Civ A No 00–674 (US, DC for the District of Columbia, 2001 and 2004): The Deputy Chief of the Indonesian Army was held individually responsible under the principle of command responsibility for a wide range of human rights abuses committed by the Indonesian military.

In sum, the (dis)qualification under the US notion act of state does not unequivocally entail a normative judgement. It appears that the authority of foreign states to ratify acts of its officials is unlimited. The interference of the foreign state on behalf of its (former) official—like that of Chile in the proceedings against Pinochet—appears to be sufficient to include the official in the protection of the FSIA. In practice the reach of the ATCA and TVPA may accordingly be limited to state officials that have fallen in disgrace or that are too unimportant for the home state to put its reputation on the line for. The Flatow Amendment evinces the unconvincing nature of the construction. Officials of states designated 'state sponsor of terrorism' qualify under the protection of the FSIA but are then responsible *with their personal estate* because of an exception to the rule of state immunity. The amendment provides that foreign officials can only be held responsible when US officials would bear responsibility in similar circumstances. However, when US officials can be sued in their personal capacity this is not an exception to the rule of state immunity but the non-applicability of the rule of state immunity and a perfect comparison between the two situations would result in the non-applicability of the FSIA to foreign state officials that can be sued in their personal capacity.[237] The current approach to the question of the applicability of the FSIA to individuals incorporates the US act of state doctrine in the rule of state immunity and the relevant case law accordingly does not reflect international law.

In conclusion it must be admitted however that although the possibility to sue individual state officials in respect of crimes committed under the colour of law in the US courts is more limited than under the proposal advanced in this study, it is positively preferable over Kelsen's act of state immunity theory.

From the perspective proposed in this study the immunity question at issue in the *Pinochet* case appears in a fundamentally different light. The rule of state immunity *ratione materiae* only applies if a state official cannot be sued in his personal capacity. As explained in chapter 3 of this study, the rule of functional immunity is a prerequisite for the applicability of the rule of state immunity.[238] States have agreed on a universal limit on the mandate of their state officials in respect of these crimes, which accordingly do not qualify as official acts for the purposes of the rule of functional immunity. Acts of torture are never committed in an official capacity *in the legal sense of that term*. Pinochet could therefore be sued in his personal capacity for the allegations of crimes against international law.[239]

[237] Cf eg *Hafer v Melo* (US, 1991) discussed in ch 3 above.

[238] It was suggested in ch 3 that it may be better to declare such suits inadmissible than to apply the rule of state immunity, cf § 2.2.2.

[239] Notably, Pinochet was not sued on the basis of vicarious responsibility, as Lord Millett rightly pointed out in *Pinochet* no 3, 179: '...Senator Pinochet is not alleged to be criminally liable because he was head of state when other responsible officials employed torture to maintain him in power. He is not alleged to be vicariously liable for the wrongdoing of his subordinates. He is

The difference with *Pinochet* no 3 is obvious. The conception of the rule of functional immunity advanced in this study reveals a direct link between that rule and the principle of individual responsibility and the principle of irrelevance of official capacity. In contrast, when the focus is on the official capacity in which an act is committed in the *factual sense of the term* it is necessary to establish an exception for crimes against international law that is not only applicable to international proceedings. Moreover, while in *Pinochet* no 3 the conception of the rule of functional immunity necessitated the conclusion that functional immunity *had* been available in civil proceedings in respect of the same allegations, the reliance on the attribution of the act to the state official in his personal capacity does not allow a distinction between civil and criminal proceedings.

The position defended in this study received support from the 2004 decision of the UK Court of Appeal in *Jones v Saudi Arabia*.[240] Contrary to the House of Lords two years later,[241] the Court of Appeal unanimously found for the claimants. The judgment does not however unequivocally state the *reasons* for the refusal to grant immunity to the individual state officials. The argumentation of the judges remains somewhat obscure because of the insistence that their conclusion is compatible with the *Pinochet* precedent. Both Mance LJ—who wrote the opinion of the court—and Lord Philips—who added an individual opinion—ultimately based the denial of immunity on the ground that no rational distinction can be made between the exercise of criminal jurisdiction and the exercise of civil jurisdiction. However, the distinction between criminal and civil jurisdiction formed exactly the thrust of *Pinochet* no 3.

At the outset, Mance LJ rejected the argument of defendants that the rule of functional immunity is co-extensive with the crime of torture. He argued that

> the requirement that the pain or suffering be inflicted by a public official does no more… than identify the author and the public context in which the author must be acting. It does not lend to the acts of torture themselves any official or governmental character or nature, or mean that it can in any way be regarded as an official function to inflict, or that an official can be regarded as representing the state in inflicting, such pain and suffering. Still less does it suggest that the official inflicting such pain or suffering can be afforded the cloak of state immunity… The whole tenor of the Torture Convention is to underline the individual responsibility of state officials for acts of torture… and I do not consider that one can derive from its definition of torture… any conclusion on the different question whether a state can assert immunity in respect of a civil claim against its officials based on allegations of systematic torture.[242]

alleged to have incurred direct criminal responsibility for his own acts in ordering and directing a campaign of terror involving the use of torture.'

[240] *Jones v Saudi Arabia and Abdul Aziz* & *Mitchell a.o. v Al-Dali a.o.* (UK, 2004).

[241] *Jones v Saudi Arabia* (UK, 2006), discussed in § 2.3.1.2 above.

[242] ibid § 71.

He then moved to the examination of the argument that the proceedings impleaded Saudi Arabia. Mance LJ based the rejection of that argument on the *Pinochet* case. He argued that the 'statements by three members of the House of Lords (Lords Hutton, Millett, and Philips) assuming or maintaining the continued existence of immunity ratione materiae in respect of a former head of state or other official in civil proceedings (even proceedings based on systematic torture)'[243] were completely obiter.[244] 'It is not easy to see', wrote Mance LJ, 'why civil proceedings against an alleged individual torturer should be regarded as involving any greater interference in or a more objectionable form of adjudication upon the internal affairs of a foreign state... Nor is it easy to see why a civil claim against an individual torturer should be regarded as indirectly impleading the foreign state in any more objectionable respect than a criminal prosecution.'[245] He concluded that '[t]here would... be considerable incongruity in a solution whereby an alleged torturer who was and remained within the jurisdiction could be prosecuted but not sued.'[246]

Lord Philips was one of the three judges in *Pinochet* no 3 who explicitly stated that Pinochet would have been immune from *civil* suit in respect of the same allegations.[247] He felt therefore obliged to explain his shift in position in an individual opinion.

His argumentation differed somewhat from that relied on by Mance LJ. He set out to restate the *Pinochet* precedent in the following terms:

> It... emerges clearly from the majority that a state cannot assert immunity *ratione materiae* in relation to a criminal prosecution for torture in as much as torture is a breach of *jus cogens* under international law. This does not merely apply to those states who are party to the Torture Convention. The Torture Convention reflects the position under public international law.
>
> ...
>
> *Pinochet* demonstrates that torture can no longer fall within the scope of official duties of a state official.[248]

He *then* asserted that

> [o]nce the conclusion is reached that torture cannot be treated as the exercise of a state function so as to attract immunity *ratione materiae* in criminal proceedings against individuals, it seems to me that it cannot logically be so treated in civil proceedings against individuals.
>
> ...

243 ibid § 57, in general § 54–7.
244 ibid § 74.
245 ibid § 75–6.
246 ibid § 81.
247 Cf p 232 above.
248 *Jones v Saudi Arabia and Abdul Aziz* & *Mitchell a.o. v Al-Dali a.o.* (UK, 2004) § 124 and § 126.

> If civil proceedings are brought against individuals for acts of torture in circumstances where the state is immune from suit *ratione personae*, there can be no suggestion that the state is vicariously liable. It is the personal responsibility of the individuals, not that of the state, which is in issue. The state is not indirectly impleaded by the proceedings.[249]

It must be concluded that both judges have engaged in a deductive argumentation on the basis of the *outcome* of the *Pinochet* case rather than in an inductive argumentation based on the theoretical conception of the rule of functional immunity that was at its basis. The decision in *Pinochet* no 3 proceeded from the assumption that the rule of state immunity *ratione materiae* in principle applied to the proceedings. Not because the decision necessarily implicates Chile but because the decision necessarily implicated the sovereign activity of Chile. The Lords did not rely on the principle of individual responsibility for crimes against international law to determine the status of the defendant before the court. Mance LJ preferred to ignore this. Lord Philips went even one step further and restated the ratio decidendi of *Pinochet* no 3 in terms that are not supported by close study of that decision. Lord Philips stated that an act cannot be official for the purposes of civil immunity and unofficial for the purposes of criminal immunity. This is very right indeed. However, the statement that *Pinochet* no 3 declared acts of torture to be unofficial simply does not hold true.[250]

By stating that civil proceedings against a state official in respect of torture allegations do not implead the home state the court has implicitly restated the rule of functional immunity in terms that are very close to those proposed in this study. Lord Philips in particular acknowledged that the state is not impleaded whenever the individual has incurred personal responsibility in respect of the alleged acts. It cannot but be admitted that the conception of the rule of functional immunity that shines through the argumentation of the judges is very different from that at the basis of *Pinochet* no 3. The immunity of state officials is no longer merely a question of state immunity *ratione materiae*. Rather, the rule of functional immunity and the concept of 'official act' acquire a distinct role. Just as this study argued in chapter 3, the rule of functional immunity for official acts is seen as a *prerequisite* for the application of the rule of state immunity to proceedings against foreign state officials. In sum, the decision of the Court of Appeal in *Jones v Saudi Arabia and Abdul Aziz* silently moved away from the concept of act of state immunity that was prevalent in *Pinochet* no 3.

It is a pity that the shift in conception of the rule of functional immunity was not admitted openly. Also in conclusion Lord Philips attempted to fit his argumentation in the mould of precedent. He stated that the principle of *Propend Finance* 'has no application if... the subject matter of the action does not rank

[249] ibid § 127 and § 128.

[250] It is in this respect noteworthy that judge Mance held the prohibition of torture *not* to be co-extensive with the rule of functional immunity (ibid § 71) while the majority of the Lords in *Pinochet* no 3 had reasoned otherwise (cf the discussion of the opinions of Lords Saville, Browne-Wilkinson, Philips, and Millett above).

as "matters of State conduct"'.[251] This conclusion assumes a room for reason in the *Propend* principle that really does not exist. A proper conclusion would have been that the principle of *Propend Finance* has been formulated in overbroad terms. Instead of the application of the rule of state immunity to proceedings against foreign state officials that have acted as an arm or mouthpiece of the foreign state, the principle espouses an act of state immunity in the sense proposed by Kelsen. The rewriting of history is not a satisfactory solution to flawed precedent.

2.3.1.4 ... That may not conclusively settle the competence of the *court*

At this point we should come back to an issue touched upon in chapter 3 of this study, namely the distinction of different types of international crimes as proposed by De Sena.[252] According to De Sena national courts in principle refrain from exercising jurisdiction over international crimes like the crime of genocide, the crime of aggression, or crimes against humanity. Since the imputability to the state constitutes the context in which the individual responsibility for these crimes necessarily inserts itself, the ascertainment of this responsibility requires an inquiry into the overall government policy of which they are, by definition, the expression. We can in this regard think of cases that require a national court to determine the legality of a particular military intervention, of the use of certain weapons in an armed conflict, or of certain strategies of warfare. Especially cases against senior government officials like the (former) head of state, (former) ministers, or (former) army commanders are likely to involve the decision of this type of question.[253] This is different with other international crimes. While the question of imputability of the act may form a constituent of the definition of the crime—as in the case of torture—and the responsibility of the state under the law of state responsibility may be inferred from the ruling, the imputability of international responsibility to the state is in substance irrelevant.

The identification of this difference by De Sena is pertinent, but this study does not agree that it relates to the rule of functional immunity. Rather, it may be seen to give rise to a residual competence issue. This study does not purport to deal with this issue in any detail—the relevance lies primarily in its articulation and its distinction from immunity rules—but one or two suggestions as to its possible substance will be made.

At the outset the issue should be distinguished from the non-justiciability rule that is sometimes propounded in national courts. In the *Buttes Gas* case the

[251] ibid § 130.

[252] Ch 3 § 2.3.

[253] The distinction is hence different from that between 'individual' and 'system' criminality as defined by Röling (cf n 18 above). While Röling saw the killing of prisoners of war, the torture of captured people to obtain information, or the killing of civilians to spread terror when ordered by the government to support the war effort as 'system criminality' (128), these examples would qualify under individualized crimes under the distinction proposed here.

House of Lords needed to take sides in an inter-state territorial dispute in order to decide a dispute between two private individuals.[254] Lord Wilberforce held:

> [T]he essential question is whether... there exists in English law a more general principle that the courts will not adjudicate upon the transactions of foreign sovereign states. Though I would prefer to avoid argument on terminology, it seems desirable to consider this principle, if existing, not as a variety of 'act of state' but one for judicial restraint or abstention... In my opinion there is, and for long has been, such a general principle, starting in English law, adopted and generalised in the law of the United States of America, which is effective and compelling in English courts. This principle is not one of discretion, but is inherent in the very nature of the judicial process.[255]

He referred to the views of the Legal Advisor to the US Department of State attached to the *amicus curiae* brief filed in the proceedings on the same issue before US courts and to the decisions of those courts.[256] In the attached letter to the Attorney-General, the Legal Advisor considered

> We believe that the political sensitivity of territorial issues, the need for unquestionable U.S. neutrality and the harm to our foreign relations which may otherwise ensue, as well as the evidentiary and jurisprudential difficulties for a U.S. court to determine such issues, are compelling grounds for judicial abstention...
>
> We do not believe that this judicial self-restraint should turn on such analytical questions as whether the so-called Act of State doctrine which is traditionally limited to governmental actions within the territory of the respective state can apply to an exercise of disputed territorial jurisdiction. It rather follows from the general notion that national courts should not assume the function of arbiters of territorial conflicts between third powers even in the context of a dispute between private parties.

The US court had considered that the determination of the questions put to it was 'constitutionally reserved to the executive branch'.[257] In addition, it had concluded that

> [t]he issue of sovereignty is political not only for its impact on the executive branch, but also because the judicial or manageable standards are lacking for its determination. To decide the ownership of the concession area it would be necessary to decide (1) the sovereignty of Abu Musa, (2) the proper territorial water limit and (3) the proper allocation of continental shelf. A judicial resolution of the dispute... is clearly impossible.[258]

[254] *Buttes Gas v Hammer* [1982] AC 888 (UK, HL, 1981).

[255] ibid 931–2.

[256] Cf *Occidental Petroleum Corporation v Buttes Gas and Oil Company* 331 F Supp 92 (US, DC for the Central District of California, 1971) affirmed by the Ct of Apps (9th Cir), 461 F 2d 1261 (1972); *Occidental of Umm al Qaywayn Inc v A Certain Cargo of Petroleum Laden Aboard the Tanker Dauntless Colocotronis* 577 F 2d 1196 (US, Ct of Apps (5th Cir), 1978).

[257] *Occidental of Umm al Qaywayn Inc v A Certain Cargo of Petroleum Laden Aboard the Tanker Dauntless Colocotronis* (US, 1978) 1203.

[258] ibid 1204. In rationalizing its finding the court conveyed a startling thesis on international law in general: 'In their external relations, sovereigns are bound by no law; they are like our ancestors before the recognition or imposition of the social contract. A prerequisite of law is a recognized superior authority whether delegated from below or imposed from above where there is no

The decision in the US courts clearly relied heavily on domestic conceptions of the relation between judiciary and executive.[259] Lord Wilberforce did acknowledge this but found that a more general principle could be seen to ultimately underlie the decision. Most pertinently, he considered that the question 'what issues are capable, and what are incapable, of judicial determination must be answered in closely similar terms in whatever country they arise, depending, as they must, upon an appreciation of the nature and limits of the judicial function'.[260] He concluded that the issues that had to be decided

> are not issues upon which a municipal court can pass. Leaving aside all possibility of embarrassment in our foreign relations... there are... no judicial or manageable standards by which to judge these issues,... the court would be in a judicial no-man's land: the court would be asked to review transactions in which four sovereign states were involved, which they had brought to a precarious settlement, after diplomacy and the use of force, and to say that at least part of these were 'unlawful' under international law.[261]

Crawford argued that the prohibition at issue in *Buttes* was of an international law character.[262] The bearing of international law principles on the questions at issue in *Buttes* is however dubious—to say the least. It must be realized that the prohibition keeps a court from deciding disputes that of itself fall within its essential jurisdiction. Since in this type of case a ruling does not directly affect the foreign state involved it may be argued that the balance of interests tips to the side of the parties to the dispute. As Singer put it:

> One would search far to find support in international law for the proposition that the courts of one country ought not to describe in apt terms the acts of the government of another country.[263]

For the purposes of this study the question needs no definite answer. The consideration of the *Buttes* type case principally serves as an example for distinction. For one, in the conflict of laws cases represented by *Sabbatino* and *Oetjen* the role of the question as to the violation of international law differs from that in *Buttes*. It was explained in chapter 2 that states may deviate from the normal conflict of

recognized authority, there is no law. Because no law exists binding these sovereigns and allocating rights and liabilities, no method exists to judicially resolve their disagreements. The ownership of the island, and derivatively its waters, has long been the subject of dispute. Were we to resolve this dispute we would not only usurp the executive power, but also intrude the judicial power beyond its philosophical limits.' (1204–05).

[259] In *Baker v Carr* the Supreme Court stressed that '[t]he nonjusticiability of a political question is primarily a function of the separation of powers.' 369 US 186 (1962) 210.

[260] *Buttes Gas v Hammer* (UK, 1981) 936.

[261] ibid 938. Cf for a case with similar problems: *Petrotimor Companhia de Petroleos SARL v Commonwealth of Australia* [2003] FCAFC 3 (Australia, Federal Court of Australia, New South Wales District Registry, 2003).

[262] J Crawford, 'Decisions of British Courts During 1982 involving Questions of Public or Private International Law' (1982) 53 BYIL 259, 265.

[263] M Singer, 'The Act of State Doctrine of the United Kingdom: An Analysis with Comparisons to United States Practice' (1981) 75 AJIL 283, 291.

law rules when a foreign law violates international law.[264] In other words, as a consequence of a finding of violation of international law acts of state may not be recognized in a foreign court. The outcome of the question determines whether a foreign state will enjoy its normal 'right', namely the application of its laws to situations that are regulated by it under the normal conflict of laws rules. The discretion of courts to set aside the normal rules calls for appropriate safeguards since a finding of violation of international law *does* affect the rights of the foreign state involved. Mann in fact acknowledged that the scope of the principle he advanced was not unlimited. The fact that foreign acts of state may be refused effect when contrary to international law does not mean, he cautioned, that courts are free to declare foreign acts of state contrary to international law. Mann argued that national courts may only refuse to give effect to foreign acts of state if there has been a clear breach of a clear international duty. Courts, he wrote, may only come to the conclusion that a foreign law amounts to an international delinquency when 'both the law and the facts are clearly established'.[265]

When the prosecution of a foreign state official requires the settlement of a controversy on the rights and obligations of the home state in terms of international law it cannot be said that such settlement only constitutes 'a preliminary to the decision of a question of private rights which in itself is subject to the competency of the Court of law'. The requirement that law and facts are clearly established hence applies with much greater force to the determination of the illegality of state action that *creates* the competence of the national court. When civil or criminal proceedings are instigated against (former) foreign state officials for crimes against international law the finding of the violation of the international law norm creates the possibility to prosecute these officials. If an act does not amount to torture but merely to 'assault and battery' the state official alleged to have committed the act can claim to have acted as the state.[266]

According to De Sena, the rare examples of national prosecution of foreign state officials for context-crimes—like the *Eichmann*,[267] *Barbie*,[268] *Demjanjuk*,[269] *Finta*,[270] and *Karadžić*[271] cases—must be understood in the context of action undertaken by the international community in respect of these crimes: the establishment of the Nuremberg Tribunal as part of the systematic dismantling of the

[264] Ch 2 § 3.2.3.

[265] FA Mann, 'International Delinquencies before Municipal Courts' (1954) 70 LQR 181, 196. See in the same sense P Weil, 'Le contrôle par les tribunaux nationaux de la licéité internationale des actes des États étrangers' (1977) 23 AFDI 9, 47.

[266] Cf *Jones v Saudi Arabia and Abdul Aziz* & *Mitchell a.o. v Al-Dali a.o.* (UK, 2004) § 94.

[267] *Attorney-General of Israel v Eichmann* (Israel, 1961), confirmed by the Supreme Court (1962).

[268] *Féderation National des Déportées et Internés Résistants et Patriotes and Others v Barbie* (France, 1983 and 1984; 1985; 1988).

[269] *Demjanjuk v Petrovsky* (US, 1985).

[270] *Regina v Finta* (Canada, 1989).

[271] *Kadic v Karadžić* (US, 1995).

overall organization of the German state, and the establishment of the ad hoc international criminal tribunal for the former Yugoslavia.

Alternatively, recalling the words of Mann, it could be said that the law and the facts of these context-crimes were clear. In this respect a parallel may be drawn to the non-justiciability doctrine. Lord Wilberforce distinguished the case of *Buttes Gas v Hammer* from cases where the question as to the situation under international law 'may... be capable of determination as a matter of fact'. The question at issue in *Buttes*, he considered, could not 'be decided simply as an issue of fact upon evidence: it calls, on the contrary, for adjudication upon the validity, meaning and effect of transactions of sovereign states'. In another relevant passage he stressed that 'it is not to be assumed that these matters have now passed into history, so that they now can be examined with safe detachment.'[272] A second case that deserves mention in this respect is the 2002 decision of the House of Lords in *Kuwait Airways Corporation v Iraqi Airways Company and Others*.[273] The case provides an important example of how consensus in the international community on the illegality of certain actions may allow national courts to also regard those actions illegal in proceedings between private persons that affect the rights of foreign states. The dispute between the two companies required passing on the legality of the invasion and annexation of Kuwait by Iraq in 1990. The Lords rejected the non-justiciability argument advanced by Iraqi Airways Company (IAC). They relied on the string of Security Council resolutions condemning the annexation to corroborate the proposition that it was 'plain beyond argument' that that seizure and assimilation 'were flagrant violations of rules of international law of fundamental importance'.[274] The conclusion of Lord Nicholls reads in relevant part:

> A breach of international law of this seriousness is a matter of deep concern to the worldwide community of nations. This is evidenced by the urgency with which the UN Security Council considered this incident and by its successive resolutions. Such a fundamental breach of international law can properly cause the courts of this country to say that, like the confiscatory decree of the Nazi government of Germany in 1941, a law depriving those whose property has been plundered of the ownership of their property in favour of the aggressor's own citizens will not be enforced or recognised in proceedings in this country. Enforcement or recognition of this law would be manifestly contrary to the public policy of English law. For good measure, enforcement or recognition would also be contrary to this country's obligations under the UN Charter. Further, it would sit uneasily with the almost universal condemnation of Iraq's behaviour and with the military action, in which this country participated, taken against Iraq to compel its withdrawal from Kuwait. International law, for its part, recognises that a national court may

[272] *Buttes Gas v Hammer* (UK, 1981).

[273] *Kuwait Airways Corporation v Iraqi Airways Company and Others* [2002] 2 AC 883 (UK, HL, 2002); 125 ILR 602, 677.

[274] ibid 682, § 20.

properly decline to give effect to legislative and other acts of foreign states which are in violation of international law . . .[275]

Lord Steyn, moreover, stated that although not all violations of international law trigger the public policy exception, the invasion and annexation of Iraq is a paradigm case since the prohibition of the use of force is *jus cogens*, SC resolutions under chapter VII are binding in law on all members of the UN, and 'a universal consensus' on the illegality of Iraq's aggression existed.[276]

The invasion of Kuwait by Iraq is indeed a paradigm example. It is not difficult to see how the illegality of that act under international law may be regarded an 'issue of fact upon evidence'. The condemnation of the international community was immediate and universal, and the SC quickly moved to adopt resolutions under chapter VII in which it emphatically stated the illegal nature of the invasion and annexation of Kuwait.[277] A similar international consensus was displayed in respect of the conflicts in the former Yugoslavia and Rwanda—when the SC decided to establish international criminal tribunals to prosecute those responsible for the crimes committed, and most prominently after the defeat of Nazi Germany—with the dismantling of the German state and the Nuremberg trials.[278] In addition, certain controversial questions may become less so with the passing of time. For example, after regime changes many countries in South America have launched inquiries into the human rights abuses allegedly committed by the military regimes in the 1970s and 1980s and the atrocities committed in Argentina and Chile can now be safely stated as facts upon evidence.[279] As Lord Browne-Wilkinson rightly held in *Pinochet* no 3, '[t]here is no real dispute that during the period of the . . . Pinochet regime appalling acts of barbarism were committed in Chile and elsewhere in the world: torture, murder and the unexplained disappearance of individuals, all on a large scale.'[280]

Recent controversies as regards the exercise of universal jurisdiction can be seen to be caused by a disregard for this residual competence issue. The case instituted against General Tommy Franks, the commander of the US troops in Iraq,

[275] ibid 685, § 29.

[276] ibid 709, § 113, 711–12, § 114 (*per* Lord Steyn).

[277] Cf also *Petrotimor Companhia de Petroleos SARL v Commonwealth of Australia* (Australia, 2003) § 63, where the court held that 'the facts in the present case are much closer to those in *Buttes* than to those in the *Kuwait* case' because in *Kuwait* 'the breach of international law had been determined by the Security Council acting under the United Nations Charter'.

[278] See for the establishment of the ICTY, SC Resolution 827 (1993); and for the establishment of the ICTR, SC Resolution 955 (1994).

[279] Cf eg CS Nino, *Radical Evil on Trial* (1996).

[280] *Pinochet* no 3, 101. The events that took place in Chile during the military regime have been the subject of thorough investigation, both in Chile (eg *Report of the Chilean National Commission on Truth and Reconciliation (The Rettig Report)* (translation PE Berryman 1993) as well as on the international level (eg Amnesty International, United Nations). See for more information: International Commission of Jurists, *Crimes against Humanity: Pinochet Faces Justice* (1999); RJ Wilson, 'Prosecuting Pinochet: International Crimes in Spanish Domestic Law' (1999) 21 Human Rights Quarterly 927.

in respect of alleged war crimes committed by the US military in Iraq is a case in point. The complaint included, *inter alia*, the use of cluster bombs and looting protected by or under orders from the US army. The United States was furious about the instigation of criminal proceedings and threatened Belgium with various retaliation measures if the proceedings were to go ahead. While this study argues that General Franks does not enjoy functional immunity in respect of allegations of crimes against international law, the accusations against him set out to question the legality of US policy in Iraq on the basis of an interpretation of the law and the facts that is highly controversial.

In this respect the dissent of Lord Browne-Wilkinson to the 2001 Princeton Principles on Universal Jurisdiction is notable. He wrote:

> I am strongly in favour of universal jurisdiction over serious international crimes if, by those words, one means the exercise by an international court or by the courts of one state of jurisdiction over the nationals of another state with the prior consent of that latter state, i.e. in cases such as the ICC and the Torture Convention.
>
> But the Princeton Principles propose that individual national courts should exercise such jurisdiction against nationals of a state which has not agreed to such jurisdiction. Moreover, the principles do not recognise any form of sovereign immunity: Principle 5(1). If the law were to be so established, states antipathic to Western powers would be likely to seize both active and retired officials and military personnel of such Western powers and stage a show trial for alleged international crimes. Conversely, zealots in Western states might launch prosecutions against, for example, Islamic extremist for their terrorist activities. It is naïve to think that, in such cases, the national state of the accused would stand by and watch the trial proceed: resort to force would be more probable. In any event, the fears of such legal actions would inhibit the use of peacekeeping forces when it is otherwise desirable and also the free interchange of diplomatic personnel. I believe that the adoption of such universal jurisdiction without preserving the existing concepts of immunity would be more likely to damage than to advance chances of international peace.[281]

This study suggests however that universal jurisdiction and the absence of functional immunity is no open sesame to the exercise of jurisdiction over foreign state officials. The concerns of Lord Browne-Wilkinson would be met—at least in part—if states refrain from the exercise of universal jurisdiction over highly controversial allegations of crimes against international law that require a decision on the context of state policy.

The issue is—to put it mildly—not devoid of problems. The reliance on the expression of consensus through international institutions is far from ideal. The (in)actions of the international community often reflect political expediency rather than legal standards.[282] This author does not purport to offer a

[281] The Princeton Project on Universal Jurisdiction, *The Princeton Principle on Universal Jurisdiction* (2001), dissent Lord BrowneWilkinson (in fn 20), available at <http://www.princeton.edu/~lapa/unive_jur.pdf>.

[282] Cf eg P Klein, 'Responsibility for Serious Breaches of Obligations deriving from Peremptory Norms of International Law and United Nations Law' (2002) 13 EJIL 1241, 1247.

comprehensive answer. The contribution of this study is limited to the identification and articulation of the issue and its distinction from immunity law. Apart from De Sena no author or court has recognized the relevance of the distinction between isolated crimes and crimes that are necessarily inserted in the context of state policy. While De Sena thought the issue to reflect an aspect of the rule of functional immunity, this study insists that it is a *separate residual issue concerning the competence of national courts*.[283] The acknowledgement of the pertinence of the issue is a first step to the formulation of more institutionalized solutions to the problem. The international community could for example agree to give a UN organ a specific mandate to report on situations that warrant the exercise of universal jurisdiction.[284]

In conclusion, one final observation is called for. The identified residual limit on the competence of national courts casts an interesting light on the debate on the jurisdiction of the International Criminal Court over nationals of non state parties. In contrast with the ICTY and the ICTR, the ICC is not established by a resolution of the UN Security Council. The Court has been established by the Treaty of Rome and can hence only bind states that have accepted its jurisdiction. The Statute of the Court provides that the Court may exercise jurisdiction when the Security Council refers a situation to the prosecutor under Chapter VII of the Charter of the UN, or when a situation is referred to the prosecutor by either the state on the territory of which the conduct in question occurred, or the state of which the person accused of the crime is a national, is party to the statute or has accepted the court's jurisdiction, or when the prosecutor initiates an investigation into crimes committed on the territory of such state.[285] In other words, the Court may exercise jurisdiction over nationals of non state parties if these nationals are suspected of committing certain crimes within the territory of a state party. This aspect of the Court's jurisdiction has met fierce opposition.[286] Especially the

[283] Cf P De Sena (1996) 139. Also in P De Sena (1997) 367; P De Sena (1999) 964ff, discussed in ch 3 § 2.3 above. Cf also JL Brierly, 'The Nature of War Crimes Jurisdiction' in H Lauterpacht and CHM Waldock (eds), *The Basis of Obligation in International Law and Other Papers by the Late JL Brierly* (1958) 297 (original text in (1944) 2 The Norseman): 'political acts, such as the making of aggressive war, ... may well be right to punish, but ... cannot properly be made the object of legal process'.

[284] Cf in this respect the proposals regarding the determination of the occurrence of serious breaches of obligations under peremptory norms of international law as controlling the Articles on the Responsibility of States for Internationally Wrongful Acts (2001), mentioned in NHB Jørgensen, *The Responsibility of States for International Crimes* (2000) 212 and 214.

[285] Arts 12 and 13 Rome Statute of the ICC.

[286] See eg DJ Scheffer, 'The United States and the International Criminal Court' (1999) 93 AJIL 12; R Wedgwood, 'The International Criminal Court: An American View' (1999) 10 EJIL 93; G Hafner et al, 'A Response to the American View as Presented by Ruth Wedgwood' (1999) 10 EJIL 108; M Zwanenburg, 'The Statute for an International Criminal Court and the United States: Peace Without Justice?' (1999) 12 LJIL 1. Notably, the drafters of the Statute did even proceed from the position that neither the state of territoriality nor the state of nationality needed to be a party to the Statute for the Court to be able to establish jurisdiction because of the principle of universal jurisdiction, cf M Scharf, 'The ICC's Jurisdiction over the Nationals of Non-Party States: A Critique of the US Position' (2001) 64 Law & Contemporary Problems 67, 77.

United States has criticized the scope of the Court's jurisdiction and has tried to ensure the exemption of its officials operating abroad.[287]

We will not enter the intricate discussion between proponents and opponents of the jurisdictional provisions of the Rome Statute in any detail here. It is however noted that, as Judge Huber stated in the *Island of Palmas* case, 'whatever may be the right construction of a treaty, it cannot be interpreted as disposing of the rights of independent third Powers'.[288] Accordingly, if national courts are not competent to decide certain allegations of crimes against international law against foreign state officials, neither are international courts that cannot bind the home state of such official.[289] While the US attack on the ICC is overbroad—the US argues that there can be jurisdiction over its nationals unless it consents to the jurisdiction of the Court—this study suggests that some legitimate concern as to the scope of the jurisdictional provisions of the ICC Statute does exist.

2.3.2 Personal Immunity

2.3.2.1 Customary international law

It was explained in the previous section that the principle of irrelevance of official capacity secures the *responsibility of the individual* who commits crimes against international law. The principle does not however secure the *jurisdiction of the court*. In other words, the principle regards the *substantive but not the procedural* immunity of state officials.[290] The principle of individual responsibility

[287] Cf The American Servicemembers' Protection Act (ASPA) 2002 (title II of Public Law 107–206); M Benzing, 'U.S. Bilateral Non-Surrender Agreements and Art 98 of the Statute of the International Criminal Court; an Exercise in the Law of Treaties' (2004) 8 Max Planck Yearbook of United Nations Law 181; R Van Alebeek, 'From Rome to The Hague, Recent Developments on Immunity Issues in the ICC Statute' (2000) 13 LJIL 485, 488–93.

[288] *Island of Palmas (Miangas) Case* (*The Netherlands v United States*) (PCA, 1928) 842. Cf also art 34 of the Vienna Convention on the Law of Treaties (1969): 'A treaty does not create either obligations or rights for a third State without its consent', reprinted in (1969) 8 ILM 697.

[289] It should in this respect be noted that it has been argued—outside the context of the present discussion—that even when national courts *do* have jurisdiction this does not mean that this jurisdiction can be exercised by an international court since the latter exercises a more intrusive form of jurisdiction, cf M Morris, 'High Crimes and Misconceptions: The ICC and Non-Party States' (2001) 64 Law & Contemporary Problems 13, 30: 'An even remotely successful international court will have significant prestige and authority. The political repercussions of such a court's determining that a state's acts or policies were unlawful would be substantial indeed, and categorically different from the repercussions of the same verdict rendered by a national court. If a guilty verdict were passed by a national court in an official-acts case, the matter would remain a disagreement among equals, one state maintaining that an unlawful act had been committed, the other disputing its occurrence or defending its lawfulness. By contrast, were the ICC to pronounce an official act to constitute a crime, the decision would bear the authoritative weight and resulting political impact of categorically different nature.'

[290] Cf in similar sense eg The Princeton Project on Universal Jurisdiction, *The Princeton Principles on Universal Jurisdiction* (2001), available at <http://www.princeton.edu/~lapa/unive_jur.pdf>, Commentary on Principle 5; A Cassese (2002). Cf also H Fox (2002) 429–33, at 431 we read: 'Nothing specific as to immunity was included in the Nuremberg Charter, nor was there any mention of immunity in the Statutes of the International Criminal Tribunals for Yugoslavia and Rwanda.'

for crimes against international law and the principle of irrelevance of official capacity accordingly do not affect the personal immunity enjoyed by foreign diplomatic agents and foreign heads of state during their term of office.

Thinking about it, this is really almost a trite thing to say. Of course there is a difference between the responsibility of a person and the jurisdiction of the court to determine that responsibility. In fact, the whole purpose of personal immunity is to shield certain state officials from foreign jurisdiction in respect of allegations of acts for which they bear personal responsibility. The personal immunity of diplomatic agents and heads of states while in office was never an issue before the Nuremberg Tribunal and has not been given thought by commentators either. Only recently states have started to take their jurisdiction under international criminal law seriously. It is not surprising that the haphazard prosecution of a handful of elderly Nazi war criminals no longer representing the German state has not brought the question to the surface. It is fair to say that until article 27.2 of the ICC Statute the personal immunity from the jurisdiction of courts in respect of crimes against international law was a commonly overlooked issue. The question was only debated in the Commission that studied the possibility of prosecution and punishment of war criminals after the First World War. It is recalled that one of the principal reasons why the US delegates to the Commission did not agree with the report sent to the Versailles Peace Conference was the assertion of the Commission that jurisdiction could be established over incumbent heads of state.[291]

The International Law Commission is responsible for the only authority that the principle of irrelevance of official capacity also entails an exception to the personal immunities of state officials. In the commentary to article 7 of the 1996 Draft Code of Crimes against the Peace and Security of Mankind we read:

> The absence of any procedural immunity with respect to prosecution or punishment in appropriate judicial proceedings is an essential corollary of the absence of any substantive immunity or defence. It would be paradoxical to prevent an individual from invoking his official position to avoid responsibility for a crime only to permit him to invoke this same consideration to avoid the consequences of this responsibility.[292]

But why would it be paradoxical to lift the functional immunity of thousands and thousands of state officials because the idea that they are not personally responsible for these acts is outrageous, but to retain the personal immunity of a limited group of state officials while they are in office because the conduct of international diplomacy so requires? The rationale of diplomatic immunity and head of state immunity—as set out in chapter 4 of this study—applies regardless of the nature of the alleged crime or tort.[293]

[291] Cf § 1 above.

[292] YBILC 1996 ii (part 2) 27.

[293] The argument that prosecution for acts of violence 'would not hinder the diplomatic process since violence is not part of that process' confuses the functionality rationale of the rule of

In the context of the Nazi atrocities Glueck argued that head of state immunity 'is based on international comity and courtesy; and this in turn depends upon the sovereign in question conducting himself in conformity with international law as a respectable and trustworthy member of the Family of Nations. By invading neighboring countries in flagrant violation of treaty obligations and for purposes of aggression, conquest and the mass-extermination of human beings, a sovereign strips himself of any mantle of immunity he may have claimed by virtue of international comity. He outlaws himself.'[294]

This argument denies the international law status of the rule of head of state immunity. Alternatively it makes the rights (and obligations?) of international law dependent on qualifications that recall the outdated distinction between civilized nations that are part of the 'Family of Nations' and barbaric people that are not.[295] This study does not accept that personal immunity rules can be shoved aside on this argumentation.

This does not of course mean that no exception to these rules may develop. This would be a policy decision to be made by states, not a state of the law finding of judicial institutions.[296] If states agree that the interests of prosecution of these crimes outweigh the interests protected by the rules they may decide to develop an exception for crimes against international law. However, the principle of irrelevance of official capacity can in itself not be interpreted as a step in that direction. A closer look at state practice is hence required.

A string of recent judicial decisions confirms that personal immunities from foreign national jurisdiction also apply in the face of allegations of crimes against international law. The House of Lords emphasized in *Pinochet* no 3 that its reasoning did not affect the immunity of *incumbent* heads of state.[297] A few weeks earlier, the Spanish *Audiencia Nacional* had come to the same conclusion. The court held that the jurisdiction of the *Ley Orgánica del Poder Judicial*—the Law on Judicial Power—could not be exercised in criminal proceedings instigated against Fidel Castro, in respect of allegations of crimes against international law. Article 21.2 of that law provides for an exception to jurisdiction whenever rules of public international law so require. In contrast to a former head of state, a serving head of state, the court reasoned, is absolutely immune from the criminal

personal immunity with the official character of acts at the basis of functional immunity, cf for this argument SL Wright, 'Diplomatic Immunity: A Proposal for Amending the Vienna Convention to Deter Violent Criminal Acts' (1987) 5 Boston University International Law Journal 177, 184 and 206; JMT Labuschagne, 'Diplomatic Immunity as Criminal Defence: An Anthropo-legal Anachronism?' (1997) 22 South African Yearbook of International law 32.

294 S Glueck, *War Criminals, Their Prosecution & Punishment* (1944) 121–32, quotation at 122.

295 Ch 6 § 2.3.2.3 below discusses this further.

296 Cf on policy arguments § 3 below.

297 *Pinochet* no 3, eg 179 (*per* Lord Millett) and 181 (*per* Lord Philips). In 2004 two UK district judges refused to issue warrants of arrest on allegations of crimes against international law in respect of the head of state of Zimbabwe, Mugabe, and the minister of defence of Israel, Mofaz, because of the personal immunity of these foreign state officials, cf C Warbrick (2004).

jurisdiction of foreign courts.[298] In 1999, the German prosecuting authorities refused to initiate criminal proceedings against Saddam Hussein for serious human rights violations because the incumbent head of state of Iraq enjoyed personal immunity from the German criminal jurisdiction. The *Oberlandesgericht Köln* confirmed this decision.[299] In 2003 the Belgian Court of Cassation ruled that a claim against the Israeli Prime Minister Sharon was inadmissible because of the rule of head of state immunity even though the allegations concerned crimes against international law.[300] The United States courts have granted diplomatic immunity[301] and head of state immunity[302] in civil proceedings concerning crimes against international law. In France, a criminal complaint filed against Colonel Ghaddafi, the serving head of state of Libya, did not survive the claim of head of state immunity. The colonel was accused of complicity in acts of terrorism that had resulted in the destruction of a French civil aircraft in which all passengers were killed. The prosecutor argued that no head of state immunity existed with regard to this type of crimes against international law. The French Cour de Cassation disagreed. It held that

> [i]nternational custom precludes Heads of State in office from being the subject of proceedings before the criminal courts of a foreign State, in the absence of specific provisions to the contrary binding on the parties concerned... in the current state of international law the alleged crime, however serious, did not constitute one of the exceptions to the principle of the jurisdictional immunity of foreign Heads of State in office...[303]

In 2005, a Dutch court was asked to order the Dutch state to arrest US president Bush when he would visit the Netherlands for the official commemoration of the end of the Second World War.[304] Claimants argued that Bush bears 'command and aider and abettor liability' for a large amount of crimes against international law—*inter alia*, the killing of civilian population in Iraq and Afghanistan and the torture of prisoners. The court rejected the claim arguing in relevant part that the rule of head of state immunity would render such arrest illegal under international law.[305]

[298] *Fidel Castro*, no 1999/2723 (Spain, Audiencia Nacional, 1999) § 1–5 Legal Grounds, discussed in A Cassese (2002) fn 19.

[299] *Beschl v 16 May 2000* NStZ 667 (Germany, Oberlandesgericht Köln, 2000). Cf Also JMT Labuschagne, 'Immunity of the Head of State for Human Rights Violations in International Criminal Law' (2001) 26 South African Yearbook of International law 180.

[300] *Re Sharon and Yaron* (Belgium, 2003). Note that the decision was taken *after* the decision of the ICJ in the *Arrest Warrant* case, discussed p 269ff below.

[301] *Aidi v Yaron* 672 F Supp 516 (US, DC for the District of Columbia, 1987); *Tachiona v Mugabe and Mudenge* (US, 2001); *Tachiona v United States* (US, 2004).

[302] *Lafontant v Aristide* (US, 1994); *Tachiona v Mugabe and Mudenge* (US, 2001) (the Second Circuit Court of Appeals decided on grounds of diplomatic immunity only); *Abiola v Abubakar* (US, 2003); *Wei Ye v Jiang Zemin* (US, 2004).

[303] *Gaddafi* 125 ILR 490 (France, CA, Court of Cassation, 2000 and 2002) 509.

[304] *De Haagse Stadspartij e.a. v De Staat der Nederlanden* KG 05/432 (The Netherlands, Rechtbank 's-Gravenhage, Voorzieningrechter in Kort Geding, 2005).

[305] ibid § 3.6–3.7.

The position that personal immunity does not yield to the jurisdiction of national courts over crimes against international law is widely shared in doctrine[306] and has been confirmed by the International Court of Justice in the 2002 *Arrest Warrant Case* (*The Democratic Republic of the Congo (DRC) v Belgium*).[307] The distant cause for the dispute between the DRC and Belgium can be seen to lie in the Statute of the International Criminal Court. In 1999 Belgium adapted its war crimes legislation to the standards set in the ICC Statute. In a remarkable contrast with the Nuremberg Charter and all the formulations of the principle of irrelevance of official capacity that followed the Charter, article 27 of the Statute provides:

1. This Statute shall apply equally to all persons without any distinction based on official capacity. In particular, official capacity as a Head of State or Government, a member of a Government or parliament, an elected representative or a government official shall in no case exempt a person from criminal responsibility under this Statute, nor shall it, in and of itself, constitute a ground for reduction of sentence.
2. *Immunities or special procedural rules which may attach to the official capacity of a person, whether under national or international law, shall not bar the Court from exercising its jurisdiction over such a person.*[308]

Consequently, in 1999 Belgium decided to change its legislation to conform to the ICC standard. Article 5.2 of the 1993 Belgian war crimes legislation provided that

Le fait que l'accusé a agi sur l'ordre de son gouvernement ou d'un supérieur hiérarchique ne dégage pas sa responsabilité, si, dans les circonstances existantes, l'ordre pouvait manifestement entraîner la perpétration d'une infraction grave aux Conventions de Genève du 12 août 1949 et à leur premier protocole additionnel du 8 juin 1977.[309]

The 1999 legislation added a *third* paragraph to article 5:

L'immunité attachée à la qualité officielle d'une personne n'empêche pas l'application de la présente loi.[310]

[306] Cf eg A Cassese, *International Criminal Law* (2003) 271–3; H Fox (2002) 430–3; J Verhoeven, (Rapporteur Institut de Droit International), *Les immunités de juridiction et d'exécution du chef d'Etat et de gouvernement en droit international, Rapport provisoire* (2000), (2000–01) 69 AIDI 482, 517–18; The Princeton Project on Universal Jurisdiction, *Princeton Principles on Universal Jurisdiction* (2001), available at <http://www.princeton.edu/~lapa/unive_jur.pdf>, Commentary on Principle 5; B. Conforti (2002) 231.

[307] *Arrest Warrant* Case.

[308] Art 29 Rome Statute of the ICC (emphasis added).

[309] Loi du 16 juin 1993 relative à la répression des infractions graves aux Conventions internationales de Genève du 12 août 1949 et aux Protocoles I et II du 8 juin 1977, Moniteur Belge, 5 August 1993.

[310] In translation: 'The immunity attributed to the official capacity of a person, does not prevent the application of the present Act.' Loi de 1993 telle que modifiée par la loi du 10 février 1999 relative à la répression des violations graves du droit international humanitaire Art 5 para. 3, Loi relative à la répression des infractions graves de droit international humanitaire, 10 February 1999, Moniteur Belge, 23 March 1999, reproduced in (1999) 38 ILM 918, 924 (§ 2 was rephrased in

The new legislation hence did not recognize *any* immunity—nor *substantive*, nor *procedural*—in respect of allegations of crimes against international law. On the basis of this law, Belgium instigated several criminal investigations into the acts of foreign state officials whose position would arguably normally give rise to immunity *ratione personae* from the Belgian jurisdiction, like the Israeli Prime Minister Ariel Sharon and the Cuban leader Fidel Castro.[311]

In response to the issuance and circulation of an international arrest warrant by Belgium for the Congolese minister of foreign affairs Yerodia, the DRC filed an application with the International Court of Justice complaining that Belgium had violated its rights by not respecting the immunity *ratione personae* of its minister of foreign affairs.[312] Belgium relied on the principle of irrelevance of official capacity as found in the Nuremberg Charter and the ICC Statute and argued that accordingly 'immunities accorded to incumbent Ministers for Foreign Affairs can in no case protect them where they are suspected of having committed war crimes or crimes against humanity'.[313]

The Court found for the applicant. It held the immunity from criminal jurisdiction of ministers of foreign affairs *ratione personae* to be absolute.[314] In particular, it pointed out that it had

> carefully examined State practice, including national legislation and those few decisions of national higher courts, such as the House of Lords or the French Court of Cassation. It has been unable to deduce from this practice that there exists under customary international law any form of exception to the rule according immunity from criminal jurisdiction and inviolability to incumbent Ministers for Foreign Affairs, where they are suspected of having committed war crimes or crimes against humanity.
>
> The Court has also examined the rules concerning the immunity or criminal responsibility of persons having an official capacity contained in the legal instruments creating international criminal tribunals, and which are specifically applicable to the latter [refers to article 7 Nuremberg Charter and progeny]. It finds that these rules likewise do not enable it to conclude that any such exception exists in customary international law in regard to national courts.
>
> Finally, none of the decisions of the Nuremberg and Tokyo international tribunals, or of the International Criminal Tribunal for the Former Yugoslavia, cited by Belgium deal with the question of the immunities of incumbent Ministers for Foreign Affairs before national courts. The Court accordingly notes that those decisions are in no way at variance with the findings it has reached above.[315]

similar terms but with the additional reference to the crime of genocide and crimes against humanity as defined in the 1999 Act). Cf also Belgium, Juge d'instruction VanderMeersch, *Ordonnance du 6 novembre 1998*, 308.

311 Cf also SR Ratner, 'Belgium's War Crimes Statute: A Postmortem' (2003) 97 AJIL 888.

312 *Arrest Warrant* Case.

313 ibid 23, § 56.

314 It is recalled that this study disagrees with the Court's position that the immunity of ministers of foreign affairs is the same as that of heads of state, see ch 4 § 2.2.2.3 of this study for a critique on the Court's reasoning on the scope of the rule.

315 *Arrest Warrant* Case, 24, § 58.

Accordingly, the Court concluded that issuance and circulation of the arrest warrant had violated the rights of the DRC under international law.[316]

It was argued earlier that in the quoted paragraph the Court set out to distinguish between procedural and functional immunity rules. This was explicated in one of the following paragraphs in which the Court stated that '[i]mmunity from criminal jurisdiction and individual criminal responsibility are quite separate concepts. While jurisdictional immunity is procedural in nature, criminal responsibility is a question of substantive law.'[317] In this reading of the judgment the Court hence did recognize the customary international law status of the principle of irrelevance of official capacity but did not regard this principle to affect rules of personal immunity.

Judge Van den Wyngaert rejected the view that the said 'immunity clauses' only regarded the substantive but not the procedural immunity of state officials:

> At the heart of [the principle of irrelevance of official capacity] is the debate about individual versus State responsibility, not the discussion about the procedural or substantive nature of the protection for government officials. This can only mean that, where international crimes such as war crimes and crimes against humanity are concerned, immunity cannot block investigations or prosecutions to such crimes, regardless of whether such proceedings are brought before national or before international courts.
>
> . . .
>
> In adopting the view that the non-impunity clauses in the relevant international instruments only address substantive, not procedural immunities, the International Court of Justice has adopted a purely doctrinal proposition, which is not based on customary or conventional international law or on national practice and which is not supported by a substantial part of legal doctrine.[318]

According to Judge Van den Wyngaert 'most authorities do not mention the distinction at all and even reject it.'[319] However, she only refers to the ILC commentary to article 7 to support this assertion. As explained earlier, the distinction between substantive and procedural immunities is far more than 'a doctrinal proposition'. In fact, it is the proposition that official capacity is *not* only irrelevant for the *responsibility* of an official but also for the *jurisdiction* of the court that requires support from state practice for it to attain the status of more than a doctrinal proposition.

It is interesting to note that in fact Judge Van den Wyngaert did not argue that the principle curtailed the personal immunity of defendants *directly*. Rather, she

[316] ibid 29–30, § 71. Cf ch 4 § 2.3 above for a critical discussion of the question whether the international circulation violated the immunity the minister enjoyed in *other* countries.

[317] ibid 25, § 60.

[318] *Arrest Warrant* Case, Dissenting Opinion Judge Van den Wyngaert, 158 and 159, § 31 and § 33. Cf also the dissent of Judge Al-Khasawneh, 97, § 5. The dissent of Judge Al-Khasawneh did not rely on the scope of the rule of personal immunity but on the invalidiation of that rule by *jus cogens* and was accordingly discussed in § 2.2 above.

[319] ibid 158, § 30.

seemed to argue that the interests in preventing impunity *outweigh* the interests protected by rule of personal immunity. With all respect, this author believes that that reasoning confuses a policy argument for a state of the law argument. As the elaboration on this issue in the Separate Opinion of Judges Higgins, Kooijmans and Buergenthal evinces, the interests in the prosecution of war criminals *are* balanced against the interests protected by personal immunity; this balancing act is however not relevant for a court determining the scope of the rule of personal immunity but is part of the policy decision to be taken by states as to what the scope of that rule *should* be. The judges observed that while for now '[t]he law of privileges and immunities... retains its importance since immunities are granted to high State officials to guarantee the proper functioning of the network of mutual inter-State relations, which is of paramount importance for a well-ordered and harmonious international system', but suggested that 'the weights on the two scales are not set for all perpetuity'.[320] As said earlier, however, judges can only establish a changing balance through the inductive approach. While the law may of course develop through judicial interpretation—judicial decisions are never value-free in that respect—judges cannot engage in the balancing act themselves in defiance of clear state practice. Their decision should reflect what the law *is*, not what the law *should be*.

In response to the decision of the Court Belgium again changed its war crimes legislation. The third paragraph of article 5 came to read as follows:

> L'immunité attachée à la qualité officielle d'une personne n'empêche l'application de la présente loi que dans les limites établies par le droit international.[321]

When a few months later the war crimes law was incorporated in the general Belgian penal code and code of penal procedure article 5 was split up and formulated in less uncertain terms.[322] The second paragraph of article 5 is now part of the penal code.[323] While article 1*bis* of the code of penal procedure reads:

> § 1. Conformément au droit international, les poursuites sont exclues à l'égard:
> — des chefs d'Etat, chefs de gouvernement et ministres des Affaires étrangères étrangers, pendant la période où ils exercent leur fonction, ainsi que des autres personnes dont l'immunité est reconnue par le droit international;

[320] *Arrest Warrant* Case, Joint Separate Opinion of Judges Higgins, Kooijmans, and Buergenthal, 85, § 75. Cf in general 84–5, § 70–5 and § 3 of this chapter below.

[321] In translation: 'International immunity derived from a person's official capacity does not prevent the application of the present law except under those limits established under international law.' 'Loi de 1993 telle que modifiée par la loi du 23 avril 2003 relative à la répression des violations graves du droit international humanitaire et l'art 144 ter du Code judiciaire, reproduced in (2003) 42 ILM 749, 755. Criminal actions that had already been instigated were after the decision of the ICJ declared inadmissible. Cf eg *Re Sharon and Yaron* (Belgium, 2003).

[322] Loi du 5 août 2003 relative à la répression des infractions graves au droit international humanitaire, reproduced in (2003) 42 ILM 1258.

[323] ibid art 12 at 1265–66 adding art 136octies.2 to the Code Pénal.

—des personnes qui disposent d'une immunité, totale ou partielle, fondée sur un traité qui lie la Belgique.

§ 2. Conformément au droit international, nul acte de contrainte relatif à l'exercice de l'action publique ne peut être posé pendant la durée de leur séjour, à l'encontre de toute personne ayant été officiellement invitée à séjourner sur le territoire du Royaume par les autorités belges ou par une organisation internationale établie en Belgique et avec laquelle la Belgique a conclu un accord de siège.[324]

Today only one state claims the right to subject foreign heads of state to its jurisdiction. While the United States recognizes the doctrine of head of state immunity they do not recognize that international law imposes limitations on the jurisdiction of the United States in this regard. As with the rule of state immunity the US asserts that 'head of state immunity is a matter of grace and comity, rather than a matter of right'.[325] After the AEDPA introduced a terrorist-state exception to the FSIA and the so-called 'Flatow Amendment' to that exception was accepted the United States courts decided that they could very well withhold that grace and comity from the heads of state of states designated state sponsor of terrorism.[326] In *Flatow v Islamic Republic of Iran* the court reasoned as follows:

The Flatow Amendment overrides the common law doctrine of head of state immunity, as it expressly provides for the application of 28 U.S.C. §1605(a)(7)'s exception to immunity to '[a]n official, employee, or agent of a foreign state... acting within the scope of his or her office, employment, or agency.' This provision was directed at those individuals who facilitate terrorist acts which cause the injury or death of American citizens. The provision does not qualify or in any way limit its application only to non-heads of state. Given that state sponsorship of terrorism is a decision made at the highest levels of government, unless the Flatow Amendment is interpreted as abrogating head of state immunity under the limited circumstances of 28 U.S.C. §1605(a)(7), the provisions cannot give full effect to Congressional intent, and the federal cause of action created by the two amendments would be irreparably and unreasonably hobbled. This Court therefore concludes that

[324] In translation:

'1. In accordance with international law there shall be no prosecution with regard to:
—Heads of State, heads of government, and foreign ministers of foreign affairs, during their term of office, and any other person whose immunity is recognized by international law.
—Persons who have immunity, full or partial, based on a treaty by which Belgium is bound.

2. In accordance with international law, no act of coercion involving the bringing of criminal proceedings may be initiated during the time of their stay, against any person officially invited to stay in the territory of the Kingdom by the Belgian authorities or by an international organization established in Belgian [sic] and with which Belgium has concluded a headquarters agreement.' Ibid art 13 art 13 at p 1265 adding art 1*bis* to the Code de Procédure Pénale. Cf also art 16 of the Dutch Wet van 19 juni 2003 houdende regels met betrekking tot ernstige schendingen van het internationaal humanitair recht ('Wet Internationale Misdrijven'), Staatsblad 2003, nr 270.

[325] *Lafontant v Aristide* (US, 1994), citing *Hilton v Guyot* 159 US 113 (US, S Ct, 1895) 163–4.

[326] For Flatow Amendment cf p 251–252 above, for the exception in general ch 6, p 354–7 below.

the defense of head of state immunity is not available in actions brought pursuant to 28 U.S.C. §1605(a)(7) and 28 U.S.C.A. §1605 note.[327]

A 2003 decision of the district court for the Southern District of New York has given an interesting twitch to the discussion. The case of *Smith and Soulas v The Islamic Emirate of Afghanistan and Iraq* concerned a tort claim of relatives of two victims of the terrorist attack on the World Trade Centre in New York on 11 September 2001 against, *inter alia*, the then head of state of Iraq Saddam Hussein.[328] The court recalled that one of the requirements of the Flatow Amendment is that '[n]o action shall be maintained under this action if an official, employee, or agent of the United States, while acting within the scope of his or her office, employment, or agency would not be liable for such acts if carried out within the United States.' It concluded that since 'a claim against a U.S. president for the conduct identical to that alleged against Saddam Hussein would be barred because of the president's absolute immunity from damages for conduct associated with the exercise of his official duties... the plaintiffs cannot satisfy this element as against Saddam Hussein and so the claim against him must be dismissed.'[329]

This is of course only a stopgap for the fundamentally problematic nature of the FSIA terrorist-state exception. Head of state immunity is a rule of international law that imposes obligations on all states in respect of the heads of state of all other states. The US approach is comparable to that of Glueck introduced earlier in this section. The unilateral tampering with the rule to suit US foreign policy goals violates international law and is unacceptable.

In chapter 4 of this study it was explained that courts and scholars disagree on the scope of head of state immunity from civil jurisdiction. In conclusion it must be noted that this uncertain scope triggers discussion on the question whether foreign heads of state may be sued for damages on allegations of crimes against international law. Of course, the diplomatic immunity protecting foreign state officials on diplomatic missions shields foreign heads of state from enforcement measures or service of process while abroad on an official visit. However, such enforcement measures are not always necessary to instigate civil proceedings, and heads of state may moreover travel abroad on private visits as well. It is recalled that this author opines that immunity from civil jurisdiction should at least be available in respect of all acts related to the exercise of the functions of head of state. Were immunity to be limited to 'official acts' that qualify under the functional immunity rule the exercise of the function of head of state could become seriously impeded by civil actions related to allegations of crimes against international law.

[327] *Flatow v Islamic Republic of Iran* 999 (US, 1998).

[328] *Smith and Soulas v The Islamic Emirate of Afghanistan and Iraq* 262 F Supp 2d 217 (US, DC for the Southern District of New York, 2003).

[329] ibid referring to *Nixon v Fitzgerald* 457 US 731 (US, S Ct, 1982) 749.

2.3.2.2 A critical intermezzo: Personal immunities before international courts

At this point an intriguing question presents itself. *If national courts cannot exercise jurisdiction over state officials protected by personal immunity, why would this be any different for international courts?* Recent judicial and academic thinking on the question tends to distinguish national courts from international courts: while personal immunities continue to apply unabatedly in *national courts*, it is argued that they do not prevent the exercise of jurisdiction by *international courts*. This author begs to disagree.

The jurisdiction of international courts over diplomatic agents is indeed evident. Diplomatic agents only enjoy personal immunity from the jurisdiction of the state to which they are accredited or through which they transit. Other states can freely exercise their adjudicative jurisdiction over these agents, so can international courts.[330] Head of state immunity, however, applies *erga omnes* and independent of the presence of the head of state on foreign territory.[331] It is therefore not immediately clear how that immunity can be circumvented by the decision of a group of states to establish an international court *if the home state is not bound by that agreement*. In fact, close examination of the issue will prove that the jurisdiction of international courts over heads of state is not unqualified. In addition, a second issue troubles the prosecution of individuals clothed with personal immunity, whether applicable *erga omnes* or not. An international court that cannot exercise jurisdiction *in absentia* must always rely on the arrest and surrender of suspects by states. In this respect, personal immunity shields heads of state and diplomatic agents representing states not bound by the statute of an international court from the jurisdiction of international courts *in practice*.

The two issues will be discussed here in turn. Subsequently, the decision of the SCSL in *Prosecutor v Taylor* will be discussed on the basis of the legal framework set out.[332] The central question in that case was whether the issuance and circulation of an arrest warrant for an incumbent head of state by the Special Court violated the rule of head of state immunity. Without much ado the question was shoved aside. We will see, however, that it is highly questionable whether international law allowed the SCSL to issue and circulate the warrant for the arrest of the incumbent head of state of Liberia.

Let us start with the first issue—that of the jurisdiction of international courts over individuals clothed with personal immunity from foreign national jurisdiction. It may be clear that a reliance on the principle of irrelevance of official

[330] On the assumption of course that the jurisdiction of the court over the diplomatic agent is not only based on the jurisdiction from the receiving state. Moreover, the jurisdiction of the international court to request arrest and surrender are limited, cf p 281 below. Cf also the *Oshima* Case decided by the Tokyo Tribunal, in BVA Röling and CF Rüter (eds), *The Tokyo Judgment, The International Military Tribunal for the Far East, 29 April 1946–12 November 1949* (1977) 456.

[331] It is noted that in the *Arrest Warrant* case the ICJ held this *erga omnes* personal immunity also to apply to ministers of foreign affairs. This study disagrees. Cf ch 4 § 2.2.2.3 above.

[332] *Prosecutor v Charles Ghankay Taylor* (SCSL, 2004).

capacity as included in the instruments establishing international tribunals is not coherent as that principle does not regard procedural immunities.[333] Most scholars therefore attempt to establish that personal immunities do not apply to international courts *as of principle*. Gaeta argued in this respect that

> [s]trictly speaking, under international law individuals are only entitled to enjoy personal immunities vis-à-vis the authorities of the State where they are authorized to discharge official functions (the 'receiving or territorial State'). Clearly, these immunities cannot be relied upon before the ICC, hence they cannot preclude the exercise of the Court's jurisdiction.[334]

This argument does not however extend to head of state immunity which applies *erga omnes*. A more popular argument asserts that the *par in parem* rationale that underlies personal immunities clearly only applies between states.[335] Whatever the exact reasoning, the fact is that commentators—and judges as we will see at the discussion of the case of *Prosecutor v Taylor* below—eagerly parrot the proposition.

However, as one perceptive commentator recently noted '[t]he view that international law immunities may never be pleaded in proceedings instituted before international courts and tribunals oversimplifies the matter.'[336] Since until the ICC Statute there was no state practice on the issue, a coherent proposition on the scope of the rule must reason within the parameters of rules and principles of international law. The argument that personal immunity does not apply before international courts because the *par in parem* rationale does not apply to international courts reasons in a circle.[337] The fundamental question that requires a clear

[333] Cf for such reliance eg C Wickremasinghe (2003) 407; B Stern (2003) 73, 86; C Ragni, 'Immunity of Heads of State: Some Critical Remarks on the Decision of the Special Court for Sierra Leone in the *Charles Taylor* Case' (2004) 14 Italian Yearbook of International Law 273, 281; T Stein, 'Limits of International Law Immunities for Senior State Officials in Criminal Procedure', in C Tomuschat and J-M Thouvenin (eds), *The Fundamental Rules of the International Legal Order, Jus Cogens and Obliogations Erga Omnes* (2006) 249, 251ff.

[334] P Gaeta (2002) 991. Cf also eg J Verhoeven, (Rapporteur Institut de Droit International), *Les immunités de juridiction et d'exécution du chef d'Etat et de gouvernement en droit international, Rapport provisoire* (2000), 69 AIDI (2000–01) 482, 518.

[335] Cf eg P Gaeta (2003) 194; S Meisenberg, 'Die Anklage under der Haftbefehl gegen Charles Ghankay Taylor durch den Sondergerichtshof für Sierra Leone' (2004) 17 Humanitäres Völkerrecht 30, 38; B Stern (2003) 73, 75 and 85–6; R Jennings, 'The Pinochet Extradition Case in the English Courts' in L Boisson de Chazournes and V Gowlland-Debbas (eds), *The International Legal System in Quest of Equity and Universality: Liber Amicorum Georges Abi-Saab* (2001) 677, 692 Cf also without explanation C Dominicé (1999) 307. It is furthermore noted that the Commentary to Principle 5 of the *Princeton Principles of Universal Jurisdiction* (2001)—while recognizing that the principle of irrelevance of official capacity regards *substantive* immunities and applies to national and international courts alike—also explicitly states that personal immunities continue to apply 'to proceedings before *national* tribunals' (emphasis added), available at <http://www.princeton.edu/~lapa/unive_jur.pdf>. Cf for early support for the argument Q Wright, 'War Criminals' (1945) 39 AJIL 257, 269.

[336] D Akande (2004) 416.

[337] Moreover, if we take the personal immunity of a head of state to have a 'functional necessity' rationale—as the ICJ did in the *Arrest Warrant* case—the argument can be made that 'proceedings

answer in a coherent proposition is why states would be able to do together what they cannot do individually. The statement that two states cannot circumvent the right to immunity of a third state by establishing an international criminal court is uncontroversial. But if two states cannot do so, why would sixty?[338]

The principle that a treaty cannot abrogate the rights of states not bound by it is central to our investigation.[339] States cannot establish a court with judicial powers over third states or their officials that would violate international law had these states acted individually. Accordingly, international courts may only have jurisdiction over state officials normally protected by an immunity *ratione personae* applying *erga omnes* if the court has the power to bind the state they represent.

Hence, the US delegates to the Commission established by the Allied Powers after the First World War to study the possibility of prosecution and punishment of war criminals were right to oppose the conclusion of the Commission that '[a]ll persons belonging to enemy countries, however high their position may have been, without distinction of rank, including Chiefs of States, who have been guilty of offences against the laws and customs of war or the laws of humanity, are liable to criminal prosecution.'[340]

The ICTY and the ICTR derive their power to bind states from their establishment by a Security Council Resolution under Chapter VII of the UN Charter.[341] While pursuant to articles 24 and 25 of the UN Charter action of the Security Council binds UN member states irrespective of whether it concerns pacific settlement of disputes under Chapter VI or action with respect to threats to the peace, breaches of the peace and acts of aggression under Chapter VII, the Security Council can *only* dispose of the sovereign rights of UN member states when acting under Chapter VII of the Charter.[342] The establishment of an international

before both national and international criminal courts may hamper the discharge of official functions and endanger the smooth conduct of international relations', M Frulli, 'The Question of Charles Taylor's Immunity, Still in Search of a Balanced Application of Personal Immunities?' (2004) 2 JICJ 1118, 1128.

[338] Cf D Akande (2004) 417. Cf also MA Tunks, 'Diplomats or Defendants? Defining the Future of Head of State Immunity' (2002) 52 Duke Law Journal 651, 665 fn 75: 'no other country has jurisdiction over a third party's head of state, and consequently, no two states (or group of states) may agree by treaty to waive the immunity of a third party's head of state without that other nation's consent'.

[339] Cf the words of Judge Huber quoted at n 288 above.

[340] Cf p 206 above.

[341] SC Resolution 808 (1993); SC Resolution 955 (1994) respectively.

[342] Art 24.1 of the UN Charter reads: 'In order to ensure prompt and effective action by the United Nations, its Members confer on the Security Council primary responsibility for the maintenance of international peace and security, and agree that in carrying out its duties under this responsibility the Security Council acts on their behalf'. And art 25 UN Charter reads: 'The Members of the United Nations agree to accept and carry out the decisions of the Security Council in accordance with the present Charter'. Art 2.7 of the Charter provides: 'Nothing contained in the present Charter shall authorize the United Nations to intervene in matters which are essentially within the domestic jurisdiction of any state or shall require the Members to submit such matters to settlement under the present Charter; but this principle shall not prejudice the application of enforcement measures under Chapter Vll'. Cf Z Deen-Racsmány, 'Prosecutor v Taylor, The Status

court with jurisdiction over state officials irrespective of personal immunities by Security Council Resolution hence requires the Chapter VII signature.

Notably, the Security Council can of course always decide to oblige states to accept the jurisdiction of an international court over individuals clothed with personal immunity *subsequent to the court's establishment* in a separate resolution adopted under Chapter VII.[343] Article 13 sub b of the ICC Statute is notable in this respect. The article provides that the Court may exercise jurisdiction if '[a] situation in which one or more of such crimes appears to have been committed is referred to the Prosecutor by the Security Council acting under Chapter VII of the Charter of the United Nations.' If the Security Council decides to refer a situation to the Court it may also decide that personal immunities of officials of UN member states are no impediment for the exercise of the Court's jurisdiction.

States can of course *consent* to the exercise of jurisdiction over their officials by an international court. This is the principle behind the jurisdiction of the International Criminal Court—which is a treaty-based organization.

At the time of writing the ICC Statute binds a hundred or so states.[344] The Statute must hence be careful not to violate the rights of about the same number of states that have not consented to the jurisdiction of the Court. Article 27.2 falls short in this respect. The article provides that

> [i]mmunities or special procedural rules which may attach to the official capacity of a person, whether under national or international law, shall not bar the Court from exercising its jurisdiction over such a person.

In other words, personal immunities are declared *a priori* inapplicable before the ICC. Article 98 of the Statute—discussed below—only impedes the prosecution of officials of non party states clothed with personal immunity *in practice—not in theory*. If the Court were to have jurisdiction to prosecute *in absentia* there would—from the perspective of the Statute—be no impediment to the exercise of jurisdiction over a head of state of a non party state suspected of having committed crimes within the jurisdiction of the court on the territory of a state party to the Statute. Akande noted in this respect:

> [W]hile Article 27 provides that a state official's possession of international immunity shall not bar the *ICC* from exercising jurisdiction, Article 98 directs the Court not to take action that would result in the violation by *states* of their international obligations to accord immunity to foreign officials.[345]

of the Special Court of Sierra Leone and its Implications for Immunity' (2005) 18 LJIL 299, 307ff for a more elaborate discussion of this issue.

343 Cf also the text at n 323 and 324 above.

344 In December 2007 105 states had ratified the Statute. Cf <http://www.icc-cpi.int/asp/statesparties.html>.

345 D Akande (2004) 420.

In less objective but broadly similar terms Triffterer put it as follows:

> [A] failure to proceed successfully according to Article 98 may *in practice and contrary to the wording of Article 27,* 'bar the Court from exercising its jurisdiction over such a person', if the Court cannot secure the attendance of the person in any other way because the Rome Statute does not provide a trial *in absentia*.[346]

This is in fact the only correct interpretation of the Statute. Arguing that because of article 98, article 27.2 *is* limited to nationals of state parties would be trying to fit a square peg in a round hole. Accordingly, article 27.2 violates international law in that it negates the personal immunity from the jurisdiction of the ICC of officials of non party states.

The discussion throws an interesting light over an obiter dictum of the International Court of Justice in the *Arrest Warrant* case. The Court held that

> an incumbent... Minister for Foreign Affairs may be subject to criminal proceedings before *certain* international courts... Examples include the International Criminal Tribunal for the Former Yugoslavia, and the International Criminal Tribunal for Rwanda, established pursuant to Security Council resolutions under Chapter VII of the United Nations Charter, and the future International Criminal Court created by the 1998 Rome Convention. The latter's Statute expressly provides, in Article 27, paragraph 2, that '[i]mmunities or special procedural rules which may attach to the official capacity of a person, whether under national or international law, shall not bar the Court from exercising its jurisdiction over such a person.[347]

Notably, the Court limited its observation to *certain* international criminal courts. It emphasized the juridical basis of the ICTY and ICTR that makes establishment of jurisdiction over persons clothed with personal immunity possible. The scope of the statement as regards the ICC is however controversial. Surely the Court did not mean to say that the ICC can establish jurisdiction over all incumbent heads of state because article 27.2 says so? Arguably the ICJ only meant to emphasize the possibility of conventional waiver of personal immunity. A benign interpretation of the statement allows the assertion that the ICJ recognized that article 27.2 only has consequences for ICC party states. We will see later that this somewhat ambiguous obiter statement is at the basis of some very definite assertions as to the non-applicability of personal immunity before *all* international courts. This study rejects that interpretation. *If* the obiter in the *Arrest Warrant* case stands for something it is for the proposition that personal immunity is *not a priori inapplicable* before international courts.

Even if the argument that personal immunities do not apply before international tribunals *were* to be accepted, there is the additional issue of the personal

[346] O Triffterer, 'Irrelevance of Official Capacity: Article 27' in O Triffterer (ed), *Commentary on the Rome Statute of the International Criminal Court: Observers' Notes, Article by Article* (1999) 501, 513 (emphasis added).

[347] *Arrest Warrant* Case, 25–6, § 61 (emphasis added).

immunity from arrest and surrender by national jurisdictions. For the arrest of suspects, as well as all other acts within the exclusive territorial competences of a state, international criminal courts depend heavily on the cooperation and assistance of states. In this respect, Cassese's metaphor for the ICTY—which he described as 'a giant without arms and legs [that] needs artificial limbs to walk and work'[348]—is equally apposite to the ICC.

Because of their Chapter VII-based powers, the ICTY and the ICTR can oblige all UN member states to cooperate, in particular by executing arrest warrants. As the Secretary-General of the UN put it in respect of the ICTY:

> [A]n order by a Trial Chamber for the surrender or transfer of persons to the custody of the International Tribunal shall be considered to be the application of an enforcement measure under Chapter VII of the Charter of the United Nations.[349]

Pursuant to article 103 UN Charter the duty to cooperate applies irrespective of interstate obligations under personal immunity rules.[350]

A treaty-based organization like the ICC however can not affect the rights and obligations of non party states. Of course, the Security Council can always decide to oblige states to arrest and surrender individuals clothed with personal immunity to the jurisdiction of an international court in a resolution adopted under Chapter VII of the UN Charter, for example when it would refer a situation to the Prosecutor under article 13 sub b of the ICC Statute.[351]

The treaty-based jurisdiction of the ICC means in the first place that the ICC Statute cannot oblige non party states to cooperate with the court. Part 9 of the Statute—regulating the cooperation and assistance of states—does indeed make clear that only states parties can be obliged to cooperate with the Court. Article 86 provides that 'States Parties shall, in accordance with the provisions of this Statute, cooperate fully with the Court in its investigation and prosecution of crimes within the jurisdiction of the Court.' Article 87.1 sub a provides that '[t]he Court shall have the authority to make requests to States Parties for cooperation.' In particular, article 89.1 provides that '[t]he Court may transmit a request for the arrest and surrender of a person . . . to any State on the territory of which

[348] A Cassese, 'On the Current Trend towards Criminal Prosecution and Punishment of Breaches of International Humanitarian Law' (1998) 9 EJIL 1, 13.

[349] Report of the Secretary-General Pursuant to Paragraph 2 of Security Council Resolution 808 (1993), UN Doc S/25704 (1993) reprinted in (1993) 14 HRLJ 201, § 125–6.

[350] Art 103 UN Charter reads as follows: 'In the event of a conflict between the obligations of the Members of the United Nations under the present Charter and their obligations under any other international agreement, their obligations under the present Charter shall prevail'. Cf A Ciampi, 'The Obligation to Cooperate' in A Cassese, P Gaeta and JRWD Jones (eds), *The Rome Statute of the International Criminal Court* (2002) 1607, 1631; B Swart, 'Arrest and Surrender' in A Cassese, P Gaeta and JRWD Jones (eds), *The Rome Statute of the International Criminal Court* (2002) 1639, 1680–81; P Gaeta (2002) 989.

[351] Cf S Villalpando and L Condorelli, 'Can the Security Council Extend the ICC's Jurisdiction?' in A Cassese, P Gaeta and JRWD Jones (eds), *The Rome Statute of the International Criminal Court* (2002) 571. Cf also A Ciampi (2002) 1611–12; B Swart (2002) 1677 (on art 13).

that person may be found and shall request the cooperation of that State in the arrest and surrender of such a person. States Parties shall, in accordance with the provisions of this Part and the procedure under their national law, comply with requests for arrest and surrender.' This obligation is explicated in article 59.1 that provides that '[a] State Party which has received a request for provisional arrest or for arrest and surrender shall immediately take steps to arrest the person in question in accordance with its laws and the provisions of Part 9.' As regards non party states article 87.5 sub a provides: 'The Court may invite any State not party to this Statute to provide assistance under this Part on the basis of an ad hoc arrangement, an agreement with such State or any other appropriate basis.'

However, *the obligations of states parties to the Statute may also not violate the rights of non party states*. Since the Court also purports to exercise its jurisdiction over nationals of non party states and article 27.2 provides that there exist no immunities from the jurisdiction of the Court, the personal immunity of officials of non party states from the jurisdiction to arrest and surrender of states party needed to be secured in the Statute. Article 98.1 therefore provides that

> [t]he Court may not proceed with a request for surrender or assistance which would require the requested State to act inconsistently with its obligations under international law with respect to the State or diplomatic immunity of a person or property of a third State, unless the Court can first obtain the cooperation of that third State for the waiver of the immunity.[352]

In other words, the ICC cannot oblige a state party to cooperate when that state party would have to violate the personal immunity of a national of a non party state to comply.[353]

It should be realized that article 98 should not only secure the obligations of state parties to non state parties, it should secure the obligations of the Court *itself* towards non state parties. Akande supported this assertion with the following argument:

> since the ICC operates in effect by 'delegation' from (or in the place of) its states parties, the immunity of officials of nonparties applies not only in relation to states parties, but

[352] Cf also Rule 195 of the Rules of Procedure and Evidence, ICC-ASP/1/3. There has been some debate on whether the provision secures the personal immunity of nationals of *all* states or of nationals of non-party states only. The arguments for the latter interpretation are forceful. In particular, states party to the Statute have lost the right to prevent surrender of their nationals to the Court on the basis of an immunity rule that runs counter to art 27.2 of the Statute and in fact to the aim of state parties—as stated in the preamble—to put an end to impunity and to ensure that the most serious crimes do not go unpunished Preamble § 4 and 5. Cf for a comprehensive discussion of arguments: P Gaeta (2002) 993–6; S Wirth (2002) 452–4; D Akande (2004) 421–30.

[353] It is notable in this respect that the implementation legislation of certain party states seems to disregard this. The Canadian 'Crimes against Humanity and War Crimes Act 2000' inserts the following § 6 into chapter 18 of the Extradition Act 1999: 'no person who is the subject of a request for surrender by the International Criminal Court…may claim immunity under common law or by statute from arrest or extradition under this Act' (chapter 24 § 48 War Crimes Act). Cf also New Zealand, International Crimes and International Criminal Court Act 2000 no 26, § 31.1. Cf for an example of correct implementation UK, International Criminal Court Act 2001 section 23.1.

also in relation to the ICC itself. Thus, the Court itself is prevented by international law from taking steps that would amount to a violation of those immunities.[354]

A more direct argument would be that as an international organization the court is obliged to respect the rules of international law.[355] In any event, the Court itself violates the rights of non party states under personal immunity rules when it requests a party state to arrest and surrender a national of a non party state protected under these rules. *The Statute must hence be careful not to grant powers to the Court that may violate the rights of non party states.*

Are the rights of non party states under personal immunity rules adequately secured by article 98.1? The decision of the ICJ in the *Arrest Warrant* case warrants the question whether the Statute does not still allow the Court to take action that can violate customary international law on personal immunities.

The ICJ held the *issuance* of the arrest warrant by Belgium to violate the immunity of Yerodia because the warrant orders 'all bailiffs and agents of public authority...to execute this arrest warrant' and was hence enforceable in Belgium.[356] In addition, however, the Court engaged the question whether the *international circulation* of the warrant constituted a separate violation of the immunity. The arrest warrant was communicated to Interpol in June 2000 but Belgium did not request an Interpol red notice until after the abdication of Yerodia as minister for foreign affairs. Belgium argued that the circulation of the warrant did not violate the sovereignty of DRC because the warrant had no legal effect on foreign territory. The Court did not agree with the criterion relied on by Belgium. Since the circulation of the arrest warrant was 'to establish a legal basis for the arrest of Mr. Yerodia...abroad and his subsequent extradition to Belgium' the 'nature and purpose' of the warrant was such that it 'effectively infringed' the immunity of Yerodia. The Court considered that even in the absence of 'further steps' by Belgium the 'mere international circulation of the warrant...could have resulted...in his arrest while abroad'. The circulation of the warrant was therefore held to constitute a violation of the rights of DRC.[357] Judges Higgins, Kooijmans and Buergenthal further explained in their Separate Opinion that '[a]n international arrest warrant, even though a Red Notice has not yet been linked...is already a statement of willingness and ability to act and as such may be perceived as a threat so to do at a moment of Belgium's choosing.'[358]

The criterion of the ICJ is a strict one—arguably too strict this author admits.[359] What are the consequences of this approach for the proceedings before international courts? Upon close consideration the consequences are

[354] D Akande (2004) 421.

[355] Cf eg HG Schermers and NM Blokker, *International Institutional Law* (4th edn, 2003) 1002, § 1579.

[356] *Arrest Warrant* Case, 29, § 70.

[357] ibid 29–30, § 70–1.

[358] ibid Joint Separate Opinion Judges Higgins, Kooijmans and Buergenthal, 84, § 69.

[359] Cf ch 4 § 2.3 for a more elaborate discussion of the issue.

arguably not limited to the power to *circulate* arrest warrants—as it is in respect of arrest warrants issued by national courts. Since the issuance of an arrest warrant by an international court is *by definition* to establish a legal basis for arrest outside the jurisdiction of the court and the subsequent surrender to the court, it can be argued that the nature and purpose of issuance is the same as that of circulation in the *Arrest Warrant* case and that accordingly the distinction between issuance and circulation is blurred. Or, the arguments that supported the finding that the circulation of the arrest warrant for Yerodia violated his immunity from foreign jurisdictions arguably applies to the *issuance* of an arrest warrant by an international court.

The ICC Statute arguably fails to comply with this strict criterion. Article 98.1 does not prevent the Pre-Trial Chamber from issuing a warrant of arrest of such a person under article 58. In this respect the absence of the possibility to *indict* individuals before formulating an arrest warrant is notable.[360]

Before we move to the discussion of the *Taylor* case a final—but not unimportant—observation is called for. In addition to the two issues of principle troubling the exercise of jurisdiction over state officials clothed with personal immunity by international courts, there is a *third*, more technical issue that must be taken into account. For an international court to be able to exercise jurisdiction irrespective of personal immunity rules, the statute that regulates the court's jurisdiction must contain a provision to that effect. It is recalled that a provision concerning the irrelevance of official capacity for the *responsibility* of suspects does not suffice in this respect. An article 27.2–like provision is indispensable.[361] It is in this respect, for example, questionable whether the ICTY had jurisdiction to indict Milosević while he was the incumbent head of state of the Federal Republic of Yugoslavia.[362] The question was never put to the ICTY. The Trial Chamber has only been asked to consider whether the Tribunal lacked competence because of the status of Milosević as a *former* head of state—an argument that could easily be rejected under article 7.2 of the Statute.[363] However, since the ICTY Statute does not provide that personal immunities do not apply before the Tribunal Milosević was not amenable to the jurisdiction of the ICTY at the time the initial indictment was formulated.

The 2004 decision of the Appeals Chamber of the SCSL in *Prosecutor v Taylor* advances the, in this study, disputed position on the *first* issue, fails to recognize

[360] Cf in contrast arts 18 and 19 ICTY Statute.

[361] Cf p 269 above. Cf for an apparently different view D Akande, (2004) 417.

[362] Milosević was head of state from the FRY from July 1997 until October 2000. The ICTY first indicted him on 22 May 1999.

[363] *Prosecutor v Milosević* (ICTY, 2001) § 26–34. Milosević did argue that the Tribunal 'does not have jurisdiction over the person of President Milosevic', but the *amici curiae* and the Court interpreted this argument as a denial of the validity of art 7.2 of the ICTY Statute. This argument was rejected, cf n 48 above.

the pertinence of the *second* issue, and completely ignores the *third* issue.[364] Let us take a closer look at the facts of the case, the influential submissions of Sands and Orentlicher as *amici curiae* of the Court, and the reasoning and conclusions of the Court in order to substantiate that assertion.[365]

In 2002 the SCSL was established by an agreement between the Secretary General of the United Nations and Sierra Leone pursuant to Security Council Resolution 1315 (2000).[366] Resolution 1315 stated 'that the situation in Sierra Leone continues to constitute a threat to international peace and security in the region' and that 'persons who commit or authorize serious violations of international humanitarian law are individually responsible and accountable for those violations and that the international community will exert every effort to bring those responsible to justice in accordance with international standards of justice, fairness and due process of law'. The Security Council requested 'the Secretary-General to negotiate an agreement with the Government of Sierra Leone to create an independent special court consistent with this resolution'. It further 'recommends... that the special court should have personal jurisdiction over persons who bear the greatest responsibility for the commission of [crimes against humanity, war crimes and other serious violations of international humanitarian law, as well as crimes under relevant Sierra Leonean law committed within the territory of Sierra Leone], including those leaders who, in committing such crimes, have threatened the establishment of and implementation of the peace process in Sierra Leone'.

The Secretary-General proposed to establish a Special Court that in contrast to the ICTY and ICTR would not be established by a Security Council resolution but by treaty and that is consequently 'a sui generis court... not anchored in any existing system (i.e. United Nations administrative law or the national law of the State of the seat)'. The Secretary-General underlined that the Special Court did not have primacy over national courts in third states and 'lacks the power to request the surrender of an accused from any third State and to induce the compliance of its authorities with any such request'. He further suggested that '[i]n examining measures to enhance the deterrent powers of the Special Court, the Security Council may wish to consider endowing it with Chapter VII powers for the specific purpose of requesting the surrender of an accused from outside the jurisdiction of the Court.'[367] In 2002 the Agreement on the Establishment

[364] *Prosecutor v Charles Ghankay Taylor* (SCSL, 2004). It is noted that on the basis of the same facts Liberia did also file an application seeking to bring proceedings against Sierra Leone before the ICJ. The Court cannot however engage the application since Sierra Leone has not accepted the jurisdiction of the Court. Cf Press Release 2003/26 (available at <http://www.icj-cij.org>).

[365] P Sands and A Macdonald (2004); D Orentlicher (2004) (on file with the author).

[366] Security Council Resolution 1315 (2000) of 14 August 2000, UN Doc. S/RES/1315.

[367] *Report of the Secretary-General on the establishment of a Special Court for Sierra Leone*, 2 October 2000, UN Doc S/2000/915, § 9–11.

of a Special Court for Sierra Leone was concluded.[368] The Statute of the Special Court was annexed to the Agreement. The Court was given jurisdiction to prosecute individuals suspected of crimes against humanity, violations of common article 3 of the Geneva Conventions and of Additional Protocol II, other serious violations of international humanitarian law, and certain crimes under Sierra Leonean law.[369] Article 1.1 of the Statute reads:

> The Special Court shall...have the power to prosecute persons who bear the greatest responsibility for serious violations of international humanitarian law and Sierra Leonean law committed in the territory of Sierra Leone since 30 November 1996, including those leaders who, in committing such crimes, have threatened the establishment of and implementation of the peace process in Sierra Leone.

And article 6.2 provides that

> [t]he official position of any accused persons, whether as head of State or Government or as a responsible government official, shall not relieve such person of criminal responsibility nor mitigate punishment.

It should further be noted that the Security Council has not taken up the suggestion of the Secretary-General to enhance the powers of the Court through a Chapter VII resolution. The Council has merely called on states and in particular on the government of Liberia to 'cooperate fully' with the Court, without putting a Chapter VII signature on that request.[370]

In March 2003 the Court issued an indictment and arrest warrant for Charles Taylor—then incumbent head of state of Liberia. The indictment accused Taylor of the commission of crimes against humanity and grave breaches of the Geneva Conventions. It alleged that he 'resourced and directed rebel forces, encouraging them in campaigns of terror, torture and mass murder, in order to enrich himself from a share in the diamond mines that were captured by the rebels'.[371] The transmission of the warrant in June 2003 to the authorities of Ghana, where Taylor was visiting, failed to secure his arrest. Before abdicating in August 2003, Taylor filed an application to quash the indictment and to set aside the warrant for his arrest in July 2003 on the ground that as the head of state of Liberia he is immune from the jurisdiction of the Court. In particular it was argued on his behalf that:

(a) Citing the judgment of the International Court of Justice ('ICJ') in the case between the *Democratic Republic of the Congo v Belgium* ('*Yerodia*' case), as an incumbent Head of State at the time of his indictment, Charles Taylor enjoyed absolute immunity from criminal prosecution;

[368] Agreement between the United Nations and the Government of Sierra Leone on the Establishment of a Special Court for Sierra Leone (2002), available at <http://www.sc-sl.org>.

[369] Cf arts 2–5 of the Statute of the Special Court for Sierra Leone, available at <http://www.sc-sl.org>.

[370] Cf SC Resolutions 1478 (2003); 1470 (2003); 1436 (2003); 1408 (2002), 1400 (2002). Cf Z Deen-Racsmány (2005) 307ff for a discussion of the legal basis of these resolutions.

[371] *Prosecutor v Charles Ghankay Taylor*, (SCSL, 2004) § 5.

(b) Exceptions from diplomatic immunity can only derive from other rules of international law such as Security Council resolutions under Chapter VII of the United Nations Charter ('UN Charter');
(c) The Special Court does not have Chapter VII powers, therefore judicial orders from the Special Court have the quality of judicial orders of a national court;
(d) The indictment against Charles Taylor was invalid due to his personal immunity from criminal prosecution…[372]

While the initial submissions did not clearly distinguish between the jurisdiction to try an incumbent head of state and the jurisdiction to circulate an arrest warrant, the applicant asserted in an additional submission that the issuance of the arrest warrant violated 'the sovereignty of Ghana' and 'the principle of international law providing for immunity from criminal proceedings in foreign jurisdictions of an incumbent Head of State'.[373] The complaint was hence directed at two distinct issues. The SCSL was held to have no jurisdiction over incumbent heads of state since it is not 'an international criminal court of the kind referred to [sic] the *Yerodia* case', and it was held that the SCSL 'acted in excess of jurisdiction in transmitting the indictment and warrant of arrest'.[374]

The Prosecution responded, in relevant part, with the following arguments:

(d) The *Yerodia* case concerns the immunities of an incumbent Head of State from the jurisdiction of the courts of another State;
(e) Customary international law permits international criminal tribunals to indict acting Heads of state and the Special Court is an international court established under international law.
(f) The lack of Chapter VII powers does not affect the Special Court's jurisdiction over Heads of State. The International Criminal Court ('ICC'), which does not have Chapter VII powers, explicitly denies immunity to Heads of State for international crimes.[375]

The position of the prosecution on the additional submission of the applicant does not transpire from the text of the decision.

Both *amici curiae* rejected the arguments of the defence. Orentlicher limited her observations to what we have called the *first* issue troubling the exercise of jurisdiction over persons with personal immunity by international courts. Without much ado she found that the SCSL has jurisdiction to prosecute a sitting head of state. On the basis of two considerations of the ICJ in the *Arrest Warrant* case she argued that international criminal tribunals now have jurisdiction over serving heads of state. She relied on paragraphs 58 and 61 of the decision quoted earlier in this chapter to argue subsequently that

> the rule that denies even incumbent heads of state immunity from prosecution before international criminal tribunals is hardly confined to courts by or with the imprimatur of

[372] ibid § 6.
[373] ibid § 12 sub d.
[374] ibid § 14.
[375] ibid § 9.

the Security Council. For purposes of the distinction drawn by the ICJ between national and international courts, relevant jurisprudence has implicitly defined 'international criminal courts' broadly.[376]

She referred to the diverse juridical bases of the Nuremberg Tribunal, the International Military Tribunal for the Far East, the ICTY and ICTR and the ICC. Orentlicher pointed out that the authority of the Security Council to act on behalf of UN Member States is not confined to actions taken under Chapter VII of the UN Charter. The Security Council, she argued, has acted 'on behalf of all Members of the United Nations' when it requested the Secretary-General to negotiate the Agreement. She moreover noted that the Secretary-General had emphasized that the SCSL 'is established outside the national court system' and noted several other points that corroborate that. Because the Special Court is properly characterized as 'an international criminal court' Orentlicher concluded that Taylor was not entitled to claim procedural immunity from the jurisdiction of the SCSL and that the indictment did not violate the rule of head of state immunity.

Sands reasoned in much the same vein. He argued—referring to the Versailles Treaty, as well as the principle of irrelevance of official capacity in the Nuremberg Charter and its progeny—that '[a]s regards the international courts and tribunals which have been established . . . practice has been consistent, in that no serving head of state has been recognised as being entitled to rely on jurisdictional immunities.'[377] He pointed out in particular that '[t]he ICC was not established pursuant to Security Council Resolution, so the question of Chapter VII powers does not arise. As a treaty-based organisation it is similar to the Special Court for Sierra Leone'.[378] Just like Orentlicher, Sands relied on paragraphs 58 and 61 of the *Arrest Warrant* case to argue that the ICJ distinguished between national courts and international courts for the purpose of the applicability of the rule of personal immunity.[379] He concludes:

The general tendency points towards the view that in respect of international courts there exists no [sic] a prior entitlement of a State to claim immunity . . . International practice and a majority of academic commentary supports the view that before an international criminal court or tribunal (whether or not it has been established under Chapter VII of the UN Charter) may exercise jurisdiction over a serving head of state and that such person is not entitled to claim immunity under customary international in respect of international crimes.[380]

376 ibid D Orentlicher (2004) (on file with the author) text with n 50 and 51 and quotation at text with n 60. Cf for § 58 and 61 of the *Arrest Warrant* Case p 242 and 243 above.

377 ibid P Sands and A Macdonald (2004), § 2. Cf § 2–9.

378 ibid § 11.

379 ibid § 43–4.

380 ibid § 55 and 56.

'The opposite view' he argued, 'relies on a particular reading of the Yerodia judgment, and on an assumption—that international law grants immunities in relation to international courts—which does not appear to rest on established or identified state practice. The approach is also not supported by the Statute of the ICC, which implies a distinction between the right to exercise jurisdiction on the one hand, and the right to expect cooperation from a Party to the Statute or a third State, on the other hand'.[381]

Accordingly, Sands stated,

> the nature of the Special Court is of central importance in determining whether it can lawfully issue and then circulate internationally an indictment or international arrest warrant against a serving head of state... In order to determine its nature, it is necessary to review the basis upon which the Special Court was established, before comparing the legal basis and capacities of the Special Court with other international criminal tribunals.[382]

While the Security Council when dealing with the Court has not acted under Chapter VII, Sands pointed out that 'Chapter VII is not a sine qua non for obligations to arise from Security Council action: in our submission Chapter VII powers may not be relevant at all to the question of the Court's exercise of jurisdiction'.[383] As Orentlicher, Sands emphasizes that

> [t]here can be no doubt that Security Council resolution 1315 is binding... Other resolutions calling on all states, and in particular the government of Liberia to cooperate fully with the Special Court are also binding. In respect of Chapter VII the Special Court is in no different position from the ICC. Yet all three tribunals—the ICTY, the ICTR, and the ICC—were envisaged by the ICJ in the Yerodia case to have jurisdiction over a serving head of state... This confirms that the possession of Chapter VII powers cannot be essential for the question of immunity.

Since the SCSL is an international court with 'jurisdiction... broadly similar to that of the ICTY, the ICTR and the ICC, including in relation to the provisions confirming the absence of entitlement of any person to claim immunity' it has jurisdiction to prosecute a sitting head of state.[384]

The Appeals Chamber proceeded from the proposition that 'the sovereign equality of states does not prevent a head of State from being prosecuted before an international criminal tribunal or court'.[385] It relied in this respect on the principle of irrelevance of official capacity as found in the instruments establishing international courts ever since article 7 was included in the Nuremberg Charter,[386] and on the distinction between national courts and international courts evinced in the *Arrest Warrant* case.[387]

[381] ibid § 55. [382] ibid § 58.
[383] ibid § 75. [384] ibid § 76.
[385] *Prosecutor v Charles Ghankay Taylor* (SCSL, 2004) § 52, cf also § 51.
[386] ibid § 43–9. [387] ibid § 50.

Consequently, the Court observed at the outset that 'the issues in this motion turn to a large extent on the legal status of the Special Court'.[388] Subsequently, it set out to establish that it is irrelevant for the status of the SCSL whether it was established under Chapter VII of the UN Charter or not. The Court recalled that in Resolution 1315 'the Security Council reiterated that the situation in Sierra Leone continued to constitute a threat to international peace and security in the region' and emphasized that the powers of Security Council under article 39 and 41 of the Charter 'are wide enough to empower the Security Council to initiate, as it did by Resolution 1315, the establishment of the Special Court by Agreement with Sierra Leone'.[389] It then explained that '[w]here the Security Council establishes a court as a measure to maintain or restore international peace and security it may or may not, at the same time, contemporaneously, call upon the members of the United Nations to lend their cooperation to such court as a matter of obligation' but that the Security Council can also decide to require members of the United Nations to lend their cooperation under Chapter VII—and hence as a matter of obligation—*subsequently* to the establishment of the Court 'should subsequent events make that course prudent.'[390] Accordingly, the Court asserted, 'the absence of the so-called Chapter VII powers does not by itself define the legal status of the Special Court'. Rather, for the determination of the legal status of the Court

> [i]t is to be observed that in carrying out its duties under its responsibility for the maintenance of international peace and security, the Security Council acts on behalf of the members of the United Nations. The Agreement between the United Nations and Sierra Leone is thus an agreement between *all* members of the United Nations and Sierra Leone. This fact makes the Agreement an expression of the will of the international community. The Special Court established in such circumstances is truly international.[391]

The Court adopted the conclusions of Sands. In particular it stated that

> the Special Court is not a national court of Sierra Leone and is not part of the judicial system of Sierra Leone exercising judicial powers of Sierra Leone ... The competence and jurisdiction *ratione materiae* and *ratione personae* are broadly similar to that of the ICTY and the ICTR and the ICC, including in relation to the provisions confirming the absence of entitlement of any person to claim immunity ... Accordingly, there is no reason to conclude that the Special Court should be treated as anything other than an international tribunal or court, with all that implies for the question of immunity for a serving Head of State.[392]

The Court and the *amici* rightly concluded that Chapter VII powers are irrelevant for the status of the SCSL as an international court. However, this study disagrees with the fundamental proposition underlying this conclusion that the status of

388 ibid § 34. 389 ibid § 37.
390 ibid § 38. 391 ibid § 38.
392 ibid § 41. Cf P Sands and A Macdonald (2004), § 118 sub 7–8.

international court is relevant for the question whether there is jurisdiction over persons clothed with personal immunity. The *amici curiae* and the Court rely entirely on a mistaken interpretation of the scope of the traditional irrelevance of official capacity principle and in particular on the very feeble fundament of the ICJ decision in the *Arrest Warrant* case. At the risk of sounding like a broken record player it should once more be emphasized that the principle of irrelevance of official capacity only regards the substantive immunity of state officials and is applicable in national and international proceedings alike. Paragraph 58 of the *Arrest Warrant* decision does *not* state that this principle does not apply to national courts. Rather it states that this principle does not warrant the conclusion that an exception to personal immunity from national court proceedings exists. Arguably, the ICJ merely set out to distinguish substantive from procedural immunities. Moreover, paragraph 61 of the *Arrest Warrant* case did *not* state that personal immunity does not apply before international courts; it only stated that the rule did not apply before *certain* international courts.

The briefs of the *amici* and the decision of the Court parrot the proposition developed in recent doctrine that the rule of personal immunity does not apply before international courts *as of principle*. The suggestion that the rule of personal immunity from the jurisdiction of international courts lacks support in state practice is however the world on its head. This study asserts that the rule applies *a priori* before international courts. It is the opposite position that requires support in state practice to be tenable.

An international court may have the power to exercise jurisdiction over individuals normally protected by personal immunity if the state of nationality has agreed to the jurisdiction of that court, if the court has Chapter VII powers, or if the Security Council so determines in a resolution adopted under Chapter VII subsequent to the court's establishment. It is interesting to note in this regard that Sands *did* state that '[i]f the Special Court had not been established pursuant to Security Council resolution the situation may be materially different: for example, two States may not be [sic] establish an international criminal court for the purpose, or with the effect, or circumventing the jurisdictional limitations incumbent on national courts as adjudged by the ICJ in the Yerodia case.'[393] Neither Sands, Orentlicher nor the Court explain how the exercise of jurisdiction by an international court established by two states differs from the exercise of jurisdiction by an international court established by sixty states.

Let us move now to the question of whether the arrest warrant violated the rule of head of state immunity from *national* jurisdiction. Taylor had argued in this respect that the issuance of the arrest warrant violated 'the principle of international law providing for immunity from criminal proceedings in foreign jurisdictions of an incumbent Head of State'.[394] The brief of Orentlicher and the

[393] P Sands and A Macdonald (2004) § 78.
[394] Cf n 373 above.

decision of the Appeals Chamber itself, did not acknowledge what this study has labelled the *second* issue troubling the prosecution of individuals clothed with personal immunity by international courts.[395] Only Sands distinguished the two principal issues of the complaint.

According to Sands the immunity from the jurisdiction of national courts only limits the *enforceability* of arrest warrants of international courts against states, *not* the jurisdiction to issue and circulate an arrest warrant. This view, he alleged, is supported by article 98.2 of the ICC Statute that 'does not appear to govern the procedures relating to the issuance by the Pre-Trial Chamber of a warrant of arrest or a summons to appear (under Article 58 of the Statute), which procedures are subject to Article 27 of the Statute'.[396] Sands admitted that the ICJ regarded the circulation of the Belgian arrest warrant for the minister of foreign affairs of the DRC to violate the personal immunity of that minister *regardless* of the legal effect of the warrant on foreign territory.[397] He however points the SCSL to the 'powerful' dissenting opinions on this issue[398] and argues moreover that the case should be distinguished because it concerned the issuance and circulation of an arrest warrant by a *national* court that did not have jurisdiction over the suspect. Did the Court not state expressly that 'before certain international courts' personal immunities did not represent a bar to criminal jurisdiction?[399] Since 'the international circulation of the arrest warrant did not per se require Ghana to give effect to it' Sands did not consider that the issuance and circulation of the arrest warrant violated the personal immunity of Taylor from national jurisdictions.[400]

This study agrees with the suggestion that the decision of the ICJ on the violation of immunity by the issuance and circulation of non-binding warrants is not necessarily correct. It is a pity that the SCSL did not recognize the distinct nature of the question. A second judicial opinion on it is most welcome.

It should finally be noted that only Sands recognized the relevance of the question whether the Statute of the SCSL allows the exercise of jurisdiction over individuals clothed with personal immunity—what this study has termed the *third* issue. Sands admitted that '[l]ike the ICTY and ICTR, the Statute of the Special Court does not contain an equivalent provision to Article 27(2) of the Rome Statute.' However, he quickly disposes of the possible problem with the argument that 'the practice of the ICTY makes it clear that the Statute of that Court (Article 7(2) of which is identical to Article 6(2) of the Statute of the Special Court) is

[395] The Appeals Chamber only—briefly—discussed the argument that the circulation of the arrest warrant violated the sovereignty of Ghana: *Prosecutor v Charles Ghankay Taylor* (SCSL, 2004) § 57.

[396] P Sands and A Macdonald (2004) § 15 and § 97.

[397] ibid § 96.

[398] ibid § 99–101.

[399] ibid § 96. Moreover—under reference to the Joint Separate Opinion of Judges Higgins, Kooijmans and Buergenthal in the *Arrest Warrant* case—Sands suggested that after Taylor ceased to be head of state 'the illegal consequences attaching to the arrest warrant also ceased', § 106–7.

[400] ibid § 92ff.

sufficient to permit the indictment of a serving head of state such as Milosevic'.[401] Sands further referred to article 1.1 of the Statute that states that the SCSL has power 'to prosecute persons who bear the greatest responsibility...including those leaders who, in committing such crimes, have threatened the establishment of and implementation of the peace process in Sierra Leone'. He argued that foreign heads of state are not excluded from this definition and that accordingly the Statute allows the exercise of jurisdiction over them.[402]

This study disagrees. The principle of irrelevance of official capacity does not regard the rule of personal immunity. A provision like article 27.2 ICC Statute is indispensable for an international tribunal to derive jurisdiction from its Statute over persons normally clothed with personal immunity. The reliance on the instigation of proceedings against Milosević attributes way too much authority to an incident the legality of which has not even been examined by the ICTY itself. While article 1.1 may not *exclude* foreign heads of state, the more pertinent question is whether it suffices to *include* foreign heads of state. This study would argue that more is required to preclude the applicability of the well-established rule of personal immunity of foreign heads of state.

The decision of the SCSL and the opinions of *amici curiae* on the vexed question as to the relevance of personal immunities to prosecutions before international criminal courts fail to convince. The Nuremberg Charter and its progeny do not shed light on the question, and the decision of the ICJ in the *Arrest Warrant* case does not support a straightforward distinction between national and international courts in this respect. At this stage in the development of thinking on the question judges and doctrine should adopt a critical stance as regards the instances of state practice that *are available*. The reference to the ICC in paragraph 61 of the *Arrest Warrant* case, the inclusion of article 98 in part 9, and the indictment of Milosević by the ICTY should prompt critical analysis rather than definite statements on the scope of the law. In the absence of state practice, a coherent proposition on the influence of the rule of personal immunity on prosecutions before international courts must be based on an inquiry into the framework of relevant rules and principles of international law. This section has argued that the outcome of such inquiry should be:

1. that personal immunities that apply *erga omnes* are *a priori* applicable to international courts;
2. that international courts can exercise their jurisdiction over persons clothed with this immunity when the state that is represented by such person is bound by the power of the court;
3. that is, provided that the relevant statute contains a provision similar to article 27.2 ICC Statute;

[401] ibid § 80. [402] ibid § 81–9.

4. that international courts must anyway be careful not to violate the personal immunity from national jurisdictions with the issuance and circulation of an arrest warrant.

2.3.2.3 Conventional law

It should in conclusion be noted that while the rule of diplomatic immunity and the rule of head of state immunity continue to shield diplomatic agents and foreign heads of state from jurisdiction in respect of allegations of crimes against international law states can of course *waive* the personal immunity of their state officials.

The already discussed article 27.2 of the Rome Statute is a case in point. We should further consider article 4 of the 1948 Genocide Convention. The article provides that

> [p]ersons committing genocide or any of the other acts enumerated in article III shall be punished, whether they are constitutionally responsible rulers, public officials or private individuals.

The article has a somewhat limited impact since the convention limits the obligation to prosecute suspects of genocide to the state in the territory of which the act was committed. It does however logically apply to diplomatic agents and foreign heads of state suspected of committing genocide within the territory of the forum state. As far as states party to the convention are concerned they may be considered to have waived their rights under the personal immunity rules normally protecting these officials as far as another state party is exercising its jurisdiction in conformance with the convention.

A similar provision is lacking in other international criminal law conventions. Notably, the 2006 International Convention for the Protection of All Persons from Enforced Disappearance[403] does not contain an immunity provision even though an earlier draft of the Convention and the 1992 Declaration on the Protection of all Persons from Enforced Disappearance did both explicitly exclude the immunity defence (except for immunity granted under the Vienna Convention on Diplomatic Relations).[404] Instead, Article 5 of the Convention provides that '[t]he widespread or systematic practice of enforced disappearance constitutes a crime against humanity as defined in applicable international law and shall attract the consequences provided for under such applicable international law', leaving any possible developments in the field of immunity law to general international customary law.

[403] International Convention for the Protection of All Persons from Enforced Disappearance, 20 December 2006, A/RES/61/177 (not yet in force).

[404] Declaration on the Protection of all Persons from Enforced Disappearance, 18 December 1992, A/RES/47/133, art 16; Draft International Convention for the Protection of All Persons from Enforced Disappearance, E/CN.4/Sub.2/1998/19 Annex, art 10.2.

However, the decision of the House of Lords in *Pinochet* no 3 warrants the question whether conventional undertakings to prosecute certain crimes should be interpreted to constitute a waiver even without an explicit provision to that effect. Lord Goff, for example, did not see how the ratification of the Torture Convention could be interpreted to have affected the rule of functional immunity but not the rule of personal immunity. His dissenting opinion reads in this respect:

> [I]t is not suggested that it is inconsistent with the convention that immunity ratione personae should be asserted; if so, I find it difficult to see why it should be inconsistent to assert immunity ratione materiae.[405]

This observation raises a critical question. Is the basis of the majority decision consistent with the argument that serving heads of state continue to enjoy immunity for acts of torture? Do the relevant provisions of the Torture Convention warrant a different conclusion for serving heads of state than for former heads of state? Fox has argued in this respect that 'there is nothing in article 1 [Torture Convention] to confine its scope to a former head of State; the retention of immunity in favour of a serving head of state then becomes equally inconsistent with the *aut dedere aut punire* scheme of the convention'.[406]

A rational distinction *does* however exist. In the first place, the reliance on the Torture Convention for the establishment of a basis for the exercise of universal jurisdiction—by Lords Hope and Philips—*only* served to give free way to an argument that was limited to the rule of functional immunity. More importantly, the argument that the rule of functional immunity is co-extensive with the definition of torture under the Convention—advanced by Lords Browne-Wilkinson and Saville—does not apply to the rule of personal immunity. While under the reasoning advanced by Lords Browne-Wilkinson and Saville the obligations under the Convention *always* clash with the obligations under the rule of functional immunity, the obligations under the Convention will only exceptionally clash with the obligations under personal immunity rules. The Convention

[405] *Pinochet* no 3, 127 (*per* Lord Goff of Chievely).

[406] H Fox (1999) 700. Cf also CA Bradley and JL Goldsmith, 'Pinochet and International Human Rights Litigation' (1999) 97 Michigan Law Review 2129, 2144; P Burns and S McBurney, 'Impunity and the United Nations Convention against Torture: A Shadow Play without an Ending' in C Scott (ed), *Torture as Tort, Comparative Perspectives on the Development of Transnational Human Rights Litigation* (2001) 275, 286; S Villalpando, 'L'affaire Pinochet: beaucoup de bruit pour rien? L'apport au droit international de la décision de la Chambre des Lords du 24 mars 1999 (2000) 104 RGDIP 393, 419; R Wedgewood (2000) 841 ('one could read the Torture Convention even more vigorously to exclude immunity for sitting heads of state'). Cosnard has argued that 'en fondant la non-immunité sur le *jus cogens*, cet équilibre devient difficile à réaliser sans hausser le principle de l'immunité des chefs d'État en exercise au niveau de règle impérative.': 'Quelques observations sur les décisions de la Chambre des Lords du 25 Novembre 1998 et du 24 Mars 1999 dans l'affaire Pinochet' (1999) 103 RGDIP 309, 321. Cf in a similar vein P De Sena (1999) 952–3. This consideration does however not cut ice since none of the Lords based the denial of immunity on the concept of *jus cogens*.

hence does not exclude personal immunities by implication, and states cannot be assumed to have waived their rights under personal immunity rules without any indication to that effect.

It is noted in comparison that the ICJ has held with regard to the local remedies rule that it is 'unable to accept that an important principle of customary international law should be held to have been tacitly dispensed with, in the absence of any words making clear an intention to do so'.[407] Equally it should not be assumed that states tacitly dispense with their rights under personal immunity rules by ratifying a treaty that provides for mandatory universal jurisdiction over a certain crime.

This is corroborated by the reasoning of the ICJ in the *Arrest Warrant* Case. The Court emphasized that 'the rules governing the jurisdiction of national courts must be carefully distinguished from those governing jurisdictional immunities: jurisdiction does not imply absence of immunity, while absence of immunity does not imply jurisdiction. Thus, although various international conventions on the prevention and punishment of certain serious crimes impose on states obligations of prosecution or extradition, thereby requiring them to extend their criminal jurisdiction, such extension of jurisdiction in no way affects immunities under customary international law, including those of Ministers for Foreign Affairs. These remain opposable before the courts of a foreign state, even where those courts exercise such jurisdiction under these conventions.'[408]

What *can* be said though is that the conventional undertaking to prosecute limits the freedom of states to grant individuals *more* immunity than required or normal under customary international law.[409] It is for example questionable whether the promise of full immunity to encourage the abdication of high foreign state officials is compatible with conventional *aut dedere aut judicare* obligations.[410]

3 Policy Arguments: The (In)Compatibility of the Rule of Personal Immunity and the Obligation to Prosecute

Personal immunity rules are not directly affected by the developments in international criminal law. The debate on an exception to personal immunity for

[407] *Elettronica Sicula SpA (ELSI)* (*United States of America v Italy*) ICJ Reports 1989 14, 42, § 50.

[408] *Arrest Warrant* Case, 24–5, § 59.

[409] The status of immunities granted under Status of Forces Agreements (SOFA's) is here not discussed. Such agreements are certainly accepted and normal state practice.

[410] It is in this respect recalled that in the US head of state immunity is commonly recognized to apply to former heads of state as well, cf *Abiola v Abubakar* (US, 2003), and *Wei Ye v Jiang Zemin* (US, 2004). Cf this to the discussion on the conclusion of art 98.2 agreements with the US by states party to the ICC. Eg M Benzing (2004).

crimes against international law hence should be conducted on the essentially different level of policy arguments. The issue of debate is then not what the scope of the rules of personal immunity *is* but what that scope *should be*. States could decide to change the rules when they agree that the interests in the administration of justice outweigh the interests protected by the rules. Judges Higgins, Kooijmans, and Buergenthal rightly considered in their Joint Separate Opinion in the *Arrest Warrant* case that 'the weights on the two scales are not set for all perpetuity'.[411]

Policy arguments cannot be relied on by courts or scholars determining the scope of the rule. Rather, they should guide states in their law-making activity. Accordingly, when Gaeta argues that personal immunities should not be granted when, although the State to which the organ belongs *does have* jurisdiction over the crimes allegedly committed by that organ, nevertheless the receiving State has compelling reasons to believe either that the sending State will not prosecute the crimes' except when the foreign official is the head of state because 'to bring to trial a Head of State might jeopardize the structure and functioning of the foreign State, since he discharges important and sensitive constitutional functions,[412] this can only be accepted as a suggestion for change; not as a declaration of law.[413] It was in this respect argued earlier that the reasoning of dissenting Judge Van den Wyngaert in the *Arrest Warrant* case was not appropriate.[414]

This study limits the discussion of policy arguments to those particularly forceful arguments that point to a clash of the obligations under personal immunity rules with the obligations under international criminal law. As said before, the obligation to prosecute does not exist under customary international *criminal* law.[415] Moreover, conventional undertakings to prosecute certain crimes in principle do not extend to individuals that are exempted from the jurisdiction of the ratifying state.[416] Policy arguments of this kind are therefore not available.

4 Conclusions

When the UK Divisional Court was asked to decide whether General Pinochet enjoyed immunity from the jurisdiction of UK courts it unanimously decided that the former head of state of Chile was protected by immunity from the jurisdiction of the English courts. The judges held that there could be no limitation to

411 *Arrest Warrant* Case, Joint Separate Opinion of Judges Higgins, Kooijmans and Buergenthal, 85, § 75. Cf in general 84–5, § 70–5.

412 P Gaeta (2002) 986–9, quotation at 987.

413 The denial of justice argument is therefore further discussed in ch 6 § 3 of this study.

414 Cf p 271–2 above.

415 There may be an obligation to exercise *territorial* jurisdiction over certain acts but that is more an obligation under international human rights law. The effect thereof will therefore be discussed in ch 6 § 3.4 below.

416 Cf p 294–5 above.

immunity based on the nature of the crimes committed. Lord Bingham rationalized his decision with the following question: 'If the former sovereign is immune from process in respect of some crimes where does one draw the line?'[417]

International law draws this line, however, in unequivocal terms. Since state officials incur personal responsibility for crimes against international law committed on orders of their government, they can be sued in their personal capacity before foreign national courts and international courts in respect of these crimes. The principle of individual responsibility for crimes against international law forms the universal limit on the mandate of state officials. Crimes against international law can never be committed under the cloak of state authority and the rationale of the rule of functional immunity hence does not extend to such proceedings. Accordingly, cases against foreign state officials on allegations of crimes against international law do not implead the state. The theory of individual responsibility for certain violations of international law bares the limits of the state immunity doctrine.

This does not mean, however, that courts can always establish competence when foreign state officials are sued on allegations of crimes against international law. The finding that crimes against international law have been committed *creates* the competence of the court. Competence may therefore be lacking when allegations rely on the context of state policy—as in the case of crimes against humanity, apartheid, genocide and the unlawful use of force and aggression—and the legal qualification of that policy is highly controversial.

The House of Lords reasoned differently in the *Pinochet* case. Since the Lords proceeded from the conception of the rule of functional immunity as protecting the sovereign acts of the home state from foreign interference, the principles of individual responsibility for crimes against international law and irrelevance of official capacity did not have the direct influence on the scope of the rule that is proposed in this study. Lords Browne-Wilkinson and Saville based the denial of immunity on the specific terms of the Torture Convention only; Lord Hutton—and maybe Lord Millett—saw an exception to the rule of act of state immunity to apply in criminal proceedings regarding crimes against international law; Lord Hope saw an exception to the rule of act of state immunity to apply in criminal proceedings regarding crimes against international law *codified in a convention establishing universal jurisdiction*; and according to Lord Philips the rule of functional immunity did not apply to crimes committed outside the territory of the forum state at all and he considered therefore that the establishment of universal jurisdiction through the Torture Convention was not limited by the rule of functional immunity. *Pinochet* no 3 is a weak precedent for functional immunity decisions in future cases regarding allegations of crimes against international

[417] *R v Bow Street Metropolitan Stipendiary Magistrate and others, ex p Pinochet Ugarte* (UK, 1998) § 63.

law because of the reliance on the act of state immunity rule and the terms of the Torture Convention.

This study asserts that the rule of state immunity applies only when the state is the direct or indirect defendant in the proceedings. Only when a foreign state official does not bear personal responsibility for the allegations can it be said that the foreign state is the factual defendant in a case. Otherwise, state immunity becomes act of state immunity. The 2004 decision of the UK Court of Appeal in *Jones v Saudi Arabia and Abdul Aziz* was a tacit but sure deviation from the *Pinochet* precedent. Recognizing the influence of the principle of individual responsibility on the applicability of the rule of state immunity *ratione materiae* the case implicitly recognized the distinction between that rule and the rule of functional immunity.

The personal immunities of diplomatic agents and heads of state remain unaffected by the principles of individual responsibility and irrelevance of official capacity. Personal immunity is procedural rather than substantive in character and a change of the law can therefore only be effected by a change in state practice on these rules. A recent string of judicial decisions—with the *Arrest Warrant* case as prominent example—has confirmed that such a change has not yet taken place. It has in this respect been argued that '[t]he Pinochet decision [might be] little more than a pyrrhic victory for human rights, providing dictators with the strongest possible incentive to keep on dictating.'[418] In a more critical vein, Bianchi noted that 'one would be left with the impression that it is power more than law which protects office holders and that no matter whether they place themselves well beyond the legitimate boundaries of their official authority, they will be protected by law as long as they retain their power, whereas they will be left to their fate once that power comes to an end.'[419] However, it is exactly the point of the law of personal immunity that it is unconcerned with the nature of the allegations. When the law protects certain individuals in power this does not mean that power substitutes the law.

As far as personal immunities apply *erga omnes* this limit applies with equal force to international courts and tribunals. States cannot abrogate the rights of other states through international agreement and cooperation. The decision of the SCSL in the *Taylor* case fails to convince. In any event, international courts must be careful that their arrest warrants do not violate the personal immunity of suspects from national jurisdictions. States can of course waive the personal immunity of their officials, as they did for example in the ICC Statute and the Genocide Convention.

[418] J Klabbers, 'The General, The Lords and the Possible End of State Immunity' (1999) 68 Nordic Journal of International Law 85, 89. Cf similarly AD Mitchell, 'Leave your Hat on? Head of State Immunity and Pinochet' (1999) 25 Monash University Law Review 225, 251–2.

[419] A Bianchi (1999) 261.

The ICJ has been presented with another opportunity to clarify some of the issues discussed in this chapter. The Republic of the Congo has seized the Court in respect of a dispute it has with France over, *inter alia*, the immunity of its Minister of the Interior and of its head of state in respect of criminal proceedings in France based on allegations of crimes against humanity and torture committed in the Congo.[420] These allegations were brought to the attention of the French judiciary by a complaint filed on 5 December 2001 on behalf of several human rights organizations. On the basis of this complaint a French investigating judge has initiated an investigation. The Congo further claims that when its head of state was on an official visit to France, the investigating judge issued a warrant to police officers 'instructing them to take testimony from him'.[421] France disputes this latter allegation, stating that the investigating judge sought to obtain evidence from the Congolese head of state through the diplomatic channel—a procedure that is laid down in article 656 of the French Code of Criminal Procedure.

On the basis of these facts, Congo alleges two separate violations of immunity rules. In the first place, it alleges 'violation of the principle that a State may not, in breach of the principle of sovereign equality among all members of the United Nations, as laid down in Article 2, paragraph 1, of the Charter of the United Nations, exercise its authority on the territory of another State... by arrogating to itself the power to prosecute and try the Minister of the Interior of a foreign State for crimes allegedly committed in connection with the exercise of his powers for the maintenance of public order in his country'. Second, it alleges 'violation of the criminal immunity of a foreign Head of State—an international customary rule recognized by the jurisprudence of the Court'.[422] Although it is not stated with so many words, it may be clear that the first allegation asks the Court to inquire into the rule of functional immunity of foreign state officials while the second allegation sees to the rule of personal immunity of foreign heads of state.

It is unlikely that the Court will depart from its decision in the *Arrest Warrant* case as far as the second allegation is concerned. However, it may shed some light on the controversies that have developed in doctrine following that decision. The question that has arisen in respect of the criminal proceedings against the Minister of the Interior is for the first time before the learned judges of the Court. It will be interesting to see how the Court defines the legal issue. Will it acknowledge the separateness of functional and state immunity? And, will it agree with this author that no immunity issue arises when allegations of crimes

[420] The Court is also asked to speak out on the requirements for the exercise of universal jurisdiction—the question it skilfully curbed in the *Arrest Warrant* case. Cf *Certain Criminal Proceedings in France* (*Republic of the Congo v France*) available at <http://www.icj-cij.org>.

[421] *Certain Criminal Proceedings in France* (*Republic of the Congo v France*) (Provisional measures) (2003) § 16, available at <http://www.icj-cij.org>.

[422] ibid § 1.

against international law are at issue? Should this be so, the Court will have to deal with the question—identified but not comprehensively dealt with in this study in section 2.3.1.4 above—whether in the absence of immunity barriers national courts may still violate aspects of the principle of the sovereign equality of states when proceedings against a foreign state official require a decision on the (il) legality of activity or policy of the home state.

6

The Immunity of States and Their Officials in Light of the Fundamental Rights of Individuals under International Law

1 Introduction

The developments in international law over the past sixty years or so reflect a paradigm shift. International law is no longer limited to the regulation of the behaviour of states as against other states but extends to the regulation of behaviour of states as against their own citizens and within their own borders. Jenks noted already in 1958 that 'the emphasis of the law is increasingly shifting from the formal structure of the relationship between States and the delimitation of their jurisdiction to the development of substantive rules on matters of common concern vital to the growth of an international community and to the individual well-being of the citizens of its member States'.[1] The shift from the classical 'international law of co-existence' to an 'international law of cooperation' has continued ever since, with the developments in international human rights law as a conspicuous example.[2] While in the beginning of the twentieth century the mistreatment by a state of its own citizens—even on the scale of the Armenian massacres—was commonly agreed to be a matter within the domestic jurisdiction of the state, today the protection of human rights is considered 'a matter of priority for the international community'.[3]

Human rights in the sense of rights of individuals as against states did not as such feature in the pre-1945 international legal order. Of course, the concept of human rights can be traced back to the 1215 Magna Carta, the philosophical writings of Locke and Rousseau, and the 1776 US Constitution and the 1789 French Déclaration des Droits de l'Homme et du Citoyen. The natural law terminology often used in respect of these rights—the US Constitution speaks of

[1] CW Jenks, *The Common Law of Mankind* (1958) 17. Cf also PC Jessup, *A Modern Law of Nations* (1948) 2; W Friedmann (1964).

[2] W Friedmann, ibid 60.

[3] Preamble to the Vienna Declaration and Programme of Action of the World Conference on Human Rights (adopted by 171 states on 23 June 1993, UN Doc A/CONF.157/23, 12 July 1993). Cf on the Armenian massacres JL Brierly, 'Matters of Domestic Jurisdiction' (1925) 6 BYIL 8, 18.

'inalienable rights', the Déclaration of 'les droits naturels, inaliénables et sacrés de l'homme'—is irrelevant however for the question of whether these rights form part of *international* law.[4] Only since states agreed to make these rights a matter of international concern can we speak of international human rights law. The Second World War is a watershed in this respect. When the scale and horror of the Nazi atrocities came to light, disbelief, shock, and anger united the world. Scholars argued in favour of an international Bill of Rights and states agreed that the protection of these rights could no longer be left to the whims of individual states.[5]

Before that time there had been occasional attempts to regulate state behaviour that causes human suffering and to ensure protection of interests of human beings within the international legal system. The most prominent example is early international humanitarian law—*jus in bello*, the law of armed conflict, or the law of war as it was initially termed—that set out to regulate state conduct in interstate warfare and was briefly discussed in the previous chapter. These rules did not, however, grant rights to individuals. The individual was, to use the words of Lauterpacht, 'an object of international compassion' rather than 'a subject of international right'.[6] Another glaring difference with modern human rights law was that the rules only applied in times of war, not in times of peace, and moreover only in interstate conflict, not in internal conflict. With the very limited exception of certain conventional obligations to respect minorities and to abolish slave trade and slavery it can be safely stated that a state's treatment of its own nationals was a matter exclusively within the domestic jurisdiction of that state and as such outside the realm of international law.[7]

This changed in the wake of the Second World War. Human rights were allocated a prominent position in the Charter of the United Nations, signed by 44 states in San Francisco on 26 June 1945.[8] Article 1 of the Charter states that one of the purposes of the United Nations is '[t]o achieve international co-operation in solving international problems of an economic, social, cultural or humanitarian character, and in promoting and encouraging respect for human rights and

[4] Cf also the preamble of the Universal Declaration of Human Rights (General Assembly Resolution 217A of 10 December 1948), that refers to 'the inherent dignity and of the equal and inalienable rights of all members of the human family' and the preamble of the above-mentioned 1993 Vienna Declaration Programme of Action of the World Conference on Human Rights that refers to 'all human rights derive from the dignity and worth inherent in the human person'.

[5] See for early advocates of an international bill of rights eg: H Lauterpacht, *An International Bill of the Rights of Man* (1945); HG Wells, *The Rights of Man* (1940); HG Wells, *The New World Order* (1940) 139–43; Q Wright, 'Human Rights and World Order', in *The Third Report of the Commission to Study the Organization of Peace* (1943); American Law Institute, *Statement of Essential Human Rights* (1945), reproduced in American Law Institute, *Seventy-Fifth Anniversary 1923–1998* (1998) 261.

[6] H Lauterpacht, *International Law and Human Rights* (1950) 4.

[7] L Oppenheim, *International Law, A Treatise* (1905) i 346–7; JL Brierly, *The Law of Nations, An Introduction to the International Law of Peace* (6th edn, 1963) 291–2.

[8] Charter of the United Nations (1945), reproduced in I Brownlie, *Basic Documents in International Law* (5th edn, 2002) 2.

for fundamental freedoms for all without distinction as to race, sex, language, or religion' and a joined reading of article 55 and 56 establishes the duty of member states to secure 'universal respect for, and observance of, human rights and fundamental freedoms'.[9] Within the context of the United Nations the rights of individuals as against the state were articulated in non-binding instruments (like the 1948 Universal Declaration of Human Rights, the 1968 Proclamation of Tehran of the International Conference on Human Rights, and the 1993 Vienna Declaration and Programme of Action of the World Conference on Human Rights, and countless GA and CS Resolutions[10]) and in binding instruments (like the 1966 International Covenant on Civil and Political Rights (ICCPR), and the 1966 International Covenant on Economic, Social and Cultural Rights[11]). In addition, conventions and declarations have been adopted on the regional level. The European Convention on Human Rights and Fundamental Freedoms (ECHR), the American Convention on Human Rights and the African Charter on Human and Peoples' Rights all oblige member states to respect the classical human rights.[12]

The Second World War also gave an impetus to international humanitarian law. With the adoption of the four Geneva Conventions in 1949—today ratified by over 190 states—the discipline has more than firmly established itself. With a large part of the rules now applying in *internal* conflicts as well, international humanitarian law has moreover acquired a genuinely humanitarian character.

International human rights law and international humanitarian law have without doubt changed the outlook of the international legal order. The traditional bilateral approach to rights and obligations has been complemented by

[9] Cf *Legal Consequences for States of the Continued Presence of South Africa in Namibia (South West Africa) notwithstanding Security Council Resolution 276 (1970)* (Advisory Opinion), ICJ Reports 1971 16, 56–7 for the interpretation of these articles as establishing legal obligations in spite of the somewhat vague language used Cf also E Schwelb, 'The International Court of Justice and the Human Rights Clauses of the Charter' (1972) 66 AJIL 337.

[10] Universal Declaration of Human Rights, GA Resolution 217 A (III) (1948), reprinted in I Brownlie and GS Goodwin-Gill (eds), *Basic Documents on Human Rights* (4th edn, 2002) 68; Proclamation of Teheran, Final Act of the International Conference on Human Rights, Teheran (1968), UN Doc A/CONF32/41 at 3 (1968); Vienna Declaration and Programme of Action of the World Conference on Human Rights (1993), UN Doc A/CONF157/23 (1993); and many declarations of the UN General Assembly and the Security Council, cf I Brownlie and GS Goodwin-Gill (eds), ibid.

[11] International Covenant on Civil and Political Rights (1966) 999 UNTS 171, reprinted in I Brownlie and GS Goodwin-Gill (eds), ibid, 182; International Covenant on Economic, Social and Cultural Rights (1966) 993 UNTS 3, reprinted in I Brownlie and GS Goodwin-Gill, 172.

[12] European Convention for the Protection of Human Rights and Fundamental Freedoms (1950), reprinted in I Brownlie and GS Goodwin-Gill, ibid, 398; American Convention on Human Rights (1969), reprinted in I Brownlie and GS Goodwin-Gill, ibid, 671; African Charter on Human and Peoples' Rights (1981), reprinted in I Brownlie and GS Goodwin-Gill, ibid, 728. Also more specialized treaties are concluded on a regional level; like eg the European Convention for the Prevention of Torture and Inhuman or Degrading Treatment or Punishment (1987), reprinted in I Brownlie and GS Goodwin-Gill, ibid, 493.

multilateral thinking in terms of community interest.[13] In its 1951 Advisory Opinion in the *Genocide* case the ICJ commented that the purpose of the 1948 Genocide Convention 'is purely humanitarian and civilising... the contracting States do not have any interests of their own; they merely have... a common interest'.[14] In a similar vein, the European Court of Human Rights has emphasized on several occasions that the European Convention creates 'over and above a network of mutual, bilateral undertakings, objective obligations which... benefit from a "collective enforcement".'[15]

The protection of community interests required rethinking of some of the parameters of the international legal system. The concepts '*jus cogens* norms' and '*erga omnes* obligations' can be seen to accommodate the secondary rules of the international legal order to the reality of rules protecting community interests.

If the obligations under human rights law could be escaped unilaterally or in agreement with other states the interests of the community would be vulnerable to the quirks of individual states. The concept of *jus cogens* was first recognized by states in the 1969 Vienna Convention on the Law of Treaties.[16] Article 53 of the convention reads:

> A treaty is void if, at the time of its conclusion, it conflicts with a peremptory norm of general international law. For the purposes of the present Convention, a peremptory norm of general international law is a norm accepted and recognised by the international community of States as a whole as a norm from which no derogation is permitted and which can be modified only by a subsequent norm of general international law having the same character.

This provision is complemented by article 64 of the Convention that reads as follows:

> If a new peremptory norm of general international law emerges, any existing treaty which is in conflict with that norm becomes void and terminates.

Although the idea of peremptory norms in the international legal system was the subject of fierce debate at the Convention,[17] and has since received many critical

[13] Cf S Rosenne, 'Bilateralism and Community Interest in the Codified Law of Treaties' in W Friedmann et al (eds), *Transnational Law in a Changing Society: Essays in Honor of Philip C Jessup* (1972) 202; B Simma, 'Bilateralism and Community Interest in the Law of State Responsibility' in Y Dinstein and M Tabory (eds), *International Law at a Time of Perplexity—Essays in Honour of Shabtai Rosenne* (1989) 821; B Simma, 'From Bilateralism to Community Interest in International Law' (1994-VI) 250 RdC 217.

[14] *Reservations to the Convention on the Prevention and Punishment of the Crime of Genocide* (Advisory Opinion), ICJ Reports 1951 15, 23.

[15] *Ireland v United Kingdom* Series A–25; 2 EHRR 25, 103 (ECHR, 1978) § 239.

[16] Vienna Convention on the Law of Treaties (1969), 1155 UNTS 331. Cf also the Vienna Convention on the Law of Treaties between States and International Organizations or Between International Organizations (1986), UN Doc A/Conf 129/15 (1986), art 53.

[17] Cf J Sztucki, *Jus Cogens and the Vienna Convention on the Law of Treaties, a Critical Appraisal* (1974).

reviews in doctrine,[18] it is now well settled that international law knows a group of core norms from which no derogation is possible—also termed 'the public order of the international community'.[19] The notion is recognized by the ICJ,[20] other international courts and tribunals,[21] as well as by national courts dealing with questions of international law.[22]

The question which norms qualify as such is much more controversial. The statement of the ILC in the comment to its 1966 Draft Convention that 'there is no simple criterion by which to identify a general rule of international law as having the character of *jus cogens*' still holds true today.[23] Some have argued in favour of a broad interpretation so that the concept covers human rights in general.[24] But most agree that only core norms of human rights are included. The German *Bundesverfassungsgericht* stated in 1965 that '[t]he quality of such peremptory norms will only be attributed to those legal rules, deeply rooted in the legal conviction of the community of States, which are indispensable for the existence of international law and an international legal order and the observance of which can be demanded by all members of the community of States.'[25] This is reflected in the words of Crawford who described the category of norms as 'those substantive rules of conduct that prohibit what has come to be seen as intolerable because

[18] Cf especially P Weil, 'Towards Relative Normativity in International Law?' (1983) 77 AJIL 413. Cf moreover G Schwarzenberger, 'International Jus Cogens?' (1965) 43 Texas Law Review 455; M Virally, 'Réflexions sur le "jus cogens"' (1966) 12 AFDI 5; T Meron, 'On a Hierarchy of International Human Rights' (1986) 80 AJIL 1; A Weisburd, 'The Emptiness of the Concept of *Jus Cogens*, as Illustrated by the War in Bosnia-Herzegovina' (1995) 17 Michigan Journal of International Law 1.

[19] H Mosler, 'The International Society as a Legal Community' (1974–IV) 140 RdC 3, 33. In his first report on the Law of Treaties H Lauterpacht referred in this regard to 'such overriding principles of international law which may be regarded as principles of international public policy (*ordre international public*)', YBILC 1953 ii 90, 90. See for other definitions J Sztucki (1974) 77. Cf for support in doctrine eg: I Brownlie 488–90; R Jennings and A Watts (1992) i 7–8; L Hannikainen, *Peremptory Norms (Jus Cogens) in International Law* (1988); A Verdross, 'Jus Dispositivum and Jus Cogens in International Law' (1966) 60 AJIL 55.

[20] See *Armed Activities on the Territory of the Congo* (*Democratic Republic of the Congo v Rwanda*) (2006), *inter alia* § 64, available at <http://www.icj-cij.org>. Cf also *Case Concerning Military and Paramilitary Activities in and against Nicaragua*, (ICJ, 1986) 100; ICJ, *Reservations to the Convention on the Prevention and Punishment of the Crime of Genocide* (ICJ, 1951) 23–4; ICJ, *Legality of the Threat or Use of Nuclear Weapons* (Advisory Opinion), ICJ Reports 1996 225, 257. Cf GA Christenson, 'The World Court and *Jus Cogens*' (1987) 81 AJIL 93; J Sztucki (1974) 12–22; FA Mann (1973) 399.

[21] Cf eg *Al-Adsani v United Kingdom* 273 (ECHR, 2001) (further referred to as *Al-Adsani*); *Prosecutor v Furundžija* (ICTY, 1998) § 153.

[22] Cf eg *Assessment of Aliens for War Taxation Case* 43 ILR 3 (Germany, Federal Constitutional Court, 1965) 8–9; and recently *R v Bow Street Metropolitan Stipendiary Magistrate and others, ex p Pinochet Ugarte (Amnesty International and others intervening)* (UK, 1999) (further referred to as *Pinochet* no 3).

[23] YBILC 1966 ii 169, 247–8.

[24] Cf eg Dissenting Judge Tanaka in *South West Africa Cases* (*Ethiopia v South Africa*; *Liberia v South Africa*) (ICJ, 1966) 298.

[25] *Assessment of Aliens for War Taxation Case* (Germany, 1965) 8–9.

of the threat it presents to the survival of States and their peoples and the most basic human values.'[26] Brownlie writes that '[t]he least controversial examples of the class are the prohibition of the use of force, the law of genocide, the principle of racial non-discrimination, crimes against humanity, and the rules prohibiting trade in slaves and piracy'.[27] For the purposes of this study the question which norms qualify under the category of *jus cogens* is not terribly important. Rather, the focus is on what the consequences of such categorization are, or: what is the scope of application of the concept of *jus cogens*?

Also the traditional rules on accountability, responsibility and enforcement as applicable to interstate relations based on essentially reciprocal rights and obligations fit community thinking uncomfortably. Not surprisingly many human rights instruments not only lay down the standards to which states commit themselves but provide for specific control and implementation mechanisms. State parties to the ECHR, for example, have a right to complain of violations of the Convention by any other state party irregardless of the nationality of the alleged victim as 'an alleged violation of the public order of Europe'.[28] The violation complained of hence may concern a law or practice *in abstracto* as well as a concrete violation 'without having to justify an interest deriving...from the fact that a measure they complain of has prejudiced one of their own nationals'.[29]

When no special treaty-based enforcement mechanisms are available multilateral rules are likely to remain ineffective. The *South West Africa* cases conspicuously evidenced the need to rethink traditional rules on standing in the law of state responsibility.[30] The cases concerned applications filed by Ethiopia and Liberia asking the ICJ to affirm the status of South West Africa as a territory under mandate and to declare that South Africa's administration of South West Africa violated several articles of the Mandate Agreement and article 22 of the Covenant of the League of Nations, in particular because of the practice of Apartheid. South Africa argued, *inter alia*, that Ethiopia and Liberia had no standing to pursue the claim since their legal rights or interests were not at issue. While the ICJ in the 1962 decision on preliminary questions had rejected this argument,[31] the 1966 judgment effectively overturned this decision and the merits of the case were never decided.[32] It was considered that applicants' claim of *locus standi* 'amounts to a plea that the Court should allow the equivalent of

[26] J Crawford, *The International Law Commission's Articles on State Responsibility, Introduction, Text and Commentaries* (2002) 246.

[27] I Brownlie (2003) 488–9.

[28] *Austria v Italy* (*Pfunders* case) 4 Yearbook on the European Convention on Human Rights 1961 116 (EComHR, 1961) 140.

[29] *Ireland v United Kingdom* (ECHR, 1978) 103, § 239.

[30] *South West Africa Cases* (*Ethiopia v South Africa*; *Liberia v South Africa*) (Preliminary Objections), ICJ Reports 1962 319; *South West Africa Cases* (*Ethiopia v South Africa*; *Liberia v South Africa*) (ICJ, 1966).

[31] *South West Africa Cases* (ICJ Reports 162) 335–42. Cf especially the Separate Opinion of Judge Jessup, 387, 424–433.

[32] *South West Africa Cases* (1966).

an "*actio popularis*", or right resident in any member of a community to take legal action in vindication of a public interest. But, although a right of this kind may be known to certain municipal systems of law, it is not known to international law as it stands at present.'[33]

In the *Barcelona Traction* case the ICJ intimated that different rules on standing did indeed apply when obligations of states towards the international community as a whole are at issue. Reaffirming the nationality of claims requirement in the field of diplomatic protection the Court considered in a famous obiter dictum that

> an essential distinction should be drawn between the obligations of a State towards the international community as a whole, and those arising vis-à-vis another State in the field of diplomatic protection. By their very nature the former are the concern of all States. In view of the importance of the rights involved, all States can be held to have a legal interest in their protection; they are obligations *erga omnes*.
>
> Such obligations derive, for example, in contemporary international law, from the outlawing of acts of aggression, and of genocide, as also from the principles and rules concerning the basic rights of the human person, including protection from slavery and racial discrimination.[34]

While the exercise of diplomatic protection is restricted by the nationality-of-claims principle, the Court considered that states have a legal interest in the protection of certain core norms regarding the treatment of individuals, even when the (possible) victims of a certain (impending) violation of these norms are not their nationals.[35]

Although the Court focused on obligations rather than on the category of norms they derive from, it is obvious that it had the most fundamental norms of international law in mind when it held that all states have a legal interest in their protection. As the Court held, *erga omnes* obligations arise when *in view of the importance of the rights involved* all states can be held to have a legal interest in their protection.[36] It is often maintained that *jus cogens* norms and obligations

[33] Ibid 47. Cf for criticism on the case eg J Dugard, 'The Court's Judgment and the 1966 South West Africa Cases, Second Phase' (1966) 83 SALJ 429; R Higgins, 'The International Court and South West Africa: The Implications of the Judgment' (1966) 42 International Affairs 575; E Schwelb, 'The Actio Popularis and International Law' (1972) 2 Israel Yearbook of Human Rights 46. Cf in general J Dugard (ed), *The South West Africa/Namibia Dispute, Documents and Scholarly Writings on the Controversy between South Africa and the United Nations* (1973).

[34] *The Barcelona Traction, Light and Power Company, Limited* (*Belgium v Spain*) (ICJ, 1970) 32.

[35] Often the dictum is held to mean that the nationality of claims principle does not apply when certain core norms of international law are violated. However, the dictum makes clear that states would not be exercising diplomatic protection with regard to non-nationals when invoking their legal interest, but rather would be protecting the rights of the international community as a whole.

[36] Cf also *East Timor* (*Portugal v Australia*) (Judgment), ICJ Reports 1995 90, 102, § 29: 'Portugal's assertion that the right of peoples to self-determination... has an *erga omnes* character, is irreproachable. The principle of self-determination ... is one of the essential principles of contemporary international law'.

erga omnes are sides of the same coin. Bassiouni, for example, commented that '[j]us cogens refers to the legal status that certain international crimes reach, and obligations erga omnes pertains to the legal implications arising out of a certain crime's characterization as jus cogens.'[37] However, the Court's dictum clearly does no more than establishing that a certain degree of importance of rights is a sufficient condition for the obligations deriving from them to apply *erga omnes* but cannot sustain an argument that makes the link a necessary one. Rather it seems that obligations may be owed *erga omnes* either because of their intrinsic multilateral nature or because the importance of the rights involved gives them a multilateral aspect—the obligations owed to the international community as a whole; even though a substantial part of *erga omnes* obligations will fit both categories.[38] Clearly, any link between *jus cogens* norms and *erga omnes* obligations is limited to the latter category.

The question to be answered in this chapter is how the development of international human rights law relates to the immunity of states and their officials under international law. Since the rule of functional immunity regards non-personal responsibility and is related to the rule of state immunity as far as the presumption of authority is concerned, our inquiry focuses on state immunity and the personal immunity of diplomatic agents and foreign heads of state.

The tension between the two bodies of law is twofold. In the first place, immunity rules may conflict with fundamental rights of individuals. It is, in fact, not surprising that the increase of criticism on the absolute state immunity rule coincided with the increased attention for human rights after the Second World War. It was repeatedly noted that the grant of immunity to foreign states in respect of claims that were otherwise within the competence of the court denied justice to private individuals.[39] In 1951 Lauterpacht pointedly phrased the tension in the following terms:

> At a period in which in enlightened communities the securing of the rights of the individual—in all their aspects, against the state has become a matter of special and significant effort, there is no longer a disposition to tolerate the injustice which may arise whenever the state—our own state or a foreign state—screens itself behind the shield of immunity in order to defeat a legitimate claim.[40]

[37] MC Bassiouni, 'International Crimes: Jus Cogens and Obligatio Erga Omnes' (1996) 25 Law & Contemporary Problems 63, 68. Cf also A De Hoogh, *Obligations Erga Omnes and International Crimes, A Theoretical Inquiry into the Implementation and Enforcement of the International Responsibility of States* (1996) 55.

[38] Several scholars have noted that *erga omnes* obligations could exist which derive from norms not of a *jus cogens* character, cf T Meron, *Human Rights Law-Making in the United Nations* (1987) 187; M Byers, 'Conceptualising the Relationship between Jus Cogens and Erga Omnes Rules' (1997) 66 Nordic Journal of International Law 211, 237.

[39] Cf ch 2 § 2.3.1 above.

[40] H Lauterpacht (1951) 235.

It could be argued *a contrario* that under a restrictive approach the grant of state immunity does *not* amount to a denial of justice. This silent assumption was challenged only some fifty years later when three individuals filed three distinct complaints before the European Court of Human Rights (ECHR) arguing that the dismissal of their claim against foreign states on the basis of the rule of state immunity by the national courts of the United Kingdom and Ireland respectively had violated their right of access to court under article 6.1 of the ECHR. One of these cases was that of *Al-Adsani v United Kingdom*.[41] Mr Al-Adsani, both a UK and Kuwaiti national, had attempted to initiate proceedings before the UK courts in order to obtain damages from the government of Kuwait for acts of torture allegedly committed by Kuwaiti security forces on Kuwaiti territory. Al-Adsani claimed to have been subjected to various forms of severe torture by security guards in retaliation of a personal conflict with a relative of the Emir of Kuwait. The UK courts granted state immunity to Kuwait and refused to hear his case. The Strasbourg Court was almost unanimous in its decision that article 6.1 is never violated when the immunity rule applied reflects a rule of international law.

A second, essentially distinct perspective on the research question focuses on the right of the respondent state (official) in view of the nature of the disputed acts. Whereas before it was debated whether the grant of state immunity or diplomatic immunity violated human rights, in the 1980s the focus of debate became whether immunity was available when human rights had been violated.[42]

In contrast with international law rules under the traditional law of co-existence material state practice is not the basis of international human rights law. The law sets standards of behaviour, it does not necessarily reflect the actual behaviour of states. In fact, the violation of human rights norms is rife—as Röling bitterly noted 'the road to hell is paved with good conventions'.[43] While some international human rights instruments allow individuals to complain of the violation of their rights on the international level, it is fair to say that victims of human rights violations are in principle dependent on national courts for the enforcement of the rights ensured to them on the international level. Since redress in the courts of the state that has allegedly violated the rights is often illusory victims have started to rely on the concept of universal jurisdiction as developed in criminal law to instigate proceedings for damages in the national courts of foreign states—in US courts in particular.[44]

[41] *Al-Adsani*. The other two cases were *Fogarty v United Kingdom* (ECHR, 2001); *McElhinney v Ireland* (ECHR, 2001).

[42] It should be noted that the argument that there is no state immunity in respect of particular serious violations of international law had already been advanced in *De Haas v De Staat Indonesië* NJ 1962, No 74 (The Netherlands, Hoge Raad, 1962). The court rejected the argument without reasons.

[43] BVA Röling, 'The Law of War and the National Jurisdiction since 1945' (1960–II) 100 RdC 323, 445.

[44] This study does not engage the question whether individuals can bring claims in respect of violations of humanitarian law. It is irrelevant for the purposes of our study whether the cases in which this second perspective on the research question presents itself are necessarily based on international human rights law or whether norms of international humanitarian law may underlie these cases as well.

The case of *Filartiga v Peña-Irala* discussed in chapter 5 of this study illustrates this development.[45] The case launched the Alien Tort Claims Act—passed into oblivion after its enactment in 1789—into the modern world of transnational human rights litigation. The Act provides that '[t]he district courts shall have original jurisdiction of any civil action by an alien for a tort only, committed in violation of the law of nations or a treaty of the United States.'[46] The consideration that international should be interpreted 'not as it was in 1789, but as it has evolved and exists among the nations of the world today'[47] opened up the US judicial system to a wide range of extraterritorial conflicts. The US courts have for example been asked to rule on allegations of torture and rape during the war in the former Yugoslavia orchestrated by the Serbian leader Karadžić;[48] allegations of torture of prisoners in Ethiopia;[49] allegations of human rights violations committed by the former President of the Philippines during his term of office;[50] and allegations of human rights abuses committed in furtherance of a gas pipeline project in Burma.[51] The observation that '[a]s a moth is drawn to the light, so is a litigant drawn to the United States'[52] has proved particularly apposite in respect of transnational human rights litigation.[53] The US Supreme Court has admittedly—to keep with the metaphor—dimmed the light somewhat with its 2004 decision in the *Alvarez-Machain* case. It decided that the ATCA only applies to a narrow class of international norms that can be established with sufficient specifity.[54] However, with the door—as the court put it—'ajar but subject to vigilant doorkeeping'[55] the light keeps shining through.

When victims of human rights abuse abroad tried to sue foreign states under the Act they had to find a way to get round the state immunity defence. They tried—without success—to squeeze their cases in the terms of the territorial tort

[45] *Filartiga v Peña-Irala* (US, 1980).

[46] 28 USC § 1350 (1982), originally the Judiciary Act of 1789, ch. 20 § 9 (b), 1 Stat 73, 77.

[47] *Filartiga v Peña-Irala* (US, 1980) 881, citing *Ware v Hylton* 3 US 199 (US, S Ct, 1796).

[48] *Kadic v Karadžić* (US, 1995).

[49] *Abebe-Jira v Negewo* 72 F 3d 844 (US, Ct of Apps (11th Cir), 1996).

[50] eg *Hilao v Marcos* (US, 1994).

[51] *Doe v UNOCAL* 963 F Supp 880 (US, DC for the Central District of California, 1997); 110 F Supp 2d 1294 (2000); and 395 F 3d 932 (Ct of Apps (9th Cir), 2002).

[52] *Smith Kline and French Laboratories Ltd. v Bloch* [1983] 2 All ER 72 (UK, CA, 1983) 74.

[53] In 1992 the TVPA was enacted to remedy the gap left by the ATCA as regards the protection of US nationals. Section 2 of the Act provides, in part, as follows: (a) Liability—An individual who, under actual or apparent authority, or colour of law, of any foreign nation—

(1) subjects an individual to torture shall, in a civil action, be liable for damages to that individual; or
(2) subjects an individual to extrajudicial killing shall, in a civil action, be liable for damages to that individual's legal representative, or to any person who may be a claimant in an action for wrongful death.

[54] *Sosa v Alvarez-Machain* (US, 2004), cf ch 5 § 1 above.

[55] ibid 1402.

exception or the commercial act exception to state immunity,[56] but also argued on principle that there *is* no immunity for human rights violations. The arguments rely not on the substantive human rights provisions but rather on the institutional and conceptual changes in the international legal order brought about by international human rights law. Do immunity rules apply in respect of violations of *jus cogens* norms and *erga omnes* obligations?

Since the European Court of Human Rights regarded the international law character of state immunity decisive for the question of whether the right of access of court is violated the controversy between the parties focused on the requirements of international law. Al-Adsani argued that international law did not oblige the UK to grant immunity to Kuwait because the rule of state immunity is trumped by the *jus cogens* norm that prohibits torture. The Court rejected the argument. It did concede that the acts complained of in the domestic proceedings can properly be categorized as torture within the meaning of article 3 of the Convention.[57] And it moreover conceded that the right to be free from torture is a fundamental value of democratic society permitting no exception in any circumstances.[58] It concluded however that

> [n]otwithstanding the special character of the prohibition of torture in international law, the Court is unable to discern in the international instruments, judicial authorities or other materials before it any firm basis for concluding that, as a matter of international law, a State no longer enjoys immunity from civil suit in the courts of another State where acts of torture are alleged.[59]

[56] Cf for the use of the territorial tort exception in human rights cases eg C Schreuer, 'The Impact of International Institutions on the Protection of Human Rights in Domestic Courts' (1978) 4 Israel Yearbook of Human Rights 60, 61; CH Schreuer (1988) 61; A Bianchi, 'Overcoming the Hurdle of State Immunity in the Domestic Enforcement of International Human Rights' in B Conforti and F Francioni (eds), *Enforcing International Human Rights in Domestic Courts* (1997) 405, 427. The territorial tort exception is however usually of no avail because '[t]he lingering effects of a personal injury suffered overseas can not be sufficient to satisfy the direct effect requirement of the FSIA', *Princz v Federal Republic of Germany* 26 F 3d 1166 (US, Ct of Apps for the District of Columbia Circuits, 1994) 1173. Cf also a.o. *Jafari v Islamic Republic of Iran* 539 F Supp 209 (US, DC for the Northern District of Illinois, 1982); *McKeel v Islamic Republic of Iran* 722 F 2d 582 (US, Ct of Apps (9th Cir), 1983); *Persinger v Islamic Republic of Iran* 729 F 2d 835 (US, Ct of Apps for the District of Columbia Circuits 1984); *Berkovitz v Islamic Republic of Iran* 735 F 2d 329 (US, Ct of Apps (9th Cir), 1984); *Frolova v Union of Soviet Socialist Republics* 761 F 2d 360 (US, Ct of Apps (7th Cir), 1985); *Martin v Republic of South Africa* 836 F 2d 91 (US, Ct of Apps (2nd Cir), 1987); *Denegri v Republic of Chile* WL 91914 (1992) (US, DC for the District of Columbia, 1992); *Cicippio v Islamic Republic of Iran* 30 F 3d 164 (US, Ct of Apps for the District of Columbia Circuits, 1994); *Bouzari and Others v Islamic Republic of Iran* 124 ILR 428 (Canada, Ontario Superior Court of Justice, 2002), and the 2004 decision of the Court of Appeal for Ontario in that case, available at <http://www.ontariocourts.on.ca/decisions/2004/june/bouzariC3829.htm> 5.

For the commercial act exception cf eg *Nelson v Saudi Arabia* 507 US 349 (US, S Ct, 1993); *Garb v Poland* 207 F Supp 2d 16 (US, DC for the Eastern District of New York, 2002) 37; *Hwang Geum Joo v Japan* 172 F Supp 2d 52 (US, DC for the District of Columbia, 2001), affirmed Ct of Apps for the District of Columbia Circuits, 332 F 3d 679 (2003).

[57] *Al-Adsani* 290, § 58.

[58] ibid § 59.

[59] ibid 290, § 61.

The Court referred to a report of the Working Group on Jurisdictional Immunities of States and their Property of the International Law Commission that acknowledged that

> while national courts had in some cases shown some sympathy for the argument that States were not entitled to plead immunity where there had been a violation of human rights norms with the character of *jus cogens*, in most cases (including those cited by the applicant in the domestic proceedings and before the Court) the plea of sovereign immunity had succeeded.[60]

Eight of the seventeen judges dissented however on this pivotal part of the decision. They agreed with Al-Adsani that the rule of state immunity could not be invoked to avoid the consequences of the violation of the hierarchically higher rule that prohibits torture.[61]

The two perspectives approach the research question on a fundamentally different level. The argument that immunity rules do not apply when core human rights have been violated is a state of the law argument. It argues that international law does not oblige states to grant state immunity or personal immunity in such circumstances. The argument that immunity rules are incompatible with fundamental rights of individuals is a policy argument. It does not argue what the state of the law *is* but what it *should be*. This chapter sets out to examine the cogency of both state of the law and policy arguments in the debate on a human rights exception, in sections 2 and 3 respectively. The nature and the scope of the rule of state immunity and the rule of personal immunity and the nature and the scope of the rules and principles of international human rights law determine the parameters of coherent legal argument.

2 State of the Law Arguments

2.1 Introduction

Does international law oblige national courts to grant immunity to a foreign state or its officials sued in respect of allegations of serious human rights violations committed within that state's own territory, or within the territory of the forum state but in the exercise of discretionary functions or as part of an armed conflict? What is the state of international law on this question?

[60] ibid § 62, referring to the Appendix to the 1999 Report of the Working Group of the International Law Commission on Jurisdiction Immunities of States and their Property, annexed to the Report of the ILC on the work of its fifty-first session. Cf in similar vein the dissenting Supreme Court judges in the Greek case of *Prefecture of Voiotia v Federal Republic of Germany* (Greece, 2000).

[61] Cf § 2.2 below.

Two lines of inquiry must be pursued. International human rights law may have effect on the *validity* as well as the *scope* of immunity rules. The first line of inquiry examines the argument that regardless of its scope the rule of state immunity or personal immunity is invalidated by hierarchically higher *jus cogens* norms of international human rights law. State practice is not determinative on the issue since the argument operates by definition on a conceptual level. The second line of inquiry entails more difficult questions as to the epistemology of international law. Is the absence of state practice determinative on the question whether a human rights exception exists?

The second inquiry therefore compels a distinction between state immunity and personal immunity. Personal immunity rules are voluntary rules of customary international law. Coherent arguments on the scope of the rule cannot ignore a general and consistent state practice. The rationale of the rules is but the material cause of the customary practice that has formed the rule. Accordingly, the argument that a certain application of the rule is not necessary to secure the undisturbed exercise of diplomatic activities is flawed. In the absence of supporting state practice arguments in favour of a human rights exception to personal immunity rules necessarily take the form of policy arguments. Equally, the reliance on the rationale of existing exceptions to the rule only supports a change of the law; it is not determinative of change. In disregard of this contention, Gaeta reasoned that since certain exceptions to diplomatic immunity are introduced in order to avoid risking a denial of justice '[o]ne could rely upon the rationale behind this *traditional* exception to the personal immunities rules in order to establish whether there are possible exceptions to these rules in the case of international crimes'.

By reference to the denial of personal immunities to officials of a sending state that also have the nationality of the receiving state she argued that 'personal immunities should not be granted when, although the State to which the organ belongs *does have* jurisdiction over the crimes allegedly committed by that organ, nevertheless the receiving State has compelling reasons to believe either that the sending State will not prosecute the crimes...'[62] This author would not accept this argument as a state of the law argument. Rather, the risk of denial of justice forms a policy argument for change and can ultimately be the material cause of a new exception established in a general and consistent state practice—as will be further argued in section 3 of this chapter.

The rule of state immunity, however, is subject to fundamentally distinct considerations. It is undeniable that state immunity practice does not support a human rights exception. Just two national courts have ever denied a foreign state sued in respect of human rights violations committed within the context of exercising state authority under international law. The Greek Supreme Court has ordered Germany to pay damages for the human rights abuses committed

[62] P Gaeta (2002) 986–8, quotation at 987.

by German occupation troops against the civilian population of the Greek town of Distomo in 1944,[63] while the Italian Supreme Court has denied Germany immunity in respect of a claim of an Italian citizen that was forced to work in the German war industry during the second World War after being captured and deported by the German occupying forces.[64] In addition several courts in the US and the UK have expressed support for a human rights exception, but have held to be bound by the strictures of national immunity legislation.[65]

The second instance of state immunity practice that supports a human rights exception is the 1996 US Antiterrorism and Effective Death Penalty Act (AEDPA) that amended the FSIA to include an exception for certain human rights violations.[66] It provides redress for US nationals who seek money damages against a foreign state 'for personal injury or death that was caused by an act of torture, extrajudicial killing, aircraft sabotage, hostage taking, or the provision of material support or resources... for such an act if such act or provision of material support is engaged in by an official, employee, or agent of such foreign state while acting within the scope of his or her office, employment, or agency'. However, the amendment only applies to countries designated 'state sponsor of terrorism'

[63] *Prefecture of Voiotia v Federal Republic of Germany* (Greece, 2000) 202. Cf for the 1997 decision of the Court of First Instance of Leivadia, (1997) 50 Revue Hellénique De Droit International 595; and the case note by I Bantekas in (1998) 92 AJIL 765. It is noted that the decision was never executed. The Greek Minister of Justice refused to authorize the enforcement of the decision against the German state—a mandatory step in the enforcement process. An enforcement procedure before the Greek courts was nevertheless started—without success. The victims of the Distomo massacre then complained in Strasbourg that, *inter alia*, their rights under art 6.1 of the ECHR were violated On the reasoning set out in § 3.2.2.3 of this chapter the European Court of Human Rights dismissed the complaint, cf *Kalogeropoulou a.o. v Greece and Germany* (ECHR, 2002), available at <http://www.echr.coe.int>.

[64] *Ferrini v Repubblica Federale di Germania* (Italy, 2004).

[65] Cf eg *Siderman de Blake v Republic of Argentina* (US, 1992). Cf also *Controller and Auditor General v Davison* [1996] 2 NZLR 278 (New Zealand, CA of Wellington, 1996). The ICTY has hinted that state immunity may not be available in human rights cases although it did not explicitly say so and its reasoning could also be limited to cases against individual state officials. It wrote: 'a State say, taking national measures authorising or condoning torture or absolving its perpetrators through an amnesty law. If such a situation were to arise, the national measures, violating the general principle and any relevant treaty provision, would produce the legal effects discussed above and in addition would not be accorded international legal recognition. Proceedings could be initiated by potential victims if they had locus standi before a competent international or national judicial body with a view to asking it to hold the national measure to be internationally unlawful; or the victim could bring a civil suit for damage in a foreign court, which would therefore be asked inter alia to disregard the legal value of the national authorising act.' ICTY, *Prosecutor v Furundžija* (1998) § 155.

[66] § 1605 (7) FSIA. Antiterrorism and Effective Death Penalty Act, PubLNo 104–32, 110 Stat. 1214 (1996). In the past, legislative attempts to include a state-sponsored terrorist exception had been unsuccessful. S. 2465, 101st Cong, 2nd Sess (1990); HR 2357, 102nd Cong, 2nd Sess (1992); HR 934, 103rd Cong, 2nd Sess (1994); S 825, HR 2363, 103rd Cong, 1st Sess (1993). When the claims of US relatives of the victims of the bombing of Pan Am flight 103 over Lockerbie instigated in US courts against the—allegedly responsible—Libyan government were dismissed on immunity grounds the US government decided that these victims should be able to get redress in American courts.

by the State Department at the time the act occurred. Currently five states are so designated—Cuba, Iran, North Korea, Sudan, and Syria—and US courts have accepted jurisdiction over several human rights claims against these states.[67]

Reliance on the absence of state practice supporting a human rights exception does not however convincingly dispose of the question. In chapter 2 it was explained that arguments on the scope of the rule of state immunity based on reason or logic do not necessarily exceed the parameters of accepted international legal theory on custom ascertainment.[68] Accordingly, state of the law arguments on a human rights exception require discussion on their merits.

Human rights-based arguments concerning the scope of the rule of state immunity divide in two categories. It may be argued that no immunity is available for human rights violations under the traditional *acta jure gestionis—acta jure imperii* reasoning, or it may alternatively be argued that no immunity is available for human rights violations in spite of the *acta jure imperii* character of the violations.

It must, at the outset, be noted that both arguments suffer from a severe form of circularity: they contain an assumption of what is to be proved while it is exactly the question who may undertake a legal assessment of the accuracy of this assumption that divides opinion. The assertion that national courts may assess whether a foreign state has violated human rights norms whenever a foreign state has violated human rights norms is clearly unconvincing. The arguments in fact imply that states do not enjoy immunity as against an *allegation* of human rights violation. In contrast to the by now accepted exceptions to state immunity, a negative finding on the merits of a claim of *jus cogens* violations committed by a foreign state within its territorial borders necessarily entails a violation of the horizontal

[67] Cf *Alejandre v Republic of Cuba*, 996 F Supp 1239 (US, DC for the Southern District of Florida, 1997); *Flatow v Islamic Republic of Iran* (US, 1998); *Rein v Socialist People's Libyan Arab Jamahiriya*, 995 F Supp 325 (US, DC for the Eastern District of New York, 1998) and Ct of Apps 2nd Cir, 162 F 3d 748 (1998); *Cicippio v Islamic Republic of Iran*, 18 F Supp 2d 62 (US, DC for the District of Columbia, 1998); *Anderson v Islamic Republic of Iran*, 90 F Supp 2d 107 (US, DC for the District of Columbia, 2000); *Eisenfeld v Islamic Republic of Iran*, 2000 WL 1918779 (US, DC for the District of Columbia, 2000); *Daliberti v Republic of Iraq*, 97 F Supp 2d 38 (US, DC for the District of Columbia, 2000), and DC for the District of Columbia, 146 F Supp 2d 19 (2001); *Higgins v Islamic Republic of Iran*, CA No 99–377-CKK (US, DC for the District of Columbia, 2000); *Elahi v Islamic Republic of Iran*, 124 F Supp 2d 97 (US, DC for the District of Columbia, 2000); *Sutherland v Islamic Republic of Iran*, 151 F Supp 2d 27 (US, DC for the District of Columbia, 2001); *Jenco v Islamic Republic of Iran*, 154 F Supp 2d 27 (US, DC for the District of Columbia, 2001); *Cronin v Islamic Republic of Iraq*, 238 F Supp 2d 222 (US, DC for the District of Columbia, 2002); *Smith and Soulas v Islamic The Emirate of Afghanistan and Iraq* (US, 2003). Cf for overviews: SD Murphy, 'Contemporary Practice of the United States', (2001) 95 AJIL 132; WP Hoye, 'Fighting Fire with... Mire? Civil Remedies and the New War on State-Sponsored Terrorism', (2002) 12 Duke Journal of Comparative and International Law 105.

[68] See ch 2 § 3.3.2.1 above. Cf for the argument that arguments of legal logic are *not* valid and that state practice is necessary F De Vittor, 'Immunità degli Stati dalla giurisdizione e tutela dei diritti umani fondamentali', (2002) 85 RDI 573, 587.

division of competences between national courts. The problematic nature of any exception that is based on the nature of the rules violated rather than the activity complained of was recognized by Goff J in his 1975 decision in the *I Congreso del Partido* case. He rejected the suggestion that states are not immune when they have violated international law because 'the sovereign is immune from process precisely because the domestic court will not adjudicate upon his actions'.[69]

2.2 The Normative Hierarchy Theory: Voidance of the Rule of State Immunity in View of Human Rights Law?

At times we find a state of the law argument in support of a human rights exception that is based on the *validity* rather than the *scope* of the immunity rule. The normative hierarchy argument portrays the problem of immunity of states and their officials and human rights as a clash of two sets of rules. Since core human rights norms qualify as *jus cogens* while the immunity rule is only a non-peremptory norm of international law, the argument runs, the first set of rules trumps the latter. When states or state officials have violated *jus cogens* norms they can not therefore rely on state immunity to shield them from the courts.[70] The argument does not assert that the rule of state immunity and the rule of personal immunity have *changed* under influence of the *jus cogens* concept but reflects a straightforward reliance on the concept as hierarchical higher rules of international law invalidating rules that are in conflict with it.

The argument was discussed in the 1992 US case *Siderman de Blake v Republic of Argentina*.[71] The case tells the gruesome story of an Argentinean business family that suffered brutal torture, persecution, and illegal expropriation of their personal and business assets at the hands of the Argentinean government. Plaintiffs asserted that Argentina did not enjoy immunity with regard to the claim based on the torture allegations since torture qualifies as *jus cogens* under international law. Although plaintiffs argued their case under the type of reasoning set out below at the discussion of the case of *Princz v Germany* and related case law—the court restated the argument as follows:

> This argument begins from the principle that jus cogens norms 'enjoy the highest status within international law,' and thus 'prevail over and invalidate... other rules of international law in conflict with them'. The Sidermans argue that since sovereign immunity

[69] UK, Queen's Bench Division, *I Congreso del Partido* (1975–77), [1978] QB 500, 532.

[70] Eg B Conforti, (2002) 253; A (1999) 237; A Bianchi (1997) 427; M Karagiannakis, 'State Immunity and Fundamental Human Rights', (1998) 11 LJIL 9, 19; M Reimann, 'A Human Rights Exception to Sovereign Immunity: Some Thoughts on Princz *v* Federal Republic of Germany', (1995) 16 Michigan Journal of International Law 403, 421; K Bartsch and B Elberling, 'Jus Cogens vs State Immunity, Round Two, The Decision of the European Court of Human Rights in the *Kalaogeropoulou et al v Greece and Germany* (2002)' (2003) 4 German Law Journal, available at <http://www.germanlawjournal.com>; A Orakhelashvili (2006) 340ff.

[71] *Siderman de Blake v Republic of Argentina* (US, 1992).

itself is a principle of international law, it is trumped by jus cogens. In short, they argue that when a state violates jus cogens, the cloak of immunity provided by international law falls away, leaving the state amenable to suit.[72]

The court proved sympathetic to the argument, acknowledging that '[a]s a matter of international law [it] carries much force'.[73] It concluded however with regret that the FSIA did not allow it to entertain the claim.

The plaintiff in the UK case *Al-Adsani v Kuwait* similarly relied on the hierarchy of norms argument to dismiss the immunity claim of the state defendant with regard to the torture allegations at issue.[74] The Court of Appeal rejected the plaintiff's submission and refused to hear the case. The judges did not unanimously accept the *Siderman* precedent. While Stuart-Smith LJ did refer extensively to the *Siderman* decision, he implied that there was no discrepancy between the 1978 State Immunity Act and international law on this point. Ward LJ on the other hand expressed support for the principle of the normative hierarchy argument. He emphasized that his decision was based on the 'as plain as plain can be' strictures of the SIA only.[75]

Al-Adsani took his case to Strasbourg. He complained that the refusal of the UK courts to hear his case amounted to a violation of his right of access to court under article 6.1 ECHR. As will be explained in more detail in section 3.2 below the decision of the European Court of Human Rights came to pivot on the scope of the rule of state immunity under international law. Al-Adsani repeated his argument that there was no immunity under international law in respect of torture claims since the *jus cogens* norm of torture trumps the rule of state immunity.

The Court agreed with the applicant that the prohibition of torture is a peremptory norm of international law.[76] It did not however accept that *therefore* the rule of state immunity does not apply in respect of torture allegations. It considered that

> [n]otwithstanding the special character of the prohibition of torture in international law, the Court is unable to discern in the international instruments, judicial authorities or other materials before it any firm basis for concluding that, as a matter of international law, a State no longer enjoys immunity from civil suit in the courts of another State where acts of torture are alleged.[77]

In particular, it pointed out that the case should be distinguished from the *Pinochet* case because it concerned not criminal but civil liability.[78]

[72] ibid 718. Cf n 112 below for the conflation of this argument with the non-sovereign act argument.
[73] ibid.
[74] *Al-Adsani v Kuwait* 107 ILR 536 (UK, CA, 1996). Cf p 309 above for the facts of this case.
[75] ibid 549. Cf also *Jones v Saudi Arabia and Abdul Aziz* (UK, 2003), especially § 32–3.
[76] *Al-Adsani* 290–1, § 59–61.
[77] ibid 291, § 61.
[78] ibid.

The decision rested on a narrow majority. Eight of the seventeen judges did embrace the normative hierarchy argument of the applicant.[79] The dissenting opinion of Judges Rozakis and Caflisch reasoned that

> The acceptance... of the *jus cogens* nature of the prohibition of torture entails that a State allegedly violating it cannot invoke hierarchically lower rules (in this case, those on State immunity) to avoid the consequences of the illegality of its actions. In the circumstances of this case, Kuwait cannot validly hide behind the rules on State immunity to avoid proceedings for a serious claim of torture made before a foreign jurisdiction; and the courts of that jurisdiction (the United Kingdom) cannot accept a plea of immunity, or invoke it *ex officio*, to refuse an applicant adjudication of a torture case. Due to the interplay of the *jus cogens* rule on prohibition of torture and the rules on State immunity, the procedural bar of State immunity is automatically lifted, because those rules, as they conflict with a hierarchically higher rule, do not produce any legal effect. In the same vein, national law which is designed to give domestic effect to the international rules on State immunity cannot be invoked as creating a jurisdictional bar, but must be interpreted in accordance with and in the light of the imperative precepts of *jus cogens*.

The dissent moreover criticizes the distinction relied on by the majority between criminal and civil proceedings. The distinction, it was argued,

> is not consonant with the very essence of the operation of *jus cogens* rules. It is not the nature of the proceedings which determines the effects that a *jus cogens* rule has upon another rule of international law, but the character of the rule as a peremptory norm and its interaction with a hierarchically lower rule. The prohibition of torture, being a rule of *jus cogens*, acts in the international sphere and deprives the rule of sovereign immunity of all its legal effects in that sphere. The criminal or civil nature of the domestic proceedings is immaterial. The jurisdictional bar is lifted by the very interaction of the international rules involved...

The Italian Supreme Court expressed support for the arguments of the minority in the 2004 *Ferrini* case.[80] Although—as will be discussed in section 2.3.2.3 below—the court based its denial of immunity in that case primarily on a different line of argumentation.

It was already argued in the introductory chapter of this study that the arguments used by both sides of the debate fail to convince. The *form* of the argument of the court and the *substance* of the argument of the dissenters is incoherent.

The court was not asked to ascertain the scope of the rule of state immunity. Al-Adsani did not argue that the rule of state immunity had changed; he argued that the rule was void of legal effect. The invalidation of rules that are incompatible with rules of a *jus cogens* character is a conceptual process independent of

[79] Cf the dissenting opinion of Judges Rozakis and Caflisch joined by Judges Wildhaber, Costa, Cabral Barreto, and Vajic, ibid. Judge Loucaides expressed support for this dissent but preferred to base his dissent on a different ground. Judge Ferrari Bravo did not state his reasons for dissenting very clearly so only seven judges expressed express support for the argument.

[80] *Ferrini v Repubblica Federale di Germania* (Italy, 2004) § 9.1.

developments in state practice.[81] In fact, because of the conceptual nature of the argument it can equally be advanced in respect of personal immunity rules.[82] A convincing rebuttal of the argument advanced by Al-Adsani requires discussion of its merits.

The substance of the argument is however problematic. It requires sliding from the prohibition of certain conduct to a jurisdictional rule allowing enforcement of that prohibition in foreign national courts. Since it is the substantive prohibition that has *jus cogens* status rather than the tools that may be available under international law to enforce that prohibition, the two rules at issue in the *Al-Adsani* case operate on different levels. In the absence of a clash between the two sets of rules, the *jus cogens* quality of the one cannot possibly trump the other.[83] Rather than arguing that *jus cogens* norms invalidate *conflicting* rules of international law the argument implies that the violation of *jus cogens* norms renders *all* non-peremptory rules of international law void. Not only the rule of state immunity but *all* non-peremptory rules that regulate responses to violations of international law as well as the secondary rules of invocation and establishing of state responsibility would no longer apply when *jus cogens* rules are violated. The argument hence exceeds the normal operation of the *jus cogens* concept and cannot succeed on this basis.

The argument would only be coherent if the right of access to court—assuming that it applies to the facts of a case—were to be of a *jus cogens* character. It is generally agreed that it is not. We will see in section 3.2 below that the right of access *may* be violated by immunity rules. The related argument against immunity however operates on the level of policy arguments. The violation entails the responsibility of the forum state to the private individual and may be an incentive to change—it does not however affect the scope of the immunity rule by itself.[84]

It may in addition be argued—as was done in chapter 2 of this study—that the rule of state immunity as we know it today is a *jus cogens* norm *avant la lettre*.

[81] Cf in similar terms A Orakhelashvili (2006) 344.

[82] Cf also ch 5 § 2.2 above.

[83] Cf H Fox (2002) 525; A Zimmerman, 'Sovereign Immunity and Violations of International *Jus Cogens*—Some Critical Remarks' (1995) 16 Michigan Journal of International Law 433, 437; J Bröhmer (1997) 194; C Maierhöfer, 'Der EGMR als "Modernisierer" des Völkerrechts? Staatenimmunität und ius cogens auf dem Prüfstand' (2002) 29 Europäische Grundrechte Zeitschrift 391, 397; F De Vittor (2002) 589; T Giegerich, 'Do Damages Claims Arising from *Jus Cogens* Violations Override State Immunity from the Jurisdiction of Foreign Courts?' in C Tomuschat and J-M Thouvenin (eds), *The Fundamental Rules of the International Legal Order, Jus Cogens and Obliogations Erga Omnes* (2006) 203, 227. K Bartsch and B Elbering disagree. In their opinion there inheres not only a right to enforcement in international human rights law but this is right also of a *jus cogens* character if the original right is: 'Jus Cogens vs State Immunity, Round Two, The Decision of the European Court of Human Rights in the *Kalaogeropoulou et al v Greece and Germany* (2002)' (2003) 4 German Law Journal. Cf also *Jones v Saudi Arabia* (UK, 2006), § 14, § 17, § 44ff.

[84] The argument based on the right to a remedy is even weaker. Even if the right were to be of a *jus cogens* character—which it is generally agreed it is not at this moment—it will only clash with immunity rules in exceptional cases, cf § 3.3 below.

The delimitation of the essential competences of states on the basis of their sovereign independence and equality is at the basis of the international legal order. The consequence of a clash between the rule and a *jus cogens* rule is therefore not self-evident—to say the least.

2.3 The Scope of the Rule of State Immunity in View of Human Rights Law

2.3.1 A Human Rights Exception within *the Rationale of the Rule of State Immunity?*

2.3.1.1 Introduction

Many proponents of a human rights exception to state immunity have cast their arguments within the parameters of the restrictive rule of state immunity. They argue that the rationale of the rule applies poorly to human rights violations. Before it is examined whether human rights arguments may fit the *acta jure imperii—acta jure gestionis* distinction, we first examine the arguments of two scholars that have restated the parameters of the restrictive rule in distinct terms in order to subsequently develop their arguments *within* 'traditional' immunity reasoning.

2.3.1.2 Bröhmer: A proposal based on the functional sovereignty rationale

In a comprehensive study on state immunity and human rights published in 1997 the German scholar Bröhmer formulated a somewhat baffling proposal for a human rights exception to the rule of state immunity.[85] Roughly, the proposal amounts to the abolition of state immunity for isolated human rights violations while immunity for massive human rights violations is preserved. How did Bröhmer rationalize the exception, and in particular, how did he rationalize the distinction?

It is noted that Bröhmer purported to base his proposal on the normal requirements of international law in the field. It was stated at the outset that state immunity can only be justified insofar as the exercise of jurisdiction would violate the sovereignty of the foreign state. Bröhmer suggested that an examination of existing exceptions would reveal when the exercise of jurisdiction would violate foreign sovereignty and when it would not. Two criteria were identified on which existing exceptions to immunity are arguably based: the option of a state to engage in a certain act and the calculability of the state's liability risk beforehand. These criteria, he argued, should equally guide the analysis of a possible human rights exception to immunity rules and their application 'to governmental acts in violation of international human rights law does not support the view

[85] J Bröhmer (1997).

that such violations must be immunity protected'.[86] Bröhmer concluded that although it is difficult to pre-calculate precisely the liability risk of intentional torts, this is compensated by the 'option' criterion since '[v]iolations of fundamental human rights are marked by the fact that the violating state has full control over its actions.'[87]

Interestingly enough, the author then leaves the path he had set out to follow by proposing to distinguish between two types of human rights violations on the basis of their nature and the quantitative effects. The distinction between 'isolated' and 'indiscriminate' human rights violations is apparently devised to comply with a third criterion controlling exceptions to state immunity, namely the extent of interference with the functional sovereignty of foreign states. Bröhmer argued that 'individualised violations of human rights need not be immunity protected because such claims pose no real threat to the sovereignty of states whereas mass violations of human rights should remain immunity protected because of the devastating effects on the functional immunity of states and the threat to the international peace of justice which could arise from such proceedings'.[88] In the case of mass violations '[t]he sum of the individual damages will often exceed the financial capacity of states and thus jeopardise their functional sovereignty.'[89]

For borderline cases a procedure labelled as 'filing of bankruptcy' in human rights cases was introduced: if a state proves that there are too many victims and that the cumulative effect of their possible claims could imperil its functional sovereignty, immunity should be granted.[90] On the basis of this distinction Bröhmer proposed the following human rights exception to immunity:

A Foreign State shall not be immune from the jurisdiction of the forum State to adjudicate

A. If the cause of action relates to death or personal injury and the act or omission, whether governmental in nature or not, which caused the death or injury also constitutes a violation of such fundamental international human rights, which are part of the *jus cogens* body of international law, *e.g.* the prohibition of torture and extrajudicial killing, and if
    1. the act or omission of the Foreign State which caused the death or personal injury was aimed at the injured or killed individual and if
    2. the act or omission of the Foreign State that caused the death or personal injury is not in violation of other norms of international law designed to protect large groups of individuals, *e.g.* the prohibition of genocide and if

[86] ibid 204.
[87] ibid 200.
[88] ibid 211–12.
[89] ibid 205. It was moreover argued that since '[v]iolations of international law in the context of a war are by nature directed against the enemy community and not against the individual members of the community as such' claims based on such violations were by definition excluded from a human rights exception for isolated human rights violations (206).
[90] ibid 212–14.

3. the act or omission of the Foreign State which caused the death or personal injury did not occur in the context of an armed conflict between states.

B. In exceptional circumstances a Foreign State shall be immune from the jurisdiction of the forum State to adjudicate despite the applicability of section A.1. above
   1. if the Foreign State presents a prima facie case that the exercise of jurisdiction in this matter could lead to an unforeseeable number of similar claims in the forum state or other states which to settle individually could seriously interfere with the Foreign State's ability to discharge its public functions or if
   2. the Foreign State establishes to the satisfaction of the tribunal that it has submitted the matter either to a respective international institution with jurisdiction to review the allegations and provide the plaintiff with adequate compensation or to some other effective international dispute settlement mechanism.[91]

This proposal—though admittedly original—contains several flaws. Even if we accept the two criteria as premises, the internal coherency of the argument leaves something to be desired. When the criteria underlying other exceptions to immunity should equally apply to a possible human rights exception it remains unclear why the functional sovereignty of the foreign state should form an additional criterion when the latter type of exception is developed. Surely, the possibility that the failure of an economic enterprise or, for that matter, the damages awarded in US courts as regards individual human rights violations, exceed the financial capacity of a small state is not unthinkable. Moreover, the reliance on 'the functional aspect of sovereignty, i.e. the ability of states to perform their functions and pursue their objectives, which could be threatened if the financial resources of states had to be spent to cover liability claims incurred in various forums all over the world' seems to confuse immunity from jurisdiction with immunity from execution. Bröhmer did try to link the functionality test to the two criteria stating: 'The higher the liability risk, the more difficult it will be to argue that the state really *opted* to take that risk.'[92] It remains unclear, however, why a similar limitation does not apply to the commercial activity exception. More importantly, the reasoning only serves to reveal the feeble construction on which the proposal is based.

The problem with the proposal is in fact not as much its relative as its absolute incoherency. The authority for the two criteria on which the argument is based is flimsy. In fact, examination of state practice does not reveal that either of them has any bearing on the restrictive theory of immunity and an argument to the opposite would require more study to convince. Bröhmer reformulated the rationale of the state immunity rule in complete disregard of the widely accepted decisive criterion of the nature of the activity the court is asked to declare illegal. Especially the ironic solution for borderline cases where a state may be granted immunity when it proves before the court that it treated many other individuals

[91] ibid 214–15. Cf for support of the proposal J-F Flauss, 'Droit des immunités et protection internationale des droits de l'homme' (2000) 10 RSDIE 299, 312.
[92] ibid 198.

in the manner complained of by the claimant evidences that the nature of the activity engaged in by the state is not regarded relevant for the operation of the immunity rule. The horizontal division of competences between national courts precludes courts from exercising jurisdiction over foreign states when the claim is based on state authority that under international law principles a state must be able to exercise independently of and without interference by other states. The interference with sovereignty is hence measured according to the nature of the activity on which the claim is based rather than the intention with which the damage was inflicted or the scale of the damages caused. The argument that the exercise of jurisdiction over individualized human rights violations 'has no greater impact on the sovereignty of the defendant state than the exercise of jurisdiction in cases concerning commercial activities of that state'[93] negates the essence of the principle of non-interference in the exclusive competences of a foreign state. Bröhmer asserted that there is no violation of the sovereignty of a foreign state if jurisdiction is exercised over a claim against a foreign state for damages relating to injurious behaviour not occurring in interstate-armed conflict that was aimed at the claimant and that violated a norm protecting the individual rather than a group. As such, a claim for damages for torture in a foreign prison would supposedly qualify under the proposed human rights exception. Even as a claim for damages for torture by foreign government forces of opposition or union leaders. The exercise of jurisdiction by a foreign national court over such claims would however always require interference in the exercise of competences a foreign state should be able to exercise independently. The proposal here is rejected as based on a contorted concept of state immunity. Although the attempt to take the edge of the human rights exception to make it more palatable is laudable, this author remains unconvinced by the suggestion that the proposed exception stays within the parameters of the traditional immunity concept.

2.3.1.3 Caplan: A proposal based on the rationale of collective benefit of state relations

In the 2003 volume of the AJIL Caplan advanced a proposal for a human rights exception that stands out from the standard doctrinal approach.[94] Just like Bröhmer, Caplan purported to argue within the normal parameters of the rule of state immunity. And even more so than Bröhmer, Caplan proceeded from a radical rethinking of these parameters. He depicted the rule of state immunity as the product of two conflicting principles of international law—the principle of adjudicatory jurisdiction and the principle of sovereign equality. State immunity, he argued, operates as an exception to the principle of state jurisdiction. Caplan reverted to the decision of the US Supreme Court in *The Schooner Exchange* to

[93] ibid 208.

[94] LM Caplan, 'State Immunity, Human Rights and Jus Cogens: A Critique of the Normative Hierarchy Theory' (2003) 97 AJIL 741.

support his thesis.[95] It is recalled that Chief Justice Marshall stated that '[t]he jurisdiction of the nation within its own territory is necessarily exclusive and absolute' and that '[a]ll exceptions, therefore, to the full and complete power of a nation within its own territories, must be traced up to the consent of the nation itself. They can flow from no other legitimate source.' Marshall explained that states 'have consented to a relaxation in practice . . . of that absolute and complete jurisdiction within their respective territories which sovereignty confers' because their 'mutual benefit is promoted by intercourse with each other'. Or, the forum state 'is understood to waive the exercise of a part of that complete exclusive territorial jurisdiction'.

Caplan argued that state immunity 'derives from the forum state's waiver of adjudicatory jurisdiction with the aim of promoting mutually beneficial interstate relations.' He concluded that accordingly, state immunity is not 'a fundamental state right by virtue of the principle of sovereign equality' but a suspension of the 'right of adjudicatory jurisdiction as a practical courtesy to facilitate interstate relations' agreed to by the forum state as a matter of customary international law. To further support his argument Caplan relied on the *Arrest Warrant* case. He recalled that the ICJ had stated that immunity is granted to foreign ministers 'to ensure the effective performance of their functions on behalf of their respective States' and 'to protect the individual concerned against any act of authority of another State which would hinder him or her in the performance of his or her duties'.[96] Caplan considered this rationale for state immunity identified by the ICJ to be 'entirely consistent with the findings in *The Schooner Exchange*'.[97]

In addition—in what may be called an obiter consideration—Caplan stated that the restrictive state immunity theory is 'antithetical' to the fundamental right approach. If state immunity were indeed a fundamental right 'it would never be susceptible to theoretical division along public/private lines'.[98]

Having reformulated the nature of the rule of state immunity Caplan set out to determine the scope of the rule. Since the forum state has agreed to waive its adjudicatory jurisdiction in order to 'enhance, not jeopardize, relations between states'[99] it may refuse state immunity to foreign state activity that fails to promote 'mutual benefit' among nations. Caplan argued that 'international law requires state immunity only as to state activity that collectively benefits the community of nations'.[100] He concluded that 'conduct of a foreign state that does not conform with the development of beneficial interstate relations falls outside the state immunity "agreement" and thus is not immune by virtue of international

[95] *The Schooner Exchange v M'Faddon* (US, 1812), cf ch 2 § 2.2.3.1 above.

[96] *Arrest Warrant of 11 April 2000* (ICJ, 2002) (further referred to as *Arrest Warrant* Case) 21 and 22, § 53 and § 54.

[97] LM Caplan (2003) 758–9.

[98] ibid 754.

[99] ibid 744.

[100] ibid 744.

custom'.[101] Especially conduct that harms the interests of the forum state—like human rights abuses against its nationals—should be seen to fail this standard. In sum, Caplan reformulated the basic test for distinguishing between immune and non-immune transactions. This test, he argued, 'should not be whether the state conduct is public or private, as the theory of restrictive immunity requires, but whether such conduct would substantially harm the vital interests of the forum state.'[102]

The theory of Caplan epitomizes the consequences of the failure to distinguish voluntary and necessary immunity rules as anticipated in chapter 2 of this study. The fundamental right theory and the exception to adjudicatory jurisdiction theory are complementary rather than mutually exclusive theories. Caplan described the theory as it applies to voluntary immunity rules. The reasoning of Chief Justice Marshall is not however, as Caplan argued, equally applicable when a foreign state is sued in national proceedings for alleged human rights abuses outside the forum state.[103] The immunity for *acta jure imperii* does not clash with the adjudicatory jurisdiction of the forum state because the essential competence of states—and hence the jurisdiction of their courts—is inherently limited by the sovereignty of other states. These two types of immunity rules coincide with the two theories and exist alongside each other—as was so aptly described by Anzilotti.[104] Chapter 2 warned that the terminology used to formulate the restrictive state immunity theory may induce conflation of two distinct concepts. And in fact, Caplan relied on the statements of distinguished scholars that state immunity is the exception rather than the rule to come to the conclusion that '[a]s a logical matter, a foreign state cannot be entitled to immunity without the prior existence of a jurisdictional anchor to establish the court's competence.'[105] The argument that state immunity from jurisdiction presupposes the existence of jurisdiction is hence based on terminology rather than on substance.

Modern state immunity law consists almost entirely of the necessary state immunity concept. The diplomatic immunity of certain foreign office holders that was at issue in the *Arrest Warrant* case can in no way be likened to the immunity of foreign states and Caplan's reliance on that case is totally out of place. The theory advanced by Caplan is hence based on a misconception of the nature and scope of the law of state immunity.[106]

[101] ibid 777.

[102] ibid 777.

[103] ibid 747.

[104] Cf for the full argument ch 2 § 2.3.2 above. § 3.2 of that chapter rebuts the argument that a fundamental right theory can only explain an *absolute* approach to state immunity.

[105] LM Caplan (2003) 754–7, quotation at 754.

[106] It can moreover be questioned whether the argument is convincing when Caplan's parameters *are* accepted. In the first place it is not entirely clear how Caplan imagined his argument to work in light of accepted principles of custom ascertainment. At 759 he hints at the argument that only state practice that reflects the rationale is supported by *opinio juris*. This is not immediately convincing since states have indicated quite clearly that they feel obliged to grant immunity in respect of *acta jure imperii*. Secondly, the argument slides from 'immunity necessary to promote

2.3.1.4 A proposal based on the *acta jure imperii–acta jure gestionis* distinction

Most proponents of a human rights exception to the state immunity rule do cast their arguments in terms of the traditional distinction between *acta jure gestionis* and *acta jure imperii*. To test the coherency of the arguments we must examine whether their reasoning properly reflects the rationale of state immunity underlying this distinction.

Proponents of the human rights exception usually tout the argument that acts violating *jus cogens* norms cannot qualify as sovereign acts under the restrictive state immunity rule. It is asserted that '[t]he existence of a system of rules that states may not violate implies that when a state acts in violation of such a rule, the act is not recognized as a sovereign act. When a state act is no longer recognized as sovereign, the state is no longer entitled to invoke the defense of sovereign immunity.'[107] Since '[t]he international community would not respect a state's sovereign independence as the source of a right to harm its citizens in terrible ways' and 'states, too, are clearly prohibited from extreme human rights violations and cannot claim that such behaviour falls within its sovereign domain' it is submitted that 'the reasons for sovereign immunity apply poorly to the case of extreme human rights violations'.[108] Whatever the exact formulation, the gist of the argument is that acts grossly violating core human rights norms are never performed under sovereign authority because states *have* no authority to violate these norms and that consequently these violations are not sovereign acts. A related argument is that since 'immunity is granted in part in order to avoid the possibility that the courts of one state will interfere with the affairs of another' and human rights protection 'is no longer a purely internal matter of any individual

mutual beneficial interstate relations' to 'acts necessary to promote mutual beneficial interstate relations.'

[107] AC Belsky et al, 'Implied Waiver under the FSIA: A Proposed Exception to Immunity for Violations of Peremptory Norms of International Law' (1989) 77 California Law Review 365, 394. Cf for similar arguments eg: A Bianchi (1999) 262; P Lieberman, 'Expropriation, Torture, and Jus Cogens under the Foreign Sovereign Immunities Act: Siderman de Blake v. Republic of Argentina' (1993) 24 University of Miami Inter-American Law Review 503, 535; S Mathew, Princz v. Federal Republic of Germany: A Violation of Customary International Law' (1995) 16 Whittier Law Review 911, 933; JA Gergen, 'Human Rights and the Foreign Sovereign Immunities Act' (1996) 36 VJIL 765, 783; SA Richmann, 'Siderman de Blake v. Republic of Argentina: Can the FSIA Grant Immunity for Violations of Jus Cogens Norms?' (1993) 19 Brooklyn Journal of International Law 967, 979; A Orakhelashvili (2006) 325. Paust was the first to develop this type of argument but he extended his reasoning to *all* violations of international law: JJ Paust, 'Federal Jurisdiction Over Extraterritorial Acts of Terrorism and Nonimmunity for Foreign Violators of International Law under the FSIA' (1983) 23 VJIL 191; JJ Paust, 'Draft Brief Concerning Claims to Foreign Sovereign Immunity and Human Rights: Nonimmunity for Violations of International Law Under the FSIA' (1985) 8 Houston Journal of International Law 49.

[108] HM Osofsky, 'Foreign Sovereign Immunity from Severe Human Rights Violations: New Directions for Common Law Based Approaches' (1998) 11 New York International Law Review 35, 52. Cf in a similar sense Redress, *Immunity v. Accountability, Considering the Relationship between State Immunity and Accountability for Torture and Other Serious International Crimes* (2005) 46–51.

state but recognized today as a concern of the community of all nations', the exercise of jurisdiction over foreign states that have allegedly violated human rights within their territory does not violate the sovereignty of foreign states.[109]

The US courts have expressed some sympathy for the argument. In *Siderman de Blake v Republic of Argentina* the plaintiffs argued that Argentina could not rely on the FSIA in respect of the torture allegations since no state immunity could be available for acts that violate human rights norms that qualify as *jus cogens*. The court agreed that

> [i]nternational law does not recognize an act that violates jus cogens as a sovereign act. A state's violation of the jus cogens norm prohibiting official torture therefore would not be entitled to the immunity afforded by international law.[110]

It felt, however, constrained to decide the case on national law rather than international law considerations. In *Argentine Republic v Amerada Hess Shipping Corporation* the Supreme Court had rejected the argument that there is an exception to state immunity for violations of international law. It emphasized that the FSIA provides 'the sole basis for obtaining jurisdiction over a foreign state in our courts'.[111] Accordingly, the court in the *Siderman* case considered:

> Unfortunately, we do not write on a clean slate. We deal not only with customary international law, but with an affirmative Act of Congress, the FSIA. We must interpret the FSIA through the prism of Amerada Hess. Nothing in the text or legislative history of the FSIA explicitly addresses the effect violations of jus cogens might have on the FSIA's cloak of immunity.
>
> ...
>
> In Amerada Hess, the Court had no occasion to consider acts of torture or other violations of the peremptory norms of international law, and such violations admittedly differ in kind from transgressions of jus dispositivum, the norms derived from international agreements or customary international law with which the Amerada Hess Court dealt. However, the Court was so emphatic in its pronouncement 'that immunity is granted in those cases involving alleged violations of international law that do not come within one of the FSIA's exceptions,'...and so specific in its formulation and method of approach...that we conclude that if violations of jus cogens committed outside the United States are to be exceptions to immunity, Congress must make them so. The

[109] M Reimann (1995) 422. It should be noted that Reimann limited his proposal to claims of nationals of the forum state. Cf also M Karagiannakis (1998) 21; J-F Flauss, 'Droit des immunités et protection internationale des droits de l'homme' (2000) 10 RSDIE 299, 308.

[110] *Siderman de Blake v Republic of Argentina* (US, 1992) 718.

[111] *Argentine Republic v Amerada Hess Shipping Corporation* 488 US 428 (US, S Ct, 1989) 434. The Court of Appeals 2nd Circuit had accepted the argument: *Amerada Hess Shipping Corporation v Argentine Republic* 830 F 2d 421 (1987) 425. Cf also *Von Dardel v Union of Soviet Socialist Republics* 623 F Supp 246 (US, DC for the District of Columbia, 1985) 254, overturned after the decision of the Supreme Court: *Von Dardel v USSR* (II) 736 F Supp 1 (US, DC for the District of Columbia, 1990).

fact that there has been a violation of jus cogens does not confer jurisdiction under the FSIA.[112]

In 1989 Belsky had argued that since under international law *jus cogens* violations are not recognized as sovereign acts, US courts should interpret a *jus cogens* violation as an implied waiver of state immunity under section 1605(a)(1) FSIA.[113] This reasoning squeezes the *jus cogens* argument to fit the strictures of the FSIA. Hugo Princz, a US national who became a victim of Nazi Germany, put the reasoning to the test in the case of *Princz v Federal Republic of Germany*.[114] The argument that Germany had impliedly waived its immunity when it violated *jus cogens* norms however was rejected by the court. It held the *jus cogens* theory of implied waiver to be incompatible with the 'intentionality requirement implicit in § 1605(a)(1)'. It insisted that '[a]n implied waiver depends upon the foreign government's having at some point indicated its amenability to suit.'[115]

Judge Wald dissented. She argued that under international law there is no state immunity for human rights violation—'when a state thumbs its nose at [a *jus cogens* norm] ... [it] cannot be performing a sovereign act entitled to immunity'. Under reference to the *Charming Betsy* doctrine she concluded that '[t]he only way to reconcile the FSIA's presumption of foreign sovereign immunity with international law is to interpret sec. 1605(a)(1) of the Act as encompassing the principle that a foreign state implicitly waives its right to sovereign immunity in United States courts by violating jus cogens norms.'[116]

In subsequent cases plaintiffs have stubbornly relied on the implied waiver provision, arguing that the majority opinion in *Princz* is no (longer) good law and

[112] *Siderman de Blake v Republic of Argentina* (US, 1992) 718–9, referring to *Argentine Republic v Amerada Hess Shipping Corporation* (US, 1989) 436 and 439. It is noted that the court in this case—as in fact several courts in later cases—conflates two arguments. On the one hand it said that the argument of the plaintiffs was that violations of *jus cogens* norms do not qualify as sovereign acts, on the other it said that the plaintiffs argued that *jus cogens* norms *trumped* the rule of state immunity, cf § 2.2 above. Caplan has argued that the two arguments are 'nearly identical in concept' LM Caplan (2003) 768. This author disagrees. If human rights violations do not qualify as sovereign acts then there *is* no state immunity and hence no rule to be trumped

[113] AC Belsky et al (1989) 365. Cf for support of this construction eg S Mathew (1995) 931; J Rabkin, 'Universal Justice: The Role of Federal Courts in International Civil Litigation', (1995) 95 CLR 2120; P Lieberman (1993); SA Richmann, (1993) 978; WF Pepper, 'Iraq's Crimes of State against Individuals, and Sovereign Immunity' (1992) 18 Brooklyn Journal of International Law 313, 369. The implied waiver argument is not in itself a substantive argument against state immunity when human rights are violated but is rather an instrument that enables the development of arguments in favour of a human rights exception within the strictures of the national legislation. Cf differently eg J Bröhmer (1997) 190.

[114] *Princz v Federal Republic of Germany* (US, 1994). It is noted that the Siderman's *had* in fact already argued in this vein (Brief for Appellant 35–42, *Siderman de Blake v Argentina* (US, 1992). The court however interpreted the argument differently.

[115] *Princz v Federal Republic of Germany* (US, 1994) 1174. Cf on the narrow scope of the implied waiver provision also *Frolova v Union of Soviet Socialist Republics* (US, 1985) 377.

[116] ibid 1182–3 (Wald J, dissenting). Cf *Murray v The Schooner Charming Betsy* 6 US (2 Cranch) 64 (US, S Ct, 1804) 118: 'an act of Congress ought never to be construed to violate the law of nations if any other possible construction remains'.

that the reasoning of Judge Wald's dissent should be adopted instead. While the courts have consistently held that 1605(a)(1) FSIA cannot be relied on as a tool to interpret the FSIA in accordance with changing international state immunity law,[117] they have at times repeated the concern of the *Siderman* court that the FSIA may not be in conformance with international law on this point. In *Smith v Socialist People's Libyan Arab Jamahiriya* the court considered that Belsky developed the *jus cogens* argument 'persuasively' and held that '[t]he contention that a foreign state should be deemed to have forfeited its sovereign immunity whenever it engages in conduct that violates fundamental humanitarian standards is an appealing one.' The court shielded behind the strictures of the FSIA to explain the grant of state immunity to states that allegedly violated *jus cogens* norms. 'The issue we face', it held, 'is not whether an implied waiver derived from a nation's existence is a good idea, but whether an implied waiver of that sort is what Congress contemplated by its use of the phrase "waive[r] ... by implication" in section 1605(a)(1) of the FSIA.'[118]

The deduction of waiver from the violation of *jus cogens* norms clearly stretches the principle too far. In fact, the argument does not even pretend that a violating state has the intention to waive immunity, but is rather of a conceptual nature, relying on a consequence allegedly inherent in the concept of *jus cogens.* Many scholars acknowledged the uncomfortable fit of the implied waiver exception to the *jus cogens* argument. As Reimann argued, the problem with the decision in *Princz* is not that it is *wrong* but that it is *right*.[119] Several scholars have therefore proposed to include a new exception to the FSIA tailored to grant US courts jurisdiction over *jus cogens* violations of foreign states.[120]

The argument that acts that violate *jus cogens* norms do not qualify as sovereign acts was relied on by the lower court in the Greek case *Prefecture of Voiotia v Federal Republic of Germany*.[121] The court ordered Germany to pay damages of approximately 30 million dollars for the atrocities committed by the German

[117] The exact reasoning does differ somewhat from case to case, cf eg *Denegri v Republic of Chile* (US, 1992); *Smith v Socialist People's Libyan Arab Jamahiriya* 101 F 3d 239 (US, Ct of Apps (2nd Cir), 1996); *Cabiri v Government of the Republic of Ghana* 165 F 3d 193 (US, Ct of Apps (2nd Cir), 1999); *Sampson v Federal Republic of Germany* 250 F 3d 1145 (US, Ct of Apps (7th Cir), 2001); *Hwang Geum Joo v Japan* (US, 2001), affirmed by the Court of Appeals for the District of Columbia Circuit (2003); *Garb v Poland* (US, 2002) 37.

[118] *Smith v Socialist People's Libyan Arab Jamahiriya* (US, 1996). Cf *Sampson v Federal Republic of Germany* (also US, 2001) 1156.

[119] M Reimann (1995) 417.

[120] Cf eg J Jacobson, 'Trying to Fit a Square Peg into a Round Hole: The Foreign Sovereign Immunities Act and Human Rights Violations' (1998) 19 Whittier Law Review 757; JA Gergen, (1996); HM Osofsky (1998); M Reimann, ibid; GM Ziman, 'Holding Foreign Governments Accountable for Their Human Rights Abuses: A Proposed Amendment to the Foreign Sovereign Immunities Act of'1976' (1999) 21 Loyola of Los Angeles International and Comparative Law Journal 185.

[121] *Prefecture of Voiotia v Federal Republic of Germany* (1997) 50 Revue Hellénique De Droit International 595 (Greece, Court of First Instance Leivadia, 1997). Cf also I Bantekas, (1998) 92 AJIL 765, 766 and 767.

occupation forces against the people of the Greek village Distomo on 10 June 1940. That day German forces killed over 200 civilians and destroyed civilian property as retaliation for actions of Greek partisan fighters. The court further supported its decision arguing that Germany had impliedly waived its immunity when it violated *jus cogens* norms. It is noted that such an argument is even less convincing in a national legal system where there *is* no immunity in respect of non-sovereign acts. In the absence of national legislation with a limitative list of exceptions the implied waiver argument is not only unsound, but also unnecessary since a non-existing immunity does not need to be waived.

In appeal the Supreme Court confirmed the argument albeit with a possibly qualifying twist. The Supreme Court emphasized that Germany had acted on Greek territory. Referring to the US *Letelier* case it argued that the territorial tort exception to state immunity applied independent of the *jure gestionis* or *jure imperii* character of an act. It then argued that the exception to the territorial tort exception for acts of foreign armed forces does not apply to acts that are directed to the civilian population and are not related to the interstate armed conflict. In particular, the court argued, the exception does not apply to acts of an occupation force that constitute an abuse of sovereign power like the murders committed in the village of Distomo. In conclusion it confirmed the conclusion of the lower court that the acts of the German forces were not of a *jure imperii* character since they violated peremptory norms of international law. It also confirmed the argument of the lower court that the violation of *jus cogens* norms constitutes an implied waiver of immunity. The decision of the Supreme Court reasons in two minds. Why did the court think it necessary to argue along the lines of the territorial tort exception if it agreed with the lower court that a violation of *jus cogens* is never a *jure imperii* act? The decision could be interpreted as limiting the *jus cogens* argument to acts performed on the territory of the forum state.

It must, at this point, moreover be noted that two subsequent Greek decisions qualify the *Voiotia* decision. In the first place did a 2002 decision of the Greek Supreme Court distinguish immunity from jurisdiction from immunity from execution. The court refused to allow execution of the decision of the lower court.[122] More importantly, the court referred a subsequent case dealing with the question of immunity from jurisdiction in case of allegations of *jus cogens* violations to the special Supreme Court dealing with questions of interpretation of international law (the *Anotato Eidiko Dikasterio*). That court—albeit with only a slight majority—did not agree with the decision of the Supreme Court in

[122] *Judgments nos 36/2002 and 37/2002* (Greece, S Ct, 2002). Applicants complained in Strasbourg that this decision violated their right of access to court under art 6.1 of the ECHR: *Kalogeropoulou et al v Greece and Germany* (ECHR, 2002), available at <http://www.echr.coe.int>. This argument was rejected by the European Court of Human Rights on the basis of the reasoning set out in § 3 of this chapter.

Prefecture of Voiotia v Federal Republic of Germany. It held that foreign states are immune in all proceedings concerning acts of its armed forces.[123]

So how does the argument fare in light of the findings of chapter 2 of this study? That chapter analysed the rule of state immunity in order to identify the parameters of coherent legal argument on the scope of the rule. It was explained that the *acta jure imperii–acta jure gestionis* distinction secures the independent exercise of exclusive competences that a state has with regard to its territory as part of the essence of statehood. If a state could extend its adjudicative jurisdiction over another state's exercise of police powers—or the collecting of taxes, law-making or administering of justice for that matter—declaring the foreign state's activity legal or illegal or ordering the foreign state to do or refrain from doing something in its regard, this would infringe the independence of a foreign state. The notion 'sovereign act' as operative in the field of state immunity is thus essentially neutral—not normative. The argument that *jus cogens* violations do not qualify as sovereign acts targets the law of state immunity from a mistaken perspective on the role of sovereignty within that law. A blinkered focus on the nature of the act as the controlling principle, detached from the rationale underlying the *jure imperii–jure gestionis* distinction, fails to provide a convincing basis of argument.[124]

At first blush, the argument that exercise of jurisdiction over *jus cogens* violations of foreign states within their own territory does not interfere with the sovereignty of that state because such violations are today no longer a purely internal matter but recognized as a concern of the community of nations may seem to escape this criticism. The argument is admittedly more sophisticated in its reliance on the rationale of the rule of state immunity rather than on the sovereign–non sovereign act mantra. It suffers however from the same defect since it confuses the principle of non-interference with the principle of domestic jurisdiction. Foreign states enjoy immunity in cases regarding the exercise of sovereign powers *not* because that state is free to do what it pleases within its borders, but because the exercise of foreign judicial authority over sovereign activity would interfere with the independent exercise of exclusive state authority.

Both arguments moralize the concept of sovereignty. This may be seen to form part of a larger movement that sets out to counter what in turn may be

[123] *Judgment no 6/2002* (Greece, Special S Ct, 2002), discussed in M Panezi, 'Sovereign Immunity and Violations of *Jus Cogens* Norms' (2003) 56 Revue Hellénique de Droit International 199.

[124] Another example of such focus can be found in R Higgins, 'The Role of Domestic Courts in the Enforcement of International Human Rights: The United Kingdom' in B. Conforti and F Francioni (eds), *Enforcing Human Rights in Domestic Courts* (1997) 37, 53. The author asserted that torture could not be entered into in the exercise of sovereign authority 'because acts in the exercise of sovereign authority (*acta iure imperii*) are those which can only be performed by states, but not by private persons. Property deprivation might fall in this category; torture would not.' This argumentation not only severs the rationale of the rule from its formulation but moreover relies on the test developed to give expression to this formulation within the domestic legal order, severing the two concepts even further.

called the 'immoralization' of sovereignty that characterized nineteenth-century international legal theory. One notable critic of typical nineteenth-century sovereignty thinking was Brierly. He argued that the concept of sovereignty had gradually been distorted 'into a principle of international disorder' and was used 'to prove that by their very nature states are above the law'.[125] He cautioned that 'sovereignty is one of those concepts [that] become our tyrants rather than our servants when they are treated as real existences and developed with disregard of their consequences to the limit of their logic'[126] and considered that 'the outworn theories of sovereignty have become anachronisms in the modern world'.[127] Now that the concept is freed from many archaic shackles, it seems that the opposite danger looms. It is not uncommon to find academics proclaiming 'the end of sovereignty' and the words of the ICTY that '[i]t would be a travesty of law and a betrayal of the universal need for justice, should the concept of State sovereignty be allowed to be raised successfully against human rights'[128] are eagerly quoted in support of a diversity of ambitious proposals in the field of human rights law. A brief examination of this phenomenon serves a better understanding of the reasoning of proponents. Clearly, this is not the place—nor is this author qualified—to engage in a historical and philosophical debate on the controversial notion of sovereignty. As 'it is doubtful whether any single word has ever caused so much intellectual confusion' a modest approach is preferred.[129] The objective is to establish that the concept of external sovereignty underlying the horizontal division of competences is essentially unrelated to the concepts of *jus cogens* norms and domestic jurisdiction.

When Bodin wrote in his famous *Les Six Livres de la Republique* that sovereignty 'est la puissance absolue et perpétuelle d'une République' his perspective on the state was essentially internal.[130] The question how the sovereignty of a state related to the sovereignty of other states was not regarded. When later Hobbes gave the sovereign his radical absolutist traits writing that 'it appeareth plainly... that the sovereign power... is as great as possibly men can be imagined to make it' he was similarly concerned with the relation between the sovereign and his people only.[131] It is also in this internal perspective that we should see the theory of sovereignty of the people, as developed for example by Locke and Rousseau. Hobbes did consider the consequence of distinct sovereignties

[125] JL Brierly, *The Law of Nations, An Introduction to the International Law of Peace* (H Waldock (ed) 6th edn 1963) 10.

[126] JL Brierly, 'The Sovereign State Today' in H Lauterpacht and CHM Waldock (eds), *The Basis of Obligation in International Law, and Other Papers by the late James Lesly Brierly* (1958) 348, 349.

[127] JL Brierly, 'International Law: Some Conditions of Its Progress' in H Lauterpacht and CHM Waldock (1958), ibid 327, 328.

[128] *Prosecutor v Tadić* (ICTY, 1995) § 58.

[129] P Malanczuk (ed), *Akehurst's Modern Introduction to International Law* (7th edn, 1997) 17.

[130] J Bodin, *Les Six Livres de la République* (1576) first book, chapter VIII.

[131] T Hobbes, *Leviathan* (1651), chapter XX. Bodin qualified his definition of sovereignty, asserting that all power is subject 'aux loix de Dieu, et de nature, et à plusieurs loix humaines communes à tous peuples.' ibid.

occupying different parts of the world—albeit in a realist vein, rather than one of legal theory. He wrote that

kings and persons of sovereign authority, because of their independence, are in continual jealousies, and in the state and posture of gladiators having their weapons pointing and their eyes fixed on one another; that is, their forts, and garrisons, and guns upon the frontiers of their kingdoms, and continual spies upon their neighbours; which is a posture of war.[132]

It is exactly the wish to transform this state of nature in a less antagonistic situation of co-existence of independent states that underlies the contemporary international legal order. It has been argued that since '[t]he notion at the root of sovereignty is superiority' the term is ill-fitted to describe the state in its relations with other states.[133] However, external sovereignty as a concept of international law does not regard absolutist power of states in the international legal order. It is but the other side of the medal of internal sovereignty when recognized by other states. In fact, it is a necessary incident of the co-existence of and cooperation between territorial sovereign states *on a basis of juridical equality rather than on a basis of superiority.* The notion external sovereignty serves to secure the independent exercise of the competences attributed to the state under international law and guarantees states the right to respect for one's statehood. Judge Alvarez famously wrote in the *Corfu Channel* case that

[b]y sovereignty, we understand the whole body of rules and attributes which a State possesses in its territory, to the exclusion of all other States, and also in its relation with other States.[134]

However, it may be more instructive to say that international law recognizes a bundle of competences that all states possess—including a body of exclusive territorial competences—and that the notion of sovereignty serves to establish that states have the right to exercise these competences independently and on a basis of equality with other states. As Judge Huber explained in the *Island of Palmas* case:

Sovereignty in the relations between States signifies independence. Independence in regard to a portion of the globe is the right to exercise therein, to the exclusion of any other State, the functions of a State.[135]

[132] T Hobbes (1651) chapter VIII.

[133] JL Brierly, 'The Shortcomings of International Law' (1924) 5 BYIL 4, 12. Cf also L Henkin, 'The Mythology of Sovereignty' in RSJ MacDonald (ed), *Essays in honour of Wang Tieya* (1994) 351, 352.

[134] *Corfu Channel Case* (ICJ, 1949), Individual Opinion Judge Alvarez 39, 43.

[135] *Island of Palmas Case* (PCA, 1928) 838. Crawford used a combination of the two definitions: '[i]n its most common modern usage, sovereignty is the term for the "totality of international rights and duties recognized by international law" as residing in an independent territorial unit—the State', J Crawford, *The Creation of States in International Law* (1979) 26 quoting the *Reparation of Injuries Case.*

It was argued in chapter 2 that several necessary principles inhere in the premise of an international community based on the independence and equality of states. In fact, the principle that '[e]very State has the right to independence and hence to exercise freely, without dictation by any other State, all its legal powers, including the choice of its own form of government' is clearly mirrored in the principle that '[e]very State has the duty to refrain from intervention in the internal or external affairs of any other State'.[136] This principle of non-intervention underlies the limit on the judicial competence of states with regard to the exercise of exclusive competences by other states. Another principle that logically follows from the independence and equality of states is that the creation of obligations under international law in principal depends on the consent of the obligor. This principle applies to both primary and secondary norms and equally underlies the international dispute settlement rule.

In the nineteenth century the principal objective of states was to regulate their interstate relations and develop some rules in fields where their claims to sovereignty risked collision. The reality of co-existing antagonistic territorial sovereign states inspired the development of the law of diplomatic relations, the law of treaties, the law of the sea and war law. All that was not regulated by international law remained in the domestic jurisdiction of states. At this stage of the development of international law it was undisputed that international law was unconcerned with a state's treatment of its own nationals. As Brierly noted in 1925:

> Australian immigration is a matter of domestic jurisdiction, but so too were the Armenian massacres.[137]

Things have clearly changed. The experience of the world wars made states aware of the existence of common interests that cannot be achieved or protected unilaterally but only through multilateral co-operation. The cooperation between states in the realization of common interests required the establishment of multilateral forums to discuss these interests, and multilateral institutions to effectively enforce the obligations undertaken. The protection of human rights is the single most important example of such a common interest and today an extensive body of international human rights law with control and enforcement mechanisms exists. No state may claim that the massacre of nationals within its territory is a matter outside the reach of international law and essentially within its domestic jurisdiction.

The consideration of the PCIJ in *Nationality Decrees issued in Tunis and Morocco* that '[t]he question whether a certain matter is or is not solely within the jurisdiction of a state is an essentially relative question; it depends upon

[136] Arts 1 and 3 of the 1949 ILC Draft Declaration on Rights and Duties of States, YBILC 1949 286, 287.
[137] JL Brierly (1925) 18.

the development of international relations'[138] evinces the relative nature of the concept of domestic jurisdiction. Though the reluctance of states to regulate behaviour within national borders on the international level may be prompted by the wish to exercise sovereign powers as they see fit; in theory there is no difference between opposition to the development of international human rights law and opposition to, for example, the development of a regime of the high seas. The relation between the principle of domestic jurisdiction and the principle of external sovereignty is hence that the latter gives states—in principle—control over the scope of the former.

In the common perception the relation has however become less relative. The idea that sovereignty is 'the right of a State to pursue whatever policies it wishes within its own borders'[139] is persistent. As a logical consequence the development of international human rights norms is often seen as limiting the sovereignty of states. Higgins for example considered that '[s]overeignty... is the entitlement of a state to act as it wished at the international level—the ability to resist intervention from the international community... Sovereignty is a relative concept in international affairs that changes through time, and it has become commonplace to say that there has been tremendous erosion in the concept of sovereignty, relating particularly to the areas of human rights and now possibly humanitarian intervention.'[140] In a similar vein another scholar compared the modern concept of sovereignty to Swiss cheese 'with holes in it of different shapes and locations. These holes represent elements that have been extracted from a state's sovereignty... The various holes correspond to the commitment for example, to human rights, disarmament, population, environment, and the like.'[141] Thus, sovereignty acquires a normative quality.

This line of reasoning is troublesome. Brierly aptly remarked that the word sovereignty 'is often used as though it means freedom from restraint whatsoever' but that in fact '"independent" does not mean freedom from law, but merely freedom from control by other states'.[142] Article 14 of the Draft Declaration on the

[138] *Nationality Decrees issued in Tunis and Morocco* Advisory Opinion PCIJ Series B No 4 (1923) 23.

[139] Quoted in JD Van der Vyver, 'Sovereignty and Human Rights in Constitutional and International Law' (1991) 5 Emory International Law Review 321, 393.

[140] American Society of International Law, 'The Transformation of Sovereignty, Theme Panel IV: The End of Sovereignty? Remark by R Higgins' (1994) 88 ASIL Proceedings 71, 73–4. Cf also *Prosecutor v Tadić* (ICTY, 1995) § 55: 'Dating back to a period when sovereignty stood as a sacrosanct and unassailable attribute of statehood, this concept recently has suffered progressive erosion at the hands of the more liberal forces at work in the democratic societies, particularly in the field of human rights'; A Cassese, *International Law in a Divided World* (1986) 148: international human rights law may seem to be 'competing—if not at loggerheads—with the traditional principles of respect for sovereign Equality of States and non-interference...'.

[141] American Society of International Law, 'The Transformation of Sovereignty, Theme Panel III: Multiple Tiers of Sovereignty: The Future of International Governance, Remarks by RS Lee' (1994) 88 ASIL Proceedings 51, 52.

[142] JL Brierly, *The Law of Nations, An Introduction to the International Law of Peace* (H Waldock (ed) 6th edn 1963) 130.

Rights and Duties of States provides that '[e]very state has the duty to conduct its relations with other states in accordance with international law and with the principle that the sovereignty of each state is subject to international law.' The widespread notion that 'sovereignty is limited by the rules of international law'[143] disregards that this limited meaning is in fact *inherent* in the concept of external sovereignty. International legal obligations do not limit the sovereignty of states; they limit the exercise of sovereign rights. As the PCIJ remarked in the *SS Wimbledon* case: 'conventions place [...] a restriction upon the exercise of the sovereign rights of the State, in the sense that it requires them to be exercised in a certain way'. The decision to thus limit a state's freedom however can only be taken by the state itself. As the Court pointed out, 'the right of entering into international engagements is an attribute of state sovereignty'.[144] In his separate opinion in the *German Customs Regime* case Judge Anzilotti explained that '[i]ndependence... is really no more than the normal condition of States according to international law; it may also be described as *sovereignty (suprema potestas)* or *external sovereignty*, by which is meant that the State has over it no other authority than that of international law.'[145]

The Armenian massacres were indeed in the domestic jurisdiction of Turkey. Any attempt to call that state to account on the international level would have infringed Turkish sovereignty because in fact states had not yet agreed on the formulation of international principles and procedures applicable to the situation. The statement, that international scrutiny of states' conduct vis-à-vis their own citizens was precluded by the doctrine of domestic jurisdiction, hence confuses cause and consequence: scrutiny was not precluded by the doctrine of domestic jurisdiction but by the unwillingness of states to extend international law to these matters.[146] The comment that what began 'as an attempt to guarantee freedom from foreign oppression is perverted into a veil to be drawn over domestic oppression' is undeniably correct.[147] However, it should be realized that this bitter taste of immorality attached to sovereignty is an essentially relative fact. The development of international human rights standards and international organs entrusted with supervisory and enforcement powers has taken place within the original parameters of external sovereignty of states.

The concept of sovereignty protected by—or structurally underlying—the international law rule of state immunity concerns the exclusive competence of states within their territory rather than non-accountability with regard to the exercise of this jurisdiction. Hence, the horizontal division of competences

143 JD Van der Vyver (1991) 421.

144 *Case of the SS 'Wimbledon'* PCIJ Series A no 1 1923) 25.

145 *Customs Régime between Germany and Austria (Protocol of March 19th, 1931)* (Advisory Opinion) PCIJ Series A/B no 41 (1931) 37, Individual Opinion Judge Anzilotti 55, 57.

146 Cf for the former statement eg A Bianchi (1997) 405.

147 AV Lowe, 'Peace without Justice; Reconsidering the Law on the Use of Force' in *Perestroika and International Law* (WE Butler (ed) 1990) 281, 284.

between national courts is in principle unrelated to the concept of domestic jurisdiction. It is not relevant whether international legal standards apply to the activity at hand and whether the matter is a purely internal one or not; immunity protects the independent exercise of exclusive competences of states from interference by other states and is neutral—not normative—in its operation. The bundle of exclusive territorial competences has not been affected by developments in international human rights law.

It has at times been advanced that the argument that violations of *jus cogens* rules do not qualify as sovereign acts for the purpose of the state immunity rule is corroborated by the cases of *Letelier v Chile*[148] and *Liu v China*[149] decided in the US courts.[150] It has however been explained in chapter 2, and again in the introduction of this chapter that the normative limit on the discretionary function exception to the territorial tort exception follows from the fact that a state can only exercise its sovereign power on the territory of another state within the limits of that state's consent. The principles developed in these cases can not therefore be transposed to the exercise of sovereign power within a state's own borders.

The same is true for the reasoning developed to limit the functional immunity of foreign state officials as discussed in the previous chapter. In the *Eichmann* case the court held that it was impossible for a state to sanction the 'odious acts' of which Eichmann was accused and that these acts were accordingly 'completely outside the "sovereign" jurisdiction of the State that ordered or ratified their commission, and therefore those who participated in such acts must personally account for them and cannot shelter behind the official character of their task or mission'.[151] Proponents of the human rights exception often rely on this in support of their 'limited sovereignty' argument.[152] However, the limited cloak of state sovereignty in personal liability questions does in no way limit the scope of state sovereignty itself.

This study hence embraces the much criticized obiter dictum of the US Supreme Court in the *Nelson* case in which it argued that torture allegations against a foreign state basically concern the abuse of police power by the foreign government and that 'however monstrous such abuse undoubtedly may be, a foreign state's exercise of the power of its police has long been understood for purposes of the restrictive theory as peculiarly sovereign in nature'.[153] It is perplexing

[148] *Letelier v Chile* (US, 1980).

[149] *Helen Liu v The Republic of China* (US, 1989).

[150] Cf eg JA Gergen (1996) 783–4; P Lieberman, (1993) 503, 536.

[151] *Attorney-General of Israel v Adolf Eichmann* (Israel, 1962) 309–10.

[152] Cf eg SA Richmann (1993); Judge Wald in her dissent in *Princz v Federal Republic of Germany* (US, 1994) 115; *Prefecture of Voiotia v Federal Republic of Germany* (Greece, 1997). Cf also I Bantekas (1998) 92 AJIL 765, 766.

[153] *Nelson v Saudi Arabia* (US, 1993). In a similar vein, the Ontario Superior Court of Justice argued in the Canadian *Bouzari* case that 'exercises of police, law enforcement and security powers are inherently exercises of governmental authority and sovereignty'. *Bouzari and Others v Islamic Republic of Iran* (Canada, 2002) 435; The Court of Appeal for Ontario agreed with the conclusion

that lower courts have only relied on the *Nelson* case to reject the argument that certain activity qualified under the commercial act exception,[154] but have not considered this clear statement of the highest court conclusive precedent precluding the argument that *jus cogens* violations do not qualify as sovereign acts.

This study also embraces part of the dissenting opinion of four judges of the Greek Supreme Court in the case of *Prefecture of Voiotia v Federal Republic of Germany*.[155] Four judges argued that the acts of the German forces qualified under the armed conflict exception to the territorial tort exception. They asserted that that exception reflects that the use of force is the paradigm *acta jure imperii*. The massacre of the civilian population of Distomo, they concluded, cannot be severed from the armed conflict between the Greek resistance and the German forces. It has been argued that the dissenting judges arguably 'missed [the point] that the tort exception to state immunity may well be interpreted as cutting across the traditional distinction between private and public acts'.[156] Arguably, that criticism misses the rationale of the territorial tort exception. It was argued in chapter 2 of this study that the territorial tort exception with the discretionary function and armed conflict exception in fact reflects the *acta jure imperii–acta jure gestionis* distinction.[157] The dissenting judges were right to point out that acts committed as part of the armed conflict were of a *jure imperii* character and therefore outside the reach of the territorial tort exception.[158]

In sum, the international regulation of the exercise of exclusive competence means that the sovereignty of states is subjected to, rather than limited by, international law. If this distinction is disregarded the concept of domestic jurisdiction may acquire a twisted role in the theory on state immunity. When Crawford argued that the division of competences between national courts was encapsulated in the term domestic jurisdiction he did caution that '[t]he term is ambiguous because a jurisdiction may cease to be 'domestic' *vis-à-vis* an international forum such as the United Nations General Assembly, while remaining domestic *vis-à-vis* another municipal legal system—and vice versa.' As a consequence 'the existence of a rule of international law which provides a basis for legitimate criticism in an international forum of the acts of State B within its territory . . . does not as such prevent those acts being matters of State B's domestic jurisdiction *vis-à-vis*

of the lower court but did not reason in a similar vein, cf *Bouzari and Others v Islamic Republic of Iran* (Canada, CA for Ontario, 2004) § 51–5.

[154] Cf n 56 above.

[155] *Prefecture of Voiotia v Federal Republic of Germany* (Greece, 2000).

[156] M Gavouneli and I Bantekas (2001) 202.

[157] Cf ch 2 § 3.2.1 and 3.2.2 above.

[158] It is noted that the Italian Supreme Court explicitly rejected the argument that violations of *jus cogens* norms do not qualify as sovereign acts, *as well as* the argument that such violations constitute an implied waiver of immunity: *Ferrini v Repubblica Federale di Germania* (Italy, 2004) § 7 and § 8.2.

the courts of State A'[159] This caveat does admittedly prevent the straightforward reliance on the concept of domestic jurisdiction to limit immunity whenever a (peremptory) rule of international law applies—as proposed by others—but is in fact only a stopgap masking the unsatisfactory nature of the original argument.[160] Domestic jurisdiction is in fact not a relative notion in the sense argued by Crawford. Rather, the absolute fact that something is not within the domestic jurisdiction of states means that the international law rules—customary or treaty-based—on accountability and responsibility become applicable and the different actors in the international legal order—like states, international organizations, international tribunals—possess different competences in this system of secondary rules.

In fact, the focus of the discussion on a possible human rights exception to state immunity should be on this system of secondary rules rather than on the sovereign–non sovereign act mould of the horizontal division of competences. The development of international legal standards as regards the exercise of exclusive competences of states and the finding that 'the matter, ceasing to be one solely within the domestic jurisdiction of the State, enters the domain governed by international law'[161] compels the conclusion that the enforcement of these standards should be—as far as it is not in the normal competence of national courts—in accordance with the secondary rules of the international legal system.

2.3.2 *A Human Rights Exception* in Spite of *the Rationale of the Rule of State Immunity?*

2.3.2.1 Introduction

Since the rule of state immunity for *acta jure imperii* is *a priori* indifferent to a normative hierarchy of rules of international law, coherent arguments in favour of a human rights exception to state immunity cannot rely on the traditional reasoning underlying the divisions of competences but must establish that the secondary rules of the international legal order have developed to include *new* competences for national courts. This section examines the influence of the concepts of *erga omnes* obligations and *jus cogens* norms on the system of secondary rules of the law of state responsibility. It will be argued that several developments in the field—like the rise and fall of the concept of international crimes of state and the decision of the ICJ in the *East Timor* case—caution against a reliance on the concepts of *jus cogens* norms and *erga omnes* obligations for more than they can bear. Any deviation of the normal division of competences between courts should either logically follow from the normal application of customary

[159] J Crawford, 'International Law and Foreign Sovereigns: Distinguishing Immune Transactions' (1983) 54 BYIL 75, 83.

[160] Cf for a straightforward reliance n 109 above.

[161] *Nationality Decrees Issued in Tunis and Morocco* (PCIJ, 1923) 26.

international law, or should be agreed to by states in express and clear terms in conventional law.

2.3.2.2 That vain thing of rights of individuals under international law?

It is at times asserted that since there is no right without a remedy,[162] an exception to state immunity for human rights violations is *inherent* in international human rights law. The national courts of the violating state will often not provide solace to the victims and in the absence of access to an international enforcement mechanism victims must necessarily have access to foreign national courts. As Bröhmer argued, '[a] subjective right is characterised by the fact that the holder of the right has the possibility to enforce that right' and since effective international procedures are lacking, the procedural side of international human rights law materializes through national remedies.[163] Or, as Flauss argued, international human rights law is only effective if there are no lacunas in the law of state responsibility.[164]

The argument recalls the teleological reasoning of dissenting Judge Tanaka in the second phase of the *South West Africa* cases.[165] The judge criticized the finding of the majority that Ethiopia and Liberia did not have standing to complain that South Africa's administration of South West Africa violated the Mandate Agreement and the Covenant of the League of Nations. Instead of a 'formalistic' interpretation of the law he proposed a 'teleological or sociological and conceptual' interpretation of international law.

Without expressing a preference here for the one or the other view[166] it should be realized that the comparison to an inherent limit on state immunity is imperfect. It confuses the position of states and individuals within international human rights law. The source of confusion is the somewhat muddled theory on the position of the individual in international law. The issue cannot be discussed here in the detail it deserves but even at the risk of oversimplification it is thought important to discuss it briefly.

International human rights law is concerned with the rights of individuals. This has led commentators to argue that—in defiance of traditional positivist thinking—individuals are not comparable to 'stocks and shares and ships' or

[162] Cf *Ashby v White* 2 Ld Raym. 938 (UK, CA, 1703) 953, dissenting opinion Holt, CJ: 'it is a vain thing to imagine a right without a remedy'.

[163] J Bröhmer (1997) 206. Cf also WF Pepper (1992) 363; W Adams, 'In Search of a Defence of the Transnational Human Rights Paradigm: May *Jus Cogens* Norms be invoked to Create Implied Exceptions in Domestic State Immunity Statutes' in C Scott (ed), *Torture as Tort, Comparative Perspectives on the Development of Transnational Human Rights Litigation* (2001) 247, 250.

[164] J-F Flauss (2000) 306.

[165] *South West Africa Cases* (ICJ, 1966), Dissenting Opinion Judge Tanaka 248, 278. Cf ch 2 p 94 above.

[166] It cannot but be admitted that the consideration of the ICJ in the *Barcelona Traction* case that obligations owed to the international community as a whole are '[b]y their very nature ... the concern of all States' is very similar to the reasoning of Judge Tanaka, *The Barcelona Traction, Light and Power Company, Limited* (ICJ, 1970) 32.

other objects of international law but are properly called *subjects of international law.*[167] The ICJ held in its 1949 advisory opinion in the *Reparations for Injuries* case that an entity with international legal personality 'is a subject of international law and capable of possessing international rights and duties, and . . . has capacity to maintain its rights by bringing international claims.'[168] While many commentators have jumbled the concepts of 'subject of international law' and 'international legal person',[169] with Raič it is probably correct to say that the Court set out to distinguish the two.[170] In other words, it is possible to be a bearer of international rights without having the capacity to bring an international claim to enforce these rights.

Having said that, it must be realized that it is not the lack of procedural capacity that distinguishes the position of individuals in the international legal order from that of states.[171] The rights of individuals recognized under international law are in principle enforced within the national legal systems of the states that undertake the protection of these rights. The recognition of these rights on the international level does not entail the *grant of a right to individuals*, it entails the *grant of a right to states.* In fact, the common articulation of the rights in natural law terms evinces that the individuals are considered to have always possessed these rights. States grant each other the right to monitor the compliance of their behaviour with the agreed norms. Since this right would be a vain thing in the absence of a remedy in the international legal system it is indeed arguable that

[167] DP O'Connell, *International Law* (1970) i 83. Cf eg H Lauterpacht (1947b); CA Nørgaard, *The Position of the Individual in International Law* (1962); J Crawford, *The Creation of States in International Law* (1979) 25; PK Menon, 'The Subjects of Modern International Law' (1990) 3 Hague Yearbook of International Law 30, 32; PH Kooijmans, 'The Security Council and Non-State Entities as Parties to Conflicts' in K Wellens (ed), *International Law: Theory and Practice, Essays in Honour of Eric Suy* (1998) 333, 338; R Jennings and A Watts(1992) i 847–9. Cf for early doctrine R Knubben, *Die Subjekte des Völkerrechts* (1928) 527; J Spiropoulos, *L'individu en droit international* (1927); M Siotto-Pintor, 'Les sujets du droit international autres que les États' (1932–III) 41 RdC 245; H Lauterpacht, *Private Law Sources and Analogies of International Law* (1927) 73; H Kelsen, *General Theory of Law and the State* (1945). Cf for the positivist view L Oppenheim (1905) i 200; D Anzilotti, *Cours de droit international* (1929) 134; For a general overview see CA Nørgaard (1962).

[168] *Reparation for Injuries Suffered in the Service of the United Nations* (Advisory Opinion), ICJ Reports 1949 174, 179.

[169] Cf R Jennings and A Watts (1992) i 119; I Brownlie (2003) 57–8.

[170] D Raič, *Statehood and the Law of Self-Determination* (2002) 13.

[171] For example the oft-quoted words of Lauterpacht seem to suggest this: 'The position of the individual as subject of international law has often been obscured by the failure to observe the distinction between the recognition, in an international instrument of rights ensuring the benefit of the individual and the enforceability of these rights at his instance. The fact that the beneficiary of rights is not authorized to take independent steps in his own name to enforce them does not signify that he is not a subject of the law or that the rights in question are vested exclusively in the agency which possesses the capacity to enforce them. Thus in relation to the current view that the rights of the alien within foreign territory are the rights of his state and not his own, the correct way of stating the legal position is not that the state asserts its own exclusive right but that it enforces, in substance, the right of the individual who, as the law now stands, is incapable of asserting it in the international sphere', H Lauterpacht (1950) 27.

enlarged rules on standing inhere in the regulation of human rights on the international level. The right of the individual, however, exists in the national legal system. The right to a remedy as provided in most human rights treaties is therefore the equivalent of the remedy of states on the international level.[172]

The access of individuals to an international enforcement mechanism *does* greatly enhance the effectiveness of the agreement between states. Individual incidental violations are not readily discernable without a right to individual petition and states are moreover reluctant to bring claims in respect of such violations. The right to an *international* remedy does however not *inhere* in the recognition of these rights on the international level, it is the right to a *national* remedy that does.

2.3.2.3 *Jus cogens* rules, *erga omnes* obligations, and the secondary rules of international law

In the 2004 *Ferrini* case the Italian Supreme Court decided that a foreign state did not enjoy immunity from jurisdiction in respect of *jus cogens* violations.[173] The reasoning of the court is somewhat ambiguous. In the first place, like the Greek court, the Italian court reasoned in two minds. It emphasized the fact that the tortious activity took place within Italian territory, while its principal argument is not limited to territorial torts but relies explicitly on the qualification of the activity in terms of international law. Second, the reasoning of the court remains underdeveloped. Although the court did express support for the minority opinion in the *Al-Adsani* case before the European Court of Human Rights, its argumentation was not limited to the 'standard' hierarchy of norms argument.[174] Rather, it primarily relied on a 'systematic interpretation' of the rule of state immunity to come to its conclusion. The rule of state immunity, the court argued, is part of a system and has to be interpreted in accordance with other norms that form part of the same legal order. Legal norms, it explained, complement one another and condition each other's application.[175]

The court mentioned several factors that influenced its interpretation of the scope of the rule of state immunity. In the first place, it recalled that the acts complained of qualified as international crimes, which it defined as violations of fundamental human rights that are protected by non-derogable norms. Such violations, the court continued, require a different reaction from other states than other violations of international law. Referring to the ILC Articles on State Responsibility, the court recalled that states may not recognize as lawful

[172] Cf § 3.3 below.

[173] *Ferrini v Repubblica Federale di Germania* (Italy, 2004). See for comments on this case A Bianchi, 'Ferrini v. Federal Republic of Germany' (2005) 99 AJIL 242; P De Sena and F De Vittor, 'State Immunity and Human Rights: The Italian Supreme Court Decision on the *Ferrini* Case' (2005) 16 EJIL 89; A Gattini (2005).

[174] ibid § 9.1.

[175] ibid § 9.

situations created by the commission of *jus cogens* violations, are prohibited from assisting in maintaining such situations, and are obliged to bring such situations to an end through lawful means. The court then stated that the respect for inviolable human rights is a fundamental principle of the international legal order that cannot but affect the scope of other principles that have traditionally inspired that order. In particular, the court held, the principle affects the principle of the equality of states that underlies the rule of state immunity. *Jus cogens* violations require a different reaction than other violations of international law. Since the grant of state immunity in respect of allegations of *jus cogens* violations does not favour the protection of *jus cogens* norms but rather forms an obstacle to their protection, the argument seems to run, it must be rejected.

In addition, the court recalled that the rule of functional immunity knows an exception in respect of international crimes.[176] Since functional immunity exists, the court argued, in order to prevent an indirect implication of foreign states, there is no reason to sustain state immunity in cases where there is no functional immunity.

It is time to take a closer look at the concepts relied on in the *Ferrini* judgment. Ever since the reference to peremptory norms in the Vienna Convention on the Law of Treaties and the mention of obligations *erga omnes* in the 1970 *Barcelona Traction* case scholars have hotly debated the question whether distinct rules on state responsibility apply when norms of an *erga omnes* or *jus cogens* character are at issue. This section will describe relevant developments in the field on the basis of the ILC Articles on the Law of State Responsibility—adopted by the ILC in their final version in 2001.[177] Although these articles have as yet not reached the status of convention they reflect many rules of customary international law and provide a useful frame of reference.

It must, however, first be questioned whether the exercise of adjudicative jurisdiction over foreign states with regard to their violations of international law can be justified under the rules on countermeasures—as is at times suggested.[178] Countermeasures are measures that 'would otherwise be contrary to the international obligations of the injured State *vis-à-vis* the responsible State if they were not taken by the former in response to an internationally wrongful act by the latter in order to procure cessation and reparation.'[179] This definition compels a preliminary observation as to the position of non-injured states that are recognized to have a legal interest in compliance under article 48 of the ILC Articles on State

[176] ibid § 11.

[177] ILC Articles on the Responsibility of States for Internationally Wrongful Acts (2001), UN Doc A/56/10, 2001.

[178] Cf eg J Kokott, 'Mißbrauch und verwirkung von Souveränitätsrechten bei gravierenden Völkerrechtsverstoßen' in U Beyerlin et al (eds), *Recht zwischen Umbruch und Bewahrung, Festschrift für Rudolf Bernhardt* (1995) 135, 148–9. J Bröhmer, *State Immunity and Human Rights Violations* (1997) 159 and 192 rejects the argument, *inter alia*, because it entails acknowledging that the denial of immunity in human rights cases is normally a violation of international law.

[179] J Crawford (2002) 281.

Responsibility. Article 54 provides that the rules on countermeasures applicable to injured states do not prejudice the rights of article 48 states 'to take lawful measures... to ensure cessation of the breach and reparation in the interest of the injured State or the beneficiaries of the obligation breached'. The provision is an empty shell since no definition of what constitutes lawful measures is available. Crawford admits that—apart from institutional reactions in the framework of international organizations—'[a]t present there appears to be no clearly recognised entitlement of States referred to in article 48 to take countermeasures in the collective interest.'[180] In sum, the argument is *a priori* limited to human rights violations against nationals of the forum state.[181]

But even in this limited form the argument proves incoherent. Some of the principal characteristics of these measures fit an institutionalized exception to immunity rules uncomfortably—to say the least. Countermeasures are essentially exceptional ad hoc measures that require careful tailoring to the particulars of each case and hence a case-by-case assessment. Before countermeasures may be lawfully taken states shall call on the responsible state to cease the internationally wrongful conduct and to pay reparation and shall notify that state of any decision to take countermeasures and offer to negotiate.[182] Moreover, states must in any case fulfil their obligations under any dispute settlement procedure applicable between it and the responsible state.[183] Since diplomatic protection is the procedure that states have agreed upon for the settlement of disputes relating to the violation of rights of their nationals by another state, it seems that states are obliged to attempt settlement of the dispute under the rules of diplomatic protection first. An exception to immunity rules based on the rules on countermeasures should hence be contingent on the fruitless result of the fulfilment of the obligations resting on the executive of the forum state as well as the fulfilment of the requirements of the local remedies rule.

More fundamentally, countermeasures have a temporary or provisional character. As Crawford pointed out: 'Their aim is the restoration of a condition of legality as between the injured State and the responsible State, and not the creation of new situations which cannot be rectified whatever the response of the latter State to the claims against it.'[184] Therefore, countermeasures should in principle be reversible.[185] Although this obligation is not absolute, when states have the choice between several lawful and effective measures, they are required to select one which permits resumption of performance of the obligations suspended.[186]

[180] ibid 305. Cf M Akehurst, 'Reprisals by Third States' (1970) 44 BYIL 1; JA Frowein, 'Reactions by Not Directly Affected States to Breaches of Public International Law' (1994–IV) 248 RdC 345.

[181] Cf also T Giegerich (2006) 232ff.

[182] Art 52.1. Cf J Crawford (2002) 297.

[183] Art 50.2(a). Cf J Crawford, ibid 291.

[184] J Crawford, ibid 286.

[185] Cf also *Gabčíkovo-Nagymaros Project* (*Hungary v Slovakia*), ICJ Reports 1997 3, 56–7.

[186] J Crawford (2002) 287.

It may be clear that the non-grant of immunity—in violation of international obligations—in order to force reparation on the responsible state is because of the necessary link between reparation paid and the obligation suspended in essence incompatible with the concept countermeasure.

It should finally be noted that it is controversial whether obligations under immunity rules can be suspended under the rules on countermeasures to begin with. Riphagen, for one, argued under reference to the ICJ's decision in the *Diplomatic and Consular Staff* case that

> one might say that in every set of rules of international law, providing for immunity is of necessity a 'self-contained régime' inasmuch as it deals with the separation of sovereignties of states in cases where those states, so to speak, share the same environment. The conditions under which such sharing may take place, the scope of the resulting immunities, and the conditions under which the sharing may be terminated form an indivisible régime, within which there is no place for countermeasures against an 'internationally wrongful act'. Indeed immunity has no meaning unless, within its scope, the state enjoying it whatever it does, is free from interference by the state granting it.[187]

The argument has much force indeed. It recalls the general problem of circularity underlined in section 2.1 of this chapter.

Let us now turn to the provisions relating to peremptory norms and *erga omnes* obligations. In 1976 Rapporteur Ago relied on the *Barcelona Traction* case as 'an important factor in support of the theory which advocates two different regimes of international responsibility depending on the content of the international obligation breached'.[188] He also relied on the concept of *jus cogens* norms to defend this thesis arguing that 'it would be hard to believe that the evolution of the legal consciousness of States with regard to the idea of the inadmissibility of any derogation from certain rules has not been accompanied by a parallel evolution in the domain of State responsibility.'[189] Ago's proposal resulted in the introduction of a distinction between international delicts and international crimes in the Draft Articles on State Responsibility in what finally became known as the (in)famous article 19.[190] Article 19.2 provided that '[a]n internationally wrongful act which results from the breach by a State of an international obligation so essential for

[187] W Riphagen, 'State Responsibility: New Theories of Obligation in Interstate Relations' in RSJ Macdonald and DM Johnston (eds), *The Structure and Process of International Law* (1983) 581, 606. Cf *United States Diplomatic and Consular Staff in Tehran* (ICJ, 1980) 40.

[188] R Ago (Special Rapporteur ILC), Fifth report on State Responsibility, YBILC 1976 ii (part one) 3, 29 (more in general p. 24–54). Cf also R Ago, 'Le délit international' (1939–II) 68 RdC 415 for an early expression of this idea. Ago was not the first Rapporteur to consider these issues, cf eg FV Garcia-Amador (Special Rapporteur ILC), Report on International Responsibility, YBILC 1956 ii 173, 183. See for an overview of the legislative history of art 19 M Spinedi, 'International Crimes of State, The Legislative History' in JHH Weiler, et al (eds), *International Crimes of State, A Critical Analysis of the ILC's Draft Article 19 on State Responsibility* (1989) 7.

[189] R Ago, ibid 32.

[190] Ibid 54 (art 18).

the protection of fundamental interests of the international community that its breach is recognized as a crime by that community as a whole constitutes an international crime.' The controversy that developed became the most persistent and divisive of the whole state responsibility project and article 19 developed into the principal stumbling block for a successful completion of the topic.

This is obviously not the place to set out the intricate debate between proponents and opponents of the concept of international crimes of state.[191] Put boldly, an important element of the opposition to article 19 was that it could not live up to the promises it held, or, as one scholar poetically noted, the introduction of the notion state crimes in article 19 is like offering a 'decaffeinated coffee'.[192] States were not willing to develop a penal regime of responsibility applicable to violations singled out as international crimes. Crawford points out that all elements—or ingredients to stick to the metaphor—that one might expect to attach to the notion of crime, like a proper definition of the crimes; procedures for investigation; a system of due process; and especially appropriate sanctions, were missing.[193] In fact, it was not at all clear how the legal position of a state that committed an international crime differed from that of a state that committed an international delict. States only agreed that the distinction had consequences for the legal position and obligations of all *other* states.[194]

[191] See for an overview a.o. JHH Weiler, et al (eds), *International Crimes of State, A Critical Analysis of the ILC's Draft Art 19 on State Responsibility* (1989); PM Dupuy, 'A General Stocktaking of the Connections between the Multilateral Dimension of Obligations and Codification of the Law of State Responsibility' (2002) 13 EJIL 1053; M Spinedi, 'From One Codification to Another: Bilateralism and Multilateralism in the Genesis of the Codification of the Law of Treaties and the Law of State Responsibility' (2002a) 13 EJIL 1099; L-A Sicilianos, 'The Classification of Obligations and the Multilateral Dimension of the Relations of International Responsibility' (2002) 13 EJIL 1127; E Wyler, 'From "State Crime" to Responsibility for "Serious Breaches of Obligations under Peremptory Norms of General International Law"' (2002) 13 EJIL 1147; CJ Tams, 'Do Serious Breaches Give Rise to Any Specific Obligations of the Responsible State?' (2002) 13 EJIL 1161; DW Bowett, 'Crimes of State and the 1996 Report of the International Law Commission on State Responsibility' (1998) 9 EJIL 163; G Abi-Saab, 'The Uses of Article 19' (1999) 10 EJIL 339; G Gilbert, 'The Criminal Responsibility of States' (1990) 39 ICLQ 345; PM Dupuy, 'The Institutionalization of International Crimes of State' in JHH Weiler et al (eds), *International Crimes of State, A Critical Analysis of the ILC's Draft Art 19 on State Responsibility* (1989) 170; K Zemanek, 'New Trends in the Enforcement of *Erga Omnes* Obligations' (2000) 4 Max Planck Yearbook of United Nations Law 1; NHB Jørgensen (2000).

[192] J Barboza, 'State Crimes: A Decaffeinated Coffee' in L Boisson de Chazournes and V Gowlland-Debbas (eds), *The International Legal System in Quest of Equity and Universality* (2001) 357. Cf in defence of notion of state crime A Pellet, 'Can a State Commit a Crime? Definitely, Yes!' (1999) 10 EJIL 425; G Abi-Saab, 'The Concept of "International Crimes" and its Place in Contemporary International Law' in JHH Weiler, et al (eds), *International Crimes of States, A Critical Analysis of the ILC's Draft Article 19 on State Responsibility* (1989) 141.

[193] J Crawford (2002) 18.

[194] Cf arts 52–3 of the set of Draft Articles provisionally adopted on first reading in 1996, UN Doc. /51/10, 1996. Art 40.3 moreover provides that if the internationally wrongful act constitutes an international crime all other states qualify as injured state; but art 40.2.e.iii makes clear that this consequence is not particular to international crimes but applies more in general to infringement of rights created for the protection of human rights and fundamental freedoms. It should also be noted that art 45.2.c provided that satisfaction may take the form of 'damages reflecting the gravity

In defence of article 19 it has been argued that the distinction between international delicts and international crimes was never modelled on any domestic law analogy but rather served to express the idea that an aggravated regime of state responsibility attaches to acts that affect essential interests of the international community.[195] Crawford—the final Rapporteur on the project—rejected this justification noting that 'the appeal of the notion "international" crime cannot be dissociated from general human experience'.[196] In 1998 he proposed to set aside article 19 for the time being and focus on other possible solutions.[197]

The final version of the Articles adopted in 2001 abandons the unwieldy—and indeed unnecessary[198]—concept of international crimes and restores the original concepts underlying *jus cogens* norms and *erga omnes* obligations in two separate sets of rules corresponding with two different aspects of the law of state responsibility. The concept of peremptory norms is used in its original meaning of non-derogability, as well as to set out certain—for now, limited—legal consequences that attach to serious breaches of these norms; while the concept of multilateral obligations is translated in special rules on the invocation of responsibility for the violation of such obligations. The disappearance of the notion of crimes of state is mourned by some.[199] Since the substantive elements of the old draft related to the concept have all survived—and indeed for the most part improved—this can only be explained by the symbolic force of the term that at least implied the sanction of the qualification.

The non-derogable character of peremptory norms is first reflected in the articles dealing with self-defence, distress and other circumstances precluding wrongfulness where article 26 provides that '[n]othing in this Chapter precludes the wrongfulness of any act of a State which is not in conformity with an obligation arising under a peremptory norm of general international law.' Furthermore, the rules on countermeasures include article 50.1 that provides that countermeasures shall not affect

(a) the obligation to refrain from the threat or use of force as embodied in the Charter of the United Nations;

of the infringement' in case of 'a gross infringement of the rights of the injured State'—a concept not linked to the definition of international crimes in art 19.

195 Cf eg G Abi-Saab (1999) 351.

196 J Crawford (Special Rapporteur ILC), First Report on State Responsibility, Yearbook ILC 1998 ii part one, § 81. See different G Abi-Saab, ibid 346 who argues that 'legal terms detach themselves from their municipal moorings to acquire specific contours and import, more consonant with the structure and functions of international law'.

197 Report of the ILC on the work of its fiftieth session (1998), YB ILC 1998 ii (part two) 77.

198 Cf J Crawford, 'Revising the Draft Articles on State Responsibility' (1999) 10 EJIL 435, 443. Ironically enough the 'father' of art 19 himself had noted: 'we are interested not so much in determining whether the responsibility... does or does not entail "criminal" international responsibility as in determining whether such responsibility is or is not "different" from that deriving from the breach of other international obligations of the State.' R Ago (Special Rapporteur ILC), Fifth report on State Responsibility, YBILC 1976 ii (part one) 3, 33, fn 154.

199 Cf G Abi-Saab (1999).

(b) obligations for the protection of fundamental human rights;
(c) obligations of a humanitarian character prohibiting reprisals;
(d) other obligations under peremptory norms of general international law.

Article 41 sets out some particular consequences of serious breaches of peremptory norms—defined in article 40.2 as 'a gross or systematic failure by the responsible State to fulfil the obligation' arising under a peremptory norm of international law. It provides that:

1. States shall cooperate to bring to an end through lawful means any serious breach within the meaning of article 40.
2. No State shall recognize as lawful a situation created by a serious breach within the meaning of article 40, nor render aid or assistance in maintaining that situation.
3. This article is without prejudice to the other consequences referred to in this Part and to such further consequences that a breach to which this Chapter applies may entail under international law.

The notion 'serious breach of a peremptory norm' has replaced the notion 'international crime'. Crawford explains that '[f]actors which may establish the seriousness of the violation would include the intent to violate the norm; the scope and number of violations, and the gravity of their consequences for the victims.'[200] Apart from the difference in symbolic force between the two notions, it is notable that the Articles no longer distinguish between, at the outset, different types of internationally wrongful acts but rather specify some additional consequences that attach to particular serious breaches. Rather than implying the existence of two separate regimes of responsibility the assumption is that of a principally unitary regime.

The additional consequences—for now—are limited. It is telling that the article that originally provided that a serious breach may give rise to aggravated damages encountered so much criticism that it was deleted from the final draft.[201] Article 41 is only a very cautious step towards a differentiation in the content of a state's responsibility depending on the character of the norm violated. In fact, the article only specifies the obligations resting on *other* states. Although the violating state can expect other states to react more forcefully to its internationally wrongful act, this in no way affects rights it would otherwise have or imposes on it obligations it would otherwise not have.

Crawford has admitted that the positive duty of cooperation may not codify existing law and that paragraph 1 may therefore amount to the progressive development of international law.[202] The two obligations of paragraph 2, on the other hand, do reflect international practice. States are obliged to refrain from

[200] J Crawford (2002) 247.
[201] ibid 36.
[202] ibid 249.

recognition—formal or de facto—as lawful situations created by a serious breach as well as from rendering aid or assistance in maintaining such situations.[203] The most obvious example would be the obligation not to recognize another state's acquisition of sovereignty over territory through violation of the prohibition of aggression or through the denial of the right of self-determination of peoples.[204] For example, the ICJ in its advisory opinion on *Namibia (South West Africa)* considered that 'the termination of the Mandate and the declaration of the illegality of South Africa's presence in Namibia are opposable to all States in the sense of barring *erga omnes* the legality of a situation which is maintained in violation of international law'.[205] One conspicuous example moreover can be found in the resolutions issued by the Security Council in reaction to Iraq's invasion and annexation of Kuwait in 1990. After the Security Council had condemned the invasion as a breach of the peace and demanded the immediate Iraqi withdrawal (Resolution 660) it called upon all states not to recognize any regime set up by Iraq (Resolution 661) and eventually decided that the annexation had no legal validity and was null and void and called upon all states not to recognize the annexation and to refrain from any action which might be interpreted as an indirect recognition of the annexation (Resolution 662).

The concept of obligations *erga omnes* is translated in special rules on the invocation of the international responsibility of a state. Article 42 sets out the basic rule. It provides that:

A State is entitled as an injured State to invoke the responsibility of another State if the obligation breached is owed to:

(a) that State individually; or
(b) a group of States including that State, or the international community as a whole, and the breach of the obligation;
  (i) specially affects that State; or
  (ii) is of such a character as radically to change the position of all the other States to which the obligation is owed with respect to the further performance of the obligation.

[203] Cf eg *Prosecutor v Furundžija* (ICTY, 1998) § 155.

[204] Cf Declaration of Principles of International Law Concerning Friendly Relations and Co-operation Among States in Accordance with the Charter of the United Nations, GA Res 2625 (XXV) first principle paragraph 10. As the ICJ considered in the *Nicaragua Case* (merits) the unanimous consent of states to this declaration 'may be understood as an acceptance of the validity of the rule or set of rules declared by the resolution by themselves'. *Case Concerning Military and Paramilitary Activities in and against Nicaragua* (ICJ, 1986) 100.

[205] *Legal Consequences for States of the Continued Presence of South Africa in Namibia* (ICJ, 1971) 56. Resolutions of the Security Council and the General Assembly concerning the situation in Rhodesia and the Bantustans in South Africa reflect a similar duty: cf SC Res 216 (1965); GA Res 31/6A (1976), endorsed by SC Res 402 (1976); GA Res 32/105N (1977); GA Res 34/93G (1979).

Article 48 complements this rule by setting out the circumstances under which a state that does not qualify as injured state under article 42 may still invoke the responsibility of another state. It provides as follows:

1. Any State other than an injured State is entitled to invoke the responsibility of another State in accordance with paragraph 2 if:
   (a) the obligation breached is owed to a group of States including that State, and is established for the protection of a collective interest of the group; or
   (b) the obligation breached is owed to the international community as a whole.
2. Any State entitled to invoke responsibility under paragraph 1 may claim from the responsible State:
   (a) cessation of the internationally wrongful act, and assurances and guarantees of non-repetition in accordance with article 30; and
   (b) performance of the obligation of reparation in accordance with the preceding articles, in the interest of the injured State or of the beneficiaries of the obligations breached.
3. The requirements for the invocation of responsibility by an injured State under articles 43, 44 and 45 apply to an invocation of responsibility by a State entitled to do so under paragraph 1.

While article 42 (b) reflects the direct interest of states in the breach of a multilateral obligation—either because a state is specially affected by the breach or because the nature of the obligations undertaken is such that each parties' performance is effectively conditioned upon and requires the performance of each of the others—article 48 reflects the indirect interest of states in objective multilateral obligations. States acting in the collective interest under article 48 have a more limited range of rights than injured states under article 42.[206]

The inclusion of a *locus standi* concept that takes account of the trend to develop objective multilateral obligations was as such not too controversial. Indeed, as Weil rightly noted 'la théorie de l'obligation erga omnes répond à une nécessité du monde international d'aujourd'hui'.[207] Traditional international law regulated the behaviour of states in their relations with each other. The absence of direct interstate aspects in the behaviour required under human rights rules requires debilateralization of relations of responsibility in their regard. Subparagraph (a) of article 48.1 concerns this category of obligations, sometimes referred to as obligations *erga omnes partes*.[208] Moreover, the hierarchy of norms thinking that has been introduced in international law through the concept of *jus cogens* norms has triggered the idea that some norms are so important that the obligations arising

[206] Cf also art 54: 'This chapter does not purport to regulate the taking of countermeasures by states other than the injured State. It is, however, without prejudice to the right of any State identified in article 48 (1) to take lawful measures, against a responsible State to ensure cessation of the breach and reparation in the interest of the injured State or of the beneficiaries of the obligation breached.'

[207] P Weil, 'Le droit international en quête de son identité, Cours général de droit international public' (1992–VI) 237 RdC 9, 290.

[208] J Crawford (2002) 277.

under such norms are owed to the international community as a whole and that all states have a legal interest in their protection. This idea lies at the basis of subparagraph (b).

Although in practice a considerable overlap exists between the two categories it is not difficult to find examples of obligations that fit one category but not the other. In the first place it is clear that collective interest obligations may be undertaken within a group of a limited number of states, as is the case with regional conventions like the ECHR. More essentially, there exist obligations that are multilateral in nature but that are not necessarily considered more important than rules of a strictly bilateral nature. One can think for example of the obligations arising from certain rules on the law of the seas, like prohibitions regarding pollution of the high seas, or, those customary human rights rules not of a non-derogable character like the freedom of religion. Second, examples can also be found of obligations 'that are the concern of all States' because of 'the importance of the rights involved' but that are not of an inherent multilateral character. The multilateral character of obligations arising from the prohibition of aggression, for example, stems from the fundamental importance of the rule rather than from its intrinsic non-bilateral quality. The category of 'obligations of a State towards the international community as a whole' is hence of an essentially different nature than the category of pure community interest obligations.

It should finally be noted that the multilateral character of an obligation breached does not mean that no state qualifies as an injured state under article 42. Apart from the situations explicitly provided for in article 42 (b), it may be clear that breach of the obligations referred to in article 48.1(b) that have a clear interstate aspect—like the prohibition of aggression—usually means that article 42(a) is equally applicable. Moreover, the breach of a multilateral obligation referred to in article 48.1 may at the same time constitute a breach of a purely bilateral obligation, as for example an obligation the performance of which is the subject of diplomatic protection.

Although the ideas underlying article 48 are relatively uncontroversial, some aspects of the final version have provoked scholarly debate. For one, several commentators have criticized the absence of a link between the concept of peremptory norms and the generality of standing under article 48.[209] The argument that this is exactly one of the important *improvements* of the final ILC Articles is however persuasive. Crawford admits that '[t]he examples which the International Court has given of obligations towards the international community as a whole all concern obligations which, it is generally accepted, arise under peremptory norms of general international law.' And that '[l]ikewise the examples of peremptory norms given by the Commission in its commentary to what became article 53

[209] Cf eg PM Dupuy (2002) 1075. See for the related argument that arts 40, 41, 42, and 48 should all have referred to obligations owed to the international community as a whole L-A Sicilianos (2002) 1141.

of the Vienna Convention [on the law of treaties] involve obligations to the international community as a whole.'[210] However the reality that '*jus cogens* rules necessarily apply *erga omnes*'[211] and the fact that *jus cogens* norms and obligations owed to the international community as a whole are in practice concepts covering the same group of rules does not sustain a formal link between the two concepts. A generalized legal interest in compliance of certain obligations does not derive from the non-derogable quality of the norms these obligations arise from per se but from the fact that these non-derogable norms protect the public order of the international community.[212] It is moreover noted that a formal link between a serious breach of peremptory norms and standing to invoke responsibility is even less desirable: while peremptory norms are at least identifiable with a special category of *erga omnes* obligations, namely those obligations owed to the international community as a whole; the category of breaches with which articles 40 and 41 are concerned is more limited in scope than that defined in article 48.1(b).

So how do the findings of this brief excursion relate to our research question? It must at the outset be pointed out that the reliance on the concept of international crimes in the *Ferrini* case is remarkable, to say the least. While the concept is accepted within the context of individual responsibility under international law, its use in relation to states is, as we saw above, far from uncontroversial. More importantly, the provisions of the ILC Articles do not offer a fertile soil for the assertion of competence of national courts over violations of *jus cogens* norms or obligations *erga omnes*. In brief it can be said that the concepts have affected the traditional view that state responsibility is not graded to gravity and that invocation of responsibility is reserved to the state whose individual right has been violated.[213]

The concept of obligations *erga omnes* is reserved for arguments related to the legal interest of states in compliance with certain norms. The concept secures enlarged standing of states in *existing* international procedures and enforcement mechanisms and offers a policy argument in favour of strengthening and developing these procedures and mechanisms. Apart from the enlarged rules on standing the concept offers, together with the *jus cogens* concept, a basis for the principle of universal jurisdiction over violations of these norms.[214] This jurisdictional basis should however not be confused with the question of competence of the court. The reasoning that '[i]f all states may be deemed to have a legal interest

[210] J Crawford (2002) 244.

[211] M Byers (1999) 200.

[212] One could of course envisage a central role for the concept of 'public order of the international community' in arts 40, 41 and 48. However, the category of obligations *erga omnes* with which art 48.1(a) is concerned would still escape this uniform approach. It is probably preferable to set out the link between the articles in a separate interpretative statement.

[213] Cf for the traditional view D Anzilotti, *Teoria generale della responsabilità dello stato nel diritto internazionale* (1902) 84ff.

[214] Cf *Prosecutor v Tadić* (ICTY, 1995) § 59; *Prosecutor v Furundžija* (ICTY, 1998) § 156.

in the protection of the fundamental rights of the human being, the exercise of jurisdiction over foreign states violating such rights is to be admitted in light of the greater interest that the international community has in the protection of such values'[215] suffers from such confusion.

A *jus cogens* exception to state immunity should be based on the particular consequences accepted to attach to breaches of peremptory norms. Such consequences are however only accepted as regards *serious* breaches and are more importantly limited in scope. In the first place article 41.1 lays down—*de lege ferenda*—a positive duty for states to cooperate to bring to an end through lawful means any such breach. The provision however does not allow states to use means that they normally would not have but rather obliges the use of those means regularly available. At the risk of stating the obvious, civil proceedings in the national courts of one state—apart from the fact that they usually concern a claim for damages rather than cessation of the breach—do not suddenly qualify as lawful means falling under the obligation.

The obligation laid down in article 41.2 not to recognize as lawful a situation created by a serious breach, nor render aid or assistance in maintaining that situation is at times relied on in the argumentation in favour of a human rights exception. It has been argued that the grant of state immunity supports illegality,[216] or even that the grant of state immunity makes the forum state an 'accomplice to the act'.[217] Also Bianchi has noted that 'to uphold the claim of immunity would have the undesirable effect of supporting the unlawfulness of the foreign state's acts'.[218] In the Greek case *Prefecture of Voiotia v Federal Republic of Germany* the Court of First Instance reasoned that '[t]he recognition of immunity by a national court for an act that is contrary to jus cogens would be tantamount to collaboration by that national court in an act that is strongly condemned by the international community'.[219] And as we saw earlier, the Italian Supreme Court also alluded to this provision in the *Ferrini* case.

These arguments are however not persuasive. In the first place, the grant of state immunity is neutral as to the lawfulness of the behaviour of the foreign state complained of. Moreover, immunity for acts committed in the exercise of

[215] A Bianchi (1997) 437. SA Richmann (1993) 985 takes the confusion even a step further. He argued that states not only have the right to use universal jurisdiction but that 'customary international law obliges [them] to use it. It is an obligation erga omnes... each state, according to this doctrine, is legally obliged or compelled to protect certain rights, since all states are interested parties.... Thus, under the erga omnes doctrine, each state has an obligation to protect peremptory norms of international law due to their shared interest in that protection.'

[216] JJ Paust (1983) 226.

[217] AC Belsky et al (1989) 401, fn 198: 'If a domestic court grants sovereign immunity to a state that has violated a rule of jus cogens, it is recognizing a sovereign right which does not exist. The tribunal could be viewed as violating the principle of nonrecognition and thus be considered an accomplice to the act.'

[218] A Bianchi (1997) 437.

[219] See the case note by I Bantekas in (1998) 92 AJIL 765, 766. Cf also *Prosecutor v Furundžija* (ICTY, 1998) § 155.

state authority under international law is not a protection of otherwise existing jurisdiction but a necessary division of competences between courts. The obligation of non-recognition is, as Lauterpacht explained, 'based on the view that acts contrary to international law are invalid and cannot become a source of legal rights for the wrongdoer'.[220] This rationale translates poorly to the grant of state immunity in respect of allegations of acts contrary to international law. The immunity of states from foreign jurisdiction in respect of *acta jure imperii* does not emanate from the violation of international law. The fact that the immunity appears to follow the act since it is only *invoked* when the act is challenged may confuse. The relation between the right and the violation is however not different from the right to non-interference and the violation of international human rights law.

In sum, while the two concepts have expanded the rights and duties of other states to take action against certain breaches of international law it cannot be argued that *jus cogens* norms are afforded 'superior means of enforcement' and that therefore the exercise of jurisdiction over allegations of *jus cogens* violations is justifiable.[221] It cannot be convincingly argued that the concept of *jus cogens* rules and *erga omnes* obligations have limited the rights of states under the law of state immunity.

In this respect one radical argument advanced by several scholars can equally not be sustained. The argument runs as follows:

> [w]here a nation violates jus cogens... it steps outside the boundaries drawn by the international community for itself. It thus forfeits the privileges accorded to the members. In other words, as an outlaw, it has no claim to deference and respect... There may have been a time when sovereign immunity was granted unconditionally. Today it should be considered a privilege contingent on compliance with at least the most fundamental rules which the community of nations has set for itself. It makes no sense to recognize unconditionally binding norms of international law and at the same time shield the perpetrators who violate these norms from legal action.[222]

In other words, outlaw—or pariah—states do no longer enjoy the rights and privileges of sovereign states under international law.

This idea also seems to be reflected in the terrorist state exception in the US FSIA.[223] The US concept of 'rogue states' underlies the 1996 amendment of

[220] H Lauterpacht, *Recognition in International Law* (1947a) 420.

[221] Cf for the argument K Bartsch and B Elbering (2003) as well as the scholars mentioned earlier in this section.

[222] M Reimann (1995) 423. M Rosen, 'The Alien Tort Claims Act and the Foreign Sovereign Immunities Act: A Policy Solution' (1998) 6 Cardozo Journal of International and Comparative Law 461, 514; J Kokott (1995) 148. This was also the argument relied on by the lower court in the *Princz* case. Judge Sporkin reasoned that a 'government which stands in the shoes of a rogue nation like the likes of Nazi Germany is estopped from asserting U.S. law in this fashion'. 813 F supp 22 (DC for the District of Columbia, 1992) 26. Cf also Brief of Amici Curiae The Anti-Defamation League et al., quoted in *Princz v Federal Republic of Germany* (US, 1994) 1173.

[223] Cf § 2.1 above.

the FSIA to include an exception for human rights abuses and terrorist activity which applies only to foreign states designated 'state sponsor of terrorism' by the executive.[224]

It may be clear that there is no basis whatsoever for the sweeping argument that states that violate *jus cogens* norms forfeit their right to rely on the rule of state immunity altogether. The idea of outlaw states that cannot invoke rights under primary or secondary rules of international law recalls outdated distinctions between civilized nations that are part of the 'Family of Nations' and barbaric people that are not.[225] Statehood is an absolute, not a relative notion. More importantly, the concepts of *jus cogens* norms and *erga omnes* obligations operate not to oust violating states from the international legal order but rather attempt to provide tools to effectively deal with community interests and particularly heinous acts threatening those interests *within* that order and as against sovereign states forming part of it.

This study asserts that the terrorist state exception to the FSIA causes the United States to violate its obligations under international law. Much seems changed since Chief Justice Marshall observed in 1825 that '[n]o principle of general law is more universally acknowledged than the perfect equality of nations.'[226] The entertainment of claims against 'rogue' states for payment of damages suffered as a result of human rights violations and terrorist acts is illegal under international law.[227]

This opinion is shared by the US Departments of State and Justice. The Departments strongly opposed the provisions of the AEDPA that amended the FSIA to include the exception. In hearings on these provisions the Department of State's representative considered that '[f]undamental principles of sovereignty and international law are implicated in determining the extent to which foreign states should be responsible to private persons in the courts of other states.'[228]

[224] Cf P Minnerop, 'Rogue States—State Sponsors of Terrorism?' (2002) 3 German Law Journal.

[225] Cf J Lorimer, *Institutes of the Law of Nations* (1883) i 101–3; L Oppenheim, (1905) i 30–4. Cf also FR Téson, 'The Kantian Theory of International Law' (1992) 92 CLR 53. In the eighteenth century international law was considered only to apply to European states cf JJ Moser, *Grund-Sätze des Europäischen Völcker-Rechts in Kriegs-Zeiten* (1752); GF Von Martens, *Précis du Droit des Gens Moderne de l'Europe* (3rd edn, 1821); KG Günther, *Europäisches Völkerrecht in Friedenszeiten* (1787) i. Cf in general B Kingsbury, 'Sovereignty and Inequality' (1998) 9 EJIL 599.

[226] *The Antelope* 23 US (10 Wheat) 66 (US, S Ct, 1825) 122.

[227] The problematic nature of the exception is only compounded by the ease with which the courts accept the rogue states to be responsible for terrorist activity. A case that pointedly illustrates this is *Smith and Soulas v The Islamic Emirate of Afghanistan and Iraq* (US, 2003). The court in this case condemns the state of Iraq to pay 64 million dollars to the relatives of two victims of the terrorist attack on the World Trade Centre in New York on 11 September 2001.

[228] Foreign Terrorism and US Courts: Hearings before the Subcommission on Courts and Administrative Practice of the Senate Commission on the Judiciary, 103rd Congress 2nd Session 13 (1994) (Statement of JS Borek, Deputy Legal Advisor to the US State Department). Cf also the statement of S Schifter (Legal Advisor of the Department of Justice). Cf also F De Vittor, (2002) 607; WP Hoye, 'Fighting Fire with … Mire? Civil Remedies and the New War on State-Sponsored Terrorism' (2002) 12 Duke Journal of Comparative and International Law 105, 137ff.

The Department of State stated that other states limited the exception to state immunity in respect of tort claims to acts committed within the forum state and that it was unaware of 'any instance in which a state permits jurisdiction over such tortious conduct of a foreign state without territorial limitations.'[229] The Department of State cautioned that '[i]f we deviate from that practice and assert jurisdiction over foreign states for acts that are generally perceived by the international community as falling within the scope of immunity, this would tend to erode the credibility of the FSIA. We have made substantial efforts over the years to persuade foreign states to participate in our judicial system—to appear and defend in actions against them under the FSIA. That kind of broad participation serves the interests of all. If we expand our jurisdiction in ways that cause other states to question our statute, this could undermine the broad participation we seek. It could also diminish our ability to influence other countries to abandon the theory of absolute immunity and adopt the restrictive view of sovereign immunity, which the United States has followed for over forty years.'[230]

The irony of the US terrorist state exception is striking. In the first place, the US lags behind in the efforts of the international community to enhance the effectiveness of international human rights law on the international level. As Slaughter and Bosco aptly noted '[t]he juxtaposition of this increased involvement of US courts in foreign affairs with the continued American refusal to participate in bodies like the International Criminal Court creates the image of a country happy to haul foreign defendants into its own courts while stubbornly resisting even the remote possibility that its own citizens might be called to account.'[231] Second, the US courts have not proven particularly avid to test the acts of the United

Others have argued that the act does not go far *enough*, cf eg D Mackusick, 'Human Rights vs. Sovereign Rights: The State Sponsored Terrorism Exception to the Foreign Sovereign Immunities Act' (1996) 10 Emory International Law Review 741, 769; N Roht-Arriaza, 'The Foreign Sovereign Immunities Act and Human Rights Violations: One Step Forward, Two Steps Back?' (1998) 16 Berkeley Journal of International Law 71, 81; RT Micco, 'Putting the Terrorist-Sponsoring State in the Dock: Recent Changes in the Foreign Sovereign Immunities Act and the Individual's Recourse against Foreign Powers' (2000) 14 Temple International and Comparative Law Journal 109, 142.

229 ibid.

230 ibid. In 2000 the FSIA was again amended to enhance the possibilities to execute judgements under the terrorist state exception (Victims of Trafficking and Violence Protection) Act of 2000, PubLNo 106–386, § 2002 (The Justice for Victims of Terrorism Act), 114 Stat. 1464, 1542–3; 28 USC § 1610). The amendment made it, *inter alia*, possible to attach 'blocked' property of foreign states pursuant to section 602 of the Foreign Assistance Act of 1961 and the International Emergency Economic Powers Act but allowed the President to waive the provision that makes blocked assets available for attachment, § 1610(f)(3). In light of the above considerations it is unsurprising that President Clinton moved quickly to issue a blanket waiver on the same day the Act entered into force: Presidential Determination No 2001–03, 65 Fed Reg. 66483 (28 October 2000). Cf WP Hoye (2002) for a more detailed discussion of the issue.

231 A Slaughter and D Bosco, 'Plaintiff's Diplomacy' (2000, issue 5) 79 Foreign Affairs 102, 115. Cf also CH Schreuer (1988) who noted that '[a]ssumption of jurisdiction over human rights violations of other States without the forum State's participation in [human rights] treaties and submission to their procedures must create the impression that the primary motive behind such action is not a concern for human rights but the pursuit of partisan political ends.'

States *itself* to the same international law norms. Third, it is clear that the United States claims a right for itself that it is not prepared to recognize when exercised by other states. The pandemonium that broke loose when Belgium threatened to prosecute US officials for allegations of war crimes in Iraq will only be greater when a foreign state allows a civil claim to proceed against the US in respect of these acts. Finally, it must be noted that the theory and practice of the exception is at odds with the original rationale of the Alien Tort Claims Act—the cradle of all transnational tort litigation in the US. In 1789 the Act was enacted to signal to the world that the newly founded United States was a respectable member of the international community poised to abide by the rules of international law. The Act was in particular considered necessary to prevent conflicts with other states over the protection of their nationals in the US legal system.[232] In sharp contrast, the terrorist state exception fits the unilateralist approach of the United States to international law issues. It is not designed to live up to the requirements of international law. It is designed to live up to the wants of the US domestic public opinion in defiance of the requirements of international law. The US manifests its superpower status through the use of 'superpower courts'.[233]

In his dissent in the 1992 decision of the US Supreme Court in *US v Alvarez-Machain* Justice Stevens wisely cautioned that the revenge for crimes does not allow the trampling of the law.[234] His quotation of Thomas Paine provides some final food for thought in conclusion of this section:

> an 'avidity to punish is always dangerous to liberty' because it leads a Nation 'to stretch, to misinterpret, and to misapply even the best of laws'. [...] 'He that would make his own liberty secure must guard even his enemy from oppression; for if he violates this duty he establishes a precedent that will reach to himself.[235]

It is, in conclusion, noted that the findings of this section are also supported by a quick glance at two other rules of secondary international law on the exercise of jurisdiction over states. Both the local remedies rule and the international dispute settlement rule apply unabated to cases concerning allegations of *jus cogens* violations.

Complaint procedures under human rights instruments are in principle only open to individuals that have exhausted the remedies afforded by the state that allegedly violated the rights secured by the instrument. Also the local remedies rule in the field of diplomatic protection applies irregardless of the nature of the violation concerned. This is only different when the local remedies available

[232] Cf eg WR Casto, 'The Federal Court's Protective Jurisdiction over Torts Committed in Violation of the Law of Nations' in RG Steinhardt and A D'Amato (eds), *The Alien Tort Claims Act: An Analytical Anthology* (1999) 119; A D'Amato, 'The Alien Tort Statute and the Founding of the Constitution' in RG Steinhardt and A D'Amato ibid 169; A-M Burley, 'The Alien Tort Statute and the Judiciary Act of 1789: A Badge of Honor' in RG Steinhardt and A ibid 257.

[233] A Slaughter and D Bosco (2000) 115.

[234] *US v Alvarez-Machain* 504 US 655 (US, S Ct, 1992) (dissent Stevens J).

[235] ibid 688, quoting PS Foner (ed), *The Complete Writings of Thomas Paine* (1945) ii 588.

provide no reasonable possibility of an effective remedy, or when the violation complained of also constitutes a direct injury to the state of nationality of the victim.[236]

In the 1995 *East Timor* case the ICJ was asked to consider the relation between *erga omnes* obligations and the international dispute settlement rule. Portugal argued that Australia failed to observe the obligation to respect, *inter alia*, the right of the people of East Timor to self-determination and the rights of Portugal as Administering Power by concluding a treaty with Indonesia concerning delimitation, exploration and exploitation of the continental shelf in the area of the Timor Gap. In order to decide the dispute the Court was however required to rule on the lawfulness of the entry in and continuing presence of Indonesia—not a party to the proceedings—in East Timor. In fact, Australia asserted that the claim was only brought against it because, in contrast with Indonesia, it had accepted the compulsory jurisdiction of the Court under the optional clause. The Court concluded that a decision on the claim would infringe the international dispute settlement rule under the principle laid down in the 1954 *Monetary Gold* case. In that case, the Court emphasized the 'well-established principle of international law embodied in the Court's Statute, namely, that the Court can only exercise jurisdiction over a State with its consent' and established that that means that not only the parties to the proceedings before it, but also third states whose rights form the subject matter of the decision must have accepted its jurisdiction.[237] The Court resolutely rejected Portugal's argument that the *Monetary Gold* principle did not apply to the facts of this case because the rights which Australia allegedly breached were rights *erga omnes*. It considered that although the right of peoples to self-determination had indeed an *erga omnes* character,

> the *erga omnes* character of a norm and the rule of consent to jurisdiction are two different things. Whatever the nature of the obligations invoked, the Court could not rule on the lawfulness of the conduct of a State when its judgment would imply an evaluation of the lawfulness of the conduct of another State which is not a party to the case. Where this is so, the Court cannot act, even if the right in question is a right *erga omnes*.[238]

Notably, the argument does not expressly rely on the nature of the obligations of *Indonesia* that would be implicated in a decision on the claim. Moreover, it

[236] Cf on this J Dugard (Special Rapporteur ILC), Second and Third Report on Diplomatic Protection, (2001 and 2002), UN Doc A/CN.4/514 (2001) and A/CN.4/523 (2002); K Doehring, 'Local Remedies, Exhaustion of' (1997) 3 Encyclopedia of International Law 238; CF Amerasinghe, *Local Remedies in International Law* (1990). Cf also arts 48 and 44 of the ILC Articles on State Responsibility.

[237] *Case of the Monetary Gold Removed from Rome in 1943* (ICJ, 1954) 32. Cf also *Military and Paramilitary Activities in and against Nicaragua (Nicaragua v United States of America)* (Jurisdiction and Admissibility), ICJ Reports 1984 169, 431; *Certain Phosphate Lands in Nauru* (*Nauru v Australia*) (Preliminary Objections), ICJ Reports 1992 240, 261–2, § 55: question is whether the determination of the state's responsibility is a prerequisite for a decision to be taken on the claim at issue.

[238] *East Timor* (ICJ, 1995) 102, § 29.

could be argued that the Court did not consider the influence of the concept of *jus cogens* on the international dispute settlement rule. To attempt to thus limit the significance of the ruling is clutching at straws. The statement of the Court is unambiguous in its rejection of a link between the character of a norm and the rule of consent to jurisdiction. Moreover, the right to self-determination is widely acknowledged to have *jus cogens* status and also the Court confirmed that it is 'one of the essential principles of contemporary international law'.[239]

In fact, in the 2006 decision in *Armed Activities on the Territory of the Congo (Democratic Republic of the Congo v Rwanda)* the Court removed all doubts stating that 'the fact that a dispute relates to compliance with a norm having [*jus cogens*] character...cannot of itself provide a basis for the jurisdiction of the Court to entertain that dispute. Under the Court's Statute that jurisdiction is always based on the consent of the parties.'[240]

The *East Timor* case establishes, as one scholar aptly put it, that 'the allegation of breach of an obligation *erga omnes*... is no "open sesame" to universal judicial action.'[241] The decision in *Congo v Rwanda* confirms that the same is true for the allegation of a breach of a *jus cogens* norm.

2.3.2.4 Conventional law

In addition to principled argumentation relying on the particular serious nature of certain human rights violations, scholars and plaintiffs have developed the more pragmatic argument that certain treaty obligations of states regarding the protection of human rights are incompatible with the invocation of immunity when such rights have been violated. States, they argue, have *waived* their rights under the law of state immunity by accession to the convention.[242] It must be realized that only the conventional obligations of the *defendant* state can amount to a coherent state of the law argument. The obligations of the defendant state under the human rights treaty must evidence an acceptance of the jurisdiction of foreign national courts—or a waiver of immunity under more traditional state immunity reasoning. A clash of obligations of the *forum* state under a human rights treaty with its obligations under the law of state immunity only gives rise to a forceful policy argument against the grant of state immunity. This type of argument is discussed in section 3 of this chapter.[243]

239 ibid.

240 *Armed Activities on the Territory of the Congo* (ICJ, 2006) § 64.

241 D Alland, 'Countermeasures of General Interest' (2002) 13 EJIL 1221, 1235.

242 Cf eg A Bianchi (1997) 423ff; KC Randall, *Federal Courts and the International Human Rights Paradigm* (1990) 96; JJ Paust (1985); JJ Paust (1983); WF Pepper (1992) 377; HG Schermers, 'Diplomatic Immunity in Modern International Law' in E Denters and N Schrijver (eds), *Reflections on International Law from the Low Countries* (1998) 156, 163.

243 It should be noted that Section 1604 of the US FSIA does limit the scope of the rule of state immunity on the basis of pre-existing conventional obligations of the US. It provides that the rule of state immunity is '[s]ubject to existing international agreements to which the United States is a party at the time of enactment of this act.'

The argument that states waive their immunity by signing and ratifying human rights treaties was first tested in *Frolova v Union of Soviet Socialist Republics*.[244] Plaintiff in this case had argued that the Soviet Union had implicitly waived its state immunity defence when it signed the United Nations Charter and the Helsinki Accords.[245] The court set out to emphasize that 'courts rarely find that a nation has waived its sovereign immunity, particularly with respect to suits brought by third parties, without strong evidence that this is what the foreign state intended' and that 'waiver would not be found absent a conscious decision to take part in the litigation'.[246] It resolutely rejected the argument, holding that there was 'absolutely no evidence from the language, structure or history of the agreements at issue that implies a waiver of the U.S.S.R.'s sovereign immunity'. The 'vague, general language' of the agreements did not support the argument. It cannot be concluded, the court held, that states anticipated the exercise of jurisdiction by US courts when they signed the agreements.[247] This strict interpretation was confirmed by the Supreme Court in *Argentine Republic v Amerada Hess Shipping Corporation*. The court held that a foreign state does not 'waive its immunity under [the act] by signing an international agreement that contains no mention of a waiver of immunity to suit in the United States courts or even the availability of a cause of action in the United States.'[248]

Interest in the implied waiver argument has been revived by the decisive role accorded to the 1984 Convention against Torture in the decision of the House of Lords in the *Pinochet* case.[249] Fox wondered in this regard why the obligation to provide 'fair and adequate compensation to the victim'—article 14 of the Torture Convention—is not equally inconsistent with the retention of a plea of state immunity.[250]

Three observations are warranted. In the first place, it must be realized that the obligation to provide a remedy for human rights violations does not apply to violations committed by foreign state officials abroad. Human rights treaties oblige a state at most to provide remedies for human rights violations committed within its jurisdiction, or by its state officials. An early draft of article 14 of the Torture

[244] *Frolova v Union of Soviet Socialist Republics* (US, 1985).

[245] ibid 376. Section 1605(1)(a) FSIA.

[246] ibid 377.

[247] ibid 378. Cf differently *Von Dardel v Union of Soviet Socialist Republics* (US, 1985).

[248] *Argentine Republic v Amerada Hess Shipping Corp* (US, 1989) 442. Cf also *Denegri v Republic of Chile* (US, 1992); *Siderman de Blake v Republic of Argentina* (US, 1992); *Smith v Socialist People's Libyan Arab Jamahiriya* (US, 1996); *Princz v Federal Republic of Germany* (US, 1994); *Von Dardel v Union of Soviet Socialist Republics* (US, 1990); *Hwang Geum Joo v Japan* (US, 2001); *Sampson v Federal Republic of Germany* 975 F Supp 1108 (US, DC for the Northern District of Illinois, 1997).

[249] *Pinochet* no 3, cf ch 5 § 2.3.1.2 above.

[250] H Fox (1999) 700. The article provides that '[e]ach State Party shall ensure in its legal system that the victim of an act of torture obtains redress and has an enforceable right to fair and adequate compensation, including the means for as full rehabilitation as possible. In the event of the death of the victim as a result of an act of torture, his dependants shall be entitled to compensation.'

Convention had explicitly limited the obligation to acts of torture 'committed in any territory under its jurisdiction'. Most commentators agree that the phrase was omitted because it was superfluous. The limitation, they argue, is implicit in the article and the Convention.[251] The latter position finds support in the 2004 decision of the Canadian Court of Appeal for Ontario in *Bouzari and Others v Islamic Republic of Iran*.[252] Bouzari had argued that Canada has an obligation to provide an exception to state immunity for civil actions for torture committed abroad by a foreign state under article 14 of the Torture Convention. The court accepted the opinion of Greenwood—who had been asked to give expert evidence on international law—that article 14 only requires Canada to provide a civil remedy for torture committed within its jurisdiction. It pointed out that while the text of the Convention itself provides no conclusive answer, state practice, including the *travaux préparatoires* of the Convention, is clear on the territorial character of the obligation.[253] Accordingly, the obligation to provide a remedy would only apply to acts of foreign state officials committed within the territory of the forum state.

In its 2006 decision in the case of *Jones v Saudi Arabia* the House of Lords reasoned along the lines of the *Bouzari* case when it held that article 14 'requires a private right of action for damages only for acts of torture committed in territory under the jurisdiction of the forum state'.[254]

Second, the right to a remedy should be clearly distinguished from the right of access to court. The remedy provided must be effective to ensure compliance with the prohibition to violate human rights but does not necessarily entail access to the judicial authorities of a state.[255] Accordingly, while the right to a remedy may

[251] See A Byrnes, 'Civil Remedies for Torture Committed Abroad: An Obligation under the Convention against Torture?' in C Scott (ed), *Torture as Tort, Comparative Perspectives on the Development of Transnational Human Rights Litigation* (2001) 537, 542–9. Cf also JF Murphy, 'Civil Liability for the Commission of International Crimes as an Alternative to Criminal Prosecution' (1999) 12 Harvard Human Rights Journal 1, 27 and 36; R Garnett, 'The Defence of State Immunity for Acts of Torture' (1997) 18 Australian Yearbook of International Law 97, 109–10. On ratifying the Convention, the United States issued an interpretive declaration indicating that it understood article 14 to require a state to provide a private right of action for damages only for acts of torture committed within the jurisdiction of that state, see (1991) 12 Human Rights Law Journal 276. Cf however the Recommendations of the Committee against Torture in its Concluding Observations on Canada in 2005, CAT/C/CR/34/CAN, § 5, sub f.

[252] *Bouzari and Others v Islamic Republic of Iran* (Canada, 2004). Cf also the 2002 decision of the Ontario Superior Court of Justice in the case, 124 ILR 427.

[253] ibid § 69–82. Cf also 124 ILR 427, 438–41.

[254] *Jones v Saudi Arabia* (UK, 2006) § 25, and also § 46, 56–7. Cf also A Byrnes (2001) 540 fn 9. It is noted that the Court of Appeal had phrased it slightly different. The court wrote that 'art 14(1) is dealing with (no more than) a right of redress in the legal system of the state...by whose official...the alleged act of torture was committed', implying that the question where the torture was committed is irrelevant, *Jones v Saudi Arabia and Abdul Aziz* and *Mitchell a.o. v Al-Dali a.o.* (UK, 2004) § 21.

[255] Cf *Leander v Sweden* Series A–116, 9 EHRR 433 (ECHR, 1987) 457. Cf also *Z and Others v United Kingdom* 34 EHRR 97 (ECHR, 2001) 141.

be violated when there is no access to court because of the rule of state immunity, there is no *direct* clash between the immunity and the right.

Finally, it is recalled that the reasoning of the Lords in the *Pinochet* case was based on the specific definition of the crime of torture. The Lords argued that there could be no immunity in regard to the crime *only* because it is *by definition* committed in an official capacity. Since the definition of the crime is co-extensive with the definition of official immunity the Lords concluded that the Torture Convention would be a dead letter if functional immunity were to exist in respect of the allegation of torture.[256] Accordingly, they concluded, the states that agreed to this obligation must have done so under the understanding that functional immunity would not apply. It is fair to say that *had* the Convention regarded a crime that can also be committed by private individuals the undertaking to prosecute the crime on the basis of universal jurisdiction would not have similarly constituted an implied waiver.

These three factors contrast the conventional obligation to exercise universal jurisdiction over the crime of torture with the conventional obligation to provide a remedy for violations of human rights in general committed within the jurisdiction of, or under the responsibility of the forum state. The obligation to provide a remedy is not co-extensive with the immunities of states and their officials under international law. This author therefore agrees with the US courts that the argument that states that accept a conventional obligation to protect human rights, and more in particular the right to a remedy in respect of violations of these rights, therewith accept the exercise of foreign national jurisdiction in respect of allegations that they have violated these obligations is not tenable. It severely overstretches the concept of implied waiver.[257]

[256] The Lords formulated their arguments in seven individual opinions that make it impossible to individuate one ratio decidendi. In fact, only some Lords qualified the ratification of the Torture Convention as an implied waiver of immunity cf further ch 5 § 2.3.1.2 above. Cf further on the difference between obligations in criminal and civil proceedings: *Von Dardel v Union of Soviet Socialist Republics* (US, 1990) (on the Vienna Convention on the Prevention and Punishment of Crimes against Internationally Protected Persons, including Diplomatic Agents (1973); *Hwang Geum Joo v Japan* (US, 2001) (on the Potsdam Declaration (1945).

[257] Cf in a similar vein F De Vittor (2002) 581–4; M Karagiannakis (1998) 20. It is noted in comparison that the ICJ has held with regard to the local remedies rule that it is 'unable to accept that an important principle of customary international law should be held to have been tacitly dispensed with, in the absence of any words making clear an intention to do so': *Elettronica Sicula SpA (ELSI)* (ICJ, 1989) 42, § 50. The baffling nature of the argument may be illustrated by reference to the ECHR. The right of individual petition (art 34 ECHR) only became an integral part of the Convention after 1998. The effect of the implied waiver construction would be that member states were free not to accept the right of individual petition under the specifically developed conventional enforcement mechanism designed with an eye to an independent and marginal review of the conduct of member states but automatically accepted a previous non-existing competence of the national courts of all other member states over that conduct.

2.4 Concluding Observations

International human rights law and the related concepts of *jus cogens* norms and *erga omnes* obligations have not affected the rule of state immunity. The absence of state practice is not in itself a sufficient rebuttal of the argument that a human rights exception to state immunity exists. In the Harvard Law Review of 1897 Mr Justice Holmes recounted the tale of a Vermont judge before whom a suit was brought by one farmer against another for breaking a churn. The judge 'took time to consider, and then said that he had looked through the statutes and could find nothing about churns, and gave judgment for the defendant.'[258] The argument that there is no human rights exception to state immunity because there is no state practice supporting such an exception suffers from a comparable rigidity towards the epistemology of the law. In chapter 2 of his study it was argued that reason and interpretation *are* essential tools of judges. Especially the rule of state immunity which is said to find its basis in the principle of sovereign equality rather than in the practice of states requires judges to look beyond state immunity practice.

However, the Court of Appeal for Ontario *was* right to point out in the *Bouzari* case that 'the extent of the prohibition against torture as a rule of jus cogens is [not] determined... by any particular view of what is required if it is to be meaningful'.[259] Arguments of proponents of a human rights exception to state immunity prove incoherent after critical analysis of the parameters of the rule of state immunity, the concepts of *jus cogens* norms and *erga omnes* obligations and international human rights law.

Both the hierarchy of norms argument, and the secondary rules argument fail to convince. In respect of the latter argument it is good to recall the words of Judge Tanaka in his dissent in the *South West Africa Cases*.[260] While the judge cautioned against a too formalistic interpretation of international law he did underline that he did not propose to deduce rules from mere necessity or desirability but from the *raison d'être* and the theoretical construction of the system of relevant rules. His proposal explicitly acknowledged the limits of voluntarism, setting out to construe the 'reasonably assumed intention' of states.[261]

In conclusion we should examine one of the arguments of the Italian Supreme Court in the *Ferrini* case that has not yet been discussed on its merits.[262] The court argued that functional immunity exists in order to prevent an indirect implication of foreign states, and that there is therefore no reason to sustain state immunity in cases concerning international crimes when it is widely accepted

[258] OW Holmes, 'The Path of the Law' (1897) 10 HLR 456, 474–5.
[259] *Bouzari and Others v Islamic Republic of Iran* (Canada, 2004) § 90.
[260] *South West Africa Cases* (ICJ, 1966) Dissenting Opinion Judge Tanaka, 248.
[261] ibid 277–8.
[262] *Ferrini v Repubblica Federale di Germania* (Italy, 2004).

that there is no functional immunity in respect of such crimes.[263] The argument had previously been advanced by Bianchi in response to the *Pinochet* case. He asserted that 'once it is held that no plea of immunity is available to state officials for crimes against international law which presuppose or require state action, the immunity of the state can be easily circumvented by bringing criminal proceedings against state officials'.[264] Since 'the immunity *ratione materiae* of state officials is necessary not to circumvent the immunity of the state', he argued, the absence of functional immunity can only mean the absence of state immunity.

Reading chapters 3 and 5 of this study reveals the fallacy of this argument. Only when a suit against a foreign state officials *is in fact a suit against the state* does the rule of functional immunity apply. When foreign state officials are sued in respect of crimes against international law they cannot say that they performed those acts as the arm of the state. Foreign state officials can be sued in their personal capacity in respect of crimes against international law. Functional immunity is absent exactly because the state is *not* indirectly impleaded in such claims. A claim in respect of the same acts directed against the state itself is therefore of a fundamental different character.

In conclusion it is noted that states may of course decide to give the *jus cogens* concept more body. As Crawford notes, 'the legal regime of serious breaches is... in a state of development'.[265] Proposals *de lege ferenda* to enhance the influence of the concept of *jus cogens* norms and *erga omnes* obligations on the law of state responsibility are therefore welcome. An example thereof can be found in the First Report on Diplomatic Protection submitted by Rapporteur Dugard to the International Law Commission in 2000.[266] While states have, in principle, discretion in the exercise of diplomatic protection on behalf of their nationals, the Rapporteur proposed the following article to be included:

1. Unless the injured person is able to bring a claim for such injury before a competent international court or tribunal, the State of his/her nationality has a legal duty to exercise diplomatic protection on behalf of the injured person upon request, if the injury results from a grave breach of a *jus cogens* norm attributable to another State.
2. The State of nationality is relieved of this obligation if:
   (a) The exercise of diplomatic protection would seriously endanger the overriding interests of the State and /or its people;
   (b) Another State exercises diplomatic protection on behalf of the injured person;

[263] ibid § 11.

[264] A Bianchi, 'Immunity versus Human Rights: The *Pinochet* Case' (1999) 10 EJIL 237. Cf also A Bianchi, 'Individual Accountability for Crimes against Humanity: Reckoning with the Past, Thinking of the Future' (1999) 19 SAIS Review 97, 113. Another scholar wrote in this regard that 'holding individuals rather than states liable for human rights violations contains an element of hypocrisy', HM Osofsky (1998) 40 and 52.

[265] J Crawford (2002) 253.

[266] JR Dugard (Special Rapporteur ILC), First Report on Diplomatic Protection (2000), UN Doc A/CN.4/506 (2000), art 4 and commentary.

(c) The injured person does not have the effective and dominant nationality of the State.

3. States are obliged to provide in their municipal law for the enforcement of this right before a competent domestic court or other independent national authority.

The proposal received a tepid response from the Commission. The general view was, as we read in the annual report on the work of the ILC to the General Assembly, that the issue was not yet ripe for codification.[267] Although the article was dropped from the project, the discussions within the ILC may contribute to changes in state practice in times to come.

This section ends with two cautionary remarks in respect of the possibility that the *jus cogens* concept were to become a tool to distinguish immune from non-immune acts of foreign states in the future. As was already pointed out in the introduction of this section, the criterion of *jus cogens* violations suffers from a severe form of circularity. Contrary to other tools of distinction, it anticipates the outcome of the inquiry into the merits of the case. In addition, one can wonder whether the lifting of procedural rights of defendants accused of horrible misdeeds is a desirable option. Faced with the seriousness of the allegations as a criterion for immunity decisions, Röling has pointed out that the need for the protection of the law is greatest in the face of severe indignation.[268]

3 Policy Arguments: The (In)Compatibility of Immunity Rules and the Fundamental Rights of Individuals

3.1 Introduction

The debate on a human rights exception to state immunity and personal immunity may also be conducted on the essentially different level of policy arguments. A clash of the obligations owed to other states under immunity rules with the obligations owed to private individuals under rules of international human rights law provides a forceful policy argument in favour of a restriction of the immunity rules. Policy arguments *precede* changing state practice and the consequent change in the scope of the rule. The issue of debate is not what the scope of the immunity rule *is* but what that scope *should be*. It is recalled here that in this study the term policy argument should be understood from the perspective of immunity law. The arguments discussed below are of course state of the law arguments as far as the scope of human rights law is concerned. Private individuals asserting them in court may obtain a result similar to that which could have been obtained

[267] See the Report of the ILC on the work of its 52th session (2000), UN Doc A/55/10 (2000), § 450ff.

[268] Note of BVA Röling to *De Haas v De Staat Indonesië* NJ 1962, no 74 (The Netherlands, Hoge Raad, 1962) 291.

with a successful state of the law argument on the immunity rule. Since judges may decide that the obligation owed to the private individual should prevail over the obligation owed to the foreign state, a successful policy argument of this kind may result in the non-application of the immunity rule. If not, the forum state is in any case obliged to compensate the private individual whose human rights were violated.

This section examines the compatibility of state immunity and personal immunity with the right to a fair trial, the right to a remedy and the right to effective protection. The exact scope and content of the respective rights may differ as between the various human rights treaties in which they feature. Since a detailed examination of the different provisions and respective interpretations thereof and the inquiry into the scope of customary international law on these rights would stray us too far from the research question, this study approaches the issue in principle from the perspective of the European Convention on Human Rights.

3.2 The Right to a Fair Trial

3.2.1 Introduction

Article 6.1 of the European Convention on Human Rights provides as follows:

> In the determination of his civil rights and obligations or of any criminal charge against him, everyone is entitled to a fair and public hearing within a reasonable time by an independent and impartial tribunal established by law.

For the purposes of this study it is important to point out that the article has been interpreted to guarantee individuals a right to equality of arms,[269] as well as a right of access to court.[270]

It was explained in the introduction to this chapter that the argument that the grant of state immunity violates the right to a fair trial—and in particular the right of access to court—is a revival of the criticism that was once developed against the absolute state immunity approach. The grant of absolute immunity to foreign states was generally felt to entail a 'denial of justice' to private individuals. This feeling underlay the indignation of the hapless owners of the schooner *Exchange* describing their plight to the court:

> Your own citizens plundered. Your national rights violated. Your courts deaf to the complaints of the injured. Your government not redressing their wrongs, but giving sanction to their spoliators. The argument of our opponents allows no remedy to the citizen, although dispossessed of his property, within the limits of our own territory. Although

[269] *Neumeister v Austria* Series A–8, 1 EHRR 91 (ECHR, 1968); *X v Federal Republic of Germany* (1963) 6 Yearbook on the European Convention on Human Rights 520 (EComHR, 1963) 574.

[270] *Golder v United Kingdom* Series A–18, 1 EHRR 524 (ECHR, 1975).

the ship should have been seized in the Delaware, and converted into a public armed vessel, we are supposed to have no redress.[271]

The early adherence to a restrictive approach was often rationalized from the perspective of the right of the individual to have his case heard. As the Mixed Tribunals of Egypt noted when in 1920 a commercial dispute was brought before it, 'l'immunité de juridiction dans ce cas serait la négation de la justice puisqu'elle priverait du secours de celle-ci les individus dont les intérêts se trouvent en conflit avec les intérêts privés du dit Etat.'[272]

The argument was equally relied on by the criticasters of the adherence to the absolute approach. Lauterpacht, for example, noted that a claim to immunity often

> consists in an unwarranted—and often petty—refusal to satisfy what would otherwise be a good and enforceable legal claim. It amounts, in fact, to a denial of justice... It is this essential incompatibility of the doctrine of jurisdictional immunity with the principle of the subjection of the sovereign state to the rule of law which explains the strength—we might say the vehemence—of the opposition to the maintenance of that doctrine and the fact that only a diminishing minority of writers are willing to support it. It is this factor rather than the expansion of the activities of the state and the unfairness of its competition with the less privileged private individual that is the paramount feature of the situation.[273]

Criticism on the absolute approach was at times formulated in terms of article 6 ECHR. In 1968 Pahr, for example, argued that state immunity violates the right to a fair trial and the right to equality of arms in particular. The rule, he argued, allows foreign states the advantage of their own courts while private individuals bear the burden of litigation in an unfamiliar legal system and language contrary to the normal jurisdictional rules.[274]

Some scholars argue that the restrictive approach to the state immunity *still* raises an issue under article 6 ECHR. In 1997 Bröhmer, for example, asserted that there is no meaningful difference between *acta jure imperii* and *acta jure gestionis* for the purposes of article 6.1 and concluded boldly that '[t]here is no room for the immunity privilege under the Convention.'[275] The question to be answered in this section is whether the denial of justice argument is indeed equally coherent as against the restrictive rule of state immunity as we know it today.

[271] *The Schooner Exchange v M'Faddon* (US, 1812) 128.

[272] *Hall v Bengoa* (Egypt, 1920) 272.

[273] H Lauterpacht (1951) 236. Cf also JF Lalive, (1953) 219; R Jennings and A Watts (eds) (1992) i 342; Institut de Droit International (Rapporteur I Brownlie), Contemporary Problems Concerning the Jurisdictional Immunity of States, Plenary Session (1992), Observation of Lauterpacht, (1992) 64–II AIDI 214, 234.

[274] WP Pahr, 'Die Staatenimmunität und Artikel 6 Absatz 1 der Europaische Menschenrechtkonvention' in *Mélanges offerts à Polys Modinos, Problèmes des droits de l'homme et de l'unification européenne* (1968) 222. Cf also J-F Lalive(1953) 217; HG Schermers (1998) 156.

[275] J Bröhmer (1997) 163–188, in particular 165, 185–6, and 187. Bröhmer based his conclusion also on an analysis of art 13 ECHR, discussed in § 3.3 below.

In addition, this section will examine whether the comprehensive personal immunity of diplomatic agents and foreign heads of state is compatible with the right to a fair trial. At about the same time that Lauterpacht formulated his criticism on the rule of absolute state immunity, Holland wrote that

> the recognition of diplomatic immunity in English law clearly infringes the rule of law, in that it necessitates an exception being made to the doctrine that all men should be equal before the law and subject to the same laws administered in the same courts.[276]

This immunity, he added, 'may cause great hardship to individuals'.[277] In the beginning of the twentieth century Italian courts did not recognize diplomatic immunity for non-official acts because, as the Court of Cassation of Rome put it, such a comprehensive immunity is contrary to justice.[278] While today a comprehensive rule of diplomatic immunity is part of customary international law it *can* be questioned whether that rule is compatible with the individual's right to a fair trial.

In comparison, it is interesting to note that the Supreme Court of Chile decided in 1988 that diplomatic and consular immunities could no longer prevent the exercise of the constitutional right of access to court to safeguard rights and guarantees protected in the constitution.[279] In particular, the court held that rights protected under the constitution prevail over these immunities because they have a superior status.[280] After an intervention of the Chilean Ministry of Foreign Affairs the Supreme Court was forced to clarify and amend its decisions. The court declared that its ruling

> in no way affects the immunity of jurisdiction referred to in the Vienna Convention on diplomatic and consular relations... since the recourse... does not involve in itself sanctions of a criminal, civil or administrative character, this immunity thereby being a bar to the adoption of coercive measures against the diplomatic agent... [and] taking into consideration the provisions of those Conventions all reports and enquiries ought to be undertaken through the Ministry of Foreign Affairs.[281]

[276] DC Holland, 'Diplomatic Immunity in English Law' (1951) 4 Current Legal Problems 81, 106.

[277] ibid.

[278] *Comina v Kite* (Italy, 1922) 174.

[279] *Walter Szurgelies Hoyer et al. v First Counsellor of the Embassy of the Federal Republic of Germany* (Chile, S Ct, 1988) and *Manfred Gerhard Skrabs et al v Consul of the Federal Republic of Germany* (Chile, S Ct, 1988), discussed in FO Vicuna, 'Diplomatic and Consular Immunities and Human Rights' (1999) 40 ICLQ 34.

[280] The argument should be distinguished from the hierarchy of norms argument discussed in § 2.2 above. It is not argued that there *is* no immunity available. Rather, the court relies on the hierarchy of norms to decide which of the two competing rules prevails and which rule is to be violated.

[281] Chile, S Ct (1988), discussed (and trans) in FO Vicuna, (1999) 40 ICLQ 34, 41. Vicuna argued that the decision distinguished between immunity from jurisdiction and immunity from enforcement. This author disagrees. The court excludes the exercise of jurisdiction over diplomatic

This rectification however *only* regards the prevalence of the right of access to court over the rule of diplomatic immunity. It does not detract from the conclusion of the court that the state has *clashing obligations* under the two rules. In view of the substantial prejudice caused to private individuals the inquiry into the compatibility of article 6.1 with immunity rules warrants a reconsideration of prevailing state practice on diplomatic immunities.

The European Court of Human Rights was asked to decide whether the restrictive approach to state immunity violates article 6 ECHR in three cases recently before it. The applicants in *McElhinney v Ireland*,[282] *Al-Adsani v United Kingdom*,[283] and *Fogarty v United Kingdom*[284] all complained that the application of the rule of state immunity to proceedings instigated by them against foreign states before the courts of the respondent states had violated their right of access to court under article 6.1 of the Convention. The Court decided the three cases on the basis of roughly identical considerations. It ruled that the rule of state immunity did indeed raise an issue under article 6.1, but found the rule to have a legitimate aim and to constitute a proportional restriction of applicant's right of access to court. Put bluntly, the Court argued that the grant of state immunity to foreign states under rules of *international* law never violates the right of access to court under article 6.1 of the Convention.

This section sets out to critically discuss the Court's reasoning in these three cases on the basis of an analysis of the relation between the obligations of states under immunity rules and the obligation of states under article 6.1 of the Convention. Can it indeed be said that these obligations clash and that hence article 6.1 is always applicable? And, as far as it is applicable, is the Court's reasoning on the balance between the interests protected by article 6.1 and the interests protected by immunity rules convincing? On the basis of the nature and scope of the rule of state immunity as set out in chapter 2 of this study and the nature and scope of personal immunity rules as set out in chapter 4 of this study, *and* on the basis of the general framework for testing the legitimacy and proportionality of restrictions of the rights under article 6.1 developed by the Convention organs in earlier jurisprudence, both these questions will be answered in the negative. Although the conclusion that article 6.1 is not violated may be correct in itself, it will be argued that the decisions have a feeble foundation. The Court, it seems, has preferred to ignore the complexity of immunity rules in the assessment of the applicability of article 6.1, and has reduced its control over the margin of appreciation to practically fictitious in its assessment of the question of the article's breach..

agents altogether. It is the special nature of the cause of action at hand that allowed a distinction from the exercise of jurisdiction.

282 *McElhinney v Ireland* (ECHR, 2001).

283 *Al-Adsani*.

284 *Fogarty v United Kingdom* (ECHR, 2001).

3.2.2 The Strasbourg Framework for Access to Court Complaints

3.2.2.1 Introduction

The judgments of the Court in *McElhinney v Ireland*, *Al-Adsani v UK*, and *Fogarty v UK* built on the legal framework developed by the Strasbourg institutions to test right of access to court complaints. The framework divides in two principal queries. In the first place it must be questioned whether article 6.1 is applicable to the facts of the case. Is there a restriction on the access to court to have a claim relating to civil rights and obligations determined? If so, it remains to be seen next whether the restriction violates the right of access to court. The right of access is not absolute but calls 'by its very nature... for regulation by the state, regulation which may vary in time and place according to the needs and resources of the community and of individuals.'[285] Restrictions must however not be such that 'the very essence of the right is impaired'. They must moreover have a 'legitimate aim' and there must be 'a reasonable relationship of proportionality' between the restriction and the aim sought to be achieved.[286] In other words, even if article 6.1 applies it may be that the article is not violated because the restriction imposed by the respondent state complies with the requirements of article 6.1.

3.2.2.2 Applicability

In the history of Strasbourg jurisprudence we find two distinct arguments challenging the applicability of article 6.1 to immunity rules.

The most common argument is that the immunity rule places a limit on the substantive right of individuals. When there is no civil right to be determined there can arise no issue under article 6.1. Thus, the Commission argued in its 1979 decision in *Agee v United Kingdom* that

> Article 6(1) must be interpreted with due regard to parliamentary immunity as traditionally recognised in the States parties to the Convention... In the present case the applicant cannot complain in the United Kingdom courts of the statements made in Parliament in view of the doctrine of Parliamentary privilege, which forms part of United Kingdom law. This affords absolute protection to persons making such statements. Although a person's rights under domestic law to protection of his reputation generally constitute 'civil rights' within the meaning of Art. 6(1), the applicant does not have any right in United Kingdom law to protection of his reputation insofar as it may be affected by the statements complained of. Art. 6(1) does not therefore guarantee the right to take proceedings in respect of these statements, since the applicant has no 'civil right' to protection of his reputation against them.[287]

This argument accommodates the scope of the substantive right of the individual to the rule of parliamentary immunity. It relies on the conventional wisdom

[285] *Golder v United Kingdom* (ECHR, 1975) 537.
[286] *Ashingdane v United Kingdom* Series A–93, 7 EHRR 528 (ECHR, 1985) 546.
[287] *Agee v United Kingdom* DR 7, 164 (EComHR, 1976) 175.

that article 6 applies to domestic law as one finds it. It is not possible to create by way of interpretation a substantive right which has no legal basis whatsoever in the domestic law of the state concerned. As the Court formulated it in *H v Belgium*, 'Article 6(1) extends only to "*contestations*" (disputes) over (civil) "rights and obligations" which can be said, at least on arguable grounds, to be recognized under domestic law; it does not in itself guarantee any particular content for (civil) "rights and obligations" in the substantive law of the Contracting States.'[288] Complaints concerning the absence of a remedy under national law will therefore in general not raise an issue under article 6. In *Powell and Rayner v United Kingdom*, for example, the Court rejected the argument that the statutory bar on the right of action in nuisance in respect of aircraft noise of Section 76.1 of the UK Civil Aviation Act was in violation with their right of access to court. Since applicants could not claim to have a substantive right under English law to obtain relief for exposure to aircraft noise there was no civil right recognized under domestic law to attract the application of article 6.1.[289]

An absolute deference to this distinction may however render the right of access to court toothless. Often, procedural limitations to access can easily be cast in the form of a limitation of the substantive content of a civil right.[290] The Court has therefore ruled in the case of *Fayed v United Kingdom* that

> [w]hether a person has an actionable domestic claim may depend not only on the substantive content, properly speaking, of the relevant civil right as defined under national law but also on the existence of procedural bars preventing or limiting the possibilities of bringing potential claims to court. In the latter kind of case Article 6(1) may have a degree of applicability. Certainly the Convention enforcement bodies may not create by way of interpretation of Article 6(1) a substantive civil right which has no legal basis in the State concerned. However, it would not be consistent with the rule of law in a democratic society or with the basic principle underlying Article 6(1)—namely that civil claims must be capable of being submitted to a judge for adjudication—if, for example, a State

[288] *H v Belgium* Series A–127-B, 10 EHRR 229 (ECHR, 1987) 346. Cf also the case of *Sporrong and Lönnroth v Sweden* in which the Commission said: 'whether a right is at all at issue in a particular case depends primarily on the legal system of the State concerned It is true that that the concept of a "right" is itself autonomous to some degree. Thus it is not decisive for the purposes of Art 6 para. 1 that a given privilege or interest which exists in a domestic legal system is not classified or described as a "right" by that system. However, it is clear that the Convention organs should not create by way of interpretation of Art 6 para 1 a substantive right which has no legal basis whatsoever in the State concerned', Commission Report (1980) § 150; *James v United Kingdom* Series A–98, 8 EHRR 123 (ECHR, 1986) 157–158; *Lithgow and Others v United Kingdom* Series A–102, 8 EHRR 329 (ECHR, 1986) 393; *Holy Monasteries v Greece* Series A–301–A, 10 EHRR 9 (ECHR, 1995) 50.

[289] *Powell and Rayner v United Kingdom* Series A–172, 12 EHRR 355 (ECHR, 1990) 366.

[290] FJ Hampson, 'Restrictions on Rights of Action and the European Convention on Human Rights: The Case of *Powell and Rayner*' (1990) 61 BYIL 279, 288, pointed out that the distinction allowed states to deny rights to a certain group of individuals, 'for example, if a legislative provision were to deny to all women the right to bring actions in defamation, ... they [would have] no cause of action in domestic law. Article 6 would therefore be inapplicable to the issue since there was no "civil right" which fell to determined'.

could, without restraint or control by the Convention enforcement bodies, remove from the jurisdiction of the courts a whole range of civil claims or confer immunities from civil liability on large groups or categories of persons.[291]

It recognized that '[i]t is not always an easy matter to trace the dividing line between procedural and substantive limitations of a given entitlement under domestic law. It may sometimes be no more than a question of legislative technique whether the limitation is expressed in terms of the right or its remedy.'[292] The jurisprudence of Commission and Court does however not excel in clarity on the question what instruments Strasbourg has to pierce the veil of form to determine the substantive nature of a rule.

In *Dyer v UK* the Commission recognized the 'real threat to the rule of law [that] could emerge if a State were arbitrarily to remove the jurisdiction of civil courts to determine certain classes of civil action'.[293] It pointed out that the removal of jurisdiction could not only be effected through procedural bars but also through substantive immunities from liability. Since article 6.1 'must be read in the light of the rule of law referred to in the preamble, of which the principle whereby a civil claim must be capable of being submitted to a judge, is an integral part' Convention organs must be allowed some control on the removal of jurisdiction of courts to determine certain classes of civil claim and the conferral of immunities from liability on certain groups in respect of their actions.[294] The applicant in *Dyer* complained that the exclusion of Crown liability in tort in respect of injuries arising out of service in the armed forces under section 10 of the Crown Proceedings Act 1947 violated his right of access to court under article 6.1. The Commission undertook to examine whether the section 'constitutes an arbitrary limitation of the applicant's substantive civil claims'. It emphasized the special nature and risks of military service and noted that the alternative invalidity pension leaves those covered by the rule often better protected than normal law. The limitation was therefore held not to be arbitrary and article 6.1 was found not to apply. The approach is somewhat puzzling. The Commission developed a test that resembles that formulated later by the Court in *Ashingdane* for the compliance with article 6.1, but now as a sort of preliminary test for the applicability of article 6.1 to limitations that are substantive in form.[295] Article 6 is not applicable, rather than not violated when the limitations satisfy the set criteria.

[291] *Fayed v United Kingdom* Series A–294–B, 18 EHRR 393 (ECHR, 1994) 429.

[292] ibid 430. Lord Hoffmann stated in the *Matthews* case that the question is 'a slippery one', *Matthews v Ministry of Defence* [2003] 1 AC 1163 (UK, HL, 2003) § 33.

[293] *Dyer v United Kingdom* appl no 10475/83, DR 39, 246 (EComHR, 1984) 252 (citing the Commission Report in the *Ashingdane* case). Cf also *Pinder v United Kingdom* 7 EHRR 464 (EComH, 1984) and *Ketterich v United Kingdom* 5 EHRR 465 (EComHR, 1982).

[294] ibid.

[295] In the 2003 decision of the House of Lords in the case of *Matthews v Ministry of Defence*, (UK, 2003), Lord Bingham of Cornhill did not appreciate the approach of the Commission in the *Dyer*, *Pinder* and *Ketterich* cases. He questioned 'whether the Commission was right to ask

The Court however has not unequivocally approved the approach of the Commission. Although the Court referred to the *Dyer* case in its somewhat Delphic statement in *Fayed* that article 6.1 may have 'a degree of applicability' in certain cases, it stuck to traditional interpretations of these concepts when it came to qualifying a rule as either procedural or substantive in character in *Osman v UK* and *Z v UK*.[296]

The facts underlying the *Osman* case were the following. Applicants had filed a claim of negligence against the police in the UK courts because the police had failed to appreciate and act on a series of clear warning signs that the person that eventually murdered their husband and father posed a serious threat to the Osman family. A court confronted with a claim of negligence is required to find that the facts of the case disclose a breach of duty of care owed by the defendant to the plaintiff which has caused harm to the latter, the constituent elements of a duty of care being the following: whether the damage is foreseeable; whether there exists a relationship of proximity between the parties; and whether it is fair, just and reasonable to impose a duty of care in the circumstances. Since the House of Lords in *Hill v Chief Constable of West Yorkshire*[297] had ruled that the last criterion shields the police from liability in the context of the investigation and suppression of crime, the applicants' claim of negligence was rejected.[298]

The Osman family filed a complaint in Strasbourg. They argued that the exclusionary rule developed by the House of Lords operated as an absolute immunity to negligence actions against the police and asked the Court to find that such immunity violated their right of access under article 6.1 of the Convention. The respondent state argued that the rule qualified the substantive right and that hence no issue under article 6.1 arose.

The Court stressed that the contested rule did not 'automatically doom to failure such a civil action at the outset but in principle allows a domestic court to make a considered assessment on the basis of the arguments before it as to whether a particular case is or is not suitable for the application of the rule' and that *therefore* 'the applicants must be taken to have had a right' for the purpose of applicability of article 6.[299]

"whether section 10 of the 1947 Act constitutes an arbitrary limitation of the applicant's substantive civil claims"...when in truth the applicant had no substantive civil claim' (§ 16).

296 *Osman v United Kingdom* 29 EHRR 245 (ECHR, 1998); *Z and Others v United Kingdom* 34 EHRR 97 (ECHR, 2001). In the case of *Fayed v United Kingdom* the Court considered it not necessary to decide whether the restriction was substantive or procedural in character since the compliance test would have to take place anyway under art 8, *Fayed v United Kingdom* (ECHR, 1994) 430–1.

297 *Hill v Chief Constable of West Yorkshire* [1989] AC 53 (UK, HL, 1988).

298 *Osman and another v Ferguson and another* [1993] 4 All ER 344 (UK, CA, 1992).

299 *Osman v United Kingdom* (ECHR, 1998) 312–13, § 138 and 139. Read in conjunction with the Court's reasoning on the issue of compliance with art 6.1 this conclusion may raise some eyebrows. Cf at n 324 below.

The case of *Z v UK* was more straightforward.[300] Applicants had filed a claim of negligence against the social services arguing that these had failed to protect them from serious ill-treatment by their mother. The House of Lords decided that there was no duty of care owed by the social services to the children.[301] It held it to be not fair, just and reasonable to hold local authorities liable in negligence in situations in which they were charged with the task of protecting society from wrongdoings of others. In the determination of the applicability of article 6.1 the Court attached great importance to the fact that at the moment that the claim was filed no rule on the liability of the social services for negligence existed. The House of Lords decided 'a serious and genuine dispute about the existence of the right asserted by the applicants under the domestic law of negligence'.[302]

The *Osman* and the *Z and Others* cases seem to imply that rules that categorically exclude liability of the police or the social services would *not* raise an issue under article 6.1. This interpretation would overrule the cautionary approach advanced by the Commission in *Dyer*. It is argued here that the Court has at least indicated in the *Fayed* case that *Dyer* must be seen to complement the inquiry at issue in *Osman* and *Z*. In these latter two cases a substantive right of action could be seen to exist *without* having recourse to the technique developed in the *Dyer* case. Had this first inquiry left the applicants without a substantive right of action they could have argued that this right was withheld from them on arbitrary grounds. The applicability of article 6.1 should be determined by piercing the veil of form through an objective examination into the nature of the limitation allegedly in violation of article 6.1.

Under influence of this case law the Commission silently retreated from the position defended in *Agee v United Kingdom*.[303] In its reports in the cases of *Waite and Kennedy v Germany* and *Beer and Regan v Germany* it argued that 'the immunity from jurisdiction, accorded to members of diplomatic or consular missions of foreign States in the exercise of public functions or international organisations...does not exclude the existence of substantive rights under domestic law and cannot be regarded as delimiting the very substance of any such rights'. Rather, the Commission argued, 'the rules on immunity from jurisdiction of, inter alia, international organisations prevent claims concerning substantive rights, which exist as such under German law, from being raised and enforced against the privileged persons in German court proceedings, unless they waive their immunity. In these circumstances, it is merely a procedural bar preventing the possibilities of bringing potential claims to court.'[304]

[300] *Z and Others v United Kingdom* (ECHR, 2001).

[301] *X and Others v Bedfordshire County Council* [1995] 3 All ER 353 (UK, HL, 1995).

[302] *Z and Others v United Kingdom* (ECHR, 2001) 135, § 89.

[303] Cf n 287 above.

[304] *Waite and Kennedy v Germany* Report (EComHR, 1997) § 53 and 55; *Beer and Regan v Germany* Report (EComHR, 1997) § 39 and § 41, available at <http://www.echr.coe.int/echr>. The issue of applicability of art 6.1 was not discussed by the Court (*Waite and Kennedy v Germany* 30 EHRR 261 (ECHR, 1999) § 49 and *Beer and Regan v Germany* 33 EHRR 54 (ECHR, 1999) §39).

It may hence be concluded that when the *McElhinney*, *Al-Adsani*, and *Fogarty* cases came before the Court article 6.1 was generally agreed to be applicable to immunity rules that limited the exercise of otherwise available jurisdiction over otherwise available civil rights and obligations.

Strasbourg jurisprudence features a second argument against the applicability of article 6.1 to certain immunity rules. It has been argued that international immunity rules limit the jurisdiction of the national court and are hence not covered by the Convention. In its 1984 decision in *Spaans v The Netherlands* the Commission argued that the immunity of international organizations did not give rise to an issue under the Convention since that rule meant that the disputed acts did not occur within the jurisdiction of the respondent state.[305] The Commission had been asked to find that the immunity of the Iran-US Claims Tribunal from jurisdiction of the Dutch courts in proceedings instigated by an employee of the Tribunal to challenge his dismissal violated the right of access to the courts under article 6.1. The Commission held that it must

> first decide whether the Netherlands can be held responsible for the alleged violations of the Convention in the present case. Under Article 1 of the Convention the High Contracting Parties to the Convention undertake to secure the rights and freedoms defined in Section I of the Convention to everyone within their jurisdiction. The question is, therefore, whether the applicant, being an employee of the Iran-United States Claims Tribunal, was within the jurisdiction of the Netherlands.

It continued:

> Because of the immunity enjoyed by the Tribunal, the administrative acts are not acts which occur within the jurisdiction of the Netherlands within the meaning of Article 1 of the Convention and thus do not engage the responsibility of the Netherlands under the Convention.
>
> The Commission notes that it is in accordance with international law that States confer immunities and privileges to international bodies like the Iran-United States Claims Tribunal which are situated in their territory. The Commission does not

In a decision taken *after* the three judgments under consideration in this section the Court has indicated that the *Agee* case is no longer good law. In the case of *A v United Kingdom* (ECHR, 2002), the Court was asked to find the rule of parliamentary immunity to be in violation of the right of access to court under art 6.1. In respect of the question of the applicability of art 6.1 the Court pointed out that subsequent to the decision in *Agee* it has been established that 'whether a person has an actionable domestic claim so as to engage Article 6 § 1 may depend not only on the substantive content of the relevant civil right, as defined under national law, but also on the existence of procedural bars preventing or limiting the possibilities of bringing potential claims to court.' (933, § 62 and 63) It considered that the rule of parliamentary immunity 'is framed not in terms of a substantive defence to civil claims, but rather in terms of a procedural bar to the determination by a court of any claim which derives from words spoken in Parliament' (933, § 64). Although the Court considered it unnecessary to settle the issue (933–4, § 65), this statement makes clear that the Court sympathizes with the argument of applicants that the parliamentary immunity in libel actions was a procedural rather than a substantive limit.

[305] *Spaans v The Netherlands* DR 58, 119 (EComHR, 1988) 122.

consider that such a restriction of national sovereignty in order to facilitate the working of an international body gives rise to an issue under the Convention.

Consequently, the application was rejected as incompatible *ratione personae* with the provisions of the Convention within the meaning of article 27.2 ECHR.[306]

The Commission did however qualify this argument at the next occasion it had to rule on the applicability of article 6.1 to the immunity of an international organization. Van der Peet, an employee of the European Patent Office (EPO) in Munich, complained that the grant of immunity from jurisdiction to the EPO in proceedings instigated by him before the German courts to challenge a series of administrative decisions of the EPO dismissing his repeated requests for leave of absence, violated his right of access to court under article 6.1 of the Convention.[307] The Commission observed that

it is in accordance with international law that States confer immunities and privileges to international bodies which are situated in their territory, and that such a restriction of national sovereignty in order to facilitate the working of an international body does not, *in principle*, give rise to an issue under the Convention.

These two words change the entire outlook of the Commission's approach. They imply that under certain circumstances, however hypothetical, an issue may arise. The Commission explains that

the transfer of powers to an international organisation is not incompatible with the Convention provided that within that organisation fundamental rights will receive an equivalent protection.[308]

It then noted that disputes about administrative acts affecting employees of the EPO are referred to the Administrative Tribunal of the International Labour Organisation. In addition, the application was held incompatible *ratione materiae* with the provisions of the Convention since disputes relating to the recruitment, employment and retirement of civil servants—permanent staff of international organizations included—are as a general rule outside the scope of article 6.1.

The reasoning of the Commission is obscure—to say the least. It seems the Commission thought to avoid a possibly intrusive inquiry into the nature of the protection offered within the international organization by foreclosing a violation of article 6.1 through a relatively uncontroversial finding of

306 ibid. Art 27.2 ECHR provided at the time as follows: 'The Commission shall consider inadmissible any petition submitted under Article 25 which it considers incompatible with the provisions of the present Conventions, manifestly ill-founded, or an abuse of the right of petition.'

307 *Van der Peet v Germany* appl no 26991/95 (EComHR, 1996).

308 Referring to *M and Co v FRG* DR 64, 138 (EComHR, 1990) 145 and *Heinz v Contracting States Also Parties to the European Patent Convention* DR. 76A 125 (EComHR, 1994) 127–8. In these cases the Commission decided that 'a transfer of powers does not necessarily exclude a State's responsibility under the Convention with regard to the exercise of the transferred powers. Otherwise the guarantees of the Convention could wantonly be limited or excluded and thus be deprived of their peremptory character.'

incompatibility *ratione materiae*. It could do this, however, but after explaining *how* the Convention could play a role in the first place since it had so avidly argued the opposite in *Spaans*. The application of the 'transfer of powers' doctrine to the immunity of international organizations makes *Van der Peet* recall the reasoning developed in *Dyer v UK*.[309] While article 6.1 is in principle not applicable to the immunity of international organizations the article *can* be violated nevertheless. Not because the state has not granted access to its courts—the acts of the international organization are still considered outside the jurisdiction of the state—but because it has transferred powers to an international organization within which the right of access to court does not receive equivalent protection.[310] The cases the Commission relied on—*M and Co v FRG* and *Heinz v Contracting States Also Parties to the European Patent Convention*—make clear that a violation of the Convention arises when an international organization violates a Convention right and that right can in addition not be said to receive an equivalent protection within the international organization in general.

In its reports in the cases of *Waite and Kennedy v Germany* and *Beer and Regan v Germany* the Commission went out of its way to distinguish the facts of these cases from *Spaans*.[311] It argued that under the exceptional circumstances at hand the immunity of the international organization did raise an issue under article 6.1. The applicability of article 6.1 was decided under the classic consideration that the immunity of the international organization did not limit the substance of the right of the applicant. The Commission hence made sure not to abandon the position it took in *Spaans* even though its reasoning on this point was not particularly convincing.[312] Since the applicability of article 6.1 was not contested before the Court the argument against the applicability of article 6 developed in *Spaans* and qualified in *Van der Peet* had not yet been clearly overturned when McElhinney, Al-Adsani, and Fogarty filed their complaint in Strasbourg.

3.2.2.3 Compliance

In an obiter dictum in the *Golder* case the Commission stated without much ado that parliamentary and diplomatic immunity were justifiable restrictions of

[309] See p 372 above.

[310] It has been argued that the 'transfer of powers' doctrine is ill-suited to describe the effect of the immunity of international organizations since it considers a limitation of powers rather than a transfer and that moreover the argument was completely obiter since the Commission could have settled the issue with conclusion of incompatibility *ratione materiae*, cf RA Lawson, *Het EVRM en de Europese Gemeenschappen, Bouwstenen voor een aansprakelijkheidsregime voor het optreden van internationale organisaties* (1999) 443–4. However, the host state can in fact be seen to transfer its powers to adjudicate a certain category of disputes that would normally arise within its essential competence to the international organization. Moreover, as said before, the compatibility *ratione materiae* could *only* be examined *because* the Commission had explained how an issue under art 6.1 could arise in the first place.

[311] *Waite and Kennedy v Germany* Report (EComHR, 1997) § 51–2; *Beer and Regan v Germany* Report (EComHR, 1997) § 37–8.

[312] Cf RA Lawson (1999) 445.

the right of access to court.[313] This must have inspired the respondent state in the *Waite and Kennedy* and *Beer and Regan* cases to argue before the Commission that 'the right of access to court is subject to inherent limitations which include the traditional and generally recognized principle of parliamentary and diplomatic immunity and also the immunity of international organisations'.[314]

The notion of inherent limitations to article 6.1 however does not agree with the adamant insistence of the Strasbourg institutions in its post-*Golder* jurisprudence that limitations on the right of access must always comply with certain criteria in order to be compatible with article 6.1. In the *Ashingdane* case the Court ruled that limitations must not restrict the access in such a way that the very essence of the right is impaired, that they must always pursue a legitimate aim, and that the means used must be proportional to that aim.[315] The Commission was indeed quick to correct the respondent state by pointing out that for limitations to the right of access to be permissible under article 6.1 they must comply with the standard requirements formulated in *Ashingdane*. It considered that the aim of the immunity of international organizations was to contribute to their proper functioning and accepted this as a legitimate aim.[316] In respect of the proportionality requirement it used the same reasoning it had used in their applicability argument in *Van der Peet*. The Commission considered the grant of immunity to international organizations to be proportional only when 'within that organisation fundamental rights will receive an equivalent protection'.[317]

In the proceedings before the Court the respondent state did not repeat the arguments it had relied on before the Commission but conformed to the *Ashingdane* structure of a compliance argument under article 6.1.[318] The Court agreed with the respondent state and found the immunity from jurisdiction granted to the international organization to have a legitimate objective. It noted that

> the attribution of privileges and immunities to international organisations is an essential means of ensuring the proper functioning of such organisations free from unilateral interference by individual governments.

[313] *Golder v UK* (EComHR, 1973). See also the separate opinion of Judge Fitzmaurice in *Golder v UK* (ECHR, 1975). In fn 17 the judge stated that 'a right of access cannot make that the courts must have unlimited jurisdiction (eg the case of diplomatic and parliamentary immunity)'. It is noted that in *N, C, F and AG v Italy* DR 84-A, 84 (EComHR, 1995) 88, the Commission still relied on its decision in *Golder* in support of the conclusion that diplomatic immunity was a justified limitation to the right of access.

[314] *Waite and Kennedy v Germany* Decision (EComHR, 1997) and *Beer and Regan v Germany* Decision (EComHR, 1997) both available at <http://www.echr.coe.int/echr>.

[315] *Ashingdane v United Kingdom* (ECHR, 1985) 546–7, § 57.

[316] *Waite and Kennedy v Germany* Report (EComHR, 1997) § 70–1; *Beer and Regan v Germany* Report (EComHR, 1997) § 56–7 available at <http://www.echr.coe.int/echr>.

[317] ibid § 73–4; § 59–60.

[318] *Waite and Kennedy v Germany* (ECHR, 1999) § 50ff; *Beer and Regan v Germany* (ECHR, 1999) § 40ff. Cf also *Lenzing v United Kingdom* DR 94A, 136 (EComHR, 1998).

The immunity from jurisdiction commonly accorded by States to international organisations under the organisations' constituent instruments or supplementary agreements is a long-standing practice established in the interest of the good working of these organisations. The importance of this practice is enhanced by a trend towards extending and strengthening international cooperation in all domains of society.[319]

However, the Court formulated the obligations of a host state under article 6.1 in essentially different terms than the Commission had. The Court first stated the competing interests that must be weighed in order to come to a proportional solution:

[W]here States establish international organisations in order to pursue or strengthen their cooperation in certain fields of activities, and where they attribute to these organisations certain competences and accord them immunities, there may be implications as to the protection of fundamental rights. It would be incompatible with the purpose and object of the Convention, however, if the Contracting States were thereby absolved from their responsibility under the Convention in relation to the field of activity covered by such attribution. It should be recalled that the Convention is intended to guarantee not theoretical or illusory rights, but rights that are practical and effective. This is particularly true for the right of access to the courts in view of the prominent place held in a democratic society by the right to a fair trial.[320]

The 'material factor' in determining the proportionality of giving precedence to the interest of the international organization over that of individuals—or to the obligations under the one rule over that under the other—is 'whether the applicants had available to them reasonable alternative means to protect effectively their rights under the Convention'.[321] Since the international organization *in casu* did provide for various—not apparently ineffective—modes of dispute settlement, their immunity from German jurisdiction did not impair the essence of applicants' right of access and was not disproportionate. The fact that applicants' original claim could only succeed under German law and not under the substantive provisions of the regulations applied in the alternative dispute settlement procedures does not affect this conclusion since the principle of proportionality cannot compel access of applicants to the substantive guarantees under national legislation.[322]

It is important to point out that the Court did not repeat the condemnation of 'blanket immunity rules' it had advanced only four months earlier in the *Osman* case.[323] In that case the Court considered the rule that excluded actions against the police in negligence in the investigation and suppression of crime to be in violation of article 6.1. It did not accept the argument of the respondent state that

[319] ibid § 63; § 53.
[320] ibid § 67; § 57.
[321] ibid § 68; § 58.
[322] ibid § 69–73; § 59–63.
[323] *Osman v United Kingdom* (ECHR, 1998). The facts of that case were set out on p 373 above.

the exclusionary rule of liability is not of an absolute nature since its application may yield to other public policy considerations. It considered that the national court had *interpreted* the rule as a watertight defence for the police.[324] It concluded that applicants had suffered a disproportionate restriction on their right of access to court because 'the application of the rule in this manner without further enquiry into the existence of competing public interest considerations only serves to confer a blanket immunity on the police for their acts and omissions during the investigation and suppression of crime and amounts to an unjustifiable restriction on an applicant's right to have a determination on the merits of his or her claim against the police in deserving cases'.[325] The decision in *Osman* implied that for an immunity rule to be proportional for the purposes of article 6.1 'it must be open to a domestic court to have regard to the presence of other public interest considerations which pull in the opposite direction to the application of the rule'.[326]

Clearly, most immunity rules are blanket immunity rules. The immunity rule at issue in *Waite and Kennedy* and *Beer and Regan* is no exception. The position that such rules are by definition in violation of article 6.1 is, to put it mildly, unorthodox. It is argued here that as long as a proper balance of competing public policy interests *underlies* a blanket immunity rule, the rule is proportionate to its aim and article 6.1 not violated. In other words, it is not relevant whether courts are allowed to balance the interests involved in their determination of the scope of the rule; it is the scope of the rule that must reflect a proper balance for it to be in accordance with article 6.1.

It seems that the Court has realized the consequences of its bold statement in *Osman* in the short period between its decision in that case and its decisions in *Waite* and *Beer*. The blanket immunity of the international organizations was weighed against the interests of the applicants to have access to the courts.

[324] ibid 316, § 150. This finding is somewhat puzzling in light of the Court's considerations on the issue of applicability of art 6.1. Cf n 299 above.

[325] ibid 316, § 151 (emphasis added). It is noted that in *Z v United Kingdom* (ECHR, 2001) (facts discussed at p 374 above) the Court withdrew from its qualification of the exclusion of liability under the English law of negligence in the *Osman* case. It stated explicitly that the 'reasoning in the Osman judgment was based on an understanding of the law of negligence . . . which has to be reviewed in the light of the clarifications subsequently made by the domestic courts and notably the House of Lords'. It pronounced itself 'satisfied that the law of negligence as developed in the domestic courts . . . includes the fair, just and reasonable criterion as an intrinsic element of the duty of care and that the ruling of law concerning that element in this case does not disclose the operation of an immunity . . . the inability of the applicants to sue the local authority flowed not from an immunity but from the applicable principles governing the substantive right of action in domestic law'. In such case, the Court explained, there is no issue under art 6.1 because there is no restriction on access to court (138, § 100). It concluded that '[t]he applicants may not therefore claim that they were deprived of any right to a determination on the merits of their negligence claims. Their claims were properly and fairly examined in light of the applicable domestic legal principles concerning the tort of negligence.' (138, § 101). It may however be clear from the quotations mentioned in the previous footnote that the Court did very well realize that the rule was not absolute. It explicitly considered that it was the way in which the UK courts applied the rule that violated art 6.1.

[326] *Osman v United Kingdom* (ECHR, 1998) 316, § 151.

Since alternative means to protect the rights under the Convention effectively were available to applicants, their interests were outweighed by those of the international organization and the international community at large. Although the Court did not say it with so many words, *Waite and Kennedy* and *Beer and Regan* arguably overturn *Osman* on this point.

In sum, even though the Court settled for the less demanding 'reasonable alternative means to protect' rather than 'equivalent protection'[327] and even though it engaged in a very marginal review of the alternative means for redress provided for within the international organization,[328] it has confirmed that limitations on the right of access by immunity rules must not impair the very essence of the right, must have a legitimate aim, and must be proportional to that aim.

3.2.3 McElhinney v Ireland, Al-Adsani v United Kingdom, *and* Fogarty v United Kingdom

3.2.3.1 Introduction

In 2001 the European Court of Human Rights passed judgment in three applications challenging the rule of state immunity under article 6.1 of the Convention. While the domestic proceedings in which a foreign state defendant had been granted state immunity were distinct on the facts, the arguments relied on by applicants and respondent states and the Court's analysis thereof followed a largely identical pattern.

The case of *McElhinney v Ireland* was brought in response to the decision of the Irish courts to grant immunity to the United Kingdom in proceedings pending before it.[329] The facts underlying the proceedings were the following. When the applicant—an Irish national—had accidentally driven his car into a checkpoint barrier between Northern Ireland and Ireland, one of the British soldiers manning the checkpoint was hit and fired at the car in response. The applicant alleged that he did not realize he hit the soldier and did not stop because he feared the shots fired at him formed a terrorist attack. He continued to drive for two miles into Irish territory. When he pulled over, the soldier that had followed him from the checkpoint was in a state of 'blind panic' and allegedly aimed his gun at him and pulled the trigger twice, although the shots did not fire because the gun jammed. McElhinney lodged an action in the Irish courts against the individual soldier and the British Secretary of State for Northern Ireland for damages in respect of his allegation that the soldier had wrongfully assaulted him. Because

[327] This difference seems to at times escape the attention of commentators on the cases, cf eg P Pustorino, 'Immunità giurisdizionale delle organizzazioni internazionali e tutela dei diritti fondamentali: le sentenze della Corte Europea nei casi *Waite et Kennedy* e *Beer et Regan*' (2000) 83 RDI 132; A Reinisch, 'Case Note *Waite and Kennedy* and *Beer and Regan*' (1999) 93 AJIL 933.

[328] Cf for criticism on this point a.o. P Pustorino, ibid 147–50; A Reinisch, ibid 937; J-F Flauss (2000) 322; H Tigroudja, 'L'immunité de juridiction des organisations internationales et le droit d'accès à un tribunal' (2000) 11 Revue Trimestrielle des Droits de l'Homme 83, 87.

[329] *McElhinney v Ireland* (ECHR, 2001).

of the rule of state immunity, however, he was held not to be entitled to bring an action in the Irish courts. In the proceedings before the European Court of Human Rights the applicant claimed that the refusal to entertain his claim for damages for personal injury following the allegedly tortious behaviour of a UK soldier on Irish territory violated his right of access to court under article 6.1 ECHR.

The facts of the UK case of *Al-Adsani v Kuwait* were set out earlier in this chapter.[330] When Al-Adsani failed to get a decision on his claim for damages for torture from the UK courts because of the grant of state immunity to Kuwait, he filed a complaint in Strasbourg arguing that the United Kingdom had violated his right of access to court.

In *Fogarty v UK* the applicant also argued that her right of access to court had been violated by the grant of state immunity in respect of a claim filed by her in the UK courts, this time to the United States.[331] Ms Fogarty had brought a claim against the US on the allegation that she had been discriminated against in the selection procedures for two secretarial positions at the US Embassy in London. Fogarty had previously worked for the Embassy and contended that the refusal to re-employ her was a consequence of the sex discrimination claim she had successfully brought with regard to facts relating to that previous position.

All three applicants argued that the grant of immunity to the foreign state constituted a *disproportionate restriction* of their right of access to court under article 6.1. The arguments of both applicants and respondent states were structured to fit the two queries of applicability of, and compliance with, article 6.

3.2.3.2 Applicability

The controversy on the applicability of article 6.1 was framed in similar terms in all three cases, albeit with a slightly different focus in each of them. In *McElhinney* the government argued that article 6.1 did not apply because the rule of state immunity in respect of fundamental acts *jure imperii* 'affected the substantive content of the right claimed and was not merely a procedural bar', whereas the applicant argued that the rule did operate as a procedural bar to the exercise of his rights.[332] In *Al-Adsani* the government claimed that article 6 'could not extend to matters outside the State's jurisdiction, and that as international law required an immunity in the present case, the facts fell outside the jurisdiction of the national courts and, consequently, Article 6'. The applicant rebutted. He observed that torture is a civil wrong in English law and that the UK does assert jurisdiction over civil wrongs committed abroad in certain circumstances. Since the courts did accept jurisdiction over his claims against the individual defendants it was clear that his claim against Kuwait was rejected not because of the nature of the

[330] *Al-Adsani*. Cf p 309 above.
[331] *Fogarty v United Kingdom* (ECHR, 2001).
[332] *McElhinney*, 329–30, § 21–2.

claim but because of the identity of the defendant and that article 6.1 was therefore applicable.[333] In *Fogarty* the government contended that article 6.1 did not apply because the applicant had 'no actionable domestic claim'. The rule of state immunity, it argued, 'removed the dispute from the competence of the national courts, which could not assert jurisdiction over the internal affairs of foreign diplomatic missions'. The applicant, on the other hand, argued that the right she had under domestic law to be free from sex discrimination was not extinguished by the rule of state immunity; the rule simply prevented the courts from examining the dispute.[334]

The Court dealt with these arguments in three identical considerations. It first recalled that

> Article 6 § 1 does not itself guarantee any particular content for 'civil rights and obligations' in the substantive law of the Contracting States. It extends only to *contestations* (disputes) over 'civil rights and obligations' which can be said, at least on arguable grounds, to be recognised under domestic law.
>
> Whether a person has an actionable domestic claim may depend not only on the substantive content, properly speaking, of the relevant civil right as defined under national law but also on the existence of procedural bars preventing or limiting the possibilities of bringing potential claims to court. In the latter kind of case Article 6 § 1 may be applicable. Certainly the Convention enforcement bodies may not create by way of interpretation of Article 6 § 1 a substantive civil right which has no legal basis in the State concerned. However, it would not be consistent with the rule of law in a democratic society or with the basic principle underlying Article 6 § 1—namely that civil claims must be capable of being submitted to a judge for adjudication—if, for example, a State could, without restraint or control by the Convention enforcement bodies, remove from the jurisdiction of the courts a whole range of civil claims or confer immunities from civil liability on large groups or categories of persons.[335]

The Court then proceeded to qualify the respective immunity rules applied in the three cases as a procedural rather than a substantive bar. In *McElhinney* the Court reasoned as follows:

> The proceedings which the applicant intended to pursue were for damages for assault, trespass to the person, negligence and breach of duty. Such an action is well known to Irish law. The Court does not accept the Government's plea that because of the operation of State immunity the applicant did not have a substantive right under domestic law. It notes that an action against a State is not barred *in limine*: if the defendant State chooses to waive immunity, the action will proceed to a hearing and judgment. The grant of

[333] *Al-Adsani*, 286–7, § 44–5.

[334] *Fogarty*, 309–10, § 22–3.

[335] *McElhinney*, 330, § 23 (referring to *Z and Others v the United Kingdom* (ECHR, 2001) 134–5, § 87) and § 24 (referring to *Fayed v United Kingdom* Series (ECHR, 1994) 429–30, § 65); *Al-Adsani*, 287, § 46–7; *Fogarty*, 310, § 24–5.

immunity is to be seen not as qualifying a substantive right but as a procedural bar on the national courts' power to determine the right.[336]

In a similar vein it considered that the actions relied on by Al-Adsani and Fogarty are well known to UK law, that the action against Kuwait and the United States are not barred *in limine*, and that the grant of immunity was therefore to be seen as a procedural bar on the national courts' power to determine the right rather than as qualifying a substantive right.[337] Consequently, the Court was satisfied that there existed a serious and genuine dispute over civil rights and that article 6.1 was applicable to all three proceedings.[338]

3.2.3.3 Compliance

In all three cases the respondent state asserted to have acted in accordance with generally recognized principles of public international law and that hence—if article 6.1 *was* found to apply to the facts of the case—the limitations on the right of access to court were proportionate restrictions pursuing a legitimate aim.[339] In *McElhinney* the respondent state argued moreover that the applicant had an alternative means of recourse since he could have instituted proceedings in Northern Ireland. Also in *Al-Adsani* the respondent state submitted that traditional means of redress for this kind of wrong were available to the applicant—namely diplomatic representations or an inter-State claim.

The applicants in *McElhinney* and *Al-Adsani* submitted that the limitation imposed did not serve a legitimate aim and was disproportionate. McElhinney argued that the immunity granted to the UK no longer existed in international law. He especially emphasized that the UK itself did not consider it necessary to grant immunity to foreign governments in similar situations. As regards the alternative remedy, he pointed out that his claim was for damages sustained in an incident on Irish territory and that Ireland as *locus delicti* was hence the appropriate forum for his action. Al-Adsani argued that state immunity was no longer a valid defence against torture allegations. In particular, he asserted that the conclusions of the *Pinochet* case equally applied in civil proceedings. He moreover underlined that the UK had refused to assist him in the pursuit of his claim through diplomatic channels. The applicant in *Fogarty* did concede that the limitation concerned a legitimate aim but argued that it was disproportionate because, *inter alia*, the immunity applied was not required under international law and no alternative means of redress was available to her since the United States was not prepared to exercise jurisdiction.

[336] *McElhinney*, 330, § 25.

[337] *Al-Adsani*, 287, § 48; *Fogarty*, 310–11, § 26.

[338] *McElhinney*, 330–1, § 26; *Al-Adsani*, 287, § 49; *Fogarty*, 311, § 27.

[339] Cf for the arguments of the parties *McElhinney*, 331ff, §27ff; *Al-Adsani*, 287ff, § 50ff; *Fogarty*, 311ff, §29ff.

Applying the *Ashingdane* criteria to the facts of the cases before it the Court developed a novel line of reasoning that entails an unqualified deference to public international law requirements. The Court did not dwell on the legitimate aim of the limitations at hand. In all three cases we find the following consideration:

[S]overeign immunity is a concept of international law, developed out of the principle *par in parem non habet imperium*, by virtue of which one State shall not be subject to the jurisdiction of another State. The Court considers that the grant of sovereign immunity to a State in civil proceedings pursues the legitimate aim of complying with international law to promote comity and good relations between States through the respect of another State's sovereignty.[340]

International law was then *again* relied on to find compliance with the requirements of the principle of proportionality. Under reference to article 31.3 (c) of the Vienna Convention on the Law of Treaties, the Court considered that in the interpretation of the Convention account is to be taken of 'any relevant rules of international law applicable in the relations between the parties'. It continued:

The Convention, including Article 6, cannot be interpreted in a vacuum. The Court must be mindful of the Convention's special character as a human rights treaty, and it must also take the relevant rules of international law into account ... The Convention should so far as possible be interpreted in harmony with other rules of international law of which it forms part, including those relating to the grant of State immunity.

It follows that measures taken by a High Contracting Party which reflect generally recognised rules of public international law on State immunity cannot in principle be regarded as imposing a disproportionate restriction on the right of access to court as embodied in Article 6 § 1. Just as the right of access to court is an inherent part of the fair trial guarantee in that Article, so some restrictions on access must likewise be regarded as inherent, an example being those limitations generally accepted by the community of nations as part of the doctrine of State immunity.[341]

Hence, the Court limited its review of the proportionality of the limitations to the question whether the rules applied in the national court proceedings reflected generally recognized rules of public international law.

Only one Judge explicitly dissented from the *approach* outlined by the Court. In all three cases Judge Loucaides relied on the *Osman* case when he argued that

a blanket immunity which is applied by a court in order to block completely the judicial determination of a civil right without balancing the competing interests, namely those connected with the particular immunity and those relating to the nature of the specific claim which is the subject matter of the proceedings, amounts to a disproportionate restriction on the right of access to court.

340 *McElhinney*, 333, § 35; *Al-Adsani*, 289, § 54; *Fogarty*, 313, § 34.

341 *McElhinney*, 333, § 36 (referring to *Loizidou v Turkey* 23 EHRR 513 (ECHR, 1996) 526, § 43) and 333–4, § 37; *Al-Adsani*, 289, § 55–6; *Fogarty*, 313–4, § 35–6.

He elaborated the underpinnings of his argument holding that:

In present democratic society an absolute immunity from judicial proceedings appears to be an anachronistic doctrine incompatible with the demands of justice and the rule of law.

The international law immunities originated at a time when individual rights were practically non-existent and when States needed greater protection from possible harassment through abusive judicial proceedings. The doctrine of State immunity has in modern times been subjected to an increasing number of restrictions, the trend being to reduce its application in view of developments in the field of human rights which strengthen the position of the individual...

It is correct that Article 6 may be subject to inherent limitations, but these limitations should not affect the core of the right. Procedural conditions such as time-limits, the need for leave to appeal etc. do not affect the substance of the right. But completely preventing somebody from having his case determined by a court, without any fault on his part and regardless of the nature of the case, contravenes, in my opinion, Article 6 § 1 of the Convention.[342]

The approach set out in the majority opinion required the Court to examine whether the three disputed applications of the rule of state immunity reflected international law requirements. Since the applicants all relied on a different exception to the rule, the reasoning of the Court diverges on this point.

In *McElhinney v Ireland* the Court considered that although

there appears to be a trend in international and comparative law towards limiting State immunity in respect of personal injury caused by an act or omission within the forum State... this practice is by no means universal.

In addition it pointed out that

the trend may primarily refer to 'insurable' personal injury, that is incidents arising out of ordinary road traffic accidents, rather than matters relating to the core area of State sovereignty such as the acts of a soldier on foreign territory which, of their very nature, may involve sensitive issues affecting diplomatic relations between States and national security.

The Court concluded that it could not be said

that Ireland is alone in holding that immunity attaches to suits in respect of such torts committed by *acta jure imperii* or that, in affording this immunity, Ireland falls outside any currently accepted international standards... it is not possible, given the present state of the development of international law, to conclude that Irish law conflicts with its general principles.[343]

In conclusion the Court noted moreover that the applicant could have brought an action in Northern Ireland against the United Kingdom Secretary of State for

[342] *McElhinney*, Dissenting Opinion of Judge Loucaides, 340, 340–1. Cf also *Al-Adsani*, 301, 301; *Fogarty*, 317, 319.

[343] *McElhinney*, 334, § 38.

Defence as already pointed out by UK government lawyers in the proceedings before the Irish courts.[344]

Four judges dissented—five if we include the dissent of principle of Judge Loucaides. Judges Caflisch, Cabral Barreto, and Vajic concluded in their dissenting opinion that the exception to state immunity for territorial torts causing personal injury as laid down in article 12 of the ILC Draft on Jurisdictional Immunities of States and their Property reflects the law as it is at present.[345] They added that

> even if one were not prepared to admit as much, that Article is, at the very least, the expression of a remarkable convergence of tendencies in contemporary international law. This convergence is sufficiently powerful to suggest, at any rate, that at present there is no international *duty*, on the part of States, to grant immunity to other States in matters of torts caused by the latter's agents.

The restriction of the right of access to court hence could not be justified by reference to the international law of state immunity. The limitation hence constituted a disproportionate restriction of the right of access to court.[346]

Judge Rozakis formulated his opinion in a separate dissent. He considered that at the time that McElhinney's case was before the Irish courts

> international law . . . allowed a State to invoke sovereign immunity in order to bar access to a court without flagrantly violating general international law. Yet, the fact that the law on sovereign immunity was—and still is—at a stage of transition, and that the clear preference of the international community was—and is—to limit it in specific States' actions, has a weighty impact on the proportionality test under the Convention.

This fact was seen to make the invocation of the interests of the state 'rather weak'. On the other side of the scale, three distinct factors added to the weight of the interests of McElhinney. In the first place, the judge emphasized that nationality 'usually creates a jurisdictional bond between a person and his State and, in international law, a *prima facie* obligation on the State to protect him'. Secondly, he pointed out that 'the assault against the applicant occurred within Irish territory, a matter which further reinforces the jurisdictional bond'. And finally the judge considered the practical difficulties of bringing proceedings in the United Kingdom not to be 'altogether irrelevant or negligible'. Judge Rozakis argued that these factors 'seriously weaken the Court's argument that the applicant had reasonable alternative means to protect effectively his right under the Convention'. He moreover pointed out that the situation of McElhinney differed fundamentally from that of the individual in the *Waite and Kennedy* case. Whereas the

[344] *McElhinney*, 334, § 39.

[345] *McElhinney*, Dissenting Opinion of Judges Caflisch, Cabral Barreto, and Vajic, 336, 336–40. Judge Loucaides subscribed to this conclusion but preferred to base his dissent on the more fundamental issue set out above.

[346] ibid 340. Oddly, the judges write that 'the Court, in our view, should have held Article 6 § 1 to apply to the present case'.

latter case concerned a person working within an international organization and a dispute for which internal proceedings existed of which the person was aware when he signed his employment contract, McElhinney 'did not have any link with [UK] jurisdiction—other than the incidental link of the national origin of the defendant—or any kind of allegiance and loyalty to that foreign jurisdiction'. Weighing the interests of the state against the interests of the applicant in this case he concluded that 'the applicant was unduly deprived of his right of access to a court and that the deprivation was disproportionate and impaired the very essence of this right'. In sum, while the Judge did not dissent from the approach of the Court he did argue that when as regards a particular application of the rule of state immunity there is some doubt as to the requirements of international law, the interests of the individual to have access to the court *should* be balanced against the interests protected by the application of the rule.

Judge Loucaides even went one step further. In an obiter consideration he argued that the availability of an alternative remedy in the courts of the foreign state should not be taken into account at all when weighing the interest of the individual to have access to court:

> I believe that when a complaint is made for a breach of the Convention, the complaint should be examined by the Court by reference only to the legal system of the respondent State. Any defects or other problems relating to such a system cannot be remedied by reference to the legal system of any other High Contracting Party, whether neighbouring to the respondent State or not. Therefore, the fact that the applicant in this case had the possibility of a judicial remedy in the United Kingdom in respect of his grievance should be irrelevant to the issue before the Court, which was solely and exclusively whether the applicant had access to the courts in Ireland in respect of the same complaint. I think it is unfair as well as odd to expect the applicant to have recourse to another State as a solution to his problem of lack of access to a court in his own country, against which his complaint was directed.

The reasoning of the Court in *Al-Adsani v UK* has been discussed in earlier parts of this chapter. It is recalled that a narrow majority of nine to eight judges found that in international law there was no exception to the rule of state immunity when acts of torture are alleged.[347] The Court hence concluded that the grant of immunity to Kuwait had not been an unjustified restriction of the right of access to court. The minority judges argued that the *jus cogens* nature of the prohibition of torture meant that states could not invoke hierarchically lower rules, like the rule of state immunity, to avoid the consequences of the violation of this prohibition.[348] They therefore concluded that the applicant's right of access to court *had* been violated.

[347] Cf § 2.2 above.

[348] *Al-Adsani*, Dissenting Opinion of Judges Rozakis and Caflisch Joined by Judges Wildhaber, Costa, Cabral Barreto, and Vajic, 297. Judge Loucaides pointed out that although he did agree with the dissenting opinion written by Judges Rozakis and Caflisch he preferred to adopt the same argument he used in his dissents in McElhinney and Fogarty (that any form of 'blanket immunity' is a

In *Fogarty v UK* the Court found that the relevant limitation of the right of access to court did not exceed the margin of appreciation allowed to states and that accordingly no violation of article 6.1 had taken place. It first considered that

> there appears to be a trend in international and comparative law towards limiting State immunity in respect of employment-related disputes. However, where the proceedings relate to employment in a foreign mission or embassy, international practice is divided on the question whether State immunity continues to apply and, if it does so apply, whether it covers disputes relating to the contracts of all staff or only more senior members of the mission. Certainly, it cannot be said that the United Kingdom is alone in holding that immunity attaches to suits by employees at diplomatic missions or that, in affording such immunity, the United Kingdom falls outside any currently accepted international standards.[349]

Subsequently, it pointed out that the controversy *anyhow* did not extend to the type of proceedings at issue since

> the proceedings which the applicant wished to bring did not concern the contractual rights of a current embassy employee, but instead related to alleged discrimination in the recruitment process. Questions relating to the recruitment of staff to missions and embassies may by their very nature involve sensitive and confidential issues, related, *inter alia,* to the diplomatic and organisational policy of a foreign State. The Court is not aware of any trend in international law towards a relaxation of the rule of State immunity as regards issues of recruitment to foreign missions.[350]

Judge Loucaides wrote the only dissent.[351] It was explained earlier that the Judge disagreed on the principle of the approach chosen by the Court. In what was technically an obiter consideration Judge Loucaides went on to argue that if the competing interests *are* weighed the immunity granted to the United States does not pass the *Ashingdane* criteria. He underlined that 'it has not been established that there is in actual fact a rule of customary international law in support of the State immunity invoked by the respondent Government'. Since the rule involved is no longer supported by a 'widespread and consistent practice'—indeed the government itself had conceded that it concerned a 'highly controversial issue'—it could not be said to reflect an obligation under international law. Considering that the claim of the applicant was an allegation of a violation of a human right, and considering the fact that there was no alternative means of redress in respect of the

disproportionate limitation of art 6.1 ECHR) as the main reasoning for finding a violation of art 6.1, Dissenting Opinion Judge Loucaides, 301. See also the Dissenting Opinion of Judge Ferrari Bravo, 300.

349 *Fogarty*, 314, § 37.

350 *Fogarty*, 314–15, § 38.

351 *Fogarty*, Dissenting Opinion of Judge Loucaides, 317. The Judge's dissent on this issue forced him moreover to find that the applicant's claim in England involved the determination of a civil right for the purposes of art 6.1, a question left open by the majority who decided that, even if art 6 was assumed to apply, there had been no violation by the court.

applicant's complaint, Judge Loucaides concluded that the balance weighing the conflicting interests tips to the side of the applicant.

3.2.4 The Right of Access to Court and State Immunity and Personal Immunity: A Critical Discussion of the McElhinney, Al-Adsani *and* Fogarty *Cases*

3.2.4.1 Introduction

The brief overview of the legal framework in which a complaint of violation of the right of access to court inserts itself helps us put the arguments of the parties, the Court and the dissenting judges in the cases of *McElhinney v Ireland*, *Al-Adsani v UK* and *Fogarty v UK* in perspective. This section first examines whether the decision on the applicability of article 6.1 on the basis of the standard distinction between substantive and procedural limits properly reflects the nature of the rule of state immunity.[352] It will be argued that it does not. Three situations should be distinguished when testing immunity rules under article 6.1 and the three cases can be seen to each represent a different situation. Second, it will be examined whether the decision on the compliance with article 6.1 properly reflects the nature of the obligations put on states under the article. It will be argued that the decisions of the Court also fall short on this point. The Court does not consider how states may make the obligations states have under rules of public international law compatible with its obligations under the Convention, but rather approaches the former obligations as inherent limitations of the latter.

3.2.4.2 Applicability

The arguments of the applicants in *McElhinney*, *Al-Adsani*, and *Fogarty* on the applicability of article 6.1 and the decision of the Court on this point relied on the distinction between procedural and substantive limitations. The Court agreed with the applicants that article 6.1 was applicable because the rule of state immunity does not limit the substantive rights of individuals but is a procedural bar to the jurisdiction of the court. It argued that the substantive rights relied on by the applicants in the national proceedings were not extinguished by the rule of state immunity. Rather, this rule prevented the national courts from determining those rights. This is, according to the Court, clear from the fact that the defendant state may waive its immunity and that actions of the applicants were hence not barred *in limine*.

Without much ado this conclusion shoved the somewhat unconventional argument advanced by the respondent states in the *Al-Adsani* and *Fogarty* cases to the side. In the *Al-Adsani* case the UK asserted that article 6 'could not extend to

[352] An argument that is not further discussed here but which is very convincing indeed is that a complaint that the grant of state immunity violates art 6.1 fails to exhaust local remedies if the applicant has not filed a complaint for damages against the respondent state in the local courts first (art 35.1 ECHR). Cf in this sense RA Lawson (1999) 441–2.

matters outside the State's jurisdiction, and that as international law required an immunity in the present case, the facts fell outside the jurisdiction of the national courts and, consequently, Article 6'. In *Fogarty* the UK argued that there was no actionable domestic claim when the rule of state immunity 'remove[s] the dispute from the competence of the national courts, which [can] not assert jurisdiction over the internal affairs of foreign diplomatic missions'.

These arguments clearly recall the reasoning of the Commission in *Spaans v The Netherlands*. In that case, the Commission had concluded that the immunity of international organizations under international law meant that acts of the international organization were 'not acts which occur within the jurisdiction of the Netherlands'. The immunity did therefore not raise an issue under the Convention. As explained above, this argument has never really lost its precedential value, and the terse reasoning of the Court can hardly be considered a convincing rebuttal.[353]

The argument was revived by Lord Millett in the 2000 decision of the House of Lords in the case of *Holland v Lampen-Wolfe*.[354] Lord Millett rejected the argument of Ms. Holland that the grant of state immunity to the defendant would violate her right of access to court under article 6.1 ECHR, arguing that

> [a]rticle 6 requires contracting States to maintain fair and public judicial processes and forbids them to deny individuals access to those processes for the determination of their civil rights. It presupposes that the contracting States have the power of adjudication necessary to resolve the issues in dispute. But it does not confer on contracting States adjudicative powers that they do not possess. State immunity, as I have explained, is a creature of customary international law and derives from the equality of sovereign States. It is not a self-imposed restriction on the jurisdiction of its courts that the United Kingdom has chosen to adopt. It is a limitation imposed from without upon the sovereignty of the United Kingdom itself.[355]

In the 2003 decision in *Matthews v Ministry of Defence* he again emphasized that article 6.1

> presupposes that the contracting states have the powers of adjudication necessary to determine the issues in dispute. But it does not confer on contracting states adjudicative powers which they do not possess. State immunity is a creature of customary international law... It is not a self-imposed restriction on the jurisdiction of its courts which

[353] Cf § 3.2.2.2 above.

[354] *Holland v Lampen-Wolfe* (UK, 2000). Lords Cooke of Thorndon and Hobhouse of Woodborough agreed with the arguments of Lord Millett. The reliance on art 6 ECHR by applicants in UK proceedings can be explained by the strictures of the 1978 UK SIA. The unambiguous terms of the domestic immunity legislation force applicants to revert to inventive legal reasoning. Since the grant of state immunity in deviance of international law violates art 6 ECHR, the argument commonly runs, judges should allow a human rights exception to state immunity even though that is not explicitly provided for in the SIA. In order to prove that international law does not require the grant of immunity in respect of allegations of gross human rights abuses, applicants rely on the arguments against state immunity discussed in § 2 of this chapter.

[355] ibid 1588 (*per* Lord Millett).

the United Kingdom has chosen to adopt. It is a limitation imposed from without upon the sovereignty of the United Kingdom itself. It derives from the equality of sovereign states, and from the fact that the adjudication of disputes is an exercise of sovereign power: *par in parem non habet imperium*.[356]

In the 2006 decision in *Jones v Saudi Arabia* the House of Lords expressed support for this position.[357] It has to be noted that while Lord Millett did in both cases explicitly note that the substance of the prohibition *derives* from the equality of sovereign states, he argued that the adjudicative powers of states are inherently limited by *all* rules of international law that put limits on the exercise of jurisdiction by national courts.[358]

This conclusive reliance on the international law character of the state immunity rule is rejected in this study. The jurisdiction of a state is not as a general rule limited by international law immunities. Voluntary immunity rules like diplomatic immunity do not limit the essential competence of states but operate as an exception to the normal jurisdiction of the receiving or host state.

Lord Millett supported his argument with the consideration that 'the United Kingdom cannot, by its own act of acceding to the Convention and without the consent of the United States, obtain a power of adjudication over the United States which international law denies it'. He further explained that '[t]he court cannot reach a particular conclusion because it prefers the right of access to justice which the Convention affords to [the individual] to the immunity from suit which international law affords to the United States. The United States has rights too, and the court is bound to respect them. It claims immunity from the present suit. In my opinion its claim is well founded. Where the immunity is available, then for the reasons I have endeavoured to give it prevails over the Convention rights contained in article 6.'[359]

It is respectfully submitted that this argumentation misconceives the character of the obligation under article 6.1. Lord Millett mistakes the state of the law argument on the scope of article 6.1—and the policy argument against immunity—for a state of the law argument on the scope of the rule of state immunity.[360] The immunity of the United States from UK jurisdiction is quite obviously not curtailed by the obligations the UK has undertaken under the Convention. When article 6.1 is violated this only affects the responsibility of the UK towards the individual, not the immunity of the United States. The fact that the UK is obliged to grant immunity to the US does not mean that it cannot

[356] *Matthews v Ministry of Defence* (UK, 2003) § 104.

[357] *Jones v Saudi Arabia* (UK, 2006) § 14 and § 64.

[358] The distinction between internal and external limitations has found some support in doctrine, Cf E Voyakis, 'Access to Court v. State Immunity' (2003) 52 ICLQ 297, 307–10. Cf for early support for this argument H Damian (1985) 17.

[359] *Holland v Lampen-Wolfe* (UK, 2000).

[360] The germ of this misconception lies in the claim of Ms Holland who had relied on art 6.1 as an argument against the granting of immunity to the defendant. That argument could have been rejected without deciding the scope of the obligations of states under art 6.1.

have, at the same time, obligations towards private individuals to mitigate the consequences of this grant of immunity. It is in this respect important to realize that article 6.1 is applicable and not yet violated when it is acknowledged that the rule of immunity limits the right of access to court.

The idea of non-applicability of article 6.1 *does* however deserve serious consideration as far as *necessary* immunity rules are concerned. Necessary immunity rules do not prevent the court from exercising an otherwise existing jurisdiction but reflect the limits on the essential competence of the forum state. In an international community of equal and independent states the sovereignty of states is inherently limited by the sovereignty of other states. Certain disputes fall outside the essential competence of a national court.[361] The obligation to grant an individual involved in such a dispute access to court—even if just in principle—cannot rest with a state whose courts lack essential competence over the dispute. The reasoning of the respondent state in the *Fogarty* case may be seen to fit the argument advanced here quite well. In contrast with the *Al-Adsani* case the focus in *Fogarty* is on the substance of the prohibition rather than merely on its international law character.[362]

How does this argument fit the construction of the Convention? It is recalled that the Commission in the *Spaans* case relied on article 1 of the Convention to declare the application inadmissible. Article 1 of the Convention provides that '[t]he High Contracting Parties shall secure to everyone within their jurisdiction the rights and freedoms defined in Section I of this Convention.' The *Spaans* argument was later explicitly revived by Voyakis who held that 'a jurisdictional limitation imposed as a matter of general international law would seem to entail that the area covered by that limitation does not lie "within the jurisdiction" of the State party concerned'.[363]

This study prefers a different approach. Although the argumentation is not altogether unappealing, it deviates from the accepted interpretation of the rationale of article 1. If article 1 is interpreted as limiting the responsibility of the state to cases where it was within its jurisdiction to act otherwise, it acquires a troubling conceptual note. Jurisdiction in the sense of article 1 is primarily territorial. The *travaux préparatoires* of the Convention make clear that the article sets out to extend the benefits of the Convention not just to persons *residing* within the territories of the contracting states but to *all persons* that find themselves on the territories of these states.[364] In exceptional cases the area of application of the Convention exceeds that of national territory. The Court has consistently held

[361] Cf for the distinction between necessary and voluntary state immunity ch 2, p 63 of this study.

[362] Cf p 383 above. The fit is of course not a perfect one. For one, the term 'removed' does not reflect that such disputes have *never* been within the competence of the court.

[363] E Voyakis (2003) 309.

[364] Collected Edition of the *Travaux Préparatoires of the European Convention on Human Rights* iii 260. Cf *Bankovic v 17 European Member States of NATO* (ECHR, 2001) available at <http://www.echr.coe.int>, § 59–63.

that 'the responsibility of a contracting party may also arise when, as a consequence of military action—whether lawful or unlawful—it exercises effective control of an area outside its national territory'.[365] In any case, the exercise of jurisdiction within the meaning of article 1 relates to the exercise of authority over a territory and article 1 is primarily relied on to limit a state's responsibility under the Convention to violations of human rights that take place within territory that falls under the jurisdiction or effective overall control of that state. The rationale of the article is that contracting states are only responsible for violations of human rights that take place within territory over which they exercise essential competence.

It may not immediately be clear how article 1 relates to the right of access to court under article 6.1. The right of access is clearly not limited to persons or disputes that are within the territorial jurisdiction of a contracting state. Rather, it seems that the Convention applies whenever an individual seeks access to *a court that falls within the jurisdiction* of the contracting state within the meaning of article 1. In fact, this position was advanced by the court in its 2006 decision in the *Markovic* case.[366] The Court silently retreated from the *Spaans* judgement holding that 'once a person brings a civil action in the courts or tribunals of a State there indisputably exists, without prejudice to the outcome of the proceedings, a "jurisdictional link" for the purposes of Article 1.'[367] As soon as this is the case, the Convention is in principle applicable *ratione loci* and the inquiry shifts to the requirements of article 6.1: does the person have a civil right and is there an unacceptable limitation of the right of access to court in respect of the determination of that right? The argument that the *dispute* is not within the jurisdiction to adjudicate of the contracting state (or within its essential competence in our version of the argument) hence targets the applicability *ratione materiae* rather than the applicability *ratione loci* of the Convention. The limits on the essential competence of a court qualify the substantive rights of individuals within a specific national order. Article 6.1 is not applicable to immunity rules that reflect such limits. The jurisdiction at issue in that argument should not be confused with the jurisdiction within the meaning of article 1 of the Convention.

The distinction between necessary rules on the one hand and voluntary and national rules on the other does not settle the applicability question completely. When foreign states are allowed to exercise their sovereign authority on the territory of the forum state—think cross-border arrests, diplomatic or consular activities or the presence of foreign military bases—the forum state in fact accepts that disputes may arise out of acts taking place on its territory that fall outside its

[365] *Loizidou v Turkey* (Preliminary Objections), Series A–310, 20 EHRR 99 (ECHR, 1995) 130, § 62. Cf also *Cyprus v Turkey* 35 EHRR 731 (ECHR, 2001) 968–70, § 75–80; *Bankovic v 17 European Member States of NATO* ibid § 70.

[366] *Markovic and others v Italy* (ECHR, 2006) available at <http://www.echr.coe.int>.

[367] ibid § 54.

essential competence. The situation recalls the *Van der Peet* case. In that case the Commission argued that the Convention could have a limited form of applicability. Immunity of international organizations was considered compatible with article 6.1 only if the right of access to court receives an equivalent protection within the international organization.[368] The comparison is however not complete. While the immunity of international organizations removes disputes from the jurisdiction of the forum state to the jurisdiction of the international organization, the immunity of foreign states for *acta jure imperii* limits that jurisdiction. Hence, it can not be said that the forum state has *transferred powers* to the foreign state. The forum state does not limit its jurisdiction by allowing foreign states to exercise state power on their territory, but it does expose individuals within its jurisdiction to legal disputes that cannot be decided by its courts. It is still arguable that a member state can only do so without violating the Convention if reasonable alternative means of redress are available. Whether the legal system of the foreign state is a reasonable alternative will depend on the weight of the other factors that determine the interest of the individual to have access to the court. One factor is the principle of good faith, or legitimate expectation. There is arguably a big difference between individuals who consciously and voluntarily interact with an entity that is protected by immunity and individuals whose dispute arises from involuntarily contact with such entity.[369] Other factors are the nationality and place of residence of the individual and the link between the act complained of and the territory of the forum state. In other words, a remedy that is reasonable for a national of the foreign state who has a dispute over an employment contract he voluntarily concluded with that state, may not be reasonable for a national of the forum state who finds himself involuntarily in a legal relation with a foreign state because of tortious activity of that state. Or, the situation of a foreign diplomat who is employed at an Embassy in the territory of the forum state differs fundamentally from that of an individual who is accidentally shot while walking the dog past the fences of a foreign military base within the territory of the forum state. If the interests of the individual to have access to court are particularly weighty the forum state may have to ensure that appropriate remedies are available.

In sum, the examination of the relation between the rule of state immunity and the right of access to court should distinguish three distinct situations. Let us in conclusion apply these findings to the *McElhinney*, *Al-Adsani*, and *Fogarty* cases.

[368] Cf p 376–7 above.

[369] It could even be argued that individuals that voluntarily and consciously engage legal relations with foreign states that pertain to *acta jure imperii*—like certain employment contracts—have waived their right of access. Cf in respect of international organizations RA Lawson (1999) 440. An example of involuntary contact is the nuisance caused by foreign military aircraft on a foreign military basis, cf *Yamaguchi v United States* (Japan, 2002).

The rules of state immunity at issue in *Al-Adsani* and *Fogarty* were clearly no procedural bars to the exercise of jurisdiction, only the rule at issue in *McElhinney* could be qualified as such. The national courts could not have decided the disputes underlying the applications of Al-Adsani and Fogarty without violating the independence and equality of a foreign state. The disputes did not fall within the essential competence of the UK courts. The Court has failed to recognize the qualitative difference between voluntary and necessary immunity rules. The concept of waiver—considered by the Court to be conclusive evidence of the procedural nature of the rule of state immunity—is not particularly helpful as far as necessary immunity rules are at issue. 'Waiver' of 'immunity' enjoyed under the necessary rule in fact *creates* an exceptional basis of jurisdiction for the foreign national court.[370] The tersely developed conclusion of the Court is based on a simplified version of the complex reality of state immunity law. It was argued in chapter 2 of this study that the use of the term immunity from jurisdiction for the restrictive rule of state immunity may confuse. It underlies the popular circular argument that state immunity presupposes jurisdiction because the term immunity from jurisdiction indicates that jurisdiction precedes immunity. The reasoning of the Court reflects this confusion. Had the Court proceeded from substance instead of form it would have found that in two of the three cases under consideration the disputes brought before the national court were not within the essential competence of that court.

In the *Al-Adsani* case this finding settles the question. Article 6.1 is not applicable to the facts of the case and the application is inadmissible *ratione materiae.* In the *Fogarty* case, however, the foreign state was *allowed* to perform sovereign activity within the territory of the UK. The circumstances of the case are however such that article 6.1 is not applicable. Fogarty has interacted voluntarily and consciously with the United States and should have understood that the legal aspects of that interaction were not within the competence of the UK courts.

The *McElhinney* case is admittedly not the most straightforward example of an immunity rule constituting a procedural bar to the exercise of jurisdiction rather than a substantive qualification of the right. It was argued in chapter 2 of this study that states that grant state immunity in situations that qualify under the territorial tort exception do not apply international law. However, it was explained that the territorial tort exception finds a limit in the discretionary function exception and the vertical division of competences between national courts and international dispute settlement procedures, the epitome being the applicability of the laws of war.[371] Did the act of the UK soldier on Irish territory qualify under the exception for acts of foreign armed forces? It is argued here that it did not. That exception should be understood from the perspective of

[370] Cf ch 2 § 3.3.1 above.

[371] The territorial tort exception does not apply regardless of the *acta jure imperii–acta jure gestionis* distinction—as is at times argued—but is in fact a proper reflection of that distinction. Cf for the argument ch 2 § 3.2.1 above.

the vertical division of competences and requires that the illegality of the act of a soldier under the national law of the forum state is of no importance in view of the exclusive applicability of international law. It is argued here that that was not the case in the shooting incident in the *McElhinney* case. Therefore, the disputed immunity rule was not a necessary rule of international law. In contrast to the other two cases before the Court, the restriction at issue in the *McElhinney* case raises an issue under article 6.1 of the Convention.

3.2.4.3 Compliance

Does the rule of state immunity have a legitimate aim and is there a reasonable relationship of proportionality between the rule and that aim? This study takes issue with the Court's answer to this question on two distinct levels. In the first place it is asserted that the Court's general approach to the compliance test fails the standard it has itself developed in its earlier jurisprudence. The Court's handling of the second prong of the article 6.1 inquiry arguably suffers the consequences of its generous conclusion on the first. In a clear attempt to limit the obligations of states under article 6.1 in respect of the rule of state immunity the international law character of the rule was relied on as providing the legitimate aim of the restriction *and* as securing its proportionality.[372] Second, this study disagrees with the Court's approach to the question of whether the rule of state immunity at hand has in fact an international law character.

The Court has basically decided that immunity rules of an international law character never violate article 6.1. Such rules, it argued, should be regarded as "inherent" restrictions on the right of access to court.[373] The approach to the issue of compliance perplexes. International law requirements provide a legitimate aim for the limitation *and* are conclusive in any inquiry into its proportionality? Did the proportionality test not essentially require courts to weigh competing interests in order to prevent the undue reliance on those interests that provided the legitimate aim? The Court did not consider it necessary to balance the interests protected by the rule of state immunity with the interests of the individual to have its claim heard. It effectively assumed that rules of international law always reflect a proper balance of these interests. The test of restrictions under the *Ashingdane* criteria is thus reduced to a paper tiger.

This is unacceptable. The concept of 'inherent limitations to article 6.1' is not compatible with the principle that exceptions to Convention rights must reflect a proper balance of interests.[374] All restrictions must be effectively tested under

[372] Cf also the subsequent decision in *Kalogeropoulou et al v Greece and Germany* (ECHR, 2002).

[373] The reasoning of the Court recalls that of the Italian Constitutional Court in the *Russel* case: *Soc. Immobiliare Soblim v Russel* (1979) 62 RDI 797.

[374] It should moreover be noted that the Court did not distinguish between the grant of immunity in accordance with international law that existed at the moment that states signed the European Convention and applications that may have developed later, or are still to develop. Surely it is not

the *Ashingdane* criteria, bearing in mind that restrictions to the rights under the Convention such as that safeguarded by Article 6 should be interpreted strictly and narrowly. In each case before the Court, the interests of the individual to have access to the court—a principle that 'ranks as one of the universally "recognised" fundamental principles of law'[375]—should be weighed against the interests protected by the rule of state immunity at hand. If the interests of the individual outweigh those of the state, the forum state has two competing obligations: the obligation to grant immunity in accordance with international law and the obligation to grant access to court in accordance with international human rights law. If it chooses to violate the obligation owed to the private individual it incurs responsibility for the individual's damages.

It is, in the first place pointed out that the weight of the interest protected by the restriction—the general interest of the community—should be determined by the *rationale* of the immunity rule. The international law character of a rule is an indication of the importance attached to this rationale by states but an independent inquiry remains necessary. It is in this respect for example possible to distinguish the weighty *ne impediatur legatio* rationale that underlies diplomatic immunity from the archaic protection of dignity rationale that underlies head of state immunity. If a certain immunity rule does *not* reflect requirements under international law it may still protect a valuable interest. However, the weight of the interest is likely to be less than that of the interests protected by immunity rules of an international law character.[376]

It must subsequently be ensured that the interests protected by the immunity rule are not *outweighed* by the interests of the individual in access to court.[377] The Court itself has stated in *Waite and Kennedy v Germany* that the availability of alternative effective remedies is the material factor in this balancing exercise.[378] Judge Loucaides argued in his dissent in the *McElhinney* case that the existence of an alternative remedy abroad is irrelevant for the question of whether there

possible for states to agree to increase the scope of state immunity under voluntary rules without raising any issue under the Convention?

[375] *Golder v United Kingdom* (ECHR, 1975) 535–6, § 35.

[376] If states agree to *increase* the scope of immunity under conventional or customary international law to include cases that could previously be heard by the courts it can also be questioned whether the interests protected by that application of the rule are particulary weighty. In this respect it is interesting to note that ratification of the UN Convention on Jurisdictional Immunities of States and their Property (2004) may entail for several states the obligation to grant immunity in cases where they previously did not.

[377] It will be clear from the discussion of the *Osman* case in § 3.2.2.3 above that this author does not share the position of Judge Loucaides on the question of proportionality. The Judge argued that any immunity that at the application stage did not leave room for deviation of the rule on the basis of counterweighing interests violates art 6.1. This study argues that this is only so if the rule does not reflect a proper balance between the various competing interests involved in a specific case. Cf different I Pingel, 'Droit d'accès aux tribunaux et exception d'immunité: La Cour de Strasbourg persiste' (2002) 106 RGDIP 893, 906.

[378] Cf also *Jones v Saudi Arabia and Abdul Aziz* and *Mitchell a.o. v Al-Dali a.o.* (UK, 2004) § 85–6.

is a violation of the right of access to court. That cannot however be sustained. That that possibility may at times not be enough to tip the balance of interests to the side of the foreign state when the interests of the individual to have access to the court are particularly weighty in view of other factors, or when the interests of the state are particularly trivial—as was indeed the case in *McElhinney*—does not mean that it is no factor to begin with.

In contrast to the rule of immunity of international organizations, the rule of state immunity may seem not to entail the risk of denial of justice since an alternative remedy is naturally available, namely the national courts of the foreign state. This remedy is however often illusory. The burden of litigating in a foreign country, in a foreign language and within a foreign legal system may render the alternative remedy unavailable in practice. Furthermore, the foreign legal system may not recognize the rights and interests protected within the legal system of the forum state.[379]

Whether the alternative remedy is a reasonable alternative will also depend on the weight of the other factors that determine the interest of the individual to have access to the court. One such factor is the principle of good faith, or legitimate expectation. The interest to have access to court of individuals who consciously and voluntarily interact with an entity that is protected by immunity is not as weighty as that of individuals whose dispute arises from involuntary contact with such entity. In this respect, the distinction that Judge Rozakis drew in his dissenting opinion in *McElhinney* between the employees of an international organization in the cases of *Waite and Kennedy* and *Beer and Regan* and *McElhinney* is convincing. The other factors identified by the Judge—the nationality of the victim and the link between the violation and the territory of the forum state—are also factors of influence. As stated above, a remedy that is reasonable for a national of the foreign state who has voluntarily entered a contract with that state may not so be reasonable for a national of the forum state who finds himself involuntarily in a legal relation with a foreign state because of tortious activity of that state. Also the importance of the right that is allegedly infringed may be taken into account. In particular, the fact that proceedings regard the alleged violation of Convention rights adds weight to the interests of the individual to have access to court.[380] In order to determine the compliance of the state immunity rule at issue in the case of *McElhinney v Ireland* with article 6.1 it is hence necessary to balance the competing interests involved in that rule. It was already explained that the application of the state immunity rule did not reflect an obligation that Ireland has under international law. Judges Caflisch, Cabral Barreto, and Vajic concluded in their dissenting opinion that the limitation '*hence* constituted a

[379] Cf eg JF Lalive (1953) 221; J Salmon and S Sucharitkul, 'Les Missions Diplomatiques Entre Deux Chaises: Immunité Diplomatique ou Immunité d'État?' (1987) 33 AFDI 163, 179.

[380] Cf § 3.3 and § 3.4 below for additional arguments against immunity when the violation of Convention rights is at issue.

disproportionate restriction of the right of access to court'.[381] This conclusion is unsatisfactory. It only *adds* to the problematic nature of the approach of the Court to the compliance test. The inquiry into the international law nature of the rule thus *replaces* the inquiry into the balance of the competing interests. Better is the approach of Judge Rozakis who recognized that the absence of a clear requirement of international law weakens the interests in support of the immunity rule that must still be weighed against the interests of the individual to have access to the court. In a case like *McElhinney* where *all* factors added weight to the interest of the individual to have access to the court, *and* the interest supporting the restriction was weak because it did not reflect an obligation under international law the balance cannot but tip to the side of the applicant. This author therefore believes that the Court should have found that Ireland violated article 6.1.

It should at this point be stressed that the oft-heard argument that states are free to grant other states or foreign state officials as much immunity as they like is debatable from the perspective of the fundamental rights of individuals recognized in international law. Human rights law may limit the freedom of states to grant more immunity than required.[382] In this respect it is also interesting to briefly note article 9 of the Resolution of the Institut de Droit International on the Immunities from Jurisdiction and Execution of Heads of State and of Government in International Law. The article provides that '[n]othing in this Resolution prohibits a State from unilaterally granting to a foreign Head of State, in conformity with international law, larger immunities than those laid down by the present provisions.'[383] At the plenary debate on the proposals of Rapporteur Verhoeven, Schermers expressed opposition to this provision. He stated that 'immunities, as an exception to the normal application of the law, should be as limited or restricted as possible.' He proposed to either amend the provision to provide that 'States should grant no more privileges or immunities than required by the present provisions' or to delete the article altogether.[384] While the article explicitly provides that national law immunities should be in accordance with international law, this author agrees with Schermers that the signal given by the article is unfortunate.

We should finally consider whether the interests protected by the comprehensive personal immunities of diplomatic agents and foreign heads of state warrant

[381] Dissenting Opinion Judges Caflisch, Cabral Barreto, and Vajic (emphasis added).

[382] Cf in this respect *Harbhajan Singh Dhalla v Union of India* (India, 1986), discussed in ch 2 § 2.2.2 above.

[383] Institut de Droit International, Resolution on Immunities from Jurisdiction and Execution of Heads of State and of Government in International Law (Résolution sur les immunités de juridiction et d'exécution du chef d'Etat et de gouvernement en droit international) (2001), (2000–01) 69 AIDI 743.

[384] Institut de Droit International (Rapporteur J Verhoeven), Les immunités de juridiction et d'exécution du chef d'Etat et de gouvernement en droit international, Plenary Session (2001), (2000–01) 69 AIDI 601, 663.

the substantial limitation of the rights of private individuals. The outcome of the test is not static. The weight accorded to the fundamental rights of individuals may change with time. Grotius wrote in 1625 that 'the security of ambassadors is a matter of greater importance than the punishment of an offense. For an ambassador may be punished by the one who sent him, if the latter so chooses. And if he refuses, he may, as a supporter of crime, be compelled by war to inflict punishment.'[385] Until the 1940 case of *De Meeüs v Forzano*[386] Italian courts struck the balance differently. The Italian Court of Cassation of Rome stated in *Comina v Kite* that an absolute rule of diplomatic immunity is contrary to justice.[387]

Also Fiore disagreed with the common practice of granting diplomatic agents virtually absolute immunity from jurisdiction.[388] 'Comment admettre', he wondered, 'qu'un Ministre public puisse contracter des dettes en ne pas payer ses créanciers, qu'il puisse consentir des obligations et ne pas accomplir ses engagements? Qu'il puisse, en vivant dans un pays, invoquer à son profit l'application des lois civiles dans ses rapports evec les habitants de ce pays et ensuite refuser d'admettre l'application des ces mêmes lois, en invoqquant le privilège des son immunité?'[389] In a similar vein, Fiore rejected diplomatic immunity from penal jurisdiction for crimes committed in a private capacity.[390]

When the International Court of Justice concluded in the *Arrest Warrant* case that the personal immunity of a minister of foreign affairs does not yield to developments in international criminal law Judges Higgins, Kooijmans, and Buergenthal explained in their Joined Separate Opinion that '[t]he law of privileges and immunities . . . retains its importance since immunities are granted to high State officials to guarantee the proper functioning of the network of mutual inter-State relations, which is of paramount importance for a well-ordered and harmonious international system.' However, they cared to add that 'the weights on the two scales are not set for all perpetuity'.[391]

It should however be realized that the perspective of the judges of the ICJ is essentially different from that of the judges of the ECHR. The ICJ only determines the scope of the rule of state immunity. They therefore limit their appraisal of the influence of human rights law (or international criminal law in this case) to the balance struck by states. They do not balance the weights on the scale themselves. The ECHR, however, must determine whether a particular immunity rule

[385] H Grotius, *De Jure Belli ac Pacis* (1625), trans by LR Loomis (1949) ii 197.

[386] *De Meeüs v Forzano* (Italy, 1940) 94 (my translation): 'costituiscono il substrato materiale necessario per lo svolgimento delle attività pubbliche'.

[387] Cf *Comina v Kite* (Italy, 1922) 174.

[388] P Fiore, *Nouveau droit international public, suivant les besoins de la civilisation moderne* (2nd edn, 1885) ii 559–63 and 569–71.

[389] ibid 559.

[390] ibid 569–71.

[391] *Arrest Warrant* Case, Joint Separate Opinion of Judges Higgins, Kooijmans, and Buergenthal, 85, § 75.

violates the right of access to court. While only states can change the rule, the ECHR may provide them with a policy argument for change when it finds that the rule does not reflect a proper balance of the interests involved. Arguably, a reconsideration of the balance struck between the interests of states on the one hand and the rights and interests of individuals on the other is called for today.

Especially the part of head of state immunity that exceeds the *ne impediatur legatio* rationale of diplomatic immunity should be subjected to a critical review. It is very arguable indeed that the interests of private individuals to have their dispute with a foreign head of state heard may outweigh the interest of protecting the dignity of a foreign head of state. But also the rule of diplomatic immunity should be subjected to close scrutiny. While ultimately the comprehensive immunity may be necessary to ensure the effective functioning of diplomatic agents, it can at least be questioned whether states undertake sufficient action to limit the prejudice the immunity causes to private individuals.

As said earlier, the interest of the private individual to have his case heard is especially weighty when the dispute arises from activity of diplomatic agents that is closely linked to the territory of the forum state and that arises from accidental contact between the individual and a diplomatic agent. There may in addition be factors related to the alternative forum that determine the weight of the interest. In addition to the factors named above it should be realized that diplomatic immunity is at times abused by states. In the case of premeditated state crime the remedies available within the courts of the sending state are likely to be illusory.

On the other hand, the interests protected by the rule of diplomatic immunity are indisputably weighty. The International Court of Justice stated in the *Teheran Hostages Case* that 'the institution of diplomacy, with its concomitant privileges and immunities, has withstood the test of centuries and proved to be an instrument essential for effective co-operation in the international community, and for enabling States, irrespective of their differing constitutional and social systems, to achieve mutual understanding and to resolve their differences by peaceful means'.[392] Hurst explained that '[t]he duties which a foreign diplomatic representative has to perform are in many cases far from easy and his communications far from welcome to the State to which they are made. If the diplomatic representative were at the mercy of interruptions which might be caused to his task by an unscrupulous abuse of powers of the local administration and of the machinery which must exist in every State for the settling of disputes between private persons, it might be impossible for him to carry out his duties.'[393]

Obviously, the danger of abuse of state power by the receiving state can only be curbed by a comprehensive immunity. However, the interests of private

[392] *United States Diplomatic and Consular Staff in Tehran* (ICJ, 1979) 19, § 39.

[393] C Hurst, 'Diplomatic Immunities' in *International Law, The Collected Papers of Sir Cecil Hurst* (1950) 169, 174 (Trans of C Hurst, 'Les Immunités Diplomatiques' (1926–II) 12 RdC 115, 122).

individuals can be protected by measures *other* than a general restriction of the scope of diplomatic immunity. In the first place, restrictions can be introduced on a regional level. The risk of undue interference is limited within a group of like-minded democratic states like, for example, those members of the European Union. Schermers, for one, has proposed a European convention abolishing diplomatic immunity.[394] Alternatively, states could attempt to limit the negative consequences of the application of the comprehensive immunity rule. For example, Hurst argued already in 1929 that states have an obligation to their own nationals to refrain from an undue increase in the number of individuals entitled to such immunity within their territory.[395] It should in this respect be noted that in preparation of the text of the 1961 Vienna Convention on Diplomatic Relations several proposals were made with a view to limit the negative impact of diplomatic immunity on the fundamental rights of individuals. For one, it was suggested that the following article be included:

A diplomatic agent shall be justiciable in the courts of the sending State. The competent tribunal shall be that of the seat of the Government of the sending State, unless some other is designated under the law of that State.[396]

The proposal was however opposed by states that did not want to change their laws to include jurisdiction over facts taking place abroad and did not secure sufficient support.[397]

Furthermore, the Netherlands submitted a proposal to make diplomatic immunity for civil claims arising from motor traffic accidents 'subject to the condition that such action can be brought directly against an insurance company before a court of the receiving State'.[398] Also that proposal was rejected, but it is interesting to note that in several states it is in fact explicitly required for diplomats to have liability insurance against risks arising from their participation in the traffic and often it is provided that insurance companies cannot take advantage of the diplomatic immunity of its client.[399]

A non-binding Resolution annexed to the Convention provides a third indication that the drafters of the Convention were concerned for the interests of private individuals. The Resolution refers to 'the deep concern expressed during the deliberations of the Conference that claims of diplomatic immunity might, in

394 HG Schermers (1998) 156, 161.

395 CJB Hurst, 'Diplomatic Immunities—Modern Developments' (1929) 10 BYIL 1, 5.

396 YBILC 1957 i 105 (proposal François).

397 UN Doc 4/114 add 4, add 2 4/116, 58.

398 UN Doc A/Conf/C 1/L 186/Re*v* 1 (1961); UN Doc A/Conf 20/14, pp 166–72. Cf E Kerley, 'Some Aspects of the Vienna Conference on Diplomatic Intercourse and Immunities' (1962) 56 AJIL 88, 120.

399 Cf E Denza (1998) 233 for the examples of the United Kingdom, the United States, Canada and Belgium. She also notes that the fact that The Netherlands did not ratify the Vienna Convention until 1984 was in large part due to its discontent regarding the question of motor accident claims, 236.

certain cases, deprive persons in the receiving State of remedies to which they are entitled by law' and recommends 'that the sending State should waive the immunity of members of its diplomatic mission in respect of civil claims of persons in the receiving State when this can be done without impeding the performance of the functions of the mission, and that, when immunity is not waived, the sending State should use its best endeavours to bring about a just settlement of the claims'.[400]

While states have proven sympathetic to the plights of private individuals, the only effective step that some of them have taken to protect the interests of private individuals is the obligatory insurance of motor vehicles. It is therefore questionable whether they comply with their obligations under article 6.1 ECHR. This author suggests that states should give their obligations under this article more serious thought. One measure that they could take to ensure the rights of their citizens is to oblige sending states to assume responsibility for damages caused by their diplomatic agents[401] and grant citizens a right to diplomatic protection.

One final issue that needs consideration in this regard is the suggestion that it is fair to have *the receiving state bear the consequences of the law of diplomatic immunity instead of the private individual*. The particular nature of the rule of diplomatic immunity makes a proper balancing of the interests of private individuals and states for the purpose of the determination of the proper *scope of the rule* impossible. While in a case at hand the interests of the individual may outweigh those of the state, a limitation of the scope of the rule of diplomatic immunity would undermine the whole edifice of diplomatic immunity. Accordingly, in such cases the grant of diplomatic immunity violates the rights of the individual while there is *no policy argument in favour of change of the scope of diplomatic immunity*. The grant of diplomatic immunity may then be seen to entail the responsibility of the receiving state under article 6.1 ECHR. In this respect the French cases of *Dame Burgat et autres* and *Tizon et Millet* are notable.[402] The case of *Dame Burgat* concerned a dispute over a raise of the rent in accordance with the law between a landlord and his tenant who was the wife of the permanent representative of Honduras at UNESCO in Paris. The court attached great importance to the fact that the rental contract was concluded twenty years earlier when the woman was still married to her previous husband. It was therefore, the court stressed, not foreseeable for the landlord that his tenant would at some point be accorded diplomatic status and it concluded that France was responsible for the damages suffered by the application of the rule of diplomatic immunity to the dispute.

[400] Non-binding Annex to the Vienna Convention on Diplomatic Relations: Resolution no II Consideration of Civil Claims, UN Doc A/Conf 20/10/Add 1.

[401] The Holy See proposed in Vienna to have sending state pay damages caused by its diplomatic agents: UN Doc A/Conf/14 in UNConference I 175–6.

[402] *Dame Burgat et autres* (1977) 104 JDI 630 (France, Conseil d'Etat, 1976); *Tizon et Millet* (1985) 31 AFDI 928 (France, Conseil d'Etat, 1984).

It explained that 'la responsabilité de l'Etat se trouve engagée sur le fondement du principe de l'égalité des citoyens devant les charges publiques'.[403]

The case of *Tizon et Millet* concerned the refusal of the state to execute a judgment establishing a debt owed by an individual protected by diplomatic immunity to two French merchants. The *Conseil d'Etat* did not regard the French state responsible for the damages suffered by the two merchants as a consequence of the application of the law of diplomatic immunity because the prejudice was not sufficiently serious and the claimants had not exhausted all available civil remedies before proceeding to public law. The responsibility of the receiving state, the court stressed, 'ne saurait constituer qu'une ultima ratio'.[404] The judgment clearly intimates that the state would have been responsible *had* the prejudice been serious and *had* all remedies been exhausted.

Both Schermers and Tanzi have advanced proposals to this effect,[405] and in the US legislation based on this principle was put to Congress—but failed to secure sufficient support.[406] The idea deserves serious consideration. With the two conditions formulated by the *Conseil d'Etat* as minimum requirements, this author supports the suggestion that diplomatic immunities may unduly infringe the rights of private individuals. The interests protected by these immunities are beyond dispute. It is however not said that the handful of individuals that suffer denial of justice as a consequence should bear the financial burden themselves. Since it is the community as a whole that stands to benefit from diplomatic intercourse it is arguable that it is the community that should pay its price.

In conclusion it is argued in this study that even if the parameters of the Court's approach to the compliance test *were* accepted, the terms of its inquiry—and in the *McElhinney* case also the outcome—fail to convince. The Court had to establish that the three disputed applications of the state immunity rule reflected requirements of international law. The relevant reasoning of the Court and of the dissenting judges in *Al-Adsani v UK* was critically discussed earlier in this chapter.[407] Here we will take a brief look at the reasoning in *Fogarty* and *McElhinney*.

The inquiry into the state of state immunity law in the *Fogarty* and *McElhinney* cases compares somewhat meagrely to that undertaken in the *Al-Adsani* case. The Court limited itself to the finding that the respondent states were 'not alone' in holding that immunity attaches to suits by employees at diplomatic missions and in respect of territorial torts respectively and decided that both applications of the

[403] ibid 631.

[404] *Tizon et Millet* (France, 1984) 929.

[405] HG Schermers (1998) 162; A Tanzi (1991) 189.

[406] The so-called *Solarz Bill* included 'the principle that whenever a person is injured or suffers financial loss due to action by a foreign state official covered by the immunity statute, that person can apply for redress from the United States Government'. Cf Diplomatic Privileges and Immunities, Hearings and Markup Before the Subcommittee on International Operations of the House Committee on International Relations, 95th Congress 1st session 1977 45.

[407] Cf § 2.2 above.

rule did not 'fall outside any currently accepted international standards'.[408] This study argues that while this scope of the rule argumentation was acceptable in the *Fogarty* case, it is out of place in the *McElhinney* case. This is due to the essential different role of state practice in the ascertainment of international law requirements in the two cases. This criticism builds on the findings of chapter 2 of this study.[409]

States agree that employment disputes involving foreign states may fall outside their essential competence. The obligation to respect the independence and equality of other states imposes this limit. The exact contours of the obligation are however blurred. The principle can be derived from logic but only a uniform and consistent state practice can establish its outer limits. As long as states disagree on these contours, the various applications of the rule that argue convincingly in terms of the principle are all acceptable interpretations of the requirements of international law. When practice is divided and several states adopt one particular interpretation of the requirements of international law it can hence indeed be said that those states apply international law requirements. The Court's reasoning on this point in *Fogarty* is therefore satisfactory.[410]

The disagreement of states on the territorial tort exception is of an entirely different character. States that grant state immunity in situations qualifying under the territorial tort exception cannot convincingly argue in terms of the principle of independence and equality of states. This application of the rule of state immunity can only be said to be required by international law if it is established through a consistent and uniform state practice. In other words, this application of the rule can only be a voluntary rule of international law. For the purpose of ascertaining the requirements of international law inconsistent state practice hence has the role it normally has in the ascertainment of customary international law. A divided practice can only lead to the conclusion that international law does not require the particular application of the rule and that, accordingly, the rule has the character of *national* law. The fact that the application does not violate international law is irrelevant for the inquiry. The Court's conclusion in *McElhinney* hence fails to convince. It should have concluded that Ireland was not obliged to grant state immunity to the United Kingdom.

3.2.5 Conclusions and Final Observations

This section has argued that the argument that the rule of state immunity violates the right of access to court of individuals finds its limit in the distinction between necessary and voluntary state immunity. The argument has no force as against state immunity for *acta jure imperii*. The right of access applies to immunity rules

[408] *McElhinney*, 334, § 38; *Fogarty*, 314, § 37.

[409] Cf ch 2 § 3.3.2.1 above.

[410] It is *hence* argued that Judge Loucaides misconceived the role of state practice when he argued that the application of the rule did not reflect international law requirements because it was not supported by a widespread and consistent state practice.

that reflect international law voluntary immunity and national law immunity. Only when the forum state has consented to the exercise of foreign state power on its territory has the right of access to court a degree of applicability.

If an individual has a prima facie right of access to court the forum state has the obligation to ensure that restrictions on that right do not impair the very essence of the right, have a legitimate aim and are proportional to that aim. The exact obligation depends on the weight of the interests protected by the restriction and the weight of the interest of the individual to have access to court. It was explained that the international law character of a certain application of the state immunity rule adds to the interests protected by the rule but does not of itself decide the balancing exercise. If the interests of the individual outweigh those protected by the immunity rule the right of access to court is violated and the state whose courts have granted the immunity is responsible for the violation. If a state wants to fulfil both its obligations under a voluntary immunity rule and the right of access to court it must make sure that the interests of the individual are sufficiently protected without access to the courts of the forum state. If it fails to do this it should compensate the individual.

Accordingly, this study respectfully disagrees with the judgments of the European Court of Human Rights in the *McElhinney*, *Al-Adsani*, and *Fogarty* cases. While this study equally concludes that there was no violation of article 6.1 in the *Al-Adsani* case and the *Fogarty* case, the reasons on which this conclusion rest are fundamentally different from those relied on by the Court. The Court concluded—and only judge Loucaides dissented—that immunity rules that have the character of *international law* always comply with the *Ashingdane* criteria. This study argued that article 6.1 is not applicable to begin with to disputes concerning acts of torture allegedly committed within the territory of the defendant and certain employment disputes. As regards the *McElhinney* case this study also concludes differently on the question of violation of article 6.1. While the Court reasoned in the same terms in all three cases, this study argued that since article 6.1 indeed applies to the case the interests protected by the restriction and the interests of the individual to have access to court must be properly balanced. The Court has made a mockery of the compliance criteria for restrictions on the right of access. The assertion that the right of access is never violated by restrictions under rules of international law denies the right an independent meaning. This study concluded that the interests of McElhinney clearly outweighed those protected by the immunity rule—also in view of the rule's *national law* character—and that article 6.1 had therefore been violated.

The Court has elaborated this idea of 'inherent limitations' in subsequent cases concerning immunity of members of parliament and members of the judiciary. In *A v United Kingdom* the Court concluded that 'a rule of parliamentary immunity, which is consistent with and reflects generally recognised rules within signatory States, the Council of Europe and the European Union, cannot in principle be regarded as imposing a disproportionate restriction on the right of access to a court'. It reiterated its finding that '[j]ust as the right of access to a court is an inherent part of the fair trial guarantee in that Article, so some restrictions on access must likewise be regarded as inherent, an example being those limitations generally accepted by signatory States as part of the doctrine of parliamentary immunity'.[411] However, contrary to the three cases on the rule of state immunity discussed in this section the Court *did* discuss the weight of the respective interests. It emphasized the importance of the principle of parliamentary immunity and it pointed out that individuals are not entirely without means of redress and that several mechanisms control the activities of the members of parliament.[412] In the case of *Ernst v Belgium* the Court again reiterated that there are certain inherent limitations to the right of access to court, like state immunity and parliamentary immunity.[413] To see whether the immunity of members of the judiciary is also compatible with article 6.1 of the Convention, 'il importe' according to the Court 'd'examiner si les requérants disposaient d'autres voies raisonnables pour protéger efficacement leurs droits garantis par la Convention'.[414]

In sum, the Court indicated in these cases that inherent limitations always reflect a positive outcome of a test under the *Ashingdane* criteria. The notion of inherent limitations is thus not much more than the notion of limitations inherent in the right of access to court that do not impair the very essence of that right, have a legitimate aim, and are proportional. In *McElhinney*, *Al-Adsani*, and *Fogarty* the Court has not dared to question the established institution of state immunity (or diplomatic immunity for that matter). As a consequence, this author believes the safeguards of article 6.1 not to be 'practical and effective' as far as immunity rules are concerned.[415] It is hoped that the Court will soon get a chance to retrace its overcautious steps.

3.3 The Right to a Remedy

Article 13 of the European Convention on Human Rights provides that

> [e]veryone whose rights and freedoms as set forth in the Convention are violated shall have an effective remedy before a national authority notwithstanding that the violation has been committed by persons acting in an official capacity.

[411] *A v United Kingdom* (ECHR, 2002) 937, § 83. Cf also *Cordova v Italy (no 1 and 2)* 45 EHRR 43 (ECHR, 2003) § 60–1.

[412] *A v United Kingdom* (ECHR, 2002) 937 § 79ff and 938 § 86.

[413] *Ernst v Belgium* 39 EHRR 35 (ECHR, 2003) § 52.

[414] ibid § 53.

[415] In *Soering v UK* A–161, 11 EHRR 439 (ECHR, 1989) 467, § 87 the Court considered that '[i]n interpreting the Convention regard must be had to its special character as a treaty for the collective enforcement of human rights and fundamental freedoms... Thus the object and purpose of the Convention as an instrument for the protection of individual human beings require that its provisions be interpreted and applied so as to make its safeguards practical and effective.'

The Court has explained on many occasions that the article 'requires the provision of a domestic remedy to deal with the substance of an "arguable claim" under the Convention and to grant appropriate relief'. While states have 'some discretion as to the manner in which they conform to [this obligation]', the remedy must 'be "effective" in practice as well as in law'.[416]

The Court has held moreover that when rights as fundamental as the right to life or the prohibition against torture, inhuman and degrading treatment under articles 2 and 3 of the Convention are at stake the notion of effective remedy entails 'a thorough and effective investigation capable of leading to the identification and punishment of those responsible and including effective access for the complainant to the investigatory procedure'.[417]

We saw in section 2.3.2.2 of this chapter that it is occasionally argued that the obligation to provide a remedy for human rights violations clashes with the obligation states owe to foreign states under the law of state immunity. Bianchi, for example, held that '[t]o argue that states which ratify international human rights treaties providing for a right to a remedy have implicitly accepted to subject to the judicial scrutiny of their domestic courts the conduct of foreign states is a perfectly tenable interpretation.'[418] Bröhmer developed and advanced the argument in respect of article 13 of the Convention. He argued that when a right under the Convention has been violated *all* contracting states are obliged to provide a remedy, even when the violation has been committed by a non-Convention state.[419]

This study argued however that the force of the argument is limited. And as far as article 13 ECHR is concerned it may not be coherent at all. In the first place it is commonly agreed that the obligation that corresponds to the right to a remedy rests solely on the state within whose jurisdiction the alleged violation of a fundamental right has taken place. Our area of inquiry is therefore reduced to the violations of Convention rights by foreign states or foreign state officials within the territory of the forum state that are covered by the law of state immunity. In chapter 2 of this study it was explained that the scope of the law of state immunity knows a normative limit as far as acts on foreign territory are concerned, since the discretion of the foreign state to exercise its sovereign power depends on the extent of the consent of the state on whose territory it acts. This is not to say that acts of foreign states on foreign territory that violate human rights can *never* qualify as *acta jure imperii*. We can think of the practice of refusal of visa by a foreign embassy on the basis of discriminatory grounds. And what about the operation of a prison camp by a state on the territory of another state? Article 14 Torture

[416] Cf eg *Z and Others v United Kingdom* (ECHR, 2001) 140–1, § 108; *Assenov and Others v Bulgaria* 28 EHRR 652 (ECHR, 1998) 704, § 117; *Aydin v Turkey* 25 EHRR 251 (ECHR, 1997) 300, § 103; *Aksoy v Turkey* 23 EHRR 553 (ECHR, 1996) 592–593, § 95.

[417] *Aksoy v Turkey* (ECHR, 1996) 593, § 98; *Assenov and Others v Bulgaria* (ECHR, 1998); *Z and Others v United Kingdom* (ECHR, 2001) 141, § 109; *Kaya v Turkey* 28 EHRR 1 (ECHR, 1998) 50–1, § 107.

[418] A Bianchi (1997) 424.

[419] J Bröhmer (1997) 171–7 and 186–8, especially 177.

Convention and in fact customary international law would seem to oblige a state that allows another state to exploit a prison on its territory to provide a remedy for the claims of prisoners that allege that they are tortured by the foreign state.

It was however argued in section 2.3.2.3 that this obligation does not clash with the obligations under the law of state immunity and the law of diplomatic immunity. The remedy provided must be effective to ensure compliance with the prohibition to violate human rights but does not necessarily entail access to the judicial authorities of a state. Accordingly, while the right to a remedy may be violated when there is no access to court because of the rule of state immunity, there is no direct clash between the immunity and the right.

As said, special considerations apply to article 13 ECHR. It is widely believed that the article obliges a state to provide a remedy *only in respect of claims under the Convention against that state.*[420] In other words, the obligation would not extend to violation of the substantive rights of the Convention within its jurisdiction but only to violations of the Convention as such. Article 13 only applies when there is an arguable claim *under the Convention*. While it is arguable that the article does apply when a member state violates the Convention on the territory of another member state, the article does not require remedies against non-member states.[421]

3.4 The Right to Effective Protection

International human rights law does not only prohibit states to interfere with the fundamental rights of individuals, it also entails the positive obligation to secure the effective protection of these rights within their jurisdiction.[422] Individuals have a right to effective protection of their fundamental rights.

One obligation corresponding to this right is the obligation of the state to ensure that its civil and criminal law provide effective deterrence against the violation of fundamental rights. In the context of the European Convention on Human Rights the case of *X and Y v The Netherlands* illustrates this point.[423] A gap in Dutch law made it impossible to prosecute a person suspected of raping a mentally disabled girl. The Court considered that the positive obligations of states under article 8 of the Convention 'may involve the adoption of measures designed to secure respect for private life even in the sphere of the relations of individuals between themselves'.[424] While states in principle enjoy a margin

[420] Cf T Barkhuysen, *Article 13 EVRM: Effectieve Nationale Rechtsbescherming by Schendingen van Mensenrechten* (1998) 73–110; RA Lawson (1999) 459–60; F De Vittor, (2002) 596. Cf different A Clapham, *Human Rights in the Private Sphere* (1993) 240–4.

[421] The fact that there is no remedy against private individuals may mean that the state has violated its positive obligations under the Convention cf § 3.4 below.

[422] Cf in general E Klein (ed), *The Duty to Protect and to Ensure Human Rights* (1999).

[423] *X and Y v The Netherlands* (ECHR, 1985). Cf also *MC v Bulgaria* 40 EHRR 20 (ECHR, 2003) § 166 and *Siliadin v France* 43 EHRR 16 (ECHR, 2005) § 112.

[424] ibid 239–40, § 23.

of appreciation as regards the choice of means to secure compliance with these obligations and '[r]ecourse to the criminal law is not necessarily the only answer', the Court decided that at times the protection afforded by civil law is insufficient. When 'fundamental values and essential aspects of private life are at stake... [e]ffective deterrence is indispensable... and it can be achieved only by criminal-law provisions'.[425] Because Dutch legislation did not provide effective deterrence to protect the fundamental rights of a certain group of individuals the Netherlands was held responsible for a violation of article 8 of the Convention.[426]

In addition, the right to effective protection is generally agreed to entail an obligation on the state to bring those who violate human rights within its territorial borders to justice. Orentlicher was one of the first—and certainly one of the most prominent—authors to point this out.[427] She argued that 'authoritative interpretations' of comprehensive human rights treaties as the ECHR, the ICCPR and the ACHR 'make clear... that these treaties require States Parties generally to investigate serious violations of physical integrity... and to bring to justice those who are responsible.'[428] She explained that 'prosecution and punishment are the most effective—and therefore only adequate—means of ensuring a narrow class of rights that merit special protection'.[429]

Of the bodies interpreting the scope of the obligations of states under the three Conventions just mentioned, the European Court of Human Rights has been the most cautious in reading an obligation to prosecute in the ECHR. The Court *has* argued that '[t]he obligation to protect the right to life under [article 2] read in conjunction with the State's general duty under Article 1 of the Convention to "secure to everyone within their jurisdiction the rights and freedoms defined in [the] Convention", requires by implication that there should be some form of effective official investigation when individuals have been killed as a result of the use of force by, *inter alios*, agents of the State.'[430] In *Assenov and Others v Bulgaria* it went a small step further when it found that 'where an individual raises an arguable claim that he has been seriously ill-treated by the police or other such agents of the State unlawfully and in breach of Article 3, that provision, read in conjunction with the State's general duty under Article 1 of the Convention to 'secure to everyone within their jurisdiction the rights and freedoms defined in... [the] Convention', requires by implication that there should be an effective official investigation. This investigation, as with that under Article 2, should be capable of leading to the identification and punishment of those responsible...

[425] ibid 240 and 241, § 24 and 27.

[426] Cf also *A v United Kingdom* (ECHR, 1998) 629–30, § 22.

[427] DF Orentlicher, 'Settling Accounts: The Duty to Prosecute Human Rights Violations of a Prior Regime' (1991) 100 YLJ 2537.

[428] ibid 2568.

[429] ibid.

[430] *McCann and Others v United Kingdom* Series A–324, 21 EHRR 97 (ECHR, 1995) 163, § 161. Cf also *Kaya v Turkey* (ECHR, 1998) 44, § 86; *Yaşa v Turkey* 28 EHRR 408 (ECHR, 1998) 447–8, § 98.

If this were not the case, the general legal prohibition of torture and inhuman and degrading treatment and punishment, despite its fundamental importance...would be ineffective in practice and it would be possible in some cases for agents of the State to abuse the rights of those within their control with virtual impunity.' The decision in *Kiliç* moreover lends support for the argument that a 'lack of accountability' renders a criminal law system ineffective for the purposes of the Convention.[431]

The United Nations Human Rights Committee has interpreted the prohibition of torture under article 7 of the ICCPR to entail the obligation to investigate complaints about ill-treatment effectively and to hold those found guilty responsible.[432] In *Muteba v Zaire* the Committee held the state to be 'under an obligation to...conduct an inquiry into the circumstances of the torture, to punish those found guilty of torture and to take steps to ensure that similar violations do not occur in the future'.[433] In a similar vein the Inter-American Court of Human Rights has held that 'states must prevent, investigate and punish any violation of the rights recognized by the Convention'.[434]

It stands to reason that immunity rules are hard to reconcile with both aspects of the obligation to provide effective protection. Is there effective deterrence to prevent the violation of fundamental rights by person or entities that know themselves outside the reach of the civil and criminal law of the state in which they operate because of immunity laws?[435] This is a very serious question indeed. It is no secret that diplomatic agents never have a problem finding a parking space. It is not unthinkable that they also feel less restrained committing crimes of a more serious nature. In 1965 Schermers already cautioned that immunity from penal jurisdiction may favour the commission of illegal acts because the threat of punishment is not felt.[436] Notably, this is not necessarily because privileges and immunities are *abused*; recklessness may cause serious threats to fundamental rights as well.

When diplomatic agents are used to carry out terrorist attacks, when states are allowed to execute arrests or even exploit prison camps within the territory of another state and—to name an example not within the direct scope of this

[431] *Assenov and Others v Bulgaria* (ECHR, 1998) 701, § 102; *Kiliç v Turkey* (ECHR, 2000) § 75.

[432] General Comment No 20 in relation to article 7 ICCPR (1992), Report of the Human Rights Committee, UN Doc A/47/40 (1992), Annex VI (pp 193–5).

[433] *Muteba v Zaire*, Communication no 124/1982, UN Doc A/39/40 (1984) (HRC).

[434] *Velásquez Rodríguez* Case Series C no 4 (Inter-American Court of Human Rights, 1988) § 174. Cf also the following reports of the Inter-American Commission on Human Rights: Report 26/92 (EL Salvador), Report 29/92 (Uruguay) and Report 24/92 (Argentina), reprinted in (1993) 14 Human Rights Law Journal 167; Report 36/96 (Chile) (1996), § 111.

[435] The consideration on the normative limit of the rule of state immunity in such situations applies equally here.

[436] HG Schermers, 'L'immunité devant le droit pénal, en particulier en ce qui concerne les infraction aux règles de la circulation' in *Le Droit Pénal International, Recueil d'Études en Hommage à JM van Bemmelen* (1965) 174, 181.

study—when international organizations are allowed to engage in potentially hazardous activities like the exploitation of a nuclear plant, the international law rules on immunities from jurisdiction may very well be incompatible with the fundamental rights of individuals.[437] In sum, the argument that the right to effective protection and the law of state immunity are incompatible as far as serious human rights violations within the jurisdiction of the forum state are concerned is very persuasive. When there is no possibility for civil or penal suit in respect of acts that violate international human rights law it can be questioned whether the state provides effective deterrence to the commission of such acts in its territory.[438]

3.5 Conclusion

States that grant foreign states and their officials immunity from jurisdiction may violate their obligations to private individuals under human rights law. The tension between the right of access to court, the right to a remedy, and the right to effective protection however should not be overstated. Coherent policy arguments based on the tension between fundamental rights and state immunity must proceed from a thorough understanding of both bodies of law.

One important conclusion of the examination of the right of access to court is that—contrary to common belief—states are not free to grant as much state immunity as they wish.[439] In this respect the recent observation of the Japanese Supreme Court that 'it is not appropriate to grant immunity from civil suit for acts *jure gestionis*' aptly reflects the influence of the fundamental rights of individuals.[440] In addition, the argument that states violate their obligations under

[437] In 2004 the Dutch prosecutor was ordered to abandon the criminal proceedings against the nuclear research basis of EURATOM (European Atomic Energy Community, party of the EU institutions) in Petten because of the rule of immunity of international organizations. The prosecutor alleged that several environmental rules regarding, *inter alia*, the storage of hazardous materials had been violated. The alleged recklessness and flaws in the safety culture are not necessarily the direct consequence of the immunity rule but it can be questioned whether the absence of effective deterrence and effective control is compatible with the obligation of the Dutch government to protect the fundamental rights of its citizens within its territory. Cf eg De Volkskrant, 4 December 2004.

[438] The only place where this author has found support for this argument is RA Lawson (1999). Schermers did allude to this when he argued in 1965 that diplomatic immunity from penal jurisdiction may favour the commission of illegal acts because the threat of punishment is not felt, cf HG Schermers (1965) 181. RC Slye, 'The Legitimacy of Amnesties under International Law and General Principles of Anglo-American Law: Is a Legitimate Amnesty Possible?' (2002) 43 VJIL 173, 197–201 has argued in a similar vein that amnesties may violate the obligation of states to protect and ensure the fundamental rights of individuals.

[439] Cf for common belief eg CH Schreuer (1988) 6; S Sucharitkul (1982) 253; R Jennings (1988) 9; J Crawford (1983) 78; Report no 24, § 41.

[440] Japanese courts have started indicating support for the restrictive approach to the rule, see especially *Yamaguchi v United States* (S Ct, 2002). Cf also *Harbhajan Singh Dhalla v Union of India* (India, 1986) discussed in ch 2 § 2.2.2 of this study.

article 6.1 ECHR because they fail to limit the prejudice caused to the interests of private individuals by personal immunities is a strong one.

Furthermore, states must realize that they must provide effective deterrence against the commission of human rights violations within their territorial jurisdiction and must ensure an effective remedy to victims of such violations. The grant of state immunity in respect of human rights violations committed on its soil may not always be compatible with these obligations.

In general it is arguable that states should limit the number of privileged persons on its territory in accordance with the functionality rationale underlying the immunities shielding these persons from their jurisdiction—if not, the interests in favour of immunity are not readily discernable and the forum state may violate its obligations towards private individuals.

As said, the perspective on immunity rules developed in this section is essentially different from that discussed under section 2 of this chapter. While the judges of the ICJ can limit their inquiry to the weight accorded by states to the respective interests as reflected in the scope of the immunity rule, the judges of the ECHR are asked to engage an independent inquiry into the weight of the respective interests on the scale. When the immunity rule is not proportional, national judges are confronted with two conflicting obligations. Accordingly, when Lord Millett argued in *Holland v Lampen-Wolfe* that the right of access to court could not be violated by the rule of state immunity since the foreign state had a right to that immunity he failed to do justice to the character of the argument before him.

In the absence of a clash between the obligations under the law of state immunity and the law of human rights law, arguments in favour of the human rights exception are much less forceful. The debate then focuses on what the rights of individuals *should be* rather than what their rights *are*. On this level of argumentation several courts and scholars have pointed to the possible negative consequences of a human rights exception. It has for example been argued that national courts risk being flooded with transnational human rights litigation, or that the political settlement of human rights may be hindered.[441] The central question is whether states should in time limit the scope of state immunity and diplomatic immunity to ensure the rights of private individuals. It is noted in this respect that the ECHR considered in the case of *Kalogeropoulou v Greece and Germany* that a development of customary international law to this effect in the future is not precluded.[442]

This study is not concerned with this level of the debate. It is only underlined that arguments that favour this development should reflect a thorough

[441] *Al-Adsani v Government of Kuwait* (UK, 1996) 544 (*per* Stuart-Smith LJ); A Slaughter and D Bosco (2000) 113; R Garnett, (1997); I Diaz, 'A Critique of Proposals to Amend the Foreign Sovereign Immunities Act to Allow Suits Against Foreign Sovereigns for Human Rights Violations' (2001) 32 University of Miami Inter-American Law Review 137.

[442] *Kalogeropoulou et al v Greece and Germany* (ECHR, 2002).

understanding of the nature of the law of state immunity. In particular, arguments that fail to distinguish between voluntary and necessary immunity rules fail to convince. The common argumentation that the current state immunity rule favours commercial interests over public interests—'if contract, why not tort?'—suffers from this conflation of distinct concepts.[443] Also the argument that 'in no way can torture rightly be considered a legitimate or protectable "police", "law enforcement" or "sovereign" activity' misconceives the nature of today's rule of state immunity.[444] Scholars that rely on the theory developed by Lauterpacht in the 1950s to argue in favour of the human rights exception make a similar mistake.[445] Both proponents and opponents of the human rights exception tend to present the issue as one of possible further restriction of the rule of state immunity continuing the path that started with the commercial activity exception. The depiction of the human rights exception as just another exception to state immunity that states may choose to develop through state practice disregards the qualitative difference between voluntary and necessary immunity rules. While the restriction of voluntary immunity is indeed a question of weighing and balancing the various interests, restriction of necessary immunity entails a more fundamental change of the pillars of the international legal order.[446]

4 Conclusions

This chapter set out to test the coherency of the various arguments in the debate on the human rights exception in light of the parameters of the rule of state immunity and international human rights law. In order to do that it was necessary to first structure the debate by classifying types of argument. Human rights based arguments against the law of state immunity operate on two distinct levels. Arguments on the first level focus on the right of the respondent state to invoke the rule of state immunity in proceedings concerning allegations of human rights

[443] Cf for the argument HH Koh, 'Transnational Public Law Litigation' (1991) 100 YLJ 2347, 2365; WF Pepper (1992) 348; R Wai, 'The Commercial Activity Exception to Sovereign Immunity and the Boundaries of Contemporary International Legalism' in C Scott (ed), *Torture as Tort, Comparative Perspectives on the Development of Transnational Human Rights Litigation* (2001) 213, 241.

[444] Cf eg BS Thornton, 'International Human Rights in American Courts: The Case of Nelson v. Saudi Arabia' (1992) 86 ASIL Proceedings 324, remarks by JJ Paust, 327.

[445] Cf eg A Bianchi (1997) 420.

[446] In their Separate Opinion in the *Arrest Warrant* case Judges Higgins, Kooijmans and Buergenthal wrote that the meaning of *acta jure imperii* and *acta jure gestionis* was 'not carved in stone... it is subject to a continuously changing interpretation which varies with time reflecting the changing priorities of society.' *Arrest Warrant* Case, Separate Opinion Judges Higgins, Kooijmans, and Buergenthal, 84–5, § 72. In the opinion of this author this consideration implies more relativity in the rationale of state immunity than there is. If states agree to a human rights exception to the rule of state immunity they accept an exception to state immunity for *acta jure imperii* rather than limiting the scope of this concept.

violations. These state of the law arguments assert that international human rights law and the related conceptual changes in the international legal order have curtailed states' rights under the law of state immunity. Arguments on the second level focus on the rights of private individuals and the corresponding obligations of the forum state. These policy arguments set out to establish a clash of the obligations of the forum state under the law of state immunity and the law of human rights. They assert the responsibility of the forum state for the violation of the rights of the individual who is denied a day in court and may provide an incentive to change the scope of the rights of states under the law of state and diplomatic immunity.

One important conclusion of the chapter is that both the form and substance of arguments in favour and against the exception suffer from the underdeveloped theory on the law of state immunity. The debate on the human rights exception to state immunity rules bears the deadweight of history. Proponents do not recognize the rationale of the rule of state immunity. They consider sovereignty to be a normative concept, related to the archaic protection of kings and princes and to nineteenth-century absolutist states. The research question is somewhat demagogically restated as a choice 'between serving the convenience of governments or pursuing justice for the victims of their crimes'.[447] In addition, arguments in favour attribute well-nigh mythical qualities to the concepts of *jus cogens* norms, *erga omnes* obligations, universal jurisdiction, and the rights of individuals under international law. Proponents fail to acknowledge that their arguments do not fit the international legal order as it *is* but rather argue that that order *should change*. Opponents, on the other hand, fail to discuss these arguments on the merits, reasoning in a formalistic vein instead. The absence of state practice supporting an exception is considered conclusive evidence of the state of the law. Reason is however an acceptable tool for the determination of the scope of the rule of state immunity and the *trump* argument must anyway be discussed on its merits since it is a conceptual process, unconcerned with state practice. In addition, the danger of confusion with a state of the law argument looms in the approach of opponents to the policy arguments in favour of a human rights exception. It is recalled that in the case of *Holland v Lampen-Wolfe* Lord Millett argued that the right of access to court could not be violated by the rule of state immunity since the foreign state had a right to that immunity.

This chapter has argued that international law immunity rules are not affected by the developments in international human rights law. There are no coherent state of the law arguments in favour of a human rights exception. There *is* however some tension between the rule of state immunity and diplomatic immunity and the fundamental rights of individuals. The tension between immunity rules and fundamental rights of individuals is a forceful policy argument for the reconsideration of certain applications of immunity. The right of access to court

[447] JF Murphy (1999) 56.

is applicable to national law and voluntary immunity rules, and it may be applicable to necessary immunity rules when foreign states are allowed to exercise state power on the territory of the forum state. In those cases, the immunity rule must have a legitimate aim and be proportional to that aim in order not to violate the right of access to court. The community interests protected by the rule must not be outbalanced by the interests of the individual to have access. If they *are*, the forum state is responsible to the individual for a violation of his right of access to court. As far as diplomatic immunity is concerned it is arguable that the scope of the rule should not be changed but that it is the forum state rather than the private individual that should bear the negative consequences of the application of the rule. There may, moreover, be tension between the right to a remedy and immunity for violations of human rights by foreign states and their officials on the territory of the forum state. Finally, the effective deterrence to the commission of human rights violations required by the right to effective protection may be at odds with the grant of state immunity and diplomatic immunity in respect of allegations of violations of human rights committed on the territory of the forum state.

The room for coherent argument in favour of a reconsideration of the grant of immunity to foreign states on the basis of international human rights law is narrow. It is unfortunate that in the current debate the handful of coherent—and forceful—arguments are veiled by the radical attack on the rule of state immunity. Simma and Alston wrote that 'the temptation to adapt or re-interpret the concept of customary international law in such a way as to ensure that it provides the "right" answers is strong, and to some, irresistible'.[448] The attempts by human rights lawyers to fit a square peg into a round hole has cast a shadow over *all* human rights based arguments against state immunity and risks an inflation of human rights law. Ironically the human rights movement may thus harm rather than promote the effective protection of the fundamental rights of individuals. The following words of Fitzmaurice still hold true today:

> The truth is that the intellectual distaste, which, as a jurist, we feel for the idea of Utopia, and many other of the kind, is that it solves too much. It disposes of difficulties not by dealing with them on their merits, but by creating conditions in which they must automatically disappear—in short be transcended... Our task as international jurists is not to imagine conditions in which the Gordian knot would be cut by the fading out of the independent nation-State, but to make the international system work in the world of the nation-State.[449]

[448] B Simma and P Alston, 'The Sources of Human Rights Law: Custom, Jus Cogens, and General Principles' (1992) 12 Australian Yearbook of International Law 82.

[449] G Fitzmaurice, 'The Future of Public International Law and of the International Legal System in the Circumstances of Today' in *Livre du centenaire de l'Institut de Droit International 1873–1973: Evolution et perspective du droit international* (1973) 196, 258.

7

Conclusion

International human rights law and international criminal law have changed the outlook of the international legal order. Over the past fifty years or so, states have developed a body of fundamental rights and obligations of individuals that deserve protection and surveillance on the international level. Many of the norms protected by international human rights law and international criminal law form part of what is sometimes called the 'international public order'. They are considered fundamental to the existence of the international legal order and are therefore non-derogable—or *jus cogens*. It is agreed that the law of state responsibility attaches certain aggravated consequences to serious breaches of peremptory norms. The community interest in the observance of these norms moreover has consequences for the rules on standing in the law on state responsibility. The obligations under these norms are owed towards the international community as a whole—obligations *erga omnes*—and all states have a legal interest in their protection. The importance of these norms also has consequences for individual perpetrators. When certain behaviour qualifies as a crime against international law individuals incur direct responsibility under international law. The international community may bring individual perpetrators to justice before international tribunals and national courts can adjudicate these crimes on the basis of universal jurisdiction.

Since human rights violations often occur under the veil of state authority national courts asked to adjudicate upon the human rights violations allegedly committed by foreign states and their officials have stumbled upon the traditional international law rules on jurisdictional immunity. Are the well-established immunity rules that shield states and their officials from the adjudicative jurisdiction of other states and that are rooted in the classic inter-state system of international law affected by the relatively recent developments in international human rights law and international criminal law? This was the question with which this study commenced. The conclusion of this study—again in an obviously constraining nutshell—is that the scope of immunity rules *should* be reconsidered in light of the developments over the past fifty years. The rule of functional immunity does not apply in the face of allegations of crimes against international law, and the rule of state immunity and the rules on personal immunity may clash with the fundamental rights of individuals under international law. However, an unqualified attack on all immunity rules harms rather than furthers the cause of human rights. The discussion on the influence of international human rights law and international criminal law on the immunities of foreign states and (former) foreign state officials cannot be conducted on the basis of black and white arguments. A coherent discourse on the topic should reflect the nuances of the nature and scope of the different immunity rules and should not confuse policy for state of the law arguments.

In order to adequately deal with the research question it has proven crucial to first clearly distinguish the three relevant immunity concepts: state immunity, functional immunity and personal immunity. The immunities attaching to states, to (former) state officials and to specific categories of state officials like diplomatic agents and heads of state all have a different rationale, a different nature and a different scope.

Chapter 2 of this study took issue with the common view that the restrictive state immunity is a continuation of the absolute immunity rule with certain exceptions accepted to it through a general and consistent state practice. It was argued that absolute state immunity has never been a rule of international law. More importantly, it was argued that there is not only a quantitative but also a qualitative difference between absolute and restrictive state immunity. The restrictive rule of state immunity reflects the inherent limit on the essential competence of states that agree to co-exist with other states in an international community based on the principles of independence and equality. Unlike absolute state immunity, restrictive state immunity is hence not an immunity from an otherwise existing jurisdiction in the traditional sense of the word. This finding also explains why the restrictive immunity rule is a rule of international law in spite of the substantial lack of uniformity in the way states interpret and apply that rule. It is not general and consistent state practice that forms the law; it is the principle of independence and equality of states.

This, it was argued, has consequences for the epistemology of the law. In a discussion on the scope of the rule of state immunity arguments based on reason and logic *are* legitimate. It also has consequences for the substance of arguments against the rule. The borderline between absolute and restrictive immunity reflects the distinction between voluntary and necessary immunity rules. For one, the connotation of archaic privileges attaches to the immunity on one side of the line, but not the other.

Chapter 3 examined that functional immunity of (former) foreign state officials. Such officials are not responsible in their personal capacity for acts they commit as arm or mouth of the state. Only the state can be held responsible for these official acts. As long as a state official performs an act in the context of state authority under international law foreign courts must presume that the act was committed on behalf of the home state—a presumption that may of course be defeated by the home state.

Two important points were made in this respect. In the first place, it was explained that there is an inherent limit on the presumption of authority in the case where foreign state officials have acted outside the territory of their home state, since the authority of the home state then depends on the scope of the consent of the forum state. Second, it was argued that the development of the concept of individual responsibility of state officials for crimes against international law should be understood in terms of an *a priori* and general defeat of the presumption of authority. States have agreed on the international level that certain acts can never be cloaked by state authority. They have developed universally applicable normative limits on the authority of state officials, just as normative limits are provided within most national legal systems.

The chapter emphasized that the 'act of state' concepts prevalent in the law of state responsibility and the law of state immunity should not be confused with the act of state concept that controls the rule of functional immunity. Acts that clearly exceed the mandate of a state official can be attributed to the state under the law of state responsibility—also when that mandate *can* be determined by the forum state because for example the act was committed on its territory and in excess of its consent. Also the act of state concept of the rule of state immunity must be distinguished. It is true that the rule of state immunity may apply to suits involving foreign state officials. However, this application *follows* the applicability of the rule of functional immunity. Only if a state official bears no personal responsibility can it be said that a suit against him is an official capacity suit and hence in fact a suit against the foreign state (this study did however put some caveats in this respect). The rule of functional immunity is hence the prerequisite for the application of the rule of state immunity. Whether or not the act is a sovereign act of state is irrelevant for this preliminary question. State officials may be functionally immune in respect of acts that do not qualify under the law of state immunity.

Chapter 4 examined the personal immunity of foreign diplomatic agents and foreign heads of state. In contrast with the rule of state immunity and the rule of functional immunity, these are immunities from jurisdiction proper. The rules apply independently from the essential competence of the forum or the individual responsibility of the defendant. The rules are moreover conspicuous examples of voluntary customary international law that relies on state practice and *opinio juris* for its formation. The *ne impediatur legatio* rationale only *explains* the course of state practice. The chapter primarily focused on some of the controversial issues as to the material and formal scope of these rules. In particular, it was argued that the immunity of heads of government and ministers of foreign affairs is less extensive than that of heads of state. These former immunities belong to the law of diplomatic immunity and only apply whenever these individuals travel abroad on official business.

The distinction of the three immunity concepts by reference to the notions of lack of essential competence, absence of personal responsibility, and immunity from jurisdiction allowed a reasoned distinction of the effects of international human rights law and international criminal law on their scope. The study has divided the research question in two separate inquiries. In the first place the present state of the law was examined. Has the scope of immunity of states and (former) state officials been affected by the said developments? Subsequently, it was examined whether the immunities—in as far as unaffected—clash with international law on the fundamental rights and obligations of individuals. If such a clash can be identified, a forceful policy argument in favour of changing the regime regarding the immunities of foreign states and their officials can be formulated. As long as immunity rules do not accommodate clashing human rights law states are faced with two competing obligations and violate international law whichever obligation they choose to prioritize. The discussion of these inquiries was divided in two parts. Chapter 5 analysed the interplay between international criminal law—the *obligations of individuals* under international law—and the immunity of foreign state officials, while chapter 6 analysed the interplay between international human rights law—the *rights of individuals* under international law—and the immunity of states and their officials.

Chapter 5 argued that the principles of individual responsibility for crimes against international law and irrelevance of official capacity directly affect the scope of the rule of functional immunity. The acceptance of individual responsibility for crimes against international law defeats the presumption that individuals have acted *as the state* whenever they act within the context of state authority under international law. Functional immunity ends where individual responsibility begins and crimes against international law hence do not qualify as official acts (or acts of state) under the rule of functional immunity. Since the principle defines the scope of the rule of functional immunity rather than that it provides an exception to that rule it is impossible to distinguish international courts from national courts for the purpose of its application.

It was, however, stipulated that despite the absence of functional immunity national courts may lack the competence to deal with certain allegations against foreign state officials. Judicial scrutiny of the acts of foreign states when that constitutes a preliminary to decision of a question of private rights and obligations, *which is in itself subject to the competency of the court*, can be distinguished from such scrutiny when that is *determinative of the competency of the court*. If the absence of functional immunity depends on the decision of highly controversial questions of international law regarding the activity or policy of foreign states the decision on these questions creates the competence of the court. This issue is not clear-cut and this study has not purported to comprehensively deal with all its aspects. It was merely proposed that there is a grey area in between the law of state immunity and the act of state and non-justiciability doctrines. In the absence of guidance by international law doctrine, courts that are reticent to engage these questions will frame their decision in terms of immunity law. This is unfortunate because it veils the fact that the incompetence only applies when the responsibility of the state official cannot be established in isolation of the larger question of state responsibility, and then only if that larger question is 'controversial'.

Personal immunity is subject to fundamentally different considerations. The principle of irrelevance of official capacity secures the responsibility of the individual that commits crimes against international law. It does not however secure the jurisdiction of the court. In other words, the principle regards the substantive but not the procedural immunity of state officials. Since state practice nor conventional law provides for a human rights exception to personal immunity rules, and the *jus cogens* character of the violated norms does not affect the procedural rule, it cannot but be concluded that no such exception exists under international law. It was further argued that there are no obligations under international criminal law that clash with obligations under personal immunity rules. Consequently, within the context of the inquiry undertaken in chapter 5 no forceful policy arguments against the rule could be identified.

The chapter furthermore repudiated the popular proposition that personal immunities do not prevent the exercise of jurisdiction by international courts. While states can of course agree to allow an international tribunal to exercise jurisdiction over its state officials normally protected by personal immunity, they cannot dispose of the immunity of foreign state officials. Only the UN Security Council acting on the basis of Chapter VII of the Charter can do so.

Finally, chapter 6 examined the research question from the perspective of international human rights law. It was concluded in chapter 2 that arguments based on reason and logic *are* valid in the discussion on the scope of the law of state immunity. Consequently, it was argued that the argument that no human rights exception to state immunity exists since there is no general and consistent state practice in that regard fails to convince. Human rights-based arguments require consideration on their merits. Upon a close analysis of the possible arguments this study however came to the conclusion that human rights law has not affected the scope or the validity of state immunity law.

This does not mean that there is no friction between human rights law and the law of state immunity or personal immunities. States may have conflicting obligations under the two bodies of law. This study examined whether the right to a fair trial, the right to a remedy and the right to effective protection are compatible with state immunity and personal immunity. It concluded that voluntary immunity rules, and even more so immunity rules of a national law character, may not always be compatible with the fundamental rights of individuals. In addition a state may violate its obligations towards its citizens if it consents to the exercise of state authority by a foreign state on its territory without safeguarding private individuals from the prejudice caused by the immunity that is attached to the exercise of such authority. The clash of obligations provides a forceful policy argument in favour of the reconsideration of certain applications of immunity rules.

In the course of this study many instances of national jurisprudence—cases like *Pinochet*, *Jones*, *Leivadia*, *Ferrini*, and *Siderman*—of international jurisprudence—cases like *Al-Adsani*, *McElhinney*, *Fogarty*, *Arrest Warrant*, and *Taylor*—of national legislation—like the US-state sponsored terrorism exception in the FSIA and the Belgian war crimes legislation—and of international documents—like the ICC Statute and the Resolution on head of state immunity of the Institut de Droit International—were examined and critically discussed. This conclusion will not repeat the detailed analyses and conclusions that were advanced in their regard. Only the three cases that were introduced in chapter 1 of this study as 'the central pieces of the décor in which our examination takes place' warrant a final word.

At the outset this author would like to put the achievements of the three eminent courts that have decided these cases beyond question. The decisions have sparked new initiatives of human rights defenders by revealing the possibilities and the limits of transnational justice, and the argumentation and the cutting insights of the judges have inspired the minds of countless scholars around the world. The critique developed in this study should at all times be understood to stem from this inspiration.

Both the *Pinochet* case and the *Arrest Warrant* case pivoted on the question of whether immunity *is* available in proceedings concerning allegations of crimes against international law. The principal question in the *Pinochet* case was whether the rule of functional immunity protects a former head of state from foreign criminal jurisdiction in respect of allegations of torture. This study concurred with the *outcome* of the *Pinochet* case but begged to disagree with the *terms on which the decision is premised*. In chapter 5 we saw that the six individual opinions of the majority differ substantially as to the reasons for the denial of immunity. In an inevitable generalization it can be said that the Lords approached the functional immunity of Pinochet as the state immunity *ratione materiae* of Chile and that the refusal of immunity was largely based on the specific terms of the 1984 Torture Convention. This study argued that Pinochet did not enjoy functional immunity since he could be sued in his personal capacity for the allegations of crimes against international law. Such crimes are not official acts for functional immunity purposes for which only the state incurs responsibility.

In the *Arrest Warrant* case the ICJ was asked to decide whether the issuance and international circulation of an arrest warrant for an incumbent minister of foreign affairs violates the personal immunity of that minister. This study agrees with the position of the Court that an exception to personal immunities rules needs support in state practice. Nevertheless, this study concluded differently on the proper *outcome* of the case. The principal reason was that it did not agree with the Court's approach to the formulation of the scope of the immunity rule applicable to ministers of foreign affairs. Ministers of foreign affairs are only protected from foreign criminal jurisdiction when they are abroad on official visits and the disputed arrest warrant made an explicit exception for that situation. It must be questioned moreover whether the international circulation of an arrest warrant constitutes an independent violation of the immunity rule if third states are not obliged to give effect to that warrant.

In the *Al-Adsani* case the European Court of Human Rights was asked to approach the relation between immunity and human rights from the essentially distinct perspective of policy arguments. A complaint under the Convention is in principle unconcerned with the question of whether immunity is available. Rather, it is argued that the grant of immunity violates the obligations of the forum state under the European Convention on Human Rights. In this case, the applicant had argued that the grant of state immunity had violated his right of access to court under article 6.1 of the Convention. It was only because of the Court's approach to this principal question that the question as to the influence of human rights law on the state of immunity law became relevant. The Court argued that immunity rules that have the character of international law do not violate article 6 because they always have a legitimate aim and are always proportional to that aim. Accordingly, the state of the law became the decisive point. This study has criticized the decision of the Court on both accounts—even though it agrees with the Court on the *outcome* of the case.

The applicant argued that the particular application of the rule of state immunity was not required by international law. The foreign state concerned had been accused of violations of *jus cogens* norms and the applicant argued that these norms trumped the rule of state immunity. Eight of the seventeen judges embraced the normative hierarchy argument and concluded that article 6.1 had indeed been violated. The majority disagreed. It argued that the thesis of the applicant was not supported by state practice. Since international law did indeed require national courts to grant foreign states state immunity in respect of allegations of *jus cogens* violations, the Court concluded that article 6.1 had not been violated.

This study does not accept the reasoning of the Court as to the state of the law. The hierarchy of norms argument relies on a conceptual process independent of developments in state practice. More in general, the discussion as to the state of immunity law allows arguments based on reason and logic without lapsing into natural law reasoning. A convincing rebuttal of arguments against state immunity based on international human rights law and related changes in the international legal order require discussion on their merits.

More fundamental, however, is the criticism as to the principal question put to the Court. This study argued that the rule of state immunity in respect of allegations of human rights violations committed within the territory of the defendant state does not raise an issue under the Convention. However, *if* an immunity rule *does* raise an issue under the Convention—as all voluntary immunity rules and national law immunity rules do—only a proper balancing of the various interests involved can determine the compatibility of the immunity rule with the right of access to court. The reasoning of the Court makes a mockery of the compliance criteria for restrictions on the right of access to court. Human rights have an autonomous meaning that fits the concept of inherent limitations—to which the approach of the Court can be said to boil down—very uncomfortably.

In the years to come the question as to the relation between international human rights law, international criminal law, and immunity rules will undoubtedly be debated within national and international court buildings. Today the questions dealt with in this study have engaged the minds of only a handful of national judges around the world. With the increasing interest in the application of international criminal law at the national level, and the rise in transboundary human rights litigation it is however to be expected that more and more judges will have to inquire into the effect of international human rights law or international criminal law on immunity rules. To ensure the coherence and the consistency of the application of international law by national authorities the guidance of international courts is most welcome.[1]

A couple of distinctions should be kept in mind when looking to international courts for guidance. In the first place, the three immunity concepts that were examined in this study require separate discussion. Second, it must be realized that courts may approach our research question from two essentially distinct perspectives—that of state of the law and policy arguments.

Let us first consider the scope of the rule of state immunity. In 1999 the Working Group of the International Law Commission on Jurisdictional Immunities of States and their Property noted that the state-sponsored terrorism exception in the US FSIA and the decision of the House of Lords in the *Pinochet* case were 'a recent development relating to immunity which should not be ignored'.[2] In 2001 the European Court of Human Rights concluded that there is no 'firm basis' in state practice 'for concluding that, as a matter of international law, a State no longer enjoys immunity from civil suit in the courts of another State where acts of torture are alleged'.[3] Greek and Italian courts have allowed the exercise of jurisdiction over claims against foreign states that concern their *acta jure imperii* when these acts violate *jus cogens* in 2000 and 2004 respectively.

The European Court of Human Rights is the only international court that has until now engaged this particular aspect of our research question. However, in proceedings before that Court the question as to the nature and scope of the rule of state immunity plays only an auxiliary role. A thorough inquiry into the

[1] In addition, completion of codification initiatives of international bodies like the International Law Commission—that decided in 2006 to include the topic of 'Immunity of State officials from foreign criminal jurisdiction' in its long-term programme of work, ILC Report on the work of the fifty-eighth session (2006), A/61/10, p 425, § 257 and Annex A, Immunity of State officials from foreign criminal jurisdiction, p 436–54—and the Institut de Droit International—that in 1995 created the Third Commission to work on the topic of 'The Fundamental Rights of the Person and the Immunity from Jurisdiction in International Law'—will undoubtedly also further these goals.

[2] International Law Commission, Report of the Working Group on Jurisdiction Immunities of States and their Property (1999), Appendix, Annex to the Report of the ILC on the work of its fifty-first session.

[3] *Al-Adsani v United Kingdom* (ECHR, 2001) 290, § 61; 123 ILR 24.

law of state immunity and an authoritative statement on the relation between human rights law and state immunity of the International Court of Justice is hence called for. The states that have recently disagreed on the interpretation of the rule of state immunity—Germany, Greece, and Italy—could have asked the ICJ to engage the question. Even though not all have accepted the jurisdiction of the ICJ under the optional protocol, they could have consented to the exercise of jurisdiction, just like France has done in *Certain Criminal Proceedings in France* (*Republic of the Congo v France*).[4]

At this point, this author wishes to underline that while this study has not argued in favour of a restriction of state immunity rules on the basis of the *jus cogens* nature of certain human rights norms, this is not to say that a serious effort of the international community to ensure that individuals have a remedy in respect of violations of such norms is not called for. Efforts to strengthen existing international mechanisms—like the UN Human Rights Committee—or to expand the use of institutions like the UN Compensation Commission, that processes claims of individuals who suffered damage as a consequence of Iraq's invasion and occupation of Kuwait, would be most welcome.

As far as the interpretation of the scope of the rules of functional and personal immunity are concerned, further guidance of the ICJ may in fact not be too far away. A case that pivots on the relation between the immunity of state officials and international criminal law, is at the time of writing of this study, pending before the Court. With *Certain Criminal Proceedings in France* (*Republic of the Congo v France*) the Court has an opportunity to clarify several questions that were raised by its not always unambiguous reasoning in the *Arrest Warrant* case. In particular, it will have to engage the question of functional immunity and international criminal law. This question allows it to shed some light on what it meant exactly with the public—private capacity distinction that has stirred academic debate so much. It is furthermore to be hoped that it will, in an obiter consideration, clarify the question of personal immunity rules before international courts.

Finally, it must be admitted that the guidance of the European Court of Human Rights, on the essentially distinct question of whether fundamental rights of individuals may clash with immunity rules in the 2001 *Al-Adsani* case, was unambiguous. The question is therefore not whether the Court will clarify its standpoint in the years to come, but rather whether it will be willing to reconsider it. This study has suggested that the position of the dissenting judges in the *Al-Adsani* case is not the only possible alternative. The recognition that the undertakings of states under international human rights law may warrant reconsideration of some—but not all—applications of immunity rules is in the view of this author urgently called for.

[4] When the 2004 UN Convention on Jurisdictional Immunities of States and their Property comes into force, disputes between state parties concerning the application of the Convention may eventually be brought before the ICJ (article 27.2).

Bibliography

Abi-Saab, G, 'The Concept of "International Crimes" and its Place in Contemporary International Law', in JHH Weiler, et al (eds), *International Crimes of States, A Critical Analysis of the ILC's Draft Article 19 on State Responsibility* (1989) 141

Abi-Saab, G, 'The Uses of Article 19' (1999) 10 EJIL 339

Adams, W, 'In Search of a Defence of the Transnational Human Rights Paradigm: May *Jus Cogens* Norms be Invoked to Create Implied Exceptions in Domestic State Immunity Statutes' in C Scott (ed), *Torture as Tort, Comparative Perspectives on the Development of Transnational Human Rights Litigation* (2001) 247

Ago, R, 'Le délit international' (1939–II) 68 RdC 415

Akande, D, 'International Law Immunities and the International Criminal Court' (2004) 98 AJIL 407

Akehurst, M, 'Reprisals by Third States' (1970) 44 BYIL 1

Akehurst, M, 'Jurisdiction in International Law' (1972–73) 46 BYIL 145

Alland, D, 'Countermeasures of General Interest' (2002) 13 EJIL 1221

Allen, EW, *The Position of Foreign States before Belgian Courts* (1929)

Allen, EW, *The Position of Foreign States before National Courts* (1933)

Amerasinghe, CF, *Local Remedies in International Law* (1990)

Anzilotti, D, *Teoria generale della responsabilità dello stato nel diritto internazionale* (1902)

Anzilotti, D, 'L'esenzione degli stati stranieri dalla giurisdizione' (1910) 5 RDI 477

Anzilotti, D, 'Case Comment' (1912) 6 RDI 501

Anzilotti, D, 'Case Comment' (1915) 9 RDI 217

Anzilotti, D, *Cours de droit international* (1929)

Apollis, G, 'L'affaire du "Rainbow Warrior"' (1987) 91 RGDIP 10

Badr, GM, *State Immunity: An Analytical and Prognostic View* (1984)

Balladore Pallieri, G, *Diritto internazionale pubblico* (8th edn, 1962)

Bank, R, 'Der Fall Pinochet: Aufbruch zu neuen Ufern bei der Verfolgung von Menschenrechtsverletzungen?' (1999) 59 ZaöRV 677

Bantekas, I, 'Case Comment', (1998) 92 AJIL 765

Barboza, J, 'State Crimes: A Decaffeinated Coffee' in L Boisson de Chazournes and V Gowlland-Debbas (eds), *The International Legal System in Quest of Equity and Universality* (2001) 357

Barker, JC, 'State Immunity, Diplomatic Immunity and Act of State: A Triple Protection against Legal Action?' (1998) 47 ICLQ 950

Barker, JC, 'The Future of Former Head of State Immunity After Ex Parte Pinochet' (1999) 48 ICLQ 937

Barkhuysen, T, *Article 13 EVRM: Effectieve Nationale Rechtsbescherming by Schendingen van Mensenrechten* (1998)

Bartoš, M, 'Le statut des missions speciales de la diplomatie ad hoc' (1963–I) 108 RdC 425

Bartsch, K and Elberling, B, 'Jus Cogens vs State Immunity, Round Two, The Decision of the European Court of Human Rights in the *Kalaogeropoulou et al v Greece and Germany* (2002)' (2003) 4 German Law Journal, available at <http://www.germanlawjournal.com>

Bass, PE, 'Ex-Head of State Immunity: A Proposed Tool of Foreign Policy' (1987) 97 YLJ 299

Bassiouni, MC, 'International Crimes: Jus Cogens and Obligatio Erga Omnes' (1996) 25 Law & Contemporary Problems 63

Baxter, RR, 'So-Called "Unprivileged Belligerency": Spies, Guerrillas and Saboteurs' (1951) 28 BYIL 323

Belsky, AC et al, 'Implied Waiver under the FSIA: A Proposed Exception to Immunity for Violations of Peremptory Norms of International Law' (1989) 77 California Law Review 365

Benzing, M, 'U.S. Bilateral Non-Surrender Agreements and Article 98 of the Statute of the International Criminal Court; an Exercise in the Law of Treaties' (2004) 8 Max Planck Yearbook of United Nations Law 181

Best, G, *Humanity in Warfare: The Modern History of the International Law of Armed Conflicts* (1980)

Bevans, CI (ed), *Treaties and other International agreements of the United States of America, 1776–1949* (1968–76)

Bhuta, N, 'Justice Without Borders? Prosecuting General Pinochet' (1999) 23 Melbourne University Law Review 499

Bianchi, A, 'Overcoming the Hurdle of State Immunity in the Domestic Enforcement of International Human Rights' in B Conforti and F Francioni (eds), *Enforcing International Human Rights in Domestic Courts* (1997) 405 (original publication Bianchi, A, 'Denying State Immunity to Violators of Human Rights' (1994) 46 Austrian Journal of Public and International Law 195)

Bianchi, A, 'Immunity versus Human Rights: The *Pinochet* Case' (1999) 10 EJIL 237

Bianchi, A, 'Individual Accountability for Crimes against Humanity: Reckoning with the Past, Thinking of the Future' (1999) 19 SAIS Review 97

Bianchi, A, 'Ferrini v. Federal Republic of Germany' (2005) 99 AJIL 242

Binschedler-Robert, D, 'A Reconsideration of the Law of Armed Conflicts' in *The Law of Armed Conflicts: Report of the Conference on Contemporary Problems of the Law of Armed Conflict, 1969* (1971) 1

Bishop, WW, 'New United States Policy Limiting Sovereign Immunity' (1953) 47 AJIL 93

Blum, JM and Steinhardt, RG, 'Federal Jurisdiction over International Human Rights Claims: The Alien Tort Claims Act after *Filártiga v Peña-Irala*' in RG Steinhardt and A D'Amato (eds), *The Alien Tort Claims Act: An Analytical Anthology* (1999) 49

Bodin, J, *Les Six Livres de la République* (1576)

Borchard, EM, 'Governmental Liability in Tort' (1924–25) 34 YLJ 1

Bothe, M, 'Die strafrechtliche Immunität fremder Staatsorgane' (1971) 31 ZaöRV 246

Bowett, DW, 'Crimes of State and the 1996 Report of the International Law Commission on State Responsibility' (1998) 9 EJIL 163

Bradley, CA, and Goldsmith, JL, 'Pinochet and International Human Rights Litigation' (1999) 97 Michigan Law Review 2129

Brierly, JL, 'The Shortcomings of International Law' (1924) 5 BYIL 4

Brierly, JL, 'Matters of Domestic Jurisdiction' (1925) 6 BYIL 8

Brierly, JL, 'Règles générales du droit de la paix' 58 (1936–IV) RdC 1

Brierly, JL, 'The Nature of War Crimes Jurisdiction' in H Lauterpacht and CHM Waldock (eds), *The Basis of Obligation in International Law and Other Papers by the Late JL Brierly* (1958) 297 (original text in (1944) 2 The Norseman)

Brierly, JL, 'The Sovereign State Today' in H Lauterpacht and CHM Waldock (eds), *The Basis of Obligation in International Law, and Other Papers by the late JL Brierly* (1958) 348

Brierly, JL, 'International Law: Some Conditions of Its Progress' in H Lauterpacht and CHM Waldock (eds), *The Basis of Obligation in International Law, and Other Papers by the late JL Brierly* (1958) 327

Brierly, JL, *The Law of Nations, An Introduction to the International Law of Peace* (H Waldock (ed) 6th edn, 1963)

Brinton, JY, 'Suits against Foreign States' (1931) 25 AJIL 50

Bröhmer, J, *State Immunity and Human Rights Violations* (1997)

Bröhmer, J, 'Diplomatic Immunity, Head of State Immunity, State Immunity: Misconceptions of a Notorious Human Rights Violator' (1999) 12 LJIL 361

Brownlie, I, *The Rule of Law in International Affairs, International Law at the Fiftieth Anniversary of the United Nations* (1998)

Brownlie, I, *Principles of Public International Law* (6th edn, 2003)

Buffard, I, and Kriebaum, U, 'Der Fall Pinochet: Für und wider die Immunität (I Buffard, Argumente für die Immunität)' in W Karl and U Brandl (eds), *Völker- und Europarecht* (2000) 25

Burley, A-M, 'The Alien Tort Statute and the Judiciary Act of 1789: A Badge of Honor' in RG Steinhardt and A D'Amato (eds), *The Alien Tort Claims Act: An Analytical Anthology* (1999) 257

Burns, P, and McBurney, S, 'Impunity and the United Nations Convention against Torture: A Shadow Play without an Ending' in C Scott (ed), *Torture as Tort, Comparative Perspectives on the Development of Transnational Human Rights Litigation* (2001) 275

Byers, M, 'Al-Adsani *v* Government of Kuwait and Others' (1996) 67 BYIL 537

Byers, M, 'Conceptualising the Relationship between Jus Cogens and Erga Omnes Rules' (1997) 66 Nordic Journal of International Law 211

Byers, M, *Custom, Power and the Power of Rules, International Relations and Customary International Law* (1999)

Byrnes, A, 'Civil Remedies for Torture Committed Abroad: An Obligation under the Convention against Torture?' in C Scott (ed), *Torture as Tort, Comparative Perspectives on the Development of Transnational Human Rights Litigation* (2001) 537

Caflisch, L, 'La Pratique Suisse en matière de droit international public 1998, no 7.2' (1999) 9 RSDIE 682

Caflisch, L, 'Immunité de Juridiction et Respect des Droits de l'Homme' in L Boisson de Chazournes and V Gowlland-Debbas (eds), *The International Legal System in Quest of Equity and Universality* (2001) 651

Cahier, P, *Le droit diplomatique contemporain* (1962)
Calvo, C, *Le droit international théorique et pratique* (3rd edn, 1881)
Calvo, C, *Le droit international théorique et pratique* (5th edn, 1896)
Caplan, LM, 'State Immunity, Human Rights and Jus Cogens: A Critique of the Normative Hierarchy Theory' (2003) 97 AJIL 741
Carnegie, AR, 'Jurisdiction over Violations of the Laws and Customs of War' (1963) 39 BYIL 402
Cassese, A, *International Law in a Divided World* (1986)
Cassese, A, 'On the Current Trend towards Criminal Prosecution and Punishment of Breaches of International Humanitarian Law' (1998) 9 EJIL 1
Cassese, A, 'The Martens Clause: Half a Loaf or Simply Pie in the Sky?' (2000) 11 EJIL 187
Cassese, A, 'When May Senior State Officials Be Tried for International Crimes? Some Comments on the *Congo v Belgium* Case' (2002) 13 EJIL 853
Cassese, A, *International Criminal Law* (2003)
Cassese, A, 'The Belgian Court of Cassation v. the International Court of Justice: the *Sharon and others* Case' (2003) 1 JICJ 437
Casto, WR, 'The Federal Court's Protective Jurisdiction over Torts Committed in Violation of the Law of Nations' in RG Steinhardt and A D'Amato (eds), *The Alien Tort Claims Act: An Analytical Anthology* (1999) 119
Cavaglieri, A, 'Règles générales du droit de la paix' (1929–I) 26 RdC 311
Cavaglieri, A, *Corso di diritto internazionale* (2nd edn, 1932)
Charney, JI, 'Universal International Law' (1993) 87 AJIL 529
Charpentier, J, 'L'affaire du Rainbow Warrior' (1985) 31 AFDI 210
Chinkin, CM, 'Regina v. Bow Street Stipendiary Magistrate, Ex parte Pinochet Ugarte (No. 3)' (1999) 93 AJIL 703
Chrétien, A, *Principes de droit international public* (1893)
Christenson, GA, 'The World Court and *Jus Cogens*' (1987) 81 AJIL 93
Ciampi, A, 'The Obligation to Cooperate' in A Cassese, P Gaeta and JRWD Jones (eds), *The Rome Statute of the International Criminal Court* (2002) 1607
Clapham, A, *Human Rights in the Private Sphere* (1993)
Cohn, EJ, 'Waiver of Immunity' (1958) 34 BYIL 260
Collums, HD, 'The *Letelier* Case: Foreign Sovereign Liability for Acts of Political Assassination' (1981) 21 VJIL 251
Condorelli, L, 'Case Comment' (1976) 2 Italian Yearbook of International Law 339
Condorelli, L, 'Le immunità diplomatiche e I principi fondamentali della Costituzione'(1979) 24–I Giurisprudenza Costituzionale 455
Condorelli, L, 'L'imputation à l'État d'un fait internationalement illicite: solutions classiques et nouvelles tendances' (1984–VI) 189 RdC 9
Conforti, B, *Diritto internazionale* (3rd edn, 1987)
Conforti, B, *Diritto internazionale* (6th edn, 2002)
Cosnard, M, *La soumission des États aux tribunaux internes: Face à la théorie des immunités des États* (1996)
Cosnard, M, 'Quelques observations sur les décisions de la Chambre des Lords du 25 Novembre 1998 et du 24 Mars 1999 dans l'affaire Pinochet' (1999) 103 RGDIP 309
Crawford, J, *The Creation of States in International Law* (1979)

Crawford, J, 'Execution of Judgments and Foreign Sovereign Immunity' (1981) 75 AJIL 820

Crawford, J, 'Decisions of British Courts During 1982 involving Questions of Public or Private International Law' (1982) 53 BYIL 259

Crawford, J, 'International Law and Foreign Sovereigns: Distinguishing Immune Transactions' (1983) 54 BYIL 75

Crawford, J, 'Revising the Draft Articles on State Responsibility' (1999) 10 EJIL 435

Crawford, J, *The International Law Commission's Articles on State Responsibility, Introduction, Text and Commentaries* (2002)

Dahm, G, 'Völkerrechtliche Grenzen der Inländischen Gerichtsbarkeit gegenüber ausländischen Staaten' in *Festschrift für Arthur Nikisch* (1958) 153

D'Amato, A, 'Trashing Customary International Law' (1987) 81 AJIL 101

D'Amato, A, 'The Alien Tort Statute and the Founding of the Constitution' in RG Steinhardt and A D'Amato (eds), *The Alien Tort Claims Act: An Analytical Anthology* (1999) 169

Damian, H, *Staatenimmunität und Gerichtszwang, Grundlagen und Grenzen der völkerrechtlichen Freiheit fremder Staaten von inländischer Gerichtsbarkeit in Verfahren der Zwangvollstreckung oder Anspruchsicherung* (1985)

Decaux, E, 'Le statut du chef d'État déchu' (1980) 26 AFDI 101

De Cuvelier, A, 'De l'incompétence des tribunaux nationaux a l'égard des gouvernements étrangers' (1888) 20 RDILC 109

Deen-Racsmány, Z, 'Prosecutor *v* Taylor, The Status of the Special Court of Sierra Leone and its Implications for Immunity' (2005) 18 LJIL 299

Dellapenna, JW, *Suing Foreign Governments and their Corporations* (1988)

De Hoogh, A, *Obligations Erga Omnes and International Crimes, A Theoretical Inquiry into the Implementation and Enforcement of the International Responsibility of States* (1996)

De Louter, J, *Het stellig volkenrecht* (1910)

Denza, E, *Diplomatic Law, A Commentary on the Vienna Convention on Diplomatic Relations* (2nd edn, 1998)

Denza, E, 'Ex Parte Pinochet: Lacuna or Leap?' (1999) 48 ICLQ 949

De Paepe, P, 'De la compétence civile à l'égard des Etats étrangers et de leurs agents politiques, diplomatiques, ou consulaires' (1895) 22 JDIP 31

De Sena, P, *Diritto internazionale e immunità funzionale degli organi statali* (1996)

De Sena, P, 'Immunity of State Organs and Defence of Superior Orders as an Obstacle to the Domestic Enforcement of International Human Rights' in B Conforti and F Francioni (eds), *Enforcing Human Rights in Domestic Courts* (1997) 367

De Sena, P, 'Immunità di ex-capi di Stato e violazioni individuali del divieto di tortura: sulla sentenza del 24 Marzo 1999 della Camera dei Lords nel caso *Pinochet*' (1999) 82 RDI 933

De Sena, P and De Vittor, F, 'State Immunity and Human Rights: The Italian Supreme Court Decision on the *Ferrini* Case' (2005) 16 EJIL

De Vattel, E, *Le droit de gens ou principes de la loi naturelle, appliqués à la conduite & aux affaires des nations & des souverains* (1758), translated by CG Fenwick (*The Law of Nations* 1983)

De Visscher, C, 'Les Gouvernements étrangers en justice, Reconnaissance internationale et immunités' (1922) 49 RDILC 300

De Visscher, P and Verhoeven, J, 'L'immunité de juridiction de l'État étranger dans la jurisprudence belge et le projet de convention du Conseil de l'Europe' in *L'immunité de juridiction et d'exécution des Etats* (1969) 37

De Vittor, F, 'Immunità degli Stati dalla giurisdizione e tutela dei diritti umani fondamentali' (2002) 85 RDI 573

Diaz, I, 'A Critique of Proposals to Amend the Foreign Sovereign Immunities Act to Allow Suits Against Foreign Sovereigns for Human Rights Violations' (2001) 32 University of Miami Inter-American Law Review 137

Dickinson, A, Lindsay, R and Loonan, JP (eds), *State Immunity, Selected Materials and Commentary* (2004)

Dinstein, Y, *Consular Immunity from Judicial Process, With Particular Reference to Israel* (1966a)

Dinstein, Y, 'Diplomatic Immunity from Jurisdiction *Ratione Materiae*' (1966b) 15 ICLQ 76

Dinstein, Y, 'Unlawful Combatants and War Criminals' in Y Dinstein and M Tabory (eds), *International Law at a Time of Perplexity, Essays in Honour of Shabtai Rosenne* (1989) 103

Doehring, K, 'Local Remedies, Exhaustion of' (1997) 3 Encyclopedia of International Law 238

Doehring K, and Ress, G, 'Diplomatische Immunität and Drittstaaten, Überlegungen zur erga omnes Wirkung der diplomatische Immunität und deren Beachtung im Fall der Staatensukzession' (1999) 37 Archiv des Völkerrechts 68

Dominicé, C, 'Quelques observations sur l'immunité de juridiction pénale de l'ancien chef d'Etat' (1999) 103 RGDIP 297

Donnarumma, MR, *La diplomazia ad hoc* (1968)

Donnarumma, MR, 'La Convention sur les missions speciales' (1972) 8 RBDI 34

Donovan, DF and Roberts, A, 'The Emerging Recognition of Universal Civil Jurisdiction' (2006) 100 AJIL 142

Dörr, O, 'Statliche Immunität auf dem Rückzug?' (2003) 41 Archiv des Völkerrechts 201

Drachsler, LM, 'Some Observations on the Current Status of the Tate Letter' (1960) 54 AJIL 790

Dugard, J, 'The Court's Judgment and the 1966 South West Africa Cases, Second Phase' (1966) 83 SALJ 429

Dugard, J (ed), *The South West Africa / Namibia Dispute, Documents and Scholarly Writings on the Controversy between South Africa and the United Nations* (1973)

Dugard, J, *International Law, A South African Perspective* (2000)

Dupuy, PM, 'The Institutionalization of International Crimes of State' in JHH Weiler et al (eds), *International Crimes of State, A Critical Analysis of the ILC's Draft Article 19 on State Responsibility* (1989) 170

Dupuy, PM, *Droit international public* (5th edn, 2000)

Dupuy, PM, 'A General Stocktaking of the Connections between the Multilateral Dimension of Obligations and Codification of the Law of State Responsibility' (2002) 13 EJIL 1053

Dworkin, R, *Taking Rights Seriously* (1977)

Fairman, C, 'Some Disputed Applications of the Principle of State Immunity' (1928) 22 AJIL 566

Fassbender, B, 'Case Comment' (1998) 92 AJIL 74
Feldman, MB, 'The United States Foreign Sovereign Immunities Act in Perspective: A Founders View' (1986) 35 ICLQ 302
Feldman, M, 'Foreign Governments in United States Courts' (1991) 85 ASIL Proceedings 251
Fenwick, CG, 'The Progress of International Law During the Past Forty Years' (1951–II) 79 RdC 1
Finch, GA, 'Jurisdiction of Local Courts to Try Enemy Persons for War Crimes' (1920) 14 AJIL 218
Finch, GA, 'The Nuremberg Trial and International Law' (1947) 41 AJIL 20
Fiore, P, *Nouveau droit international public suivant les besoins de la civilisation moderne* (1869, trans by P Pradier-Fodéré)
Fiore, P, *Nouveau droit international public, suivant les besoins de la civilisation moderne* (2nd edn, 1885)
Fitzmaurice, G, 'State Immunity from Proceedings in Foreign Courts' (1933) 14 BYIL 101
Fitzmaurice, G, 'The Future of Public International Law and of the International Legal System in the Circumstances of Today' in *Livre du centenaire de l'Institut de Droit International 1873–1973: Evolution et perspective du droit international* (1973) 196
Fitzpatrick, J, 'The Future of the Alien Tort Claims Act of 1978: Lessons from in Re Marcos Human Rights Litigation' (1993) 67 St John's Law Review 491
Fitzpatrick, J, 'The Claim to Foreign Sovereign Immunity by Individuals Sued for International Human Rights' (1994) 15 Whittier Law Review 465
Flauss, J-F, 'Droit des immunités et protection internationale des droits de l'homme' (2000) 10 RSDIE 299
Fox, H, 'Employment Contracts as an Exception to State Immunity: Is All Public Service Immune?' (1995) 66 BYIL 97
Fox, H, 'The Pinochet Case No. 3' (1999) 48 ICLQ 687
Fox, H, 'Access to Justice and State Immunity' (2001) 117 LQR 10
Fox, H, *The Law of State Immunity* (2002)
Fox, WTR, 'Competence of Courts in Regard to "Non-Sovereign" Acts of Foreign States' (1941) 35 AJIL 632
Frey, LS, and Frey, ML, *The History of Diplomatic Immunity* (1999)
Freyria, C, 'Les limites de l'immunité de juridiction et d'exécution des Etats étrangers' (1951) 40 RCDIP 207, 449
Friedmann, W, *The Changing Structure of International Law* (1964)
Frowein, JA, 'Reactions by Not Directly Affected States to Breaches of Public International Law' (1994–IV) 248 RdC 345
Frulli, M, 'The ICJ Judgment on the Belgium *v* Congo Case (14 February 2002): a Cautious Stand on Immunity from Prosecution for International Crimes' (2002) 3 German Law Journal, available at <http://www.germanlawjournal.com>
Frulli, M, 'The Question of Charles Taylor's Immunity, Still in Search of a Balanced Application of Personal Immunities?' (2004) 2 JICJ 1118
Gabba, CF, 'De la compétence des tribunaux à l'égard des souverains et des Etats étrangers', (1890) 17 JDIP 27
Gaeta, P, 'Official Capacity and Immunities', in A Cassese, P Gaeta, JRWD Jones (eds), *The Rome Statute of the International Criminal Court: A Commentary* (2002) 975

Gaeta, P, '*Ratione Materiae* Immunities of Former Heads of State and International Crimes; The *Hissène Habré* Case', (2003) 1 JICJ 186
Garner, JW, 'Punishment of Offenders against the Laws and Customs of War', (1920) 14 AJIL 70
Garnett, R, 'State Immunity in Employment Matters', (1997) 46 ICLQ 81
Garnett, R, 'The Defence of State Immunity for Acts of Torture', (1997) 18 Australian Yearbook of International Law 97
Gattini, A, 'War Crimes and State Immunity in the *Ferrini* Decision', (2005) 2 JICJ 224
Gavouneli, M and Bantekas, I, 'Prefecture of Voiotia v. Federal Republic of Germany', (2001) 95 AJIL 198
Gentili, A, *De Legationibus Libri Tres* (1594), trans by GJ Laing (Three Books on Embassies, 1924)
Geny, F, *Méthode d'interprétation et sources en droit privé positif* (2nd edn, 1919)
Gergen, JA, 'Human Rights and the Foreign Sovereign Immunities Act', (1996) 36 VJIL 765
Giegerich, T, 'Do Damages Claims Arising from *Jus Cogens* Violations Override State Immunity from the Jurisdiction of Foreign Courts?' in C Tomuschat and J-M Thouvenin (eds), *The Fundamental Rules of the International Legal Order, Jus Cogens and Obliogations Erga Omnes* (2006) 203
Gilbert, G, The Criminal Responsibility of States, (1990) 39 ICLQ 345
Glueck, S, *War Criminals, Their Prosecution & Punishment* (1944)
Gore-Booth (ed), *Satow's Guide to Diplomatic Practice* (5th edn, 1979)
Grotius, H, *De Jure Belli ac Pacis* (1625), trans by LR Loomis (1949)
Günther, K G, *Europäisches Völkerrecht in Friedenszeiten* (1787)
Hackworth, GH, *Digest of International Law* (1941) ii
Hafner G et al, 'A Response to the American View as Presented by Ruth Wedgwood' (1999) 10 EJIL 108
Haggenmacher, P, 'La doctrine des deux éléments du droit coutumier dans la pratique de la cour international' (1986) 90 RGDIP 5
Hall, WE, *A Treatise on International Law* (7th edn, 1917)
Halleck, H, *International Law* (3rd edn, 1893)
Hampson, FJ, 'Restrictions on Rights of Action and the European Convention on Human Rights: The Case of *Powell and Rayner*' (1990) 61 BYIL 279
Hannikainen, L, *Peremptory Norms (Jus Cogens) in International Law* (1988)
Henkin, L, 'The Mythology of Sovereignty' in RSJ MacDonald (ed), *Essays in Honour of Wang Tieya* (1994) 351
Hereshoff Bartlett, CA, 'Liability for Official War Crimes' (1919) 35 LQR 177
Higgins, R, 'The International Court and South West Africa: The Implications of the Judgment' (1966) 42 International Affairs 575
Higgins, R, 'Certain Unresolved Aspects of the Law of State Immunity' (1982) 29 NILR 265
Higgins, R, *Problems & Process, International Law and How We Use It* (1994)
Higgins, R, 'The Role of Domestic Courts in the Enforcement of International Human Rights: The United Kingdom' in B Conforti and F Francioni (eds), *Enforcing Human Rights in Domestic Courts* (1997) 37
Highet K et al, 'Lafontant v. Aristide' (1994) 88 AJIL 528

Hill, DJ, *A History of Diplomacy in the International Development of Europe* (1911) i

Hill, TH, 'A Policy Analysis of the American Law of Foreign State Immunity' (1981) 50 Fordham Law Review 155

Hobbes, T, *Leviathan* (1651)

Holland, DC, 'Diplomatic Immunity in English Law' (1951) 4 Current Legal Problems 81

Holmes, OW, 'The Path of the Law' (1897) 10 HLR 456

Hoye, WP, 'Fighting Fire with... Mire? Civil Remedies and the New War on State-Sponsored Terrorism' (2002) 12 Duke Journal of Comparative and International Law 105

Hurst, C, 'Diplomatic Immunities' in *International Law, The Collected Papers of Sir Cecil Hurst* (1950) 169 (Trans of C Hurst, 'Les Immunités Diplomatiques' (1926–II) 12 RdC 115)

Hurst, CJB, 'Diplomatic Immunities—Modern Developments' (1929) 10 BYIL 1

Hyde, CC, *International Law, chiefly as interpreted and applied by the United States* (1945) ii

Iwasawa, Y, 'Japan's Interactions with International Law: The Case of State Immunity' in N Ando (ed), *Japan and International Law: Past, Present and Future* (1999) 123

Jacobson, J, 'Trying to Fit a Square Peg into a Round Hole: The Foreign Sovereign Immunities Act and Human Rights Violations' (1998) 19 Whittier Law Review 757

Jenks, CW, *The Common Law of Mankind* (1958)

Jennings, RY, 'The *Caroline* and *McLeod* Cases' (1938) 32 AJIL 82

Jennings, RY, 'What is International Law and how do we tell it when we see it?' in BS Markesinis and JHM Willems (eds), *The Cambridge-Tilburg Law Lectures, Third Series 1980* (1980) 1

Jennings, R, 'The Identification of International Law' in B Cheng (ed), *International Law: Teaching and Practice* (1982) 3

Jennings, R, *The Place of the Jurisdictional Immunity of States in International and Municipal Law; Vortrag vor dem Europa-Institut der Universität des Saarlandes, Saarbrücken, 6 November 1987* (1988)

Jennings, R, 'The Pinochet Extradition Case in the English Courts' in L Boisson de Chazournes and V Gowlland-Debbas (eds), *The International Legal System in Quest of Equity and Universality: Liber Amicorum Georges Abi-Saab* (2001) 677

Jennings, R and Watts, A (eds), *Oppenheim's International Law* (9th edn, 1992)

Jescheck, H-H, *Die Verantwortlichkeit der Staatsorgane nach Völkerstrafrecht, eine Studie zu den Nürnberger Prozessen* (1952)

Jessup, PC, 'Has the Supreme Court Abdicated One of its Functions?' (1946) 40 AJIL 168

Jessup, PC, *A Modern Law of Nations* (1948)

Jones, TH, 'Judicial Bias and Disqualification in the Pinochet Case' (1999) Public Law 391

Jørgensen, NHB, *The Responsibility of States for International Crimes* (2000)

Joyner, CC, 'Arresting Impunity: The Case for Universal Jurisdiction in Bringing War Criminals to Accountability' (1996) 59 Law & Contemporary Problems 153

Kalshoven, F, 'The Position of Guerrilla Fighters under the Law of War' (1972) 11 Revue de Droit Pénal Militaire et de Droit de la Guerre 73

Kamto, M, 'Une troublante "immunité totale"' du ministre des affaires étrangères' (2002) 35 RBDI 518

Karagiannakis, M, 'State Immunity and Fundamental Human Rights' (1998) 11 LJIL 9
Kelsen, H, 'Théorie du Droit International Coutumier' (1939) 1 Revue Internationale de la Théorie du Droit 253
Kelsen, H, 'Collective and Individual Responsibility in International Law with Particular Regard to the Punishment of War Criminals' (1943) 31 California Law Review 530
Kelsen, H, *Peace Through Law* (1944)
Kelsen, H, *General Theory of Law and State* (1945)
Kelsen, H, 'Will the Judgment in the Nuremberg Trial Constitute a Precedent in International Law?' (1947) 1 ILQ 153
Kelsen, H, 'Collective and Individual Responsibility for Acts of State in International Law' (1948) Jewish Yearbook of International Law 226
Kelsen, H, *Principles of International Law* (1952)
Kelsen, H, *Principles of International Law* (RW Tucker (ed) 2nd edn, 1966)
Kerley, E, 'Some Aspects of the Vienna Conference on Diplomatic Intercourse and Immunities' (1962) 56 AJIL 88
Kingsbury, B, 'Sovereignty and Inequality' (1998) 9 EJIL 599
Kirgis, FL, 'Custom on a Sliding Scale' (1987) 81 AJIL 146
Kirgis, FL, 'Alien Tort Claims, Sovereign Immunity and International Law in US Courts' (1988) 82 AJIL 323
Kiss, A-C, *Répertoire de la pratique française en matière de droit international public* (1965)
Kissinger, HA, 'The Pitfalls of Universal Jurisdiction' (July/August 2001) Foreign Affairs 86
Klabbers, J, 'The General, The Lords and the Possible End of State Immunity' (1999) 68 Nordic Journal of International Law 85
Klein, E (ed), *The Duty to Protect and to Ensure Human Rights* (1999)
Klein, P, 'Responsibility for Serious Breaches of Obligations Deriving from Peremptory Norms of International Law and United Nations Law' (2002) 13 EJIL 1241
Knubben, R, *Die Subjekte des Völkerrechts* (1928)
Kobrick, ES, 'The Ex Post Facto Prohibition and the Exercise of Universal Jurisdiction over International Crimes' (1987) 87 CLR 1515
Koh, HH, 'Transnational Public Law Litigation' (1991) 100 YLJ 2347
Kokott, J, 'Mißbrauch und verwirkung von Souveränitätsrechten bei gravierenden Völkerrechtsverstoßen' in U Beyerlin et al (eds), *Recht zwischen Umbruch und Bewahrung, Festschrift für Rudolf Bernhardt* (1995) 135
Kokott, J, 'Zum Spannungsverhältnis zwischen nationality rule und Menschenrechtsschutz bei der Ausübung diplomatischer Protektion', in G Ress and T Stein (eds), *Der diplomatische Schutz im Völker- und Europarecht* (1996) 45
Kooijmans, PH, *The Doctrine of the Legal Equality of States: An Inquiry into the Foundations of International Law* (1964)
Kooijmans, PH, 'The Security Council and Non-State Entities as Parties to Conflicts' in K Wellens (ed), *International Law: Theory and Practice, Essays in Honour of Eric Suy* (1998) 333
Koskenniemi, M, *From Apology to Utopia, The Structure of International Legal Argument* (1989)
Koskenniemi, M, 'The Pull of the Mainstream' (1990) 88 Michigan Law Review 1946

Kunz, JL, 'Privileges and Immunities of International Organizations' (1947) 41 AJIL 828
Kunz, JL, 'The Nature of Customary International Law' (1953) 47 AJIL 662
Kunz, JL, 'The Nottebohm Judgment (Second Phase)' (1960) 54 AJIL 536
Labuschagne, JMT, 'Diplomatic Immunity as Criminal Defence: An Anthropo-legal Anachronism?' (1997) 22 South African Yearbook of International Law 32
Labuschagne, JMT, 'Immunity of the Head of State for Human Rights Violations in International Criminal Law' (2001) 26 South African Yearbook of International Law 180
Lalive, J-F, 'L'immunité de juridiction des États et des organisations internationales' (1953–III) 84 RdC 205
Lauterpacht, H, *Private Law Sources and Analogies of International Law* (1927)
Lauterpacht, H, *An International Bill of the Rights of Man* (1945)
Lauterpacht, H, *Recognition in International Law* (1947a)
Lauterpacht, H, 'The Subjects of the Law of Nations' (1947b) 63 LQR 438
Lauterpacht, H, *International Law and Human Rights* (1950)
Lauterpacht, H, 'Sovereignty over Submarine Areas' (1950) 27 BYIL 376
Lauterpacht, H, 'The Problem of Jurisdictional Immunities of Foreign States' (1951) 28 BYIL 220
Lauterpacht, H, *International Law: Collected Papers* (1970)
Lawson, RA, *Het EVRM en de Europese Gemeenschappen, Bouwstenen voor een aansprakelijkheidsregime voor het optreden van internationale organisaties* (1999)
Lawyer, V, 'Birth and Death of Governmental Immunity' (1966) 15 Cleveland-Marshall Law Review 529
Lee, LT, *Consular Law and Practice* (2nd edn, 1991)
Le Fur, L, 'Règles générales du droit de la paix' (1935–IV) 54 RdC 5
Levie, HS, *The Code of International Armed Conflict* (1986)
Lewis, CJ, *State and Diplomatic Immunity* (3rd edn, 1990)
Lieberman, P, 'Expropriation, Torture, and Jus Cogens under the Foreign Sovereign Immunities Act: Siderman de Blake v. Republic of Argentina' (1993) 24 University of Miami Inter-American Law Review 503
Liebman, ET, 'Case Comment' (1926) 18 RDI 257
Lininger, T, 'Overcoming Immunity Defenses to Human Rights Suits in U.S. Courts' (1994) 7 Harvard Human Rights Journal 177
Lissitzyn, OJ, 'The Treatment of Aerial Intruders in Recent Practice and International Law' (1953) 47 AJIL 559
Lissitzyn, OJ, 'Sovereign Immunity as a Norm of International Law' in *Essays in Honour of Philip Jessup* (1972) 188
Loening, E, *Die Gerichtsbarkeit über fremde Staaten und Souveräne* (1903)
Lorimer, J, *Institutes of the Law of Nations* (1883)
Lowe, AV, 'Peace without Justice; Reconsidering the Law on the Use of Force' in WE Butler (ed), *Perestroika and International Law* (1990) 281
Lowe, V, 'Jurisdiction' in MD Evans (ed), *International Law* (2003) 329
Lyons, AB, 'The Conclusiveness of the "Suggestion" and Certificate of the American State Department' (1947) 24 BYIL 116

Mackusick, D, 'Human Rights vs. Sovereign Rights: The State Sponsored Terrorism Exception to the Foreign Sovereign Immunities Act' (1996) 10 Emory International Law Review 741

Maierhöfer, C, 'Der EGMR als "Modernisierer" des Völkerrechts? Staatenimmunität und ius cogens auf dem Prüfstand' (2002) 29 Europäische Grundrechte Zeitschrift 391

Malanczuk P (ed), *Akehurst's Modern Introduction to International* Law (7th edn, 1997)

Malintoppi, A, 'Su l'esenzione giurisdizionale degli agenti diplomatici' (1954) 37 RDI 118

Malintoppi, A, 'Attività imputabile a Stato estero e responsabilità personale dell'individuo-organo' (1955) 38 RDI 84

Mallory, JL, 'Resolving the Confusion over Head of State Immunity: The Defined Rights of Kings' (1986) 86 CLR 169

Mann, FA, 'The Sacrosanctity of the Foreign Act of State' (1943) 59 LQR 42 and 155

Mann, FA, 'The Present Legal Status of Germany' (1947) 1 ILQ 314

Mann, FA, 'International Delinquencies before Municipal Courts' (1954) 70 LQR 181

Mann, FA, 'The Doctrine of Jurisdiction in International Law' 111 (1964–I) RdC 1

Mann, FA, *Studies in International Law* (1973)

Mann, FA, 'The Doctrine of Jus Cogens in International Law' in *Festschrift für Ulrich Scheuner* (1973) 399

Manner, G, 'The Legal Nature and Punishment of Criminal Acts of Violence Contrary to the Laws of War' (1943) 38 AJIL 407

Marek, K, 'Le problème des sources du droit international dans l'arrêt sur le plateau continental de la mer du Nord' (1970) 6 RBDI 55

Mathew, S, 'Princz v. Federal Republic of Germany: A Violation of Customary International Law' (1995) 16 Whittier Law Review 911

McLachlan, C, '*Pinochet* Revisited' (2002) 51 ICLQ 959

McNair, Lord, *International Law Opinions* (1956) i

Meisenberg, S, 'Die Anklage under der Haftbefehl gegen Charles Ghankay Taylor durch den Sondergerichtshof für Sierra Leone' (2004) 17 Humanitäres Völkerrecht 30

Menon, PK, 'The Subjects of Modern International Law' (1990) 3 Hague Yearbook of International Law 30

Meron, T, 'International Responsibility of States for Unauthorized Acts of their Officials' (1957) 23 BYIL 85

Meron, T, 'On a Hierarchy of International Human Rights' (1986) 80 AJIL 1

Meron, T, *Human Rights Law-Making in the United Nations* (1987)

Micco, RT, 'Putting the Terrorist-Sponsoring State in the Dock: Recent Changes in the Foreign Sovereign Immunities Act and the Individual's Recourse against Foreign Powers' (2000) 14 Temple International and Comparative Law Journal 109

Miele, M, *L'immunità giurisdizionale degli organi stranieri* (2nd edn, 1961)

Migliorino, L, 'Giurisdizione dello Stato territoriale rispetto ad azione non autorizzate di agenti di Stati stranieri' (1988) 71 RDI 784

Minnerop, P, 'Rogue States—State Sponsors of Terrorism?' (2002) 3 German Law Journal

Mitchell, AD, 'Leave your Hat on? Head of State Immunity and Pinochet' (1999) 25 Monash University Law Review 225

Morelli, G, *Diritto processuale civile internazionale* (2nd edn, 1954)

Morelli, G, 'Immunità dalla giurisdizione e competenza giurisdizionale' (1958) 41 RDI 126

Morelli, G, *Nozioni di diritto internazionale* (7th edn, 1967)

Morris, M, 'High Crimes and Misconceptions: The ICC and Non-Party States' (2001) 64 Law & Contemporary Problems 13

Moser, JJ, *Grund-Sätze des Europäischen Völcker-Rechts in Kriegs-Zeiten* (1752)

Mosler, H, 'The International Society as a Legal Community' (1974–IV) 140 RdC 3

Murphy, JF, 'Civil Liability for the Commission of International Crimes as an Alternative to Criminal Prosecution' (1999) 12 Harvard Human Rights Journal 1

Murphy, SD, 'Contemporary Practice of the United States' (2001) 95 AJIL 132

Niboyet, JP, 'Les immunités de juridiction en droit français, des états étrangers engagés dans des transactions privées' (1936) 43 RGDIP 525

Niboyet, JP, 'Immunité de juridiction et incompétence d'attribution' (1950) 39 RCDIP 139

Nino, CS, *Radical Evil on Trial* (1996)

Nollkaemper, A, 'Concurrence between Individual Responsibility and State Responsibility in International Law' (2003) 52 ICLQ 615

Nørgaard, CA, *The Position of the Individual in International Law* (1962)

Nys, E, *Le droit international: les principes, les théories, les faits* (1904)

O'Connell, DP, *International Law* (1970)

Ogdon, M, *Juridical Bases of Diplomatic Immunity, A Study in the Origin, Growth and Purposes of the Law* (1936)

O'Keefe, R, 'Customary International Crimes in English Courts' (2001) 72 BYIL 293

Oppenheim, L, *International Law, A Treatise* (1905)

Oppenheim, L, *International Law, A Treatise* (2nd edn, 1912)

Oppenheim, L (ed), *The Collected Papers of John Westlake* (1914)

Oppenheim, L, *International Law, A Treatise* (AD McNair (ed) 4th edn, 1926)

Oppenheim, L, *International Law, A Treatise* (H Lauterpacht (ed) 6th edn, 1940)

Oppenheim, L, *International Law: A Treatise* (H Lauterpacht (ed) 7th edn, 1952)

Orakhelashvili, O, *Peremptory Norms in International Law* (2006)

Orentlicher, DF, 'Settling Accounts: The Duty to Prosecute Human Rights Violations of a Prior Regime' (1991) 100 YLJ 2537

Orentlicher, D, *Submission of the Amicus Curiae on Head of State Immunity (in SCSL, Appeals Chamber, Prosecutor v. Charles Ghankay Taylor SCSL–2003–01–I, Decision on Immunity from Jurisdiction* (2004)

Osofsky, HM, 'Foreign Sovereign Immunity from Severe Human Rights Violations: New Directions for Common Law Based Approaches' (1998) 11 New York International Law Review 35

Outry, J, *Verletzung der Schweizerischen Gebietshoheit durch verbotene Handlungen für einen fremden Staat* (1951)

Pahr, WP, 'Die Staatenimmunität und Artikel 6 Absatz 1 der Europaische Menschenrechtkonvention' in *Mélanges offerts à Polys Modinos, Problèmes des droits de l'homme et de l'unification européenne* (1968) 222

Palmisano, G, 'Sulla Decisione Arbitrale Relativa alla Seconda Fase del Caso "Rainbow Warrior"' (1990) 73 RDI 874

Panebianco, M, *Giuridisdizione interna e immunità degli Stati stranieri* (1967)

Panezi, M, 'Sovereign Immunity and Violations of *Jus Cogens* Norms' (2003) 56 Revue Hellénique de Droit International 199
Paust, JJ, 'Federal Jurisdiction Over Extraterritorial Acts of Terrorism and Nonimmunity for Foreign Violators of International Law under the FSIA' (1983) 23 VJIL 191
Paust, JJ, 'Draft Brief Concerning Claims to Foreign Sovereign Immunity and Human Rights: Nonimmunity for Violations of International Law Under the FSIA' (1985) 8 Houston Journal of International Law 49
Pellet, A, 'Can a State Commit a Crime? Definitely, Yes!' (1999) 10 EJIL 425
Pepper, WF, 'Iraq's Crimes of State against Individuals, and Sovereign Immunity' (1992) 18 Brooklyn Journal of International Law 313
Perassi, T, 'Su l'esenzione degli agenti diplomatici dalla giurisdizione' (1940) 32 RDI 95
Perassi, T, *Lezioni di diritto internazionale* (1955)
Phillimore, GG, 'Immunité des États, au point de vue de la juridiction ou de l'exécution forcée' (1925–III) 8 RdC 413
Phillimore, R, *Commentaries upon International Law* (3rd edn, 1889)
Phillipson, C, *The International Law and Custom of Ancient Greece and Rome* (1911)
Pingel, I, 'Droit d'accès aux tribunaux et exception d'immunité: La Cour de Strasbourg persiste' (2002) 106 RGDIP 893
Pingel-Lenuzza, I, *Les immunités des Etats en droit international* (1997)
Pradier-Fodéré, P, *Traité de droit international public européen et américain suivant les progrès de la science et de la pratique contemporaines* (1906)
Provinciali, R, *L'immunità giurisdizionale degli stati stranieri* (1933)
Pugh, RC and McLaughlin, J, 'Jurisdictional Immunities of Foreign States' (1966) 41 New York University Law Review 25
Pustorino, P, 'Immunità giurisdizionale delle organizzazioni internazionali e tutela dei diritti fondamentali: le sentenze della Corte Europea nei casi *Waite et Kennedy* e *Beer et Regan*' (2000) 83 RDI 132
Quadri, R, *La giurisdizione sugli stati stranieri* (1941)
Quadri, R, *Diritto internazionale pubblico* (5th edn, 1968)
Rabkin, J, 'Universal Justice: The Role of Federal Courts in International Civil Litigation' (1995) 95 CLR 2120
Ragni, C, 'Immunity of Heads of State: Some Critical Remarks on the Decision of the Special Court for Sierra Leone in the *Charles Taylor* Case' (2004) 14 Italian Yearbook of International Law 273
Raič, D, *Statehood and the Law of Self-Determination* (2002)
Randall, KC, 'Universal Jurisdiction under International Law' (1988) 66 Texas Law Review 785
Randall, KC, *Federal Courts and the International Human Rights Paradigm* (1990)
Ratner, SR, 'Belgium's War Crimes Statute: A Postmortem' (2003) 97 AJIL 888
Redress, *Universal Jurisdiction in Europe, Criminal Prosecutions in Europe since 1990 for war crimes, crimes against humanity and genocide* (1999)
Redress, *Immunity v. Accountability, Considering the Relationship between State Immunity and Accountability for Torture and Other Serious International Crimes* (2005)
Reimann, M, 'A Human Rights Exception to Sovereign Immunity: Some Thoughts on Princz *v* Federal Republic of Germany' (1995) 16 Michigan Journal of International Law 403

Reinisch, A, 'Case Note *Waite and Kennedy* and *Beer and Regan*' (1999) 93 AJIL 933

Renault, L, 'Un litige international devant la cour de cassation de France' (1881) 13 RDILC 22

Renault, L, 'De l'application du droit pénal aux faits de guerre' (1918) 25 RGDIP 5

Reydams, L, '*In re* Pinochet, Belgian Tribunal of First Instance of Brussels' (1999) 93 AJIL 700

Reydams, L, *Universal Jurisdiction, International and Municipal Legal Perspectives* (2003)

Richmann, SA, 'Siderman de Blake v. Republic of Argentina: Can the FSIA Grant Immunity for Violations of Jus Cogens Norms?' (1993) 19 Brooklyn Journal of International Law 967

Riphagen, W, 'State Responsibility: New Theories of Obligation in Interstate Relations' in RSJ Macdonald and DM Johnston (eds), *The Structure and Process of International Law (*1983) 581

Roht-Arriaza, N, 'The Foreign Sovereign Immunities Act and Human Rights Violations: One Step Forward, Two Steps Back?' (1998) 16 Berkeley Journal of International Law 71

Röling, BVA, 'The Law of War and the National Jurisdiction since 1945' (1960–II) 100 RdC 323

Röling, BVA, 'The Significance of the Laws of War' in A Cassese (ed), *Current Problems of International Law, Essays on UN Law and on the Law of Armed Conflict* (1975) 133

Röling, BVA, *The Tokyo Judgment, The International Military Tribunal for the Far East, 29 April 1946–12 November 1949* (1977) 456

Romano, CPR, and Nollkaemper, A, 'The Arrest Warrant Against the Liberian President, Charles Taylor' (June 2003) ASIL insights, <http://www.asil.org/insights/insight110.htm>

Rosas, A, *The Legal Status of Prisoners of War: A Study in International Humanitarian Law Applicable in Armed Conflict* (1976)

Rosen, M, 'The Alien Tort Claims Act and the Foreign Sovereign Immunities Act: A Policy Solution' (1998) 6 Cardozo Journal of International and Comparative Law 461

Rosenne, S, 'Bilateralism and Community Interest in the Codified Law of Treaties' in W Friedmann et al (eds), *Transnational Law in a Changing Society: Essays in Honor of Philip C Jessup* (1972) 202

Rousseau, C, *Le droit des conflits armés* (1983)

Ryan, MH, 'The Status of Agents on Special Missions in Customary International Law' (1978) 16 Canadian Yearbook of International Law 157

Salmon, J, *Manuel de droit diplomatique* (1994)

Salmon, J and Sucharitkul, S, 'Les missions diplomatiques entre deux chaises: immunité diplomatique ou immunité d'État ?' (1987) 33 AFDI 163

Salmon, J, 'Libres propos sur l'arrêt de la C.I.J. du 14 Février 2002 dans l'affaire relative au *mandat d'arrêt du 11 Avril 2000 (RDC c Belgique)*' (2002) 35 RBDI 512

Sands, P and Macdonald, A, *Submissions of the Amicus Curiae on Head of State Immunity (in SCSL, Appeals Chamber, Prosecutor v Charles Ghankay Taylor SCSL–2003–01–I, Decision on Immunity from Jurisdiction* (2004), available at <http://www.icc-cpi.int/library/organs/otp/Sands.pdf>

Schabas, WA, *An Introduction to the International Criminal Court* (2nd edn, 2004)

Schachter, O, 'International Law in Theory and Practice: General Course in Public International Law' (1982–V) 178 RdC 21

Scharf, M, 'The ICC's Jurisdiction over the Nationals of Non-Party States: A Critique of the US Position' (2001) 64 Law & Contemporary Problems 67

Scheffer, DJ, 'The United States and the International Criminal Court' (1999) 93 AJIL 12

Schermers, HG, 'L'immunité devant le droit pénal, en particulier en ce qui concerne les infraction aux règles de la circulation' in *Le Droit Pénal International, Recueil d'Études en Hommage à JM van Bemmelen* (1965) 174

Schermers, HG, 'Diplomatic Immunity in Modern International Law' in E Denters and N Schrijver (eds), *Reflections on International Law from the Low Countries in Honour of Paul de Waart* (1998) 156

Schermers, HG, and Blokker, NM, *International Institutional Law* (4th edn, 2003)

Schick, FB, 'The Nuremberg Trial and the International Law of the Future' (1947) 41 AJIL 770

Schindler, D and Tomon, J (eds), *The Laws of Armed Conflict: A Collection of Conventions, Resolutions and other Documents* (4th edn, 2004)

Schreuer, C, 'The Impact of International Institutions on the Protection of Human Rights in Domestic Courts' (1978) 4 Israel Yearbook of Human Rights 60

Schreuer, C, 'The Waning of the Sovereign State: Towards a New Paradigm for International Law?' (1993) 4 EJIL 447

Schreuer, CH, *State Immunity: Some Recent Developments* (1988)

Schwarzenberger, G, 'The Problem of an International Criminal Law' (1950) 3 Current Legal Problems 263

Schwarzenberger, G, 'International Jus Cogens?' (1965) 43 Texas Law Review 455

Schwelb, E, 'The Actio Popularis and International Law' (1972) 2 Israel Yearbook of Human Rights 46

Schwelb, E, 'The International Court of Justice and the Human Rights Clauses of the Charter' (1972) 66 AJIL 337

Seidl-Hohenveldern, I, 'Immunität ausländischer Staaten in Strafverfahren und Verwaltungsstrafverfahren' in H Conrad, et al (eds), *Gedächtnisschrift Hans Peters* (1967) 915

Seyersted, F, 'Jurisdiction over Organs and Officials of States, the Holy See and Intergovernmental Organisations' (1965) 14 ICLQ 31

Sicilianos, L-A, 'The Classification of Obligations and the Multilateral Dimension of the Relations of International Responsibility' (2002) 13 EJIL 1127

Simma, B, 'Bilateralism and Community Interest in the Law of State Responsibility' in Y Dinstein and M Tabory (eds), *International Law at a Time of Perplexity—Essays in Honour of Shabtai Rosenne* (1989) 821

Simma, B, 'From Bilateralism to Community Interest in International Law' (1994–VI) 250 RdC 217

Simma, B and Alston, P, 'The Sources of Human Rights Law: Custom, Jus Cogens, and General Principles' (1992) 12 Australian Yearbook of International Law 82

Sinclair, I, 'The Law of Sovereign Immunity, Recent Developments' (1980–II) 167 RdC 113

Singer, M, 'The Act of State Doctrine of the United Kingdom: An Analysis with Comparisons to United States Practice' (1981) 75 AJIL 283

Siotto-Pintor, M, 'Les sujets du droit international autres que les États' (1932–III) 41 RdC 245

Slaughter, A and Bosco, D, 'Plaintiff's Diplomacy' (2000, issue 5) 79 Foreign Affairs 102

Slye, RC, 'The Legitimacy of Amnesties under International Law and General Principles of Anglo-American Law: Is a Legitimate Amnesty Possible?' (2002) 43 VJIL 173

Sørensen, M, *Les sources du droit international: étude sur la jurisprudence de la Cour Permanente de Justice Internationale* (1946)

Spinedi, M, 'International Crimes of State, The Legislative History' in JHH Weiler, et al (eds), *International Crimes of State, A Critical Analysis of the ILC's Draft Article 19 on State Responsibility* (1989) 7

Spinedi, M, 'From One Codification to Another: Bilateralism and Multilateralism in the Genesis of the Codification of the Law of Treaties and the Law of State Responsibility' (2002a) 13 EJIL 1099

Spinedi, M, 'State Responsibility *v* Individual Responsibility for International Crimes: *Tertium Non Datur*?' (2002b) 13 EJIL 895

Spiropoulos, J, *L'individu en droit international* (1927)

Stein, T, 'Limits of International Law Immunities for Senior State Officials in Criminal Procedure', in C Tomuschat and J-M Thouvenin (eds), *The Fundamental Rules of the International Legal Order, Jus Cogens and Obligations Erga Omnes* (2006) 249

Steinberger, H, 'Zur Rechtsprechung des Bundesverfassungsgerichts zu Fragen der Immunität fremder Staaten' in B Börner, H Jahrreiß, K Stern (eds), *Einigkeit und Recht und Freiheit: Festschrift für Karl Carstens* (1984) ii 889

Stern, B, 'La Coutume au coeur du droit international, quelques réflexions' in *Mélanges offerts à Paul Reuter, Le droit international: unité et diversité* (1981) 479

Stern, B, 'Case Note' (1999) 93 AJIL 700

Stern, B, 'Immunities for Heads of State: Where Do We Stand?' in M Lattimer and P Sands (eds), *Justice for Crimes against Humanity* (2003) 73

Sucharitkul, S, *State Immunities and Trading Activities in International Law* (1959)

Sucharitkul, S, 'Immunities of Foreign States before National Authorities' (1976–I) 149 RdC 87

Sucharitkul, S, 'Developments and Prospects of the Doctrine of State Immunity, Some Aspects of Codification and Progressive Development' (1982) 29 NILR 252

Sur, S, *La coutume internationale, sa vie, son oeuvre* (1990)

Swart, B, 'Arrest and Surrender' in A Cassese, P Gaeta and JRWD Jones (eds), *The Rome Statute of the International Criminal Court* (2002) 1639

Sztucki, J, *Jus Cogens and the Vienna Convention on the Law of Treaties, a Critical Appraisal* (1974)

Tams, CJ, 'Do Serious Breaches Give Rise to Any Specific Obligations of the Responsible State?' (2002) 13 EJIL 1161

Tanzi, A, *L'immunità dalla giurisdizione degli agenti diplomatici* (1991)

Tenékidès, G, 'Droit international et communautés fédérales dans la Grèce des cités' (1956–II) 90 RdC 469

Téson, FR, 'The Kantian Theory of International Law' (1992) 92 CLR 53

Thornton, BS, 'International Human Rights in American Courts: The Case of Nelson v. Saudi Arabia' (1992) 86 American Society of International Law Proceedings 324

Tigroudja, H, 'L'immunité de juridiction des organisations internationales et le droit d'accès à un tribunal' (2000) 11 Revue Trimestrielle des Droits de l'Homme 83

Tomonori, M, 'Case Note on *Yamagughi v United States*' (2003) 97 AJIL 406

Tomonori, M, 'The Individual as Beneficiary of State Immunity: Problems of the Attribution of *Ultra Vires* Conduct' (2003) 29 Denver Journal of International Law and Policy 101

Tomuschat, C, 'Obligations Arising for States Without or Against Their Will' (1993–IV) 241 RdC 195

Triffterer, O, 'Irrelevance of Official Capacity: Article 27' in O Triffterer (ed), *Commentary on the Rome Statute of the International Criminal Court: Observers' Notes, Article by Article* (1999) 501

Trooboff, PD, 'Foreign State Immunity: Emerging Consensus on Principles' (1986–V) 200 RdC 235

Tunks, MA, 'Diplomats or Defendants? Defining the Future of Head of State Immunity' (2002) 52 Duke Law Journal 651

Van Alebeek, R, 'The *Pinochet* Case: International Human Rights Law on Trial' (2000) 71 BYIL 29

Van Alebeek, R, 'From Rome to The Hague, Recent Developments on Immunity Issues in the ICC Statute' (2000) 13 LJIL 485

Van Bynkershoek, C, *De Foro Legatorum Liber Singularis* (1721), trans by GJ Laing (1946)

Van der Vyver, JD, 'Sovereignty and Human Rights in Constitutional and International Law' (1991) 5 Emory International Law Review 321

Van Elst, R, 'Implementing Universal Jurisdiction Over Grave Breaches of the Geneva Conventions' (2000) 13 LJIL 815

Van Hecke, G, 'Notes Critiques sur la Théorie de la Non-Justiciabilité' in *Nouveaux itinéraires en droit: Hommage à François Rigaux* (1993) 517

Van Hoof, GJH, *Rethinking the Sources of International Law* (1983)

Van Panhuys, HF, 'In the Borderland between the Act of State Doctrine and Questions of Jurisdictional Immunities' (1964) 13 ICLQ 1193

Van Praag, L, *Juridiction et droit international public, La juridiction nationale d'après droit international public coutumier en temps de paix* (1915)

Van Praag, L, 'Vonnis en Beslag tegen een Vreemden Staat' Weekblad van het Recht [1917] 10036, 3:1–4:1

Varughese George, S, 'Head of State Immunity in the United States Courts: Still Confused After All These Years' (1995) 64 Fordham Law Review 1051

Verdross, A, *Die völkerrechtswidrige Kriegshandlung und der Strafanspruch der Staaten* (1920)

Verdross, A, *Völkerrecht* (1937)

Verdross, A, 'Jus Dispositivum and Jus Cogens in International Law' (1966) 60 AJIL 1966 55

Verdross, A, and Simma, B, *Universelles Völkerrecht, Theorie und Praxis* (3rd edn, 1984)

Vicuna, FO, 'Diplomatic and Consular Immunities and Human Rights' (1999) 40 ICLQ 34

Villalpando, S, 'L'affaire Pinochet: beaucoup de bruit pour rien? L'apport au droit international de la décision de la Chambre des Lords du 24 mars 1999' (2000) 104 RGDIP 393

Villalpando, S, and Condorelli, L, 'Can the Security Council Extend the ICC's Jurisdiction?' in A Cassese, P Gaeta and JRWD Jones (eds), *The Rome Statute of the International Criminal Court* (2002) 571

Virally, M, 'Réflexions sur le "jus cogens"' (1966) 12 AFDI 5

Von Bar, L, *The Theory and Practice of Private International Law* (2nd edn, 1892), trans by GR Gillespie

Von Martens, GF, *Précis du Droit des Gens Moderne de l'Europe* (3rd edn, 1821)

Von Pufendorf, S, *Elementorum jurisprudentiae universalis libri duo* (1672), trans by W Abbott Oldfather (Oxford 1931)

Voskuil, CCA, 'State Immunity and the Law of Civil Procedure and Execution in the Netherlands' in TD Gill and WP Heere (eds), *Reflections on Principles and Practice of International Law* (2000) 223

Voyakis, E, 'Access to Court v. State Immunity' (2003) 52 ICLQ 297

Wai, R, 'The Commercial Activity Exception to Sovereign Immunity and the Boundaries of Contemporary International Legalism' in C Scott (ed), *Torture as Tort, Comparative Perspectives on the Development of Transnational Human Rights Litigation* (2001) 213

Warbrick, C, 'Immunity and International Crimes in English Law' (2004) 53 ICLQ 769

Waters, M, *The Ad Hoc Diplomat: A Study in Municipal and International Law* (1963)

Watts, A, 'The Legal Position in International Law of Heads of State, Heads of Government and Foreign Ministers' (1994–III) 247 RdC 13

Wedgwood, R, 'The International Criminal Court: An American View' (1999) 10 EJIL 93

Wedgwood, R, 'International Criminal Law and Augusto Pinochet' (2000) 40 VJIL 829

Weil, P, 'Le contrôle par les tribunaux nationaux de la licéité internationale des actes des États étrangers' (1977) 23 AFDI 9

Weil, P, 'Towards Relative Normativity in International Law?' (1983) 77 AJIL 413

Weil, P, 'Le droit international en quête de son identité, Cours général de droit international public' (1992–VI) 237 RdC 9

Weiler, JHH et al (eds), *International Crimes of State, A Critical Analysis of the ILC's Draft Article 19 on State Responsibility* (1989)

Weisburd, A, 'The Emptiness of the Concept of *Jus Cogens*, as Illustrated by the War in Bosnia-Herzegovina' (1995) 17 Michigan Journal of International Law 1

Weiss, A, *Traité élémentaire de droit international privé* (1886)

Weiss, A, 'Compétence ou incompétence des tribunaux à l'égard des États étrangers' (1923–I) 1 RdC 521

Wells, HG, *The New World Order* (1940)

Wells, HG, *The Rights of Man* (1940)

Whomersley, CA, 'Some Reflections on the Immunity of Individuals for Official Acts' (1992) 41 ICLQ 848

Wickremasinghe, C, 'Immunities Enjoyed by Officials of States and International Organizations' in MD Evans (ed), *International Law* (2003) 387

Wilson, RJ, 'Prosecuting Pinochet: International Crimes in Spanish Domestic Law' (1999) 21 Human Rights Quarterly 927

Wirth, S, 'Immunities, Related Problems, and Article 98 of the *Rome Statute*' (2002) 12 Criminal Law Forum 429

Wirth, S, 'Immunity for Core Crimes? The ICJ's Judgment in the *Congo v. Belgium* Case' (2002) 13 EJIL 877

Wolfman, N, 'Sovereigns as Defendants' (1910) 4 AJIL 373

Wortley, BA, 'The Interaction of Public and Private International Law Today' (1954–I) 85 RdC 239

Wright, Q, 'Human Rights and World Order' in *The Third Report of the Commission to Study the Organization of Peace* (1943)

Wright, Q, 'War Criminals' (1945) 39 AJIL 257

Wright, Q, 'The Law of the Nuremberg Trial' (1947) 41 AJIL 38

Wright, SL, 'Diplomatic Immunity: A Proposal for Amending the Vienna Convention to Deter Violent Criminal Acts' (1987) 5 Boston University International Law Journal 177

Wyler, E, 'From "State Crime" to Responsibility for "Serious Breaches of Obligations under Peremptory Norms of General International Law"' (2002) 13 EJIL 1147

Zemanek, K, 'New Trends in the Enforcement of *Erga Omnes* Obligations' (2000) 4 Max Planck Yearbook of United Nations Law 1

Ziman, GM, 'Holding Foreign Governments Accountable for Their Human Rights Abuses: A Proposed Amendment to the Foreign Sovereign Immunities Act of 1976' (1999) 21 Loyola of Los Angeles International and Comparative Law Journal 185

Zimmerman, A, 'Sovereign Immunity and Violations of International *Jus Cogens*—Some Critical Remarks' (1995) 16 Michigan Journal of International Law 433

Zitelman, E, *Internationales Privatrecht* (1897)

Zwanenburg, M, 'The Statute for an International Criminal Court and the United States: Peace Without Justice?' (1999) 12 LJIL 1

Index

UNIVERSITY OF GREENWICH LIBRARY

Lightning Source UK Ltd.
Milton Keynes UK
UKOW050917180912

199185UK00005B/12/P

9 780199 232475